Rick Steves®

R O M E

Rick Steves & Gene Openshaw

CONTENTS

Post-Pandemic Travels: Expect a Warm Welcome...and a Few Changes
Research for this guidebook was limited by the COVID-19 outbreak, and the long-term impact of the crisis on our recommended destinations is unclear. Some details in this book will change for post-pandemic travelers. Now more than ever, it's smart to reconfirm specifics as you plan and travel. As always, you can find major updates at RickSteves.com/update.

Welcome to Rick Steves' Europe

Travel is intensified living—maximum thrills per minute and one of the last great sources of legal adventure. Travel is freedom. It's recess, and we need it.

I discovered a passion for European travel as a teen and have been sharing it ever since—through my tours, public television and radio shows, and travel guidebooks. Over the years, I've taught millions of travelers how to best enjoy Europe's blockbuster sights—and experience "Back Door" discoveries that most tourists miss.

Written with my talented co-author, Gene Openshaw, this book offers you a balanced mix of Rome's brutal but *bella* sightseeing: breathtaking ancient and religious sights, world-class museums, and lively people zones. It's selective: Rather than listing all of Rome's many sights, we recommend only the best. And it's in-depth: Our self-guided museum tours and city walks provide insight into Rome's vibrant history and today's living, breathing culture.

We advocate traveling simply and smartly. Take advantage of our money- and time-saving tips on sightseeing, transportation, and more. Try local, characteristic alternatives to expensive hotels and restaurants. In many ways, spending more money only builds a thicker wall between you and what you traveled so far to see.

We visit Rome to experience it—to become temporary locals. Thoughtful travel engages us with the world, as we learn to appreciate other cultures and new ways to measure quality of life.

Judging by the positive feedback we receive from our readers, this book will help you enjoy a fun, affordable, and rewarding vacation—whether it's your first trip or your tenth.

Buon viaggio! Happy travels!

Rick Steves

ROME

Rome is magnificent and overwhelming at the same time. It's a showcase of Western civilization, with astonishingly ancient sights and a modern vibrancy.

Two thousand years ago the word "Rome" meant civilization itself. Everything was either civilized (part of the Roman world) or barbarian. Today, Rome is Italy's political capital, the spiritual capital of a billion Roman Catholics, and an open-air museum of the evocative remains of the capital of what was the greatest empire in the history of humanity.

As you peel through Rome's fascinating and jumbled layers, you'll find the marble ruins of ancient times, tangled streets of the medieval world, early Christian churches, grand Renaissance buildings and statues, Baroque fountains and church facades, 19th-century apartments, 21st-century traffic, and nearly three million people. And then, of course, there are Rome's stupendous sights.

Visit St. Peter's, the greatest church on earth, and scale Michelangelo's 448-foot-tall dome. Learn something about eternity at the huge Vatican Museums, where the story of creation is as bright as when Michelangelo first painted it in the restored Sistine Chapel. Ramble among the rabble and rubble, doing the "Caesar Shuffle" through ancient Rome's Colosseum and Forum, mentally resurrecting those tumble-down stones. Peer into the eyes of Roman busts at the National Museum of Rome, and savor Bernini's lifelike sculptures at the sumptuous Borghese Gallery. Wander through the surrounding Villa Borghese Gardens, Rome's biggest public park.

*Marveling at St. Peter's Basilica,
savory saltimbocca alla romana
(veal wrapped with proscuitto)*

Take a spin on the ancient Appian Way and clamber through the catacombs.

To experience the intimacy of Rome, buy a picnic at a farmers market, attend a church service, cheer at a soccer match, or find a little square peppered with pizzerias.

When the museums close and the crowds thin, Rome relaxes. The city, so monumental by day, becomes intimate and approachable. Its neighborhoods feel more like villages, and its famous squares become places to simply hang out.

Do as the Romans do. Early in the evening, join the promenade—called the *passeggiata*—up and down the main streets. After a sociable stroll, take a break for an *aperitivo*—a before-dinner drink.

Dine well at least once, though even a modest dinner can easily become the evening's entertainment. Settle into a seat at a rickety sidewalk table on an atmospheric piazza with the rust-colored facade of Rome as your backdrop. The table is yours for the night. You'll have a front-row view of Rome unwinding as you enjoy your meal.

Roman cuisine, strongly flavored and unpretentious, features meats, fish, some fried foods, and fresh vegetables. Roman specialties are *spaghetti alla carbonara* (the egg-and-bacon sauce was created here) and *saltimbocca alla romana* ("jump in the mouth" veal).

Skip your restaurant's dessert in Rome—instead, wander

The Evening Stroll: The *Passeggiata*

Throughout Italy, early evening is time to stroll—it's the ritual *passeggiata*. The streets of central Rome are safe and inviting for a walk at dusk, and there's no better way to feel the city's pulse. It seems like everyone is out—people-watchers, shoppers, tourists, families, fashionistas, and flirts on the prowl—making the scene.

As I walked with my Roman friends, they explained the ritual of the promenade: In a more genteel small town, the *passeggiata* comes with sweet whispers of "*bella*" and "*bello*" ("pretty" and "handsome") as the boys and girls eye each other. But in big-city Rome, where the ritual is called the *struscio* (meaning to rub), the admiration is a little cruder and oriented toward consumption—they say "*buona*" and "*buono*," roughly meaning "tasty."

If you want to be elegant, join the *passeggiata* in the area around the Spanish Steps, where chic people window-shop in front of upscale boutiques. For a more come-as-you-are vibe, head to Piazza Popolo or Via del Corso. Working-class youth from the suburbs converge in these spots, like American kids once gathered at the mall.

You can be a spectator, sipping a drink at a sidewalk table, but it's more fun to stroll along with everyone else. It's the perfect way to start a night in Rome. Later in this book I outline the two best walks: the early evening "Dolce Vita Stroll" down Via del Corso with Rome's beautiful people, and the after-dark "Heart of Rome Walk" from Campo de' Fiori to the Spanish Steps, lacing together the city's Baroque and bubbly nightspots. ▪

Strolling at dusk at Piazza Navona, a people-watching perch at the Pantheon, window-shopping as you walk

Throwing coins in the Trevi Fountain, sun shining on a peaceful piazza

the medieval back lanes, find a gelato shop, and jostle with kids to get a scoop. Walking down a cobbled street, gently illuminated as if by torchlight, it's easy to imagine you're rubbing shoulders with the past. In the squares, youngsters kick soccer balls until midnight and splashing fountains are bathed in velvety lighting. Sit so close to a bubbling fountain that traffic noise evaporates. Marvel at the ramshackle elegance that softens this brutal city for those who were born here—and can't imagine living anywhere else. These are the flavors of Rome, best enjoyed after dark.

Rome can be romantic...but hard on the unprepared. If you're careless, you could get pickpocketed. And if you have the wrong attitude, you'll be frustrated by the kind of chaos that only an Italian can understand. On a recent visit, my cabbie struggled with the traffic and said, "*Roma chaos.*" I responded, "*Bella chaos.*" He agreed.

Make it easy on yourself. If you choose a comfortable hotel for a refuge, pace yourself, enjoy a siesta during midday heat, organize your sightseeing, and take sensible precautions to protect your valuables, you'll love Rome. Soon you'll be the one at the Trevi Fountain throwing in a coin to ensure your return.

Rome by Neighborhood

Rome is a sprawling city—it takes an hour to walk from Termini Station to the Vatican—but its major sights cluster in convenient zones. You'll save lots of time if you thoughtfully group your sightseeing, walks, and dining. Think of Rome as a collection of neighborhoods, huddling around major landmarks, and it becomes manageable.

TOP NEIGHBORHOODS

Ancient Rome

In ancient times, this was home to the grandest buildings of a city of a million people. Today, the best of the classical sights stand in a line from the Colosseum (huge stadium) to the ruined Roman Forum (main square and marketplace) over Capitoline Hill to the Pantheon (Roman temple turned into a church).

Luckily, it's possible to knock off these top symbols of Rome's magnificence in one great day of sightseeing. Just link the biggies together in what I call the "Caesar Shuffle." With extra time, visit the Capitoline Museums' ancient art.

Just north of this area, between Via Nazionale and Via Cavour, is the atmospheric and trendy Monti district.

Pantheon Neighborhood

The Pantheon anchors the neighborhood I like to call the "Heart of Rome," which includes the atmospheric squares of Campo de' Fiori and Piazza Navona, the dramatic Trevi Fountain, and several historic churches. My "Heart of Rome Walk" ties these sights together. The walk is worthwhile doing day and night, for the different but always lively ambience.

Vatican City

Located west of the Tiber River, this is a compact world of its own, with two great, massive sights: St. Peter's Basilica, the finest church on earth, has Michelangelo's *Pietà* and huge dome, which you can climb for sky-high views. And the Vatican Museums, a showcase for the best art of Western civilization, host Michelangelo's glorious Sistine Chapel.

Opposite: *Pantheon's dome*
This page: *The Roman Forum,
She-Wolf (Capitoline Museums),
bridge over the Tiber, Michelangelo's Sistine Chapel*

The popular Spanish Steps in better times (sitting no longer allowed), seeing eye to eye at the National Museum of Rome, a café break, exploring the Ancient Appian Way

North Rome

This modern, classy area hosts the celebrated Spanish Steps, an elegant grid of trendy shopping streets (between the main drag—Via del Corso—and the Spanish Steps), and the Borghese Gallery (gorgeous Bernini sculptures) set within the fun-on-a-sunny-day Villa Borghese Gardens. My "Dolce Vita Stroll" starts in the vast square called Piazza del Popolo.

East Rome

This neighborhood around Termini Station boasts the stunning National Museum of Rome (ancient Roman sculpture) and includes Piazza della Repubblica, many recommended hotels, and convenient public-transportation connections. Just to the south and east is the area I call "Pilgrim's Rome," with several prominent churches.

Trastevere

Trastevere is the colorful, wrong-side-of-the-river neighborhood with a village feel. Its red pastel buildings are draped with green ivy, Vespas rule the streets, and locals frequent mom-and-pop cafés. Trastevere is the city at its crustiest... and perhaps most "Roman." It's short on sights, but long on atmosphere and worth a wander.

South Rome

Anchoring the city to the south is the funky Testaccio neighborhood (with a Roman pyramid, fun market, foodie restaurants, and lively nightlife). Farther south is the 1930s suburb of E.U.R. (Mussolini's planned district) and the Ancient Appian Way, home of Rome's underground catacombs.

Day Trips

When you're ready to explore beyond Rome, here are three good day-trip options:

Ostia Antica is an ancient, excavated seaport, similar to Pompeii but much closer—only 30 minutes from Rome.

The town of Tivoli offers two sights: the sprawling Hadrian's Villa (built by Emperor Hadrian in the second century AD) and the 16th-century Villa d'Este, with a lush garden awash with pools, waterfalls, and fountains.

For a long but unforgettable day trip, visit the lively, gritty city of Naples and ancient ruins of Pompeii.

Planning and Budgeting

The best trips start with good planning. Here are ideas to help you decide when to go, design a smart itinerary, set a travel budget, and prepare for your trip. For my best general advice on sightseeing, accommodations, restaurants, and more, see the Practicalities chapter.

PLANNING YOUR TIME

As you read this book and learn about your options...

Decide when to go.

Rome's best travel months (also its busiest and most expensive) are April, May, June, September, October, and early November. These months combine the convenience of peak season with pleasant weather.

The most grueling thing about travel in Rome is the summer heat in July and August, when temperatures can soar to the high 90s and pricier hotels discount their rooms. Fortunately, air-conditioning is the norm in all but the cheapest hotels (though it's generally available only from June through September).

Spring and fall can be cool, and many hotels do not turn on their heat. Rome is fine in winter—cool and crisp with temperatures in the 40s and 50s (see the climate chart in the appendix). Street life stays in full swing all year, as restaurants set up heaters to warm outdoor tables, and nativity scenes grace churches through January. Off-season has none of the sweat and stress of the tourist season, but sights may have shorter hours, lunchtime breaks, and fewer activities. Confirm your sightseeing plans locally, especially when traveling off-season.

Work out a day-by-day itinerary.

The following day-plans offer suggestions for how to maximize your sightseeing, depending on how many days you have. You can adapt these itineraries to fit your own interests. To find out what days sights are open, check the "Daily Reminder" in the Orientation chapter.

Rome in a Day

Some people actually "do" Rome in a day. Crazy as that sounds, if all you have is a day, it's one of the most exciting days Europe has to offer. Start at 8:30 at the Colosseum. Then explore the Forum (skip the Palatine Hill), hike over Capitoline Hill, and cap your "Caesar Shuffle" with a Pantheon visit. After a quick lunch, taxi to the Vatican Museums, then head to St. Peter's Basilica (open until 19:00 April-Sept). Taxi to Campo de' Fiori for dinner, then finish your day lacing together the famous floodlit spots (following my "Heart of Rome Walk").

Note: This busy plan is possible only if you reserve entry times for the Vatican Museums and the Colosseum in advance.

Make time for people-watching and sightseeing (Capitoline Museums).

Piazza Navona, atmospheric Campo de' Fiori, Baths of Diocletian, Mount Vesuvius looming over Pompeii

Rome in Two to Three Days

On the first day, do the "Caesar Shuffle" from the Colosseum (book ahead) to the Roman Forum, then over Capitoline Hill (visiting the Capitoline Museums), and on to the Pantheon. After a siesta, add some sightseeing to suit your interest. In the evening enjoy a sound-and-light show at the Imperial Forum and/or a colorful stroll in Trastevere or the Monti district. On the second day, see Vatican City (St. Peter's, dome climb, Vatican Museums—book ahead). Have dinner near the atmospheric Campo de' Fiori, and then walk to the Trevi Fountain and Spanish Steps (following my "Heart of Rome Walk"). With a third day, add the Borghese Gallery (reservations required) and more sights.

Rome in Seven Days

Rome is a great one-week getaway. Its sights can keep even the most fidgety traveler well entertained for a week.

Day 1: Do the "Caesar Shuffle" from the Colosseum to the Forum, Capitoline Museums, Victor Emmanuel Monument viewpoint, and Pantheon. Spend the late afternoon doing the "Heart of Rome Walk."

Day 2: In the morning, visit the National Museum of Rome and the nearby Baths of Diocletian. In the afternoon do my Jewish Ghetto Walk followed immediately by my Trastevere Walk. Enjoy dinner in Trastevere.

Day 3: At Vatican City, visit St. Peter's Basilica, climb the dome, and tour Vatican Museums. Spend the early evening shopping and enjoying the local *passeggiata* by doing the "Dolce Vita Stroll."

Day 4: Side-trip to Ostia Antica (closed Mon). In the evening, you could repeat my "Heart of Rome Walk" to enjoy the after-dark scene.

Day 5: Visit the Borghese Gallery (reservation required) and the churches I call "Pilgrim's Rome": San Giovanni in Laterano, Santa Maria Maggiore, and San Clemente.

Day 6: Day-trip to Naples and Pompeii.

Day 7: You choose—Hadrian's Villa near Tivoli, Appian Way with catacombs, E.U.R., Testaccio sights, a food tour, shopping, Galleria Doria Pamphilj, Castel Sant'Angelo, or more time at the Vatican.

PLANNING YOUR BUDGET

Run a reality check on your dream trip. You'll have major transportation costs in addition to daily expenses.

Flight: A round-trip flight from the US to Rome costs about $900-1,500, depending on where you fly from and when.

Public Transportation: For a one-week visit, allow $60-100 for taxis (can be shared by up to 4 people); if you opt for buses and the Metro, figure about $30 per person. Day-trip destinations range from a few dollars to get to Tivoli or Ostia Antica to about $90 for second-class train tickets to Naples and Pompeii (book a month in advance for deals). For a one-way trip between Rome's main airport and the city center, allow $15 per person by train or about $55 by taxi.

Budget Tips: To cut your daily expenses, take advantage of the deals you'll find throughout Rome and mentioned in this book.

Daily Expenses Per Person

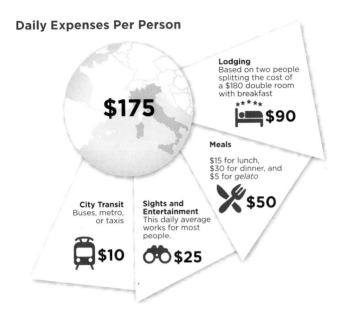

$175

Lodging
Based on two people splitting the cost of a $180 double room with breakfast

$90

Meals
$15 for lunch, $30 for dinner, and $5 for *gelato*

$50

City Transit
Buses, metro, or taxis

$10

Sights and Entertainment
This daily average works for most people.

$25

Use Rome's public transportation, and visit sights by neighborhood for efficiency. Enjoy Rome's free sights and experiences (people-watching counts).

Some businesses—especially hotels and walking-tour companies—offer discounts to my readers (look for the RS% symbol in the listings in this book).

Book your rooms directly with the hotel. Some hotels offer a discount if you pay in cash and/or stay three or more nights (check online or ask). Rooms cost less outside of peak season (roughly Nov-March). And even seniors can sleep cheap in hostels (some have double rooms) for about $30 per person. Or check Airbnb-type sites for deals.

It's no hardship to eat cheap in Rome. You can get tasty, inexpensive meals at delis, bars, takeout pizza shops, ethnic eateries, and at Italian restaurants, too. Cultivate the art of picnicking (but avoid major sights).

When you splurge, choose an experience you'll always remember, such as a food-tasting tour or sound-and-light show. Minimize souvenir shopping—how will you get it all home? Focus instead on collecting wonderful memories.

BEFORE YOU GO

You'll have a smoother trip if you tackle a few things ahead of time. For more information on these topics, see the Practicalities chapter and RickSteves.com, which has helpful travel tips and talks.

Make sure your travel documents are valid. If your passport is due to expire within six months of your ticketed date of return, you need to renew it. Allow up to six weeks to renew or get a passport (www.travel.state.gov). You may also need to register with the European Travel Information and Authorization System (ETIAS).

Arrange your transportation. Book your international flights. Overall, Kayak.com is the best place to start searching for flights. If you're traveling beyond Rome, figure out your transportation options. You can buy train tickets as you go, get a rail pass, rent a car, or book a cheap flight. (You can wing it in Europe, but it may cost more.) Drivers: Consider bringing an International Driving Permit (sold at AAA offices in the US, www.aaa.com) along with your license.

Book rooms well in advance, especially if your trip falls during peak season or any major holidays or festivals.

Reserve ahead for key sights. While Rome has plenty of crowds, only a few sights merit booking in advance: the Colosseum, Vatican Museums, Roman Forum, and Borghese Gallery. Only the Borghese Gallery actually requires advance booking, but reservations are absolutely essential for all of them. It's easy, and if you don't do it, you'll be frustrated by long and time-consuming lines any time of year. Clear instructions are in this guidebook. For all other sights, you can simply show up, pay, and enjoy.

Consider travel insurance. Compare the cost of the insurance to the cost of your potential loss. Check whether your existing insurance (health, homeowners, or renters) covers you and your possessions overseas.

Call your bank. Alert your bank that you'll be using your debit and credit cards in Europe. Ask about transaction fees, and get the PIN number for your credit card. You don't need to bring euros along; you can withdraw euros from cash machines in Europe.

Use your smartphone smartly. Sign up for an international service plan to reduce your costs, or rely on Wi-Fi in Europe instead. Download any apps you'll want on the road, such as maps, translators, and Rick Steves Audio Europe (see sidebar).

Pack light. You'll walk with your luggage more than you think. I travel for weeks with a single carry-on bag and a day pack. Use the packing checklist in the appendix as a guide.

Rick's Free Video Clips and Audio Tours

Travel smarter with these free, fun resources:

Rick Steves Classroom Europe, a powerful tool for teachers, is also useful for travelers. This video library contains over 400 three- to five-minute clips excerpted from my public television series. Enjoy these videos as you sort through options for your trip and to better understand what you'll see in Europe. Just enter a topic (city name, historical event, etc.) into the search bar for a list of everything I've filmed on a subject. Check it out at Classroom.RickSteves.com.

Rick Steves Audio Europe, an app for Apple and Android mobile devices, makes it easy to download my audio tours and listen to them offline as you travel. In this book, these audio tours include my Heart of Rome Walk, Trastevere Walk, Jewish Ghetto Walk, and Naples Walk plus tours of the Pantheon, St. Peter's Basilica, Roman Forum, Colosseum, Sistine Chapel, Vatican Museums, Ostia Antica, Naples' Archaeological Museum, and Pompeii (look for the 🎧 in this book).

The app also offers insightful travel interviews from my public radio show with experts from Europe and around the globe. Find it in your app store or at RickSteves.com/AudioEurope.

Travel Smart

If you have a positive attitude, equip yourself with good information (this book), and expect to travel smart, you will.

Read—and reread—this book. To have an "A" trip, be an "A" student. Note opening hours of sights, closed days, crowd-beating tips, and whether reservations are required or advisable. Check out the latest at www.ricksteves.com/update.

Be your own tour guide. As you travel, get up-to-date info on sights, reserve tickets and tours, reconfirm your hotel, and check any transit connections. Visit the local tourist information office (TI).

Outsmart thieves. Pickpockets abound in crowded places where tourists congregate. Treat commotions as smoke-screens for theft. Keep your cash, credit cards, and passport secure in a money belt tucked under your clothes; carry only a day's spending money in your front pocket. Don't set valuable items down on counters or café tabletops, where they can be quickly stolen or easily forgotten.

Minimize potential loss. Keep expensive gear to a minimum. Bring photocopies or take photos of your important documents (passport and cards) to aid in replacement if they're lost or stolen. Back up photos and files frequently.

Beat the summer heat. If you wilt easily, choose a hotel with air-conditioning. Start your day early, take a mid-day siesta at your hotel, and resume your sightseeing later. Churches offer a cool haven to recharge (though dress modestly—no bare shoulders or shorts). Take frequent gelato breaks. Join the *passeggiata*, when locals stroll in the cool of the evening.

Guard your time and energy. Taking a taxi can be a good value if it saves you a long wait for a cheap bus or an exhausting walk across town. To avoid long lines, follow my crowd-beating tips, such as making advance reservations, getting a pass, or sightseeing early or late.

Be flexible. Even if you have a well-planned itinerary, expect changes, strikes, closures, sore feet, bad weather, and so on. Your Plan B could turn out to be even better.

Attempt the language. Many Italians—especially in the tourist trade and in big cities like Rome—speak English, but if you learn some Italian, even just a few phrases, you'll get more smiles and make more friends. Practice the survival

Opposite: Guard at Vatican City
This page: Beating the summer heat at the Spanish Steps, connecting with locals at a farmers market

phrases near the end of this book, and even better, bring a phrase book.

Connect with the culture. Interacting with locals carbonates your experience. Enjoy the friendliness of the Roman people. Ask questions; most locals are happy to point you in their idea of the right direction. Set up your own quest for your favorite piazza, church, or gelato. Break out of the tourist track and explore. When an opportunity pops up, make it a habit to say "yes."

Rome...here you come!

ORIENTATION TO ROME

Today's Rome sprawls over about 500 square miles, but the city center within the ancient Aurelian Wall is all you need to know—and that's only four square miles. The old core, with most of the tourist sights, sits inside a diamond formed by Termini train station (in the east), the Vatican (west), Villa Borghese Gardens (north), and the Colosseum (south). The Tiber River snakes through the diamond from north to south. At the center of the diamond is Piazza Venezia, a busy square and traffic hub.

This chapter offers helpful hints and details on Rome's tourist services, a rundown of your options for getting around, and recommendations for organized tours. For an overview of the city's neighborhoods and detailed day-plans, see the previous chapter.

Overview

TOURIST INFORMATION

Rome has about a dozen small city-run tourist information offices scattered around town that sell city maps and sightseeing passes. The largest TIs are at Fiumicino Airport (Terminal 3, daily 8:00-21:00) and Termini train station (daily 8:00-18:45, exit by track 24 and walk 100 yards down along Via Giovanni Giolitti). Little kiosks (most open daily 9:30-19:00) are on Via Nazionale (at Palazzo delle Esposizioni), between the Trevi Fountain and Pantheon (at the corner of Via del Corso and Via Minghetti), near Piazza Navona (at Piazza delle Cinque Lune), and in Trastevere (at Piazza Sidney Sonnino). A larger information center is directly across from the Forum entrance, on Via dei Fori Imperiali (see page 177). There are also offices at Tiburtina train station and Ciampino Airport.

The TI's website is www.turismoroma.it, but a better site for practical information is www.060608.it. That's also the number for

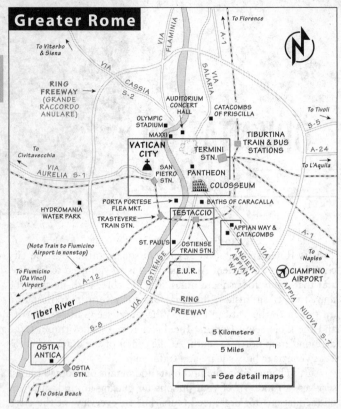

Rome's **call center**—the best source of up-to-date tourist information, with English speakers on staff (answered daily 9:00-19:00, tel. 06-0608, press 2 for English).

Your hotel will have a freebie map and may also have a booklet with up-to-date listings of the city's sights and hours. To find the city's many small streets and alleys, map apps work better than paper maps. If you do want a paper map, you'll find better quality ones at bookstores than at newsstands. See "Getting Around Rome" later in this chapter for recommended public transport maps.

Some English-language **websites,** oriented to those staying longer in Rome, provide insight into events and daily life in the city: www.inromenow.com (light tourist info on lots of topics) and www.wantedinrome.com (events and accommodations).

ARRIVAL IN ROME

For a rundown of Rome's train stations and airports, see the Rome Connections chapter.

HELPFUL HINTS

Sightseeing Tips: Despite the huge crowds inundating Rome, you'll only find lines a problem at **St. Peter's Basilica** (go early or late to minimize), **Vatican Museums** (easy to avoid by booking in advance online), and the **Colosseum** and **Roman Forum** (book online and go early morning or late afternoon). The exquisite **Borghese Gallery** requires a ticket with timed entry purchased in advance.

Even with a reservation, these sights can be very crowded. If that's not for you, remember that Rome has many other historical treasures, such as the **Capitoline Museums** and the **Baths of Caracalla,** with fewer to no crowds.

The **Roma Pass** is only worthwhile if you want a public transit pass (covers 2 or 3 days of transit, entry to 1 or 2 sights, and discounts at others—but you'll still need a Colosseum and a Borghese Gallery reservation).

Decorum: Rome has begun enforcing strict laws to protect its historical treasures from visitors who may not appreciate their significance to Roman life. Be respectful. Don't climb on ruins, picnic at (or on) ancient or historic sights, or dip your hand in the Trevi Fountain—fines can be expensive.

Bookstores: Borri Books, a large chain store at Termini station, sells English-language books (open daily). A few small, independent bookstores have a more personal touch: The **Anglo-American Bookshop** has great art and history sections (closed all day Sun and Mon morning, a few blocks south of Spanish Steps at Via della Vite 102—see map on page 83, tel. 06-679-5222). In Trastevere, the **Almost Corner Bookshop** stocks an extensive Italian-interest section (Via del Moro 45—see map on page 387, tel. 06-583-6942, Dermot from Ireland), and the **Open Door Bookshop** carries the only used books in English in town (closed Sun, Via della Lungaretta 23—see map on page 387, tel. 06-589-6478).

Laundry: Coin launderettes are common in Rome. Your hotelier can direct you to the closest one. The **Wash & Dry Lavarapido** chain has a branch near Piazza Barberini (Mon-Sat 9:00-21:00, closed Sun, Via degli Avignonesi 17—see map on page 380, tel. 06-4201-3158). The Funny Palace Hostel's **Splashnet,** two blocks from Termini, offers full-serve laundry for about the same price (see details on page 385).

Travel Agencies: Instead of making a trip to a train station or purchasing online, you can get train tickets and rail pass-related reservations and supplements at travel agencies (at little or no additional cost). Your hotelier will know of a convenient agency.

Best Views: You have good choices: from the rooftop of the Victor Emmanuel Monument (take the Rome from the Sky elevator

Daily Reminder

Sunday: These sights are closed: the Vatican Museums (except the last Sun of the month, when it's free and more crowded), Villa Farnesina (except the second Sun of the month), Catacombs of San Sebastiano, and Testaccio Market. In the morning, the Porta Portese flea market opens, and the old center is delightfully quiet. Much of the Appian Way is closed to traffic and fun to stroll.

Monday: Many sights are closed, including the National Museum of Rome, Borghese Gallery, Catacombs of Priscilla, Montemartini Museum, Etruscan Museum, MAXXI, some Appian Way sights (Tomb of Cecilia Metella and the Circus and Villa of Maxentius), and Ostia Antica.

    Major sights that are open include the Colosseum, Forum, Vatican Museums, Capitoline Museums, Ara Pacis, and the Museum of the Imperial Forums (includes Trajan's Market and Trajan's Forum). Churches are open as usual. The Baths of Caracalla close early in the afternoon.

Tuesday: All sights are open in Rome. This isn't a good day to side-trip to Naples because its Archaeological Museum is closed.

Wednesday: All major sights are open, except the Catacombs of San Callisto. St. Peter's Basilica is typically closed in the morning for a papal audience.

Thursday/Friday: All sights are open.

Saturday: Most sights are open in Rome, except for the Synagogue and Jewish Museum.

to the top); from the top of the dome of St. Peter's Basilica; and from the top of Castel Sant'Angelo. One of the best views of the Roman Forum is from the Farnese Gardens viewpoint on Palatine Hill. Another is on Capitoline Hill—from two free overlooks plus the Tabularium (underground galleries) that is part of the Capitoline Museums.

Best Hangouts: The city's most atmospheric squares are Campo de' Fiori and Piazza Navona, interesting day and night. For monuments, it's the Trevi Fountain. The Monti neighborhood, near the Roman Forum, is a popular gathering spot in the evening (particularly Piazza della Madonna dei Monti) and a delight to explore any time of day.

DEALING WITH (AND AVOIDING) PROBLEMS

Theft Alert: While violent crime is rare in the city center, petty theft is rampant. Pickpockets troll through the tourist crowds around the Colosseum, Forum, Vatican, and all train and Metro stations. Always use your money belt. Keep nothing important in your pockets. If you carry a backpack, never leave it unattended and try to keep it attached to your body in some way (even when you're seated for a meal).

Be particularly on guard in crowds (such as those at the Trevi Fountain or in front of a famous painting in a church) and wear your day pack in front, especially when boarding and leaving buses and subways. You'll find less crowding and commotion—and less risk—waiting for the end cars of a subway rather than the middle cars. Thieves are particularly thick on the Metro and the crowded and made-for-tourists buses #40 and #64.

Thieves strike when you're distracted. Don't trust kind strangers or be deceived by appearance: Sneaky thieves may pose as businessmen or tourists, moms with babies, or gangs of children.

Scams abound: Always be clear about what paper money you're giving someone, demand clear and itemized bills, and count your change. Don't give your wallet to self-proclaimed "police" who stop you on the street, warn you about counterfeit (or drug) money, and ask to see your cash. If a bank machine eats your ATM card, see if there's a thin plastic insert with a tongue hanging out that thieves use to extract it.

Beggars: Throughout Rome, you may encounter downtrodden-looking people asking for money. Know that social services are available to them, and give at your own discretion.

Reporting Losses: To report lost or stolen items, file a police report (at Termini Station, with *polizia* at track 11 or with Carabinieri at track 20; offices are also at Piazza Venezia and at the corner of Via Nazionale and Via Genova). For information on how to replace a passport or report lost or stolen credit cards, see page 541.

Pedestrian Safety: Your main safety concern in Rome is crossing streets without incident. Use caution. Some streets have pedestrian-crossing signals (red means stop—or jaywalk carefully; green means go...also carefully; and yellow means go...extremely carefully, as cars may be whipping around the corner). But just as often, multilane streets have crosswalks with no signals at all. And even when there are traffic lights, they are provisional: Scooters don't always stop at red lights, and even cars exercise what drivers call the "logical option" of not stopping if they see no oncoming traffic. Each year, as noisy gasoline-powered scooters are replaced by electric ones, the streets get quieter (hooray) but more dangerous for pedestrians.

Follow locals like a shadow when you cross a street (or spend a good part of your visit stranded on curbs). When you

ORIENTATION

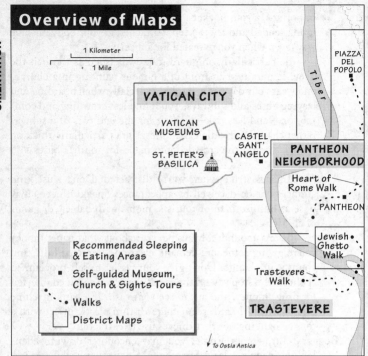

Overview of Maps

1 Kilometer

1 Mile

VATICAN CITY

VATICAN MUSEUMS ■

ST. PETER'S BASILICA

CASTEL SANT' ANGELO ■

Tiber

PIAZZA DEL POPOLO

PANTHEON NEIGHBORHOOD

Heart of Rome Walk

PANTHEON

Jewish Ghetto Walk

Trastevere Walk

TRASTEVERE

Recommended Sleeping & Eating Areas

■ Self-guided Museum, Church & Sights Tours

• Walks

☐ District Maps

To Ostia Antica

do cross alone, don't be a deer in the headlights. Find a gap in the traffic and walk with confidence while making eye contact with approaching drivers—they won't hit you if they can tell where you intend to go.

Staying/Getting Healthy: The siesta is a key to survival in summertime Rome. Lie down and contemplate the extraordinary power of gravity in the Eternal City. I drink lots of cold, refreshing water from Rome's many drinking fountains (the Forum has three) which are handy for refilling your bottle and staying hydrated.

Every neighborhood has a **pharmacy** (marked by a green cross). The 24-hour Farmacia Piram is several blocks down from Piazza della Repubblica at Via Nazionale 228 (tel. 06-488-4437). Pharmacies stay open late in Termini Station (daily 7:30-22:00, along northeast side of station, enter from Via Marsala), at Piazza dei Cinquecento 51 (Mon-Fri 7:00-23:30, Sat-Sun 8:00-23:00, next to Termini Station on the corner of Via Cavour—see map on page 410, tel. 06-488-0019), and in the Pantheon neighborhood (Farmacia Senato, between Piazza Navona and the Pantheon, Mon-Fri 7:30-24:30, Sat from 8:30, Sun 12:00-23:00, Corso del Rinascimento 50—see map on page 398).

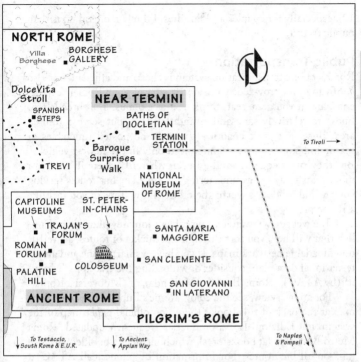

NORTH ROME
Villa Borghese • BORGHESE GALLERY

DolceVita Stroll

• SPANISH STEPS

NEAR TERMINI

BATHS OF DIOCLETIAN

TERMINI STATION

To Tivoli →

• Baroque Surprises Walk

• TREVI

• NATIONAL MUSEUM OF ROME

CAPITOLINE MUSEUMS

ST. PETER-IN-CHAINS

↓ TRAJAN'S FORUM

ROMAN FORUM •

SANTA MARIA • MAGGIORE

• SAN CLEMENTE

COLOSSEUM

• PALATINE HILL

SAN GIOVANNI • IN LATERANO

ANCIENT ROME

PILGRIM'S ROME

↓ To Testaccio, South Rome & E.U.R.

↓ To Ancient Appian Way

To Naples & Pompeii ↓

Embassies and hotels can recommend English-speaking **doctors.** Consider MEDline, a 24-hour private home-medical service; doctors speak English and make calls at hotels for about €150 (tel. 06-808-0995, www.soccorso-medico.com). Another private clinic is International Medical Services, Via Firenze 47, tel. 06-488-2371. Anyone is entitled to emergency treatment at public hospitals. The hospital closest to Termini Station is Policlinico Umberto I (entrance for emergency treatment on Via Lancisi, translators available, Metro: Policlinico).

GETTING AROUND ROME

You can see a lot of Rome on foot, and I've grouped your sightseeing into walkable neighborhoods. Make it a point to visit sights in a logical order. Needless backtracking wastes precious time.

To connect sights beyond walking distance, you can ride the Metro or a city bus, or take a taxi. As Rome is a great taxi town (most rides cost €7-

12), especially for couples and families, I'd rely more on taxis than public transit.

Public Transportation

Rome's public transportation system is cheap and efficient, but also confusing and crowded. Consider it part of your Roman experience, and if you get a seat, think of it as a bonus. The three Metro lines are relatively sane and straightforward, but serve a limited area. Buses are more chaotic—there are no posted timetables or maps, and stop names are announced only in the newest vehicles. But they run frequently and go everywhere. If you're in town for more than a day or two, mastering a couple key bus routes serving your neighborhood is worth the effort and will make you feel like a Rome pro.

The website www.atac.roma.it has a **journey planner** in English that will help you sort through the thicket of routes, as well as downloadable network maps. If you have a smartphone and an international data plan, consider downloading the free apps "Moov-it" (by ATAC), "Roma Bus" (by Movenda), or "Muoversi a Roma."

For an overview, see the color "Rome's Public Transportation" map at the back of this book. There's no official paper map of the system, but Edizioni Lozzi produces a frequently updated "Roma Metro Bus" map (at bookstores), which includes a booklet with details on all bus routes. For information by phone, call ATAC at 06-57003.

Buying Tickets

All public transportation uses the same ticket. It costs €1.50 and is valid for one Metro ride—including transfers underground—plus unlimited city buses and trams during a 100-minute period. Passes good on buses and the Metro are sold in increments of 24 hours (€7), 48 hours (€12.50), 72 hours (€18), one week (€24—about the cost of three taxi rides), and one month (€35, valid for a calendar month).

You can purchase tickets and passes from machines at Metro stations and a few major bus stops (cash/coins only), and from some newsstands and tobacco shops (*tabacchi*, marked by a black-and-white *T* sign). Tickets are not sold on board. It's smart to stock up on tickets early—that way you don't have to run around searching for an open tobacco shop when you spot your bus approaching.

Validate your ticket by sticking it in the Metro turnstile (magnetic strip-side up, arrow-side first) or in the machine when you board the bus (magnetic-strip-side down, arrow-side first)—watch others and imitate. It'll return your ticket with your expiration time printed. To get through a Metro turnstile with a transit pass or Roma Pass, press the card to the turnstile's electronic sensor pad.

On buses and trams, you need to validate your pass only on your first time using it.

If you need help from a real person, ATAC runs a small ticket office at Termini Station. Follow signs for *Metro Linea B*, then *ATAC ticket office* (Mon-Sat 7:00-20:00, Sun 8:00-20:00).

By Metro

The Roman subway system (Metropolitana, or "Metro") is simple, clean, cheap, and fast. The two lines you need to know—A and

B—intersect at Termini Station. Line A serves the Vatican area, Piazza del Popolo, Spanish Steps/ Villa Borghese, Baths of Diocletian, Termini Station, and San Giovanni in Laterano. Line B connects the Tiburtina train and bus stations with Termini, the Colosseum and Forum/Palatine Hill, Testaccio, and EUR. The Metro runs from 5:30 to 23:30 (Fri-Sat until 1:30 in the morning). The subway's first and last compartments are generally the least crowded, and the least likely to harbor pickpockets.

The partly finished line C currently serves only the suburbs.

By Bus

The Metro is handy, but it won't get you everywhere—you often have to take the bus (or tram). Bus routes are listed at each stop.

Route and system maps aren't posted, but with some knowledge of major stops, you can wing it without one. (The ATAC website has a PDF bus map that you can download, bookstores sell paper transport maps, and the ATAC journey planner is helpful.) Rome's few tram lines function for all intents and purposes identically to buses.

Buses—especially the touristy #40 and #64—are havens for thieves and pickpockets. These two lines in particular can be nose-to-armpit crowded during peak times...and while you're sniffing that guy's pit, his other hand could be busily rifling through your pockets. Assume any commotion is a thief-created distraction. If one bus is packed, there's likely a second one on its tail with far fewer crowds and thieves. Or read the signs posted at stops to see if a different, less crowded bus route can get you to or near your destination.

On buses, tickets must be inserted in the yellow box with the digital readout (magnetic-strip-side down, arrow-side first; be sure to retrieve your ticket after it's spit out). Do this as you board, otherwise you're cheating. Inspectors fine even innocent-looking tourists €50. You don't need to validate a transit pass or Roma Pass on the bus if you've already validated it elsewhere in the transit system. Bus etiquette (not always followed) is to board at the front or rear doors and exit at the middle.

Regular bus lines start running at about 5:30, and during the day major routes run every 10-15 minutes. After 23:30 (and sometimes earlier) and on Sundays, buses are less frequent. Night buses are marked with an *N* and an owl symbol on the bus-stop signs. Frustratingly, the exact frequency of various bus routes is difficult to predict (and not printed at bus stops). At major stops, an electronic board shows the number of minutes until the next buses arrive, but at most stops to find out how long you have to wait you'll need to use a mobile device to check the ATAC journey planner or apps listed earlier.

These are the most important bus routes for tourists:

Bus #64: This bus cuts across the city, linking Termini Station with the Vatican, stopping at Piazza della Repubblica (sights), Via Nazionale (recommended hotels), Piazza Venezia (near Forum), Largo Argentina (near Pantheon and Campo de' Fiori), St. Peter's Basilica (get off just past the tunnel), and San Pietro Station. Ride it for a city overview and to watch pickpockets in action. The #64 can get horribly crowded.

Bus #40: This express bus, which mostly follows the #64 route (but ends near the Castel Sant'Angelo on the Vatican side of the river), is especially helpful—fewer stops and (somewhat) fewer crowds.

The following routes conveniently connect Trastevere with other parts of Rome:

Bus #H: This express bus, linking Termini Station and Trastevere, makes a stop near Piazza Repubblica and at the bottom of Via Nazionale (for Trastevere, get off at Sonnino/S. Gallicano, just after crossing the Tiber River). It doesn't run on Sundays.

Tram #8: This tram connects Piazza Venezia and Largo Argentina with Trastevere (get off at Piazza Belli, just over the river) and runs further to the Trastevere train station.

Bus #23: This bus links the Vatican with Trastevere and Tes-

Bus Bravado

Zip around Rome like a local by learning to read the bus signs. The sign in the photo shows the three buses (#40, #60, and #64) that stop at the "Nazionale (Torino)" stop. If you're asking yourself the following questions, it's got answers.

❶ Where am I? You're at the bus stop *(fermata)* called Nazionale (Torino). There are several bus stops along Via Nazionale, identified by their cross-streets (in this case, Via Torino).

❷ Which buses stop here? Three do: #40, #60, and #64. Notice the arrow—it shows which direction the bus is headed.

❸ Where is the bus going? Bus #64, for example, starts its journey at "Termini" (Termini Station), goes to Repubblica, and then serves four stops along Via Nazionale. The stop you are at has a box around it. From here, the #64 continues to Piazza Venezia, Largo Argentina, makes several more stops, and ends its journey at Piazza Stazione San Pietro.

Scan the list to see if any of these buses stop where you want to go. If you don't see your destination, look for a major stop where you can transfer—such as Largo Argentina, Piazza Venezia, or Termini Station. Note that if your destination is listed *above* your current bus stop, you need to cross the street to catch the bus going in the other direction.

❹ When will my bus come? The bottom of the sign (not shown) lists the first and last departure times from the beginning of the route. *"lun./ven."* means it runs on weekdays, *"sab."* means Saturday, and *"fest."* means Sundays and holidays.

---

taccio, stopping at the Vatican Museums (nearest stop is on Via Leone IV), Castel Sant'Angelo (Sforza Pallavicini), Trastevere (Lungotevere de Cenci/Arenula, on opposite side of Ponte Garibaldi), Porta Portese (Sunday flea market at Emporio stop), and Piramide (Ostiense stop; Metro and gateway to Testaccio). **Bus #280** follows much the same route from Trastevere to Piramide.

Other useful routes include:

Bus #16: Termini Station, Santa Maria Maggiore, and San Giovanni in Laterano.

Bus #49: Piazza Cavour/Castel Sant'Angelo, Piazza Risorgimento (Vatican), and Vatican Museums.

Bus #62: Tiburtina, Piazza Barberini, Piazza Venezia, Piazza Pia (near Castel Sant'Angelo).

Bus #81: San Giovanni in Laterano, Largo Argentina, and Piazza Risorgimento (Vatican).

Buses #85 and #87: Piazza Navona (#87 only), Pantheon, Via del Corso (#85 only), Piazza Venezia, Forum, Colosseum, San Clemente, and San Giovanni in Laterano.

Bus #492: Travels east-west across the city, connecting Tiburtina (train and bus stations), Largo Santa Susanna (near Piazza della Repubblica), Piazza Barberini, Piazza Venezia, Largo Argentina (near Pantheon and Campo de' Fiori), Piazza Cavour (Castel Sant'Angelo), and Piazza Risorgimento (St. Peter's Basilica and Vatican).

Buses #660, #118, and #218: These run to/from the Appian Way.

Bus #714: Termini Station, Santa Maria Maggiore, San Giovanni in Laterano, Terme di Caracalla (Baths of Caracalla), and on to E.U.R.

Tram #2: Board near Flaminio Metro stop for easy access to MAXXI.

Tram #3: Zips from the Colosseum to San Giovanni in Laterano (and onward to Valle Giulia) in one direction, and to Piramide/Testaccio (and onward to Trastevere, though a 15-minute walk from the touristic heart) in the other.

Tram #19: Connects Piazza del Risorgimento and the Ottaviano Metro stop (by the Vatican Museums) to the Etruscan Museum and the Villa Borghese.

***Elettrico* Minibuses:** Cute electric minibuses take circular routes past major sights and are great for transport or simple joyriding (though they're so small, it can be hard to find a seat). They run weekdays only, 7:15-20:15. *Elettrico* #117 connects San Giovanni in Laterano, Colosseo, Via Cavour, Via Nazionale, and Trevi Fountain. *Elettrico* #119 connects Piazza Venezia, Via del Corso, Trevi Fountain, Piazza di Spagna, Piazza del Popolo, and Piazza Augusto Imperatore.

By Taxi

I use taxis in Rome more often than in other cities. They're reasonable and useful for efficient sightseeing in this big, hot metropolis. Three or four companions with more money than time should taxi almost everywhere. Taxis start at €3, then charge about €1.50 per kilometer (surcharges: €1.50 on Sun, €3.50 for nighttime hours of

22:00-6:00, one regular suitcase or bag rides free, tip by rounding up—€1 or so). Sample fares: Termini area to Vatican—€15; Termini area to Colosseum—€7; Termini area to the Borghese Gallery—€9; Colosseum to Trastevere—€12 (or look up your route at www.worldtaximeter.com).

Calling a Cab: You can always just hail a cab on the street. But Romans generally walk to the nearest taxi stand (many are marked on this book's maps) or ask a passerby or a clerk in a shop, *"Dov'è una fermata dei taxi?"* (doh-VEH OO-nah fehr-MAH-tah DEH-ee TAHK-see). Easiest of all, have your hotel or restaurant call a taxi for you. (It's routine for Romans to ask the restaurant to call a taxi when they're ready to go.) The meter starts when the call is received. To call a cab on your own, dial 06-3570, 06-4994, or 06-6645, or use the official city taxi line, 06-0609; they'll likely ask you for an Italian phone number (give them your mobile number or your hotel's).

You can also use the Free Now app, which orders an official white taxi at regular taxi rates, with the convenience of paying via the app.

Avoid Scams: Beware of corrupt taxis. First, only use official Rome taxis. They're white, with a taxi sign on the roof and a maroon logo on the door that reads *Roma Capitale*.

When you get in, make sure the meter *(tassametro)* is turned on (you'll see the meter either on the dashboard or up by the rearview mirror). If the meter isn't on, get out and find another cab. Check that the meter is reset to the basic drop charge (should be around €3, or around €5 if you phoned for the taxi). You'll rarely pay more than €12 for a ride in town. Keep an eye on the fare on the meter as you near your destination; some cabbies turn the meter off instantly when they stop and tell you a higher price.

By law, every cab must display a multilingual official price chart—usually on the back of the seat in front of you. If the fare doesn't seem right, point to the chart and ask the cabbie to explain it. When you pay the cabbie, have your wits about you. A common cabbie scam is to take your €20 note, drop it, and pick up a €5 note (similar color), claiming that's what you gave him. To avoid this scam, pay in small bills; if you only have a large bill, show it to the cabbie as you state its face value.

At the train station or airport, avoid hustlers conning naive visitors into unmarked, rip-off "express taxis" (for tips on taking a taxi from the airport, see page 446). If you encounter any problems with a taxi, making a show of writing down the taxi number (to file a complaint) can motivate a driver to quickly settle the matter.

Taxi Alternative: Uber works in Rome as it does in the US, but only at the more expensive Uber Black level.

By Bike

Riding a bicycle in Rome's traffic is best suited to serious urban bikers—use caution and never assume you have the right of way. For less stressful joy-riding, the best rides are on small streets in the city center, at the Villa Borghese Gardens, and along the Appian Way. Also, a bike path along the banks of the Tiber River makes a good 20-minute ride (easily accessed from the ramps at Porta Portese and Ponte Regina Margherita near Piazza del Popolo).

TopBike Rental & Tours is professionally run by Roman bike enthusiasts who want to show off their city. Your rental comes with a helmet, a lock, and a handy map that suggests a route and indicates less-trafficked streets. They also offer English-only guided tours around the city (4 hours) and the Appian Way (6 hours); check their website for itineraries and schedules (rental: €15/day, €25/day for electric bike, RS%—10 percent with this book, best to reserve in advance via email, bring ID for deposit; bike tours start at €45, reservations required; daily 8:30-19:00, Via Labicana 49, Metro: Colosseo—exit left and walk 10 minutes past the Colosseum, tel. 06-488-2893, www.topbikerental.com, info@topbikerental.com, ask for Florien from the Netherlands).

Cool Rent, a sidewalk operation, is cheaper but less helpful and has only basic bikes (€4/hour, €10/day, daily 9:00-20:00, Nov-March until 18:00, driver's license or other ID for deposit, 10 yards to the right as you exit the Colosseo Metro stop). A second outlet is just off Via del Corso (on Largo di Lombardi, near corner of Via del Corso and Via della Croce, mobile 328-277-3993).

You can also rent a bike at the Appian Way (see the Ancient Appian Way Tour chapter) and in the Villa Borghese Gardens (see page 77).

Tours in Rome

🎧 To sightsee on your own, download my free audio tours, including my Heart of Rome, Jewish Ghetto, and Trastevere neighborhood walks, and my tours of the Pantheon, Colosseum, Roman Forum, St. Peter's Basilica, Vatican Museums, Sistine Chapel, and Ostia Antica (see sidebar on page 21 for details).

ON FOOT

You can either hire a local to serve as your personal guide, or sign up for a group tour with a tour company, joining up to 50 fellow travelers. Private guides are good but pricey (around €180 for a three-hour tour). Tour companies are cheaper (€30/person), but quality and organization are unreliable. If you do hire a private Italian guide, consider inviting others from your hotel to join you and split the cost. This ends up costing about the same per person as going on a scheduled tour from one of the walking-tour companies listed below—and you'll likely get a better guide.

Local Guides

I've worked with and enjoyed each of these licensed independent local guides. They're native Italians, speak excellent English, and enjoy tailoring tours to your interests. Prices (roughly €60/hour) flex with the day, season, and demand. Arrange your date and price by email. **Carla Zaia** (carlaromeguide@gmail.com); **Cristina Giannicchi** (mobile 338-111-4573, www.crisromanguide.com, crisgiannicchi@gmail.com); **Sara Magister** (a.magister@iol.it); **Giovanna Terzulli** (gioterzulli@gmail.com); **Alessandra Mazzoccoli** (www.romeandabout.com, alemazzoccoli@gmail.com); and **Massimiliano Canneto** (a Catholic guide with a Vatican forte, but does all of Rome, massicanneto@gmail.com).

Francesca Caruso, who works almost full time with my tours when in Rome, has contributed generously to this book (www.francescacaruso.com, francescainroma@gmail.com); she offers private tours for €300/half-day. Popular with my readers, Francesca understandably books up quickly; if she's busy, she'll recommend one of her colleagues (at the standard €60/hour listed for guides above). At her website you can listen to the many interviews I've enjoyed with Francesca on my public radio program.

Walking-Tour Companies

Rome has many highly competitive tour companies, each offering a series of themed walks through various slices of the city. Three-hour guided walks generally cost €25-30 per person. Guides are usually native English speakers, often American expats. Before your trip, spend some time on these companies' websites to get to know your options, as each company has a particular teaching and guiding personality. Some are highbrow and more expensive. Others are less scholarly. It's sometimes required, and always smart, to book a spot in advance (easy online). Readers report that advertising can be misleading, and scheduling mishaps are common. Make sure you know what you are booking and when.

These companies are each well-established, creative, and competitive, with their various tours explained on their websites. Each offers a 10 percent discount with most online bookings for Rick Steves travelers.

Is the Pope Catholic?

Rome's tour guides, who introduce tourists to the city's great art and Christian history, field a lot of interesting questions and comments from their groups. Here are a few of their favorites:

- Oh, to be here in Rome...where our Lord Jesus walked.
- Is this where Christ fought the lions?
- Who's the guy on the cross?
- This guy who made so many nice things, Rene Sance, who is he?
- Was John Paul II the son of John Paul I?
- What's the Sistine Chapel worth in US dollars?
- How did Michelangelo get Moses to pose for him?
- What's Michelangelo doing now?
- (Upon seeing the arrow-pierced St. Sebastian) Oh, you Italians had problems with the Indians, too.

Walks of Italy (RS%—enter "RICKWALKSROME," US tel. 888/683-8670, tel. 06-9480-4888, www.walksofitaly.com).

Europe Odyssey (RS%, tel. 06-8854-2416, mobile 328-912-3720, www.europeodyssey.com, Rahul).

Through Eternity (RS%—look for "Group Tours Rome" and enter "RICKSTEVES," tel. 06-700-9336, www.througheternity.com, office@througheternity.com, Rob).

The Roman Guy (RS%—enter "ricksteves," ask about electric-assist bike tours, theromanguy.com, Sean Finelli).

Miles & Miles Private Tours, described under "Car & Minibus Tours," below, also offers walking tours (www.milesandmiles.net). They are a great value, especially if a car is used.

Tom Rankin, an American architect, offers thought-provoking architectural walks and educational tours around Italy. They're not cheap, but the small-group seminars are worth it to some for the authentic engagement in local culture (RS%, half-day: €100/person or €400/group, info@tomrankinarchitect.com, www.tomrankinarchitect.com).

Food Tours: While some of the above also offer food-oriented walking tours, I favor the food-tour companies listed on page 403.

Car and Minibus Tours

Miles & Miles Private Tours offers a number of tours, all with good English-speaking Italian driver/guides and fine air-conditioned cars and minibuses. Their basic line-up for groups of up to eight people includes a five-hour "History and Fun" tour (a fine first day by car with a broad overview and a chance to get out when you like, €350), "Squares and Fountains" (three-hour walking tour starting at Piazza Farnese, €250) and day trips from Rome into Umbria including Civita di Bagnoregio (9 hours with hotel pickup, €600). They also provide walking tours, shore excursions (from Civitavecchia and other ports), and unguided long-distance transportation; if traveling with a small group or a family from Rome to Florence, the Amalfi Coast, or elsewhere, consider paying extra for this convenience (RS%—mention Rick Steves when booking direct, then show this book; mobile 331-466-4900, www.milesandmiles.net, info@milesandmiles.net).

ON WHEELS
Hop-On, Hop-Off Bus Tours

Several different agencies run hop-on, hop-off, double-decker bus tours around Rome. These tours make the same 90-minute, eight-stop loop through the traf-fic-congested town center with about four pickups at each stop per hour. Buses provide an easy way to see the city from above the traffic (choose open or with canopy), but you'll likely feel trapped rather than entertained. The lazy recorded narration does little more than identify the sightseeing icons you drive by and misses the opportunity to fill the time with worthwhile information. You can join one (and pay as you board; usually around €20) at any stop; Termini Station and Piazza Venezia are handy hubs.

Car and Driver Service

Autoservizi Monti Concezio, run by gentle, capable, and English-speaking Ezio (pronounced Etz-io), offers private cars or minibuses with driver/guides (car—€40/hour, minibus—€45/hour, 3-hour minimum for city sightseeing, transfers between cities are more expensive, mobile 335-636-5907 or 349-674-5643, info@tourservicemonti.it).

SIGHTS IN ROME

I've clustered Rome's sights into walkable neighborhoods, some quite close together (see map on page 30). Save transit time by grouping your sightseeing according to location. For example, in one great day you can start at the Colosseum, then go to the Forum, then Capitoline Hill, and from there either to the Pantheon or back to the Colosseum (by way of additional ruins along Via dei Fori Imperiali).

When you see a □ in a listing, it means the sight is described in greater detail in one of my self-guided walks or tours. A ∩ means the walk or tour is also available as a free audio tour (via my Rick Steves Audio Europe app—see page 21). Some walks and tours are available in both formats—take your pick. This is why some of Rome's most important sights get the least coverage in this chapter—we'll explore them in greater depth elsewhere in this book.

For general tips on sightseeing, see page 544. Rome's good city-run information website, www.060608.it, lists current opening hours.

To connect some of the most central sights, follow my Heart of Rome Walk (see the next chapter), which takes you from Campo de' Fiori to the Trevi Fountain and Spanish Steps. This walk is most enjoyable in the evening—after the museums have closed, when the evening atmosphere and lit-up fountains show off Rome at its most magical. To join the parade of people strolling down Via del Corso every evening, take my "Dolce Vita Stroll" (see page 82).

Avoiding Free-Entry Crowds: State museums in Italy are free to enter once or twice a month, usually on a Sunday. Free days are actually bad news—they attract crowds. In peak season, I'd check state museum websites in advance and make a point to avoid their free days. For Rome, that means the Colosseum, Roman Forum,

Palatine Hill, Borghese Gallery, National Museum of Rome, Castel Sant'Angelo, Etruscan Museum, and Baths of Caracalla.

Ancient Rome

The core of ancient Rome, where the grandest monuments were built, is between the Colosseum and Capitoline Hill. Among the ancient forums, a few modern sights have popped up. I've listed these sights from south to north, starting with the biggies—the Colosseum and Forum—and continuing up to Capitoline Hill and Piazza Venezia. Between the Capitoline and the river is the former Jewish Ghetto. As a pleasant conclusion to your busy day, consider my relaxing self-guided walk back south along the broad, parklike main drag—Via dei Fori Imperiali—with some enticing detours to nearby sights.

SIGHTS

ANCIENT CORE

▲▲▲Colosseum (Colosseo)

This 2,000-year-old building is the classic example of Roman engineering. Used as a venue for entertaining the masses, this colossal, functional stadium is one of Europe's most recognizable landmarks. Whether you're playing gladiator or simply marveling at the remarkable ancient design and construction, the Colosseum gets a unanimous thumbs-up.

Cost and Hours: €16 combo-ticket covers the Colosseum and the Roman Forum/Palatine Hill and is valid for 24 hours. Buy it online well in advance to get a timed-entry reservation (€2 fee) for the Colosseum. Do not show up without a reserved entry. A Full Experience ticket costs €22, is valid for two consecutive days, and covers the Colosseum, Palatine Hill/Roman Forum, and all the minor sights at these archaeological areas. Open daily 8:30 until one hour before sunset—April-Aug until 19:15, Sept until 19:00, Oct until 18:30, off-season closes as early as 16:30; last entry one hour before closing, audioguide—€5.50, Metro: Colosseo, tel. 06-3996-7700, www.coopculture.it.

 📖 See the Colosseum Tour chapter or 🎧 download my free audio tour.

▲Arch of Constantine

This well-preserved arch, which stands between the Colosseum and the Forum, commemorates a military coup and, more important,

SIGHTS

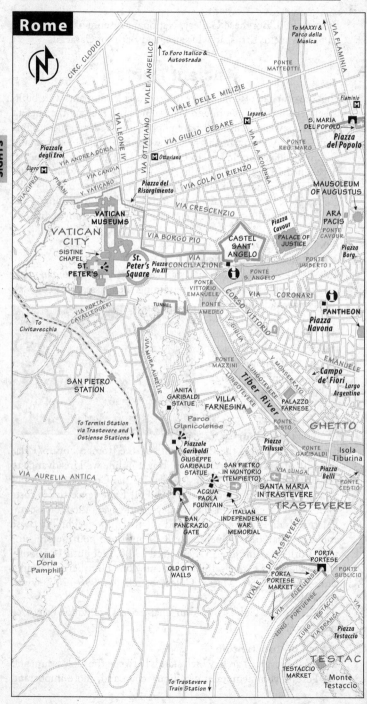

Rome

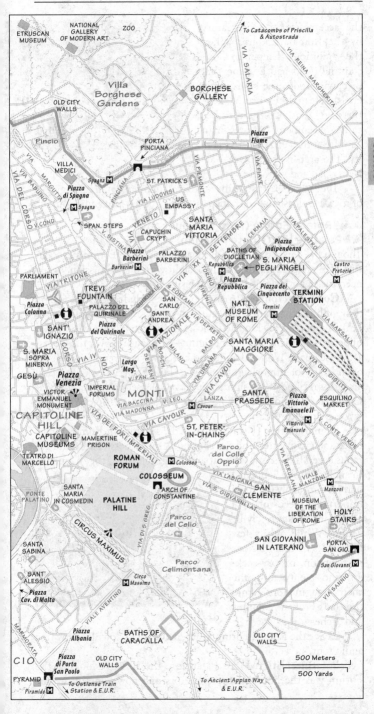

ETRUSCAN MUSEUM

NATIONAL GALLERY OF MODERN ART

ZOO

To Catacombs of Priscilla & Autostrada

VIA SALARIA

VIA REINA MARGHERITA

Villa Borghese Gardens

BORGHESE GALLERY

OLD CITY WALLS

Pincio

Piazza Fiume

VIA PIEMONTE

VIA FLAVE

PORTA PINCIANA

VILLA MEDICI

Spagna

ST. PATRICK'S

VIA LUDOVISI

US EMBASSY

SANTA MARIA VITTORIA

VIA PALESTRO

Piazza di Spagna

Spagna

VIA VENETO

SETTEMBRE

V. CERNAIA

Piazza Indipendenza

Castro Pretorio

SPAN. STEPS

V. SISTINA

CAPUCHIN CRYPT

BATHS OF DIOCLETIAN

S. MARIA DEGLI ANGELI

PARLIAMENT

VIA TRITONE

Piazza Barberini

Barberini

PALAZZO BARBERINI

VIA XX

Repubblica

Piazza Repubblica

Piazza dei Cinquecento

TERMINI STATION

VIA MARSALA

TREVI FOUNTAIN

PALAZZO DEL QUIRINALE

SAN CARLO

VIA 4 FONTANE

FIRENZE

NAT'L MUSEUM OF ROME

Termini

Piazza Colonna

QUIRINALE

SANT ANDREA

VIA NAZIONALE

VIA DEPRETIS

SANT' IGNAZIO

Piazza del Quirinale

V. BOSGHI

MILANO

BALBO

SANTA MARIA MAGGIORE

VIA GIO. GIOLITTI

S. MARIA SOPRA MINERVA

VIA IV

NOV.

Largo Mag.

SERPENTI

VIA URBANA

SANTA PRASSEDE

VIA TURATI

GESÙ

Piazza Venezia

V. PAN.

VIA CAVOUR

Piazza Vittorio Emanuele II

ESQUILINO MARKET

VICTOR EMMANUEL MONUMENT

IMPERIAL FORUMS

MONTI

VIA BACCINA

VIA MADONNA

V. LEO.

LANZA

Cavour

Vittorio Emanuele

V. CONTE VERDE

CAPITOLINE HILL

VIA DEI FORI IMPERIALI

VIA CAVOUR

ST. PETER-IN-CHAINS

CAPITOLINE MUSEUMS

MAMERTINE PRISON

Parco del Colle Oppio

Manzoni

TEATRO DI MARCELLO

ROMAN FORUM

Colosseo

VIA LABICANA

SAN CLEMENTE

VIALE MANZONI

PONTE PALATINO

SANTA MARIA IN COSMEDIN

COLOSSEUM

ARCH OF CONSTANTINE

VIA S. GIOVANNI LAT

MUSEUM OF THE LIBERATION OF ROME

HOLY STAIRS

PALATINE HILL

VIA DI S. GREG.

Parco del Celio

SAN GIOVANNI IN LATERANO

PORTA SAN GIO.

CIRCUS MAXIMUS

San Giovanni

SANTA SABINA

Parco Celimontana

VIA SANNIO

SANT' ALESSIO

Circo Massimo

OLD CITY WALLS

Piazza Cav. di Malta

VIALE AVENTINO

Piazza Albania

BATHS OF CARACALLA

OLD CITY WALLS

CIO

MARMORATA

Piazza di Porta San Paolo

OLD CITY WALLS

500 Meters

500 Yards

PYRAMID

Piramide

To Ostiense Train Station & E.U.R.

To Ancient Appian Way & E.U.R.

the acceptance of Christianity by the Roman Empire. When the ambitious Emperor Constantine (who had a vision that he'd win under the sign of the cross) defeated his rival Maxentius in AD 312, Constantine became sole emperor of the Roman Empire and legalized Christianity. The arch is free to see—always open and viewable.

The Arch of Constantine is covered in more detail on page 172 of my 📖 Colosseum Tour chapter, and 🎧 in my free audio tour.

▲▲▲Roman Forum (Foro Romano) and ▲▲Palatine Hill (Monte Palatino)

Though I've covered them with separate tours, the Forum and Palatine Hill are organized as a single sight with one admission. You'll need to see both sights in a single visit.

Cost and Hours: €16 combo-ticket includes the Colosseum (buy online in advance to secure an entry time for the Colosseum). If you plan to skip the Colosseum, you can buy a €16 Forum Super Pass, which adds minor sights—but doesn't cover the Colosseum (see page 176 for details and check www.parcocolosseo.it for open hours of minor sights). A €22 Full Experience ticket covers Forum Super Pass sights plus the Colosseum. Same hours as Colosseum, audioguide—€5, Metro: Colosseo, tel. 06-3996-7700, www.coopculture.it.

Roman Forum (Foro Romano): This is ancient Rome's birthplace and civic center, and the common ground between Rome's famous seven hills. As just about anything important that happened in ancient Rome happened here, it's arguably the most important piece of real estate in Western civilization. While only a few fragments of that glorious past remain, history seekers find plenty to ignite their imaginations amid the half-broken columns and arches.

📖 See the Roman Forum Tour chapter or 🎧 download my free audio tour.

Palatine Hill (Monte Palatino): The hill overlooking the Forum was the home of the emperors and now contains a mu-

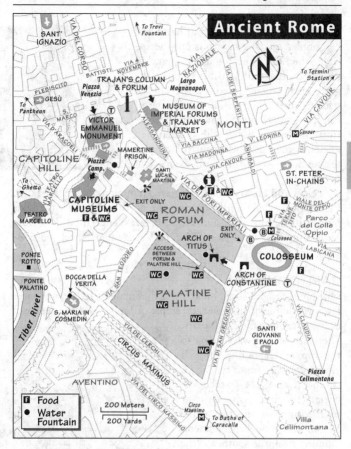

Ancient Rome

Food
Water Fountain

200 Meters
200 Yards

seum, scant (but impressive when understood) remains of imperial palaces, and a view of the Circus Maximus (if it's not blocked by ongoing archaeological work).

📖 See the Palatine Hill Tour chapter.

Bocca della Verità

The legendary "Mouth of Truth" at the Church of Santa Maria in Cosmedin—a few blocks southwest of the other sights listed here—can be crowded, with lots of mindless "selfie-stick" travelers. Stick your hand in the mouth of the gaping stone face in the porch wall. As the legend goes (and was popularized by the 1953 film *Roman Holiday,* starring Gregory Peck and Audrey

Hepburn), if you're a liar, your hand will be gobbled up. The mouth is only accessible when the church gate is open, but it's always (partially) visible through the gate, even when closed. If the church itself is open, step inside to see one of the few unaltered medieval church interiors in Rome. Notice the mismatched ancient columns and beautiful cosmatesque floor—a centuries-old example of recycling.

Cost and Hours: €0.50 suggested donation, daily 9:30-17:50, Piazza Bocca della Verità 18, near the north end of Circus Maximus, a 10-minute walk south from Piazza Venezia, bus #81 from Vatican area or #170 from Termini/Via Nazionale, tel. 06-678-7759.

CAPITOLINE HILL

Of Rome's famous seven hills, this is the smallest, tallest, and most famous—home of the ancient Temple of Jupiter and the center of city government for 2,500 years.

There are several ways to get to the top of Capitoline Hill. If you're coming from the north (from Piazza Venezia), take Michelangelo's impressive stairway to the right of the big, white Victor Emmanuel Monument. Coming from the southeast (the Roman Forum), take the steep staircase near the Arch of Septimius Severus. From near Trajan's Forum along Via dei Fori Imperiali, take the winding road. All three converge at the top, in the square called Campidoglio (kahm-pee-DOHL-yoh).

▲Piazza del Campidoglio

This square atop the hill, once the religious and political center of ancient Rome, is still the home of the city's government. In the 1530s, the pope called on Michelangelo to reestablish this square as a grand center. Michelangelo placed the ancient equestrian statue of Marcus Aurelius as its focal point—very effective. (The original statue is now in the adjacent museum.) The twin buildings on either side are the Capitoline Museums. Behind the replica of the statue is the mayoral palace (Palazzo Senatorio).

Michelangelo intended that people approach the square from

his grand stairway off Piazza Venezia. From the top of the stairway, you see the new Renaissance face of Rome, with its back to the Forum. Michelangelo gave the buildings the "giant order"—huge pilasters make the existing two-story buildings feel one-storied and more harmonious with the new square. Notice how the statues atop these buildings welcome you and then draw you in.

The terraces just downhill (past either side of the mayor's palace) offer grand views of the Forum. To the left of the mayor's palace is a copy of the famous she-wolf statue on a column. Farther down is *il nasone* ("the big nose"), a refreshing water fountain (see photo). Block the spout with your fingers, and water spurts up for drinking. Romans joke that a cheap Roman boy takes his date out for a drink at *il nasone*.

▲▲▲Capitoline Museums (Musei Capitolini)

Some of ancient Rome's most famous statues and art are housed in the two palaces that flank the equestrian statue in the Campidoglio. You'll see the Dying Gaul, the original she-wolf, and the original version of the equestrian statue of Marcus Aurelius. Admission includes access to the underground Tabularium, with its panoramic overlook of the Forum.

Cost and Hours: €15, daily 9:30-19:30, last entry one hour before closing, videoguide—€6, good children's audioguide—€4, tel. 06-0608, www.museicapitolini.org.

📖 See the Capitoline Museums Tour chapter.

▲Mamertine Prison (Carcer Tullianum Museum)

This 2,500-year-old cistern-like prison on Capitoline Hill is where, according to Christian tradition, the Romans imprisoned Saints Peter and Paul. Today it's a small but impressive archeological site using the latest technology to illustrate what you might unearth when digging in Rome: a pagan sacred site, an ancient Roman prison, an early Christian pilgrimage destination, or a medieval church. After learning the context using the included videoguide, and browsing artifacts (including the skeletons of those executed with their hands still tied behind their backs), you can walk to the bottom of this dank cistern under an original Roman stone roof—marvel at its engineering. Amid fat rats and rotting corpses, unfortunate prisoners of the emperor awaited slow deaths here. It's said that a miraculous fountain sprang up inside so Peter could convert

SIGHTS

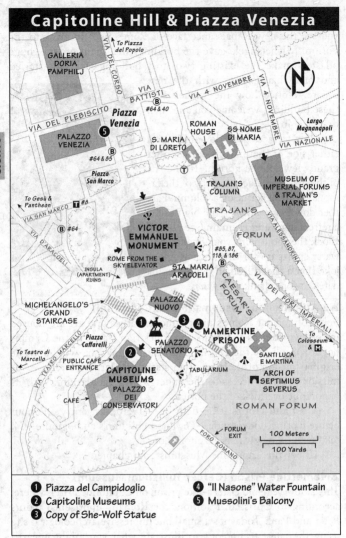

Capitoline Hill & Piazza Venezia

- 1 Piazza del Campidoglio
- 2 Capitoline Museums
- 3 Copy of She-Wolf Statue
- 4 "Il Nasone" Water Fountain
- 5 Mussolini's Balcony

and baptize his jailers, who were also subsequently martyred. This pricey sight is a good value for pilgrims and antiquities wonks.

Cost and Hours: €10, credit cards only, includes videoguide, €20 combo-ticket includes Colosseum and Roman Forum/Palatine Hill, same hours as Colosseum, Clivo Argentario 1, tel. 06-698-961, www.tullianum.org.

Santa Maria in Aracoeli Church

The church atop Capitoline Hill is old and dear to the hearts of Romans. It stands on the site where Emperor Augustus (supposedly) had a premonition of the coming of Mary and Christ standing on an "altar in the sky" *(ara coeli)*.

Cost and Hours: Free, daily 9:00-18:30, Oct-April 9:30-17:30, tel. 06-6976-3839.

Visiting the Church: Climb up the long, steep staircase from street level (the right side of the Victor Emmanuel Monument as you face it).

The church is Rome in a nutshell, where you can time-travel across 2,000 years by standing in one spot. The building dates from Byzantine times (sixth century) and was expanded in the 1200s. Inside, the mismatched columns (red, yellow, striped, fluted) and marble floor are ancient, plundered from many different monuments. The medieval world is evident in the gravestones beneath your feet. The early Renaissance is featured in beautiful frescoes by Pinturicchio (first chapel on the right from the main entrance), with their 3-D perspective and natural landscapes. The coffered ceiling celebrates the Christian victory over the Ottoman Turks (Battle of Lepanto, 1571), with thanks to Mary (in the center of the ceiling). The chandeliers in the nave hint at the elegance of Baroque. Napoleon's occupying troops used the building as a horse stable. But like Rome itself, it survived and retained its splendor.

The church comes alive at Christmastime. Romans hike up to enjoy a manger scene *(presepio)* assembled every year in the second chapel on the left. They stop at the many images of the Virgin (e.g., the statue in the marble gazebo to the left of the altar), who made an appearance to the pagan Augustus so long ago. And, most famously, they venerate a wooden statue of the Baby Jesus (Santo Bambino), displayed in a chapel to the left of the altar (go through the low-profile door and down the hall). Though the original statue was stolen in 1994, the copy continues this longtime Roman tradition. A clear box filled with handwritten prayers sits nearby.

The daunting 125-step staircase up Capitoline Hill to the entrance was once climbed—on their knees—by Roman women who wished for a child. Today, they don't...and Italy has Europe's lowest birthrate.

SIGHTS

Rome Sightseeing Tips

Rome is doing its best to cope with an ever-increasing number of visitors, but especially in peak season you'll encounter lines, crowds, and exasperating changes to ticketing and tour procedures. These tips will help you use your time and money efficiently, making the Eternal City seem less eternal and more entertaining.

Skipping the Colosseum: While it sounds like a sacrilege, a visit to the interior of the Colosseum may not be worth suffering through the mob scene. Half the thrill of the Colosseum is seeing it from outside (free and easy at any time).

Advance Tickets and Reservations: You should buy tickets online to avoid long lines at the Vatican Museums, Colosseum, and Roman Forum. The Borghese Gallery requires reservations in advance (for specifics, see the individual tour chapters).

Forum/Palatine Hill: These two sights share an admission ticket. Unless you buy a Full Experience ticket (see page 161), you must see them together on a single visit (don't exit the Forum and try to reenter at Palatine Hill).

Roma Pass: Until recently, this pass was an exciting option for tourists, as it let you go directly into the Colosseum. As that's no longer the case, the Roma Pass is little more than a glorified two- or three-day transit pass that includes entrance to one or two sights and discounts to others.

Avoiding Crowds: Can't get reservations to the main sights (or just can't stand crowds)? Keep in mind that Rome has many magnificent attractions without the hordes. Try the Palatine Hill,

JEWISH QUARTER

From the 16th through the 19th century, Rome's Jewish population was forced to live in a cramped ghetto at an often-flooded bend of the Tiber River. While the medieval Jewish ghetto is long gone, this area—between Capitoline Hill and the Campo de' Fiori—is still home to Rome's synagogue and fragments of its Jewish heritage.

📖 See the Jewish Ghetto Walk chapter or 🎧 download my free audio tour.

Baths of Caracalla, National Museum of Rome, or Trajan's Market. Even in peak season, you'll often be all alone with the wonders of the ancient world, wondering, "Where is everyone?"

Opening Hours: Rome's sights have notoriously variable hours from season to season. It's smart to check each sight's website in advance. On holidays, expect shorter hours or closures.

Churches: Many churches, which have divine art and free entry, open early (around 7:00-7:30), close for lunch (roughly 12:00-15:30), and close late (about 19:00). Kamikaze tourists maximize their sightseeing hours by visiting churches before 9:00 or late in the day; during the siesta, they see major sights that stay open all day (St. Peter's, Colosseum, Forum, Capitoline Museums, Pantheon, and National Museum of Rome). Dress modestly for churches.

Picnic Discreetly: Public drinking and eating are not allowed at major sights. To avoid a fine, choose an empty piazza or a park for your picnic.

Morning Magic: When I want to reconnect with the city, I walk through the historical center before Rome wakes up. In the early morning, I've never met more than six people at the Trevi Fountain, and Rome shows its calm, majestic face. It's a great way to get energized for the day ahead.

Miscellaneous Tips: I carry a water bottle and refill it at Rome's many public drinking spouts. Because public restrooms are scarce, use WCs at museums, restaurants, and bars.

Synagogue (Sinagoga) and Jewish Museum (Museo Ebraico)

Rome's modern synagogue stands proudly on the spot where the medieval Jewish community was sequestered for more than 300 years. The site of a historic visit by Pope John Paul II, this synagogue features a fine interior and a museum filled with artifacts of Rome's Jewish community. The only way to visit the synagogue—unless you're here for daily prayer service—is with a tour.

Cost and Hours: €11 ticket covers both, includes museum audioguide and guided tour of synagogue; Sun-Thu 10:00-18:00, Fri until 16:00; shorter hours Oct-March, closed Sat year-round and on Jewish holidays; last entry 45 minutes before closing, English tours usually at :15 past the hour, 30 minutes, confirm at ticket counter, modest dress required, on Lungotevere dei Cenci, tel. 06-6840-0661, www.museoebraico.roma.it. Walking tours of the ghetto are conducted at least once a day except Saturday.

PIAZZA VENEZIA

This vast square, dominated by the big, white Victor Emmanuel Monument, is a major transportation hub and the focal point of modern Rome. With your back to the monument (you'll get the best views from the terrace by the guards and eternal flame), look down Via del Corso, the city's axis, surrounded by Rome's classiest shopping district. In the 1930s, Benito Mussolini whipped up Italy's nationalistic fervor from a balcony above the square (it's the less-grand building on the left). He gave 64 speeches from this balcony, including the declaration of war in 1940. This Early Renaissance building (with hints of medieval showing with its crenellated roof line) was the seat of Mussolini's fascist government. Fascist masses filled the square screaming, "Four more years!"—or something like that. Mussolini created the boulevard Via dei Fori Imperiali (to your right, capped by Trajan's Column) to open up views of the Colosseum in the distance. Mussolini lied to his people, mixing fear and patriotism to push his country to the right and embroil the Italians in expensive and regrettable wars. In 1945, they shot Mussolini and hung him from a meat hook in Milan.

With your back still to the monument, circle around the left side. At the back end of the monument, look down into the ditch on your left to see the ruins of an ancient apartment building from the first century AD; part of it was transformed into a tiny church (faded frescoes and bell tower). Rome was built in layers—almost everywhere you go, there's an earlier version beneath your feet.

Continuing on, you reach two staircases leading up Capitoline Hill. One is Michelangelo's grand staircase up to the Campidoglio. The steeper of the two leads to Santa Maria in Aracoeli, a good example of the earliest style of Christian church (described earlier). The contrast between this climb-on-your-knees ramp to God's house and Michelangelo's elegant stairs illustrates the changes Renaissance humanism brought civilization.

From the bottom of Michelangelo's stairs, look right several blocks down the street to see a condominium built upon the surviving ancient pillars and arches of Teatro di Marcello.

▲Victor Emmanuel Monument

This oversized monument to Italy's first king, built to celebrate the 50th anniversary of the country's unification in 1861, was part of Italy's push to overcome the new country's strong regionalism and create a national identity. Today, the monument houses museums and a €10 elevator to a fantastic view. See the map on page 208.

The scale of the monument is over the top: 200 feet high, 500 feet wide. The 43-foot-long statue of the king on his high horse is one of the biggest eques-trian statues in the world. The king's moustache forms an arc five feet long, and a person could sit within the horse's hoof. At the base of this statue, Ita-ly's Tomb of the Unknown Soldier (flanked by Italian flags and armed guards) is

watched over by the goddess Roma (with the gold mosaic back-ground).

Cost and Hours: Monument—free, daily 9:30-18:45, a few WCs scattered throughout; Rome from the Sky elevator—€10, daily until 19:00; ticket office closes 15 minutes earlier, tel. 06-0608; follow *ascensori panoramici* signs inside the Victor Emmanuel Monument (no elevator access from street level).

Background: With its gleaming white sheen (from a recent scrubbing) and enormous scale, the monument provides a vivid sense of what Ancient Rome looked like at its peak—imagine the Forum filled with shiny, grandiose buildings like this one. It's also lathered in symbolism meant to connect the modern city and na-tion with its grand past: The eternal flames are reminiscent of the Vestal Virgins and the ancient flame of Rome. And it's crowned by glorious chariots like those that topped the ancient Arch of Con-stantine.

Locals have a love/hate relationship with this "Altar of the Nation." Many Romans say it's a "punch in the eye" and regret its unfortunate, clumsy location atop precious antiquities. Others con-sider it a reminder of the challenge that followed the creation of the modern nation of Italy: actually creating "Italians."

Visiting the Monument: The "Vittoriano" (as locals call it) is free to the public. You can simply climb the front stairs, or go inside from one of several entrances: midway up the monument through doorways flanking the central statue, on either side at street level, and at the base of the colonnade (two-thirds of the way up). Deeper into the monument, the little-visited **Museum of the Risorgimen-to** contains displays (well-described in English) on the movement and war that led to the unification of Italy (€5, tel. 06-679-3598, www.risorgimento.it; may be closed for renovation). A section on the lower east side hosts **temporary exhibits** of minor works by major artists.

SIGHTS

SIGHTS

Rome at a Glance

▲▲▲**Colosseum** Huge stadium where gladiators fought. **Hours:** Daily 8:30 until one hour before sunset: April-Aug until 19:15, Sept until 19:00, Oct until 18:30, off-season closes as early as 16:30. See page 43.

▲▲▲**Roman Forum** Ancient Rome's main square, with ruins and grand arches. **Hours:** Same hours as Colosseum. See page 46.

▲▲▲**Capitoline Museums** Ancient statues, mosaics, and expansive view of Forum. **Hours:** Daily 9:30-19:30. See page 49.

▲▲▲**Pantheon** The defining domed temple. **Hours:** Mon-Sat 8:30-19:30, Sun 9:00-18:00, holidays 9:00-13:00, closed for Mass Sat at 17:00 and Sun at 10:30. See page 67.

▲▲▲**St. Peter's Basilica** Most impressive church on earth, with Michelangelo's *Pietà* and dome. **Hours:** Church—daily April-Sept 7:00-19:00, Oct-March 7:00-18:30, often closed Wed mornings; dome—daily April-Sept 7:30-19:00, Oct-March 7:30-18:00. See page 71.

▲▲▲**Vatican Museums** Four miles of the finest art of Western civilization, culminating in Michelangelo's glorious Sistine Chapel. **Hours:** Mon-Sat 9:00-18:00. Closed on religious holidays and Sun, except last Sun of the month (open 9:00-14:00). Open Fri night mid-April-Oct by online reservation only. See page 72.

▲▲▲**Borghese Gallery** Bernini sculptures and paintings by Caravaggio, Raphael, and Titian in a Baroque palazzo. Reservations mandatory. **Hours:** Tue-Sun 9:00-19:00, Thu until 21:00, closed Mon. See page 77.

▲▲▲**National Museum of Rome** Greatest collection of Roman sculpture anywhere. **Hours:** Tue-Sun 9:00-19:45, closed Mon. See page 91.

▲▲**Palatine Hill** Ruins of emperors' palaces, Circus Maximus view, and museum. **Hours:** Same hours as Colosseum. See page 46.

▲▲**Trajan's Column, Market, and Forum** Tall column with narrative relief, forum ruins, and museum with entry to Trajan's Market. **Hours:** Forum and column always viewable; museum open daily 9:30-19:30. See page 59.

▲▲**Museo dell'Ara Pacis** Shrine marking the beginning of Rome's Golden Age. **Hours:** Daily 9:30-19:30. See page 87.

▲▲**Dolce Vita Stroll** Evening *passeggiata,* where Romans strut their stuff. **Hours:** Roughly Mon-Sat 17:00-19:00 and Sun afternoons. See page 82.

▲▲**Catacombs** Underground tombs, mainly Christian, some outside the city. **Hours:** Generally 10:00-12:00 & 14:00-17:00. See pages 90 and 122.

▲▲**Church of San Giovanni in Laterano** Grandiose and historic "home church of the popes," with one-of-a-kind Holy Stairs across the street. **Hours:** Daily 7:00-18:30. See page 102.

▲**Mamertine Prison** Ancient prison where Saints Peter and Paul were held. **Hours:** Same hours as Colosseum. See page 49.

▲**Arch of Constantine** Honors the emperor who legalized Christianity. **Hours:** Always viewable. See page 43.

▲**The Roman House at Palazzo Valentini** Remains of an ancient house and bath. **Hours:** Wed-Mon 9:30-18:30, closed Tue. See page 66.

▲**St. Peter-in-Chains** Church with Michelangelo's *Moses.* **Hours:** Daily 8:00-12:30 & 15:00-19:00, Oct-March until 18:00. See page 67.

▲**Piazza del Campidoglio** Square atop Capitoline Hill, designed by Michelangelo, with a museum, grand stairway, and Forum overlooks. **Hours:** Always open. See page 48.

▲**Victor Emmanuel Monument** Gigantic edifice celebrating Italian unity, with Rome from the Sky elevator ride up to 360-degree city view. **Hours:** Monument open daily 9:30-18:45 (shorter in winter), elevator until 19:00. See page 54.

▲**Trevi Fountain** Baroque hot spot into which tourists throw coins to ensure a return trip to Rome. **Hours:** Always flowing. See page 71.

▲**Castel Sant'Angelo** Hadrian's Tomb turned castle, prison, papal refuge, now museum. **Hours:** Daily 9:00-19:30. See page 74.

▲**Baths of Diocletian/Basilica S. Maria degli Angeli** Once ancient Rome's immense public baths, now a Michelangelo church. **Hours:** Daily 7:30-18:30, closes later May-Sept and Sun year-round. See page 91.

Best of all, the monument offers a grand, free **view** of the Eternal City. You can climb the stairs to the midway point for a decent view, or keep climbing to the base of the colonnade for a better view. For the grandest, 360-degree view—even better than from the top of St. Peter's dome—pay to ride the **Rome from the Sky** (Roma dal Cielo) elevator, which zips you to the rooftop. Once on top, you stand on a terrace between the monu-

ment's two chariots. You can look north up Via del Corso to Piazza del Popolo, west to the dome of St. Peter's, and south to the Roman Forum and Colosseum. Helpful panoramic diagrams describe the skyline, with powerful binoculars available for zooming in on particular sights. It's best in late afternoon, when it's beginning to cool off and Rome glows.

THE IMPERIAL FORUMS

Though the original Roman Forum is the main attraction for today's tourists, there are several more ancient forums nearby, known collectively as "The Imperial Forums."

As Rome grew from a village to an empire, it outgrew the Roman Forum. Several energetic emperors built their own forums complete with temples, shopping malls, government buildings, statues, monuments, and piazzas. These new imperial forums were a form of urban planning, with a cohesive design stamped with the emperor's unique personality. Julius Caesar built the first one (46 BC), and over the next 150 years, it was added to by Augustus (2 BC), Vespasian (AD 75), Nerva (AD 97), and Trajan (AD 112).

Today the ruins are out in the open, never crowded, and free to look down on from street level at any time, any day. (With the Forum Super Pass or Full Experience ticket—see page 176—you can access the Forum of Julius Caesar and the Forum of Trajan via a pathway that passes beneath Via dei Fori Imperiali.) The forums stretch in a line along Via dei Fori Imperiali, from Piazza Venezia to the Colosseum. The boulevard was built by the dictator Benito Mussolini in the 1930s—supposedly so he could look out his office window on Piazza Venezia and see the Colosseum, creating a military parade ground and a visual link between the glories of the imperial past with what he thought would be Italy's glorious imperial future. Today, the once-noisy boulevard is a pleasant walk, since it is closed to private vehicles—and, on Sundays, to all traffic.

○ Self-Guided Walk: For an overview of the archaeological area, take this walk from Piazza Venezia down Via dei Fori Impe-

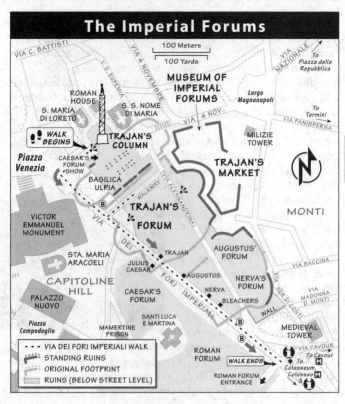

The Imperial Forums

riali to the end of the Imperial Forums. After a busy day of sightseeing, this stroll offers a relaxing way to wind down (while seeing a few more ancient wonders, but without crowds or turnstiles) on your way to Via Cavour, the Monti neighborhood for lunch or dinner, or the nearby Cavour and Colosseo Metro stops.

• Start at Trajan's Column, the colossal pillar that stands alongside Piazza Venezia.

Trajan's Column: The world's grandest column from antiquity (rated ▲▲) anchors the first of the forums we'll see—Trajan's Forum. The 140-foot column is decorated with a spiral relief of 2,500 figures trumpeting the emperor's exploits. It has stood for centuries as a symbol of a truly cosmopolitan civilization. At one point, the ashes of Trajan and his wife were held in the base, and the sun glinted off a polished bronze statue of Trajan at the

top. Since the 1500s, St. Peter has been on top. (Where's the original bronze statue of Trajan? Spaghetti pots.) Built as a stack of 17 marble doughnuts, the column is hollow (note the small window slots) with a spiral staircase inside, leading up to the balcony.

The **relief** unfolds like a scroll, telling the story of Rome's last and greatest foreign conquest, Trajan's defeat of Dacia (modern-day Romania). The staggering haul of gold plundered from the Dacians paid for this forum. The narrative starts at the bottom with a trickle of water that becomes a river and soon picks up boats full of supplies. Then come the soldiers themselves, who spill out from the gates of the city. A river god (bottom band, south side) surfaces to bless the journey. Along the way (second band), they build

roads and forts to sustain the vast enterprise, including (third band, south side) Trajan's half-mile-long bridge over the Danube, the longest for a thousand years. (Find the three tiny crisscross rectangles representing the wooden span.) Trajan himself (fourth band, in military skirt with toga over his arm) mounts a podium to fire up the troops. They hop into a Roman galley ship (fifth band) and head off to fight the valiant Dacians in the middle of a forest (eighth band). Finally, at the very top, the Romans hold a sacrifice to give thanks for the victory, while the captured armor is displayed on the pedestal.

Originally, the entire story was painted in bright colors. If you were to unwind the scroll, it would stretch over two football fields—it's far longer than the frieze around the Parthenon in Athens.

• *Now, start heading toward the Colosseum, walking along the left side of Via dei Fori Imperiali. You're walking alongside...*

Trajan's Forum: The dozen-plus gray columns mark one of the grandest structures in Trajan's Forum—the Basilica Ulpia, the largest law court of its day. Nearby stood two libraries that contained the world's knowledge in Greek and Latin. (The internet of the day, contained in two big buildings.)

Rome peaked under Emperor Trajan (ruled AD 98-117), when the empire stretched from England to the Sahara, from Spain to the Fertile Crescent. A triumphant Trajan returned to Rome with his booty and shook it all over the city. Most was spent on this forum, complete with temples, law courts, and the monumental column trumpeting his exploits. To build his forum, Trajan moved mountains or, more literally, hills. He cut away a ridge that once connected the Quirinal and Capitoline hills, creating this valley.

This was the largest forum ever, and its opulence astounded even jaded Romans. Looking at this, you can only think that for every grand monument here, there was untold hardship and suffering in the Barbarian world.

• *Most astounding of all was Trajan's Market. That's the big, semicircular brick structure nestled into the cutaway curve of Quirinal Hill. If you want a closer look, a pedestrian pathway leads you close to it.*

Trajan's Market: This structure was part shopping mall, part warehouse, and part administration building and/or government offices. For now the con-

ventional wisdom holds that at ground level, the 13 tall (shallow) arches housed shops selling fresh fruit, vegetables, and flowers to people who passed by on the street. The 26 arched windows (above) lit a covered walkway lined with shops that sold wine and olive oil. On the roof (now lined with a metal railing) ran a street that likely held still more shops and offices, making about 150 in all. (The modern wooden sidewalks below are only used after dark for the nightly sound-and-light show—see page 438.)

By now, Rome was a booming city of more than a million people. Shoppers could browse through goods from every corner of Rome's vast empire—exotic fruits from Africa, spices from Asia, and fish-and-chips from Londinium.

Above the semicircle, the upper floors of the complex housed bureaucrats in charge of a crucial element of city life: doling out free grain to unemployed citizens, who lived off the wealth plundered from distant lands. Better to pacify them than risk a riot. Above the offices, at the very top, rises a (leaning) tower added in the Middle Ages.

The market was beautiful and functional, filling the space of the curved hill perfectly and echoing the curved side of the Forum's main courtyard. (The wall of rough volcanic stones on the ground once extended into a semicircle.) Unlike most Roman buildings, the brick facade wasn't covered with plaster or marble. The architect liked the simple contrast between the warm brick and the white stone lining the arches and windows.

To walk around the market complex and see some excavated statues, you can visit the **Museum of the Imperial Forums** (described later; enter just uphill from Trajan's Column).

• *Return to the main street and continue toward the Colosseum for about 100 more yards.*

You're still walking alongside Trajan's Forum. In Trajan's day, you would have entered the forum at the Colosseum end through a triumphal arch and would have been greeted in the main square by a large statue of the soldier-king on a horse.

But none of those things remain. The ruins you see in this section are actually from the medieval era. These are the foundations of the old neighborhood that was built atop the ancient city. In modern times, that neighborhood was cleared out to build the new boulevard.

You'll soon reach a bronze **statue of Trajan** himself. Though the likeness is ancient, this bronze statue is not. It was erected by the dictator Benito Mussolini when he had the modern boulevard built. Notice the date on the pedestal—Anno XI. That would be "the 11th year of the Fascist Renovation of Italy"—i.e., 1933. Imagine Mussolini strolling proudly down this historic boulevard with his fellow fascist leader, Adolf Hitler, in 1938. Anticipating the chance to host Hitler, he made sure all the props were in place enabling him to share stories of Rome's tradition of powerful rulers.

Across the street is a similar statue of **Julius Caesar.** It marks the first of these imperial forums, **Caesar's Forum,** built by Julius in 46 BC as an extension of the Roman Forum. Near Julius stand the three remaining columns of his forum's Temple of Venus—the patron goddess of the Julian family.

• *Continue along (down the left side). If the bleachers are set up for the nightly sound-and-light show, you can take a temporary seat and ponder the view.*

As Trajan's Forum narrows to an end, you reach a statue of Emperor Augustus that indicates...

The Forums of Augustus and Nerva: The statue captures **Emperor Augustus** in his famous hailing-a-cab pose (a copy of the original, which you can see at the Vatican Museums). This is his "commander talking to his people" pose. Behind him was the Forum of Augustus. Find the four white, fluted, Corinthian columns that were part of the forum's centerpiece, the Temple of Mars. The ugly gray stone "firewall" that borders the forum's back end was built for security. It separated fancy "downtown Rome" from the workaday world beyond (today's characteristic and trendy Monti neighborhood) and protected Augustus' temple from city fires that frequently broke out in poor neighborhoods made up of wooden buildings.

Farther along is a statue of **Emperor Nerva,** trying but failing to have the commanding presence of Augustus. (In fact, he seems to be gazing jealously across Via dei Fori Imperiali at the grandeur of the Roman Forum—the Curia and Palatine Hill.) Behind Nerva, you can get a closer look at his forum. As with Augustus' Forum, the big stone wall (composed of volcanic tuff) on the far side was built to protect the "important" part of town from the fire-plagued working-class zone beyond.

Continuing a little farther (toward the Colosseum, above two Corinthian columns), find some fine marble reliefs from Nerva's Forum showing women in pleated robes parading in religious rituals.

• *You've reached the end of the Imperial Forums. You're at the intersection of Via dei Fori Imperiali and busy Via Cavour. From here, you have several options.*

Nearby: Here at the intersection stands an impressive crenellated tower. This was a medieval noble family's fortified residence—a reminder that the fall of Rome left a power vacuum, and with no central authority, it was every warlord with a fortified house and a private army for himself. Behind that (and the firewall) is the colorful neighborhood of Monti (described in the next section; it's home to a slew of fun little eateries).

Two blocks up busy Via Cavour is the Cavour Metro stop. From there, you could turn right to find St. Peter-in-Chains Church (also described in the next section).

Across Via dei Fori Imperiali is an entrance to the Roman Forum; 100 yards farther down Via dei Fori Imperiali (on the left) is a tourist information center with a handy café, info desk, and WC.

• *Our walk is over. Your transportation options include the Cavour and Colosseo Metro stops. Several buses stop along Via dei Fori Imperiali. And it's easy to hail a cab from here.*

NEAR THE IMPERIAL FORUMS

Several worthwhile sights sit north of Via dei Fori Imperiali from the Roman Forum—and offer a break from the crowds. If you'll be here in the evening, consider taking in a sound-and-light show (see page 438).

▲Museum of the Imperial Forums (Museo dei Fori Imperiali)

This museum, housed in buildings from Trajan's Market, features discoveries from the forums built by the different emperors. Although its collection of statues is not impressive compared to Rome's other museums, it's well displayed and, if you really study the descriptions and fine reconstructions, it helps put all these ruins in context. It also allows you to walk outside, atop, and amid the ruins, making this a rare opportunity to get up close to Trajan's Market and Forum (described earlier). Focus on the big picture to mentally resurrect the fabulous forums.

Cost and Hours: €14, daily 9:30-19:30, last entry one hour before closing, tel. 06-0608, www.mercatiditraiano.it. Skip the

Rome vs. Milan: A Classic Squabble

In Italy, the North and South bicker about each other, hurling barbs, quips, and generalizations. All the classic North/South traits can be applied to Milan (the business capital) and Rome (the government and religious capital). Italians like to say that people come to Milan to sin, and they go to Rome to ask for forgiveness.

The Milanesi say the Romans are lazy. Government jobs in Rome come with short hours—made even shorter by multiple coffee breaks, three-hour lunches, chats with colleagues, and phone calls to friends and relatives. Milanesi contend that "Roma *ladrona*" (Rome, the big thief) is a parasite that lives off the taxes of people up North. There's still a strong Milan-based movement promoting secession from the South.

Romans, meanwhile, dismiss the Milanesi as uptight workaholics with nothing else to live for—gray like their foggy city. Romans do admit that in Milan, job opportunities are better and based on merit. And the Milanesi grudgingly concede that the Romans have a gift for enjoying life.

While Rome is more of a family city, Milan is the place for high-powered singles on the career fast track. Milanese yuppies

slow, 1.5-hour videoguide. Enter at Via IV Novembre 94 (up the staircase from Trajan's Column).

Visiting the Museum: Start by simply admiring the main hall—three stories with marble-framed entries, fine brickwork, and high windows to allow natural light—Romans had the technology to make small panes of glass. (Cheapskates can see this much from outside the entrance without paying admission.) A caryatid (a female statue serving as a column) from the Forum of Augustus stands in the museum's entryway, alongside a bearded mask of Giove (Jupiter, the top god). In the room to the right, a bronze foot is all that's left of a larger-than-life *Winged Victory* that adorned Augustus' Temple of Mars the Avenger.

Then explore the statues and broken columns that once decorated the forums. The small rooms facing this main floor have fascinating reconstructions that help us imagine ancient Rome—a city of a million people with the grandiosity of the modern Victor Emmanuel Monument.

Upstairs circling this same main hall, you'll find a section on

mix with each other...not the city's longtime residents. Milan is seen as wary of foreigners and inward-looking, and Rome as fun-loving, tolerant, and friendly. In Milan, bureaucracy (like social services) works logically and efficiently, while in Rome, accomplishing even small chores can be exasperating. Everything in Rome—from finding a babysitter to buying a car—is done through friends.

Milanesi find Romans vulgar. The Roman dialect is considered one of the coarsest in the country. Much as they try, Milanesi just can't say "Damn your dead relatives" quite as effectively as the Romans. Still, Milanesi enjoy Roman comedians and love to imitate the accent.

The Milanesi feel that Rome is dirty and Roman traffic nerve-wracking. But despite the craziness, Rome maintains a genuine village feel. People share family news with their neighborhood grocer. Milan lacks people-friendly piazzas, and entertainment comes at a high price. But in Rome, *la dolce vita* is as close as the nearest square, and a full moon is enjoyed by all.

Julius Caesar's Forum, including baby Cupids (the son of Venus and Mars) carved from the pure white marble that would eventually adorn all of Rome. Your ticket includes any special exhibits, which are often hosted on this floor and generally have an ancient Rome theme.

The rest of the upstairs is dedicated to the Forum of Augustus. A model of the Temple of Mars and some large column fragments give a sense of the complex's enormous scale. You'll see bits and pieces of the hand of the 40-foot statue of Augustus that once stood in his forum. Take a moment to enjoy a close-up look at the practical engineering: brick-rubble arches, marble trim.

At the far end of the Augustus rooms you can go outside to a high perch for a grand overview of the forums. Walkways let you descend to stroll along the curved top of Trajan's Market. You get a sense of how inviting the market must have been in its heyday. The "market" was really a collection of streets, shops, and offices. As you walk around, you'll also enjoy expansive views of Trajan's

Forum, his column, other forums in the distance, and the modern Victor Emmanuel Monument.

Leaving the museum, enjoy a fine view down on a 2,000-year-old street of shops.

▲The Roman House at Palazzo Valentini (Le Domus Romane di Palazzo Valentini)

For a quality (air-conditioned) experience, duck into this underground series of ancient spaces at the base of Trajan's Column. The 1.5-hour tour with good English narration and evocative lighting features scant remains of an elegant ancient Roman house and bath. The highlight is a small theater where you'll learn the entire story depicted by the 2,600 figures that parade around the 650-foot relief carved onto Trajan's Column.

Cost and Hours: €12, daily 9:30-18:30, entrance is on the half-hour, 15 people per departure—reservations smart (€1.50 fee), tel. 06-2276-1280, www.palazzovalentini.it.

▲Monti Neighborhood

Tucked behind the Imperial Forums (between Trajan's Column and the Cavour Metro stop) is a quintessentially Roman district called Monti. During the day, check out Monti's array of funky shops and grab a quick lunch. In the evening, linger over a fine meal. Later at night, the streets froth with happy young drinkers.

One of the oldest corners of Rome, this was the original "suburb" (from *"subura"*—outside the sacred center). Separated from the Imperial Forums by a tall stone firewall (which stands to this day), this was the rough, fire-prone, working-class zone. And it kept that character until just a few years ago when it became trendy. Strolling around here helps visitors understand why the Romans see their hometown not as a sprawling metropolis, but as a collection of villages. Exploring back lanes, you can still find neighbors hanging out on the square and chatting, funky boutiques and fashionable shops sharing narrow streets with hole-in-the-wall hardware shops and *alimentari*, and wisteria-strewn cobbled lanes beckoning photographers. How this charming little bit of village Rome survived, largely undisturbed, just a few steps from some of Italy's most trafficked sights, is a marvel. While well-discovered by now (savvy travelers have been reading about Monti in "hidden Rome" magazine and newspaper articles for years), it's still a great place to peruse.

To explore the Monti, get to its main square, **Piazza della Madonna dei Monti** (three blocks west of the Cavour Metro). To get oriented, face uphill, with the big fountain to your right. That fountain is the neighborhood's meeting point—and after hours, every square inch is thronged with young Romans socializing and drinking. They either buy bottles of wine or beer to go at the little grocery at the top of the square or at a convenience store on nearby Via Cavour.

From this hub, interesting streets branch off in every direction. The characteristic core of the district can be enjoyed by strolling one long street with three names (Via della Madonna dei Monti, which leads from the ancient firewall on the downhill side of the ancient forums, then to the central Piazza Madonna dei Monti, before continuing uphill as Via Leonina and then Via Urbana).

Monti is an ideal place for a quick lunch or early dinner, or for a memorable meal; for recommendations, see page 391. It's also a fine place to shop, with funky and artistic shops lining streets such as Via del Boschetto, Via dei Serpenti, and Via Leonina (see page 430). Night owls will find this a good place to hang out after dark.

▲St. Peter-in-Chains Church (San Pietro in Vincoli)

A church was first built on this spot in the fifth century, to house the chains that once restrained St. Peter. Today's church, restored in the 15th century, is famous for its Michelangelo statue of Moses, intended for the (unfinished) tomb of Pope Julius II. Check out the chains under the high altar, then focus on mighty Moses. (Note this isn't the famous St. Peter's—that's in Vatican City.)

Cost and Hours: Free, daily 8:00-12:30 & 15:00-19:00, Oct-March until 18:00, modest dress required; the church is a 10-minute uphill walk from the Colosseum, or a shorter, simpler walk (but with more steps) from the Cavour Metro stop; tel. 06-9784-4950.

📖 See the St. Peter-in-Chains Tour chapter.

Pantheon Neighborhood

Besides being home to ancient sites and historic churches, the area around the Pantheon is another part of Rome with an urban village feel. Wander narrow streets, sample the many shops and eateries, and gather with the locals in squares marked by bubbling fountains. Just south of the Pantheon is the Jewish quarter, with remnants of Rome's Jewish history and culture.

PANTHEON AND NEARBY

Exploring this area is especially nice in the evening, when restaurants bustle and streets are jammed with foot traffic. For a self-guided walk in this neighborhood from Campo de' Fiori to the Trevi Fountain (and ending at the Spanish Steps), 📖 see the Heart of Rome Walk chapter or 🎧 download my free audio tour.

▲▲▲Pantheon

For the greatest look at the splendor of Rome, antiquity's best-preserved interior is a must. Built two millennia ago, this influential

SIGHTS

Pantheon Neighborhood

domed temple served as the model for Michelangelo's dome of St. Peter's and many others.

Cost and Hours: Free, Mon-Sat 8:30-19:30, Sun 9:00-18:00, holidays 9:00-13:00, audioguide—€6, tel. 06-6830-0230, www.pantheonroma.com.

📖 See the Pantheon Tour chapter or 🎧 download my free audio tour.

▲▲Churches near the Pantheon
For more on the following churches, see the latter half of my Pantheon Tour chapter. Modest dress is recommended.

The **Church of San Luigi dei Francesi** has a magnificent chapel with paintings by Caravaggio (free, daily 9:30-12:30 & 14:30-18:30 except closed Sun morning, between Pantheon and north end of Piazza Navona, www.saintlouis-rome.net). The only Gothic church in Rome is the **Church of Santa Maria sopra Minerva,** with a little-known Michelangelo statue, *Christ Bearing the Cross* (free, Mon-Fri 7:00-19:00, Sat from 10:00, Sun from 8:10; closes midday Sat-Sun; on a little square behind the Pantheon, to the east,

www.santamariasopraminerva.it). The **Church of Sant'Ignazio,**
several blocks east of the Pantheon, is a riot of Baroque illusions
with a false dome (free, Mon-Sat 7:30-19:00, Sun from 9:00, www.
chiesasantignazio.it). A few blocks away, across Corso Vittorio
Emanuele, is the rich and Baroque **Gesù Church,** headquarters
of the Jesuits in Rome (free, daily 7:00-12:30 & 16:00-19:45, interesting daily ceremony at 17:30—see page 152 for details, www.
chiesadelgesu.org).

Two blocks down Corso Vittorio Emanuele from the Gesù
Church, you'll hit **Largo Argentina,** an excavated square about
four blocks south of the Pantheon. Stroll around this square and
look into the excavated pit at some of the oldest ruins in Rome. Julius Caesar was assassinated near here. At the far (west) side of the
square is a cat refuge where volunteers try to find adoptive families for over 100 felines (visitors welcome daily 12:00-18:00, www.
gattidiroma.net).

▲Galleria Doria Pamphilj

This underappreciated art-filled palace lies in the heart of the old
city and boasts absolutely no tourist crowds. It offers a rare chance

to wander through a noble
family's lavish rooms with
the prince who calls this
downtown mansion home.
Well, almost. Through an
audioguide, the prince lovingly narrates his family's
story as you tour the palace
and its world-class art.

Cost and Hours:
€12, includes worthwhile 1.5-hour audioguide, daily 9:00-19:00,
last entry one hour before closing, closed third Wed of month, elegant café, from Piazza Venezia walk 2 blocks up Via del Corso to
#305, tel. 06-679-7323, www.dopart.it/roma.

Visiting the Galleria: A visit here is relaxing, with a chance
to sit on comfortable chairs for a few minutes in each room as the
prince (via his audioguide) tells the story. It begins upstairs in the
grand entrance hall (Salone del Poussin), wallpapered with French
landscapes. In the adjoining throne room, you'll see a portrait of
Pope Innocent X (1574-1655), patriarch of the Pamphilj (pahm-
FEEL-yee) family. His wealth and power flowed to his nephew,
who built the palace—a cozy relationship that inspired the word
"nepotism" (*nepotem* is Latin for "nephew"). The family eventually
married into English nobility, which is why today's prince speaks
the Queen's English. You'll visit the red velvet room, the green
living room, and the mirror-lined ballroom that once hosted music

by resident composers Scarlatti and Handel. Along the way, the prince tells charming family secrets, like when he and his sister were scolded for roller-skating through the palace.

Past the bookshop is the painting collection. (Major works have a number to dial up audioguide information.) Don't miss Velázquez's intense, majestic, ultrarealistic portrait of the family founder, Innocent X. It stands alongside an equally impressive bust of the pope by the father of the Baroque art style, Gian Lorenzo Bernini. Stroll through a mini-Versailles-like hall of mirrors to more paintings. In one impressive room you'll see works by Titian, Raphael, and Caravaggio.

Piazza di Pietra (Piazza of Stone)

This square, between the Pantheon and Via del Corso, is worth walking through to admire the remains of the ancient Temple of Hadrian. One huge wall from the temple survives as the facade of a 17th-century building. The temple was dedicated to the deified emperor responsible for building the Pantheon, nearby. To help you imagine the square in AD 145, look for a model of the temple in a window across the square at #36. In 1696 the city incorporated the remains of the temple into the building of Rome's central customs house. Today the building houses a meeting hall for the nearby national parliament. The holes chipped into the ancient stones could be where the marble facing (which once adorned the temple) was attached. Historians think that Dark Age scavengers dug out the metal pins the Romans used to hold the marble stones in place. Look down over the railing to see ground level—with some original paving stones—from 1,900 years ago. (The piazza is two blocks toward Via del Corso from the Pantheon.)

Welcome to Rome

A small theater has been turned into a modern exhibit offering nothing actually ancient—and that's OK. Start with a series of four high-tech dioramas (Castel Sant'Angelo, Imperial Forums, Forum of Augustus, St. Peter's Basilica) showing cleverly how each monument was built, followed by a 30-minute sweep through Roman history in a small, air-conditioned theater. Attendants fit you with headphones and let you know when the video plays next, so you won't waste any time waiting. The hourlong experience is thoughtful, smart, and fun.

Cost and Hours: €12.50, Mon-Thu 9:00-19:00, Fri-Sun 10:00-21:00, a block east of Piazza Chiesa Nuova on Corso Vittorio Emanuele II at #203, tel. 06-8791-1691, www.welcometo-rome.it.

▲Trevi Fountain

The bubbly Baroque fountain, worth ▲▲ by night, is a minor sight to art scholars...but a major nighttime gathering spot for teens on the make and tourists tossing coins. Those coins are collected daily to feed Rome's poor.

📖 See the Heart of Rome Walk chapter or 🎧 download my free audio tour.

Vatican City and Nearby

Vatican City, the world's smallest country, contains St. Peter's Basilica (with Michelangelo's exquisite *Pietà*) and the Vatican Mu-

seums (with Michelangelo's Sistine Chapel). A helpful **TI** is just to the left of St. Peter's Basilica as you're facing it (Mon-Sat 8:30-18:15, closed Sun, tel. 06-6988-2019, www.vaticanstate. va). The entrances to St. Peter's and the Vatican Museums are a 15-minute walk apart (follow the outside of the Vatican wall,

which links the two sights). The nearest Metro stop—Ottaviano— still involves a 10-minute walk to either sight. For information on Vatican tours, post offices, and the pope's schedule, see page 234.

Modest dress is technically required of men, women, and children throughout Vatican City, even outdoors. The policy is strictly enforced in the Sistine Chapel and at St. Peter's Basilica but is more relaxed elsewhere (though always at the discretion of guards). To avoid problems, cover your shoulders; bring a light jacket or cover-up if you're wearing a tank top. Wear long pants or capris instead of shorts. Skirts or dresses should extend below your knee.

▲▲▲St. Peter's Basilica (Basilica San Pietro)

There is no doubt: This is the richest and grandest church on earth. To call it vast is like calling Einstein smart.

Cost and Hours: Free, daily April-Sept 7:00-19:00, Oct-March 7:00-18:30. The church closes on Wednesday mornings during papal audiences (until roughly 13:00). Masses occur daily throughout the day. Audioguides can be rented near the checkroom (€5 plus ID, for church only, daily 8:30-17:00). The view from

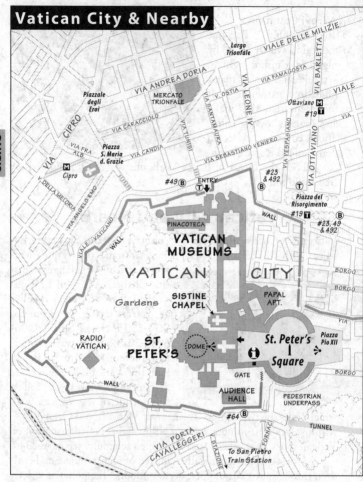

Vatican City & Nearby

the dome is worth the climb (€10 for elevator to roof, then take stairs; €8 to climb stairs all the way, cash only, allow an hour to go up and down, daily April-Sept 7:30-19:00, Oct-March 7:30-18:00, last entry one hour before closing if you take the stairs the whole way). Tel. 06-6988-2019, www.vaticanstate.va.

📖 See the St. Peter's Basilica Tour chapter or 🎧 download my free audio tour.

▲▲▲Vatican Museums (Musei Vaticani)

The four miles of displays in this immense museum complex—from ancient statues to Christian frescoes to modern paintings—culminate in the Raphael Rooms and Michelangelo's glorious Sistine Chapel.

Cost and Hours: €17, €4 online reservation fee, Mon-Sat

SIGHTS

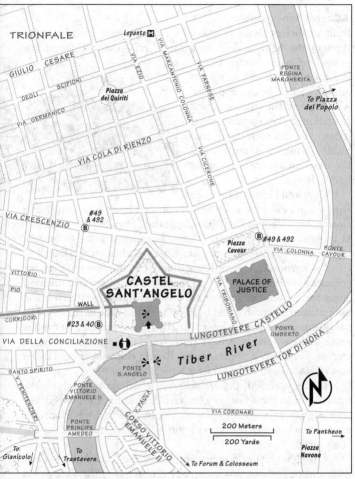

9:00-18:00, last entry at 16:00 (though the official closing time is 18:00, the staff starts ushering you out at 17:30), closed on religious holidays and Sun except last Sun of the month (when it's free, more crowded, and open 9:00-14:00, last entry at 12:30); open Fri nights mid-April-Oct 19:00-23:00 (last entry at 21:30) by online reservation only—check the website. Hours are subject to frequent change and holidays; look online for current times. Lines are extremely long—especially in the morning. Skip the ticket-buying line by buying your ticket with a reserved entry time online in advance. A €8 audioguide is available. Tel. 06-6988-4676, www.museivaticani.va.

📖 See the Vatican Museums Tour chapter. You can also 🎧 download my free Sistine Chapel and Vatican Museums audio tours.

▲Castel Sant'Angelo

Built in ancient times as a tomb for the emperor Hadrian, used through the Middle Ages as a castle, prison, and place of last

refule for popes under attack, and today a museum, this giant pile of ancient bricks is packed with history. The structure itself is striking, the opulent papal rooms are dramatic (and cool inside during the summer), and the views up top are some of the best in Rome.

Cost and Hours: €15, more with special exhibits, daily 9:00-19:30, last entry one hour before closing, near Vatican City, 10-minute walk from St. Peter's Square at Lungotevere Castello 50, Metro: Lepanto or bus #40 or #64, café, tel. 06-681-9111, www.castelsantangelo.beniculturali.it.

Background: Ancient Rome allowed no tombs—not even the emperor's—within its walls. So Emperor Hadrian grabbed the most commanding position just outside the walls and across the river and built a towering tomb (c. AD 139) well within view of the city. His mausoleum was a huge cylinder (210 by 70 feet) topped by a cypress grove and crowned by a huge statue of Hadrian himself riding a chariot. For nearly a hundred years, Roman emperors (from Hadrian to Caracalla, in AD 217) were buried here.

In the year 590, the archangel Michael appeared above the mausoleum to Pope Gregory the Great. Sheathing his sword, the angel signaled the end of a plague. The fortress that was Hadrian's mausoleum eventually became a fortified palace, renamed for the "holy angel."

Castel Sant'Angelo spent centuries of the Dark Ages as a fortress and prison, but was eventually connected to the Vatican via an elevated corridor at the pope's request (1277). Since Rome was repeatedly plundered by invaders, Castel Sant'Angelo was a handy place of last refuge for threatened popes. In anticipation of long sieges, rooms were decorated with papal splendor (you'll see paintings by Carlo Crivelli, Luca Signorelli, and Andrea Mantegna). In 1527, during a sacking of Rome by troops of Charles V of Spain, the pope lived inside the castle for months with his entourage of hundreds (an unimaginable ordeal, considering the food service at the top-floor bar).

Castel Sant'Angelo is famed as the setting of the final act of Puccini's opera *Tosca*, which takes place in 1800 during the struggle between Napoleonic France and the Kingdom of Naples for control of Rome. Napoleon won, and France controlled Rome for the next 14 years.

SIGHTS

Visiting the Castle: A one-way route circulates visitors through the medieval and then the ancient parts of the monument. Just follow the route—you can't get lost. As you enter (before the turnstile) notice the ancient ceremonial entrance with the empty, white travertine niche that once held a "Welcome to my tomb" statue of Hadrian. This is the ceremonial ramp that led to his burial spot, which you'll hike down at the end of your visit.

After the ticket booth, head upstairs to the **rampart** with its four bastions (named for the evangelists: Matthew, Mark, Luke, and John). Then climb a ramp and cross a **bridge** that traverses the sacred chamber in the center. Pause to consider that this space once held the urns containing the ashes of a hundred years of emperors.

Next, you reach a sunny courtyard with a 16th-century statue of St. Michael. Climbing to another rampart, you then pass the little 19th-century **military museum** (interesting for fans of Garibaldi and the Italian unification movement). The café (with WC) comes with dramatic views toward the dome of St. Peter's.

Next, enter medieval rooms built for the pope. The **papal library** was painted by followers of Raphael. Its fine ceiling features grotesque-style figures made trendy in the 16th century after the discovery of Nero's Golden House (his palace near the Colosseum). Next is the pope's **treasury;** imagine the huge armored box containing the loot of the medieval pope. The box—with 13 keys for extra security—was actually built into the room—too big for any invader to ever steal.

Eventually you reach the **rooftop terrace** with the statue of the Archangel Michael sheathing his sword—and one of the best views anywhere of Rome and St. Peter's Basilica. From the safety of this well-protected vantage point, the pope surveyed the city in times of siege. Look down at the bend of the Tiber River—which for 2,700 years has cradled the Eternal City.

Looking toward St. Peter's and the Vatican, find the elevated passage that gave the pope his escape route to this fortress in times of attack. Until the 1930s the real estate between you and St. Peter's was a medieval jumble. Then the dictator Mussolini bulldozed it all to make more stately buildings and the grand boulevard approaching the Vatican that you see today.

Continuing your one-way tour, you come to the **Paolina Room** (named for Pope Paul III), luxuriously painted in the 1540s as an answer to the challenges that Martin Luther and the Reformation posed to the Roman Catholic Church. The throne room and adjacent bedroom, with their exquisite ceilings, were also painted by artists from the school of Raphael.

It's all downhill from here as you descend the **ramp.** Immediately after crossing back over the chamber of emperors' urns, take a right turn. Notice the remains of a 500-year-old elevator built for a fat pope (on the left). Then spiral 400 feet down the original second-century ramp built for Hadrian's burial procession. The passage is tall enough to fit an emperor's urn. While some of the original brickwork and bits of mosaic survive, the marble veneer is long gone (notice holes in the wall that held it in place). At the end of the ramp is an old reconstruction showing the **mausoleum** as it looked in the second century and, on the right, the niche that held a statue of Hadrian.

He's gone (and in a moment you will be, too).

Ponte Sant'Angelo

The bridge leading to Castel Sant'Angelo was built by Hadrian for quick and regal access from downtown to his tomb. The three middle arches are Roman originals and a fine example of the empire's engineering expertise. The statues of angels (each bearing a symbol of the passion of Christ—nail, sponge, shroud, and so on) are Bernini-designed and textbook Baroque. In the Middle Ages, this was the only bridge in the area that connected St. Peter's and the Vatican with downtown Rome. Nearly all pilgrims passed this bridge to and from the church. Its shoulder-high banisters recall a tragedy: During a Jubilee Year festival in 1450, the crowd got so huge that the mob pushed out the original banisters, causing nearly 200 to fall to their deaths.

Today, as through the ages, pilgrims cross the bridge, turn left, and set their sights on the Vatican dome. Around the year 1600, they would have also seen a bunch of heads hanging from

the crenellations of the castle. Ponte Sant'Angelo was infamous as a place for beheadings (banditry in the countryside was rife). Locals said, "There are more heads at Castel Sant'Angelo than there are melons in the market."

North Rome

BORGHESE GARDENS AND NEARBY
▲Villa Borghese Gardens

Rome's somewhat scruffy three-square-mile "Central Park" is great for its quiet shaded paths and for people-watching plenty of

modern-day Romeos and Juliets. The best entrance is at the head of Via Veneto (Metro: Barberini, then 10-minute walk up Via Veneto and through the old Roman wall at Porta Pinciana, or catch a cab to Via Veneto—Porta Pinciana). There you'll find a cluster of buildings with a café, a kiddie arcade, and bike rental (€4/hour). Rent a bike or, for romantics, a pedaled rickshaw (*riscio*, €12/hour). Bikes come with locks to allow you to make sightseeing stops. Follow signs to discover the park's cafés, fountains, statues, lake, and prime picnic spots. Some sights require paid admission, including the Borghese Gallery (see Borghese Gallery Tour chapter), Rome's zoo (see page 423), the National Gallery of Modern Art (which holds 19th-century art; not to be confused with MAXXI, described later), and the Etruscan Museum (described later).

You can also enter the gardens from the top of the Spanish Steps (facing the church, turn left and walk down the road 200 yards beyond Villa Medici, then angle right on the small pathway into the gardens), and from Piazza del Popolo (in the northeast corner of the piazza, stairs lead to the gardens via a terrace with grand views out to St. Peter's Basilica—bikes and Segways can be rented nearby).

▲▲▲Borghese Gallery (Galleria Borghese)

This plush museum, filling a cardinal's mansion in the park, offers one of Europe's most sumptuous art experiences. You'll enjoy a collection of world-class Baroque sculpture, including Bernini's *David* and his excited statue of Apollo chasing Daphne, as well as paintings by Caravaggio, Raphael, Titian, and Rubens. The museum's mandatory reservation system keeps crowds to a manageable size.

Cost and Hours: €15, Tue-Sun 9:00-19:00, Thu until 21:00, closed Mon; free and very crowded once or twice a month when no reservations are taken, usually on a Sun. Check in advance and avoid going on a free day. Reservations are mandatory and easy to get in English online or by phone (€2-4/person booking fee, tel. 06-32810, www.galleriaborghese.it). The further in advance you reserve, the better. Admission times are strictly enforced (you'll get exactly 2 hours inside). Show up late and you won't get in. The 1.5-hour audioguide is excellent.

📖 For more on reservations, as well as a self-guided tour, see the Borghese Gallery Tour chapter.

Etruscan Museum (Museo Nazionale Etrusco di Villa Giulia)

The fascinating Etruscan civilization thrived in Italy around 600 BC, when Rome was an Etruscan town. The Villa Giulia (a once fine, now down-at-heel Renaissance palace in the Villa Borghese Gardens) hosts a museum that tells the story. The displays are clean and bright, with thorough but stilted English descriptions.

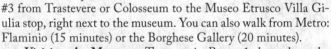

Cost and Hours: €10, Tue-Sun 9:00-20:00, closed Mon, last entry one hour before closing; free to enter once or twice a month, usually on a Sun (check in advance to avoid crowds on free days); Piazzale di Villa Giulia 9, tel. 06-322-6571, www.museoetru.it.

Getting There: Take tram #19 from Ottaviano or Lepanto Metro stations or tram #3 from Trastevere or Colosseum to the Museo Etrusco Villa Giulia stop, right next to the museum. You can also walk from Metro: Flaminio (15 minutes) or the Borghese Gallery (20 minutes).

Visiting the Museum: The map in Room 1 shows how the Etruscans held the area from Rome to Florence (modern-day Tuscany and Umbria) before the rise of Rome. Find the key Etruscan cities (Vulci, Tarquinia, Cerveteri) where the museum's treasures were unearthed. Farther along, a painted, room-sized tomb from Tarquinia (Room 8, down the spiral staircase) shows how Etruscans buried their dead, along with their possessions. Stroll through room after room of cases with vases—pottery painted either red-on-black or black-on-red. The star of the museum's sculptures is the famous "husband and wife sarcophagus" (Il Sarofago degli Sposi, Room 12)—a dead couple seeming to enjoy an everlasting banquet from atop their tomb (sixth century BC from Cerveteri).

Room 13b has a treasure: the Pyrgi Tablets, three gold sheets with inscriptions in both Etruscan and Phoenician. Texts like these have helped scholars decipher the Etruscan language. Sadly, most surviving Etruscan texts are gravestone epitaphs with a limited vocabulary—not very interesting reading. Etruscan isn't related to any other known language and its origin is a mystery.

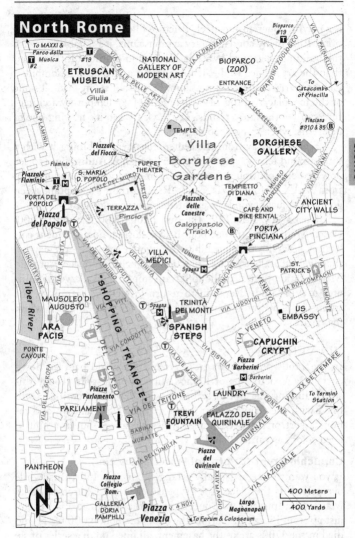

North Rome

To MAXXI & Parco della Musica

#19

ETRUSCAN MUSEUM

Villa Giulia

NATIONAL GALLERY OF MODERN ART

BIOPARCO (ZOO)

ENTRANCE

To Catacombs of Priscilla

TEMPLE

Villa Borghese Gardens

Piazzale del Fiocco

Flaminio

PUPPET THEATER

S. MARIA D. POPOLO

Piazzale Fiammino

#2

TERRAZZA Pincio

Piazzale delle Canestre

Galoppatoio (Track)

BORGHESE GALLERY

TEMPIETTO DI DIANA

CAFÉ AND BIKE RENTAL

ANCIENT CITY WALLS

PORTA PINCIANA

PORTA DEL POPOLO

Piazza del Popolo

Tiber River

PONTE CAVOUR

MAUSOLEO DI AUGUSTO

ARA PACIS

"SHOPPING TRIANGLE"

VILLA MEDICI

Spagna

TUNNEL

St. Patrick's

US EMBASSY

Spagna

TRINITÀ DEI MONTI

SPANISH STEPS

CAPUCHIN CRYPT

Piazza Barberini

Barberini

Piazza Parlamento

PARLIAMENT

LAUNDRY

To Termini Station

Piazza Collegio Rom.

TREVI FOUNTAIN

PALAZZO DEL QUIRINALE

Piazza del Quirinale

PANTHEON

GALLERIA DORIA PAMPHILIJ

Piazza Venezia

Largo Magnanapoli

To Forum & Colosseum

400 Meters

400 Yards

Upstairs on the mezzanine, pass through the long hall of small, mostly bronze objects (statuettes and mirrors). Continuing up to the second floor, ogle gold jewelry that belonged to sophisticated, luxury-loving Etruscans (Room 24). Near the exit, Room 40 displays a well-known terra-cotta statue, the *Apollo of Veio*, which stood atop Apollo's temple. The smiling god welcomes Hercules, while his mother Latona stands nearby cradling baby Apollo.

MAXXI

Rome's "National Museum of Art of the 21st Century," billed as Italy's "first national museum dedicated to contemporary creativity," is a playful concrete and steel structure filled with bizarre installations. Like many contemporary art museums, it's notable more for the building (designed by Zaha Hadid and costing €150 million) than the art inside. To me, it comes off as a second-rate Pompidou Center, Paris' modern art museum. While not to my taste, it's one of the few places in the city where fans of contemporary architecture can see the latest trends. Try to visit when it's hosting one of its events, when trendy people gather.

Since it's away from the center, consider combining it with a walk around fellow "starchitect" Renzo Piano's **Auditorium** to see how the city continues to evolve (15-minute walk to auditorium, from MAXXI follow Via Guido Reni to tram #2 stop and keep going—it's just beyond the elevated road; see page 436).

Cost and Hours: €12, Tue-Sun 11:00-19:00, Sat until 22:00, closed Mon, last entry one hour before closing; no permanent collection, several rotating exhibits throughout the year—preview on their website; take tram #2 (direction: Mancini) from the Flaminio Metro station to the Apollodoro tram stop, then walk west 5 minutes to Via Guido Reni 4a; to return (direction: Flaminio), the tram stop is 50 yards closer to MAXXI, tel. 06-320-1954, www.maxxi.art.

VIA VENETO

In the 1960s, movie stars from around the world paraded down curvy Via Veneto, one of Rome's glitziest nightspots. Today this street, linking the Borghese Gardens to Piazza Barberini, is still lined with the city's poshest hotels and the US Embassy, and retains a sort of faded Champs-Elysées elegance—but any hint of local color has turned bland.

Capuchin Crypt (Cripta dei Frati Cappuccini)

If you want to see artistically arranged bones in Italy, this (while overpriced) is the place. The crypt is below the Church of Santa Maria della Immacolata Concezione on the tree-lined Via Veneto, just up from Piazza Barberini. The bones of about 4,000 friars who died in the 1700s are in the basement, all lined up in a series of six crypts for the delight—or disgust—of the always-wide-eyed visitor.

Cost and Hours: €9, €5 for kids 17 and under, daily 9:00-19:00, modest dress required, Via Veneto 27, Metro: Barberini, tel. 06-8880-3695, www.cappucciniviaveneto.it.

Visiting the Crypt: Before the crypt, a six-room museum covers the history of the Capuchins, a branch of the Franciscan order. You'll see painting after painting of monks with brown robes and tonsure (ring-cut hair). The exhibits, featuring clothing, books, and other religious artifacts used by members of the order, are explained in English, but the only real artistic highlight is *St. Francis in Meditation,* a painting once attributed to Caravaggio (but now thought to be a contemporary copy).

For most travelers, however, the main attraction remains the morbid crypt. You'll begin with the Crypt of the Three Skeletons

(#1). The ceiling is decorated with a skeleton grasping a grim-reaper scythe and scales weighing the "good deeds and the bad deeds so God can judge the soul"—illustrating the Catholic doctrine of earning salvation through good works. The clock with no hands, on the ceiling above the aisle, is a symbol: It means that life goes on forever, once led into the afterlife by Sister Death. The chapel's bony chandelier and the stars and floral motifs made by ribs and vertebrae are particularly inspired. Finally, look down to read the macabre, monastic, thought-provoking message that serves as the moral of the story: "What you are now, we used to be; what we are now, you will be."

In the large Crypt of the Tibia and Fibula (#2), niches are inhabited by Capuchin friars, whose robes gave the name to the brown coffee drink with the frothy white cowl. (Unlike monks, who live apart from society, the Capuchins are friars, who depend on charity and live among the people, and are part of the Franciscan order.) In this chapel we see the Franciscan symbol: the bare arm of Christ and the robed arm of a Franciscan friar embracing the faithful. Above that is a bony crown. And below, in dirt brought from Jerusalem 400 years ago, are 18 graves with simple crosses.

The Crypt of the Hips (#3) is named for the canopy of wavy hipbones with vertebrae bangles over its central altar. Between crypts #3 and #4, look up to see the jaunty skull with a shoulder-blade bowtie.

In the Crypt of the Skulls (#4), look close on the central wall to find the hourglass with wings. Yes, time on earth flies.

The next room (#5) is the boneless chapel. This is part of a church, and the monks sometimes hold somber services here.

In the last room, the Crypt of the Resurrection (#6), with a painting of Jesus bringing Lazarus back to life, sets the theme of your visit: the Christian faith in resurrection.

As you leave (humming "the foot bone's connected to the..."), pick up a few of Rome's most interesting postcards—the proceeds support Capuchin mission work. Head back outside, where it's not just the bright light that provides contrast with the crypt. Within a few steps are the US Embassy, Hard Rock Café, and fancy Via Veneto cafés, filled with the poor and envious keeping an eye out for the rich and famous.

St. Patrick's Church (Chiesa di San Patrisio)

Administered by Paulist priests, St. Patrick's is the home of the American Catholic Church in Rome. The early-20th-century building isn't very historic, but the parish warmly welcomes pilgrims to the city. Mass is held in English daily, and their excellent website contains a list of convents that rent out rooms.

Hours: Mass usually held Mon-Sat at 18:00, Sun at 9:00 and 10:30; Via Boncompagni 31, near the US Embassy, Metro: Barberini—from there, it's a 10- to 15-minute walk (head up Via Veneto and turn right onto Via Boncompagni—see map on page 44); office tel. 06-8881-8727, www.stpatricksamericanrome.org.

NORTH OF THE PANTHEON

These sights are on or within a short walk of the bustling Via del Corso thoroughfare, which connects Piazza del Popolo to the heart of town. The best sight here is a walk through the neighborhood as evening falls—one of my favorite experiences in Rome.

▲▲Dolce Vita Stroll

All over the Mediterranean world, people are out strolling in the early evening in a ritual known in Italy as the *passeggiata* (see the sidebar on page 7). Rome's *passeggiata* is both elegant (with chic people enjoying fancy window shopping in the grid of streets around the Spanish Steps) and a little crude (with young people on the prowl). The major sights along this walk are covered later in this section.

Romans' favorite place for a chic evening stroll is along Via del Corso. Join in as you walk from Piazza del Popolo (Metro: Flaminio) down a wonderfully traffic-free section of Via del Corso, and up Via Condotti to the Spanish Steps. Historians can continue to Capitoline Hill. Although busy at any hour, this area really attracts crowds from around 17:00 to 19:00 each evening (Fri and Sat are best), except on Sunday, when it occurs earlier in the afternoon. Leave before 18:00 if you plan to visit the Ara Pacis (Altar of Peace), which closes at 19:30 (last entry at 18:30).

As you stroll, you'll see shoppers, flirts, and people watchers filling this neighborhood of some of Rome's most fashionable stores (mostly open until 20:00). The most elegance survives in the grid of streets between Via del Corso and the Spanish Steps. For a detailed description of shops in this area, see page 431. If you get hungry during your stroll, see page 406 for listings of neighborhood wine bars and restaurants.

SIGHTS

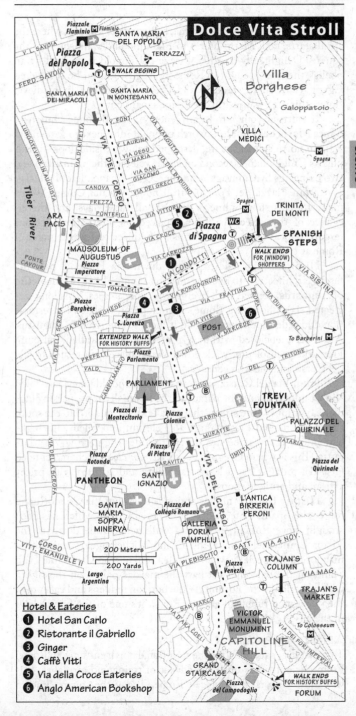

Dolce Vita Stroll

Piazzale Flaminio — Ⓜ Flaminio
SANTA MARIA DEL POPOLO
TERRAZZA
V. L. SAVOIA
Piazza del Popolo
Ⓣ ● **WALK BEGINS**
FERD. SAVOIA
SANTA MARIA DEI MIRACOLI
SANTA MARIA IN MONTESANTO
Villa Borghese
Galoppatoio

VILLA MEDICI
Ⓜ Spagna

FONT
VIA MARGUTTA
V. LAURINA
VIA GESU E MARIA
VIA DEL BABUINO
VIA SAN GIACOMO
VIA DEI GRECI

VIA DI RIPETTA
VIA DEL CORSO

CANOVA
FREZZA
PONTEFICI

Tiber River

ARA PACIS
PONTE CAVOUR

VIA VITTORIA
❷
❺
VIA CROCE
Piazza di Spagna
VIA CARROZZE
❶
VIA CONDOTTI

Spagna Ⓜ
WC

TRINITÀ DEI MONTI
SPANISH STEPS
WALK ENDS FOR (WINDOW) SHOPPERS
Ⓣ
VIA SISTINA

MAUSOLEUM OF AUGUSTUS
Piazza Imperatore

TOMACELLI

Piazza Borghese

VIA DELLA SCROFA
VIA FONT. BORGHESE

❹
Piazza S. Lorenzo
EXTENDED WALK FOR HISTORY BUFFS
Piazza Parlamento
PREFETTI
VALD.
CAMPO MARZIO

❸
VIA BORGOGNONA
VIA FRATTINA
VIA VITE
❻
POST
V. MERCEDE
V. CON.

PROPS.
VIA DUE MACELLI
To Barberini Ⓜ

TRITONE

PARLIAMENT
Piazza di Montecitorio
Piazza Colonna
CHIGI Ⓣ Ⓑ
SABINA
MURATTE
DATARIA

TREVI FOUNTAIN
PALAZZO DEL QUIRINALE
Piazza del Quirinale

VIA DELLA SCROFA
Piazza Rotonda
PANTHEON
SANTA MARIA SOPRA MINERVA

Piazza di Pietra
CARAVITA
SANT' IGNAZIO
Piazza del Collegio Romano
GALLERIA DORIA PAMPHILJ
VIA DEL CORSO

UMILTA

L'ANTICA BIRRERIA PERONI

VIA 4 NOV.

200 Meters
200 Yards

CORSO VITT. EMANUELE II
Largo Argentina

VIA PLEBISCITO
BATT. Ⓑ
Piazza Venezia
SAN MARCO Ⓑ
VIA D'ARA COELI

TRAJAN'S COLUMN
VIA MAG.
TRAJAN'S MARKET

VICTOR EMMANUEL MONUMENT
CAPITOLINE HILL
GRAND STAIRCASE
Piazza del Campidoglio
FORUM
VIA DEI FORI IMPERIALI
To Colosseum Ⓜ
WALK ENDS FOR HISTORY BUFFS

Hotel & Eateries
❶ Hotel San Carlo
❷ Ristorante il Gabriello
❸ Ginger
❹ Caffè Vitti
❺ Via della Croce Eateries
❻ Anglo American Bookshop

◒ Self-Guided Walk: To reach **Piazza del Popolo,** where the stroll starts, take Metro line A to Flaminio and walk south to the square. Delightfully car-free, Piazza del Popolo is marked by an obelisk that was brought to Rome by Augustus after he conquered Egypt. (It used to stand in the Circus Maximus.) In medieval times, this area was just inside Rome's main entry.

If starting your stroll early enough, the Baroque church of **Santa Maria del Popolo** is worth popping into (next to gate in old wall on north side of square, described below). Inside, look for Raphael's Chigi Chapel (second on left as you face the main altar) and two paintings by Caravaggio (in the Cerasi Chapel, left of altar).

From Piazza del Popolo, stroll down **Via del Corso.** While many Italians shop online or at the mall these days, and the elegance of this street has been replaced by international chains targeting local teens, this remains a fine place to feel the pulse of Rome at twilight.

Historians can side-trip right down Via Pontefici past the fascist architecture to see the massive, round-brick **Mausoleum of Augustus,** topped with overgrown cypress trees. This long-neglected sight, honoring Rome's first emperor, is slated for restoration and redevelopment. Beyond it, next to the river, is Augustus' **Ara Pacis,** enclosed within a protective glass-walled museum. From the mausoleum, walk down Via Tomacelli to return to Via del Corso and the 21st century.

From Via del Corso, window shoppers should take a left down **Via Condotti** to join the parade to the **Spanish Steps,** passing big-name boutiques. The streets that parallel Via Condotti to the south (Borgognona and Frattina) are also elegant and filled with high-end shops. A few streets to the north hides the narrow Via Margutta. This is where Gregory Peck's *Roman Holiday* character lived (at #51); today it has a leafy tranquility and is filled with pricey artisan and antique shops.

History Buffs: Another option is to ignore Via Condotti and forget the Spanish Steps. Stay on Via del Corso, which has been straight since Roman times, and walk a half-mile down to the Victor Emmanuel Monument. Climb Michelangelo's stairway to his glorious (especially when floodlit) square atop Capitoline Hill. Stand on the balcony (just past the mayor's palace on the right), which overlooks the Forum. As the horizon reddens and cats prowl the unclaimed rubble of ancient Rome, it's one of the finest views in the city.

▲Piazza del Popolo

This vast oval square marks the traditional north entrance to Rome. From ancient times until the advent of trains and airplanes, this was most visitors' first look at Rome. Today the square, known for its symmetrical design and its art-filled churches, is the starting point for the city's evening *passeggiata* (see my "Dolce Vita Stroll," earlier).

In 1480, Pope Sixtus IV recognized that the ramshackle medieval city was making a miserable first impression on pilgrims who walked here from all over Europe (similar to the Muslim pilgrimage to Mecca). He authorized city planners to appropriate property (establishing "eminent domain"), demolish old buildings, and create straight streets to accommodate traffic. This was the first of several papal campaigns to spruce up the square and make it a suitable entrance for the grand city. The German monk, Martin Luther, would have been impressed when, after walking 700 miles from Germany, he entered the city through this gate (in 1510).

Reach the square via the Flaminio Metro stop, pass through the third-century Aurelian Wall via the Porta del Popolo, and look south. The 10-story **obelisk** in the center of the square once graced the temple of Ramses II in Egypt and the Roman Circus Maximus racetrack. The obelisk was brought here in 1589 as one of the square's beautification projects. (The oval shape dates from the early 19th century.) At the south side of the square, twin **domed churches** mark the spot where three main boulevards exit the square and form a trident. The central boulevard (running between the churches) is Via del Corso, which since ancient times has been the main north-south drag through town, running to Capitoline Hill (the governing center) and the Forum. The road to the right led to the Vatican, and the road to the left led to the big pilgrimage churches of San Giovanni in Laterano and Santa Maria Maggiore. With the help of this *tridente,* pilgrims arriving without a good Rome guidebook knew just where to go. The three churches on Piazza del Popolo are all dedicated to Mary, setting the right tone.

Along the north side of the square (flanking the Porta del Popolo) are two 19th-century buildings that give the square its pleasant symmetry: the Carabinieri station and the Church of Santa Maria del Popolo.

Two large **fountains** grace the sides of the square—Neptune to the west and Roma to the east (marking the base of Pincio Hill; steps lead up to the overlook with fine views to St. Peter's and the rest of the city (a popular place for local Romeos to propose). Though the name Piazza del Popolo means "Square of the People" (and the square is a popular hangout), it probably derives from the poplar trees that once stood here.

Church of Santa Maria del Popolo

One of Rome's most overlooked churches, this features two chapels with top-notch art by Caravaggio and Bernini, and a facade built

of travertine scavenged from the Colosseum. The church is brought to you by the Rovere family, which produced two popes, and you'll see their symbol—the oak tree and acorns—throughout.

Cost and Hours: Free but bring coins to illuminate the art, daily 7:00-12:30 & 16:00-19:00, Fri-Sat open during lunchtime but often partially closed to accommodate its busy schedule of Masses; on north side of Piazza del Popolo—as you face the gate in the old wall from the square, the church entrance is to your right.

Visiting the Church: Go inside and enjoy the big view from the entrance. This Augustianian church is a fine example of Roman Renaissance architecture, exuding harmony, rhythm, and lightness as its arches lope to the front where a few rare Renaissance glass windows shine behind the altar. (Most church windows in Rome are from Baroque times, and are clear.)

Like a mini art-history class, this church exposes you to various periods: art of the 1400s, celebrating realism (in the Della Rovere Chapel); the 1500s, embracing humanism (Chigi Chapel); and the 1600s, getting emotional with Baroque and the Counter-Reformation (Cerasi Chapel).

In the **Della Rovere Chapel** (immediately right of the church entrance), Pinturicchio's *Nativity with St. Jerome* illustrates the groundbreaking mastery of realistic landscape painting typical of the Renaissance. It's a Bible scene, but it's set in 1490 Italy so that parishioners could relate to it. Enjoy the delicate and harmonious scene with a stretch of ancient Rome's brick wall included.

The **Chigi Chapel** (KEE-gee, second on the left from the entrance) was designed by Raphael and inspired (as Raphael was) by the Pantheon. Notice the Pantheon-like dome, pilasters, and capitals. Above in the oculus, God looks in, aided by angels who power the eight known planets. Raphael built the chapel for his wealthy banker friend Agostino Chigi, buried in the pyramid-shaped tomb in the wall to the right of the altar. Later, Chigi's great-grandson hired Bernini to make two of the four statues, and Bernini—in good Baroque style—delivers with theatrics. In one corner, Daniel straddles a lion and raises his praying hands to God for help. Kitty-corner across the chapel, an angel grabs the prophet Habakkuk's hair and tells him to go take some food to poor Daniel in the lion's den.

In the **Cerasi Chapel** (left of the main altar) Carracci's *Assumption of Mary* is pretty, classical, and forgettable. The highlights are the two Caravaggios on either side. Caravaggio's *Conversion of St. Paul* (from 1601) shows the future saint sprawled on his back beside his horse while his servant looks on. The startled Paul is blinded by the harsh light as Jesus' voice asks him, "Why do you persecute me?" In the style of the Counter-Reformation, Paul receives his new faith with open arms. The big butts, dirty feet, harsh foreshortening, and striking angels are all classic, melodramatic Caravaggio.

In the same chapel, Caravaggio's *Crucifixion of St. Peter* is shown as a banal chore; the workers toil like faceless animals. The light and dark are in high contrast. Caravaggio liked to say, "Where light falls, I will paint it."

▲Spanish Steps

The wide, curving staircase, culminating with an obelisk between two Baroque church towers, is one of Rome's iconic sights. But be sure not to sit on them (€250 fine). By day, the area hosts shoppers looking for high-end fashions; on warm evenings, it attracts young people in love with the city. 📖 For more about the steps, see the Heart of Rome Walk chapter or 🎧 download my free audio tour.

Shopping Triangle

The triangular-shaped area between the Spanish Steps, Piazza Venezia, and Piazza del Popolo (along Via del Corso) contains Rome's highest concentration of upscale boutiques and fashion stores. For more, see the Shopping in Rome chapter.

▲▲Museo dell'Ara Pacis (Museum of the Altar of Peace)

On January 30, 9 BC, soon-to-be-emperor Augustus led a procession of priests up the steps and into this newly built "Altar of Peace." They sacrificed an animal on the altar and poured an offering of wine, thanking the gods for helping Augustus pacify barbarians abroad and rivals at home. This marked the dawn of the Pax Romana (c. AD 1-200), a Golden Age of good living, stability, dominance, and peace *(pax)*. The Ara Pacis (AH-rah PAH-chees) hosted annual sacrifices by the emperor until the area was flooded by the Tiber River. For an idea of how high the water could get, find the measure *(idrometro)* scaling the right side of the church closest to the entrance. Buried under silt, it was abandoned and forgotten until the 16th century, when various parts were discovered and excavated. Mussolini gathered the altar's scattered parts and reconstructed them in a building here in 1938.

Today, the Altar of Peace stands in a pavilion designed by American architect Richard Meier (opened 2006). If this modern

building seems striking, perhaps that's because it's about the only entirely new structure permitted in the old center of Rome since Mussolini's day. To see what the altar looked like in its day, consider the virtual reality show—a colorful 3-D reconstruction of the altar.

Cost and Hours: €10.50, more with special exhibits, tightwads can look in through huge windows for free, daily 9:30-19:30, last entry one hour before closing; videoguide—€6; 45-minute virtual reality show—€12, runs daily May-June 20:45-23:30, last show at 22:30, generally Fri-Sat only in other months, reserve online (under "Events"), no kids under age 13; a long block west of Via del Corso on Via di Ara Pacis, on the east bank of the Tiber near Ponte Cavour, Metro: Spagna plus a 10-minute walk down Via dei Condotti; tel. 06-0608, www.arapacis.it.

◐ Self-Guided Tour: Start with the model in the museum's lobby. The Altar of Peace was originally located east of here, along today's Via del Corso. The model shows where it stood in relation to the Mausoleum of Augustus (now next door) and the Pantheon. (The Ara Pacis originally faced west; now it faces east. Be aware that some art-history books and even the Ara Pacis website may describe it using the original—and opposite—orientation.) Nearby, you'll also see a row of emperors' heads, a good film telling the story of the Ara Pacis and its recovery (press the button for English), and other exhibits.

Entrance Side: Approach the Ara Pacis and look through the doorway to see the raised altar. This simple structure has just the basics of a Roman temple: an altar for sacrifices surrounded by cubicle-like walls that enclose a consecrated space. Its well-preserved reliefs celebrate Rome's success. After a sacrifice, the altar was washed, and the blood flowed out drain holes still visible at the base of the walls. Flanking the doorway are (badly damaged) reliefs of Rome's legendary founders—Romulus and Remus (on the left, being suckled by the she-wolf) and bearded Aeneas (right), the mythical hero of Troy and Rome, who's pouring a wine offering and preparing to sacrifice a sow.

Interior: Climb the 10 steps and go inside. From here, the priest would climb the eight altar steps to make sacrifices. The walls of the enclosure are decorated with the kinds of things offered to the gods: animals (see the cow skulls), garlands of fruit, and ceremonial platters to present the offerings. Circle to the left side of the altar to find a relief showing a sacrifice in action. Priests lead the animals to slaughter. They carry swords to do the job, plates and jugs for offering food and wine, and leafy sprigs to dip into the blood and shake around.

Right (North) Side: Head back out and walk around the right side of the structure. This relief probably depicts the parade of dignitaries who consecrated the altar. Just left of center is Augustus, his body sliced in two, vertically, by a missing stone—he's the one with only half a body. Augustus wears the victor's crown of laurel leaves, having just conquered parts of Spain and Gaul. Augustus is followed by a half-dozen bigwigs and priests (with spiked hats) and the man shouldering the sacrificial ax. Next comes Agrippa (wearing the hood of a priest), Augustus' right-hand man in battles against Mark Antony and Cleopatra. Agrippa married Augustus' daughter, Julia—their little son, Gaius, tugs on his dad's toga while turning to look at Livia, Augustus' wife (a few heads farther back). When Agrippa died, Gaius was adopted and named as successor by Augustus. Gaius also died young, making the next in line Tiberius, Livia's son by a first marriage, shown standing next to his mother. Confused? Find these names and other descendants of Julius Caesar on the genealogical chart and the row of busts in the museum lobby.

Before proceeding farther around the altar, look out the window to see the overgrown Mausoleum of Augustus and his family, once capped with a dome of earth, elegant spruces, and statues of the emperor. To the left is an example of Mussolini's fascist architecture—intended to remind Italians of their imperial Roman roots. Note the travertine, brick, low-relief propaganda, stony inscriptions, Roman numerals, and cold rationality. (Locals don't like it.) This area was the Field of Mars, Rome's only neighborhood continuously inhabited since ancient times.

Back Side: The altar's back door is flanked with reliefs celebrating the two things Augustus brought to Rome: peace (goddess Roma as a conquering Amazon, right side) and prosperity (fertility goddess surrounded by children, plants, and animals, left side). For a closer look at details from the various reliefs, see the model back near the museum entrance.

Left (South) Side: Leading the parade of senators is a *lictor*—a ceremonial bodyguard—carrying the *fasces*. This bundle of sticks symbolized how unity brings strength, and it gave us the modern word "fascism." The reliefs feature the first official portrayal of women and children in a public monument.

Beneath the parade, notice the elaborate floral relief that runs all the way around the Ara Pacis. Acanthus tendrils spiral out, forming decorative garlands, intertwining with ivy, laurel, and more. Swans with outstretched wings hide among the patterns. Some 50 plants are blooming in this display of abundance. Imagine the altar as it once was, standing in an open field, painted in bright colors—a mingling of myth, man, and nature.

BEYOND THE ANCIENT WALLS
▲▲Catacombs of Priscilla (Catacombe di Priscilla)
Of the dozens of catacombs honeycombing the area just outside the ancient city walls, only five are open to the public. While most tourists and nearly all tour groups go out to the Appian Way to see the famous catacombs of San Sebastiano and San Callisto, the Catacombs of Priscilla (on the other side of town) are less commercialized and less crowded—they just feel more intimate, as catacombs should.

Cost and Hours: €8, €5 for kids 7-15, free for kids 6 and under, Tue-Sun 9:00-12:00 & 14:00-17:00, closed Mon, closed one random month a year—check website or call first, Via Salaria 430, tel. 06-8620-6272, www.catacombepriscilla.com.

Getting There: The catacombs are on the northeast edge of the city but well-served by direct buses (30 minutes from Termini or 40 minutes from Piazza Venezia) or a €15 taxi ride. From Termini, take bus #92 or #310 from Piazza Cinquecento or Metro B1 (direction: Jonio) to Libia or Sant'Agnese/Annibaliano stop. From Piazza Venezia, along Via del Corso or Via Barberini, take bus #63 or #83. Tell the driver "Piazza Crati" and "kah-tah-KOHM-bay" and you'll be let off near Piazza Crati (at the Nemorense/Crati stop). From there, walk through the little market in Piazza Crati, then down Via di Priscilla (about 5 minutes). The entrance is in the orange building on the left at the top of the hill.

Visiting the Catacombs: The Catacombs of Priscilla likely originated as underground tombs for Christians, who'd meet to worship in the wealthy Christian's home that was on this spot. As poor people couldn't generally afford a nice plot in a cemetery, they would dig graves at a generous person's home... and dig and dig.

At the Catacombs of Priscilla, you enter from a convent

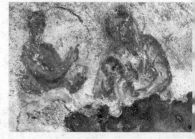

and explore the result of 250 years of tunneling that occurred from the second to the fifth centuries. Visits are by 30-minute guided tour only (English-language tours go whenever a small group gathers—generally every 20 minutes or so). You'll see a few thousand of the 40,000 niches carved here, along with some beautiful frescoes, including what is considered the first depiction of Mary nursing the Baby Jesus.

As in other catacombs, some of the tunnels date from an earlier quarry. Volcanic tuff, the stone ancient Rome was built with, works great for burial niches—it's easy to dig and dries hard when exposed to air.

📖 For more information on catacombs, see the Ancient Appian Way Tour chapter.

East Rome

NEAR TERMINI TRAIN STATION

Most of these sights are within a 10-minute walk of the train station (except for the Baroque Surprises Stroll and art exhibitions, which are a bit farther).

▲▲▲National Museum of Rome
(Museo Nazionale Romano Palazzo Massimo alle Terme)

The National Museum's main branch, at Palazzo Massimo, houses the greatest collection of ancient Roman art anywhere, including busts of emperors and a Roman copy of the Greek Discus Thrower.

Cost and Hours: €10, €12 combo-ticket covers three other branches—all skippable; free and crowded once or twice a month, usually on a Sun—check in advance and avoid going on a free day; open Tue-Sun 9:00-19:45, closed Mon, last entry one hour before closing; audioguide—€5, about 100 yards from Termini station at Largo di Villa Peretti 2, Metro: Repubblica or Termini, tel. 06-3996-7700, www.museonazionaleromano.beniculturali.it.

📖 See the National Museum of Rome Tour chapter.

▲Baths of Diocletian/Church of Santa Maria degli Angeli
(Terme di Diocleziano/Basilica S. Maria degli Angeli)

Of all the marvelous structures built by the Romans, their public baths were arguably the grandest, and the Baths of Diocletian were the granddaddy of them all. Built by Emperor Diocletian around AD 300 and sprawling over 30 acres—roughly five times the size of the Colosseum—these baths could cleanse 3,000 Romans at once. Today, tourists can visit one grand section of the baths, the former main hall. This impressive remnant of the ancient complex was later transformed (with help from Michelangelo) into the Church of Santa Maria degli Angeli.

Visiting when the great organ is played (every Sat at 18:00) is

SIGHTS

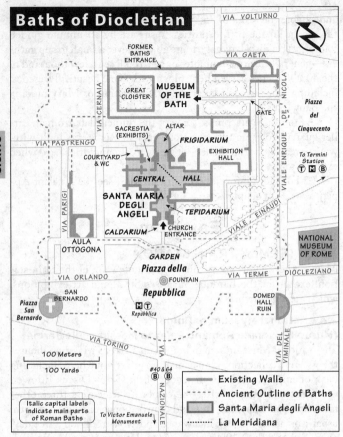

Baths of Diocletian

VIA VOLTURNO

VIA GAETA

FORMER BATHS ENTRANCE

GREAT CLOISTER

MUSEUM OF THE BATH

GATE

VIA CERNAIA

VIALE ENRIQUE DE NICOLA

Piazza del Cinquecento

VIA PASTRENGO

SACRESTIA (EXHIBITS)   ALTAR

FRIGIDARIUM

EXHIBITION HALL

To Termini Station
Ⓣ Ⓜ Ⓑ

COURTYARD & WC

CENTRAL   HALL

SANTA MARIA DEGLI ANGELI

TEPIDARIUM

VIALE E. EINAUDI

VIA PARIGI

CALDARIUM   CHURCH ENTRANCE

AULA OTTOGONA

GARDEN
Piazza della

NATIONAL MUSEUM OF ROME

VIA ORLANDO

Repubblica

FOUNTAIN

VIA TERME   DIOCLEZIANO

Piazza San Bernardo

SAN BERNARDO

Ⓜ Ⓣ
Repubblica

DOMED HALL RUIN

VIA DEL VIMINALE

VIA TORINO

100 Meters
100 Yards

VIA NAZIONALE

#40 & 64
Ⓑ   Ⓑ

Italic capital labels indicate main parts of Roman Baths

To Victor Emanuele Monument

===== Existing Walls
----- Ancient Outline of Baths
▦ Santa Maria degli Angeli
····· La Meridiana

a unique experience. Note that the nearby Museum of the Bath, which requires a separate ticket, has little to do with the Baths of Diocletian—skip it.

Cost and Hours: Free, daily 7:30-18:30, closes slightly later May-Sept and Sun year-round, entrance on Piazza della Repubblica (Metro: Repubblica), www.santamariadegliangeliroma.it.

Background: Large building projects like the baths were political security: They provided employment and fed the masses. Diocletian (ruled AD 285-305) struggled to find a system to rule his unwieldy empire. He broke it into zones ruled by four "tetrarchs." During Diocletian's "tetrarchs" period, architecture and art were grandiose, but almost a caricature of greatness—meant to proclaim to Romans that their city was still the power it had once been.

The baths were one of the last great structures built before Rome's 200-year fall. They functioned until AD 537, when barbarians attacked and the city's aqueducts fell into disuse, plunging Rome into a thousand years of poverty, darkness, and BO.

● **Self-Guided Tour:** Start outside the church. The curved brick facade of today's church was once part of the *caldarium*,

or steam room, of the ancient baths. Romans loved to sweat out last night's indulgences. After entering the main lobby (located where Piazza della Repubblica is today), they'd strip in the locker rooms, then enter the steam room. The *caldarium* had wood-fired furnaces under the raised floors. Stoked by slaves, these furnaces were used to heat the floors and hot tubs. The low ceiling helped keep the room steamy.

Entry Hall: Step into the vast and cool church. This round-domed room with an oculus (open skylight, now with modern stained glass) was once the *tepidarium*—the cooling-off room of the baths, where medium, "tepid" temperatures were maintained. This is where masseuses would rub you down and clean you off with a metal scraper called a *strigil* (Romans mostly used oils, including olive, rather than soap).

Large Transept: Step into the biggest part of the church and stand under the towering vault on the inlaid marble cross. In an-

cient times, from the *tepidarium*, Romans would have continued to this space, the **central hall** of the baths. While the decor around you dates from the 18th century, the structure dates from the fourth century.

This hall retains the grandeur of the ancient baths. It's the size of a football field and seven stories high—once even higher, since the original ancient floor was about 15 feet below its present level. The ceiling's criss-cross arches were an architectural feat unmatched for a thousand years. The eight red granite columns are original, from ancient Rome—stand next to one and feel its five-foot girth. (Only the eight in the transept proper are original. The others are made of plastered-over brick.) In Roman times, this hall was covered with mosaics, marble, and gold, and lined with statues.

From here, Romans could continue (through what is now the apse, near the altar) into an open-air courtyard to take a dip in the

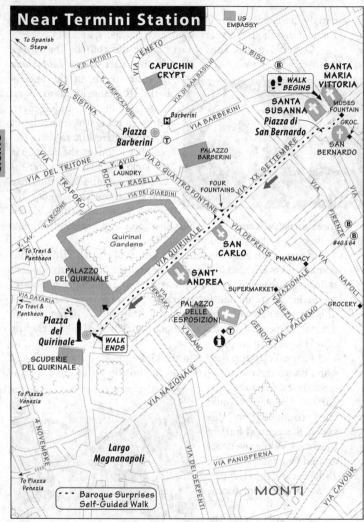

Near Termini Station

- - - Baroque Surprises
      Self-Guided Walk

vast 32,000-square-foot swimming pool (the *frigidarium*) that paralleled this huge hall. Many other rooms, gardens, and courtyards extended beyond what we see here. The huge complex was built in only 10 years (around AD 300)—amazing when you think of the centuries it took to build puny medieval cathedrals, such as Notre-Dame in Paris.

Mentally undress your fellow tourists and churchgoers, and imagine hundreds of naked or toga-clad Romans wrestling, doing jumping jacks, singing in the baths, networking, or just milling about.

The baths were more than washrooms. They were health clubs

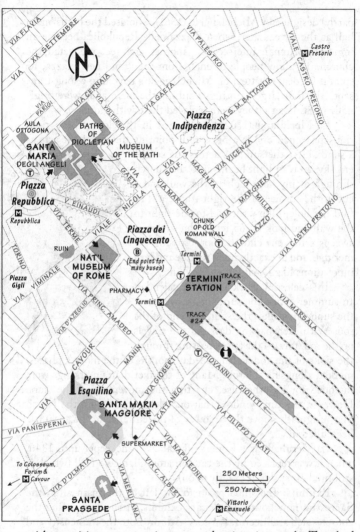

with exercising areas, equipment, and swimming pools. They had gardens for socializing. Libraries, shops, bars, fast-food vendors, pedicurists, depilatories, and brothels catered to every Roman need. Most important, perhaps, the baths offered a spacious, cool-in-summer/warm-in-winter place for Romans to get out of their stuffy apartments and schmooze or simply hang out.

Admission was virtually free, requiring only the smallest coin. Baths were open to men and women—and during Nero's reign, coed bathing was popular—but generally there were either separate rooms or separate entry times. Most Romans went daily.

Michelangelo's Church: The church we see today was (at least

SIGHTS

partly) designed by Michelangelo (1561), who used the baths' main hall as the nave. Later, when Piazza della Repubblica became an important Roman intersection, another architect renovated the church. To allow people to enter from the grand new piazza, he spun it 90 degrees, turning Michelangelo's nave into a long transept. The four large paintings flanking the main altar were originally in St. Peter's (they were replaced there with mosaics).

La Meridiana (1702): Embedded in the floor of the right transept (roped off) is a brass rod, pointing due north. It acts as a sundial. As the sun arcs across the south-ern sky, a ray of light beams into the church through a tiny hole high in the wall and a cut in the cornice of the right transept. (To find the hole, follow the rod to the right to the wall and look up 65 feet.) The sunbeam sweeps across the church floor, crossing the meridian rod at exactly noon (before modern innovations like Daylight Saving Time).

This celestial clock is also a calendar. In summer, when the sun is high overhead, the sunbeam strikes the southern end of the rod. With each passing day, the sun travels up the rod (toward the apse), passing through the signs of the zodiac (the 28-day months of the moon's phases) marked alongside the rod. Many of the meridian's markings were intended for its other use, charting the movement of the stars. However, the tiny window that once let in light from the North Star (originally above the archway of the entrance to the apse) has been filled in.

La Meridiana was Rome's official city timekeeper until 1846, when it was replaced by the cannon atop Gianicolo Hill (which is still fired every day at exactly noon).

Exhibits: The small room to the left of the main altar, the **Sacrestia,** now houses temporary exhibits, often illuminating the church's rich architectural history. Admire both the immensity and height of the ancient Roman brickwork in this room. Step outside into the courtyard and re-create the grand architecture. Notice the *exedra* (semicircular recess in a wall or building)—a motif Romans used for decoration and as a kind of stage for philosophers and orators. See the niches that once housed statues, the rectangular holes that could be used to hold wood-beam scaffolding, and the small pockmarks where iron pegs once secured the marble paneling.

Nearby: In front of the baths, **Piazza della Repubblica** was once a garden at the center of the vast, ancient complex. It was called Piazza Esedra until Italian unification (and is still called that by many Romans). The building wrapping around it is a monumental office block, typical of Italian-unification architecture of the late 19th century. The thundering Via Nazionale starts on the far side at what was an ancient door. Look down it (past the erotic nymphs of the Naiad fountain) to the Victor Emmanuel Monument. The Art Nouveau fountain of the four water nymphs created quite a stir when unveiled in the early 1900s. The nymphs were modeled after a set of twins, who kept coming to visit as late as the 1960s to remind themselves of their nubile youth. Here at the site of the ancient *thermae,* the statues bathe eternally.

▲Church of Santa Maria della Vittoria

This church houses Bernini's best-known statue, the swooning *St. Teresa in Ecstasy.*

Cost and Hours: Free (anyone collecting money at the door is not affiliated with the church), pay €0.50 for light, Mon-Sat 8:30-12:00 & 15:30-18:00, Sun 15:30-18:00, about 5 blocks northwest of Termini train station at Via XX Settembre 17, Metro: Repubblica.

Visiting the Church: Inside the church, you'll find St. Teresa to the left of the altar. Teresa has just been stabbed with God's arrow of fire. Now, the angel pulls it out and watches her reaction. Teresa swoons, her eyes roll up, her hand goes limp, she parts her lips...and moans. The smiling, cherubic angel understands just how she feels. Teresa, a 16th-century Spanish nun, later talked of the "sweetness" of "this intense pain," describing her oneness with God in ecstatic, even erotic, terms.

Bernini, the master of multimedia, pulls out all the stops to make this mystical vision real. Actual sunlight pours through the alabaster windows, and bronze sunbeams shine on a marble angel holding a golden arrow. Teresa leans back on a cloud and her robe ripples from within, charged with her spiritual arousal. Bernini has created a little stage-setting of heaven. And watching from the "theater boxes" on either side are members of the family who commissioned the work.

The church, originally a poor Carmelite church, was slathered with Baroque richness in the 17th century. (It grew popular in modern times for its part in Dan Brown's *Angels and Demons,* something that serious historians scoff at.) At the altar, in the center of the starburst, is an icon of the Virgin Mary, considered miraculous for the military victories attributed to it during the Thirty

Years' War (early 1600s). And, as the 17th century was a time when the Roman Catholic Church was threatened by Protestants, the ceiling shows Mary defeating (Protestant) snakes, who grasp scriptures translated from the pope's Latin into the evil vernacular.

Baroque Surprises Stroll on Via XX Settembre

When Pope Sixtus V developed an ambitious plan to reorganize Rome around key landmarks (c. 1580s), he transformed this formerly sleepy neighborhood near the Baths of Diocletian. Within three generations, it was a major traffic hub and the center of a new city water system. The streets were lined with grand fountains, obelisks, and churches, all decorated in the new style of the 1600s—Baroque.

➔ **Self-Guided Walk:** This half-mile walk starts in Piazza di San Bernardo (near the Church of Santa Maria della Vittoria, with Bernini's famous statue of St. Teresa, described earlier), travels down Via XX Settembre, and ends at the Palazzo del Quirinale, where you can see a distant obelisk (see map on page 94 for route). The churches we'll look at are free to enter; the hours are listed for each one, but keep in mind that they close for an early afternoon break (from 12:00 or 13:00 until 15:30 or 16:00).

• *Start at the wide square known as...*

Piazza di San Bernardo: At the end of the square is the imposing **Fountain of Moses.** After a thousand years of living on well water, the citizens of this neighborhood finally got fresh running water with the opening of this public fountain (1585-1588). It was built by Pope Sixtus V as the end point for a newly restored, 15-mile-long ancient aqueduct. From here, water was distributed to dozens of other nearby fountains. The vast undertaking was celebrated with statues by Domenico Fontana, starring Moses—renowned for miraculously bringing forth water in the desert. Take a look at the fountain's four huge columns, recycled from ancient ruins. Besides being decorative, the fountain was functional, designed to quench the thirst of visiting pilgrims and their horses.

Also on the square is the **Church of Santa Susanna.** You're looking at what was considered the first Baroque facade—see the date: MDCIII (1603). It was designed by Carlo Maderno at the same time he was working on the facade of St. Peter's. As this is Baroque rather than Renaissance, the columns are in higher relief. The structure seems to pop out at you from the center with an energy that enlivens the entire building. The architect added a new Baroque element—curves—seen in the scrollwork "shoulders." We'll see curves in spades later in this walk.

Turn 180 degrees. Opposite the Church of Santa Susanna is the circular **Church of San Bernardo** (built 1598). Why is the church round? Because it was incorporated into one of the corner towers of the Baths of Diocletian. Think of how far away the baths' central hall is (see map on page 94), and appreciate how vast that ancient health club was.

• *Now, with the Fountain of Moses at your back, walk down...*

Via XX Settembre: This is an ancient road. Pope Sixtus knew it as Via Pia, but its name now memorializes a modern military victory—the capture of Rome by Italian nationalists on September 20, 1870. As you walk, you'll pass the local "Pentagon" (the Ministry of Defense, on the left, with the stony bottom and pink top) and other governmental buildings marked by uniforms, tight security, barriers against car bombs, and Italian and European flags.

• *Soon you'll reach the very pedestrian-unfriendly intersection with...*

Via delle Quattro Fontane: This intersection, named for its four fountains, was an important waypoint for 16th-century pilgrims. Imagine poor and haggard wayfarers trudging into town with little money and bereft of a Rick Steves guidebook. They navigated by sighting the obelisks and domes that Sixtus' plan had planted around the city. Entering from the north (as most Northern European visitors did), they'd hike up the hill and pause here to drink from their choice of fountains. They could then either continue straight to the famous pilgrimage church of Santa Maria Maggiore—whose spire is visible to the left—or (spotting the obelisk down the road), head for Palazzo del Quirinale, then the residence of the pope. The intersection's fountains depict river gods relaxing in the shade. They were designed by a familiar name—Domenico Fontana, or Signor "Fountain."

• *Just past the fountain on the left side of the street (best viewed from the right side, to take in the full facade) is the...*

Church of San Carlo alle Quattro Fontane: On the facade, the distinct curves of Baroque have now evolved into undulating waves, rippling the surface of this watershed church. And the medallion on top introduces another Baroque element—the oval.

The church was designed by Francesco Borromini (c. 1640), who had served his apprenticeship at St. Peter's, carving *putti* for his cousin Maderno and building the altar canopy *(baldacchino)* for the famous Bernini. He and Bernini split on bad terms. Now Bernini's competitor, Borromini used this church as a chance to finally go solo and show his stuff.

Step inside (generally Mon-Sat 10:00-13:00, Sun 12:00-13:00, www.sancarlino.eu). The tiny interior is oval-shaped, topped with an oval dome, which is itself topped with a tiny oval lantern.

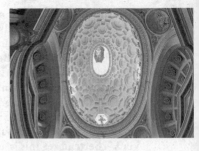

The whole upper story is a riot of wavy lines—ovals, arches, circles—that defy classical notions of symmetry. The dome is coffered with a complex mix of polygons and crosses. The dome seems to float, with no visible support, and is lit by no obvious light source.

The church looks rich. But Borromini's patrons—an order of poor monks—had little money. So the church is small and made of simple materials—brick, concrete, and plaster—but manipulated with lots of 3-D tricks. Borromini's design is brilliant: light, soft, and as if in a cloud. Light, a symbol of God, pours in from the holy dove in the cupola above (which seems higher than it is). Borromini designed everything for the tight space—notice the tidy little confessionals. And the cherubs are ever so huggable.

With this church, Borromini shocked the critics. But over the centuries, it's become classically Roman—locals fondly call it San Carlino. Borromini, who went on to contribute much to Rome's architecture, later became severely depressed and died by suicide when he stabbed himself in the chest.

• *Head one block farther down the street (which is now called Via del Quirinale). On the left is the...*

Church of Sant'Andrea al Quirinale: Often called the "Pearl of the Baroque," this exquisite church sums up the Baroque style (1661). It was designed by the most famous Baroque artist, Gian Lorenzo Bernini, as a chapel for the pope's entourage at the Palazzo del Quirinale. As it was actually used by popes, Bernini had plenty of money for the work—there's lots of marble and gold—but he needed to be pretty conventional. This feels more solid, stable, and classical than the Borromini church.

Inside, the focus is on the altar, dedicated to St. Andrew, or Sant'Andrea (Tue-Sun 9:00-12:00 & 15:00-18:00, closed Mon, www.santandrea.gesuiti.it). Bernini—the master of multimedia—uses every artistic device to tell Andrew's story. The apostle (depicted in the altar painting) is being crucified on his X-shaped cross. He gazes up toward the light. His soul seems to follow the bronze angels above him, up through a light-filled shaft. Then he reappears—now as a marble statue—above the altar. He bursts through the pediment, ascending on a cloud, into the golden light where he joins his fellow saints in the dome of heaven.

Bernini makes all these elements come together. The pink marble columns color-coordinate with the pink frame of the painting. A bronze angel rests his hand on the painting's marble frame.

The delightfully backlit cherubs at the base of the shaft playfully look down on the action. And, the suffused light filtering in from the dome brings all the colors together. Bernini combines sculpture, painting, and architecture into *"un bel composto"*—a beautiful whole.

• *Continue down Via del Quirinale, walking along the loooong extent of the Palazzo del Quirinale (on your right). The building looks somewhat bigger than it is, because the side we're walking along is just a long, skinny building enclosing the formal Quirinale Gardens (for a glimpse of them, peek past the guards when you get to the square). Keep walking toward the main entrance on Piazza di Quirinale.*

SIGHTS

Palazzo del Quirinale: The building (by Maderno and Signor Fountain) dates from 1583, but this site has housed Rome's ruling elite for 2,000 years. Ancient Roman aristocrats, Baroque-era popes, the kings of reunited Italy (after XX Settembre, 1870), and today's presidents of Italy have all resided here—it's like a combination of the White House and Versailles. The

president is elected by parliament and serves a seven-year term with mostly ceremonial duties; Sergio Mattarella, chosen in 2015, is the current office holder. Notice the three flags above the entrance: Europe, Italy, and—if he's currently at home in the palace—the personal flag of the president. The palace is tourable, but only by advance reservation (tours in Italian only, reserve at least five days in advance; www.quirinale.it).

Piazza del Quirinale: The square in front of the palace marks the summit of Quirinal Hill, the highest of Rome's fabled seven hills. The fountain in the middle of the square has colossal statues of horses and men (probably Castor and Pollux, third century); as part of his reordering of the city, Pope Sixtus V had the figures moved here around 1585 from a spot near the Baths of Constantine. The obelisk, which formerly stood in front of the Mausoleum of Augustus, was erected here in the late 1700s. Take in the views—there's a fine vista of St. Peter's Basilica in the distance. From here, a set of stairs (in the direction of the dome) leads down to the Trevi Fountain. The big road continues on to Piazza Venezia.

Art Exhibitions

Two temporary exhibition spaces near Palazzo del Quirinale show top-notch art on a rotating basis. Scuderie del Quirinale typically focuses on the great masters (Titian, Vermeer, Caravaggio), while

Palazzo delle Esposizioni favors contemporary artworks and photography.

Cost and Hours: Typically €12-15 for each, can be more for some exhibits; both open Sun-Thu 10:00-20:00, Fri-Sat 10:00-22:30 except the Palazzo is closed Mon; both may open—and stay open—much later in summer; last entry one hour before closing; Scuderie—Via XXIV Maggio 16, tel. 06-692-0428, www.scuderiequirinale.it; Palazzo—Via Nazionale 194, tel. 06-3996-7500, www.palazzoesposizioni.it.

PILGRIM'S ROME

East of the Colosseum (and south of Termini train station) are several venerable churches that Catholic pilgrims make a point of visiting. Near one of the churches is a small WWII museum.

☐ See the Pilgrim's Rome Tour chapter.

▲▲Church of San Giovanni in Laterano

Built by Constantine, the first Christian emperor, this was Rome's most important church through medieval times. A building alongside the church houses the Holy Stairs (Scala Santa), said to have been walked up by Jesus, which today are ascended by pilgrims on their knees.

Cost and Hours: Church and Holy Stairs—free, cloister—€5, chapel at Holy Stairs—€3.50 (€10 combo-ticket covers cloister, chapel, and audioguide); church open daily 7:00-18:30; Holy Stairs open Mon-Sat 6:30-19:00, Sun 7:00-19:00, Oct-March closes daily at 18:30; Piazza di San Giovanni in Laterano, Metro: San Giovanni, or bus #87; tel. 06-772-6641 (phone answered daily 8:00-13:00), www.vatican.va (search for "San Giovanni in Laterano").

Museum of the Liberation of Rome (Museo Storico della Liberazione)

This small memorial museum, near the Church of San Giovanni in Laterano, is housed in what was the prison wing of the Nazi police headquarters while Rome was occupied during World War II. The descriptions are mostly in Italian but there are information sheets in English in each room. For those interested in resistance movements and the Nazi occupation, it's a stirring visit. You'll see a few artifacts, many photos of heroes, and a couple of cells preserved as they were found on June 4, 1944, when the city was liberated.

Cost and Hours: Free but donations accepted, daily 9:00-19:00, closed Aug, just behind the Holy Stairs, look for the flags at Via Tasso 145; tel. 06-700-3866, www.museoliberazione.it.

SIGHTS

▲Church of Santa Maria Maggiore

Rome's best-surviving mosaics line the nave of this church, built as Rome was falling. The nearby Church of Santa Prassede has still more early mosaics (described in the Pilgrim's Rome Tour chapter).

Cost and Hours: Free, daily 7:00-18:45, Piazza di Santa Maria Maggiore, Metro: Termini or Vittorio Emanuele, tel. 06-6988-6800, www.vatican.va (search for "Santa Maria Maggiore").

▲Church of San Clemente

Besides visiting the church itself, with frescoes by Masolino, you can also descend into the ruins of an earlier church. Descend yet one more level and enter the eerie remains of a pagan temple to Mithras. It's one of the easiest places to fully appreciate the layers of history that lie underfoot in Rome.

Cost and Hours: Upper church—free, lower church—€10, both open Mon-Sat 9:00-12:30 & 15:00-18:00, Sun 12:15-18:00,

Via di San Giovanni in Laterano, Metro: Colosseo or bus #87, tel. 06-774-0021.

Trastevere and Nearby

Trastevere (trahs-TAY-veh-ray) is a colorful neighborhood with a medieval-village feel across *(tras)* the Tiber *(Tevere)* River. The action unwinds to the chime of the church bells. Go there and wander. This is Rome's Left Bank, the place for poets and artists.

This neighborhood was long a working-class area. Now that it's become trendy, high rents have driven out some of the color. Still, it's a great people scene, especially at night. Stroll the back streets (for restaurant recommendations, see the Eating in Rome chapter).

📖 See the Trastevere Walk chapter or 🎧 download my free audio tour.

▲Church of Santa Maria in Trastevere

One of Rome's oldest church sites, a basilica was erected here in the fourth century, when Christianity was legalized. It is said to have been the first church in Rome dedicated to the Virgin Mary. The structure you see today dates mainly from the 12th century. Its portico (covered area just outside the door) is decorated with fascinating fragments of stone—many of them lids from catacomb burial niches—and filled with early Christian symbolism. Out front on Piazza di Santa Maria, an impressive 17th-century fountain stands on the same spot where locals have been drawing water since Roman times.

Cost and Hours: Free, daily 7:30-21:00, Aug 8:00-12:00 & 16:00-21:00.

▲Villa Farnesina

Here's a unique opportunity to see a sumptuous Renaissance villa in Rome decorated with Raphael paintings. It was built in the early 1500s for the richest man in Renaissance Europe, Sienese banker Agostino Chigi. Kings and popes of the day depended on generous loans from Chigi, whose bank had more than 100 branches in places as far-flung as London and Cairo. His villa here in Rome was the meeting place of aristocrats, artists, beautiful women, and philosophers. It's a quick visit (there are only four main rooms).

Architect Baldassare Peruzzi's design—a U-shaped building with wings enfolding what used to be a vast garden—successfully blended architecture and nature in a way that both ancient and Renaissance Romans loved. Orchards and flower beds flowed down in terraces from the palace to the riverbanks. Later construction of modern embankments and avenues robbed the garden

of its grandeur, leaving it with a more melancholy charm. Inside, cavorting gods and goddesses cover the walls and ceilings, most famously Raphael's depiction of the sea nymph Galatea.

Cost and Hours: €10, includes audioguide; Mon-Sat 9:00-14:00, closed Sun except open 9:00-17:00 on second Sun of month; guided visit in English on Sat at 10:00; across the river from Campo de' Fiori, a short walk from Ponte Sisto and a block behind the river at Via della Lungara 230; tel. 06-6802-7268, www.villafarnesina.it.

◆ Self-Guided Tour: Enjoy the best bits of the villa with this commentary.

• *Begin in Room 1.*

Loggia of Galatea: Note the ceiling painted by Peruzzi, showing the position of the signs of the horoscope at the exact moment of

Agostino's birth (21:30, November 29, 1466). The room's claim to fame is Raphael's painting of the nymph Galatea (on the wall by the entrance door). She shuns the doting attention of the ungainly one-eyed giant Polyphemus (to the left, above the door, painted by another artist) and speeds away in the company of her rambunctious entourage on a chariot led by dolphins. She turns back and looks up, amused by the Cyclops' crude love song (which, I believe, was "I Only Have Eye for You"). The trigger-happy cupids and lusty,

entwined fauns and nymphs announce the pagan spirit revived in Renaissance Rome. All the painting's lines of sight (especially the cupids' arrows) point to the center of the work, Galatea's radiant face. Galatea is considered Raphael's vision of female perfection—

not a portrait of an individual woman, but a composite of his many lovers in an idealized vision.

• *Continue into Room 2.*

Loggia of Psyche: This room was painted by Raphael and his assistants. Imagine it without the glass windows, as a continuation of the garden outside, where plays were performed to entertain Agostino's guests. Raphael's two ceiling frescoes were painted to look like tapestries (complete with ruffled edges), suspended from the ceiling by garlands, making the room appear to be an open bower. Sit in the comfy chairs with your back to the garden and view the frescoes from the top. The ceiling shows episodes in the myth of a lovely mortal woman, Psyche, who caught the eye of the winged boy-god Cupid (Eros). See the loving couple at the far-left end, in the center lunette. The big ceiling fresco on the left depicts the gods of Olympus gathered to plan a series of ordeals to test whether Psyche is worthy to marry a god. (Find Hercules with a laurel wreath around his head, white beard, and club—and Dionysius pouring the wine.) The other shows the happy ending, as Cupid (boy with wings) and Psyche stand before Zeus to celebrate their wedding feast, attended by the pantheon of gods.

The whole setting—the room by the gardens, the subject of the frescoes, the fleshy bodies—has an erotic subtext. At the time, Raphael was having a passionate affair with the celebrated Fornarina (the "baker's daughter," who lived down the street). Agostino, noticing that his painter was constantly interrupting his workday to be with her, had the girl kidnapped so that Raphael would finally concentrate. But production slowed even more, as Raphael was depressed. Agostino gave up and had the Fornarina move in with Raphael to keep him company as he happily resumed work in this cheery room. The room's decoration abounds with images both phallic and yonic (the female counterpart). Next to the ripe, split-open cantaloupe (right end, in the garland above wing-footed Mercury), find the erect gourd wearing a condom.

• *Go out the room's main door and upstairs (past a fine WC at mezzanine level) to the…*

Room of the Perspectives: Peruzzi, another trendsetter, painted this room. Walls seem to open onto views and perspectives that correspond with what lies outside. The graffiti (for example, on the wall at the far end) dates from 1527, when Protestant mercenaries sent by Charles V sacked the city and wrote some not very nice things about the Catholic Church.

Agostino had his wedding banquet in this room. His parties were the talk of the town. On one occasion, he invited his guests in the (now lost) dining loggia overlooking the Tiber to toss the gold and silver dishes they had just used into the river. (The banker had nets conveniently placed just below the river's surface.)

The small chamber at the end of the Room of the Perspectives was the **bedroom.** The painting on the wall depicts the consummation of the wedding of Alexander the Great and Roxanne—showing Alexander crowning his bride. Roxanne has the features

of Agostino's bride, and the bed is the same jewel-encrusted ebony bed that received Agostino and his bride here in this room. On the entrance wall, find the three-arched ruins of the Basilica of Constantine in the Forum. The room was painted by Il Sodoma, one of the artists who was replaced by Raphael when he took over the decoration of the papal apartments at the Vatican. Had that not happened, the Raphael Rooms at the Vatican might have looked like this.

Agostino had famous affairs with the most beautiful courtesans of his day. He eventually settled down, but his wild-living descendants didn't, and—in the space of a couple of generations—the Chigi family lost its fabulous fortune.

Gianicolo Hill Viewpoint Hike

From this park atop a hill, the city views are superb, and the walk to the top holds a treat for architecture buffs. (It's easy to follow the route described below on the map on page 349.) Start at Trastevere's Piazza di Santa Maria and go south (to the left as you face the Church of Santa Maria in Trastevere) a couple of blocks through Piazza di San Calisto to Via Luciano Manara. Go right and walk until you come to the fountain at the base of the hill (on Via Goffredo Mameli). Go right, following Via Goffredo Mameli until it intersects with Via Garibaldi. Just to the left of the intersection is access to the ramp and stairs that lead to the Church of San Pietro in Montorio. To the right of the church, in a small courtyard, is the **Tempietto** by Donato Bramante. This "small temple," built to commemorate the martyrdom of St. Peter (once believed to have happened at this spot), is considered a jewel of Italian Renaissance architecture and a prototype for the design of St. Peter's dome.

From the church, go right and continue up Via Garibaldi. You'll see immediately across the street on your left the white fascist arches of the **Italian Independence War Memorial,** commemorating the 1849 battle fought here, when Giuseppe Garibaldi's forces valiantly tried to hold back the invading French army. Atop one side is the inscription *Roma o Morte* (Rome or Death), the battle cry of Garibaldi's troops.

Continuing up, as the road curves, you'll see the monumental Baroque **Acqua Paola** fountain, named after Pope Paul V of the Borghese family (if you've been to the Borghese Gallery, you'll recognize the eagle and dragons from their coat of arms). Like the Trevi Fountain, it commemorates the restoration of an aqueduct that brought water to the city and incorporates columns from the original St. Peter's Basilica. Expansive views of the Roman skyline open up on your right. You can't miss the blocky, gleaming white Victor Emmanuel Monument along with assorted domes that rise above the Roman roofscape (look straight out for the rather nondescript, shallow dome of the Pantheon). The green space beyond the roofline is the Villa Borghese Gardens, and looming in the distance are the Alban Hills (home to Frascati, a town known for its wine production, and Castel Gandolfo, summer residence of the popes).

From here, you have two choices. To return to Trastevere, retrace your steps. But a short climb farther is rewarding. If you were to continue up Via Garibaldi, you'd reach the cube-shaped **Porta San Pancrazio,** an opening in the Aurelian Walls that were extended up this hill in the third century to protect Rome's strategic water mills.

But by now your quad muscles are reminding you that you are climbing a hill—the Janiculum (Gianicolo in Italian) Hill, named after the two-faced Roman god Janus (who also gives name to the month January—looking back to the previous year and forward to the next). Leaving the fountain, cross the street and take a right through the gate with two urns up the tree-lined Passeggiata del Gianicolo and enter the hill-crowning park. You'll soon reach the large **Piazzale Giuseppe Garibaldi,** dominated by the equestrian statue of the swashbuckling military leader of the Italian unification. He enjoys a *magnifico* view of the Eternal City that you can drink in by standing at the railing on the right. A little farther along, look left to find the baby-carrying, gun-wielding, horse-riding statue of Anita Garibaldi, Giuseppe's Brazilian-born partner in battle (and in life). They had four children before her death from malaria during Garibaldi's retreat from Rome in 1849. The nearby **Manfredi Lighthouse** was built as a gift to Rome from Italian immigrants to Argentina.

From here you can follow the road that snakes its way down to the river. Or if your feet are screaming *"Roma o Morte,"* catch any northbound bus (#115 or #870) down to the river. Consider doing this hike in reverse by taking a bus (or taxi) to the top of the hill and then walking steadily downhill to Trastevere.

South Rome

These second-tier but interesting sights are strung along Metro line B, south of the city. For maximum efficiency, use this spine to quickly hop between these sights, using the following Metro stops: Piramide (Testaccio area and trains to Ostia Antica), Garbatella (Montemartini Museum), Basilica San Paolo (St. Paul's Outside the Walls), and E.U.R. Magliana (Palace of the Civilization of Labor). The color map of South Rome at the back of this book gives an overview of this area.

TESTACCIO

In the creative, postindustrial Testaccio neighborhood, you can spend a pleasant hour exploring several fascinating but lesser sights near the Piramide Metro stop, then end with a meal. (This is a quick and easy stop as you return from E.U.R., or when changing trains en route to Ostia Antica.)

In ancient times (when Rome was the first city on earth to reach a population of one million), wharves lined the banks of the Tiber River here. Back then, 90 percent of the city's food came through this area. More recently, the neighborhood was known for a huge slaughterhouse that opened in the late 19th century. Now the formerly abandoned complex is being redeveloped. Meat hooks and cattle pens have yielded to a branch of Rome's contemporary art museum (MACRO), temporary exhibition space, classrooms from a nearby university, and a weekend farmers and craft market.

Long a working-class neighborhood, Testaccio has gone trendy-bohemian. Visitors wander through an awkward mix of hipster and proletarian worlds, not noticing—but perhaps sensing—the "Keep Testaccio for the Testaccians" graffiti.

Romans come to Testaccio to enjoy its numerous tasty eateries. Thanks to its history as the neighborhood of slaughterhouses, Testaccio (more so than elsewhere in Rome) is home to restaurants that are renowned for their ability to cook up the least palatable parts of the animals...the *quinto quarto* ("fifth quarter"): tripe (stomach), lungs, brains, sweetbreads (organs), tail, and so on. While adventurous foodies (who call this "nose-to-tail" eating) seek out these dishes—and you'll find them at most restaurants here—every place also has plenty of offerings that are anything but offal.

You can pick and choose among the Testaccio sights described here or link them as a walk, using the map in this section to follow along. A late morning visit works well, ending with lunch at Testaccio's covered market or nearby restaurants. Note that the neighborhood is quiet, and many restaurants are closed on Sunday.

Testaccio can be reached by taking the Metro to Piramide, or

SIGHTS

Testaccio

Tiber River

To Trastevere

To Tiber

Eateries
1 Agustarello & Trapizzino
2 Flavio al Velavevodetto
3 Pizzeria Remo
4 Volpetti Taverna & Salumeria
5 Perilli
6 L'Oasi della Birra
7 To Eataly

S. MARIA LIBERATRICE

Piazza Testaccio

To Central Rome & Termini Station

Viale Manlio Gelsomini

Parco della Resistenza dell'8 Sett.

POST

PORTA SAN PAOLO & MUSEUM

OLD CITY WALLS

PYRAMID

WALK BEGINS

TESTACCIO MARKET

WALK ENDS

POTTERY SHARDS VIEWPOINTS

Monte Testaccio

TESTACCIO

CEMETERY ENTRANCE

KEATS

CAT HOSPITAL

Protestant Cemetery

SHELLEY

Piazzale Ostiense

Piramide

UNDERGROUND MOVING SIDEWALK

V. MARCO POLO

MACRO MUSEUM (FORMER STOCK- YARDS)

British Military Cemetery

#23 & 769

PORTA SAN PAOLO STATION (TRAINS TO OSTIA ANTICA)

Piazzale dei Partigiani

OLD CITY WALLS

PEDESTRIAN OVERPASS

OSTIENSE TRAIN STN.

To 7

STAZIONE OSTIENSE

200 Meters
200 Yards

To Montemartini Museum & St. Paul's Outside the Walls

by bus (#23 or #280 from Trastevere or the Vatican area; #83 from Piazza Venezia).

• *From the Metro station exit, look straight across the busy intersection to find the giant pyramid and the adjacent brick fortress. For a closer look at these, carefully cross the several busy lanes of traffic and head for the gap between these two landmarks.*

Pyramid of Gaius Cestius

In the first century BC, the Roman occupation of Egypt brought exotic Pharaonic styles into vogue. Stoking the fascination with Egypt even further was the love affair of Mark Antony and Cleopatra; this power couple was the ancient equivalent of Brangelina (Cleopantony?). A rich Roman magistrate, Gaius Cestius, had this pyramid built

as his tomb, complete with a burial chamber inside. Made of brick covered in marble, the 90-foot structure was completed in just 330 days (as stated in its Latin inscription). While smaller than actual Egyptian pyramids, its proportions are correct. It was later incorporated into the Aurelian Wall (explained next), and it now stands as a marker to the entrance of Testaccio. The most dramatic views of the pyramid are from inside the Protestant Cemetery (described later), on the other side of the wall.

• *Across the narrow street from the pyramid is the...*

Porta San Paolo and Museo della Via Ostiense

This formidable gate is from the Aurelian Wall, begun in the third century under Emperor Aurelian. The wall, which encircled the city, was 12 miles long and averaged about 26 feet high, with 14 main gates and 380 72-foot-tall towers. Most of what you'll see today is circa AD 400, but the barbarians reconstructed the gate later, in the sixth century.

Inside the gate is a tiny free museum, the Museo della Via Ostiense (find entrance near pyramid; Tue-Sun 9:00-13:00, closed Mon, tel. 06-574-3193). The museum offers a chance to explore the gate and a few models of Rome's ancient port, Ostia Antica; its neighbor, Porto, with its famed hexagonal harbor; and the Ostian Way, the straight Roman road that paralleled the curvy Tiber for 15 miles from Rome to the sea.

For more on the Aurelian Wall, visit the Porta San Sebastiano and Museum of the Walls (see the end of the 🕮 Ancient Appian Way Tour chapter). For more on Ostia Antica, see the 🕮 Ostia Antica chapter or 🎧 download my free audio tour.

• *Go through the gap between the pyramid and the gate on Via Raffaele Persichetti/Via Marmorata. On your right, notice the beige travertine **post office** from 1932. This is textbook Mussolini-era fascist architecture; the huge X theme in the window design celebrates the 10th anniversary of the dictator's reign.*

Take the first left, on sleepy Via Caio Cestio, and walk about 100 yards, looking on the left for the gate of the...

Protestant Cemetery

Lush and lovingly cared for, the Cemetery for the Burial of Non-Catholic Foreigners (Cimitero Acattolico per gli Stranieri al Testaccio) is a tomb-filled "park," running along the wall just beyond the pyramid. The cemetery is also the only English-style landscape (rolling hills, calculated vistas) in Rome, making it a favorite spot for a quiet stroll.

Cost and Hours: €3 suggested donation—leave in box by entrance, Mon-Sat 9:00-17:00, Sun until 13:00, WC inside, staff at info office can help you find specific graves, tel. 06-574-1900, www.cemeteryrome.it.

SIGHTS

Keats and Shelley on Mortality

Ponder mortality along with Keats and Shelley, with these excerpts from their poetry:

From Keats' "Ode to a Nightingale"

Adieu! adieu! thy plaintive anthem fades
Past the near meadows, over the still stream,
Up the hill-side; and now 'tis buried deep
In the next valley-glades:
Was it a vision, or a waking dream?
Fled is that music:—Do I wake or sleep?

From Shelley's "Adonais: An Elegy on the Death of John Keats"

I weep for Adonais—he is dead!
Oh, weep for Adonais! though our tears
Thaw not the frost which binds so dear a head!
...I am borne darkly, fearfully, afar;
Whilst, burning through the inmost veil of Heaven,
The soul of Adonais, like a star,
Beacons from the abode where the Eternal are.

Visiting the Cemetery: Originally, none of the Protestant epitaphs were allowed to mention heaven. Signs direct visitors to the graves of notable non-Catholics who have died in Rome since 1716. Many of the buried were diplomats. And many, such as the poets Percy Bysshe Shelley (1792-1822) and John Keats (1795-1821), were from the Romantic Age. They came to Italy on the Grand Tour and—"captivated by the fatal charms of Rome," as Shelley wrote—never left.

Shelley's tomb is straight ahead from the entrance, up the hill and a bit to the left, at the base of the stubby tower. It's a big, inscribed, flat slab in the ground. Like so many Romantic Age artists and writers, Shelley was enamored with Rome. In 1821 he wrote, "Go thou to Rome,—at once the Paradise, the grave, the city, and the wilderness" (from *Adonais*, his elegy on Keats' death).

Back at the entrance, with your back to the gate, head 90 degrees left to find **Keats' tomb,** near the fence in the far corner of the big park facing the pyramid. Keats died in his twenties, unrecognized. He wanted to be unnamed on a tomb that read, "Young English Poet, 1821. Here lies one whose name was writ in water." (To see Keats' tomb when the cemetery is closed, look through the

tiny peephole on Via Caio Cestio, 10 yards off Via Marmorata.)

There are cats everywhere. At the big park overlooking the pyramid, look down and to the right to find Matilde Talli's cat hospital (daily 14:00-16:00, www. igattidellapiramide.it). Volunteers use donations to care for these "Guardians of the Departed" who "provide loyal companionship to these dead."

• *Exit the cemetery through the main gate and turn left, continuing down Via Caio Cestio. Cross the wide street and head down into the sunken area ringing...*

SIGHTS

Monte Testaccio

This "hill," actually a 115-foot-tall ancient trash pile, is made of *testae*—broken shards of earthenware jars mostly used to haul oil 2,000 years ago, when this was a gritty port warehouse district. For 500 years, rancid oil vessels were discarded here. Slowly, Rome's lowly eighth hill was built. Because the caves dug into the hill are naturally air-conditioned, trendy bars, clubs, and restaurants compete with gritty car-repair places for a spot. Testaccio is one of Rome's most popular nightlife spots and, in the summer, the area around here houses Testaccio Village, a festival with concerts and techno raves.

Loop around the left side of the hill until you reach the old slaughterhouse complex. Linger here to pick out the history of this spot—the ornamentation of the building itself, the *frigorifero* (ice house adjacent), and the fine view of the shard mountain.

Within Rome, Testaccio's restaurants are known for serving menus heavy on offal—innards and other "unwanted" parts of the animals that were processed here (tripe, sweetbreads, oxtail, lungs, and so on). While the "nose to tail" foodie aesthetic has become trendy, Testaccio embraced that approach long before it was cool.

• *Circling the rest of the way around Monte Testaccio, you'll run right into the main entrance of the former stockyards and, across the street, the very modern-looking...*

Testaccio Market (Mercato di Testaccio)

The covered and colorful market is typically Italian and a focal point of the neighborhood. Locals nurture close relationships with the merchants who sell them their favorite foods. There are several cafés as well as clothing and housewares sections (open Mon-Sat until 14:00, closed Sun, WC on the north side, near the clothing stalls). Find the center (seating in a good courtyard, where the sky opens up) and look down at the ancient Roman road littered with the shards of broken amphorae.

For tips on where to eat within the market and the surrounding neighborhood, see page 413. For a better understanding of what Testaccio is all about, consider Eating Italy Food Tours' interesting, food-oriented walk (see page 403).

SOUTH OF TESTACCIO

You can ride the Metro to the Montemartini Museum and St. Paul's Outside the Walls, but if you prefer to stay above ground, buses #23 and #769 run along Via Ostiense from the Piramide Metro stop to the museum (stop: Ostiense/Garbatella) and the church (stop: Viale S. Paolo).

▲Montemartini Museum
(Musei Capitolini Centrale Montemartini)

This museum houses a dreamy collection of 400 ancient statues, set evocatively in a classic 1932 electric power plant, among generators and *Metropolis*-type cast-iron machinery. While the art is not as famous as the collections you'll see downtown, the effect is fun and memorable—and you won't encounter a single tourist. If you're tackling Rome with kids, this museum is ideal: It's uncrowded and cool, immersed in an old power plant, with art placed at kid level.

Cost and Hours: €7.50, €6.50 for kids 6-25, free for kids 5 and under, Tue-Sun 9:00-19:00, closed Mon, look for red banner marking Via Ostiense 106, a short walk from Metro: Garbatella, tel. 06-0608, www.centralemontemartini.org.

▲St. Paul's Outside the Walls
(Basilica San Paolo Fuori le Mura)

According to Christian tradition, the body of St. Paul was buried here, where a small shrine once stood. It was replaced by a much

bigger church in around AD 380—in what was the last major construction project of Imperial Rome and the largest church in Christendom until St. Peter's. That church burned in 1823, and the stately, if stark, Neoclassical church you see today was built on its footprint. Pilgrims flock here to venerate the saint, espe-

cially since forensic experts concluded in 2009 that the bones interred under the altar date from the first or second century.

Cost and Hours: Free, daily 7:00-18:30, modest dress code enforced, dry audioguide—€5 plus ID, café, Via Ostiense 186, Metro: Basilica San Paolo, exit the Metro station following *via Os-*

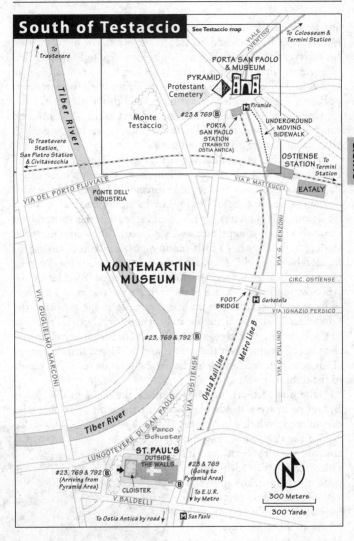

South of Testaccio

See Testaccio map

To Colosseum &
Termini Station

To Trastevere

VIALE AVENTINO

PORTA SAN PAOLO
& MUSEUM

PYRAMID
Protestant
Cemetery

Tiber River

Monte
Testaccio

#23 & 769 Ⓑ

Ⓜ Piramide

PORTA
SAN PAOLO
STATION
(TRAINS TO
OSTIA ANTICA)

UNDERGROUND
MOVING
SIDEWALK

To Trastevere
Station,
San Pietro Station
& Civitavecchia

OSTIENSE
STATION   To
          Termini
          Station

VIA P. MATTEUCCI

EATALY

VIA DEL PORTO FLUVIALE

PONTE DELL'
INDUSTRIA

VIA G. BENZONI

**MONTEMARTINI
MUSEUM**

CIRC. OSTIENSE

FOOT
BRIDGE Ⓜ Garbatella

VIA IGNAZIO PERSICO

VIA GUGLIELMO MARCONI

#23, 769 & 792 Ⓑ

VIA OSTIENSE

Ostia Rail Line

Metro Line B

VIA G. PULLINO

Tiber River

LUNGOTEVERE DI SAN PAOLO

Parco
Schuster

ST. PAUL'S
OUTSIDE
THE WALLS

#23, 769 & 792 Ⓑ
(Arriving from
Pyramid Area)

CLOISTER

#23 & 769
(Going to
Pyramid Area) Ⓑ

To E.U.R.
▼ by Metro

V. BALDELLI

To Ostia Antica by road ▼ Ⓜ San Paolo

Ⓝ

300 Meters

300 Yards

SIGHTS

tiense sign, and look for the church's round tower, the entrance is on the far side, tel. 06-6988-0800, www.basilicasanpaolo.org.

Visiting the Church: As the church is part of the Vatican, you'll start your visit by going through security (a metal detector and an X-ray machine for your bags, set up in a tent in the courtyard).

The column-lined courtyard leading up to the church is typical of early Christian churches—the first version of St. Peter's Basilica also had this kind of welcoming zone. The facade, while 19th century, is early Christian in its style—with mosaics picturing Rome and Jerusalem flanking the Lamb of God. In the courtyard's center is a statue of Paul holding his trademark sword, the instrument of his martyrdom. The palm trees, while not native to Rome, remind pilgrims of what they saw in the Holy Land. The central door of bronze and silver, from the 1930s, is dedicated to the patron saints of Rome, Peter (crucified upside-down) and Paul (beheaded).

Step inside and feel as close as you'll get in the 21st century to experiencing a monumental Roman basilica. Marvel at the ceiling, with those massive gilded-wood panels.

The marble-inlaid floor is like that of the Pantheon and typically Roman. Alabaster windows light the vast interior. It feels sterile, but in a good way—as if you're already in heaven. Along with St. Peter's Basilica, San Giovanni in Laterano, and Santa Maria Maggiore, this church is, legally speaking, part of the Vatican (you can buy Vatican stamps here and send mail). The triumphal arch leading to the altar has a fifth-century mosaic of Christ raising his hand in blessing. He's flanked by the four evangelists (in symbolic winged-animal guise) and, in white, the mysterious 24 elders of the Apocalypse. At the bottom of the arch are the two early followers of Jesus who, according to tradition, came to Rome to spread the Gospel and ended up dying for it: St. Peter (right) carries the keys to the kingdom of heaven, and St. Paul holds a sword symbolizing the piercing truth. Over the altar is a multicolored marble canopy (13th century). A 20-foot-tall Easter candlestick (c. 1170) stands to the right.

The fine 13th-century mosaic filling the dome in the apse is Byzantine in style; it was likely done by the same craftsmen who decorated St. Mark's in Venice. Notice the tiny, white, bug-like creature washing Jesus' toe. It's Honorius III, the 13th-century pope who paid for the apse renovation—reminding people of his humbleness while getting some credit at the same time (€1 illuminates the dome; machine to the right of the apse).

The church is built upon the supposed grave of St. Paul. According to tradition, Paul was decapitated two miles from this spot. His head was preserved at San Giovanni in Laterano, and his body was buried here under the altar. In 2009, archaeologists unearthed a sarcophagus with early inscriptions identifying it as Paul's, and carbon-dating on the bones inside confirmed their ancient origin. Today, you can descend a few steps in front of the central canopied altar to see the exposed end of Paul's supposed stone coffin, and look down through the glass floor to see the remains of the much smaller original fourth-century church.

Ringing the upper part of the church are round mosaic portraits of 266 popes, from St. Peter (the first one in the right transept) to the present. Find the recent popes to the right of the central altar—not in the nave, but farther to the right, under the arches of the dim right aisle. You'll see globetrotting John Paul II *(Jo Paulus II)* and progressive John XXIII, who oversaw the Vatican II reforms of the 1960s. A portrait of Pope #266, Francis, sits alongside blank medallions for future popes.

The peaceful 13th-century cloister (€4, €6 combo-ticket includes audioguide; enter from the right transept) has elegant Romanesque columns and arches, and fragments of early Christian/Roman sarcophagi, a relic chapel, and a small painting gallery.

E.U.R.

In the late 1930s, Italy's dictator Benito Mussolini planned an international exhibition—the 1942 Exhibit Universal Rome (E.U.R.)—to show off the wonders of his fascist society. But those wonders helped bring on World War II before II Duce's celebration could happen. The unfinished megaproject was completed in the 1950s, and today it houses apartment blocks,

corporate and government offices, and big, rarely visited museums.

If Hitler and Mussolini had won the war, our world might look like E.U.R. (AY-oor). Hike down E.U.R.'s wide, pedestrian-mean boulevards. Patriotic murals, aren't-you-proud-to-be-an-extreme-right-winger pillars, and stern squares decorate the soulless planned grid and sterile office blocks. Patriotic quotes are chiseled into walls. Boulevards named for Astronomy, Electronics, Social Security, and Beethoven are more exhausting than inspirational. And, not to be outdone by the ancients, Mussolini had a towering fascist-style obelisk erected in the central Piazza Marconi.

Despite its grim past, E.U.R. is now an upscale district with a mix of businessmen and women at work—and young people enjoying its trendy cafés. Because a few landmark buildings of Italian modernism are located here, E.U.R. is an important destination for architecture buffs, and the new futuristic convention center nicknamed "The Cloud" (it's meant to look like a cloud suspended in a glass box) promises to bring even more life to the area.

The Metro skirts E.U.R. with three stops (10 minutes from

SIGHTS

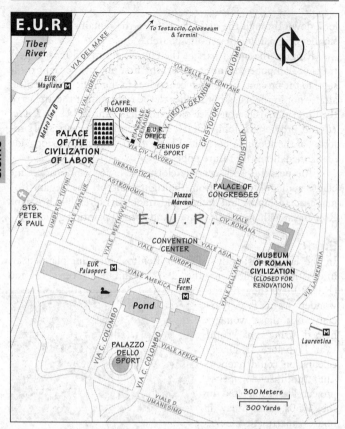

the Colosseum). Use E.U.R. Magliana for the Palace of the Civilization of Labor. Consider walking 20 minutes from the palace to the museum through the center of E.U.R.

Palace of the Civilization of Labor (Palazzo della Civiltà del Lavoro)

From the E.U.R. Magliana Metro stop, stairs lead uphill to this epitome of fascist architecture. With its giant no-questions-asked patriotic statues and its stark simplicity, this is E.U.R.'s tallest building and dominant landmark. It's understandably nicknamed the "Square Colosseum." Being intimidated by Mussolini's Palace of the Civilization of Labor (a name that reeks of dishonest corporatism—the dark power behind any fascist regime), you'll notice the obsession with powerful stonework and melodramatic statues.

The big slogan chiseled into the building declares: "The Italians: poets, artists, heroes, saints, thinkers, scientists, navigators, and explorers." The twin statues of Castor and Pollux recall ancient greatness, as nearby statues ringing the building celebrate virtues

Mussolini and Imperial Rome

Benito Mussolini incorporated much from ancient Rome during his dictatorship. His military was organized according to Roman terminology (divided into legions and run by centurions and consuls). The salute with the right arm raised, flat palm down (later used by the Nazis), was also Roman. More hygienic and quicker than a handshake, it fit the dynamic character of fascism.

While the classical values of power and discipline were stressed in the rhythmic march of military parades, convincing Italians of the need for order was a challenge even to Mussolini. He claimed it wasn't impossible to govern the Italian people...just useless.

Mussolini's title, Il Duce, meant "leader" or "guide." When chanted by crowds and carved onto monuments, it likely fueled Mussolini's belief that he was carrying out extraordinary historical missions like Caesar and Augustus before him.

For his symbol, rather than the she-wolf or eagle, Mussolini chose the ancient *fasces lictoriae*—an ax with a bundle (*fasces*) of wooden rods tied around the handle, carried by Roman officers in front of a magistrate (*lictor*) during processions as a sign of authority. (The same symbol was on the back of the old Mercury dime in America.) The symbol, which is the origin of the term "fascist," was aimed at replacing the popular view of Italy as a joyous, carefree country of mandolin-playing pizza-eaters with a new image of austerity and order.

Fascist architects built on a monumental scale (inspired by ancient monuments), with arches, bold statues, and rhetorical inscriptions—resulting in an austere and impersonal feel that Romans today generally dislike.

Despite his supposed passion for ancient Rome, Mussolini was a dreadful archaeologist. He would isolate a major monument and destroy everything around it. Sections of the imperial forums were sacrificed to build the wide street, Via dei Fori Imperiali, that goes from Piazza Venezia to the Colosseum. A famous fountain by the Colosseum that had survived almost 2,000 years was torn down without a second thought.

of proper Italian character, as if to say, "enough of the jaunty mandolins and pizzerias." After many years of standing empty, Fendi, an Italian luxury clothing and fashion company, has leased the building from the government for its headquarters. Its ground floor is a public art gallery showcasing revolving contemporary exhibits (free, daily 10:00-20:00).

Fascist Art, Architecture, and Propaganda

Standing at the Palace of the Civilization of Labor, survey the grand urban design that spreads out before you. Opposite, in the distance, is the Palace of Congresses. While the buildings and street plan of the entire area date from the fascist regime, there are two interesting stops within a couple blocks: a café and a bit of propaganda street art.

Caffè Palombini—just down the stairs and a block ahead on the left—is worth a quick visit for its architecture and marble mosaics, and the lively scene inside. In the side room to the right upon entering is some original fascist art created for this building: a multicolored marble mosaic by Eugenio Fegarotti depicting a domestic still life with E.U.R.'s buildings in the background. Today the café is a popular Roman institution; the buffet line in back is a hit with local workers for lunch (daily 7:00-22:00; good gelato, pastries, and snacks; Piazzale K. Adenauer 12, tel. 06-591-1700).

A block farther away from the palace, turn left on Via Ciro il Grande and find the bronze statue of a young boxer saluting. Originally called "The Genius of Fascism," the statue was given ancient boxing gloves and retitled "The Genius of Sport" after the war. But he still retains his fascist salute.

About ten steps beyond the boxer (just around the corner) is a fascinating 1939 stone relief showing "The Story of Rome through Construction." It celebrates the three Romes: ancient, Christian, and fascist. Trace the story from the top (Romulus and Remus plowing to define the original Rome) through the ages (constructing the ancient city, Caesar's rule, the heyday of the Colosseum, the looting of Jerusalem, the rise of St. Peter's, hoisting the obelisk, the era of Garibaldi) to the rule of Mussolini (adored by workers, women, children, and soldiers in lock-step).

To the right stretches the original office built for the 1942 exhibition. On its textbook fascist arcade a chiseled slogan proclaims: "The Third Rome will expand over other hills and along banks of the sacred river to the shores of the sea."

Museum of Roman Civilization (Museo della Civiltà Romana)

E.U.R.'s Museum of Roman Civilization, with dozens of fascinating rooms of plaster casts and models illustrating the greatness of classical Rome, is closed for renovation with no indication as to when it will reopen (www.museociviltaromana.it).

ANCIENT APPIAN WAY AND SOUTHEASTERN ROME

Southeast of the city center lie several ancient sites that make the trek here worthwhile.

Baths of Caracalla (Terme di Caracalla)

Inaugurated by Emperor Caracalla in AD 216, this massive bath complex—supplied by its own branch of an aqueduct—could accommodate 1,600 visitors at a time. Today it's just a shell—a huge shell—with all of its sculptures and most of its mosaics moved to museums.

Cost and Hours: €8; free and crowded once or twice a month, usually on a Sun—check in advance and avoid going on a free day; open Mon 9:00-14:00, Tue-Sun 9:00 until one hour before sunset: April-Aug until 19:15, Sept until 19:00, Oct until 18:30, off-season closes as early as 16:30; last entry one hour before closing, audioguide—€5, good €8 guidebook tel. 06-3996-7700, www.coopculture.it.

Getting There: Metro: Circo Massimo, then a 5-minute walk south along Via delle Terme di Caracalla; bus #714 from Termini train station or bus #118 from the Appian Way—see the end of my Ancient Appian Way Tour.

Visiting the Baths: You'll see a two-story roofless brick building surrounded by a garden, bordered by ruined walls. The two large rooms at either end of the building were used for exercise. In between the exercise rooms was a pool flanked by two small mosaic-floored dressing rooms. Niches in the walls once held statues. The baths' statues are displayed elsewhere: For example,  the immense *Toro Farnese* (a marble sculpture of a bull surrounded by people) snorts in Naples' Archaeological Museum.

This sight is dramatic in part because nothing was built around or on top of it. It's stood here, in ruins, for 1,500 years. As you enter (near the turnstile), study the four information posts with reconstructions of the complex. As you wander, keep these points in mind as you imagine the baths in their heyday:

Roman baths were more than baths and more than an athletic club. For 300 years, this was a social center offering people of various classes a chance to escape the intensity of the city and enjoy gardens, libraries, and cultural events. The huge rooms had vaulted ceilings overhead, walls veneered with colorful marble, and finely mosaicked floors. There was an entire parallel world under all this splendor—a world of darkness, heat, and suffering where slaves stoked furnaces with 10 tons of wood per day to heat all the water. (The baths stored up to 2,000 tons of firewood below its pavements.)

The Baths of Caracalla functioned until Goths severed the aqueducts in the sixth century. Consider a little nap in the shade of the Roman pine trees in front of the baths (where modern audiences sit to enjoy the grand operas staged here during the summer, www.operaroma.it).

▲Appian Way

For a taste of the countryside around Rome and more wonders of Roman engineering, take the four-mile trip from the Colosseum

out past the wall to a stretch of the ancient Appian Way, where the original pavement stones are lined by several interesting sights. Ancient Rome's first and greatest highway, the Appian Way once ran from Rome to the Adriatic port of Brindisi, the gateway to Greece. Today you can walk (or bike) some stretches of the road, rattling over original paving stones, past crumbling monuments that once edged the sides. The Tomb of Cecilia Metella and the Circus of Maxentius are the two most impressive pagan sights. Just a few hundred yards away are two major Christian catacombs (briefly described next).

📖 For more on these sights, see the Ancient Appian Way Tour chapter.

▲▲Catacombs of San Sebastiano

A guide leads you underground through the tunnels where early Christians were buried. You'll see faded frescoes and graffiti by early-Christian tag artists, as well as some pagan tombs that predate the Christian catacombs. Besides the catacombs themselves, there's a historic fourth-century basilica with the relics of St. Sebastian, the (supposedly) original Quo Vadis footprints of Christ, and an exquisite Bernini statue.

Cost and Hours: €8, includes 35-minute tour, 2/hour, Mon-Sat 10:00-17:00, closed Sun and Dec, Via Appia Antica 136, tel. 06-785-0350, www.catacombe.org.

▲▲Catacombs of San Callisto

The larger of the two sets of catacombs, San Callisto also is the more prestigious, having been the burial site for several early popes.

Cost and Hours: €8, includes 30-minute tour, at least 2/hour, Thu-Tue 9:00-12:00 & 14:00-17:00, closed Wed and late Jan-late Feb, Via Appia Antica 110, tel. 06-513-0151, www.catacombe.roma.it.

HEART OF ROME WALK

Rome's most colorful neighborhood features narrow lanes, intimate piazzas, fanciful fountains, and some of Europe's best people-watching. During the day, this walk—worth ▲▲▲—shows off the colorful Campo de' Fiori market and trendy fashion boutiques as it meanders past major monuments such as the Pantheon and the Spanish Steps.

But the sunset brings unexpected magic. A stroll in the cool of the evening is made memorable by the romance of the Eternal City at its best. Sit so close to a bubbling fountain that traffic noise evaporates. Jostle with kids to see the gelato flavors. Watch lovers straddling more than the bench. Jaywalk past *polizia* in bulletproof vests. And marvel at the ramshackle elegance that softens this brutal city for those who were born here and can't imagine living anywhere else. These are the flavors of Rome, best enjoyed after dark.

Orientation

Length of This Walk: Allow one to three hours for this mile-long walk, depending on whether you linger and tour the Pantheon.

Getting There: Campo de' Fiori is a few blocks west of Largo Argentina, a major transportation hub. Buses #40, #64, and #492, and tram #8, stop at Largo Argentina and/or along Corso Vittorio Emanuele II (a long block northwest of Campo de' Fiori). A taxi from Termini station costs about €14.

Pantheon: Free, Mon-Sat 8:30-19:30, Sun 9:00-18:00.

Tours: ♫ Download my free Heart of Rome Walk audio tour.

The Walk Begins

❶ Campo de' Fiori

Kick off this walk in one of Rome's most colorful spots, Campo de' Fiori. Depending on the time of day, the square is quite different.

In the morning, this bohemian piazza hosts a fruit-and-vegetable market. In the evening, the cafés and restaurants that line the square predominate. On weekend nights, beer-drinking young people (mostly American students) pack the medieval square, transforming it into a vast Roman street party.

With the neighborhood feel of Campo de' Fiori, it's hard to believe you're in a major capital city of nearly three million people. Rome has no skyscrapers, no central business district, and no obvious downtown. It's more a collection of urban villages, like this square. Romans jealously guard their laidback lifestyle, and nowhere is it clearer than in Campo de' Fiori.

This piazza has been the neighborhood's living room for centuries. In ancient times, it was a pleasant meadow—literally a *campo de' fiori*, or "field of flowers." Then the Romans built a massive entertainment complex, the Theater of Pompey, right next to it. The complex covered several city blocks, stretching from here to Largo Argentina (and including the spot where Julius Caesar was stabbed to death).

In medieval times, Christian pilgrims passed through the *campo* on their way to the Vatican, and a thriving market developed. As popes modernized the city in Renaissance and Baroque times, this square kept its local flavor. It's the product of centuries of unplanned urban development.

Today's Romans live amid the eclectic heritage of their ancestors. For example, at the east end of the square (behind the statue of the heretic Bruno), see how the ramshackle apartments are built right into the older parts. Find the pinkish-beige brick building, midway up, and the two white columns incorporated into it. Those ancient columns were once part of that Theater of Pompey.

Lording over the center of the square is the statue of **Giordano Bruno,** an intellectual who was burned on this spot in 1600. The pedestal shows scenes from Bruno's trial and execution, and an inscription translates, "And the flames rose up." The statue, facing a Vatican administration building, was erected in 1889, a time when the new state of Italy and the Vatican were feuding. Vatican officials protested the heretic in their midst, but they were overruled

Giordano Bruno (1548-1600)

Lauded as a martyr to free thought and reviled as an intellectual con man and heretic, the philosopher-priest Bruno has a

legacy only a Roman could love. Details of his life are sketchy, and his writings range from the sublime to the ridiculous.

The young Dominican priest was nonconformist and outspoken from the start. He had to flee Italy to avoid a charge of heresy and spent most of his adult life wandering Europe's capitals. In Geneva, he joined the Calvinists, until he was driven out for his unorthodox views. In London, he met with Queen Elizabeth I, who found him subversive. In Germany, the Lutherans excommunicated him.

In his writings, Bruno claimed to have discovered the "Clavis Magna" (Great Key) to training the human memory. He published satirical plays tweaking Church morals. He advanced the then-heretical (Copernican) notion that the earth revolved around the sun and speculated about other inhabited planets in the universe. All his works show a vast-ranging mind aware of the scientific trends of the day.

In 1593, Bruno was arrested by the Inquisition and sent to Rome, where he languished in prison for six years before being sentenced to death by fire. He replied, "Perhaps you who pronounce this sentence are more fearful than I who receive it." On February 17, 1600, the civil authorities led him to the stake on Campo de' Fiori. As they lit the fire, he was offered a crucifix to hold. He pushed it away.

by angry neighborhood locals. This district is still known for its free spirit and antiauthoritarian demonstrations.

The square is surrounded by fun eateries, and is great for people-watching. Bruno faces the bustling **Forno** (in the left corner of the square), where takeout *pizza bianca* is sold hot from the oven.

• *If Bruno did a hop, step, and jump forward, then turned left, in a block he'd reach...*

❷ Piazza Farnese

While the higgledy-piggledy Campo de' Fiori feels free and easy, the 16th-century Renaissance Piazza Farnese, named for the family whose palace dominates it, seems to stress order. The Farnese family was nouveau riche and needed to make a statement. They hired Michelangelo to help design their palace. He created the jutting roofline (the cornice), and made the window in the very center

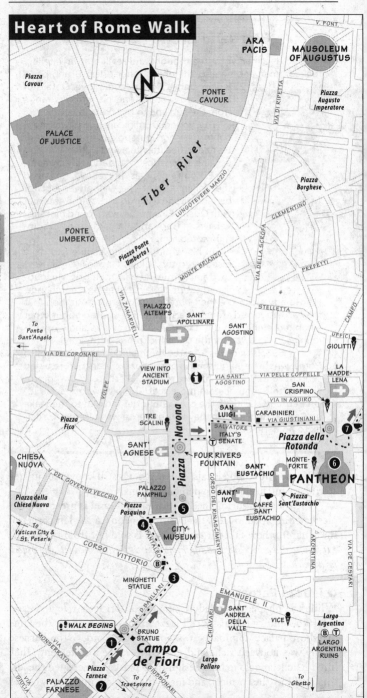

Heart of Rome Walk

HEART OF ROME

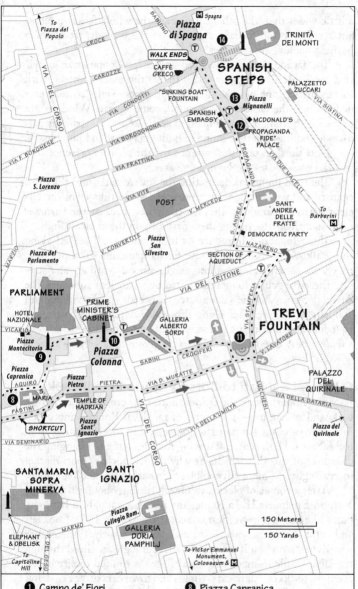

1. Campo de' Fiori
2. Piazza Farnese
3. Via dei Baullari to Corso Vittorio Emanuele II
4. Pasquino Statue
5. Piazza Navona
6. Pantheon
7. Caffè Tazza d'Oro
8. Piazza Capranica
9. Piazza di Montecitorio
10. Piazza Colonna & Via del Corso
11. Trevi Fountain
12. Palazzo di Propaganda Fide
13. Column of the Immaculate Conception
14. Spanish Steps

a little wider than the others. This gave the whole facade a pleasant symmetry and focused attention on the balcony, from where Farnese nobles gave speeches.

The facade design influenced and helped popularize a style that you'll see all along our walk. There's the main doorway, with its big rustic stone blocks. There are pilasters—half-columns embedded into the facade—some round, some square. Windows are topped with triangular pediments or semi-arches. The balcony balustrade (railing) is a type found in buildings great and humble.

Note the flags over the entrance and the security presence. The palazzo now houses the French embassy.

The twin fountains decorating the square date from the third century and were made with repurposed stone tubs from the ancient Baths of Caracalla. They ended up here because the Farneses excavated the baths, giving them first dibs on the choicest finds.

These fountains introduce us to a theme we'll see all along this walk: water. Rome is famous for its fountains. In times past, they were functional, providing neighborhoods with a water supply. These particular fountains are fed by an ancient aqueduct, the Acqua Vergine. It's the same source that feeds the Trevi Fountain and others that we'll see along this walk. After 2,000 years, the aqueduct is still bringing the water of life into the city.

• *Walk back to Campo de' Fiori, cross the square, and continue a couple of blocks down...*

❸ Via dei Baullari to Corso Vittorio Emanuele II

As you slalom through the crowds, notice the crush of cheap cafés, bars, and restaurants—the center of medieval Rome is morphing into a playground for tourists, students, and locals visiting from the suburbs. High rents are driving families out and changing the character of this district. That's why the Campo de' Fiori market increasingly sells more gifty edibles than basic fruits and vegetables.

After a couple of blocks, you reach the busy boulevard, Corso Vittorio Emanuele II. In Rome, any road big enough to have city buses like this is post-unification: constructed after 1870. Look left and right down the street—the facades are mostly 19th-century neo-Renaissance, built after this main thoroughfare sliced through the city. Traffic in much of central Rome is limited to city buses, taxis, motorbikes, "dark cars" (limos and town cars of VIPs), delivery vans, residents, and disabled people with permits (a.k.a. friends of politicians). This is one of the increasingly rare streets where any vehicle is welcome.

• *Cross Corso Vittorio Emanuele II, and enter a square with a statue of Marco Minghetti, an early Italian prime minister. Angle left at the statue, walking along the left side of the skippable City Museum of Rome,*

HEART OF ROME

down Via di San Pantaleo. A block down, at the corner, you'll find a beat-up old statue.

❹ Pasquino

Pasquino—a third-century-BC statue that was discovered near here—is one of Rome's "talking statues." For 500 years, this statue

has served as a kind of community billboard, allowing people to complain anonymously when it might be dangerous to speak up. And, to this day, you'll see old Pasquino strewn with political posters, strike announcements, and grumbling graffiti. The statue looks worn down by centuries of bitching.

Speaking of government, the road stretching out the far end of this piazza is a typical pre-unification "Papal Road"—as big as roads got before the mid-19th century. It's called the Via del Governo Vecchio—road of the old government.

• *Facing Pasquino, veer to the left and head up Via di Pasquino. You'll soon emerge into a place where all the layers of Rome are on display: ancient, medieval, Baroque, and contemporary.*

❺ Piazza Navona

This long, oblong square is dotted with fountains, busy with outdoor cafés, lined with palazzos and churches, and thronged with

happy visitors.

Piazza Navona has been a center of Roman life since ancient times. By its shape you might guess that it started out as a racetrack, part of the training grounds built here by Emperor Domitian around AD 80. That was the same year the Colosseum opened: Rome was at its peak.

But much of what we see today came in the 1600s, when the whole place got a major renovation. At the time, the popes were trying to put some big scandals behind them, and beautification projects like this were a peace offering to the public.

The first building on your left is the **Palazzo Pamphilj.** It's now the Brazilian embassy. The Pamphilj nobles were big patrons of the arts, and one of them became Pope Innocent X—the man who created the square as we see it today.

Three Baroque fountains decorate the piazza. The first fountain, at the southern end, features a Moor wrestling with a dolphin. In 17th-century Rome, Moors (North Africans) represented all that was exotic and mysterious. In the fountain at the northern end, Neptune slays a giant octopus.

The most famous fountain, though, is in the center: the **Four Rivers Fountain** by Gian Lorenzo Bernini, the man who in the mid-1600s remade Rome in the Baroque style. It's topped with an Egyptian-style obelisk—another of the themes we'll see along this walk. Obelisks were popular with Roman emperors because Egyptian society saw its rulers as divine—an idea Roman rulers liked to promote.

Get close to admire Bernini's four enormous statues at the base. As the water of the world gushes everywhere, these four burly river gods represent the four quarters of the world. Bernini enlivens the fountain with horses plunging through rocks and the exotic flora and fauna of faraway lands.

Stroll around the fountain counterclockwise and admire the gods: The good-looking figure of the Danube represents the continent of Europe. He reaches back and grabs hold of the coat of arms of Bernini's Pamphilj patron. Next comes the Ganges (for Asia), a bearded old man with an oar between his legs. Next you pass a palm tree, one of many exotic details. The Nile (for Africa) has his head covered, since the river's source was unknown back then. Uruguay's Rio de la Plata, representing the Americas, tumbles backward in shock, wondering how he ever made the top four. Notice the god's exotic facial features. Back in the 1600s, Europeans didn't have a clear idea of how to depict a Native American. The spilled coins represent the easy-to-harvest wealth of the New World.

Now, follow the Plata river god's gaze upward. He's looking at the **Church of Sant'Agnese,** which dominates the square. It was the work of Francesco Borromini, Rome's other great Baroque architect. It has Borromini's signature motif—concave lines. Notice how the inward-curving facade helps reveal the dome. Borromini's elaborate facade epitomizes the curved symmetry of the Baroque era. It's also a fine example of Baroque deception: While the facade is mammoth, the actual church interior is only as wide as the four middle columns at the entrance.

Borromini was once Bernini's student and became his great rival. But legend says that Bernini got the final word: He designed the river god Plata to look up at Borromini's church...and tumble backward, in horror. It certainly looks that way and makes a great story—but in fact, the fountain was completed before Borromini even began the church.

Piazza Navona is Rome's most interesting night scene, with street music, artists, fire-eaters, local Casanovas, ice cream, and outdoor cafés that are worthy of a splurge if you've got time to sit and enjoy Italy's human river.

• *Leave Piazza Navona directly across from* **Tre Scalini** *(famous for its tartufo, a rich, chocolate gelato concoction), and go east down Corsia Agonale, past rose peddlers and palm readers. Ahead of you (across the busy street) stands the stately Palazzo Madama, where the* **Italian Senate** *meets. (Hence, security is high.) Jog left around this building, and follow the brown* Pantheon *sign straight down Via del Salvatore.*

After a block, you'll pass (on your left) the **Church of San Luigi dei Francesi,** *with its* très *French decor and precious Caravaggio paintings (described on page 149). If it's open, pop in. Otherwise, continue along, following the crowd, as everyone seems to be heading for the Pantheon.*

As you walk, notice the basalt cobbles underfoot. This is the same stone ancient Romans cobbled their streets with, quarried from volcanic mountains south of here (like Vesuvius). The public debate lately is whether to replace them with modern pavement (more practical and comfortable) or keep them (more character and a part of the heritage). Rounding the next corner, you come to...

❻ The Pantheon

Perhaps the most magnificent building surviving from ancient Rome is this temple to the "pantheon" (literally, all the gods). It faces a piazza, as it has since ancient times, when this was an arcaded square—an elegant and shaded gathering place with covered walkways. The ancient Romans introduced the piazza culture, and you can see it thrives to this day. In antiquity, the Pantheon was above street level, approached by a staircase (the staircase survives but is buried beneath the square). Notice how the steps of the 18th-century **fountain** in the center of the square disappear into the modern pavement, and how the square slants down toward the street level of 2,000 years ago. The obelisk rising from the fountain originally decorated a temple to the Egyptian goddess Isis (wife of Osiris). Rome had an important connection to Egypt (from where much of its grain came) and was happy to have a temple here for its Egyptian residents.

The 40-foot, single-piece granite columns of the Pantheon's entrance show the scale the ancient Romans built on. The columns support a triangular Greek-style roof with an inscription that proclaims, "M. Agrippa built this." In fact, the present structure was built *(fecit)* by Emperor Hadrian (AD 120), who gave credit to the builder of an earlier temple. This impressive entranceway gives no clue that the greatest wonder of the building

is inside—a domed room that inspired later domes, including Michelangelo's St. Peter's and Brunelleschi's Duomo in Florence.

If it's open, pop into the Pantheon for a look around. Afterward, consider detouring to several interesting churches near the Pantheon (**Santa Maria sopra Minerva,** with its purely Gothic interior, and **Sant'Ignazio,** with its 3-D Baroque illusions, are just a few steps away). For details on the Pantheon and these other churches, 🕮 see the Pantheon Tour chapter or 🎧 download my free Pantheon audio tour.

If the Pantheon is closed, just stand for a while under the portico, which is romantically floodlit and moonlit at night.

• *To continue this walk, with your back to the Pantheon, veer to the right, uphill toward the yellow sign on Via Orfani that reads* Casa del Caffè—*you've reached the...*

❼ Caffè Tazza d'Oro

This is one of Rome's top coffee shops, dating back to the days when this area was licensed to roast coffee beans. Locals come here for a shot of espresso or, when it's hot, a refreshing *granita di caffè con panna* (coffee and crushed ice with whipped cream).

Circle through the interior and absorb the aroma and energy of a classic Italian café scene. To-go coffee is simply wrong here in Rome. Locals pay at the cashier, bring their receipt to the

barista, and enjoy an elegant little break. This scene is just as it was in the early 1980s, when Howard Schultz traveled to Italy and was inspired to buy a coffee business in Seattle—and set off to conquer the world. (Starbucks has three locations in less traditional Milan.)

• *From here, our walk continues past some interesting landmarks to the Trevi Fountain. To get there more directly, you could opt to take a **short-cut** by bearing right at the coffee shop onto Via de' Pastini, which leads through Piazza di Pietra (with some surviving chunks of the Temple of Hadrian—described on page 70), then across busy Via del Corso, where it becomes the touristy, pedestrianized Via delle Muratte and heads straight for the fountain.*

To stick with me for the slightly longer version, bear left at the coffee shop and continue up Via degli Orfani to the next square...

❽ Piazza Capranica

This square is home to the big, plain Florentine-Renaissance-style Palazzo Capranica (directly opposite as you enter the square). Its stubby tower was once much taller, but when a stronger government arrived, the nobles were all ordered to shorten their towers. The six-story building to the left was once an apartment building for 17th-century Rome's middle class. Like so many of Rome's churches, the church on the square—Santa Maria in Aquiro—is older than its Baroque-era facade. Notice the circular little shrine on the street corner (between the palace and the apartment building). For centuries, worshipful spots like this have made pilgrims (and, today, tourists) feel welcome.

• *Leave the piazza to the right of the palace, heading down Via in Aquiro. The street jogs to the left and into a square called...*

❾ Piazza di Montecitorio

This square, home to Italy's Parliament, is marked by an **Egyptian obelisk** from the sixth century BC. It adorned a temple in Egypt

for half a millennium before Emperor Augustus brought it to Rome as a trophy proclaiming his victory over Mark Antony and Cleopatra. Made of red granite, the obelisk stands 70 feet tall—or well over 100 feet when you include the base.

In Egypt, obelisks, with their pointed tops, were meant to look like the rays of the sun god Ra. Roman emperors used them to proclaim their own divinity. Augustus had this one taken down in Egypt, rolled on logs to the port, shipped across the Mediterranean, and hoisted up here to mark his Solarium Augusti (a shrine dedicated to the Roman god of the sun).

After the fall of Rome, centuries of debris buried the obelisk and it was forgotten. Rediscovered in the 1700s, it was re-erected by the pope—who also loved the idea of the heavens imparting divine powers to rulers on earth.

In Augustus' day, the obelisk acted as a sundial and calendar, aligned to cast a shadow across the solarium altar on the emperor's birthday. Today, the obelisk still functions as a sundial. Follow the zodiac markings in the pavement to the square's next big sight— the **Italian Parliament.**

This impressive building is where the legislature's lower chamber (the equivalent of the US House of Representatives) attempts to govern the nation. You'll see heavy security. You may also see politicians coming and going, demonstrations, and TV cameras. If some major law has just been passed, this stately building is often the backdrop for news reporters.

The palazzo has a long history of governance. Note the relief to the right of the door, showing Lady Justice. Before Italy was unified in the 19th century, the high court of the papal state met here. The building's spacious facade was designed by our old friend Bernini. It bulges in the middle, to make this small square feel grander. At either end of the facade, notice the strips of jagged stones. This rustic "back-to-nature" style was popular in the Baroque age. We'll see more fake grotto stones in a few minutes, at the Trevi Fountain.

The building caps ancient Rome's smallest hill, Montecitorio. This man-made hill was the mound of dirt dug up when Augustus built his monument to the sun.

• *One block to your right is Piazza Colonna, where we're heading next—unless you like gelato...*

A one-block detour to the left (past Hotel Nazionale) brings you to a famous Roman gelateria, Giolitti.

⑩ Piazza Colonna and Via del Corso

The square features a massive column that has stood here since the second century AD. The column's shaft is 12 feet across, al-

most 100 feet tall, and stands on a 30-foot base, which rests on a platform. It's a particularly imposing-looking column because it doesn't taper at the top. The whole thing is carved from the finest white marble in the world, from Carrara—the favorite quarry of the ancient Romans and of Michelangelo.

This isn't a single piece of marble. It's 28 cylindrical blocks stacked atop each other like a pile of 10-ton checkers. A carved frieze winds from the bottom to the top, telling the story of Emperor Marcus Aurelius heroically battling barbarians around AD 170. In the very bottom relief, find a few boats. These depict the crucial start of the campaign, when the Romans built a bridge of boats to cross the Danube River and attack.

The column is pure propaganda. Although it trumpeted Marcus's triumph, in reality, the barbarians were winning, beginning Rome's long, three-century fall. The statue of the pagan Emperor Marcus that once topped the column was eventually replaced by the Christian missionary Paul, who helped bring Christianity to Rome.

Notice the horizontal slits in the column: It's hollow, and has a spiral staircase inside. These little windows provide light.

In ancient times, Piazza Colonna was a major square with a temple to Marcus Aurelius. Today, it is still important. The big white building adjacent to the parliament houses the headquarters for the prime minister's cabinet. And the big beige building with columns and clock houses the right-wing *Il Tempo* newspaper. It's appropriately situated in what was the headquarters of the fascist party of Mussolini.

Beyond Piazza Colonna runs noisy **Via del Corso,** Rome's main north-south boulevard. In ancient times, this was the Via Flaminia, the highway that stretched from the Roman Forum to the Adriatic coast. For 2,000 years, all travelers from northern Europe first entered Rome and headed downtown on this street. In the Middle Ages, the street brought pilgrims to the Vatican.

The street was renamed "corso" for a famous medieval horse race that took place here during the crazy Carnevale season leading up to Lent. This wild tradition continued until the late 1800s, when it was cancelled after a series of fatal accidents.

In 1854, Via del Corso became one of Rome's first gas-lit streets. It still hosts some of the city's most chic stores. Every evening, the pedestrian-only stretch of the Corso is packed with people on parade, taking to the streets for their *passeggiata*. It's an ideal venue for Romans to show off what they might have purchased from those classy shops (see the "Dolce Vita Stroll" in the Sights in Rome chapter).

Before crossing the street, look left (to the obelisk marking Piazza del Popolo—the ancient north gate of the city) and right (to the Victor Emmanuel Monument).

• *Cross Via del Corso to enter a big palatial building with columns, the* **Galleria Alberto Sordi** *shopping mall. It's typical* *of the grand galleries built throughout Italy in the late 1800s, powered by the energy of a newly united and proud Italy. To the left are convenient WCs.*

Go to the right and exit out the back, where you'll continue directly to the Trevi Fountain. (If you're here after 21:00, when the mall is closed, circle around the right side of the Galleria on Via dei Sabini.) At any time, be on guard for pickpockets, who thrive in the nearby Trevi Fountain crowds. Once out the back, the tourist kitsch builds as you head up Via de Crociferi to the roar of the water, lights, and people at the...

⓫ Trevi Fountain

The Trevi Fountain is the ultimate showcase for Rome's love affair with water.

Architect Nicola Salvi conceived this liquid Baroque avalanche in 1762, cleverly incorporating the palace behind the fountain as a theatrical backdrop. Centerstage is the enormous figure known simply as the "Ocean." He symbolizes water in every form. The statue stands in his shell-shaped chariot, surfing through his wet dream. Water gushes from 24 spouts and tumbles over 30 different kinds of plants. Winged horses represent cresting waves. They're led by Tritons who blow on their conch shells. *Drammatico!*

Rome took full advantage of the abundant water brought into the city by its great aqueducts. Even in ancient times, there was a fountain here, where locals came to get their water. It was dug lower than street level to give maximum gravitational oomph to the water flow.

Now turn your back to the fountain, and locate the columns built into the Benetton shop, facing the fountain. In ancient times this was an arcaded square (like the one facing the Pantheon) where the neighborhood gathered, jugs on heads, to fetch water. But in the sixth century, invaders destroyed the aqueduct that flowed here.

Much later, in the Renaissance and Baroque eras, the old aqueduct was renovated and reopened. The Trevi Fountain (named for the three ancient roads that converged here) was built to celebrate that joyous event. After surviving for 1,000 years on poor-quality well water, Romans could once again enjoy pure water brought from the distant hills east of the city.

The square that faces the fountain has a lively atmosphere. The magic is enhanced by the fact that no streets directly approach it. You can hear the excitement as you draw near, and then—

Egyptian Obelisks

Rome has 13 obelisks, more than any other city in the world. In Egypt, they were connected with the sun god Ra (like stone sun rays) and the power of the pharaohs. The ancient Romans, keen on exotic novelty and sheer size, brought the obelisks here and set them up in key public places as evidence and celebration of their occupation of Egypt. Starting from the 1580s, Rome's new rulers—the popes—relocated the obelisks and topped most of them with Christian crosses. The obelisks came to acquire another significance that guaranteed their survival: the triumph of Christianity over all other religions.

The tallest (105 feet) and the most ancient (16th century BC) is the obelisk in Piazza San Giovanni in Laterano. It once stood in the Circus Maximus next to its sister, which now marks the center of Piazza del Popolo.

The obelisks were carved from single blocks of granite. Imagine the work, with only man and horsepower, first to quarry them and set them up in Egypt, then—after the Romans came along—to roll them on logs to the river or the coast, sail (or row) them in special barges across the Mediterranean and up the Tiber, and finally hoist them up here.

Rome wasn't above cheap imitations, however: A couple of the obelisks are ancient Roman copies. The one at the top of the Spanish Steps has spelling mistakes in the hieroglyphics.

bam!—you're there. Enjoy the scene. Lucky Romeos clutch dates while unlucky suitors clutch beers.

Romantics toss a coin over their shoulder into the fountain. Legend says it will assure your return to Rome. Over the years, more convoluted legends sprang up—two coins bring romance, three means marriage...and no coins means you're divorced and paying alimony. It's all pretty silly. But hey—it's Rome, and the world is yours. Make up your own wish. Some people pooh-pooh the idea that a coin guarantees their return. But every year I go through this tourist ritual...and so far it's working.

Take some time to people-watch (whisper a few breathy *bello*s or *bella*s) before leaving. There's a peaceful zone at water level on the far right.

• *Facing the Trevi Fountain, walk along its right side up Via della Stamperia. Cross busy Via del Tritone. Angle left as you continue about 30 yards up Via del Nazareno to #9, where you'll pass a fence on the* *left, with an exposed bit of that ancient Acqua Vergine aqueduct. At the T-intersection ahead, turn right on Via Sant'Andrea delle Fratte. You'll pass (at #16, on the right) a low-key doorway protected by security. This is the headquarters of Italy's **Democratic Party**.*

The street becomes Via di Propaganda. You'll pass alongside the...

⓬ Palazzo di Propaganda Fide

At #1, on the right, the white-and-yellow entrance marks the palace from which the Catholic Church "propagated," or spread, its message to the world. Back in the 1600s, this "Propaganda Palace" was the headquarters of the Catholic Church's P.R. department—a priority after the Reformation. The building was designed by that dynamic Baroque duo, Bernini and Borromini (with his concave lines). It flies the yellow-and-white flag signifying that it is still owned by the Vatican.

• *The street opens up into a long piazza. You're approaching the Spanish Steps. But first, pause at the...*

⓭ Column of the Immaculate Conception

Atop a tall column stands a bronze statue of Mary. She wears a diadem of stars for a halo, and stands on a crescent moon atop a globe of the earth, which is crushing a satanic serpent.

The monument celebrates the Catholic doctrine of Immaculate Conception. This was the idea that not only was Jesus born pure, but his mother Mary also was conceived without sin. The concept had been around since medieval times, but in 1854, Pope Pius IX finally proclaimed it official dogma and erected this statue in celebration.

To hammer home that the idea of Immaculate Conception had a long tradition, the architect placed Mary atop a marble column that was itself ancient. At the base sit statues of venerable and sage prophets, all in total agreement with the new doctrine. (By the way, the grand backdrop for the column is none other than the "Propaganda Palace," with its Vatican flag.)

Picture the festive scene here every December 8, the feast day of the Immaculate Conception. The pope attends, the fire department brings out a ladder truck, and fresh flowers are placed high on Mary's statue. (You may see wilted remains of a flower wreath in Mary's hand.) This is the traditional event that kicks off Rome's Christmas season—the locals all go home and decorate their trees on this December day.

To Mary's immediate left stands the Spanish embassy to the

Vatican. Rome has double the embassies of a normal capital because here countries need two: one to Italy and one to the Vatican. And because of this 300-year-old embassy, the square and its famous steps are called "Spanish."

• *Just 100 yards past Mary, you reach the climax of our walk, the...*

⓮ Spanish Steps

The wide, curving staircase is one of Rome's iconic sights. Its 138 steps lead sharply up from Piazza di Spagna. Partway up, the steps fan out around a central terrace, forming a butterfly shape. The design culminates at the top in an obelisk framed between two Baroque church towers.

For decades the steps were a favorite Roman hangout (see photo), but recently the city banned anyone from sitting on them. You can walk up and down the steps, but if you sit, you'll face a €250 fine.

At the foot of the steps is the aptly named Sinking Boat Fountain. It was built by Gian Lorenzo Bernini's father, Pietro. This fountain is powered by that same Acqua Vergine aqueduct. Because the water pressure here is low, the water can't shoot high in the air. So Bernini designed the fountain to be low key—a sinking boat filled with water.

The Piazza di Spagna has been the hangout of many Romantics over the years (Keats, Wagner, Openshaw, Goethe, and others). For British aristocrats of yesteryear, this was the culmination of their Grand Tour of Europe's famous sights. They came to Rome to contemplate the decaying ruins, enjoy the warm climate, and exercise their elite status in a foreign culture.

British poet John Keats pondered his mortality, then died of tuberculosis at age 25 in the orange building on the right side of the steps. Fellow Romantic Lord Byron lived across the square at #66. Nearby, Caffè Greco has been a favored haunt of artists and writers since 1760 (it's just down Via dei Condotti at #86, with a historic interior).

The piazza is a thriving scene both day and night. From here you can window-shop along Via Condotti, which stretches away from the steps. This is where Gucci and other big names cater to well-heeled jetsetters.

But before you head off, take a final 360-degree spin of the piazza. It features many of the themes we've enjoyed on this walk—fountains, obelisks, public spaces, statues, and gelato. Most of all, it's a glimpse at today's Rome—a city where friends and families live much the same kind of life as their ancient cousins.

• *Our walk is finished. To reach the top of the steps sweat-free, take the free elevator just inside the Spagna Metro stop (to the left, as you face the steps; elevator closes at 23:30). The nearby McDonald's (as you face the Spanish Steps, go right one block) is big and lavish, with a salad bar and WC. When you're ready to leave, you can zip home on the Metro (usually open until 23:30) or grab a taxi at the north or south ends of the piazza.*

PANTHEON TOUR

The Roman Temple and Nearby Churches

If your imagination is fried from trying to reconstruct ancient buildings out of today's rubble, visit the Pantheon, Rome's best-preserved monument. Engineers still admire how the Romans built such a mathematically precise structure without computers, fossil fuel-run machinery, or electricity. (Having unlimited slave power didn't hurt.) Stand under the Pantheon's solemn dome to gain a new appreciation for the sophistication of these ancient people.

The Pantheon is the centerpiece of this tour, and is a must-see on any visit to Rome. The second part of the tour features several interesting churches that cluster near the Pantheon, with art by Michelangelo and Caravaggio, and connections with Galileo, St. Ignatius, and the Jesuit order.

Orientation

Pantheon: Free, Mon-Sat 8:30-19:30, Sun 9:00-18:00, holidays 9:00-13:00, closed for Mass Sat at 17:00 and Sun at 10:30, www.pantheonroma.com.

Church of San Luigi dei Francesi: Free, daily 9:30-12:30 & 14:30-18:30 except closed Sun morning, good €3 booklet, on Piazza di San Luigi dei Francesi, www.saintlouis-rome.net. Bring coins to light the Caravaggios.

Gesù Church: Free, daily 7:00-12:30 & 16:00-19:45 (afternoon visits are easier as there are frequent Masses in the morning), interesting daily ceremony at 17:30, on Piazza del Gesù, www.chiesadelgesu.org.

Church of Santa Maria sopra Minerva: Free, Mon-Fri 7:00-19:00, Sat from 10:00, Sun from 8:10, closes midday Sat-Sun, Piazza della Minerva 42, www.santamariasopraminerva.it.

Church of Sant'Ignazio: Free, Mon-Sat 7:30-19:00, Sun from
9:00, on Piazza di Sant'Ignazio, www.chiesasantignazio.it.

When to Go: Don't go at midday, when the Pantheon is packed
and some of the churches are closed. If you visit the Pantheon
before 9:00, you'll have it all to yourself.

Dress Code: No visitors with skimpy shorts or bare shoulders allowed inside the Pantheon. Modest dress is recommended for
the churches nearby.

Getting There: Many buses (including #40, #64, #492, #85, and
#87) stop on the major boulevards near the Pantheon (Via del
Corso, Corso Rinascimento, and Corso Vittorio Emanuele);
from any of these it's about a three-block walk. You can also
walk from the Spagna or Barberini Metro stops in about 15
minutes.

Tours: The Pantheon has a €6, 30-minute audioguide (€10/2 people).

🎧 Download my free Pantheon audio tour.

Length of This Tour: Allow 30 minutes to see the Pantheon and at
least an hour to visit the nearby churches. If you have less time,
the essential Pantheon can be seen in a glance.

Visitor Services: The nearest WCs are at bars and cafés on the
Pantheon's square.

Eating: Restaurants abound. Several recommendations are listed
in the Eating in Rome chapter (see page 397).

Drinks: A refreshing water fountain spurts near the obelisk in Piazza della Rotonda.

For those who prefer their liquids caffeinated, two of
Rome's most venerable (and busiest) coffee shops are just steps
away: **Tazza d'Oro Casa del Caffè** (their icy *granita di caffè
con panna* is heaven on a hot day; Via degli Orfani 84) and **Bar
Sant'Eustachio** (they add sugar to their coffee drinks unless
you request otherwise; Piazza di Sant'Eustachio 82). For locations, see the "Churches Near the Pantheon" map, later in this
chapter.

The Tour Begins

• *Start the tour at the top of the square called Piazza della Rotonda, with
cafés and restaurants around the edges and an obelisk-topped fountain in
the center. You're looking at...*

The Pantheon

Exterior

The Pantheon was a Roman temple dedicated to all *(pan)* of the
gods *(theos)*. The original temple was built in 27 BC by Emperor

Augustus' son-in-law, Marcus Agrippa. In fact, the inscription below the triangular **pediment** proclaims (in Latin), "Marcus Agrippa, son of Lucio, three times consul made this." But after a couple of fires, the structure we see today was completely rebuilt by Emperor Hadrian around AD 120.

A voracious tourist, Hadrian personally visited almost every corner of his vast empire. He returned home to beautify the capital city with structures based on great buildings he'd seen abroad. Some say that Hadrian, an amateur architect, helped design the Pantheon. It was made to look like a Greek temple, with columns, crossbeams, and a pediment. The columns have leafy Corinthi-

an capitals, the Greek order that was most popular among Romans. Hadrian was such a Grecophile that he even grew a beard to look like a Greek philosopher, bucking the beardless tradition of Rome's 13 previous emperors.

Now turn your attention to the building's famous dome. Frankly, from the outside, that shallow dome isn't very impressive. But as we'll see when we go inside, the dome is what makes this building unique—and perhaps the most influential architectural design in art history. The Pantheon's dome was the model for the Florence cathedral dome, which launched the Renaissance, and for Michelangelo's dome of St. Peter's, which capped it all off. Even the US Capitol in Washington, DC, was inspired by this dome.

Wander into the ❶ **portico** with its forest of 16 enormous **columns.** They're 40 feet tall and 15 feet around, made of red-and-gray granite. Whereas many ancient columns are a stack of cylindrical

drums, these columns are each a single piece of stone. They are sequoia-huge—it takes the outstretched arms of four good-size tourists to encircle one column.

Think of the engineering problems posed by these 55-ton columns. They were quarried in faraway Egypt, shipped across the Mediterranean, transferred by barge up the Tiber, then carried overland to this spot, where they were lifted into place using only ropes, pulleys, and lots of sweaty slaves. It's little wonder that the Romans—so organized, so rational—could dominate their barbarian neighbors.

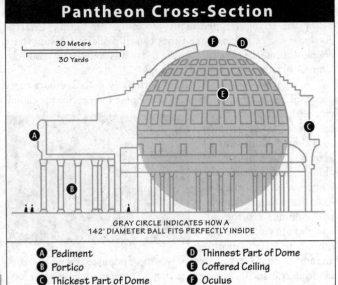

Pantheon Cross-Section

30 Meters
30 Yards

GRAY CIRCLE INDICATES HOW A
142' DIAMETER BALL FITS PERFECTLY INSIDE

- **A** Pediment
- **B** Portico
- **C** Thickest Part of Dome
- **D** Thinnest Part of Dome
- **E** Coffered Ceiling
- **F** Oculus

PANTHEON

Imagine how impressive this portico was in its heyday, when the ceiling was covered with shiny bronze plating. A scavenging pope from the Barberini family removed the metal in the 17th century, inspiring the quip, "What the barbarians didn't do, the Barberini did." Melted down, some of that bronze was used to build the huge canopy over the altar at St. Peter's.

Check out the giant doorway—it's considered original. The **❷ doors** are 23 feet tall and made of bronze. In ancient times the monumental entryway was flanked by statues of Emperor Augustus and Marcus Agrippa, the man who built the original (pre-Hadrian) Pantheon. Although much of the ancient decoration has been lost, the mathematical perfection of the interior is as fresh today as the day Hadrian himself first walked through these doors.
• *Now strut like an emperor through the giant bronze doors. Take a seat and take it all in.*

Inside the Pantheon

Once inside, your eye will be drawn upward to the magnificent, soaring dome, the largest made until the Renaissance. It is set on a circular base, and the mathematical perfection of this dome-on-a-base design is a testament to Roman engineering. The dome is as high as it is wide—142 feet. To picture it, imagine a basketball wedged inside a wastebasket so that it just touches bottom.

The dome is made from concrete, a Roman invention. It gets lighter and thinner as it reaches the top. The base of the dome is

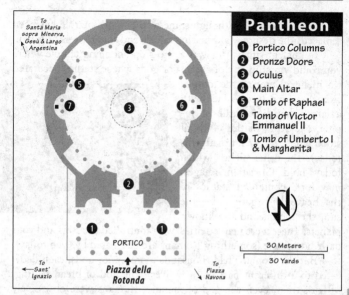

23 feet thick and made from heavy concrete mixed with travertine, while near the top, it's less than five feet thick and made with a lighter volcanic rock (pumice) mixed in. Note the square indentations in the surface of the dome. This **coffered ceiling** reduces the weight of the dome without compromising strength. The walls are strengthened by brick relieving arches ("blind" arches)—visible in the exposed brickwork in a few of the interior niches and easy to see from outside.

Both Brunelleschi and Michelangelo studied this dome before building their own, in Florence and the Vatican, respectively. (The grandiose vision for St. Peter's Basilica was to place the dome of the Pantheon atop the Forum's Basilica of Constantine.)

At the top, the ❸ **oculus** is the building's only light source. It's completely open and almost 30 feet across. Looking up, you get a sense for how, in the pagan religion, the god or gods were distant. The dome overhead probably represented the dome of heaven where the gods lived. Rather than Jesus on earth as the people's connection to God, they had a kind of scary oculus through which to ponder the heavens.

The 1,800-year-old **floor**—with 80 percent of its original stones surviving—has holes in it and slants toward the edges to let rainwater drain. Although some of the floor's marble has been replaced, the design—alternating circles and squares—is original.

In ancient times, this was a one-stop-shopping temple where you could worship any of the major gods whose statues decorated the niches. Entering the temple, Romans came face to face with a larger-than-life statue of Jupiter, the King of the Gods (it stood where the ❹ **main altar** is today). The other niches, which today hold Christian images, may have contained statues of the heavenly pagan gods—the sun, the moon, and the known

planets. These were major deities, who controlled the stars and your daily horoscope (something Romans are fascinated by even today).

But the Romans had thousands more minor gods, each dedicated to a different part of their lives—the god of bread-baking, of fruit trees, even the god of manure. Romans were obsessively superstitious, and a visit to the Pantheon was a way to appease the fickle gods lest they smite them with bad juju. The Pantheon was not only for all of the gods, but also for all of the people, one of the rare public temples that allowed ordinary Romans—not just priests—to go inside.

After the fall of Rome, the Pantheon became a Christian church (from "all the gods" to "all the martyrs"), which saved it from architectural cannibalism and ensured its upkeep through the Dark Ages. (The year 2009 was the building's 1,400th anniversary as a church.) In the seventh century, a Byzantine emperor stripped the dome's interior of its original golden-tile ceiling. The twin grilled windows just right of the altar (at 2 o'clock) are a modern re-creation of the original and, along with the inlaid marble floor, give you a sense of the colorful ancient decor. Although the decoration has changed over the years, we stand beneath the same dome and experience the same wonder as the ancients.

Tombs

Its ancient statuary long gone, today the Pantheon's interior holds decorative sculptures and the tombs of important people from more recent centuries. The building that once honored pagan gods and Christian saints now honors secular saints of the arts and the Italian nation.

The artist **Raphael** (1483-1520) lies in

a ❺ stone coffin to the left of the main altar, in a lighted glass niche (facing the altar, he's at about 11 o'clock, beneath a statue of a Madonna and Child). The Latin inscription along the top honors the man who could capture nature with a brush. It reads, *Ille hic est Raffael*... "Here lies Raphael. In life, Nature feared to be outdone by him. In the artist's death, she feared she too would die."

On the wall above the tomb (left of the Madonna statue), look for the bronze bust of the handsome painter with his flowing locks. One of the holy trinity of Renaissance artists, Raphael combined the serene grace of Leonardo with the dramatic power of Michelangelo. He perfected his craft in Florence before being called to Rome, where he worked in the Vatican Palace at the same time Michelangelo was laboring down the hall on the Sistine ceiling. Besides his artistic talents, Raphael charmed everyone with an easygoing personality that epitomized the effortless grace of the Renaissance Man. He hobnobbed equally with kings, popes, businessmen, and beautiful ladies.

In his will, Raphael asked to be buried in the Pantheon, and he himself commissioned the Madonna and Child statue above his tomb. City fathers were glad to honor the man who'd done so much to beautify Rome with paintings, frescoes, and tapestries (which you can see in today's Vatican Museum, the Villa Farnesina, and elsewhere). Now Raphael lies in the place where he once came for inspiration.

Facing each other across the rotunda are the tombs of modern Italy's first two kings, members of the House of Savoy. The Roman eagle and the inscription, *Padre della Patria*—father of his country—announces the ❻ resting place of **King Victor Emmanuel II,** the leader of Italy when it united in 1861. Before then, Italy was divided into separate states ruled by foreigners. Victor Em-

manuel, as head of the small northern Italian province of Piedmont, was the only Italian-blooded ruler. Italian nationalists rallied around Victor Emmanuel—the natural choice for their first king. They drove out the foreign rulers and made Italy a parliamentarian democracy with Victor Emmanuel as the symbolic head. If you've been to Piazza Venezia, the huge white Victor Emmanuel monument is dedicated to him and to modern Italy. (This dates from a time when relations between the state and pope were not good— the bronze used for the king's tomb came from melted-down papal cannons.)

When Victor Emmanuel died, his son became king, so opposite the "father of the homeland" is the son of the father, **Umberto I.** ❼ His burial spot is marked with a monument made of porphyry marble—it's the color purple, which has long symbolized royalty. The monument is topped with a ceremonial crown sitting atop a stone pillow. Umberto ruled during a time of great social change, as Italy made the transition from rural feudalism to industrial democracy.

Beneath Umberto's tomb lies that of his queen (and first cousin), Margherita. Her sense of fashion (and extravagant collection of pearls) made her the toast of European royalty and the bane of Italian liberals. Margherita is best known as the person for whom the classic *pizza margherita* was named in 1889. With green basil, white mozzarella, and red tomato sauce, it's the color of the Italian flag. Although great patriots, Margherita and her husband were both unbending conservatives, and Umberto was shot by an assassin in 1900.

You may see fresh flowers placed at these tombs by Italian royalists and social conservatives. There's often a white-gloved guard standing by a guestbook, where visitors can register their support for the controversial Savoy family. They lost favor after collaborating with Mussolini and the fascists. In 1943, instead of standing by his people, the Savoy king abandoned Rome to the Germans and fled. After the war, the Italians abolished the monarchy, established a republic, and proclaimed that no male Savoy could ever again set foot on Italian soil. (Savoy royals weren't allowed back into Italy until 2003.) In exile, the Savoys demonstrated a knack for bad press, insisting that Italy owed them money, despite living in stunning wealth in Switzerland.

Think of all the history this place has seen. At Rome's peak it was a temple to pagan gods. As Christianity took over the empire, the pagan priests became persona non grata and the building crumbled along with the empire. When barbarians looted the city, they carried off some exterior marble, but the structure remained intact. In 609, it was saved from further architectural cannibalism when it became a Christian church, and the Virgin Mary replaced Jupiter at the high altar.

In Renaissance times, Raphael made detailed architectural drawings of this ancient building, and was buried here. A few centuries later, the Pantheon became the final resting spot of the Italian kings who first ruled modern Italy. And these days, visitors from around the world pack the place to remember the greatness of classical Rome. If ever a building illustrated the notion that architecture is art, it's the Pantheon.

The Pantheon is the only ancient building in Rome in continuous use since its construction. (When you leave, notice that the building is sunken below current street level, showing how the rest of the city has risen on 20 centuries of rubble.)

The Pantheon also contains the world's greatest Roman column. There it is, spanning the entire 142 feet from heaven to earth—the pillar of light from the oculus.

• *Leaving the Pantheon, take a moment to enjoy the square facing it. Piazza della Rotonda has been a gathering place for 2,000 years. Its slope illustrates the literal "rise of Rome." Imagine in past centuries when there was a fish and chicken market in the portico. In an 18th-century urban beautification project, the fountain and obelisk were added. Feel the vibrancy of the piazza culture, which goes back to ancient Rome.*

Churches near the Pantheon

Many visitors just see the Pantheon and leave the neighborhood. But consider visiting one or more of these four unique churches, all less than 10 minutes' walk from the Pantheon (for locations, refer to the "Churches near the Pantheon" map). If you're budgeting your energy, here's a quick rundown on what each has to offer: San Luigi houses several stunning Caravaggio paintings. The Gesù is packed with ornate art and Jesuit history. Santa Maria sopra Minerva, Rome's only Gothic church, has a Michelangelo sculpture and St. Catherine's tomb. Finally, Sant'Ignazio is full of Baroque perspective illusions that will leave your head spinning.

CHURCH OF SAN LUIGI DEI FRANCESI

This is the national church of France *(dei francesi)* in Rome. You'll find French motifs throughout. Outside, check out the salamander (at eye level), symbol of François I, the French king who brought Leonardo (and the Renaissance) north from Italy to France. Step inside and stand on the marble inlaid fleur-de-lis in the center rear of the nave.

This is a Renaissance building with Baroque icing. The stylized fleurs-de-lis scattered throughout are emblems of French royalty. On the ceiling of the nave is France's King (a.k.a. Saint) Louis IX ascending to heaven. You'll see him again in the center chapel on the left. Joan of Arc stands (posing as usual) over your left shoulder, taking it all in just like you.

The church's highlight is the chapel in the far-left front corner, which was decorated by Caravaggio. This church makes a great little detour between the Pantheon and nearby Piazza Navona.

• *In the Caravaggio chapel, pop in a euro coin for light and look first to the left wall.*

PANTHEON

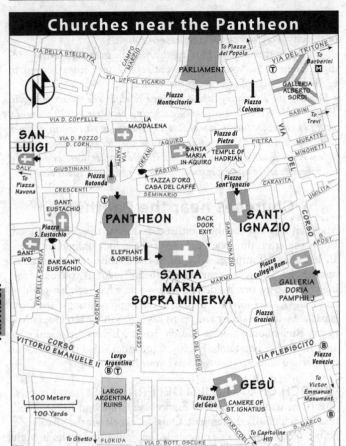

Churches near the Pantheon

(Map shows streets and landmarks including:)

VIA DELLA STELLETTA · CAMPO MARZIO · VIA UFFICI VICARIO · To Piazza del Popolo · VIA DEL TRITONE · To Barberini M · PARLIAMENT · Piazza Montecitorio · Piazza Colonna · T · GALLERIA ALBERTO SORDI · SABINI · To Trevi · VIA D. COPPELLE · LA MADDALENA · Piazza di Pietra · PIETRA · MURATTE · MINGHETTI · **SAN LUIGI** · VIA D. POZZO D. CORN. · AQUIRO · SANTA MARIA IN AQUIRO · TEMPLE OF HADRIAN · CARAVITA · UMILTA · SALV. · GIUSTINIANI · Piazza Rotonda · PASTINI · TAZZA D'ORO CASA DEL CAFFÈ · Piazza Sant'Ignazio · VIA DEL CORSO · To Piazza Navona · CRESCENTI · SEMINARIO · **SANT' IGNAZIO** · S. APOST. · SANT' EUSTACHIO · **PANTHEON** · T · BACK DOOR EXIT · Piazza S. Eustachio · ELEPHANT & OBELISK · Piazza Collegio Rom. · GALLERIA DORIA PAMPHILJ · SANT' IVO · BAR SANT' EUSTACHIO · **SANTA MARIA SOPRA MINERVA** · MARMO · Piazza Grazioli · VIA DELLA SCROFA · ARGENTINA · CESTARI · VIA DEL GESÙ · VIA PLEBISCITO · B · Piazza Venezia · CORSO VITTORIO EMANUELE II · Largo Argentina · B · T · To Victor Emmanuel Monument · **GESÙ** · LARGO ARGENTINA RUINS · Piazza del Gesù · CAMERE OF ST. IGNATIUS · B · To Ghetto · FLORIDA · VIA D. BOTT. OSCURE · D'ARACELI · To Capitoline Hill · S. MARCO

100 Meters · 100 Yards

The Calling of St. Matthew

Matthew (old man with beard) and his well-dressed, tax-collecting cronies sit in a dingy Roman tavern and count the money they've extorted. Suddenly, two men in robes and bare feet enter from the right—Jesus and Peter. Jesus' "Creation-of-Adam" hand emerges from the darkness to point at Matthew. A shaft of light extends the gesture, lighting up the face of Matthew, who points to himself, *Last Supper*-style, to ask, "You talkin' to me?"

Jesus came to convince Matthew to leave his sleazy job and preach Love. Matthew did.

In this, his first large-scale work, 29-year-old Caravaggio (1571-1610) shocked critics and clerics by showing a holy scene in a down-to-earth location. Lower-class people in everyday clothes were his models; his setting was a dive bar (which he knew well). Christ's teeny gold halo is the only hint of the supernatural, as Caravaggio makes a bold proclamation—that miracles are natural events experienced in a profound way.

• *Now look to the center wall.*

The Inspiration of St. Matthew

Matthew followed Christ's call, traveled with him, and (supposedly) wrote Jesus' life story (the Gospel according to Matthew). Here, Matthew is hard at work when he's interrupted by an angel with a few suggestions. This sets the scene in motion. Matthew kneels on a stool, which is just about to fall out of the painting and into our zone. Matthew's bald head, wrinkled face, and grizzled beard make him an all-too-human saint. Even the teen angel lacks a holy glow—he just hangs there. Caravaggio paints a dark background, then shines a dramatic spotlight on the few things that tell the story.

• *Finally, check out the right wall.*

The Martyrdom of St. Matthew

Matthew lies prone, while a truly scary man straddles him and brandishes a sword. The bystanders shrink away from this angry

executioner. Caravaggio shines his harsh third-degree spotlight on Matthew and the killer, who are the focus of the painting. The other figures swirl around them in a circle (with the executioner's arm as the radius). Matthew, who thought he had already given up everything to follow Christ, now gives up his life as well. He is as open as a crucifix, accepting his fate, and reaching for a palm frond—symbolic of victory over death. The bearded face in the background (to the left of the executioner's shoulder) is a self-portrait of Caravaggio, observing the violence without getting involved.

When the chapel was unveiled in 1600, Caravaggio's ultra-realism shocked Rome. Although he died only 10 years later, his uncompromising details, emotional subjects, odd compositions, and dramatic lighting set the tone for later Baroque painters. (For a bit more on Caravaggio, see page 305.)

GESÙ CHURCH

The center of the Jesuit order (of which Pope Francis is a member) and the best symbol of the Catholic Counter-Reformation, the Gesù (jay-zoo) is packed with overblown art and underappreciated history. Consider seeing this church en route to Capitoline Hill.

❶ Exterior

The facade looks ho-hum, like a thousand no-name Catholic churches scattered from Europe to Southern California...until you

realize that this was the first, the model for all of the others. Its scroll-like shoulders were revolutionary, breaking up the rigid rectangles of Renaissance architecture and signaling the coming of Baroque. The travertine stone facade has been cleaned but—with its sponge-like properties and Rome's pollution—it will be black again soon enough.

The adjacent building, to the right of the church—called Camere of St. Ignatius—is where Ignatius of Loyola, the founder of the Jesuits, lived, worked, and died (free, Mon-Sat 16:00-18:00, Sun 10:00-12:00).

• *Step inside the Gesù Church, grab a seat, and look up at the huge painting on the ceiling (or take advantage of the neck-saving mirror).*

❷ The Triumph of the Name of Jesus

The church's sunroof opens, and we can see right up to heaven. A glowing cross with the initials "I.H.S." (from the Latinized Greek, "Jesus Savior of Mankind," adopted as the seal of the Society of Jesus) astounds the faithful and sends the infidels plunging downward. The twisted tangle of bodies—the damned—spills over the edge of the painting's frame on the way to hell. The painted bodies mingle with 3-D stucco bodies and a riot of decoration in a classic example of Baroque multimedia (created by one of Bernini's protégés, Giovanni Battista Gaulli, better known as Il Baciccio, in the 1670s).

During the Counter-Reformation, when Catholics fought Protestants for the hearts and minds of the world's Christians, art was a powerful propaganda weapon. The moral here is clear—hell

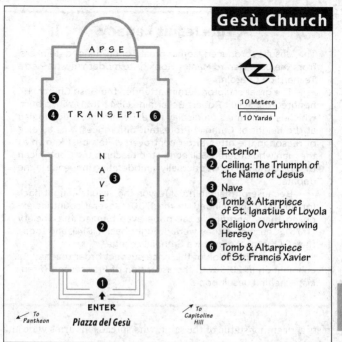

Gesù Church

APSE

⑤
④ TRANSEPT ⑥

N
A
V
E

③

②

① ENTER

Piazza del Gesù

← To Pantheon

↗ To Capitoline Hill

10 Meters
10 Yards

① Exterior
② Ceiling: The Triumph of the Name of Jesus
③ Nave
④ Tomb & Altarpiece of St. Ignatius of Loyola
⑤ Religion Overthrowing Heresy
⑥ Tomb & Altarpiece of St. Francis Xavier

PANTHEON

is the fate of Protestant heretics who dared to pervert the true teachings of Jesus.

❸ Nave

When the church was originally built (1568), the walls were white and the decor was simple. It was designed for what the Jesuits did best—teaching. The Jesuits wanted to educate Catholics to prepare them for the onslaught of pesky, probing Protestant questions. The church's nave is like one big lecture hall, with no traditional side aisles.

In the 1500s, the best way to keep Protestants from stealing your church members was to reason with them. By the 1600s, it was easier to kill them, and so the Thirty Years' War raged across Europe. The church became crusted over with the colorful, bombastic, jingoistic Baroque we see today.

• *Now look toward the left transept.*

❹ Tomb and Altarpiece of St. Ignatius of Loyola

A big altarpiece with towering columns and topped with statues of the Trinity marks the burial spot of the humble war veteran who founded the Jesuit order.

In the center of this altarpiece, you'll see a painting (by Andrea Pozzo) of Ignatius receiving his call. Behind the painting

The Jesuit Legacy

The Jesuits produced some great, open-minded thinkers, from the poet Gerard Manley Hopkins to modern mystic Pierre Teilhard de Chardin.

The great sculptor Bernini attended the Gesù Church. He honored the Jesuit Robert Bellarmine (1542-1621) with a bust, which is sometimes on display here. Bellarmine, a theologian at the height of Catholic-Protestant differences, was a voice of reason in the often bitter controversy. He's best known as the man who ordered Galileo to stop teaching the Copernican theory, although he was actually a moderating influence in the debate.

Because of their spiritual fervor, the Jesuits caught flack for being closed-minded. In the 1700s, several countries expelled them, and finally the pope even banned the Society (1773). Chastened, they were brought back (1814), and today they fill the staff of many a Catholic college.

The rehabilitation of this once-suspect order reached its culmination in 2013 with the ascension of Francesco I (Francis)—the first Jesuit pope.

rests a gleaming statue of the saint, who spreads his arms wide and gazes up, receiving a vision from on high. But you won't be able to see it unless you come after 17:30 (see sidebar).

Ignatius (1491-1556) was a Spanish soldier during the era of conquistadors. Then, at age 30, he was struck down by a cannonball. While convalescing, he was seized by the burning desire to change his life. He wandered Europe and traveled to Jerusalem. He meditated with monks. He lived in a cave. At 33, he enrolled in a school for boys to fill in the knowledge he'd missed. He studied in Paris and Rome. Finally, after almost two decades of learning and seeking, he found a way to combine his military training with his spiritual aspirations.

In 1540, the pope gave approval to Ignatius and his small band of followers—the Society of Jesus (Jesuits). These monks (technically, priests or friars), organized like a military company, vowed complete obedience to their "General" and placed themselves at the service of the pope. Their mission: to be intellectual warriors doing battle with heretics. They were in the right place at the right time—Ignatius and Martin Luther were almost exact contemporaries.

Ignatius' body lies in the small coffin beneath the statue (near

---

The Spectacle of Baroque

At 17:30 every day, a 20-minute service takes place at the Tomb of St. Ignatius in the Gesù Church, and all are welcome. During this time, a statue of Ignatius, housed behind the altar-piece painting, is unveiled.

The service starts with recorded music—"Kyrie eleison" (Lord, have mercy). Then a recorded voice (in Italian) tells the story of Ignatius and his impact, illustrated by spotlighting different parts of the tomb.

The service is squarely in the Baroque tradition—a multi-media extravaganza that combines painting, sculpture, music, words, and lighting effects. (Don't expect Hollywood-quality SFX—this is "spectacle" on a small, semi-cheesy scale.)

The ceremony is meant to tap into the heart, not the head, encouraging an emotional response to the faith. As the service unfolds, look around the church at its glorious art and architecture. Don't reflect. Be awed, amazed, moved.

At 17:45, church attendants turn a crank, and the altar-piece painting slowly lowers, revealing the gleaming statue of Ignatius in his ta-da pose. After a few closing words, the choir finishes with "Gloria in excelsis Deo" (Glory to God in the highest). Amen.

---

ground level). This simple, intense man might have been embarrassed by the lavish memorial to him, with its silver, gold, green marble, and lapis lazuli columns. Above the painting of Ignatius, a statue of God stands near a lapis lazuli globe (under the sunburst, the biggest in the world) and gestures as though to say, "Go and spread the Word to every land"...which the Jesuits tried to do.

• *Look at the marble statue group to the right of Ignatius.*

❺ *Religion Overthrowing Heresy*

This statue (and a similar one to the left of Ignatius) shows the Church as an angry nun hauling back with a whip and just spanking a bunch of miserable Protestants. The man with the serpent (Luther) is being stepped upon while the angry cherub rips pages out of a heretical book. Not too subtle.

The Jesuits earned a reputation for unfeeling dedication to truth above all else. Their weapons were words, ideas, and critical reasoning. They taught and defended the recently revamped doctrines of the

Council of Trent (a reaction against—and a response to—the Reformation, 1545-1563).

• *Now view the right transept.*

❻ Tomb and Altarpiece of St. Francis Xavier

This was also the Age of Discovery, when Spain and Portugal were colonizing and Christianizing the world, using force if necessary. Francis Xavier joined a Portuguese expedition and headed out to convert the heathens. His right hand, with which he baptized and healed, is encased in a glass reliquary above his tomb. Francis touched down in Africa, India, Indonesia, China, and Japan. Along the way, he learned new languages and customs, trying to communicate a strange, monotheistic religion to puzzled polytheists.

He had been on the road for more than a decade (1552) when he died on an island off the coast of China (see the dim painting over the altar). Thanks largely to the tireless evangelizing of zealous Jesuits such as Francis, Catholicism became a truly worldwide religion.

CHURCH OF SANTA MARIA SOPRA MINERVA

From the outside, survey the many layers of Rome: An Egyptian obelisk sits on a Baroque elephant (by Bernini) in front of a Gothic church built over *(sopra)* a pre-Christian, pagan Temple of Minerva.

Before stepping in, notice the high-water-mark plaques *(alluvione)* on the wall to the right of the door. Each time the Tiber River flooded, it left silt, which contributed to the slow and steady geological rise of Rome. Inside, you'll see that the lower parts of some frescoes were lost to floods. After the last great flood, in 1870, Rome built the present embankments along the river, finally breaking the spirit of the mighty Tiber.

Nave

This is the only Gothic church you'll see in Rome. (During the Gothic 14th century, with the pope residing in France, Rome was left to local barons and little was built.) The ceiling has pointed crisscross arches in a starry, luminous blue sky, and the nave is lit by rows of round stained-glass windows. When this Dominican church was built, Gothic was the rage in northern Europe, with large windows to let in the light—though churches in Italy were so colorful there was less emphasis on colored glass. During the

Middle Ages, Rome was almost a ghost town, and what little was built during this time was later gussied up in the Baroque style. The lack of Baroque excess in this church (in spite of its over-the-top, 19th-century renovation) is a refreshing exception. The blue ceiling studded with gold stars is similar to the one that decorated the Sistine Chapel before Michelangelo gave it an upgrade.

Main Altar

The body of St. Catherine of Siena lies under the altar (her head is in Siena). In the 1300s, this Italian nun was renowned for her righteousness and her visions of a mystical marriage with Jesus. Her impassioned letters convinced the pope to return from France to Rome, thus saving Italy from untold chaos. Behind her, two Medici popes are buried: Leo X, the son of Lorenzo the Magnificent and the man who excommunicated Martin Luther; and his cousin Clement VII. Both men were friends with Michelangelo, who was raised alongside them in the Medici household.

In 1633, a frail 70-year-old Galileo knelt at this altar on the way to his trial before the Inquisition in the church's monastery. Facing the fierce Dominican lawyers, he renounced his heretical belief that the earth moved around the sun. (Legend has it that as he walked out, he whispered, "But it *does* move.")

• *Left of the altar stands a little-known Michelangelo statue...*

Christ Bearing the Cross, 1519-1520

Note Jesus' athletic body, a striking contrast to the docile Jesus of medieval art. This sculpture shares the same bulging biceps as the Christ in Michelangelo's *The Last Judgment* in the Sistine Chapel. Christ's pose is slightly twisted, with one leg forward in typical *contrapposto* style, leaning on a large cross along with the symbols of the Crucifixion. Originally, Christ was buck naked, but later prudish Counter-Reformation censors gave him his bronze girdle.

This statue was Michelangelo's second attempt—he was forced to abandon a first effort due to a flaw in the block of Carrara marble. In this version, he left parts—including the face—to be finished by an apprentice, who took the liberty of working on and botching the feet and hands. This ineptitude led him to be replaced by yet another sculptor who finally finished the job. Michelangelo, disturbed that anyone would mess up his work, offered to redo the sculpture, but apparently the patrons were pleased. One contemporary said, "The knees alone are worth more than all of Rome together."

The tomb of the great early Renaissance painter (and Dominican brother) Fra Angelico ("Beato Angelico 1387-1455") is farther to the left (on the floor), just up the three stairs.

Over in the right (south) transept, pop in a coin for light, and enjoy a Filippino Lippi fresco showing scenes of the life of the great Dominican scholar St. Thomas Aquinas (big man in blue and white). In the central scene, Thomas—seeming to interrupt the Annunciation—presents the chapel's patron to Mary. Above, circling an ascended Mary, is a frolicking carousel of heavenly musicians—notice the delightful instruments. Meanwhile, on the right wall, Thomas displays a book to show everyone the true dogma, causing a heretic to slump defeated at his feet.

• *The Church of Sant'Ignazio is behind this church. If you're going there next, look for a little rear door (behind the Michelangelo statue) that's often open in the morning. If so, slip out that door, go down the alley, and turn left. Otherwise, exit the way you came in, refer to your map, and hike around the block.*

CHURCH OF SANT'IGNAZIO

This church is a riot of Baroque illusions. Stand in the middle of the nave and look up at the large, colorful ceiling fresco (or use the big mirror). Use the numbered fresco at right to find the following elements: ❶ St. Ignatius, whom we met in the Gesù Church, was the founder of the Jesuits, a disciplined Catholic teaching order charged with spreading the word of God around a world that was rapidly being "discovered." Here you see him (a small figure perched on a cloud in the center) having a ❷ vision of Christ with the Cross. Heavenly light from the vision bounces off his chest, and the rays beam to the four corners of the earth (including ❸ America, to the left, depicted as a bare-breasted Native American maiden spearing naked men). This fresco epitomizes pure Baroque drama, with perspective illusions that fool the eye into thinking the fresco is an extension of the church architecture. Note how the actual columns of the church are extended into the two-dimensional fresco. Now fix your eyes on the ❹ arch at the far end of the painting. Walk up the nave, and watch the arch grow and tower over you.

Before you reach the center of the church, stop at the small yellow disc (near the last row of pews) on the floor, and look up into the central (black) dome. Keeping your eye on the dome, walk under and past it. Building project runs out of money? Hire an artist to paint a fake, flat dome.

Now take a moment to survey the art in general, appreciating the tricks of the trade. For example, explore deep inside the

PANTHEON

right transept (on the left), where you'll find an explosive scene. The curtain is pulled back for the theatrical tomb of Pope Gregory XV—textbook bombastic Baroque. With trumpet fanfare and the stony curtain flapping in the spiritual wind, the pope springs with jubilation into eternal life.

As you leave, check out the permanent nativity scene *(presepe)* in the rear of the nave (to the right). Such *presepi* are a Roman tradition, with churches all over town displaying them each Christmas. This one depicts the first Christmas in Bethlehem as a classic 18th-century Neapolitan *presepe*.

Back outside, the church faces a headquarters of the Carabinieri police force (this station deals with art theft—a major problem in a country with so much to protect), forming Piazza Sant'Ignazio, a square with several converging streets that has been compared to a stage set. Sit on the church steps, admire the theatrical yellow backdrop, and watch the "actors" enter one way and exit another, in the human opera that is modern Rome.

• *From here it's a short walk to the left down Via del Seminario back to the Pantheon. Or go right, cross busy Via del Corso, and follow the crowds to the Trevi Fountain.*

COLOSSEUM TOUR

Colosseo

Rome has many layers—modern, Baroque, Renaissance, Christian. But let's face it: "Rome" is Caesars, gladiators, chariots, centurions, *"Et tu, Brute,"* trumpet fanfares, and thumbs-up or thumbs-down. That's the Rome we'll look at. Our "Caesar Shuffle" begins with the most popular relic of ancient Rome, the Colosseum. This was where Romans—whose taste for violence was the equal of modern America's—enjoyed their *Dirty Harrys* and *John Wicks*. Gladiators, criminals, and wild animals fought to the death in every conceivable scenario. It makes sense to see the Colosseum together with the Roman Forum and Palatine Hill, just next door, covered by a joint ticket, and described in the following two chapters.

Orientation

Cost: A €16 combo-ticket covers the Colosseum and the Roman Forum/Palatine Hill and is valid for 24 hours. Buy it online well in advance to get a reserved Colosseum entry time (www.coopculture.it, extra €2 booking fee); free for kids 17 and under (must present proof of age and have a ticket—also obtained online). A €22 Full Experience ticket is valid for two consecutive days and includes admission to the Colosseum (including choice of arena or underground area), Palatine Hill and Roman Forum, minor sights, and Imperial Forums.

The Colosseum is covered by the Roma Pass, but pass holders must reserve an entry time, either on the Colosseum website or by calling 06-3996-7575.

Hours: The Colosseum and the Roman Forum/Palatine Hill are open daily 8:30 until one hour before sunset: April-Aug until 19:15, Sept until 19:00, Oct until 18:30, Nov-mid-Feb until

16:30, mid-Feb–mid-March until 17:00, mid-March–late March until 17:30; last entry one hour before closing.

Free Entry: State museums in Italy, including the Colosseum, are free to enter once or twice a month, usually on a Sunday. Check in advance and avoid going on a free day, which can attract huge crowds.

Information: Call center tel. 06-3996-7700 (for tickets and tours, English spoken, open Mon-Fri 9:00-13:00 & 14:00-17:00, Sat 9:00-14:00, closed Sun); www.coopculture.it.

Reservations and Avoiding Lines: The solution to the crowded Colosseum is simple: Buy your ticket with a reserved-entry time online well in advance.

The official site is best (www.coopculture.it) but other sites may have more availability for a higher price (www.il-colosseo.it). Try to get an early-morning or late-afternoon time slot, because at midday the Colosseum can be so crowded that even reservation-holders can face ridiculously long waits. If the time-slot you want is sold out, there may be one available if you pay extra for an audio- or videoguide.

If you show up without a reservation you can suffer in the long ticket-buying line or, as a last resort, join one of the tours sold by hawkers outside the gate. (They purchase entry reservations on spec and make their money like scalpers by inflating the price and including a tour.) If you're desperate, you can join a tour to get in, then ditch it once inside. If you book a private tour in advance (see "Tours," below), the guide may be able to book your ticket and reservation.

Generally, crowds are thinner (and lines shorter) in the afternoon (especially after 16:00 in summer); this is also true at the Forum. A line typically has already formed at 8:30 when the Colosseum opens.

Getting There: The Colosseo Metro stop on line B is just across the street from the monument. Buses #51, #75, #85, #87, and #118 stop along Via dei Fori Imperiali near the Colosseum entrance (buses don't run on this street on Sun but still stop nearby), one of the Forum/Palatine Hill entrances, and Piazza Venezia. Tram #3 stops behind the Colosseum.

Getting In: The single entry point has two lines: one for those with reservations and another for the sorry lot without reservations.

Tours: A fact-filled **audioguide** is available just past the turnstiles (€5.50/1 hour). A handheld **videoguide**

senses where you are in the site and plays related clips (€6/50 minutes) but can be hard to see in bright sunlight.

🎧 Download my free Colosseum **audio tour.**

Official **guided tours** in English depart roughly hourly between 9:45 and 15:00 (€5 plus Colosseum ticket, 45-60 minutes, purchase inside Colosseum near ticket booth marked *Visite didattiche*).

A longer, interesting, but not essential 1.5-hour guided "Underground and Belvedere" tour takes you through areas that are otherwise off-limits, including the top floor and underground passageways. Advance reservations are required, either by phone or online.

Private guides stand outside the Colosseum looking for business (€25-30/2-hour tour of the Colosseum, Forum, and Palatine Hill). If booking a private guide on the spot, make sure that your tour will start right away and that the ticket you receive covers all three sights: the Colosseum, Forum, and Palatine Hill.

Length of This Tour: Allow an hour. If you're short on time, you can see the entire interior from a single viewpoint. It's not necessary to go upstairs or circle the place.

Baggage: Small bags are no problem. Larger bags and backpacks are not allowed, and there is no bag check. Spray cans and glass bottles are prohibited.

Restoration: The arena is being cleaned from top to bottom, given permanent lighting, and outfitted with new shops and services. These ongoing renovations, scheduled to last several years, may affect your visit.

Visitor Services: A WC (often crowded) is inside the Colosseum, and there are also water fountains. For tips on where to eat, drink, and find additional WCs, see the sidebar on page 170.

The Tour Begins

• *There it is! View the Colosseum from the Forum fence, across the street from the Colosseo Metro station.*

VIEWING THE EXTERIOR

Built when the Roman Empire was at its peak in AD 80, the Colosseum represents Rome at its grandest. The Flavian Amphitheater (the Colosseum's real name) was an arena for gladiator contests and public spectacles. When killing became a spectator sport, the Romans wanted to share the fun with as many people as possible, so they stuck two semicircular theaters together to create a freestanding amphitheater, the largest in the empire.

The sheer size of the Colosseum is impressive, even in our era

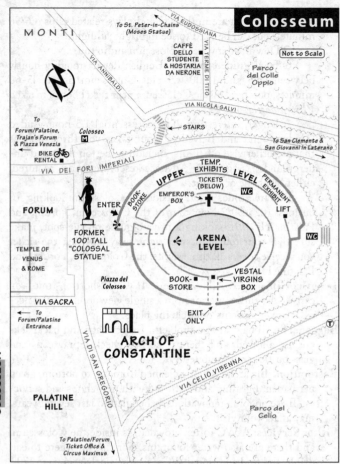

COLOSSEUM

of mega-stadiums. With four oversized stories, it's 160 feet high, nearly a third of a mile around, and makes an oval-shaped footprint that covers six acres.

Imagine the Colosseum in its glory days. The whole thing was a brilliant white, highlighted with brightly painted trim. Monumental statues of Greek and Roman gods (Zeus, Venus, Hercules), also in bright colors, stood in the arches of the middle two stories. The top of the structure was studded with wooden beams sticking straight up, to hold a canvas awning that shaded the spectators inside.

The stadium could accommodate 50,000 roaring fans (that's 100,000 thumbs). As Romans arrived for the games, they'd be greeted outside by a huge bronze statue of the emperor Nero—100 feet tall, gleaming in the sunlight—standing where the cypress trees stand today, between the Colosseum and the Metro stop.

Though the Colosseum is massive, it looks light and airy. The three lower stories are nothing but open arches, framed by half-columns. The arches are stacked right on top of each other, and all the columns line up as well, drawing your eye upward. Meanwhile, each story forms a horizontal band that wraps around the structure. This combination of horizontal and vertical makes the Colosseum appear firmly planted on the ground while reaching for the sky.

The Romans pioneered the use of concrete and the rounded arch, which enabled them to build on this tremendous scale. The exterior is a skeleton of 3.5 million cubic feet of travertine stone. (Each of the pillars flanking the ground-level arches weighs five tons.) It took 200 ox-drawn wagons shuttling back and forth every day for four years just to bring the stone here from Tivoli. The builders stacked stone blocks (without mortar) into the shape of an arch, supported temporarily by wooden scaffolding. Finally, they wedged a keystone into the top of the arch—it not only kept the arch from falling, but also could bear even more weight above. Iron pegs held the larger stones together; notice the small holes—the result of medieval peg poachers—that pockmark the sides. Only a third of the original Colosseum remains. Earthquakes destroyed some of it, but most was carted off during the Middle Ages and Renaissance as easy precut stone for other buildings.

The Colosseum's facade says a lot about the Roman personality. The Romans were engineers more than artists, so they borrowed decorative elements from the more cultured Greeks. Look closely at the half-columns that flank the arches. These ornamental columns have no structural purpose, and are done in the Greek style. At ground level, you'll see thick columns with simple capitals (the top part of the column). Moving up to the next story, the columns are thinner, with scroll-shaped capitals. On the third story, you'll find leafy capitals, and the top level has a fanciful mix of all three styles. These are the three "orders" of classical Greek architecture: sturdy Doric, scroll-shaped Ionic, and leafy Corinthian. By combining these classy Greek elements with pragmatic Roman engineering, the builders added a veneer of sophistication to this arena of death.

Of the 250 or so amphitheaters in the Roman Empire, this was the granddaddy of them all—the biggest, the most famous, and with all the top-notch gladiators. Out-of-town visitors marveled at the biggest man-made structure they'd ever seen. Over time, the Flavian Amphitheater acquired a nickname, perhaps from the "colossus" of Nero that stood outside, or maybe just because it was so darn colossal, the wonder of its age. It became...the Colosseum.

• To enter, line up in the correct queue (see "Getting In," earlier), and pass through security.

COLOSSEUM

TOURING THE INTERIOR

Once past the turnstiles, get your bearings. Signs direct you on a suggested (but not mandatory) visitors' route. It's a fine route, but you're free to see the place in almost any order you'd like. Since the whole arena is visible from everywhere—there wasn't a bad seat in the house—most of this chapter's descriptions work wherever you may wander.

Here's how I would structure my visit: After the turnstiles, walk directly to the arena and view it from ground level—near the Christian cross (see the "Colosseum" map, earlier). The cross is a good reference point, and I'd consider using the WC near here if it's not jammed. Then, climb the stairs to the permanent exhibit on the upper level. Tour the exhibit. Then step out to view the arena from that upper level. Circle the arena clockwise three-quarters of the way around. From there, enjoy a viewpoint overlooking the Arch of Constantine and Roman Forum, check out the fine bookstore, then take the stairs down to ground level and head for the exit.

Entering the Stadium

Imagine being an ancient spectator arriving for the games. Fans could pour in through ground-floor entrances; there were 76 numbered ones in addition to the emperor's private entrance on the north side. Your ticket (likely a pottery shard) was marked with your entrance, section, row, and seat number. You'd pass by concession stands selling fast food and souvenirs, such as wine glasses with the names of famous gladiators. A hallway leading to the seats was called a *vomitorium*. At exit time, the Colosseum would "vomit" out its contents, giving us the English word. It's estimated that a capacity crowd could enter and exit in just 15 minutes.

• *Wherever you spill out into the arena—upstairs or downstairs, at one side of the arena or the other—just take it all in and get oriented. The tallest side of the Colosseum (with the large Christian cross) is the north side.*

Arena

The games took place in this oval-shaped arena, 280 feet long by 165 feet wide. The ratio of length to width is close to the so-called golden ratio. Since the days of the Greek mathematician Pythagoras, artists considered that proportion (1.6 to 1) to be ideal, with almost mystical properties. The Colosseum's architects may have wanted their structure to

embody the perfect mathematical order they thought existed in nature.

When you look down into the arena, you're seeing the underground passages beneath the playing surface (which can be visited only on a private tour). The arena was originally covered with a wooden floor, then sprinkled with sand (*arena* in Latin). The bit of reconstructed floor gives you an accurate sense of the original arena level and the subterranean warren where animals and prisoners were held. As in modern stadiums, the spectators ringed the playing area in bleacher seats that slanted up from the arena floor.

Around you are the big brick masses that supported the tiers of seats.

A variety of materials were used to build the stadium. Look around. Big white travertine blocks stacked on top of each other formed the skeleton. The pillars for the bleachers were made with a shell of brick, filled in with concrete. Originally the bare brick was covered with marble columns or ornamental facing, so the interior was a brilliant white (they used white plaster for the upper-floor cheap seats).

The Colosseum's seating was strictly segregated. At ringside, the emperor, senators, Vestal Virgins, and VIPs occupied marble seats with their names carved on them (a few marble seats have been restored, at the east end). The next level up held those of noble birth. The level tourists now occupy was for ordinary free Roman citizens, called plebeians. Up at the very top (a hundred yards from the action), there were once wooden bleachers for the poorest people—foreigners, slaves, and women. While no seats survive, you can imagine the scene.

The top story of the Colosseum is mostly ruined—only the north side still retains its high wall. This was not part of the original three-story structure but was added around AD 230 after a fire necessitated repairs. Picture the awning that could be stretched across the top of the stadium by armies of sailors. The awning covered only about a third of the arena—so those at the top always enjoyed shade, while many nobles down below roasted in the sun.

Looking into the complex web of passageways beneath the

arena, imagine how busy the backstage action was. Gladiators strolled down the central corridor, from their warm-up yard on the east end to the arena entrance on the west. Some workers tended wild animals. Others prepared stage sets of trees or fake buildings, allowing the arena to be quickly transformed from an African jungle to a Greek temple. Props and sets were hauled up to arena level on 80 different elevator shafts via a system of ropes and pulleys. (You might be able to make out some small  rectangular shafts, especially near the center of the arena.) That means there were 80 different spots from which animals, warriors, and stage sets could pop up and magically appear.

The Games

The games pitted men against men, men against beasts, and beasts against beasts. The program began in the morning with a few warm-up acts. First came the animals, things like watching dogs bloody themselves attacking porcupines. Or you'd see hunters prowling through fake forests in search of prey. The Colosseum's menagerie of beasts came from all over the empire and were a sight in themselves: lions, tigers, and bears (Oh my!), crocodiles, elephants, rhinos, and hippos.

Animals were kept in cages beneath the arena floor, and at just the right moment, workers would hoist one up through a trap door into the stadium—the hunter didn't know where, when, or by what he'd be attacked. (This brought howls of laughter from the hardened fans in the cheap seats.) Nets ringed the arena to protect the crowd.

At lunchtime came Act Two. This is when criminals and POWs were executed, often in creative ways. They might be thrown to the lions—naked and unarmed. Or they were dressed up like classical heroes and forced to star in a play featuring their own death. When the "star" wandered onstage, dressed as, say, Hercules or Adonis, he'd be attacked by wild animals or by gladiators in costume, who'd kill him in the same way the legendary hero had died.

Between rounds, fans were treated to palate-cleansing gimmicks, such as a dwarf battling a one-legged man. Clowns, jugglers, and circus performers provided more comic relief.

Finally, in the afternoon, came the main event: the gladiators. Trumpets would blare, drums would pound, and the gladiators would enter the arena from the west end, parade around to the music, and pause at the south side. There, they'd acknowledge the Vestal Virgins sitting in their special box seats on the 50-yard line. (They got season tickets as a reward for their unique contribution to Roman society—chastity.) After a nod to the Virgins, the gladiators continued on to the emperor's box. There, they'd raise their weapons, salute, and shout *Ave, Caesar!*—"Hail Caesar! We who are about to die salute you!" (Though some scholars doubt they actually said that.)

These warriors had their own martial specialties. Some carried swords, protected only with a shield and a heavy helmet. Some threw the javelin. Others represented fighting fishermen, with a net to snare opponents and a trident to spear them. The gladiators were usually slaves, criminals, or poor people who saw a chance for freedom, wealth, and fame in the ring. They learned to fight in training schools, then battled their way up the ranks. The best were rewarded very much like our modern sports stars, with fan clubs, great wealth, and, yes, product endorsements.

The fight would begin. The gladiators would raise their weapons, shout, salute—and go at it. The crowd would roar. Imagine being a gladiator. Picture 50,000 screaming people around you, and imagine that they want to see you die.

If a gladiator fell helpless to the ground, his opponent would approach the emperor's box and ask: Should he live or should he die? Sometimes the emperor or master of ceremonies left the decision to the crowd, who judged how valiantly the man had fought and delivered the verdict—thumbs-up or thumbs-down. (Scholars debate exactly which gesture meant what.) The Romans thought nothing of condemning a coward to the death he deserved. After a gladiator was killed, a man dressed up like Charon—the Grim Reaper of Roman mythology—entered the arena and dragged the lifeless body away.

The Colosseum was inaugurated in AD 80 with a 100-day festival in which 2,000 men and 9,000 animals died. That's roughly one death every 5 minutes. Colosseum employees squirted perfumes around the stadium to mask the stench of blood.

Consider the value of these games in placating and controlling the huge Roman populace. In an age without a hint of a newsreel, it was hard for local Romans to visualize and appreciate the faraway conquests of their empire. The Colosseum spectacles were a way to bring home the environments, animals, and people of these conquered lands, parade them before the public, and make them real.

COLOSSEUM

Modern Amenities in the Ancient World

The area around the Colosseum, Forum, and Palatine Hill is rich in history but pretty barren when it comes to food, shelter, and WCs. Here are a few options:

The Colosseum has a crowded **WC** inside and a pay WC outside the arena's east end. If you can wait, Palatine Hill has several good WCs—at the Via di San Gregorio entrance, in the museum, near the stadium, near the entry to the Forum, and in the Farnese Gardens. The Forum has WCs at the entrance on Via dei Fori Imperiali and in the middle of the Forum (near #7 on the map on page 180).

Because **eating** options are limited, consider bringing a snack. The Colosseo Metro stop has forgettable hot sandwiches, and sells drinks. A few restaurants behind the Colosseum have expansive views but high prices and mediocre food. My recommended places are within a few blocks (no views but a better value—see page 391). The Monti neighborhood, with several recommended eateries, is just north of the Forum's Via dei Fori Imperiali entrance.

To refill your **water** bottle, stop at a fountain along the city streets, or inside the Colosseum, Forum, and Palatine Hill. There's also a high-tech water fountain next to the Colosseo Metro entrance.

A nice oasis is the free **information center** located across from the Forum entrance on Via dei Fori Imperiali and a bit east, toward the Colosseum (small café, food stand, WC; open daily 9:30-19:00). If your sightseeing takes you as far as **Capitoline Hill,** you'll find services at the Capitoline Museums, including a nice view café (see the Capitoline Museums Tour chapter).

Public buses (#85, #87, etc.) traverse Via dei Fori Imperiali between the Colosseum and Piazza Venezia, making it easy to hop on for a stop or two. For a **taxi,** use the stand near the Colosseum's southeast corner. (Taxis parked near the Colosseo Metro stop on Via dei Fori Imperiali have a bad reputation.)

Imagine never having seen an actual lion, and suddenly one jumps out to chase a prisoner in the arena. Seeing the king of beasts slain by a gladiator reminded the masses of man's triumph over nature.

And having the thumbs-up or thumbs-down authority over another person's life gave the spectators a real sense of power. Think of the psychological boost

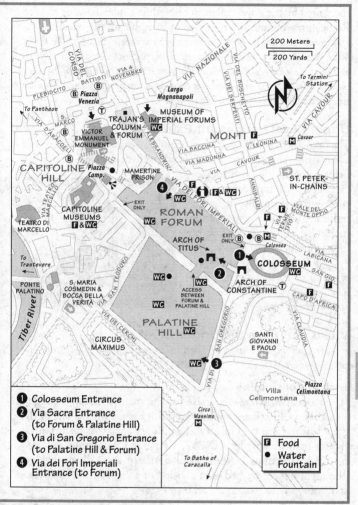

- **1** Colosseum Entrance
- **2** Via Sacra Entrance
  (to Forum & Palatine Hill)
- **3** Via di San Gregorio Entrance
  (to Palatine Hill & Forum)
- **4** Via dei Fori Imperiali
  Entrance (to Forum)

F Food
● Water
  Fountain

COLOSSEUM

the otherwise downtrodden masses felt when the emperor granted them this thrilling decision.

Did the Romans throw Christians to the lions as in the movies? Christians were definitely thrown to the lions, made to fight gladiators, crucified, and burned alive...but probably not here in this particular stadium. Maybe, but probably not.

Rome was a nation of warriors that built an empire by conquest. The battles fought against barbarians, Egyptians, and strange animals were played out daily here in the Colosseum for the benefit of city-slicker bureaucrats, who got vicarious thrills by watching brutes battle to the death. The contests were always free, sponsored by the government to bribe the people's favor or to keep Rome's growing masses of unemployed rabble off the streets.

• *With these scenes in mind, wander around, then check out the upper level. Stairs are at the east and west sides, with an elevator at the east end (accessible only to those who really need it). The upper deck offers more colossal views of the arena, plus a bookstore, temporary exhibits, and a fine permanent exhibit (near the elevator).*

Upper Level Permanent Exhibit

The permanent exhibit, with lots of ancient artifacts found here and fascinating reconstruction models (all well-described in English), helps bring to life both the ancient and medieval scene. It features intimate details, including pullies, pastimes, and seating hierarchy, and gives a close-up look at architectural details.

• *As you Rome about, be sure to find a spot at the west end of the upper deck, where you can look out over some of the sights nearby.*

Views Out from the Upper Level

• *Start your visual tour of sights outside the Colosseum with the big, white, triumphal arch.*

Arch of Constantine

If you are a Christian, were raised a Christian, or simply belong to a so-called Christian nation, ponder this arch. It marks one of the great turning points in history: the military coup that made Christianity mainstream. In AD 312, Emperor Constantine defeated his rival Maxentius in the crucial Battle of the Milvian Bridge. The night before, he had seen a vision of a cross in the sky. Constantine—whose mother and sister had already become Christians—became sole emperor and legalized Christianity. With this one battle, a once-obscure Jewish sect with a handful of followers became the state religion of the entire Western world. In AD 300, you could be killed for being a Christian; a century

later, you could be killed for not being one. Church enrollment boomed.

The restored arch is like an ancient museum. It's decorated entirely with recycled carvings originally made for other buildings. By covering it with exquisite carvings of high Roman art—works that glorified previous emperors—Constantine put himself in their league. Hadrian is featured in the round reliefs, with Marcus Aurelius in the square reliefs higher up. Originally, the emperors drove a chariot similar to the one topping the modern Victor Emmanuel Monument. Fourth-century Rome may have been in decline, but Constantine clung to its glorious past.

Surrounding Hills

Looking southwest, beyond the Arch of Constantine, you see Palatine Hill, dotted with umbrella pines. To the right of the Arch of Constantine is the road called Via Sacra ("Sacred Way"), once Rome's main street. It heads west up an incline toward the Arch of Titus (you can just make out its white top from here). That marks the top of the Forum, the religious, political, and commercial heart of ancient Rome (covered in the next chapter).

The Colosseum was built between three of Rome's legendary seven hills: Palatine (to the southwest), Esquiline (to the north), and Caelian (to the south). The Colosseum stands on land where the notorious Emperor Nero once had his sumptuous Golden House, which stretched from the Arch of Titus, across the valley, and up onto Esquiline Hill. After the house was replaced by the Colosseum, Nero's statue (or colossus) became the Colosseum's 100-foot-tall doorman.

• *Looking west, in the direction of the Forum, you'll see some ruins sitting atop a raised, rectangular-shaped hill. (You can recognize the hill by some door-like openings cut into the hill's support wall.) The ruins— consisting of an arched alcove made of brick and backed by a church bell tower—are all that remain of the once-great...*

Temple of Venus and Rome

At 100 feet tall, this temple atop a pedestal was one of the most prominent temples in Rome—and also its biggest. The size of a football field, it once cov-ered the entire hill. The style of the temple was Greek—surrounded by white columns and topped with a triangular pediment above the entrance. Today, the perimeter of the complex is still visible, marked by a few massive white columns, six feet thick.

The main ruin in the center—the tall brick arch with a cross-hatched ceiling—was once the *cella*, or sacred chamber of the temple. Here sat two monumental statues, back to back. Venus, the goddess of love, faced the Colosseum. The goddess called Roma Aeterna faced the Forum. The pair of statues symbolized the birth and eternal destiny of the race of people meant to endure forever.

The goddesses' Latin names were written in the twin *cella*s. On one side it read "Roma," and on the other, "Amor." Roma and Amor—a perfectly symmetrical palindrome, showing how Rome and Love were meant to go together. In ancient times, newlyweds ascended the staircase from the Colosseum (some parts are still visible) to the temple to ask Venus and Roma Aeterna to bring them good luck. These days, Roman couples get married at the adjacent church with the bell tower to ensure themselves love and happiness for eternity.

The temple was designed by Hadrian, the second-century emperor and amateur architect who also designed the Pantheon. Hadrian's design was critiqued by Rome's best-known architect, who complained that the huge statues would be so cramped they'd bump their heads if they stood up. Hadrian listened patiently to the criticism...then had the architect killed.

For a closer-up look at the Temple of Venus and Rome, access the ruins from within the Roman Forum.

THE COLOSSEUM'S LEGACY

With the coming of Christianity to Rome, the Colosseum and its deadly games slowly became politically incorrect. Gladiator contests continued here sporadically until they were completely banned in AD 435. Animal hunts continued a few decades longer. As the Roman Empire dwindled and the infrastructure crumbled, the stadium itself was neglected. Finally, around AD 523—after nearly 500 years of games—the last animal was killed, and the Colosseum shut its doors.

For the next thousand years, the structure was inhabited by various squatters (as illustrated very well in the permanent exhibit on the Colosseum's upper level). It was used for makeshift apartments and shops, as a church, a cemetery, and as a refuge during invasions and riots. Over time, the Colosseum was eroded by wind, rain, and the strain of gravity. Earthquakes weakened it, and a powerful quake in 1349 toppled the south side.

More than anything, the Colosseum was dismantled by Rome's citizens themselves, who carted off precut stones to be reused for the construction of palaces and churches, including St.

Peter's. The marble facing was pulverized into mortar, and 300 tons of iron brackets were pried out and melted down, resulting in the pockmarking you see today.

After centuries of neglect, a series of 16th-century popes took pity on the pagan structure. In memory of the Christians who may (or may not) have been martyred here, they shored up the south and west sides with bricks and placed the big cross on the north side of the arena.

Today, the Colosseum links Rome's glorious past with its vital present. Major political demonstrations begin or end here, providing protesters with an iconic backdrop for the TV cameras. On Good Friday, the pope comes here to lead pilgrims as they follow the Stations of the Cross.

The legend goes that as long as the Colosseum shall stand, the city of Rome shall also stand. For nearly 2,000 years, the Colosseum has been the enduring symbol of Rome, the Eternal City.

• *The Roman Forum is 100 yards to the right of the arch. You can go in through the entrance across from the Colosseum, the entrance on Via dei Fori Imperiali, or the entrance along Via di San Gregorio—see the map on page 180. If you're ready for a visit, turn to the next chapter.*

ROMAN FORUM TOUR

Foro Romano

The Forum was the political, religious, and commercial center of the city. Rome's most important temples and halls of justice were here. This was the place for religious processions, political demonstrations, elections, important speeches, and parades by conquering generals. As Rome's empire expanded, these few acres of land became the center of the civilized world.

Though I've covered them as two separate tours, the Roman Forum and Palatine Hill are organized as a single sight with one admission—meaning if you want to see both you'll need to do it in a single visit (unless you buy a Full Experience ticket; see below). The passage between the Forum and Palatine Hill is near the Arch of Titus. Don't exit the Forum through the turnstiles, hoping to walk down the street to the Palatine and re-enter; you won't be allowed in.

Orientation

Cost: A €16 combo-ticket covers the Colosseum/Forum/Palatine Hill. While it's possible to buy it at the entrance to any of these sights, you should buy your ticket online well in advance to get a reserved Colosseum entry time (www.coopculture.it, €2 booking fee).

    The €16 Forum Super Pass covers the Forum/Palatine Hill, Palatine's museum, Imperial Forums, House of Livia, and House of Augustus--but not the Colosseum. The €22 Full Experience ticket includes the Colosseum (plus choice of arena or underground area), as well as the Forum Super Pass sights, and is valid for two consecutive days.

Hours: The Roman Forum/Palatine Hill and Colosseum are all open daily 8:30 until one hour before sunset: April-Aug until 19:15, Sept until 19:00, Oct until 18:30, Nov-mid-Feb until 16:30, mid-Feb-mid-March until 17:00, mid-March-late March until 17:30; last entry one hour before closing.

Free Entry: State museums in Italy, including the Forum, are free to enter once or twice a month, usually on a Sunday. Check in advance and avoid going on a free day, which can attract huge crowds.

Information: Call center tel. 06-3996-7700, www.coopculture.it.

Avoiding Lines: Save time by buying your ticket in advance on-line. Generally, crowds are smaller in the afternoon, especially after 16:00 in summer.

Getting There: The closest Metro stop is Colosseo. Buses #51, #75, #85, #87, and #118 stop along Via dei Fori Imperiali near the Colosseum, the Forum, and Piazza Venezia (buses don't run on this street on Sun but still stop nearby).

Getting In: There are three main entrances to the Forum/Palatine Hill sight: 1) from the Colosseum (the most crowded entry)—nearest the Arch of Titus, where this chapter's guided walk starts; 2) from Via dei Fori Imperiali; and 3) from Via di San Gregorio—at south end of Palatine Hill, which is least crowded. With a Forum Super Pass or Full Experience ticket, you can also enter near Trajan's Column.

Tours: An unexciting yet informative **audioguide** helps decipher the rubble (€5/2 hours, €7 version includes Palatine Hill and lasts 3 hours, must leave ID). You must return it to where you rented it.

⌒ Download my free Roman Forum **audio tour.**

Length of This Tour: Allow 1.5 hours, plus any time you'll spend on Palatine Hill. If you have less time, end the walk at the Arch of Septimius Severus.

Services: A free information center, located across from the Via dei Fori Imperiali entrance, has a bookshop, small café, food stand, and WCs (daily 9:30-19:00). Bookstalls sell a variety of colorful books with plastic overlays that restore the ruins (official price in bookstore for larger version with DVD is €20 and for smaller version is €10—don't pay more, you're welcome to bargain).

WCs are at the Palatine Hill and Via dei Fori Imperiali ticket entrances. Within the Forum itself, there's one near #7 on the map. Others are at the base of Palatine Hill. For other WCs and suggested eateries, see the sidebar on page 170.

Plan Ahead: The ancient paving at the Forum is uneven; wear sturdy shoes. I carry a water bottle and refill it at the Forum's public drinking fountains.

Viewpoint: For fine views of the Forum (no ticket required), head

FORUM

to overlooks near the Mamertine Prison and higher up on Capitoline Hill.

Nearby: Nighttime **sound-and-light shows** illuminate Caesar's Forum and the Forum of Augustus (part of the Imperial Forums). For details, see the Nightlife in Rome chapter.

The Tour Begins

• *Whichever entrance you use, our tour begins at the Arch of Titus (Arco di Tito). It's the white triumphal arch that rises above the rubble on the east end of the Forum (closest to the Colosseum). Stand at the viewpoint alongside the arch and gaze over the valley known as the Roman Forum.*

View of the Forum

The Forum is a rectangular valley running roughly east (the Colosseum end) to west (Capitoline Hill, with its bell tower). The rocky path at your feet is the Via Sacra.

It leads from the Arch of Titus, through the trees, past the large brick Senate building, through the triumphal arch at the far end, and up Capitoline Hill. The hill to your left (with all the trees) is Palatine Hill.

Picture being here when a conquering general returned to Rome with crates of booty. The valley was full of gleaming white buildings topped with bronze roofs. The Via Sacra—the Forum's Main Street—would be lined with citizens waving branches and carrying torches. The trumpets would sound as the parade began. First came porters, carrying chests full of gold and jewels. Then, a parade of exotic animals from the conquered lands—elephants, giraffes, hippopotamuses—for the crowd to "ooh" and "ahh" at. Next came the prisoners in chains, with the captive king on a wheeled platform so the people could jeer and spit at him. Finally, the conquering hero himself would drive down in his four-horse chariot, with rose petals strewn in his path. The whole procession would run the length of the Forum and up the face of Capitoline Hill to the Temple of Saturn (the eight big columns midway up the hill—#15 on the map in this chapter), where they'd place the booty in Rome's coffers.

Then they'd continue up to the summit to the Temple of Jupiter—you can't see the temple from here (only ruins of its foundation remain—within the Capitoline Museums). Meeting the priests at the temple, they'd dedicate the victory to the king of the gods. Conquest by conquest, Rome grew from a small band of villagers huddled in this valley, to an empire stretching across Europe and beyond. The wealth of that far-flung empire flowed inward to the city of Rome.

❶ Arch of Titus (Arco di Tito)

The Arch of Titus commemorated the Roman victory over the province of Judaea (Israel) in AD 70. The Romans had a reputa-

tion as benevolent conquerors who tolerated local customs and rulers. All they required was allegiance to the empire, shown by worshipping the emperor as a god. No problem for most conquered people, who already had half a dozen gods on their prayer lists anyway. But Israelites believed in only one god, and it wasn't the emperor. Israel revolted. After a short but bitter war, the Romans defeated the rebels, took Jerusalem, destroyed their temple (leaving only a fragment of one wall's foundation—today's revered "Wailing Wall"), and brought home 50,000 Jewish slaves... who were forced to build this arch (and the Colosseum).

Roman propaganda decorates the inside of the arch, where a relief shows the emperor Titus in a chariot being crowned by the goddess Victory. (Thanks

to modern pollution, they both look like they've been through the wars.) The other side shows booty from the sacking of the temple in Jerusalem—soldiers carrying a Jewish menorah and other plunder. The two (unfinished)

plaques on poles were to have listed the conquered cities. Look at the top of the ceiling. Constructed after Titus' death, the relief shows him riding an eagle to heaven, where he'll become one of the gods.

The brutal crushing of the AD 70 rebellion (and another one 60 years later) devastated the nation of Israel. With no temple as a center for their faith, the Jews scattered throughout the world (the Diaspora). There would be no Jewish political entity again for almost 2,000 years, until modern Israel was created after World War II.

As you begin this Forum tour, see things with "period eyes." We imagine the structures in ancient Rome as mostly white, but

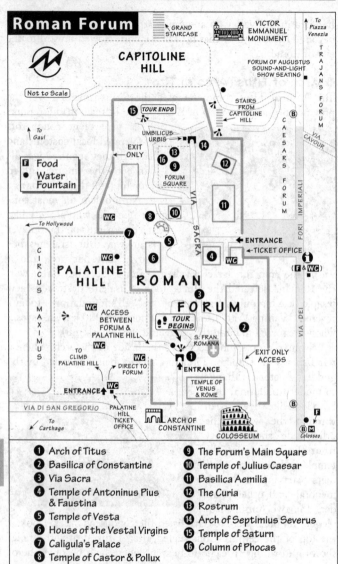

Roman Forum

GRAND
STAIRCASE

VICTOR
EMMANUEL
MONUMENT

To
Piazza
Venezia

CAPITOLINE
HILL

FORUM OF AUGUSTUS
SOUND-AND-LIGHT
SHOW SEATING

T
R
A
J
A
N
S

F
O
R
U
M

Not to Scale

15 TOUR ENDS

To
Gaul

STAIRS
FROM
CAPITOLINE
HILL

B

C
A
E
S
A
R
S

F
O
R
U
M

VIA
CAVOUR

B

UMBILICUS
URBIS

14

EXIT
ONLY

16 13

12

F Food

● Water
Fountain

FORUM
SQUARE

11

To Hollywood

WC

8

10

VIA
SACRA

ENTRANCE

TICKET OFFICE

7

5

i

C
I
R
C
U
S

M
A
X
I
M
U
S

WC

PALATINE
HILL

6

ROMAN

4

WC

(**F** & WC)

F
O
R
I

I
M
P
E
R
I
A
L
I

WC

FORUM

3

2

ACCESS
BETWEEN
FORUM &
PALATINE HILL

WC

TOUR
BEGINS

S. FRAN.
ROMANA

V
I
A

D
E
I

TO
CLIMB
PALATINE HILL

WC

DIRECT TO
FORUM

1

ENTRANCE

**EXIT ONLY
ACCESS**

ENTRANCE WC

TEMPLE OF
VENUS
& ROME

B

VIA DI SAN GREGORIO

PALATINE
HILL
TICKET
OFFICE

F

To
Carthage

ARCH OF
CONSTANTINE

COLOSSEUM

B M
Colosseo

FORUM

❶ Arch of Titus
❷ Basilica of Constantine
❸ Via Sacra
❹ Temple of Antoninus Pius
   & Faustina
❺ Temple of Vesta
❻ House of the Vestal Virgins
❼ Caligula's Palace
❽ Temple of Castor & Pollux

❾ The Forum's Main Square
❿ Temple of Julius Caesar
⓫ Basilica Aemilia
⓬ The Curia
⓭ Rostrum
⓮ Arch of Septimius Severus
⓯ Temple of Saturn
⓰ Column of Phocas

ornate buildings and monuments like the Arch of Titus were originally more colorful. Through the ages, builders scavenged stone
from the Forum, and the finest stone—the colored marble—was
cannibalized first. If any was left, it was generally the white stone.
Statues that filled the niches were vividly painted, but the organic paint rotted away as statues lay buried for centuries. Lettering
was inset bronze and eyes were inset ivory. Even seemingly intact

structures, like the Arch of Titus, have been reassembled. Notice the columns are half smooth and half fluted. The fluted halves are original; the smooth parts are reconstructions—intentionally not trying to fake the original.

And speaking of cannibalizing marble, remember that when marble burns it becomes lime, which is used to make cement. In the Middle Ages, before the historic importance of antiquity was appreciated, the Forum was surrounded by kilns used to melt marble. Much of the grandeur of ancient Rome—statues, reliefs, marble slabs—was loaded into these ovens, melted, and re-poured as concrete into the medieval city.

• *Walk down Via Sacra into the Forum. Imagine Roman sandals on these original basalt stones—the oldest street you'll ever walk. Many of the stones under your feet were walked on by Caesar Augustus 2,000 years ago. After about 50 yards, turn right and follow a path uphill to the three huge arches of the...*

❷ Basilica of Constantine (Basilica Maxentius)

Yes, these are big arches. But they represent only one-third of the original Basilica of Constantine, a mammoth hall of justice. The arches were matched by a similar set along the Via Sacra side (only a few squat brick piers remain). Between them ran the central hall, which was spanned by a roof 130 feet high—about 55 feet higher than the side arches you see. (The stub of brick you see sticking up began an arch that once spanned the central hall.) The hall itself was as long as a football field, lavishly furnished (with colorful in-laid marble, a gilded bronze ceiling, and statues), and filled with strolling Romans. At the far (west) end was an enormous marble statue of Emperor Constantine on a throne. (Pieces of this statue, including a hand the size of a man, are on display in Rome's Capitoline Museums.)

This "basilica" was not a church but a Roman hall of justice. In a society that was as legal-minded as America is today, you needed a lot of lawyers—and a big place to put them. Citizens came here to work out matters like inheritances and building permits, or to sue somebody.

FORUM

Rome: Republic and Empire (500 BC-AD 500)

Ancient Rome lasted for a thousand years, from about 500 BC to AD 500. During that time, Rome expanded from a small tribe of barbarians to a vast empire, then dwindled slowly to city size again. For the first 500 years, when Rome's armies made her ruler of the Italian peninsula and beyond, Rome was a republic governed by elected senators. Over the next 500 years, a time of world conquest and eventual decline, Rome was an empire ruled by a military-backed dictator.

Julius Caesar bridged the gap between republic and empire. This ambitious general and politician, popular with the people because of his military victories and charisma, suspended the Roman constitution and assumed dictatorial powers in about 50 BC. A few years later, he was assassinated by a conspiracy of senators. His adopted son, Augustus, succeeded him, and soon "Caesar" was not just a name but a title.

Emperor Augustus ushered in the Pax Romana, or Roman peace (AD 1-200), a time when Rome reached her peak and controlled an empire that stretched even beyond Eurail—from England to Egypt, Turkey to Morocco.

The basilica was begun by the emperor Maxentius, but after he was trounced in battle (see page 172), the victor Constantine completed the massive building. No doubt about it, the Romans built monuments on a more epic scale than any previous Europeans, wowing their "barbarian" neighbors.

• *Now backtrack downhill and stroll deeper into the Forum, turning right along the...*

❸ Via Sacra

Stroll through the trees, down this main drag of the ancient city. Imagine being an out-of-town visitor during Rome's heyday—maybe from Gaul (modern France) or Londinium (modern London). You know a little Latin, but nothing would have prepared you for the bustle of Rome—a city of a million people, by far the biggest in Europe. This street would be swarming with tribunes, slaves, and courtesans. Chariots whizzed by. Wooden stalls lined the roads, where merchants peddled their goods.

Think of all the history around you. You may pass by roped-off archaeological zones

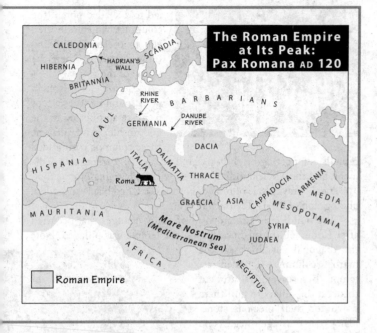

The Roman Empire
at Its Peak:
Pax Romana AD 120

CALEDONIA
HIBERNIA
HADRIAN'S WALL
SCANDIA
BRITANNIA
RHINE RIVER
B A R B A R I A N S
GERMANIA
DANUBE RIVER
GAUL
DACIA
HISPANIA
ITALIA
DALMATIA
THRACE
Roma
CAPPADOCIA
ARMENIA
MEDIA
GRAECIA
ASIA
MESOPOTAMIA
MAURITANIA
Mare Nostrum
(Mediterranean Sea)
SYRIA
JUDAEA
A F R I C A
AEGYPTUS

Roman Empire

or modern workers digging down through the millennia. The road beneath you is paved with large basalt stones. Sturdy roads like Via Sacra were part of an efficient transportation network—about 50,000 miles of paved roads in all. Roman businessmen traveled them on foot or in carts, the mail sped along in a kind of Pony Express system, and bureaucrats rode in chariots, allowing them to administer far-off lands.

On your right, you'll pass a building with a green door still swinging on its fourth-century hinges—the original bronze door to a temple that survived because it became a church shortly after the fall of Rome. This ancient temple is still in use, sometimes hosting modern exhibits. No wonder they call Rome the Eternal City.

• *Just past the ancient temple, 10 huge columns stand in front of a much newer-looking church. This colonnade was part of the...*

❹ Temple of Antoninus Pius and Faustina

The Senate built this temple to honor Emperor Antoninus Pius (AD 138-161) and his deified wife, Faustina. (The lintel's inscription calls them "*divo*" and "*divae*.") The 50-foot-tall Corinthian (leafy) columns must have been awe-inspiring to out-of-towners who grew up in thatched huts. Although the temple has been inhabited by a church, you can still see the basic layout—a staircase

FORUM

led to a shaded porch (the columns), which admitted you to the main building (now a church), where the statue of the god sat.

Picture a Roman priest climbing these steps to make an offering to the god inside. And imagine these columns with gilded capitals, supporting brightly painted statues in a triangular pediment, and the whole building capped with a gleaming bronze roof. The stately gray rubble of today's Forum is a faded black-and-white photograph of a 3-D Technicolor era.

The building is a microcosm of many changes that occurred after Rome fell. In medieval times, the temple was pillaged. Note the diagonal cuts high on the marble columns—a failed attempt by scavengers to cut through the pillars to pull them down for their precious stone. (They tried using vinegar and rope to cut the marble...but because vinegar also eats through rope, they abandoned the attempt.) In 1550, a church was

housed inside the ancient temple. The green door shows the street level at the time of Michelangelo. The long staircase was underground until excavated in the 1800s.

• *With your back to the colonnade, walk straight ahead—jogging a bit to the right to stay on the path. The dirt path leads to two sights associated with Rome's Vestal Virgins. Head for the three short columns, all that's left of the...*

❺ Temple of Vesta

This is perhaps Rome's most sacred spot. Notice that the temple remains are curved. Originally, this temple was circular, like a glorified farmer's hut—the kind Rome's first families lived in. Rome considered itself one big family, and inside this temple a fire burned, just as in a Roman home. Although we think of the Romans as decadent, in fact they prided themselves on their family values. People venerated their parents, grandparents, and ancestors, even keeping small statues of them in sacred shrines in their homes. This temple represented those family values on a large scale; its fire symbolized the "hearth" of the extended family that was Rome.

Back in those days, you never wanted your fire to go out. As long as the sacred flame burned, Rome would stand. The flame was tended by six priestesses known as the Vestal Virgins.

• *Backtrack a few steps up the path, behind the Temple of Vesta. You'll find a few stairs that lead up to a big, enclosed field with two rectangular brick pools (just below the hill). This was the courtyard of the...*

❻ House of the Vestal Virgins

The Vestal Virgins lived in a two-story building surrounding a long central courtyard with two pools at one end. Rows of statues depicting leading Vestal Virgins flanked the courtyard. This place was the model—both architecturally and sexually—for medieval convents and monasteries.

Chosen from noble families before they reached the age of 10, the six Vestal Virgins each served a 30-year term. Honored and revered by the Romans, the Vestals even had their own box seats opposite the emperor in the Colosseum. The statues that line the courtyard honor dutiful Vestals.

Their sacred duty was to be ceremonial homemakers, tending the temple-home of the goddess Vesta. They brought water from a sacred spring, cooked sacred food, polished the ritual silverware, and—most importantly—made sure the hearth fire never went out.

As the name implies, a Vestal took a vow of chastity. If she served her term faithfully—abstaining for 30 years—she was given a huge dowry and allowed to marry. But if they found any Virgin who wasn't, she was strapped to a funeral car, paraded through the streets of the Forum, taken to a crypt, given a loaf of bread and a lamp...and buried alive. Many Vestals suffered the latter fate.

• *Looming just beyond this field is Palatine Hill—the corner of which may have been...*

❼ Caligula's Palace (Palace of Tiberius)

Emperor Caligula (ruled AD 37-41) had a huge palace on Palatine Hill overlooking the Forum. It actually sprawled down the hill into the Forum (some supporting arches remain in the hillside).

Caligula was not a nice person. He tortured enemies, stole senators' wives, and parked his chariot in handicap spaces. But Rome's luxury-loving emperors only added to the glory of the Forum, with each one trying to make his mark on history.

• *Continue downhill, passing the three short columns of the Temple of Vesta, where you'll get a view of three very tall columns just beyond.*

❽ Temple of Castor and Pollux

These three columns—all that remain of a once-prestigious temple—have become the most photographed sight in the Forum. The temple was one of the city's oldest, built in the fifth century BC. It commemorated the Roman victory over the Tarquin, the notorious Etruscan king who once oppressed them. After the battle, the legendary twin brothers Castor and Pollux watered their horses here, at the Sacred Spring of Juturna (which has been excavated nearby).

As a symbol of Rome's self-governing republic, the temple was often used as a meeting place of senators, and its front steps served as a podium for free speech. The three columns are Corinthian style, featuring leafy capitals and fluting. They date from a later incarnation of the temple (first century).

• *The path spills into a flat, open area that stretches before you. This was the center of the ancient Forum.*

❾ The Forum's Main Square

The original Forum, or main square, was this flat patch about the size of a football field, stretching to the foot of Capitoline Hill. Surrounding it were temples, law courts, government buildings, and triumphal arches.

Rome was born right here. According to legend, twin brothers Romulus (Rome) and Remus were orphaned in infancy and raised by a she-wolf on top of Palatine Hill. Growing up, they found it hard to get dates. So they and their cohorts attacked the nearby Sabine tribe and kidnapped their women. After they made peace, this marshy valley became the meeting place and then the trading center for the scattered tribes on the surrounding hillsides.

Throughout Rome's long history, the square was the busiest and most crowded—and often the seediest—section of town. Besides the senators, politicians, and currency exchangers, there were even sleazier types—souvenir hawkers, pickpockets, fortunetellers, gamblers, slave marketers, drunks, hookers, lawyers, and tour guides.

Ancient Rome's population exceeded one million, more than any city until London and Paris in the 19th century. All those Roman masses lived in tiny apartments as we would live in tents at a campsite, basically just to sleep. The public space—their Forum, today's piazza—is where they did their living. Consider how, to this day, the piazza is still such an important part of any Italian town. Since Roman times, the piazza has reflected and accommodated the gregarious and outgoing nature of the Italian people.

The Forum is now rubble, but imagine it in its prime: blindingly brilliant marble buildings with 40-foot-high columns and shining metal roofs; rows of statues painted in realistic colors; processional chariots rattling down Via Sacra. Mentally replace tourists in T-shirts with tribunes in togas. Imagine the buildings towering and the people buzzing around you while an orator gives a rabble-rousing speech from the Rostrum. If things still look like just a pile of rocks, at least tell yourself, "But Julius Caesar once leaned against these rocks."

• *And speaking of Julius Caesar, at the near end of the main square (the end closest to the Colosseum) find the foundations of a temple now sheltered by a peaked wood-and-metal roof.*

❿ Temple of Julius Caesar (Tempio del Divo Giulio, or Ara di Cesare)

On March 15, in 44 BC, Julius Caesar was stabbed 23 times by political conspirators. After his assassination, Caesar's body was cremated on this spot (under the metal roof). Afterward, this temple was built to honor him. Peek behind the wall into the small apse area, where a mound of dirt usually has fresh flowers—given to remember the man who, more than any other, personified the greatness of Rome.

Caesar (100-44 BC) changed Rome—and the Forum—dramatically. He cleared out many of the wooden market stalls and

FORUM

Religion in Ancient Rome

Religion in ancient Rome was all about the *pax deorum* (peace, or pact, with the gods) that guaranteed the prosperity of the incredibly superstitious Romans. To appease the fickle gods, they performed elaborate rituals at lavish temples and shrines. Romans had a god for every moment of their days and each important event in their lives. While the Romans adopted the Greek pantheon, they also embraced the

gods from many of the people they came into contact with, sometimes using elaborate ceremonies to persuade these new gods to "move" to Rome. Scholars estimate Romans had about 30,000 gods to keep happy. In this high-maintenance religion, there was Cunina, the goddess who protected cradles; Statulinus, to help children stand up; and Fabulina, for their first words. Fornax was the oven god, Pomona the fruit-tree goddess, Sterculinus the manure god, and Venus Cloacina the sewer goddess.

Priests interpreted the will of the gods by studying the internal organs of sacrificed animals, the flight of birds, and prophetic books. A clap of thunder was enough to postpone a battle.

Astrology, magic rites, the cult of deified emperors, house gods, and the near-deification of ancestors permeated Roman life. But all these gods didn't quite do it for the Romans—they were gradually replaced by the rise of monotheistic religions from the East. In AD 313, Emperor Constantine legalized and embraced Christianity. By 390, the Christian God was the only legal god in Rome.

FORUM

began to ring the square with even grander buildings. Caesar's house was located behind the temple, near that clump of trees. He walked right by here on the day he was assassinated ("Beware the Ides of March!" warned a street-corner Etruscan preacher).

Although he was popular with the masses, not everyone liked Caesar's urban design or his politics. When he assumed dictatorial powers, he was ambushed and stabbed to death by a conspiracy of senators, including his adopted son, Brutus *("Et tu, Brute?").*

The funeral was held here, facing the main square. The citizens gathered, and speeches were made. Mark Antony stood up to say (in Shakespeare's words), "Friends, Romans, countrymen, lend me your ears. I come to bury Caesar, not to praise him." When Caesar's body was burned, his adoring fans threw anything at hand on the fire, requiring the fire department to come put it out. Later, Emperor Augustus dedicated this temple in his name, making Caesar the first Roman to become a god.

• *Continue past the Temple of Julius Caesar, to the open area between the columns of the Temple of Antoninus Pius and Faustina (which we passed earlier) and the boxy brick building (the Curia). You can view these ruins of the Basilica Aemilia from a ramp next to the Temple of Antoninus Pius and Faustina, or (if the path is open) walk among them.*

⓫ Basilica Aemilia

Notice the layout. This was a long, rectangular building. The stubby columns all in a row form one long, central hall flanked by two side

aisles. Medieval Christians required a larger meeting hall for their worship services than Roman temples provided, so they used the spacious Roman basilica as the model for their churches. Cathedrals from France to Spain to England, from Roman-

esque to Gothic to Renaissance, all have the same basic floor plan as a Roman basilica.

• *Now head for the big, well-preserved brick building with the triangular roof—the Curia. It's just to the right of the big triumphal arch at the foot of Capitoline Hill. While often closed, the building is impressive even from outside.*

⓬ The Curia (Senate House)

The Curia was the most important political building in the Forum. Since the birth of the republic, this was the site of Rome's official center of government. Three hundred senators, elected by the citizens of Rome, donned their togas, tucked their scrolls under their arms, and climbed the steps into this great hall. Inside, they gave speeches, debated policy, and created the laws of the land. They sat with their backs to the walls, surrounding the big hall on three sides, in three rows of seats. At the far end sat the Senate president—and later, the emperor—on his podium. The vast room still echoes with stirring speeches and passionate debates.

Rome prided itself on being a republic. Early in the city's history, its people threw out the king and established rule by elected representatives. Each Roman citizen was free to speak his mind and have a say in public policy. Even when emperors became the supreme authority, the Senate was a power to be reckoned with. (Note: Although Julius Caesar was assassinated in "the Senate," it wasn't here—the Senate was temporarily meeting across town.)

The present Curia building dates from AD 283, when it replaced an earlier Senate building. It's so well preserved because it was used as a church since early Christian times. In the 1930s, it was restored as a historic site.

On display inside the Curia (if it's open) are a statue and two reliefs that help build our mental image of life in the Forum long ago. The statue (with its head, arms, and feet now missing) was made of porphyry marble in about AD 100. It was a tribute to an emperor, probably Hadrian or Trajan. The relief panel on the left shows people with big stone tablets standing in line to destroy their debt records following a government amnesty. The other shows the distribution of grain (Rome's welfare system), some buildings in the background, and the latest fashion in togas. Today's marble floor is still the original from ancient times.

• *Go back down the Senate steps and find the 10-foot-high wall just to the left of the big arch, marked...*

⑬ Rostrum

Nowhere was Roman freedom of speech more apparent than at this "Speaker's Corner." The Rostrum was a raised platform, 10 feet high and 80 feet long, decorated with statues, columns, and the prows of ships.

On a stage like this, Rome's orators, great and small, tried to draw a crowd and sway public opinion. Picture the backdrop these speakers would have had—a mountain of marble buildings piling up on Capitoline Hill. Mark Antony rose to offer Caesar the laurel-leaf crown of kingship, which Caesar publicly (and hypocritically) refused—while privately becoming a dictator. Men such as Cicero—a contemporary of Julius Caesar—railed against the corruption and decadence that came with the city's newfound wealth.

Rome Falls

Remember that Rome lasted 1,000 years—500 years of growth, 200 years of peak power, and 300 years of gradual decay. The fall had many causes, among them the barbarians who pecked away at Rome's borders. Christians blamed the fall on moral decay. Pagans blamed it on Christians. Socialists blamed it on a shallow economy based on the spoils of war. (Republicans blamed it on Democrats.)

Whatever the reasons, the far-flung empire could no longer keep its grip on conquered lands, and it pulled back. Barbarian tribes from Germany and Asia attacked the Italian peninsula and even looted Rome itself in AD 410, leveling many of the buildings in the Forum. In 476, when the last emperor checked out and switched off the lights, Europe plunged into centuries of ignorance, poverty, and weak government—the Dark Ages.

But Rome lived on in the Catholic Church. Christianity was the state religion of Rome's last generations. Emperors became popes (both called themselves "Pontifex Maximus"), senators became bishops, orators became priests, and basilicas became churches. The glory of Rome remains eternal.

(Cicero paid the price: he was executed, and his head and hands were nailed to the Rostrum.)

In later years, when emperors ruled, it took real daring to speak out against the powers-that-be. Rome's democratic spirit was increasingly squelched. Eventually, the emperor and the army—not

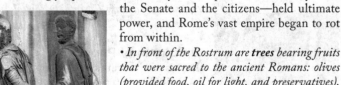

the Senate and the citizens—held ultimate power, and Rome's vast empire began to rot from within.

• *In front of the Rostrum are* **trees** *bearing fruits that were sacred to the ancient Romans: olives (provided food, oil for light, and preservatives), figs (tasty), and wine grapes (made a popular export product). Now turn your attention to the big arch to the right of the Rostrum, the...*

⑭ Arch of Septimius Severus

In imperial times, the Rostrum's voices of democracy would have been dwarfed by images of the empire, such as the huge six-

FORUM

story-high Arch of Septimius Severus (AD 203). The reliefs commemorate the African-born emperor's battles in Mesopotamia. Near ground level, see soldiers marching captured barbarians back to Rome for the victory parade. More and more, Rome's economy was based on slave power and foreign booty rather than on domestic production. And despite efficient rule by emperors like Severus, Rome's empire began to crumble under the weight of its own corruption, disease, and decaying infrastructure.

• *As we near the end of Rome's history, we're also nearing the end of our tour. Our next stop is the Temple of Saturn. You can see it from here—it's the eight big columns just up the slope of Capitol Hill. Or you could make your way to it for a closer look.*

⓯ Temple of Saturn

These columns framed the entrance to the Forum's oldest temple (497 BC). Inside was a humble, very old wooden statue of the god Saturn. The statue's claim to fame was its pedestal, which held the gold bars, coins, and jewels of Rome's state treasury, the booty collected by conquering generals.

Even older than the Temple of Saturn is the **Umbilicus Urbis,** which stands nearby (next to the Arch of Septimius Severus). A humble brick ruin marks this historic "Navel of the City." The spot was considered the center of the cosmos, and all distances in the empire were measured from here.

• *Now turn your attention from the Temple of Saturn, one of the Forum's first buildings, to one of its last monuments. Find a lone, tall column standing in the Forum in front of the Rostrum. It's fluted and topped with a leafy Corinthian capital. This is the...*

⓰ Column of Phocas

This is the Forum's last monument (AD 608), a gift from the powerful Byzantine Empire to a fallen empire— Rome. Given to commemorate the pagan Pantheon's becoming a Christian church, it was a symbolic last nail in ancient Rome's coffin. After Rome's 1,000-year reign, the city was looted by Vandals, the population of a million-plus shrank to about 10,000, and the once-grand city center—the Forum—was abandoned, slowly covered up by centuries of silt and dirt. In the 1700s, an English historian named Edward Gibbon overlooked this spot from Capitoline Hill. Hearing Christian monks singing at these pagan ruins, he looked out at the few columns poking up from the ground, pondered the decline and fall of the Roman Empire, and thought, "Hmm, that's a catchy title..."

• *Your tour is over. If you want to see Palatine Hill, don't leave the Forum complex; you won't be allowed back in without a new ticket. Instead, return to the Arch of Titus, where my Palatine Hill Tour—and this book's next chapter—begins.*

If you'd rather exit the Forum, be aware that the exact ways in and out change from year to year. Refer to your map for possible exit locations. If heading for Capitoline Hill, your best escape is likely on the west side (behind #16 on the map in this chapter).

PALATINE HILL TOUR

Monte Palatino

While many tourists consider Palatine Hill extra credit after the Forum, it offers insight into the greatness of Rome that's well worth the effort. (And, if you're visiting the Colosseum or Forum, you've got a ticket whether you like it or not.) Palatine Hill is nearly empty of tourists, but it's jam-packed with history—"the huts of Romulus," the huge Imperial Palace, a view of the Circus Maximus—but only the barest skeleton of rubble is left to tell the story. This tour—which is essentially walking through the remains of one massive palace—enables the thoughtful sightseer to bring those remains to life.

Palatine Hill is ideal for those who want to get away from the crowds and feel the romance and the melancholy of Rome's ruins. Become a 19th-century poet or a painter on the Grand Tour, meditating on the destiny of once-great civilizations, and wander through the remains of the palaces that nature has reclaimed for herself.

Although I've covered them as two separate tours, the Forum and Palatine Hill are organized as a single sight with one admission—meaning if you want to see both, you'll need to do it in a single visit unless you purchase a Full Experience ticket. The passage between the Forum and Palatine Hill is near the Arch of Titus. Don't exit Palatine Hill through the turnstiles, hoping to walk down the street to the Forum and reenter; you won't be allowed back in.

Orientation

Cost: A €16 combo-ticket covers the Colosseum/Forum/Palatine Hill. You can buy it at the Palatine entrance, but if your plans include the Colosseum, it's best to get the ticket online well in

advance to reserve a Colosseum entry time (www.coopculture.
it, €2 booking fee).

The €16 Forum Super Pass covers the Forum/Palatine
Hill, Palatine's museum, Imperial Forums, House of Livia,
and House of Augustus—but not the Colosseum. The €22
Full Experience ticket covers the Colosseum as well as the
Forum Super Pass sights, and is valid for two consecutive days.

Hours: The Roman Forum/Palatine Hill and the Colosseum have
the same hours—open daily 8:30 until one hour before sunset: April-Aug until 19:15, Sept until 19:00, Oct until 18:30,
Nov-mid-Feb until 16:30, mid-Feb-mid-March until 17:00,
mid-March-late March until 17:30; last entry one hour before
closing; www.parcocolosseo.it. Palatine Hill can be delightfully cool and peaceful at the end of the day.

Free Entry: State museums in Italy, including the Forum/Palatine
Hill, are free to enter once or twice a month, usually on a Sunday. Check in advance and avoid going on a free day, which
can attract huge crowds.

Information: Tel. 06-3996-7700, www.coopculture.it.

Getting There: The nearest Metro stop is Colosseo. Buses #51,
#75, #85, #87, and #118 stop along Via dei Fori Imperiali near
the Colosseum, the Forum, and Piazza Venezia (buses don't
run on this street on Sun but still stop nearby).

Getting In: There are three entrances to the combined Palatine/
Forum sight; see the "Palatine Hill" map in this chapter. The
easiest for our tour is the entrance on Via di San Gregorio, 150
yards from the Colosseum. Upon entering, follow the path to
the left as it winds to the top. Alternatively, if you sightsee the
Forum first, to get to Palatine Hill you must walk up from the
Arch of Titus.

Wherever you enter, our tour begins on the top of the hill
at the one big building still standing—the museum.

Tours: Audioguides cost €5/2 hours (€7 version includes Roman
Forum and lasts 3 hours, must leave ID and return the audioguide where you rent it).

Length of This Tour: Allow 1-1.5 hours. Don't miss the stadium
or the view of the Circus Maximus.

Services: WCs are rare in the Colosseum/Roman Forum/Palatine
Hill area. Your best options are here at Palatine Hill, where
you'll find WCs at the ticket office when you enter, on top
of the hill near the stadium, at the museum, near the access
point to the Forum, and hiding among the orange trees in the
Farnese Gardens. For eateries, see the sidebar on page 170.

Expect Changes: Parts of Palatine Hill are often closed off due to
ongoing archaeological work. Just see what you can, using this
chapter's map to navigate.

PALATINE HILL

The Tour Begins

• *Start on top of the hill at the Palatine Museum (Museo Palatino, #6 on the map). Once on top, it's easy to spot the museum: It's the one modern building amid the ruins.*

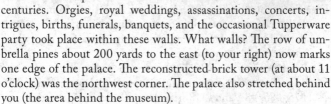

Grab a stone and sit with your back to the museum to orient yourself, facing in the direction of the Forum (roughly north).

THE IMPERIAL PALACE

You're sitting at the center of what was once a huge palace, the residence of emperors for three centuries. Orgies, royal weddings, assassinations, concerts, intrigues, births, funerals, banquets, and the occasional Tupperware party took place within these walls. What walls? The row of umbrella pines about 200 yards to the east (to your right) now marks one edge of the palace. The reconstructed brick tower (at about 11 o'clock) was the northwest corner. The palace also stretched behind you (the area behind the museum).

The area in front was the official wing of the palace; behind were the private quarters.

The palace was built by Emperor Domitian in about AD 81. It was later named the Domus Augustana because it was for centuries the house of the emperors. (In this case "Augustana" has nothing to do with Emperor Augustus but refers to emperors in general.) A poet of the day described it as so grand that it "made Jupiter jealous."

• *Now proceed, following the map for this 13-stop tour. With your back to the museum, head left to a big rectangular field with an octagonal brick design in the center—the main courtyard of the palace.*

❶ Main Courtyard (Peristilio) and Octagonal Fountain (Fontana Ottagona)

The brick octagon was a sunken fountain in the middle of an open-air courtyard. Like many fine Roman homes, this palace was built

around an oasis of peace where you could enjoy the sun, catch the precious rain, and listen to the babble of the fountain. The courtyard was lined with columns (notice the fragments) supporting an arcade for shade. Origi-

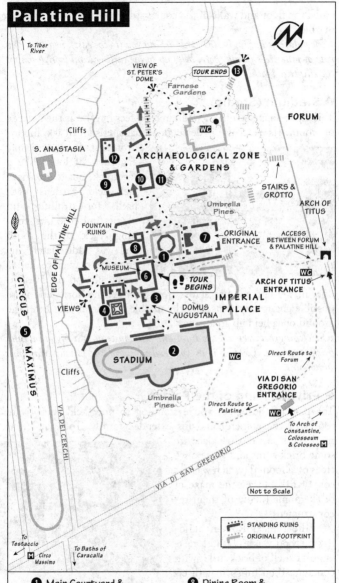

Palatine Hill

To Tiber River

VIEW OF ST. PETER'S DOME

Farnese Gardens

TOUR ENDS ⓭

FORUM

Cliffs

S. ANASTASIA

WC

⓬

ARCHAEOLOGICAL ZONE & GARDENS

ⓐ ⓑ ⓒ

STAIRS & GROTTO

Umbrella Pines

ARCH OF TITUS

FOUNTAIN RUINS

ⓗ

ⓐ

ORIGINAL ENTRANCE

ⓖ

ACCESS BETWEEN FORUM & PALATINE HILL

MUSEUM

ⓕ

ⓐ

WC

EDGE OF PALATINE HILL

TOUR BEGINS

ⓒ

ARCH OF TITUS ENTRANCE

VIEWS

ⓓ

DOMUS AUGUSTANA

IMPERIAL PALACE

CIRCUS MAXIMUS

ⓔ

STADIUM

ⓑ

WC

Direct Route to Forum

Cliffs

Umbrella Pines

VIA DI SAN GREGORIO ENTRANCE

Direct Route to Palatine

WC

To Arch of Constantine, Colosseum & Colosseo Ⓜ

VIA DEI CERCHI

VIA DI SAN GREGORIO

Not to Scale

To Testaccio
Ⓜ Circo Massimo

To Baths of Caracalla

STANDING RUINS
ORIGINAL FOOTPRINT

PALATINE HILL

❶ Main Courtyard & Octagonal Fountain
❷ Stadium
❸ Private Wing of the Palace
❹ Lower Courtyard
❺ Circus Maximus
❻ Museum & WC
❼ Throne Room
❽ Dining Room & Fountain Room
❾ House of Augustus
❿ House of Livia
⓫ Cryptoporticus
⓬ Huts of Romulus
⓭ Farnese Gardens & Forum View

nally, the floor and walls of the courtyard were faced with colorful marble.

• *The palace's stadium is 100 yards behind you (to the east), near the long row of pine trees. Walk there, belly up to the railing, and look down on the elliptical track.*

❷ Stadium (Stadio)

This cigar-shaped, sunken stadium (500 feet long) was the palace's rec room. Its exact use is debated: archaeologists call it a hippo-

drome, stadium, or simply a garden. It looks like a racetrack, but it may have just held gardens with paths for strolling and meditating. The oval running track at the south end was added later. The emperor may have had a raised box on the 50-yard

line, in the curved apse across from you. At the north end were possible changing rooms, and the marble fragments that litter the ground once held up an arcade.

• *Stretching between the stadium and the museum is a big, rambling brick structure. Explore it as you walk toward the Circus Maximus viewpoint.*

❸ Private Wing of the Palace

The part of the palace you're standing in now held the private rooms of the emperor and his extended family. Today, all that marks this part of the palace are some brick ruins and three olive trees on a mound (which was the courtyard). Survey the maze of brick rooms (many of them re-constructed).

The typical Roman build-ing method was to build a rect-angular shell of brick, fill it with concrete, then finish it with ei-ther plaster (you'll see an occasional faded fresco) or a veneer of marble. The small, round pockmarks on many walls show where the marble sheets were fastened.

The square holes in the walls held wooden beams, which were used for scaffolding during construction and maintenance, for shelves, and to support wooden floors.

Over the doorways, the bricks in the walls form the pattern of an arch. These "blind arches" were structural elements that allowed the walls to be built higher and stronger. The iron bar clamps are recent additions and hold the crumbling walls together.

The many niches and apses once held statues. Every family had their own household gods and displayed small images of these guardian spirits, as well as busts of honored ancestors.

The fragments of columns, reliefs, and sculpture scattered about suggest the wealth of this great palace. Notice surviving in-laid marble floors. The floor plan was complex—a fantasyland maze of small, private, sometimes even curved rooms.

• *Walk a little farther. In the south part of the palace (behind the museum), you can look down on the ruins of the lower story.*

❹ Lower Courtyard

This open-air courtyard has the concave-convex remains of a large fountain that must have been a marvel. Try to mentally reconstruct

the palace that surrounded this fountain. The emperors could look down on it from the upper story (where you're standing) or view it from the rooms around it on the lower story, where the emperor and his family ate their meals in private.

The lower story was built into the slope of the hill. The southern part of the palace was an extension of the hill-side, supported beneath your feet by big arches.

• *Continue to the far edge of the hill (directly behind the museum), to a viewpoint*
overlooking a long, wide grassy field—what once was the Circus Maximus.

❺ Circus Maximus

If the gladiator show at the Colosseum was sold out, you could always get a seat at Circus Max. In an early version of today's demolition derby, Ben-Hur and his fellow charioteers once raced recklessly around this oblong course.

Locate the track's various features. (Compare what you see today with the artist's reconstruction in the photo below.) Directly across from you is a sloping hillside—this once supported the bleachers. The dusty flat land at the base of the former bleachers was the track itself, stretching to your right and left. On the right end was the track's starting point. In the middle of the track you can make out a long, raised, grassy strip of land. This was what the chariots raced around. Find the lone cypress tree to the right that now marks one end of that strip. Got it? Now, imagine the scene...

The track was 1,300 feet long, while the stadium was much bigger. It seated—get this—250,000 people. The wooden bleachers once collapsed during a race, killing thousands.

The horses began at a starting gate at the west end (to your right), while the public entered at the other end. Races consisted of seven laps (about 3.5 miles total). In such a small space, collisions and overturned chariots were common. The charioteers were usually poor people who used this dangerous sport to get rich and famous. Some succeeded. Most died.

The public was crazy about the races. There were 12 per day, 240 days a year. Four teams dominated the competition—Reds, Whites, Blues, and Greens—and every citizen was fanatically devoted to one of them. (Today, 2,000 years later, Romans have a similar passion for their two soccer teams: Roma or Lazio.) Obviously, the emperors had the best seats in the house: Built into the palace's curved facade was a box overlooking the track. For their pleasure, emperors occasionally had the circus floor carpeted with designs in colored powders. (Lean over the railing to see the concave shape of the palace's southern facade.)

Picture it: rowdy crowds, lots of drinking, heroes strutting to the adoration of the masses (and that was just the Rolling Stones concert held here in 2014). The emperor watching from the balcony of his fully intact palace. Below, a quarter of a million Romans were cheering, jeering, and furiously betting. Horses raced here for about a thousand years. The track dates from 300 BC, and the spectacles continued into the Christian era, until AD 549, despite Church disapproval.

From this viewpoint, looking to the left, you can see the ruins of the Baths of Caracalla (not worth touring if you've seen Palatine) rising above the trees a half-mile away. About a mile beyond that, Appian Way led from a grand gate in the ancient wall, past the catacombs, to Brindisi. Directly across is Aventine Hill, one of Rome's original seven hills and a residential district today.

• *Turn around and head back toward the museum.*

❻ Museum (Museo Palatino)

The museum holds a small collection of statues and frescoes that helps you imagine the luxury of the imperial Palatine (requires Forum Super Pass or Full Experience ticket). While the museum is nice, it's not worth your energy if you're planning to visit the Capitoline Museums.

If you visit, enter on the lower level (note the WCs) and trace the Palatine's history from the start. In section 1, find the model of the eighth-century BC Iron Age village of Germalus. Notice the so-called Huts of Romulus that we'll see later in the tour. The rest of the lower floor uses audiovisual displays to virtually reconstruct the luxury of the palaces. In the last room, look for a map of the empire at its peak (it also tracks the sources of the ancient marble fragments on display).

Go back outside and climb the stairs to the upper floor. As you enter, turn left and go to the end of the hall to find the statue of "Magna Mater" on her throne. This goddess, called the Great Mother, brought life and fertility to the Roman people, who worshipped her at the nearby Temple of Cybele. Her arms and foot were destroyed by time, but there was always a cavity where her head should be—this was a standard Roman device in which interchangeable heads could be inserted. In this case, the Magna Mater's "head" was actually a sacred, black cone-shaped meteorite that caused astonishment when it fell from the sky.

Next comes the "Augustus" room, with frescoes, terra-cotta panels, and statues from Augustus' residence. (Take an angel selfie at the surviving wings from a Victory statue.) As you wander, look for surviving bits of paint that once brightly decorated these statues. Another room features frescos and decorative marble from Nero's house. Continuing on, find two torsos—of a tiger and a river god. Next is a room of portrait busts, including the notorious Emperor Nero ("Nerone") and the last great emperor, Trajan. And finally, back near the entrance is a large, headless, topless statue of a Muse (labeled as "muse of Dresden-Zagreb type") that once decorated the Hippodrome.

• *From the museum, begin circling the main courtyard (with its octagonal fountain) counterclockwise. Turn left with the path, into what was the throne room (marked by the squat brick wall with a stubby column on top, on your left).*

❼ Throne Room (Aula Regia)

The nerve center of an empire that controlled some 50 million people from England to Africa, this was the official seat of power. The curved apse on your left (there's now a plaque on it) marks the spot where the emperor sat on his throne for official business.

Beauty Among Rubble

As you walk through the (mostly brick) ruins, you'll also see colorful marble scraps lying all over Palatine Hill. Flashy building stone was used to boast of the power and vastness of the empire. Citizens knew that the Numidian yellow marble was from Tunisia, the veined Cipollino marble (with swirling designs like an onion) was from the island of Euboea in Greece, and the pink granite was from Aswan in Egypt. This was all sliced and laid out in fine pavement and wall designs, enjoyed by those who could only be thankful they were on the winning team.

Imagine being a Roman citizen summoned by the emperor. You'd enter the palace through the main doorway (now a gap) at the far (Forum) end of the room, having climbed up three flights of a monumental staircase. The floor and walls dazzled with colorful inlaid marble. Along the walls were 12 colossal statues of Roman gods. The ceiling was a barrel vault that towered seven stories overhead. (The vault rested atop pillars as tall as the brick tower you can see in the distance.) On either side were doorways leading to a basilica and the emperor's private temple.

You'd approach the emperor, who sat on a raised throne in the apse, dressed in royal purple, with a crown of laurel leaves on his head and a scepter cradled in his arm. Big braziers burned on either side, throwing off a flickering light. As you approached, you'd raise your arm (heil-Hitler style) to greet him, saying, *"Ave, Caesar!"* The words would echo through the great hall.

Now imagine yourself as emperor. Stand on the small white stone marking the location of the throne (a few feet in front of the plaque), and look out over your palace.

• *Continue circling the main courtyard counterclockwise until it deadends at a big field filled with pebbles.*

❾ Dining Room (Triclinium) and Fountain Room (Nymphaeum)

This field of pebbles was once the emperor's dining room. The emperor himself ate from the far right end—atop the platform with the curved apse. From here, he could look down on his subjects. The dining room floor—of fine inlaid marble—was heated by fires in a hollow space beneath floor level. (Look straight across to find the two-foot gap between the two original floors.) Slaves stoked fires from underground stoves to heat the floor with forced air.

Here, the wealthiest Romans enjoyed the spoils that poured into Rome from its vast empire. Guests could look into the adjoining room (10 steps behind you), where an elliptical-shaped **foun-**

tain (see the brick remains) spurted for their amusement. Reclining on a couch, waited on by slaves, you'd order bowls of larks' tongues or a roast pig stuffed with live birds, then wash it down with wine. If you were full but tempted by yet another delicacy, you could call for a feather, vomit, and start all over. Dancing dark-skinned slaves from Egypt or flute players from Greece entertained. If you fancied one, he or she was yours—the bedrooms were just down the hall.

Or so went the stories. In fact, many emperors were just and simple men, continuing the old Roman traditions of hard work and moderate tastes. But just as many were power-mad scoundrels who used their authority to indulge their every desire.

• *From the dining room, backtrack a few steps and work your way west through openings in the low brick wall to exit the palace. After a few dozen steps, you emerge at the entrance to the Archaeological Zone. Follow the paved path to the left as it winds downhill. Because of ongoing archaeological work, some of the following sights may not be accessible (check hours at www.parcocolosseo.it). Do your best.*

ARCHAEOLOGICAL ZONE AND GARDENS

Enter Rome's oldest area. It was here that Romulus and Remus suckled at the she-wolf's teat, that Rome's first primitive inhabitants settled, that the city's first protective wall was built, and that the first (and therefore most venerable) shrines and temples were set up. Because this was where Rome was born, it was where—later—the emperors chose to build their palaces.

• *As you descend into the zone on the paved path, you'll see the ruins of two excavated homes of Rome's first power couple—Augustus and his wife, Livia. To the right is Livia's house (fairly intact and somewhat visible from the outside). On the left is Augustus' house (largely hidden among a field of other excavations).*

Entering the houses requires the Forum Super Pass or Full Experience ticket, and they are often closed. Still, it's a fascinating place to read and ponder.

❾ House of Augustus (Casa di Augusto)

Augustus, a.k.a. Octavian, lived in this house. He was the first emperor, and the first to make his residence atop Palatine Hill, establishing the precedent. Augustus saw himself as the new Romulus, so he built a relatively small house (compared to Domitian's Domus Augustana) adjacent to the home of the mythological founder of Rome and to the oldest shrines to the gods. Augustus was a modest man who believed in traditional Roman values. His wife and daughter wove the clothes he wore. He slept in the same small bedroom for 40 years. He burned the midnight oil in his study, where he read and wrote his memoirs. Augustus set a standard for emperors' conduct that would last...until his death.

If you enter the house, you'll see that it's actually a relatively modest dwelling, dating from before Octavian became emperor, and a far cry from the later Imperial Palace that you just explored. You'll see several humble rooms with finely painted ancient frescoes. Admire the vibrant colors, fake columns and arches, fake windows that once looked out on illusionary landscapes, and the use of perspective (which 15 centuries later inspired the Renaissance). Livia and Augustus had little of the lavish marble found in most homes of the wealthy.

⑩ House of Livia (Casa di Livia)

Scholars think that these ruins were the quarters of Livia, Augustus's wife, because they found her honorific name, "Julia Augusta," inscribed on one of the lead pipes now displayed inside. From the outside, you can look down into the excavated ruins and get a sense of the place.

If you go inside, the highlight is the former entrance hall—a high-ceilinged room with a few faded frescoes in purple, yellow, blue, and white. The best-preserved ones are in the central alcove, the room known as the *tablinum*, where guests were received. The *tablinum*'s right wall depicts the god Mercury (on the right side of the scene), arriving to kill the giant Argus (left) and kidnap the nymph Io (center) so Jupiter can ravish her. Frescoes in the alcove to the right of the *tablinum* show a columned portico draped with garlands. The left alcove has delicate Pompeiian-style designs.

• *Around the back side of the House of Livia, find the entrance to the Cryptoporticus tunnel. If open, you can walk through it to the Farnese Gardens.*

⑪ Cryptoporticus

At 400 feet long, this tunnel allowed the imperial entourage to travel privately through the palace complex. The tunnel was elaborately decorated with fancy stucco (little remains). The Cryptoporticus may have been built by Emperor Nero to link the Palatine and Forum with his vast mansion, the Domus Aurea, which extended from the edge of the Forum past (what is now) the Colosseum and onto Esquiline Hill. Here, the notorious emperor Caligula is said to have been assassinated.

• *Now let's see Rome's very origins. Make your way to the downhill-most part of the zone, where a section of ruins is protected by a large metal roof. Cozy up to the railing to see ruined walls and foundations.*

⑫ Huts of Romulus (Capanne Romulee)

Looking down into this pit filled with big blocks of stone, you're gazing at the place where legend says Romulus and Remus lived,

and where even historians agree that Rome got its start. You can make out some elliptical and rect- angular shapes carved into the stony ground. These are the partial outlines of huts from about 750 BC. Some have holes that once held the wooden posts of round thatched huts. The stone was "tufo," a volcanic lava stone— soft and easy to carve into foundations and blocks for walls.

Consider how this sacred-to-Romans site was already 800 years old when emperor Augustus honored and protected it, choos- ing to build his place next door.

This is the village of Germalus, which we saw a model of in the museum, earlier. Picture the village long, long ago: a few dozen people, with their goats, dogs, and crude farm tools, eking out a living.

According to legend, Romulus and Remus were children of the first Vestal Virgin. For complicated family reasons, she was ex- ecuted and her babies set adrift on the flooding Tiber River, even- tually washing ashore at the foot of Palatine Hill. In a cave just downhill from here, a shepherd discovered them being suckled by a mother wolf. He took them home—maybe right here—and raised them as his own. When Romulus grew up, he killed his broth- er and built a square wall (Roma Quadrata) on the hilltop, thus founding the city of Rome.

For centuries, the Romans believed this myth. They honored the wolf's cave (called the "Lupercale," where every February 15 men dressed up in animal skins and whipped women), as well as the spot where Romulus was said to have lived. Lo and behold, in the 1940s, these huts were unearthed, and the legend became history. Archaeologists are still at it, and the more they dig, the more they find to confirm the legends. A nearby cave discovered in 2007—ornamented with seashells, colored marble, and a wolf mo- saic—may be that original Lupercale. (It's not open to the public.)

Here at Rome's birthplace, reflect on the rise of this great cul- ture—from thatched huts to the modest House of Augustus to the massive Imperial Palace of Domitian, with its stadium and view over the Circus Maximus. It's no wonder that the hill's name gave us our English word "palace."

• *Exit the Archaeological Zone by climbing a set of stairs (following signs to* Orti Farnesiani*). At the top are great views of the city. Now start walking through the trees of the Farnese Gardens as you make your way back toward the Forum.*

⓫ Farnese Gardens—View of the Forum Fit for an Emperor

Finish your tour with a stroll through the Renaissance gardens and pavilions of the Farnese family (built upon the ruins of the House of Emperor Tiberius). Admire the orange grove, Renaissance aviaries, exotic plants, fountains, and underground grotto. When you see the incredible view of the Forum from the end of the gardens, you'll know why Palatine Hill was Rome's best address.

• *To exit, wind down Palatine Hill into the Forum, ending up at the Arch of Titus.*

CAPITOLINE MUSEUMS TOUR

Musei Capitolini

This enjoyable museum complex claims to be the world's oldest, founded in 1471 when a pope gave ancient statues to the citizens of Rome. Many of the museum's statues have gone on to become instantly recognizable cultural icons. Perched on top of Capitoline Hill, the museum's two buildings (Palazzo dei Conservatori and Palazzo Nuovo) are connected by an underground passage that leads to the Tabularium and panoramic views of the Roman Forum. A visit here is easily as important as anything else you may do to appreciate the grandeur of the Roman Empire—and it's generally empty of tourists.

Orientation

Cost: €15

Hours: Daily 9:30-19:30, last entry one hour before closing.

Information: Tel. 06-0608, www.museicapitolini.org.

Getting There: The museum (Musei Capitolini in Italian) sits atop Capitoline Hill (Campidoglio), housed in two buildings that flank the square. Buy tickets and enter at the Palazzo dei Conservatori (on your right as you face the equestrian statue).

Tours: The €6 videoguide is good; a €4 kids audio-only version is available.

Length of This Tour: Allow two hours.

Baggage Check: Free (mandatory for bags larger than a purse).

Cuisine Art: A great view café, called **Caffè Capitolino** (daily 9:30-19:00, lunch served 12:15-15:00), is upstairs in Palazzo dei Conservatori (enter from inside museum; also has exterior public entrance—facing museum entrance, go to your right around the building to Piazzale Caffarelli and through door #4). The pavilion on the terrace outside offers full service; the

Capitoline Museums Overview

tables inside are self-service (pay first, then take receipt to bar; good salads and toasted sandwiches). Piazzale Caffarelli is a fine place for a snooze, a picnic, and a great view, though it doesn't overlook the Forum.

Starring: The original she-wolf statue, Marcus Aurelius, the Dying Gaul, the Boy Extracting a Thorn, and Forum views.

OVERVIEW

Capitoline Hill's main square (Piazza del Campidoglio), home to the museum, began as a religious center in ancient Rome, the site of a temple to the gods Jupiter, Juno, and Minerva. In the 16th century, Michelangelo transformed the square from pagan to papal, while adding a

harmonious and refined Renaissance touch. His centerpiece was the magnificent ancient statue of Emperor Marcus Aurelius. (For more on the square, and Capitoline Hill, see page 48.)

On this tour, we'll see statues and artifacts dating back to Rome's very origins. There's the original version of Marcus Aurelius, plus more images of this dynamic emperor and his bratty son. We'll stand on the site of Rome's most venerable spot, the Temple of Jupiter. And we'll see the icon that started it all—the she-wolf suckling Romulus and Remus.

The museum's layout—with two buildings connected by an underground passage—can be confusing, but this self-guided tour is easy to follow.

You'll enter at the Palazzo dei Conservatori (on your right as you face the equestrian statue), cross underneath the square (beneath the Palazzo Senatorio, the mayoral palace, not open to public), and exit from the Palazzo Nuovo (on your left).

Expect Changes: Special exhibits (sometimes an exciting value and sometimes, it seems, just an excuse to raise the price) may cause some items to shift to different rooms. Use this chapter's photos or ask a guard for help.

The Tour Begins

• *Begin at the square on top of Capitoline Hill. After your ticket is checked, enter the courtyard.*

PALAZZO DEI CONSERVATORI

In the **courtyard,** enjoy the massive chunks of Constantine: his head, hand, feet, bicep, and other bits and pieces. When intact, this giant, 30-foot statue of the emperor sitting on his throne held the place of honor in the Basilica of Constantine in the Forum. Imagine it's AD 330 as you stare up at the emperor, an abstract symbol of power. His face is otherworldly. You can't really connect. You feel like a subject rather than a citizen. You could say the concept of monarchy by divine right starts here.

Only the extremities of the massive statue survive because a statue of this size was not entirely marble. Its core was cheaper and made of more perishable material, like bricks. Appreciate the detail of the vein in his bicep. Notice also the mortise-and-tenon joint and imagine the engineering necessary to construct this Goliath.

Also in the courtyard are reliefs of conquered peoples—not in chains, but new members of an expansive empire. These represent provinces such as Gaul, Britannia, and Thracia, and date from the reign of Hadrian (second century AD), whose passion was running the empire not as something to exploit but as a commonwealth.

• *Go up the staircase (the one near the entrance, not the one in the courtyard). On the landing, find...*

Reliefs of Second-Century Imperial Grandeur

These four fine reliefs show great moments in an emperor's daily grind. Because Rome was a visual culture and used public art for

propaganda purposes, these reliefs portray typical duties a good emperor was supposed to perform: conquering, rallying the masses, and performing religious ceremonies.

Three of the four panels feature Marcus Aurelius, the emperor-philosopher who worked so valiantly to prevent Rome's fall to the barbarians. First, find the relief where he rides in on his horse, posing like the bronze statue in Piazza del Campidoglio. Marcus stretches his hand out, offering clemency to his vanquished foes.

The detail, with expressive faces and banners blowing in the wind, is impressive. Next, the emperor makes his triumphal entry into Rome on a chariot. Originally, this relief had one more figure, riding next to Marcus. It was Commodus, his wicked son (and Russell Crowe's nemesis in *Gladiator*). After his assassination, Commodus' memory was damned, so images of him were erased or chiseled out. (But, as we'll see, his memory still lives on.) In the final relief, the good emperor greets priests about to sacrifice a bull in thanks to the gods (with even the bull looking on curiously).

• *Continue up the stairs to the first floor. Go through two large frescoed rooms (Rooms 4 and 5) and continue directly ahead through a doorway to find Room 8, with the...*

Boy Extracting a Thorn
(Spinario)

He's just a boy, intent only on picking a thorn out of his foot. As he bends over to reach his foot, his body sticks out at all angles, like a bony chicken wing. He's even scuffed up, the way small boys get. At this moment,

nothing matters to him but that splinter. Our lives are filled with these mundane moments (when we'd give anything for tweezers), which are rarely captured in art.

The boy is a bronze cast with eyes once inlaid as in the adjacent bronze cast of Brutus. Take a close look at Brutus (whose descendent took part in the killing of Caesar). This wonderful bust typifies Roman character: determined, thoughtful, no-nonsense, and capable. The ivory eyes are original.

Now, look up, and appreciate the fresco that has lined this room since it was part of a municipal palace in the 16th century. It's a scene that celebrates the power and glory of ancient Rome. Find the wagonload of enemy armor and weapons and sweep 360 degrees as if joining in this triumphal parade. It's another great military victory, and the troops are bringing home precious statues of bronze and marble as plunder. There's the emperor on his four-horse chariot. The enemy prisoners are bound and ready to absorb your disdain. And after the sacrificial bulls is a chorus of trumpets and throngs of your fellow adoring citizens—all thankful to be loyal subjects of the emperor.

• *In the next room (Room 9) is the...*

Capitoline She-Wolf

The original bronze she-wolf suckles the twins Romulus and Remus. This symbol of Rome is ancient, though the wolf statue itself (long thought to be Etruscan, from the fifth century BC) was made in the 13th century, and the boys are an invention of the 15th century. Look into the eyes of the wolf. An animal looks back, with ragged ears, sharp teeth, and staring eyes. This wild animal, teamed with the wildest creatures of all—hungry babies—makes a powerful symbol for the tenacious city/empire of Rome.

• *Continue on to Room 10.*

From Michelangelo to Medusa

Along with a bust of Michelangelo made from his death mask (black, on left), this room contains Bernini's anguished bust of Medusa—with writhing snakes on her head. This goes way beyond a bad hair day. Enjoy the art-

istry of Bernini as he fashions a marble lock of hair into a writhing snake.

Then appreciate the room you're in as a piece of art in itself: Murano glass chandelier, fine painted coffered ceiling, fabric walls, inlaid marble floor, medallions celebrating papal donations to the collection, and frescoed panels set in fanciful grotesque-style decor. As a bonus, you've got Rome, including St. Peter's dome, out the window.

• *Continue straight through three small rooms: Room 12 has the Arte-mis of Efesia (Ephesus), with her extremely fertile draping of numer-ous bull testicles, breasts, or perhaps puka shells (no one knows for sure). Room 13 features Greek red-figured vases (and the elevator up to the second-floor café—need a coffee break?). Room 15 has a fourth-century chariot and an incredibly lifelike bronze horse. Continue ahead up a set of seven stairs and follow them to the next room to discover the remark-able bust of...*

Commodus as Hercules

This arrogant emperor brat used to run around the palace in animal skins pretending (or believing) he was Hercules. Here, he wears a lion's head over his own and drapes the lion's paws over his chest. This lion king made a bad emperor (ruled AD 180-192). Commo-dus earned a reputation as a good athlete and warrior, and a rough character. He hung out with low-class gladiators, and even fought in the arena himself. The fights were staged— no one was allowed to hurt the emperor— which meant that Commodus killed inno-cent people, some of them beaten to death with his beloved Hercules club. The people hated Commodus. Commodus-the-jock was also at odds with his father, the previous emperor and noted scholar and philosopher, Marcus Aurelius.

This statue dates from the late second century, a period of de-bauchery and decline. The emperor is self-indulgent. The gravitas is gone, and soon the empire will follow. Examine the statue's de-tails—the perfect curls of hair and beard, sheen of the skin, and manicured nails. Notice also the symbols of astrology, fertility, and abundance. While Commodus' memory was damned (remember how he was chiseled out of the panel downstairs), somehow this masterpiece survived.

• *As you are looking at Commodus, directly behind you is his dad, the Emperor...*

Marcus Aurelius (c. AD 176)

This is the only surviving equestrian statue of a Roman emperor. Marcus Aurelius was a Roman philosopher-emperor (ruled AD 161-180) known more for his *Meditations* than his prowess on the battlefield. His gesture is of clemency, pardoning defeated enemies. The patina of time almost drips off him. While he has the same fine hair and features of his son Commodus (see earlier), the emperor is still working for the glory of Rome rather than for the glory of himself.

Christians in the Dark Ages thought that the statue's hand was raised in blessing, which probably led to their misidentifying him as Constantine, the first Christian emperor. While most pagan statues were destroyed by Christians, "Constantine" was spared. It graced several prominent locations in medieval Rome, including the papal palace at San Giovanni in Laterano.

In 1538, this gilded bronze statue was placed in the center of the Campidoglio (directly outside the museum), and Michelangelo was hired to design the buildings around it with the statue as the centerpiece. A few years ago, the statue was moved inside and restored, while the copy you see outside today was placed on the square. (Notice that Aurelius doesn't use stirrups—an Asian invention, those newfangled devices wouldn't arrive in Europe for another 500 years.)

Also in the room are more hunks—head, hand, and a globe—of another statue of Constantine. (Or was it the Emperor Sylvestrus Stalloneus?)

• *Descend the ramp to the wall of blocks from the...*

Temple of Jupiter

This is part of the foundation of the ancient Temple of Jupiter (Giove), once the most impressive in Rome. It was located right near where you're standing. Find the scale model of the temple (1:40) to get a sense of its size and where you stand in relation to the ruins. Imagine you're standing before a wall that has stood here, crowning the capital hill of Rome, for more than 2,500 years. It is in situ; this part of the museum is built around this wall.

The King of the Gods resided atop Capitoline Hill in this once-classy 10,000-square-foot temple, which was perched on a podium and lined with Greek-style columns, overlooking downtown Rome. The most important rites were performed here, and victory parades through the Forum ended here. Replicas of this building were erected in every Roman city. The temple was begun by Rome's last king (the Tarquin), and its dedication in 509 BC marks the start of the Roman Republic.

All that remains of the temple today are these ruined foundation stones, made of volcanic tuff, an easily carved rock commonly used in Roman construction. Although there are hundreds of these blocks here, they represent only a portion of the immense foundation, which is only a fraction of the temple itself. In its prime, the temple rose two stories above our heads. Inside stood a statue of the god of thunder wielding a lightning bolt. The temple was refurbished a number of times over the centuries, often after damage by...lightning bolts.

• *By the way, a good WC is behind the wall to the left.*

Here's how to get to the next stop, the Tabularium: With your back to the old wall, find seven stairs (to the right of the ramp, in front of the gilded Hercules). Go up the steps and then straight to the end of the hall. Exiting the hall, make a U-turn right and go down the stairs you climbed earlier, all the way to the basement—the piano sotterraneo. Then cross underneath the square through the long passageway filled with ancient inscriptions (well described in English). About 20 yards before the far end, turn right and climb a set of stairs into the...

TABULARIUM

Built in the first century BC, these sturdy vacant rooms once held the archives of ancient Rome. The word Tabularium comes from "tablet," on which Romans wrote their laws.

The rooms offer a stunning head-on view over the Forum, giving you a more complete picture of the sprawl of ancient Rome. Belly up to the overlook. Panning left to right, find the following landmarks: Arch of Septimius Severus, Arch of Titus (in the distance), the lone Column of Phocas, the three columns of the Temple of Castor and Pollux, the eight columns of the Temple of Saturn (closer to you), and the three columns (closest to you) of the Temple of Vespasiano.

Now do an about-face and look up to see a huge white hunk of carved marble, an overhang from the Temple of Vespasiano. Wander around. Appreciate the towering vaulted ceiling and ancient Roman engineering. While some say Rome was built of marble, that's not quite true. The Romans baked thin bricks and also invented concrete. They built their big buildings mostly out of brick and concrete and then covered them with marble veneer.

• *Leave the Tabularium by going back down the stairs you just climbed. Turn right (passing a low-key WC), and go up three flights of stairs, entering the Palazzo Nuovo. Climb until you reach its top floor.*

PALAZZO NUOVO

• *From the top of the stairs, continue directly up and into Room 66—the "Hall of the Gaul"—with one of the museum's most famous pieces.*

Dying Gaul

A first-century BC copy of a Greek original, this was sculpted to celebrate the Greeks' victory over the Galatians. This Roman ad-

aptation shows a warrior wounded in battle. The dying Gaul holds himself upright, but barely. Minutes earlier, before he was stabbed in the chest, he'd been in his prime. Now he can only watch helplessly as his life ebbs away. His sword is useless against this last battle. With his messy hair, downcast eyes, and crumpled position, he poignantly reminds us that every victory also means a defeat.

• *The next few rooms are filled with interesting art. As you wander, take a quick look at...*

Ancient Roman Statues and Busts

In the first room (#65), a faun—carved out of red marble—glories in grapes and life, oblivious to the loss of his penis (at least he still has his tail). The statue, found among a couple dozen pieces in Hadrian's Villa, was skillfully restored. Check out the chandeliered ceilings in this room and elsewhere; this building is truly a *palazzo* (palace).

Next, the **Great Hall** (Room 64) features more sculpture from Hadrian's Villa (and elsewhere). Notice the Amazon, near the window, with her one breast uncovered in typical Amazon fashion, so that the fabric wouldn't be in the way of her archery. Standing in a classic *contrapposto* pose (weight on one leg), this is a Roman copy of a fifth-century BC Greek original by Polycletus.

Roll through two rooms lined with busts. The **Hall of Philosophers** (Room 63) celebrates Socrates, Homer, Euripides,

Cicero, and many more. The **Hall of Emperors** (Room 62, in the corner) welcomes you with Constantine's mom Helena sitting center stage, resting after her journey to Jerusalem to find Christ's cross. In this 3-D yearbook of ancient history, find the purple-chested bust of Caracalla. Infamous for his fervent

brutality, he instructed his portraitists to stress his meanness. They did it well. Directly across on the lower shelf, the biggest bust—of Emperor Decius (who ruled in the third century)—is one of the finest of late antiquity. His expression shows the concern and consternation of a ruler whose empire is in decline. In this room you can find classic expressions of confidence, brutality, and anguish—human drama through the ages. Before leaving, sample the delicate elegance of ancient Roman hairstyles for women.

• *Enter the hallway, turn right, and start down the hall. The small octagonal room on your left contains one of the museum's treasures.*

Capitoline Venus

This is a Roman copy of a fourth-century BC Greek original by the master Praxiteles. Venus, leaving the bath, is suddenly aware that someone is watching her. As she turns to look, she reflexively covers up (nearly). Her blank eyes hold no personality or emotion. Her fancy hairstyle is the only complicated thing about her. She is simply beautiful—generically erotic.

• *Head to the last room on the left before the stairs (Room 60). Among the many busts in the room, find the...*

Mosaic of Doves

Four doves perch on the rim of a bronze bowl as one drinks water from the bowl. Minute bits make up this small, exquisite work. Found in the center of a floor in one of the rooms in Hadrian's Villa, this second-century AD mosaic was based on an earlier work done, of course, by the Greeks.

We all know that ancient Rome was grand.

But the art in this museum tells us that its culture was refined as well. Before leaving, walk slowly around this last room, looking into the eyes of the characters who were the real foundation of ancient Rome.

• *To exit, head down the stairs to the ground floor, and follow signs to the* uscita. *Take a photo with the colossal river-god statue of Marforio. If you checked a bag, cross the courtyard to retrieve it.*

ST. PETER-IN-CHAINS TOUR

San Pietro in Vincoli

Michelangelo—the world's greatest sculptor—died having failed to complete his greatest work, the tomb of Pope Julius II. Today, you can visit the powerful remains of that unfinished masterpiece, including the famous statue of Moses, housed in a historic church that also contains Peter's chains.

Orientation

Cost: Free.

Hours: Daily 8:00-12:30 & 15:00-19:00, Oct-March until 18:00.

Information: Tel. 06-9784-4950.

Dress Code: Modest dress is required—no short shorts, above-knee skirts, or bare shoulders.

Getting There: The church is a 10-minute uphill walk north of the Colosseum. From the Colosseo Metro stop, take the escalator just inside the station exit (follow the brown *S. Pietro in Vincoli* sign). When you emerge, cross the pedestrian bridge and head straight up the Via della Polveriera. At the top, turn left to reach the church. There's also a staircase 50 yards east of the station.

For a shorter walk (but with steep steps), use the Cavour Metro stop; from that station, go downhill on Via Cavour a half-block, then climb the big pedestrian staircase called Via di San Francesco di Paola, which leads right to the church. If asking for directions, say "San Pietro in Vincoli" (sahn pee-AY-troh een VEEN-koh-lee). From the outside, St. Peter-in-Chains' rounded arches and columns look more like a Renaissance loggia than a church.

Length of This Tour: Allow 30 minutes.

Eating: Recommended eateries in the Monti neighborhood are listed on page 391; also consider those closer to the Colosseum (on page 393).

The Tour Begins

• *In the far-right corner of the church, you'll find a wall full of marble statues. In the center sits...*

Michelangelo's *Moses* (1515)

Moses has just returned from meeting face-to-face with God. Now he senses trouble back home. Slowly he turns to see his followers worshipping a golden calf. As his anger builds, he glares at them. His physical strength is symbolic of his moral and spiritual fortitude as a leader of his people. His powerful left leg tucks under and tenses, as if he's just about to spring up out of his chair and punish the naughty Children of Israel with the Ten Commandments under his arm. Enjoy the cascading beard, one of the greatest in art history.

And if he did stand up, this statue would be 13 feet tall, nearly the height of Michelangelo's famous *David*. This Charlton Hes-

ton-with-horns is interesting in photographs...and awe-inspiring when confronted in person. His bare, muscular arms exude power. Michelangelo completed the statue after practicing for four years painting the seated prophets on the Sistine ceiling.

Like other Michelangelo statues, *Moses* is both at rest (seated) and in motion (his tensed leg, turning head, and nervous fingers). This restlessness may reflect Michelangelo's Neo-Platonic belief that the soul is the claustrophobic prisoner of the body. Or it's the statue itself fighting to emerge from the stone around it. A fanciful legend says that Michelangelo, frustrated at trying to bring God's statue into existence, hit *Moses* with his hammer (causing the scar on *Moses*' right knee), imploring, "Now, speak!"

The horns are the crowning touch. In medieval times, the Hebrew word for "rays of light" (halo) was mistranslated as "horns." Michelangelo knew better but wanted to give the statue an air of *terribilità*, a kind of scary charisma possessed by Moses, Pope Julius II...and Michelangelo. This Moses radiates the smoldering *terribilità* of a borderline-abusive father.

Find a quiet spot and enjoy the artificial play of light mimicking the change in sunlight from dawn to dusk. Originally, there

The Tomb of Pope Julius II

Moses sits on the bottom level of a two-story marble wall filled with statues. This is a puny, cobbled-together version of what was to have been a grand tomb for Pope Julius II.

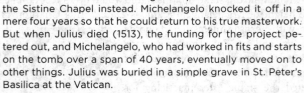

In 1505, Pope Julius II hired young Michelangelo to build his tomb, a huge monument to be placed in St. Peter's Basilica. An excited Michelangelo sketched designs for a three-story wedding-cake mountain of marble studded with 48 statues and bronze reliefs and topped with a huge statue of the egomaniacal pope. *Moses* was to have been placed on an upper level on the right-hand corner, looking away from the monument.

Michelangelo traveled to Carrara, selected 100 tons of marble for the project, and started working. Then Julius changed his mind. He ordered Michelangelo to paint the Sistine Chapel instead. Michelangelo knocked it off in a mere four years so that he could return to his true masterwork. But when Julius died (1513), the funding for the project petered out, and Michelangelo, who had worked in fits and starts on the tomb over a span of 40 years, eventually moved on to other things. Julius was buried in a simple grave in St. Peter's Basilica at the Vatican.

was a window nearby, and Michelangelo used the natural light to paint the marble with warm shades of color, from orange to pink to a delicate red.

The Tomb Today

In 1542, remnants of the tomb project were brought to the St. Peter-in-Chains church and pieced together by Michelangelo's assistants. What we see today is a far cry from the original design, which was to have been fully three-dimensional and five times as big. Some of the best statues ended up elsewhere, such as the *Prisoners* in Florence and the *Slaves* in the Louvre. Although the assistants had Michelangelo's original instruction manual, they were trying to assemble the tomb with most of the parts missing.

Moses and the Louvre's *Slaves* are the only statues Michelangelo personally completed for the project. Flanking *Moses* are the Old Testament sister-wives of Jacob, Leah (to our right) and Rachel, both begun by Michelangelo but probably finished by pupils. On the second story, a Madonna and Child stand above a reclining, thoughtful-looking Pope Julius II on a coffin.

The sheer variety of decoration we see here gives us a glimpse of the tomb's original scope—nearly 50 statues laced together with Pompeii-esque garlands and proto-Baroque scrolls.

Michelangelo went to his grave thinking that he'd wasted the best years of his life on the tomb. Today, we can only reconstruct it in our minds, imagining a monument intended to exceed (according to Giorgio Vasari) "every ancient or imperial tomb ever made."

The Church

Founded in 440, it's one of Rome's oldest, built to house Peter's chains. Though the church was greatly changed in 1475, the 20

Doric columns flanking the wide nave are from the original church. The central ceiling painting (c. 1700) shows the chains—with their miraculous curative powers in action—healing someone possessed by demons, on the steps of St. Peter's Basilica at the Vatican. Sculpted skeletons and grim reapers adorn a number of the tombs lining the side naves. These *memento mori* (Latin for "remember you must die") were popular in the 17th century and are graphic reminders of mortality, the fate that awaits rich and poor alike.

• *On the altar is a gold-and-glass case containing what tradition claims to be...*

Peter's Chains

There are actually two different sets of chains, linked together. One set is said to have held Peter when he and Paul were in the Mam-

ertine Prison in Rome (near the Forum). The other dates from when Herod jailed Peter in Jerusalem (Acts 12; see the scene frescoed on the left wall of the apse). During the night, "Peter was sleeping between two soldiers, bound with chains, while sentries were guarding the doors. And behold, an angel of the Lord appeared and a light shone in the cell. The angel struck Peter on the side and woke him, saying, 'Get up quickly.' And the chains fell off his hands." The angel led Peter, who thought he was dreaming, out of the prison to safety. (Raphael's depiction of this is in the Vatican Museums. A less-famous 1577 version by Jacopo Coppi is behind the altar, on the left wall.)

In the waning days of ancient Rome, the Jerusalem chains ended up here as a gift from the Eastern empress (as depicted in another Coppi fresco on the right wall of the apse).

According to tradition, when the Jerusalem chains arrived and were paired with the Mamertine chains, the two sets—chink!—joined together miraculously.

JEWISH GHETTO WALK

East Bank of the Tiber

For centuries, Rome's Jewish ghetto—even while a site of relentless persecution—has showcased the undying pride and solidarity of a tight-knit community. Built in 1555 on the banks of a frequently flooded bend of the Tiber River, the ghetto was the forced home of the city's Jewish population for more than 300 years, ending only with Italian unification in 1870. Although most of the old ghetto buildings were torn down long ago, the area is still a lively center of Jewish life.

Orientation

Length of This Walk: Allow about 30 minutes, plus an additional hour or more if you tour the synagogue and visit the museum. You might also plan a meal here.

When to Go: Avoid Saturday and late Friday afternoon, when the synagogue, museum, and bakery are closed.

Getting There: The Jewish ghetto is on the east bank of the Tiber River, near the river's island (Isola Tiberina) and the ancient ruins of the Theater of Marcellus (Teatro di Marcello). The walk's starting point is right across the river from Trastevere and is a 10-minute walk from Largo Argentina. Bus #23 stops nearby.

Synagogue and Jewish Museum: €11 ticket covers both, includes guided tour of synagogue and one-hour audioguide for museum; open Sun-Thu 10:00-18:00, Fri until 16:00, shorter hours Oct-March, closed Sat year-round and on Jewish holidays; last entry 45 minutes before closing, on Lungotevere dei Cenci, tel. 06-6840-0661, www.museoebraico.roma.it. Modest dress is required.

Entry to the synagogue (unless you're attending servic-

In the Ghetto

The word "ghetto" comes from the Italian *geto* (foundry) and was first used in Venice to describe the part of town where Jews lived near the copper foundry. Initially the term meant only Jewish neighborhoods, but it later came to mean any neighborhood where a single ethnic group is segregated.

es) is only by guided **tour** (included in museum admission, 30-minute English tours usually at :15 past the hour, check schedule at ticket counter).

Tours: Walking **tours** of the Jewish ghetto leave from the museum at least once a day Sun-Fri (€8, usually at 13:00, 45 minutes, no tours on Sat, www.museoebraico.roma.it). Ask for the schedule at the museum and sign up at least 30 minutes before the tour departure time (3-person minimum).

🎧 Download my free Jewish Ghetto **audio tour.**

Local Guide: Micaela Pavoncello is uniquely equipped to guide visitors through the neighborhood her family has lived in for generations (€130/2 hours, tel. 393-217-5898, www.jewishroma.com, info@jewishroma.com).

Eateries: Near the end of this tour, you'll find restaurants offering traditional Roman and Jewish fare and several places to pick up snacks, including a Jewish bakery.

Nearby: The Trastevere Walk starts near where this one does—on Ponte Fabricio (see the Trastevere Walk chapter, later).

BACKGROUND

Today, nearly half of Italy's 35,000 Jews call Rome home. Jews here have a uniquely Roman style of worship and even preserve remnants of their own Judaic-Roman dialect. That's because, unlike most of the world's Jewish people, Roman Jews are neither Sephardic (descended from Spain) nor Ashkenazi (descended from Eastern Europe). Italy's Jews came from the Holy Land before the Diaspora, some directly and some via Greece;  after Rome invaded Judaea in the first century AD, others came as POWs sold into slavery. These first Jews lived, like other foreigners, outside the city—across the river, in Trastevere.

With the fall of the Roman Empire, the status of Jews declined. As Christianity enveloped Rome, the state denied Jews

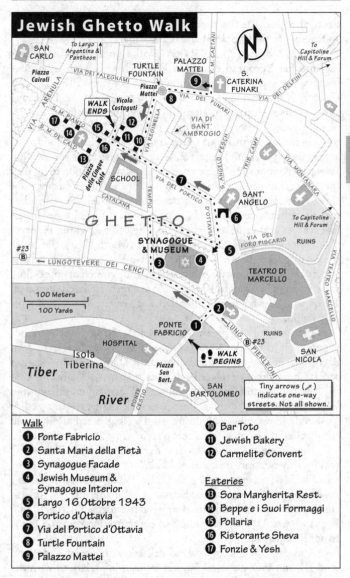

Jewish Ghetto Walk

Walk
1 Ponte Fabricio
2 Santa Maria della Pietà
3 Synagogue Facade
4 Jewish Museum & Synagogue Interior
5 Largo 16 Ottobre 1943
6 Portico d'Ottavia
7 Via del Portico d'Ottavia
8 Turtle Fountain
9 Palazzo Mattei
10 Bar Toto
11 Jewish Bakery
12 Carmelite Convent

Eateries
13 Sora Margherita Rest.
14 Beppe e i Suoi Formaggi
15 Pollaria
16 Ristorante Sheva
17 Fonzie & Yesh

their full rights as citizens, and once the pope became literally the king of Rome, the Church enforced laws that limited the spread of the Jewish faith (such as no proselytizing, no new synagogues, no intermarriage). The severity of these laws varied from pope to pope. Despite this, Rome's Jews prospered for the most part and were often held in high regard as physicians, businessmen, and confidants of popes. The community in Trastevere was even allowed to spill across to the opposite bank of the Tiber.

In 1492, Spain expelled its Jews, with similar removals following in other European countries. Rome's Jewish population doubled, swelling with refugees. Things soon got worse. The Catholic Counter-Reformation—originally set in motion to combat rising Protestantism—turned its attention to anything deemed a "heresy" or simply not Catholic, including Judaism. In 1555, Pope Paul IV forcibly moved all of Rome's Jews into the undesirable flood zone across the river from Trastevere, creating a ghetto of some 2,000 Jews packed into a miserable seven acres of mucky land. There they lived—in cramped conditions, behind a wall, with a curfew—for three centuries. They could go out by day, but had to return before the gates were locked at night. Jews were forced to wear yellow scarves and caps, and were prohibited from owning property or holding good jobs. During Carnevale (Mardi Gras), they were forced to parade down Via del Corso while Christians lined the streets and shouted insults. Through this long stretch of oppression, the synagogue was a place Jews could feel respected and dignified. It's no wonder such loving attention was given to the Jewish tools of worship.

The gates of the ghetto were opened during Napoleon's occupation of the city (1805-1814), and in 1848 they were torn down. But it was only after Italian unification in 1870—when a secular government replaced religious rule by the Vatican—that the ghetto's inhabitants were granted full rights and citizenship. When Rome became the country's capital, the city—ashamed of its shoddy Jewish quarter—destroyed the old ghetto buildings and rebuilt the district on a new street plan in a fine 19th-century style.

Then came the rise of fascism. Even though Mussolini wasn't rabidly anti-Semitic, he instituted a slew of anti-Jewish laws as he allied himself more strongly with Hitler. When Mussolini was deposed and the Nazis occupied Rome late in the war, the Jewish community was suddenly in even greater danger. Of the 10,000 Roman Jews, 2,000 were sent off to concentration camps. Only a handful came back.

A measure of healing and reconciliation came with Pope John Paul II, who took a special interest in fostering relations with the Jewish community. It was John Paul II who finally acknowledged that the Church should have intervened more forcefully to defend Jews during the Holocaust. He was also the first pope in history to enter a synagogue (here, in this neighborhood, in 1986).

Today, Rome's Jewish ghetto is not as evocative as Venice's (where the original buildings remain intact), but its school, shops, restaurants, and synagogue make it more lively.

The Walk Begins

• *Start at the north end of Ponte Fabricio, which connects central Rome with the Isola Tiberina and the neighborhood of Trastevere. You'll see the big synagogue with its square dome. The neighborhood consists of the synagogue and the several blocks behind it.*

❶ Ponte Fabricio

Ponte Fabricio is nicknamed Ponte Quattro Capi ("Bridge of the Four Heads") for its statues of the two-faced pagan god Janus. In

ancient times, it was called Pons Judaeorum ("Jews' Bridge") because foreigners, immigrants, and Jews—who weren't allowed to live in central Rome—would commute across this bridge to get into town. Some 30,000 Jews once lived in Trastevere. Look down at the river. The embankment was only built in the late 19th century. Before then, this was the worst flood zone along the Roman riverbank—just right for a ghetto for the politically powerless.

• *With your back to the river, look left to see the synagogue, with its square-domed roof. But our first stop is the little church just across the busy* street from the bridge—the beige building with an oval painting on the facade.

❷ Santa Maria della Pietà (a.k.a. San Gregorio)

When the ghetto was a walled-in town, Catholics built churches at each gate to try and spread their faith to the Jews. Every time Jews

entered or left their home, they got a little sermon from the church's facade. There was the Crucifixion in the oval painting, which reminded all that it was the "Jews" who killed Christ (who, of course, was Jewish himself). And notice the Hebrew script under the crucifix. It quotes the Jewish prophet Isaiah—"All day long, I have stretched out my hands to a disobedient and faithless nation that has lost its way" (Isaiah 65:2)—but misuses the quote to give it an anti-Semitic twist.

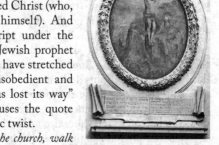

• *Turning your back to the church, walk* one block along the river and then turn right on Via del Tempio. Stand *in front of the synagogue's main entrance, reserved for worshippers. This is the best vantage point to admire the...*

❸ Synagogue Facade

Take in the impressive structure. Its warm golden stone glows. The dome on top was made square to distinguish it from a Christian church. Scan the facade for familiar Jewish iconography: a menorah, the Ten Commandments, a Star of David, palm branches, and a few inscriptions in Hebrew script.

The structure is modern (completed in 1904), but this has been the place of worship for Rome's Jews for half a millennium—since the 16th century, when Pope Paul IV forced the Jews to reside within a walled ghetto. After Rome became the capital of the newly unified Italy in 1870, Jews gained equal rights and were free to live anywhere in the city. Not long after, the original ghetto buildings were demolished and replaced with the modern blocks you see today. The Jewish community was offered better real estate for its synagogue, but chose instead to build a new "Great Synagogue" here, on the original site.

• *To visit the Jewish Museum, which includes a guided tour of the synagogue, circle around the left side of the synagogue and walk down pedestrian-only Via Catalana to the "Museo Ebraico" entrance at the far end of the building.*

❹ Jewish Museum (Museo Ebraico) and Synagogue Interior

On a single basement level, the worthwhile **museum** tells the story of Roman Jews from ancient times to today, showing off historically significant artifacts. You'll see second-century BC reliefs with Jewish symbols, finely worked religious items, and other relics of the past. A reconstructed image shows how the neighborhood looked in the 19th century, with tall buildings not unlike those in Venice's ghetto. The museum also shows a film (subtitled in English) about the Nazi occupation of Rome, along with a display of artifacts and documentation from this dark time.

Your admission includes a guided visit inside the **Great Synagogue.** Gaze up into the dome painted with the colors of the rainbow, symbolizing God's promise to Noah that there would be no more floods. The stars on the ceiling recall God's pledge that Abraham's descendants would flourish and be as many as the stars in the sky. Architects designed the structure in the Art Nouveau style, with a dash of Tiffany. The sandy color tones are a reminder of the community's desert heritage. You'll also get a brief tour of the older, smaller **Spanish Synagogue**—which once stood on a nearby square but was moved in 1932 to the ground floor of this building.

• *Just outside the museum entrance is a small square (along Via Portico d'Ottavia) dominated by a big Roman ruin. This square is called...*

❺ Largo 16 Ottobre 1943

This square is named for the day when Nazi trucks parked here and threatened to take the Jews to concentration camps unless the community came up with 50 kilos (110 pounds) of gold in 24 hours. Everyone, including many non-Jewish Romans, tossed in their precious gold, and the demand was met. The Nazis took the gold—and later, they took many of the Jews as well. Some 2,000 of the ghetto's residents were sent to concentration camps, most of them never to return.

• *The big ancient ruin is the...*

❻ Portico d'Ottavia

This monumental gateway—with columns supporting a triangular pediment—was built by soon-to-be-emperor Augustus. Once

flanked by temples and libraries, the passageway served as a kind of cultural center. After Rome's fall, the portico housed a thriving fish market. In the eighth century, the ruins of the portico were incorporated into the Church of Sant'Angelo in Pescheria. (You can find the entrance to the church behind the portico.) For centuries, this Christian church was packed every Saturday with Jews—forced by decree to listen to Christian sermons. Notice the faded bits of Christian fresco on the parts of the portico made of medieval-era brick. If you like, walk through the archway into the quiet backstreets, then return.

Find the small bridge on your right, where you can look down at the level of the street in Roman times. On the right is a fine view of the Teatro di Marcello, which predates and inspired the design of the Colosseum. One of three major theaters in the ancient city, it could hold more than 10,000 spectators. In the Middle Ages, it was converted into a fortress, and today those are luxury apartments on the top level. Beyond it is the tree-capped Capitoline Hill. You can take a short detour down the ramp into the archaeological area and enjoy the hodgepodge of ancient fragments scattered about.

JEWISH GHETTO

• Now walk along the ghetto's main street...

❼ Via del Portico d'Ottavia

This main drag is a fine place to get a taste of yesterday's ghetto and today's Rome. In general, buildings on the left side of the  street are "new" (less than 150 years old, at least), while those on the right have some old ghetto building-fronts. Imagine today's street as it was then: much narrower (as it is at the far end today). Walking down the street, notice kosher restaurants advertising artichokes *(carciofi)*, either braised *(alla romana)* or deep-fried in the "Jewish" style *(alla giudia)*. You might see posters for community events, a few men wearing yarmulkes, shops selling Judaica, and political graffiti, both pro- and anti-Israel. The Palestine Liberation Organization attacked this area in 1982, and a police presence still lingers.

After a block, you reach the center of the district. Look right, down very narrow **Via di Sant'Ambrogio,** an old surviving street.

Imagine the dense population, flood muck, and squalor of the past.

On the pedestrianized **square** ahead, older folks hang out together and shoot the breeze, sometimes even bringing their favorite chairs from home. This neighborhood has become trendy, and apartment prices are expensive. Though the Jewish community has long since dispersed all over Rome, they still come back here for activities and worship. The big tan building (on the left) houses the Jewish school.

Opposite the big school, take a one-block detour down **Via della Reginella,** where you'll find some fun shops (see page 430 in the Shopping in Rome chapter) as well as some poignant artifacts. In front of #10 (on the right), you'll see several small bronze plaques in the shape of cobbles, memorials to members of the community arrested in these homes during the Nazi occupation. These *Stolperstein* ("stumbling stones"), designed by a German artist, commemorate victims of the Holocaust and are found in front of their residences throughout the city (and the rest of Europe). At #28, notice where the six-floor buildings end and more elegant and spacious (but no taller) three-floor buildings begin...marking the end of the ghetto.

In the square (Piazza Mattei) at the end of the lane is a fun ❽ **turtle fountain**—an old Mannerist work, later embellished with turtles by Bernini. It's said that Bernini cared about the Jews and honored them with the symbol of a turtle—an ancient creature that carries all its belongings on its back.

Cross the square and jog right down Via de' Funari ("Street of the Ropemakers") to the big brick ❾ **Palazzo Mattei** (#31, on the left). Step inside from around the corner on Via Michelangelo Caetani to be reminded that very often in Rome, grim, uninviting exteriors contain unexpected treasures, like this building's court-yard. Encrusted with the family's collection of ancient Roman sculpture, it was intended to show off their wealth and refined taste. Today, the palazzo is home to the Italian Center for American Studies.

Returning to the ghetto's main drag (Via del Portico d'Ottavia), continue to ❿ **Bar Toto** (the second café on the right).

Next to the door you'll see a slot in the wall—a ghetto-era charity box for orphans that still accepts donations for worthy causes. The ancient relief below the box marks the home of a big shot who, at the start of the Renaissance age (before the ghetto's establishment in 1555), plugged this chunk of ancient Rome into his facade for prestige. A few steps farther down (before the kosher gelato shop at #1b), another bit of ancient marble depicts a lion attacking a gazelle. Also on the building is a big stone panel with a Latin inscription dated "MMCCXX." Yes, that's 2220, and no, it's not from the future. It was carved in AD 1467—marking the years since the birth of Rome in 753 BC.

At the next intersection (Piazza Costaguti), stand in the center of the white decorative design and get oriented for your next

move. To the left—on the car-filled square called Piazza delle Cinque Scole—is a recommended restaurant, **Sora Margherita** (at #30). Directly ahead of you, the main street leads to more recommended eateries, and eventually to Campo de' Fiori.

Now, let's see our final

sights. On your right, at the corner, is a tiny ❶ **Jewish bakery.** Go inside to check out the braided challah bread (Friday only), cheesecakes, almond paste-filled macaroons, and misleadingly named "Jewish pizzas" *(pizza Ebraica)*—which are actually like little €4 fruitcakes, but better tasting, with a crunchy top.

Around the corner, the curving, white-columned structure is part of a former ❷ **Carmelite convent.** Consider how Rome's Jews felt when the Church built a convent and a Catholic school here in the ghetto to preach to their children, and forced locals to attend Mass. Finally, pop through the tunnel-like passageway to the left of the convent. You emerge into a tiny courtyard ringed with tall tenements. Imagine the tight conditions of thousands of Jews living in this small seven-acre area. Think of the turbulent history of the ghetto—and the rich heritage of Rome's Jewish community.

• *The tour is over. From here, you're within walking distance of many sights in Rome. For transportation options, get out your map, and you'll see that a major transit hub—Largo Argentina—is just a couple of blocks away. Shalom.*

ST. PETER'S BASILICA TOUR

Basilica San Pietro

St. Peter's is the greatest church in Christendom. It represents the power and splendor of Rome's 2,000-year domination of the Western world. Built on the memory and grave of the first pope, St. Peter, this is where the grandeur of ancient Rome became the grandeur of Christianity.

Orientation

Cost: Free entry to basilica and crypt. Dome climb—€8 if you take the stairs all the way up, €10 to ride an elevator partway (to the roof), then climb to the top of the dome (cash only; see "Dome Climb," later in this section). Treasury Museum—€5 (includes audioguide).

Hours: The **church** is open daily April-Sept 7:00-19:00, Oct-March 7:00-18:30. It closes on Wednesday mornings during papal audiences (until roughly 13:00).

    The **dome** *(cupola)* is open to climbers daily April-Sept 7:30-19:00, Oct-March until 18:00, last entry one hour before closing.

    The **Treasury Museum** is open daily 8:30-18:30.

    The **crypt** *(grotte)* is open daily 9:00-16:00.

Visitor Information: The Vatican TI, up close to the church on the left (south) side of the square, is excellent (Mon-Sat 8:30-18:15, closed Sun, tel. 06-6988-2019, www.vaticanstate.va).

Avoiding Lines: There's often a bottleneck at the security check. The checkpoint is typically on the north side of the square, but is sometimes closer to the church or tucked under the south colonnade.

You can visit before 10:00 to avoid the worst crowds. Crowds also thin out after 16:00—just as sunbeams begin working their magic on the altar. But after 16:00, the crypt is closed, and the altar area is often roped off.

Security: Pocketknives are not allowed, and anything larger than a Swiss Army knife can be reported to the police.

Dress Code: No shorts, above-the-knee skirts, or bare shoulders (applies to men, women, and children). Attendants enforce this dress code, so carry a cover-up if necessary.

Getting There: Take the Metro to Ottaviano, then walk 10 minutes south on Via Ottaviano. The #40 express bus drops off at Piazza Pio, next to Castel Sant'Angelo—a 10-minute walk from St. Peter's. The more crowded bus #64, beloved by pickpockets, stops just outside St. Peter's Square to the south (get off the bus after it crosses the Tiber, at the first stop past the tunnel; backtrack toward the tunnel and turn left when you see the rows of columns; the return bus stop is adjacent to the tunnel). Bus #492 heads through the center of town, stopping at Largo Argentina, and gets you near Piazza Risorgimento (get off when you see the Vatican walls). A few other handy buses (see page 34) get you to the general Vatican area. A taxi from Termini train station costs about €15.

Church Services: Mass, generally in Italian, is said varyingly in the south (left) transept, the Blessed Sacrament Chapel (on right side of nave), or at the main altar. Confirm times on the signboard as you enter. Typical schedule: Mon-Sat at 8:30, 9:00, 10:00, 11:00, 12:00, and at 17:00 (in Latin, at the main altar); Sun and holidays at 9:00, 10:30 (in Latin), 11:30, 12:15, 13:00, 16:00, 16:45 (vespers), and 17:30.

Tours: Audioguides can be rented near the baggage check (€5 plus ID, for church only, daily 8:30-17:00).

⌒ Download my free St. Peter's Basilica **audio tour.**

To see St. Peter's original grave, you can take a *Scavi* (excavations) tour into the **Necropolis** under the basilica (€13, 1.5 hours, ages 15 and up only). Book at least two months in advance by email (scavi@fsp.va) for the fastest reply; go to www.scavi.va (select "Excavations Office") for details. If you get no response, it means they're booked.

Dome Climb: You can take an elevator or climb 231 stairs to the roof, then climb another 323 steps to the top of the dome. The entry to the elevator is just outside the north side of the basilica—look for signs to the *cupola*. If you're climbing the dome without your travel partner, confirm where you'll exit before you split up. For more on the dome, see the end of this chapter.

Length of This Tour: Allow one hour, plus another hour if you climb the dome (or a half-hour to the roof). With as little as

15 minutes, you could stroll the nave, glance up at the dome, down at St. Peter's resting place, and adore the *Pietà* on your way out.

Baggage Check: The free bag check (mandatory for bags larger than a purse or day pack) is inside security, but outside the basilica (to the right as you face the entrance). Pocketknives are not allowed inside the basilica.

Vatican Museums Tickets: The Vatican TI at St. Peter's often has museum tickets available for sale (with same-day, timed-entry reservations; see listing on page 233). This can be a good way to skip the ticket-buying line at the Vatican Museums (for other ticketing options, see the Vatican Museums chapter).

Services: WCs are on both sides of St. Peter's Square (by the TI and just outside security), near the baggage check down the steps by the church entrance, and on the roof. **Drinking fountains** are near the obelisk and the WCs. A **post office** is next to the TI, and a "post bus" often parks on the square.

Starring: Michelangelo, Bernini, St. Peter, a heavenly host...and, occasionally, the pope.

BACKGROUND

Nearly 2,000 years ago, St. Peter's oval-shaped "square" was the site of Nero's Circus—a huge, cigar-shaped Roman chariot racecourse. The Romans had no marching bands, so for halftime entertainment they killed Christians. This persecuted minority was forced to fight wild animals and gladiators, or they were simply crucified. Some were tarred up, tied to posts, and burned—human torches to light up the evening races.

One of those killed here, in about AD 65, was Peter, Jesus' right-hand man, who had come to Rome to spread the message of love. At his own request, Peter was crucified upside down, because he felt unworthy to die as his master had. His remains were buried in a cemetery located where the main altar in St. Peter's is today. For 250 years, these relics were quietly and secretly revered.

Peter had been recognized as the first "pope," or bishop of Rome, from whom all later popes claimed their authority as head of the Church. When Christianity was finally legalized in 313, the Christian emperor Constantine built a church on the site of Peter's martyrdom. "Old St. Peter's" lasted 1,200 years (AD 326-1500).

By the time of the Renaissance, Old St. Peter's was falling apart and was considered unfit to be the center of the Western Church. The new, larger church we see today was begun in 1506 by the architect Donato Bramante. (Bramante was in such a hurry to demolish parts of the original church that he earned the nickname "Master Ruiner.") He was succeeded by Michelangelo and a number of other architects, each with his own designs. Later, Carlo

Vatican City

The tiny independent country of Vatican City is contained entirely within Rome. (Its 100 acres could fit eight times over in New York's Central Park.) The Vatican has its own postal system, armed guards, beautiful gardens, helipad, mini train station, and radio station (KPOP). It also has two huge sights: St. Peter's Basilica and the Vatican Museums. Politically powerful, the Vatican is the religious capital of 1.2 billion Roman Catholics. If you're not a Catholic, become one for your visit.

The pope is both the religious and secular leader of Vatican City. For centuries, the Vatican was the capital of the Papal States, and locals referred to the pontiff as "King Pope." Because of the Vatican's territorial ambitions, it didn't always have good relations with Italy. Even though modern Italy was created in 1870, the Holy See didn't recognize it as a country until 1929.

Like every European country, Vatican City has its own versions of the euro coin (with a portrait of the pope), though they're usually snatched up by collectors before falling into circulation.

Vatican Gardens: To walk through the manicured Vatican Gardens (with views over Rome and a good look at St. Peter's dome), you must book a guided tour several days in advance at www.museivaticani.va (€33, 2 hours, daily except Wed and Sun, includes entry to Vatican Museums; tours usually start at 9:30 or 11:00 at Vatican Museums tour desk). On rare occasions, same-day tickets are available at the Vatican TI. A 45-minute open-bus tour through the gardens is offered in good weather (€37, includes audioguide and entry to Vatican Museums).

Post Offices: The Vatican postal service is famous for its stamps, which you can get from offices on St. Peter's Square (next to the TI), in the Vatican Museums (closed Sun), or from a "post bus" that's often parked on St. Peter's Square (open Sun). To get a Vatican postmark, you must mail your cards from Vatican post-boxes, but beware they can take a long time to reach their recipient (the stamps are good throughout Rome).

Seeing the Pope: Your best chances for a sighting are on Sunday or Wednesday. Most Sundays (though not always, especially in July or Aug), the pope gives a **blessing** at noon from his apartment on St. Peter's Square to the faithful assembled below. On most Wednesdays, the pope holds a **general audience** at 10:00 (tickets get you a closer-up spot but are not required; anyone can enjoy a look via jumbo-screens). That's when he arrives in his Popemobile and gives a short sermon from a canopied platform on the square. (In winter, it's sometimes held indoors at the big Paolo VI Auditorium, next to St. Peter's Basilica, though Pope Francis prefers the square, even in cold weather.) Note that whenever the pope appears on the square, the basilica closes and crowds are substantial—so avoid these times if you just want to sightsee. To get the pope's schedule, see www.vatican.va (select

ST. PETER'S

"Prefecture of the Papal Household" at the bottom of the page).

General Audience Tickets: For the Wednesday audience at 10:00, a (free) ticket gets you closer to the papal action. Reserve tickets (available a month or two in advance) by sending a request by mail or fax (access the form at www.vatican.va—select "Prefecture of the Papal Household" at the bottom of the page). You'll then pick up the tickets at St. Peter's Square before the audience (available Tue 15:00-19:00 and Wed 7:00-9:00; usually under Bernini's colonnade, to the right of the church).

Finally, starting the Monday before the audience, Swiss Guards hand out tickets from their station near the basilica exit (see the "St. Peter's Square" map, later). Don't go through security—just march up, ask nicely, and say *"danke."* While this is perhaps easiest, I'd reserve in advance to guarantee a ticket.

General Audience Tips: On Wednesday morning, you'll need to be dressed modestly (shoulders covered, no short shorts or tank tops—long pants or knee-length skirts are safest) and clear security (no big bags; lines tend to move more quickly on the side of the square farthest from the Metro stop). To get a seat (much less a good one), it's smart to be there a couple of hours early—there are far fewer seats than ticket holders. If you just want to see the pope, get a good photo, and don't mind standing, you can show up later (though still at least 30 minutes early) and take your place in the standing-room section in the back half of the square. The service gets underway around 9:30. Shortly thereafter, the Popemobile appears, winding through the adoring crowd (the best places—seated or standing—are near the cloth-covered wooden fences that line the Popemobile route). Around 10:00, the Pope's multilingual message begins and lasts for about an hour (you can leave at any time).

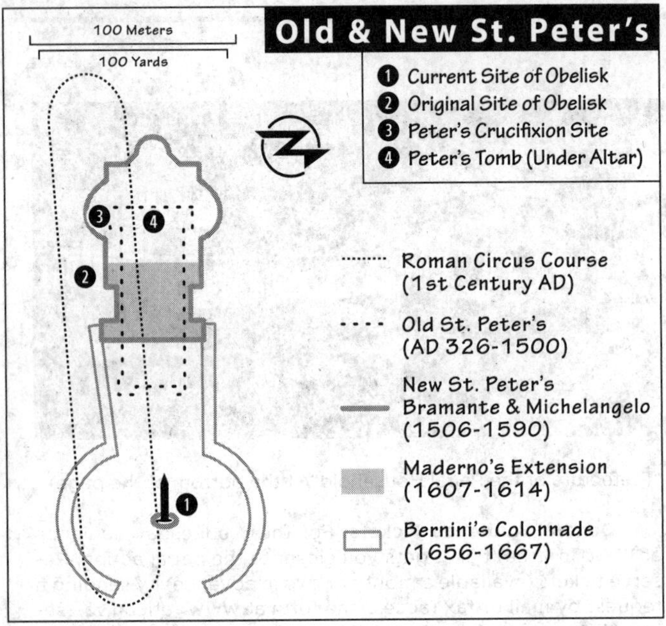

Old & New St. Peter's

1. Current Site of Obelisk
2. Original Site of Obelisk
3. Peter's Crucifixion Site
4. Peter's Tomb (Under Altar)

100 Meters
100 Yards

.... Roman Circus Course
(1st Century AD)

- - - - Old St. Peter's
(AD 326-1500)

New St. Peter's
Bramante & Michelangelo
(1506-1590)

Maderno's Extension
(1607-1614)

Bernini's Colonnade
(1656-1667)

ST. PETER'S

Maderno took Michelangelo's Greek-cross-shaped church and lengthened it, adding a long nave. As the construction proceeded, the new church rose around the old one (see diagram above). The project was finally finished 120 years, 20 popes, and 10 architects later, and Old St. Peter's was dismantled and carried out of the new church. (A few bits survive from the first church: the central door, some columns in the narthex, eight spiral columns around the tomb from the Jerusalem Temple, the venerated statue of Peter, and Michelangelo's *Pietà*.) It took another 200 years to decorate. All told, it took 320 years to create the largest church in the world in what is now the smallest country in the world.

Michelangelo designed the magnificent dome. Unfortunately, although it soars above St. Peter's, it's barely visible from the center of the square because of Maderno's extended nave. To see the entire dome, step outside the open end of the square, where in the 1930s Benito Mussolini opened up the broad boulevard, finally letting people see the dome that had been hidden for centuries by the facade. Although I don't make a habit of thanking fascist dictators, in this case I'll make an exception: *"Grazie, Benito."*

The Tour Begins

• Ideally, you should head out to the obelisk at the center of the square and read this. But let me guess—it's 95 degrees outside, right? OK, find a shady spot under one of these stone sequoias. If the pigeons have left a clean spot, sit on it. Take in the scene: the church, the dome, the obelisk, the statues, and the crowds of tourists and pilgrims.

ST. PETER'S SQUARE

St. Peter's Square, with its ring of columns, symbolizes the arms of the church welcoming everyone—believers and nonbelievers—in its motherly embrace. It was designed a century after Michelangelo by the Baroque architect Gian Lorenzo Bernini, who did much of the work that we'll see inside. Numbers first: 284 columns, 56 feet high, in stern Doric style. Topping them are Bernini's 140 favorite saints, each 10 feet tall. The "square" itself is actually elliptical, 660 by 500 feet (roughly the same dimensions as the Colosseum). Though large, it's designed like a saucer, a little higher around the edges, so that even when full of crowds (as it often is), it allows those on the periphery to see above the throngs.

The **obelisk** in the center is 90 feet of solid granite weighing more than 300 tons. It once stood about 100 yards from its current location, in the center of the circus course (to the left of where St. Peter's is today). Think for a second about how much history this monument has seen. Originally erected in Egypt more than 2,000 years ago, it witnessed the fall of the pharaohs to the Greeks and then to the Romans. Then the emperor Caligula moved it to imperial Rome, where it stood impassively watching the slaughter of Christians at the racecourse and the torture of Protestants by the Inquisition (in the yellow-and-rust building just outside the square, to the left of the church). Today, it watches over the church, a reminder that each civilization builds on the previous ones. The puny cross on top reminds us that Christian culture has cast but a thin veneer over our pagan origins.

• Ready? Venture out across the burning desert to the obelisk, which provides a narrow sliver of shade.

The Vatican is the home of the pope, and St. Peter's is where so many important events take place. Let's find a few of the sights that appear regularly on the evening news.

Face the church and find the balcony in the middle of the fa-

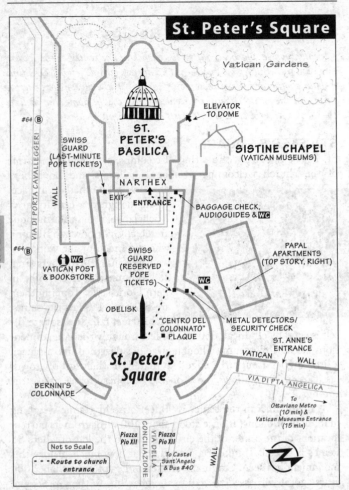

St. Peter's Square

Vatican Gardens

ELEVATOR TO DOME

SISTINE CHAPEL (VATICAN MUSEUMS)

ST. PETER'S BASILICA

SWISS GUARD (LAST-MINUTE POPE TICKETS)

WALL

VIA DI PORTA CAVALLEGGERI

#64 (B)

#64 (B)

NARTHEX

EXIT   ENTRANCE

BAGGAGE CHECK, AUDIOGUIDES & WC

VATICAN POST & BOOKSTORE

SWISS GUARD (RESERVED POPE TICKETS)

PAPAL APARTMENTS (TOP STORY, RIGHT)

WC

OBELISK

"CENTRO DEL COLONNATO" PLAQUE

METAL DETECTORS/ SECURITY CHECK

ST. ANNE'S ENTRANCE

VATICAN   WALL

St. Peter's Square

VIA DI PTA. ANGELICA

To Ottaviano Metro (10 min) & Vatican Museums Entrance (15 min)

BERNINI'S COLONNADE

Piazza Pio XII

VIA DELLA CONCILIAZIONE

Piazza Pio XII

To Castel Sant'Angelo & Bus #40

Not to Scale

- - - Route to church entrance

ST. PETER'S

cade, over the central doorway. This is where the pope appears on formal occasions such as Christmas and Easter. He pronounces a blessing in Latin to the *"Urbi et orbi"*—the city and the world.

Facing the church, pan to the right and find the gray building at about two o'clock, rising up behind Bernini's colonnade. That's the pope's official residence. His suite of rooms is on the top floor. The last window on the right is his bedroom. To the left of that window is the window of his study. Pope Francis, however, has shunned the grand papal apartments and lives instead in a modest Vatican guesthouse (upon first seeing the papal suite, he exclaimed, "You could fit 300 people in here!").

But it is from here that the pope often appears Sundays at noon. The window opens and he waves to the faithful assembled below. He gives a short sermon, says a traditional prayer in Latin called the Angelus, and blesses the crowd with a wave of his hand. The whole thing lasts about 15 minutes. If you want to see it, you don't need a ticket—just show up at the square. The pope also gives audiences on Wednesday mornings, right here in the square, seated in front of the church under an awning.

Now find the Sistine Chapel. It's just to the right of the church's facade—the small gray-brown building with the triangu-

lar roof, topped by an antenna. Look closely. That tiny pimple along the roofline midway up the left side is a chimney. That's where the famous smoke signals announce the election of each new pope (an extension is added for the occasion). White smoke means a new pope has been se-lected. If the smoke is black, a two-thirds majority hasn't been reached.

Walk to the right, five pavement plaques from the obelisk, to the off-center plaque marked *Centro del Colonnato*. From here, all Bernini's columns on the right side line up. The curved Baroque square still pays its respects to Renaissance mathematical symme-try.

• *Now make your way up toward the security checkpoint.*

Notice that there are two entrances into Vatican City: one to the left of the facade, and one to the

right, in the crook of Bernini's "arm." Guarding this small but powerful country's border crossing are merce-nary guards from Switzerland. You have to wonder if they really know how to use those pikes. Their colorful uni-forms are said to have been designed by Michelangelo, although he was not known for his sense of humor.

• *After you clear security, continue up, passing the huge statues of St. Paul (with his two-edged sword) and St. Peter (with his bushy hair and keys). Along the way, you'll pass by the dress-code enforcers and a gaggle of ticked-off tourists in too-short shorts. If you need to rent an audioguide or use the baggage check or WCs, do it now (on the right). Then enter the church narthex.*

THE BASILICA
The Narthex

The narthex (portico) is itself bigger than most churches. Its huge white columns date from the first church (fourth century). Five famous bronze doors lead into the church.

Made from the melted-down bronze of the original door of Old St. Peter's, the central door was the first Renaissance work in Rome (c. 1450). It's only opened on special occasions. The panels (from the top down) feature Jesus and Mary, Paul and Peter, and (at the bottom) how each was martyred: Paul decapitated, Peter crucified upside down.

The far-right entrance is the ❶ **Holy Door,** opened only during Holy Years (and special "Jubilee" years designated by the pope). On Christmas Eve every 25 years, the pope knocks three times with a silver hammer and the door opens, welcoming pilgrims to pass through. For Holy Year 2000, Pope John Paul II opened this door, then bricked it up again with a ceremonial trowel a year later. Above the door is a commemorative plaque that says that Pope "IOANNES PAULUS II" opened the door in the year "MM"—2000—and closed it in "MMI." Although Holy Years officially come every 25 years, Pope Francis declared the year 2016 as an "Extraordinary Jubilee of Mercy" Holy Year. So (as the plaque to the right says), this Holy Door was once again opened to welcome an extraordinary horde of pilgrims. On the door itself, note the crucified Jesus and his shiny knees, polished by pious pilgrims who touch them for a blessing.

• *Now for one of Europe's great "wow" experiences: Enter the church. Gape for a while. But don't gape at Michelangelo's famous* Pietà *(on the right). I'll cover it later in the tour. I'll wait for you at the round maroon pavement stone on the floor near the central doorway (#2 on the map).*

The Nave: Overview of the Church

Wow. The church is huge. Stand at the very back of the nave and survey the heavenly expanse. It's

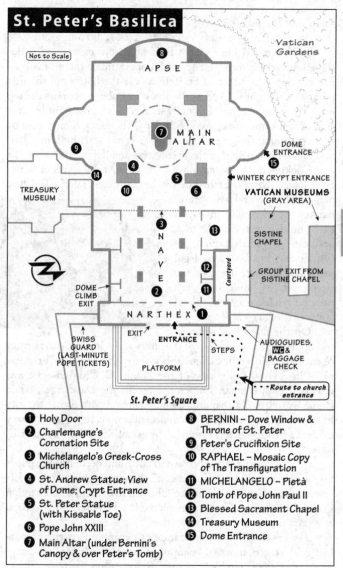

St. Peter's Basilica

Not to Scale

VATICAN MUSEUMS
(GRAY AREA)

ST. PETER'S

1. Holy Door
2. Charlemagne's Coronation Site
3. Michelangelo's Greek-Cross Church
4. St. Andrew Statue; View of Dome; Crypt Entrance
5. St. Peter Statue (with Kissable Toe)
6. Pope John XXIII
7. Main Altar (under Bernini's Canopy & over Peter's Tomb)
8. BERNINI – Dove Window & Throne of St. Peter
9. Peter's Crucifixion Site
10. RAPHAEL – Mosaic Copy of The Transfiguration
11. MICHELANGELO – Pietà
12. Tomb of Pope John Paul II
13. Blessed Sacrament Chapel
14. Treasury Museum
15. Dome Entrance

a riot of marble, gold, stucco, mosaics; columns of stone, and pillars of light. As the symbol of global Catholicism, this church is appropriately big. Size before beauty: The golden window at the far end is two football fields away. The dove in the golden window has the wingspan of a 747 (OK, maybe not quite, but it *is* big). The church covers six acres. The babies at the base of the pillars along the main hall (the nave) are adult-size. The lettering in the gold band along the top of the pillars is seven feet high. Really. The church has a capacity of 60,000 standing worshippers (or 1,200 tour groups).

The church is huge and it feels huge, but everything is designed to make it seem smaller and more intimate than it really is. For example, the statue of St. Teresa near the bottom of the first pillar on the right is 15 feet tall. The statue above her near the top looks the same size, but is actually six feet taller, giving the impression that it's not so far away. Similarly, the fancy bronze canopy over the altar at the far end is as tall as a seven-story building. That makes the great height of the dome seem smaller.

Looking down the nave, we get a sense of the splendor of ancient Rome that was carried on by the Catholic Church. The floor plan, with a central aisle (nave) flanked by two side aisles, is based on that of ancient Roman basilicas—large halls built to accommodate business and legal meetings. In fact, many of the stones used to build St. Peter's were scavenged from the ruined law courts of ancient Rome.

On the floor near the central doorway is a round slab of porphyry stone in the maroon color of ancient Roman officialdom. This is the spot where, on Christmas night in AD 800, the king of the Franks **❷ Charlemagne was crowned** Holy Roman Emperor. Even in the Dark Ages, when Rome was virtually abandoned and visitors reported that the city had more thieves and wolves than decent people, its imperial legacy made it a fitting place to symbolically establish a briefly united Europe.

St. Peter's was very expensive to build and decorate. The popes financed it by selling "indulgences," allowing the rich to buy forgiveness for their sins from the Church. This kind of corruption inspired an obscure German monk named Martin Luther to rebel and start the Protestant Reformation.

The ornate, Baroque-style interior decoration—a riot of marble, gold, stucco, mosaics, columns of stone, and pillars of light—was part of the Church's "Counter" Reformation. Baroque art and architecture served as cheery propaganda, impressing followers with the authority of the Church and giving them a glimpse of the heaven that awaited the faithful.

• *Now, walk straight up the center of the nave toward the altar.*

❸ Michelangelo's Greek-Cross Church

The plaques on the floor show where other, smaller churches of the world would end if they were placed inside St. Peter's: St. Paul's

ST. PETER'S

Cathedral in London (Londinense), Florence's Duomo, and so on.

You'll also walk over circular golden grates. Stop at the second one (at the third pillar from the entrance). This was the extent of the original Greek-cross church. Look back at the entrance and realize that if Michelangelo had had his way, this whole long section of the church wouldn't exist. The nave was extended after his death.

The church took 120 years to build (1506-1626), and the blueprint changed and evolved with each generation. The first architect, Donato Bramante, intended the church to have four equal-length arms, radiating out from the altar in a Greek cross. But after Bramante died, the project languished for decades under several different architects. Finally, Michelangelo, at age 71, was asked to take over the church project and cap it with a dome.

He agreed, intending to put the dome over Donato Bramante's original floor plan. In optimistic Renaissance times, this symmetrical arrangement symbolized perfection—the orderliness of the created world and the goodness of man (who was created in God's image). But Michelangelo was a Renaissance Man in Counter-Reformation times. The Church, struggling against Protestants and its own corruption, opted for a plan designed to impress the world with its grandeur—the Latin cross of the Crucifixion, with its nave extended to accommodate the grand religious spectacles of the Baroque period.

• *Continue toward the altar, entering "Michelangelo's church." Park yourself in front of the* ❹ *statue of St. Andrew to the left of the altar, the guy holding an X-shaped cross. (Note that the* **entrance to the crypt** *is usually here; in winter it's by the dome entrance.)*

Like Andrew, gaze up into the dome, and also like him, gasp. (Never stifle a gasp.)

The Dome

The dome soars higher than a football field on end, 448 feet from the floor of the cathedral to the top of the lantern. It glows with

light from its windows, the blue-and-gold mosaics creating a cool, solemn atmosphere. In this majestic vision of heaven (not painted by Michelangelo), we see (above the windows) Jesus, Mary, and a ring of saints, rings of more angels above them, and, way up in the ozone, God the Father (a blur of blue and red, unless you have binoculars).

When Michelangelo died (1564), he'd completed only the drum of the dome—the circular base up as far as the windows—but the next architects were guided by his designs.

Listen to the hum of visitors echoing through St. Peter's and reflect on our place in the cosmos: half animal, half angel, stretched between heaven and earth, born to live only a short while, a bubble of foam on a great cresting wave of humanity.

• *But I digress.*

Peter's Remains

Peter—the disciple of Jesus, who brought Christianity to Rome—lies buried directly beneath the altar ahead of you. Although the actual tomb is not visible, there are lots of reminders of Peter all around you. Start by looking back up at the dome. The base of the dome is ringed with a gold banner telling us in massive blue

letters why this church is so important. According to Catholics, Peter was selected by Jesus to head the church. The banner in Latin quotes from the Bible where Jesus says to him, "You are Peter *(Tu es Petrus)* and upon this rock I will build my church, and to you I will give the keys of the kingdom of heaven" (Matthew 16:18). (Every quote from Jesus to Peter found in the Bible is written out in seven-foot-tall letters that continue around the entire church.)

Peter was the first bishop of Rome. His prestige and that of the city itself made this bishopric more illustrious than all others, and Peter's authority has supposedly passed in an unbroken chain to each succeeding bishop of Rome—that is, the 260-odd popes that followed.

Under the dome, under the bronze canopy, under the altar, some 23 feet under the marble floor, rest the bones of St. Peter,

From Pope to Pope

When a pope dies—or retires—the tiny, peaceful Vatican stirs from its timeless slumber and becomes headline news. Millions of people converge on Vatican City, and hundreds of millions around the world watch raptly on TV.

JOAN. PAULUS II

The deceased pope's body is displayed in state in front of the main altar in St. Peter's Basilica. Thousands of pilgrims line up down Via della Conciliazione, waiting for one last look at their pope. On the day of the funeral, hundreds of thousands of mourners, dignitaries, and security personnel gather in St. Peter's Square. The pope's coffin is carried out to the square, where a eulogy is given.

Most popes are laid to rest in the crypt below St. Peter's Basilica, near the tomb of St. Peter and among shrines to many other popes. Especially popular popes—such as John Paul II or John XXIII—eventually find a place upstairs, inside St. Peter's itself.

While the previous pope is being laid to rest, 100-plus cardinals, representing Catholics around the globe, descend on Rome to elect a new pope. Once they've assembled, the crimson-robed cardinals are stripped of their mobile phones, given a vow of secrecy, and locked inside the Sistine Chapel. This begins the "conclave" (from Latin *cum clave,* with key). As they cast votes, their used paper ballots are burned in a stove inside the chapel. The smoke rises up and out the tiny chimney, visible to the crowds assembled in St. Peter's Square. Black smoke means they haven't yet agreed on a new pope.

Finally, the anxious crowd looks up to see a puff of white smoke emerging from the chapel. The bells in St. Peter's clock towers ring out gloriously, the crowd erupts in cheers, and Romans watching on TV hail taxis to hurry to the square.

On the balcony outside St. Peter's, the newly elected pope steps up and raises his hands, as thousands chant *"Viva il Papa."* A cardinal introduces him to the crowd, announcing his newly chosen name. "Brothers and sisters," the cardinal says in several languages, *"habemus papam."* "We have a pope."

ST. PETER'S

the "rock" upon which this particular church was built. You can't see the tomb, but you can go to the railing and look down into the small, lighted niche below the altar to see a box containing bishops' shawls—a symbol of how Peter's authority spread to other churches. Peter's tomb is just below this box.

Are the remains buried there really the bones of Jesus' apostle? According to a papal pronouncement: definitely maybe. The traditional site of his tomb was sealed when Old St. Peter's was built

ST. PETER'S

Peter, the "Fisher of Men"

According to the Bible, Peter was a fisherman chosen by Christ to catch sinners instead. This "fisher of men" had human weaknesses that have endeared him to Christians. He was the disciple who tried to walk on water—but failed. In another incident, he impetuously cut off a man's ear when soldiers came to arrest Jesus. And he even denied knowing Christ, to save his own skin. But Jesus chose him anyway and gave him his nickname—Rock (in Latin: *Petrus*).

Legend says that Peter came to the wicked city of Rome after Jesus' death to spread the gospel of love. He may have been imprisoned in the Mamertine Prison near the Roman Forum (see page 47), and other stories claim he had a vision of Christ along the Appian Way (described on page 367). Eventually, Peter's preaching offended the Nero administration. Christ's fisherman was arrested, crucified upside down, and buried here, where St. Peter's now stands.

on it in AD 326, and it remained sealed until 1940, when it was opened for archaeological study. Bones were found, dated from the first century, of a robust man who died in old age. His body was wrapped in expensive cloth. A third-century tag artist had graffitied a wall near the tomb with "Peter is here," indicating that early visitors thought this was Peter's tomb. Does that mean it's really Peter? Who am I to disagree with the pope? Definitely maybe.

Look closely at the niche. If you line up the cross on the altar with the dove in the window, you'll notice that the niche below the cross is just off-center compared with the rest of the church. Why? Because Michelangelo built the church around the traditional location of the tomb, not the actual location—about two feet away—discovered by modern archaeology.

Back in the nave sits a bronze ❺ **statue of St. Peter** under a canopy. This is one of a handful of pieces of art that were in the earlier church. In one hand he holds keys, the symbol of the authority given him by Christ, while with the other hand he blesses us. He's wearing the toga of a Roman senator. It may be that the original statue was of a senator and that the bushy head and keys were added later to make it Peter. His big right toe has been worn smooth by the lips of pilgrims and foot fetishists. Stand in line and kiss it, or, to avoid foot-and-mouth disease, touch your hand to your lips, then rub the toe. This is simply an act of reverence with no legend attached, though you can make one up if you like.

• *Circle to the right around the statue of Peter to find another stop that's popular among pilgrims: the lighted glass niche with the red-robed body of...*

❻ Pope John XXIII

Pope John XXIII, whose papacy lasted from 1958 to 1963, is nicknamed "the good pope." He is best known for initiating the landmark Vatican II Council (1962-1965) that instituted major reforms, bringing the Church into the modern age. The Council allowed Mass to be conducted in the common vernacular rather than in Latin. Lay people were invited to participate more in services, Church leadership underwent some healthy self-criticism, and a spirit of ecumenism flourished. Pope John was a populist, referring to people as "brothers and sisters"...a phrase popular today amongst popes. In 2000, during the beatification process (a stop on the way to sainthood), Church authorities checked his body, and it was surprisingly fresh. So they moved it upstairs, put it behind glass, and now old Catholics who remember him fondly enjoy another stop on their St. Peter's visit. Pope John was canonized in 2014.

After John died, he was succeeded by a more conservative pope. Then came Pope John Paul II, who leaned more liberal (we'll see his tomb later). The next pope, Benedict XVI, was more conservative. But then Benedict stunned the world by retiring from office, allowing the liberal Pope Francis to succeed him...and the pendulum swung once again. Each 21st-century pope has been influenced in some way by the changes introduced by Pope John XXIII. Each walks the delicate tightrope of defending centuries-old Catholic doctrine, while responding to a changing world.

❼ The Main Altar

The main altar (the white marble slab with cross and candlesticks) beneath the dome and canopy is used only when the pope himself says Mass. He sometimes conducts the Sunday morning service when he's in town, a sight worth seeing. I must admit, though, it's a little strange being frisked for weapons at the door to the holiest place in Christendom.

The tiny altar would be lost in this enormous church if it weren't for Gian Lorenzo Bernini's seven-story bronze canopy (God's "four-poster bed"), which "extends" the altar up-

Pope Francis I

In 2013, Cardinal Jorge Bergoglio of Argentina became Francis I, the Catholic Church's 266th pope. Signaling a new direction for the Church, his election represents three "firsts": As the first pope from the Americas, Francis personifies the 80 percent of Catholics who live outside Europe. As the first Jesuit pope—from the religious order known for education—he stands for spreading the faith through teaching. And as the first Francis—named after St. Francis of Assisi—he calls to mind that medieval friar's efforts to return a corrupt church to simple Christian values of poverty and humility.

Born in 1936, Francis grew up in Buenos Aires in a family of working-class Italian immigrants. He worked as a chemist and a high-school teacher before entering the priesthood. Ordained a Jesuit in 1969, he eventually rose to become archbishop of Buenos Aires. He first came to the world's attention in 2005, when he was the runner-up in the election of Pope Benedict. While bishop in Argentina, he worked in the worst of slums and denounced (though some say not loudly enough) Argentina's bloody dictatorship during the Dirty War of the 1970s.

PAPA FRANCESCO

Now a resident of Vatican City, Francis lives simply, staying in a Vatican guesthouse rather than the official papal apartments overlooking St. Peter's Square. He reportedly eats leftovers. When people talk about Francis, the word that comes up is often "dialogue." He's known for listening to every point of view, whether mediat-

ward and reduces the perceived distance between floor and ceiling. The corkscrew columns echo the marble ones that surrounded the altar/tomb in Old St. Peter's. Some of the bronze used here was taken and melted down from the ancient Pantheon. On the marble base of the columns are three bees on a shield, the symbol of the Barberini family, who commissioned the work and ordered the raid on the Pantheon.

Starting from the column to the left of the altar, walk clockwise around the canopy. Notice the female faces on the marble bases, about eye level above the bees. Someone in the Barberini family was pregnant during the making of the canopy, so Bernini put the various stages of childbirth on the bases. Continue clockwise to the last base to see how it came out.

Bernini (1598-1680), the Michelangelo of the Baroque era, is the man most responsible for the interior decoration of the church.

ing between dictators and union leaders, sitting down with the Orthodox Patriarch, celebrating Rosh Hashanah with Jews, visiting a mosque, or speaking well of gays and atheists. In Argentina, he was often seen sharing *mate* (the national tea) with people of every stripe. At the Vatican, his management style stresses the collegiality of the cardinals. He speaks a number of languages, including fluent Italian—the language of his parents and of the Vatican. As Francis himself has pointed out, the original Latin word for pope—*"pontifex"*—literally means "bridge builder."

But Francis is also a strong defender of traditional Catholic beliefs. No one expects major shifts under Francis in the Church's positions on abortion, gay marriage, contraception, or the celibate, male-only priesthood. He inherited a Catholic Church with many problems: financial shenanigans, charges that they've protected pedophiles, and alleged blackmailing of gay priests. And although the Catholic religion is growing worldwide, its home base—Europe—is becoming increasingly secular.

As pope, Francis has made it clear that he wants the Church to focus less on money and power, and more on the poor and the outcast. Francis is skeptical of globalization, worldliness, and unchecked capitalism, with the economic inequality they bring. He's well aware that many of Rome's homeless people camp out right by the basilica. (In fact, Francis—making a point to walk the talk—has opened up a service center just off St. Peter's Square where the local homeless can get a haircut, shower, and use the toilet.) One of his favorite Christian rituals is to literally kneel down before the poor, sick, or imprisoned, and wash their feet. Francis' personal credo, *"Miserando atque elignedo,"* focuses on how God shows "mercy"—*miserando*—and compassion by forgiving sinners and helping the downtrodden.

The altar area was his masterpiece, a "theater" for holy spectacles. Bernini did: 1) the bronze canopy; 2) the dove window in the apse, surrounded by bronze work and statues; 3) the massive statue of lance-bearing St. Longinus ("The hills are alive..."), which became the model for the other three statues in the niches around the main altar; 4) much of the marble floor decoration; and 5) the balconies above the four statues, incorporating some of the actual corkscrew columns from Old St. Peter's, said to have been looted by the Romans from the Temple of Herod (called "Solomon's Temple") in Jerusalem. Bernini, the father of Baroque, gave an impressive unity to an amazing variety of pillars, windows, statues, chapels, and aisles.

• *Approach the apse, the front area with the golden dove window.*

The Apse

Bernini's ❽ **dove window** shines above the smaller front altar used for everyday services. The Holy Spirit, in the form of a six-foot-high dove, pours sunlight onto the faithful through the alabaster windows, turning into artificial rays of gold and reflecting off swirling gold clouds, angels, and winged babies. During a service, real sunlight passes through real clouds of incense, mingling with Bernini's sculpture. This is the epitome of Baroque—an ornate,

mixed-media work designed to overwhelm the viewer. (By the way, as the basilica faces west, rather than the standard east, late in the day the light of the setting sun pours through the alabaster window.)

Beneath the dove is the centerpiece of this structure, the so-called **Throne of St. Peter,** an oak chair built in medieval times for a king. Subsequently, it was encrusted with tradition and encased in bronze by Bernini as a symbol of papal authority. Statues of four early Church Fathers support the chair, a symbol of how bishops should support the pope in troubled times—like the Counter-Reformation.

Remember that St. Peter's is a church, not a museum. In the apse, Mass is said daily for pilgrims, tourists, and Roman citizens alike. Wooden booths are available in the north transept (to the right of the main altar) for Catholics to confess their sins to a listening ear and receive forgiveness and peace of mind (daily, usually mornings and late afternoons). The faithful renew their faith, and the faithless gain inspiration. Look at the light streaming through the windows, turn and gaze up into the dome, and quietly contemplate your deity (or lack thereof).

• *To the left of the main altar is the* **south transept.** *It may be roped off for worship, but anyone can step past the guard if you say you're there "for prayer." At the far end, left side, find the dark "painting" of St. Peter crucified upside down.*

❾ Peter's Crucifixion Site

This marks the exact spot (according to tradition) where Peter was killed 1,900 years ago. Peter had come to the world's greatest city to preach Jesus' message of love to the pagan, often hostile Romans. During the reign of Emperor Nero, he was arrested and brought to Nero's Circus so all of Rome could witness his execution. When the authorities told Peter he was to be crucified just like his Lord,

Bernini Blitz

Nowhere is there such a conglomeration of works by the flamboyant genius who remade this church—and the city—in the Baroque style. Here's your scavenger-hunt list. You have 20 minutes. Go!

1. St. Peter's Square: design and statues
2. Constantine equestrian relief (right end of narthex)
3. Decoration (stucco, gold leaf, marble, etc.) of side aisles (flanking nave)
4. Tabernacle (the temple-like receptacle) inside Blessed Sacrament Chapel
5. Much of the marble floor throughout church
6. Bronze canopy *(baldacchino)* over main altar
7. St. Longinus statue (holding a lance) near main altar
8. Balconies (above each of the four statues ringing main altar) with corkscrew columns
9. Dove window, bronze sunburst, angels, "Throne," and Church Fathers (in apse)
10. Tomb of Pope Urban VIII (far end of apse, right side)
11. Tomb of Pope Alexander VII (between apse and left transept, over a doorway, with the gold skeleton smothered in jasper poured like maple syrup)

Bizarre...Baroque...Bernini.

Peter said, essentially, "I'm not worthy" and insisted they nail him on the cross upside down.

The Romans were actually quite tolerant of other religions, but they required their conquered peoples to worship the Roman emperor as a god. For most religions, this was no problem, but monotheistic Christians refused to worship the emperor even when they were burned alive, crucified, or thrown to the lions. Their bravery, optimism in suffering, and message of love struck a chord among slaves and members of the lower classes. The religion started by a poor carpenter grew, despite the occasional persecution of minorities by fanatical emperors. In three short centuries, Christianity went from a small Jewish sect in Jerusalem to the official religion of the world's greatest empire.

This and all the other "paintings" in the church are actually mosaic copies made from thousands of colored chips the size of your little fingernail. Because smoke and humidity would damage real paintings, since the 1700s church officials have replaced the paintings with mosaics (a.k.a. the "art of eternity") produced by the Vatican Mosaic Studio. Around the corner on the right (heading back toward the central nave), pause at the mosaic copy of Raphael's epic painting of ❿ *The Transfiguration*. The original is now beautifully displayed in the Pinacoteca of the Vatican Museums.

• *Back near the entrance of the church, in the far corner, behind bulletproof glass, is the sculpture everyone has come to see, the…*

⓫ *Pietà*

Michelangelo was 24 years old when he completed this *pietà*—a representation of Mary with the body of Christ taken from the cross. It was Michelangelo's first major commission (by the French ambassador to the Vatican), done for Holy Year 1500.

In Italian, *pietà* means "pity." Michelangelo, with his total mastery of the real world, captures the sadness of the moment. Mary cradles her crucified son in her lap. Christ's lifeless right arm drooping down lets us know how heavy this corpse is. His smooth skin is accented by the rough folds of Mary's robe. Mary tilts her head down, looking at her dead son with sad tenderness. Her left hand turns upward, asking, "How could they do this to you?"

Michelangelo didn't think of sculpting as creating a figure, but as simply freeing the God-made figure from the prison of marble around it. He'd attack a project like this with an inspired passion, chipping away to find what God had placed inside.

The bunched-up shoulder and rigor-mortis legs show that Michelangelo learned well from his studies of cadavers. But realistic as this work is, its true power lies in the subtle "unreal" features. Life-size Christ looks childlike compared with larger-than-life Mary, which accentuates the impression of Mary enfolding Jesus in her maternal love. Mary—the mother of a 33-year-old man—looks like a teenager (she would have been about 50), emphasizing how she was the eternally youthful "handmaiden" of the Lord, always serving him, even at this moment of supreme sacrifice. She accepts God's will, even if it means giving up her son.

The statue is a solid pyramid of maternal tenderness. Yet within this, Christ's body tilts diagonally down to the right and Mary's hem flows with it. Subconsciously, we feel the weight of this dead God sliding from her lap to the ground.

In 1972, a madman with a hammer entered St. Peter's and

began hacking away at the *Pietà*. The damage was repaired, but that's why there's now a shield of bulletproof glass in front of the sculpture.

This is Michelangelo's only signed work. The story goes that he overheard some pilgrims praising his finished *Pietà*, but attributing it to a second-rate sculptor from a lesser city. He was so enraged that he grabbed his chisel and chipped "Michelangelo Buonarroti of Florence did this" in the ribbon running down Mary's chest.

On your right (covered in gray concrete with a gold cross) is the back side of the Holy Door. It will next be opened in 2025, the next Jubilee Year. If there's a prayer inside you, ask that St. Peter's will no longer need security checks or bulletproof glass when this door is next opened.

• *In the chapel to the left is the...*

⓬ Tomb of Pope John Paul II

John Paul II (1920-2005) was one of the most beloved popes of recent times. During his papacy (1978-2005), he was the highly

visible face of the Catholic Church as it labored to stay relevant in an increasingly secular world. The first non-Italian pope in four centuries, he traveled widely. He was the first pope to visit a mosque and a synagogue. He oversaw the fall of communism in his native Poland. He survived an assassination attempt, and he publicly endured his slow decline from Parkinson's disease with great stoicism.

When John Paul II died in 2005, hundreds of thousands lined up outside the church, waiting up to 24 hours to pay their respects. At his funeral in St. Peter's Square, the crowd began chanting, insisting he be made a saint. They didn't have to wait long—he was sainted in April 2014, just nine years after his death.

The tomb has no monument—just a simple stone slab with the inscription *Ioannes Paulus PP. II (1920-2005).* St. John Paul II lies beneath a painting of the steadfast St. Sebastian—the martyr who calmly suffered the slings and arrows of outrageous Romans. Sebastian was John Paul's favorite saint.

Other Sights in the Church

You're welcome to step through the metalwork gates into the ⓭ **Blessed Sacrament Chapel** (Capella di Santissimo Sacramento), an oasis of peace reserved for prayer and meditation (on right

ST. PETER'S

side of church, about midway to the altar). Mass is sometimes said here.

The ⓮ **Treasury Museum** (Museo-Tesoro), on the left side of the nave near the altar, contains the room-size tomb of Sixtus IV by Antonio Pollaiuolo, a big pair of Roman pincers used to torture Christians, an original corkscrew column from Old St. Peter's, and assorted jewels, papal robes, and golden reliquaries—a marked contrast to the poverty of early Christians.

The foundation of Old St. Peter's, the **Crypt** (Grotte/Tombe), contains tombs of popes and memorial chapels. In summer, the crypt entrance is usually beside the statue of St. Andrew, to the left of the main altar (near #4 on the map); in winter, it's by the dome entrance. Stairs lead you down to the floor level of the previous church, where you'll pass the sepulcher of Peter. This lighted niche with an icon is not Peter's actual tomb, but part of a shrine that stands atop Peter's tomb. Nearby is the chapel where Pope John Paul II was buried before being moved upstairs in 2011. Next are the tombs of past popes, including the traditionalist Paul VI (1897-1978), who suffered reluctantly through the church's modernization. Finally, you can see a few column fragments from Old St. Peter's (a.k.a. "Basilica Costantiniana"). Continue your one-way visit until it spills you out, usually near the checkroom.

The walk through the crypt is free and quick (15 minutes)—but you won't see St. Peter's original grave unless you take a *Scavi* (excavations) tour—see "Tours" in the "Orientation" section at the beginning of this chapter.

UP TO THE DOME (CUPOLA)

A good way to finish a visit to St. Peter's is to go up to the dome for the best view of Rome anywhere. The ⓯ **entrance to the dome** is along the right (north) side of the church, but the line begins to form out front, at the church's right door (as you face the church). Look for *cupola* signs.

There are two levels: the rooftop of the church and the very top of the dome. Climb or take an elevator to the first level, on the church roof just above the facade. From the roof, you have a commanding view of St. Peter's Square, the statues on the colonnade, Rome across the Tiber in front of you, and the dome itself—almost terrifying in its nearness—looming behind you. (Depending on the routing when you visit, you might see this view from the roof only after descending from the dome.)

From the roof, you can also go inside the gallery ringing the interior of the dome and look down inside the church. Notice the dusty top of Bernini's seven-story-tall canopy far below. Study the mosaics up close—and those huge letters! It's worth the elevator ride for this view alone.

From this level, if you're energetic, continue all the way up to the top of the dome. The staircase actually winds between the outer shell and the inner one. It's a sweaty, crowded, claustrophobic 15-minute, 323-step climb, but worth it. The view from the summit is great, the fresh air even better.

Admire the arms of Bernini's colonnade encircling St. Peter's Square. Find the big, white Victor Emmanuel Monument, with the two statues on top; and the Pantheon, with its large, light, shallow dome. The large rectangular building to the left of the obelisk is the Vatican Museums complex, stuffed with art. Survey the Vatican grounds, with its mini train system and lush gardens. Look down into the square at the tiny pilgrims buzzing like electrons around the nucleus of Catholicism.

VATICAN MUSEUMS TOUR

Musei Vaticani

The glories of the ancient world displayed in a lavish papal palace, decorated by the likes of Michelangelo and Raphael...the Musei Vaticani. A conglomerate of many submuseums, the Vatican Museums hold some of the greatest art anywhere. Unfortunately, many tourists see these collections only as an obstacle between them and the grand finale, the Sistine Chapel. True, this huge, confusing, and crowded megamuseum can be a jungle—but with this book as your vine, you should swing through with ease, enjoying the highlights and getting to the Sistine just before you collapse.

With the Fall of Rome (AD 476), the Catholic ("universal") Church became the great preserver of civilization, collecting artifacts from cultures dead and dying. Renaissance popes (15th and 16th centuries) collected most of what we'll see, using it as furniture to decorate their palace (today's museum). Combining the classical and Christian worlds, they found the divine in the creations of man.

We'll concentrate on classical sculpture and Renaissance painting. But along the way (and there's a lot of along-the-way here), we'll stop to leaf through a few yellowed pages from this 5,000-year-old scrapbook of humankind.

The always crowded museum has an online reservation system and a website with up-to-date hours and information. For more on Vatican City, the small, independent country where this museum is located, see page 236.

Orientation

Cost: €17, €8 for kids 6-18, free for kids 5 and under, €4 online reservation fee, free on the last Sun of each month (when it's very crowded).

Hours: Mon-Sat 9:00-18:00, last entry at 16:00 (the staff starts ushering you out at 17:30). Closed Sun, except last Sun of the month, when it's open 9:00-14:00, last entry at 12:30. Open Fri nights, mid-April-Oct 19:00-23:00 (last entry at 21:30) by online reservation only; note that during evening visits, parts of the museum—including the Pinacoteca—are often closed.

The museum is closed on many holidays (mainly religious ones), including Jan 1 (New Year's), Jan 6 (Epiphany), Feb 11 (Vatican City established), March 19 (St. Joseph's Day), Easter Sunday and the following Monday, May 1 (Labor Day), June 29 (Sts. Peter and Paul), Aug 15 (Assumption of the Virgin), Nov 1 (All Saints' Day), Dec 8 (Immaculate Conception), and Dec 25 and 26 (Christmas). Always check the current hours and calendar on the museum website.

Individual rooms may close at odd hours, especially in the afternoon. The rooms described here are usually open.

Information: Tel. 06-6988-4676, www.museivaticani.va.

Reservations: You're crazy to come without a reservation: The Vat-

ican Museums can be extremely crowded, with waits of up to two hours just to buy tickets. Bypass these long lines by reserving an entry time online for €21 (€17 ticket plus €4 booking fee). It's easy—and it can change your day. For this chapter's sights, select the ticket called "Vatican Museums and Sistine Chapel."

Print the emailed voucher to present at the museum (see "Getting In," later). You can also receive your reservation on your mobile phone.

When to Go: The museum is generally crowded, with shoulder-to-shoulder sightseeing through much of it. The best time to visit is a weekday after 14:00—the later the better. Another good time is during the papal audience on Wednesday morning, when many tourists are at St. Peter's Square (the drawback is that St. Peter's Basilica is closed until roughly 13:00). The worst days are Saturdays, the last Sunday of the month (when the museum is free), Mondays, rainy days, and any day before or after a holiday closure.

More Line-Beating Tips: If you didn't book tickets in advance, you have a few other line-avoiding options. Booking a **guided tour** (described later, under "Tours") gets you right in—just show the guard your voucher.

You can often buy **same-day timed-entry reservations**

without a ticket-buying line at the Vatican TI in St. Peter's Square (to the left, as you face the basilica—see details in the previous chapter). The Opera Romana Pellegrinaggi (a.k.a., Roma Cristiana), a private pilgrimage tour company, also sells same-day tickets (€30, entrances almost hourly, office in front of St. Peter's Square, Piazza Pio XII 9, tel. 06-698-961, www. operaromanapellegrinaggi.org).

Hawkers peddling skip-the-line access swarm the Vatican area, offering guided tours—but museum staff advise against accepting their offers (while legitimate, the tour caliber is often low—use them only as a last resort to get in).

Dress Code: While modest dress (no shorts, above-knee skirts, or bare shoulders) is technically required throughout the Vatican Museums, this dress code is most strictly enforced inside the Sistine Chapel (and at St. Peter's Basilica). Carry a cover-up if necessary.

Getting There: The Ottaviano Metro stop is a 10-minute walk from the entrance. Bus #49 from Piazza Cavour/Castel Sant'Angelo stops at Piazza Risorgimento and continues right to the entrance. Bus #23 from Trastevere hugs the west bank of the Tiber and stops on Via Leone IV, just downhill from the entrance. Bus #492 heads from the city center past Piazza Risorgimento and the Vatican walls, and stops on Via Leone IV. Bus #64 stops on the other side of St. Peter's Square, a 15- to 20-minute walk (facing the church from the obelisk, take a right through the colonnade and follow the Vatican Wall). Or take a taxi from the city center—they are reasonable (hop in and say, "moo-ZAY-ee vah-tee-KAH-nee").

Getting In: Approaching the exterior entrance (the big white door), you'll see three lines: individuals without reservations (far left), individuals with reservations (usually shorter and faster), and groups (on the right). Make sure you get in the correct entry line. All visitors must pass through a metal detector (no pocketknives allowed).

With a reservation, show your voucher to the guard and enter via the reserved ticket-holder line. Inside, after the security check, go to any window on the left to show your voucher and pick up your ticket, then go up the steps and enter the museum. (Or, you can skip the ticket-window line by going upstairs and processing your voucher on a machine.)

Without a reservation, enter via the far left line. Once you clear security, go upstairs to buy your ticket.

Visitor Information: As you enter the main lobby of the museum, an info desk is to your left, and video screens list which rooms are open or closed. Bookstores are scattered throughout the museum, and many exhibits have English explanations. You can virtually tour the Sistine Chapel ceiling at the museum website.

Tours: An €8 **audioguide** is available at the top of the spiral ramp/escalator, and can be prepaid when you book tickets online. No ID is required to rent an audioguide. Confirm the drop-off location when renting.

∩ Download my free Vatican Museums and Sistine Chapel **audio tours.**

The Vatican offers **guided tours** in English that are easy to book on their website (€33, includes admission). Present your

confirmation voucher to a guard to the right of the entrance; then, once inside, go to the Guided Tours desk (in the lobby, up a few stairs).

For a list of **private tour** companies and guides, see page 39.

Length of This Tour: Until you expire, the museum closes, or 2.5 hours pass, whichever comes first. If you're short on time, see the octagonal courtyard *(Laocoön)*, then follow the crowd flow directly to the Sistine Chapel, sightseeing along the way.

Services: The museum's "checkroom" (to the right after security) takes only bigger bags, not day bags.

The post office, with stamps that make collectors drool, is upstairs. WCs are mainly at the entrance/exit, plus a few scattered within the collection.

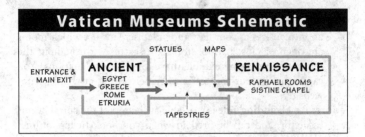

Vatican Museums Schematic

ENTRANCE &
MAIN EXIT

ANCIENT
EGYPT
GREECE
ROME
ETRURIA

STATUES   MAPS

TAPESTRIES

RENAISSANCE
RAPHAEL ROOMS
SISTINE CHAPEL

VATICAN MUSEUMS

Cuisine Art: A **$** self-service cafeteria is inside, downstairs, near the Pinacoteca. Smaller **$$** cafés are in the outdoor Pinecone Courtyard (Cortile della Pigna) and near the Sistine Chapel. All offer mediocre food at inflated prices.

Cheaper choices outside the museum include nearby supermarkets and the great Mercato Trionfale produce market on Via Andrea Doria, three blocks north of the entrance (head across the street, down the stairs, and continue straight). Inexpensive *pizza rustica* shops selling pizza by the slice line Viale Giulio Cesare and Via Candia, and good restaurants are nearby (see page 406).

Starring: World history, a pope's palace, Michelangelo, Raphael, *Laocoön*, the Greek masters, and their Roman copyists.

The Tour Begins

This heavyweight museum is shaped like a barbell—two buildings connected by a long hall. The entrance building covers the ancient world (Egypt, Greece, Rome). The building at the far end covers its "rebirth" in the Renaissance (including the Sistine Chapel). The halls there and back are a mix of old and new. Move quickly—don't burn out before the Sistine Chapel, near the end of this tour—and see how each civilization borrows from and builds upon the previous one.

• *Our tour starts in the Vatican Museums' large open-air courtyard called the "Pinecone Courtyard" (Cortile della Pigna).*

To get there, scan your ticket at the turnstiles, and then take the long escalator or spiral ramp up, up, up to a glass-covered patio. The audioguide kiosk is here. To your right are the cafeteria and the Pinacoteca painting gallery, described at the end of this chapter. To your left is the beginning of our tour.

So go left, and after 50 yards emerge into the open air of the Pinecone Courtyard...

Pinecone Courtyard (Cortile della Pigna)

Locate the big bronze ball in the center of the courtyard, and the 12-foot-tall pinecone. This vast space is the perfect place to start

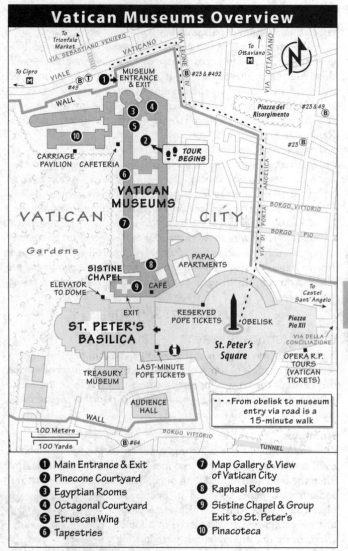

Vatican Museums Overview

1. Main Entrance & Exit
2. Pinecone Courtyard
3. Egyptian Rooms
4. Octagonal Courtyard
5. Etruscan Wing
6. Tapestries
7. Map Gallery & View of Vatican City
8. Raphael Rooms
9. Sistine Chapel & Group Exit to St. Peter's
10. Pinacoteca

your visit of this vast museum. The Pinecone Courtyard sums up the Vatican's entire collection: Pinecone—ancient. Bronze sphere—modern. And the courtyard around it—Renaissance, designed by Bramante.

The bronze pinecone is 2,000 years old. It originally stood near the Pantheon, to honor Isis, the Egyptian goddess of fertility. In Christian times, it was moved to the entrance of Old St. Peter's Church. During the Renaissance, when popes reigned supreme, it was brought here, to decorate this courtyard in what was then the pope's breezy summer palace on a hill.

The bronze ball in the center of the courtyard, by the Italian sculptor Pomodoro, arrived here in 1990. It symbolizes—well, there are many interpretations. It may represent the cosmos, or, the earth surrounded by the heavens. (Or the eternity it takes to see this huge museum.) Whatever—it's big, it's shiny, and its presence here completes the march through history: ancient, Christian, Renaissance, modern.

• *We start in the ancient world, with the Egyptian collection. To get there, face the pinecone, and turn left, backtracking through the door you just came through. Immediately after reentering the door, turn right up a flight of marble stairs to reach the first-floor Egyptian rooms (Museo Gregoriano Egizio). Enter, and don't stop until you find your mummy.*

Note: Occasionally, the stairs up to Egypt are closed off, and crowds are routed through the courtyard to a door to the right of the pinecone. If so, just follow the masses until you reach the octagonal courtyard with the Apollo Belvedere and Laocoön *figures. Tour the museum from there to the* "Sarcophagi," *where you'll find the entrance to the Egyptian rooms.*

VATICAN MUSEUMS

Ancient Wing

EGYPT (3000-1000 BC)

Egyptian art was religious, not decorative. A statue or painting preserved the likeness of someone, giving him or her a form of eternal life. Most of the art was for tombs, where they put the mummies.

• *Pass beyond the imitation Egyptian pillars to the left of the case in the center of the room, and you'll find...*

Mummies

This woman died three millennia ago. Her corpse was disemboweled, and her organs were placed in a jar like those you see nearby. Then the body was refilled with pitch, dried with natron (a natural sodium carbonate), wrapped in linen, and placed in a wood coffin, which went inside a stone coffin, which was placed in a tomb. (Remember that the pyramids were just big tombs.) Notice the henna job on her hair—in the next life, your spirit needed a body to be rooted to...and you wanted to look your best.

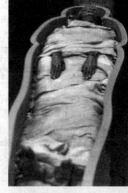

Painted inside the coffin lid is a list of what the deceased "packed" for the journey to eternity. The coffins were decorated with magical spells to protect the body from evil and to act as crib notes for the confused soul

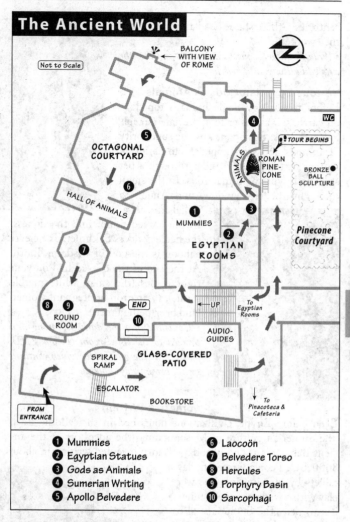

The Ancient World

Not to Scale

BALCONY
WITH VIEW
OF ROME

OCTAGONAL
COURTYARD

⑤

⑥

HALL OF ANIMALS

① MUMMIES

② EGYPTIAN ROOMS

③

ANIMALS

ROMAN
PINE-
CONE

④

WC

TOUR BEGINS

BRONZE
BALL
SCULPTURE

Pinecone
Courtyard

⑦

← UP

To
Egyptian
Rooms

⑧ ⑨
ROUND
ROOM

END

⑩

AUDIO-
GUIDES

SPIRAL
RAMP

GLASS-COVERED
PATIO

ESCALATOR

BOOKSTORE

To
Pinacoteca &
Cafeteria

FROM
ENTRANCE

VATICAN MUSEUMS

① Mummies
② Egyptian Statues
③ Gods as Animals
④ Sumerian Writing
⑤ Apollo Belvedere
⑥ Laocoön
⑦ Belvedere Torso
⑧ Hercules
⑨ Porphyry Basin
⑩ Sarcophagi

in the netherworld. In nearby cases are *shabtis,* small figurines of the deceased placed inside the tomb.
• *In the next room are...*

Egyptian Statues

Egyptian statues walk awkwardly, as if they're carrying heavy buckets, with arms straight down at their sides. Even these Roman reproductions (made for Hadrian's Villa) are stiff, two-dimensional, and schematic—the art is only realistic enough to get the job done. In Egyptian belief, a statue like this could be a stable refuge for the wandering soul of a dead person. Each was made according to an established set of proportions. Little changed over the centuries—these statues had a function, and they worked.

• *Walk through the next small room and into the curved hallway, and look for...*

Various Egyptian Gods as Animals

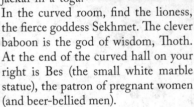

Before technology made humans top dogs on earth, it was easier to appreciate our fellow creatures. Egyptians saw the superiority of animals and worshipped them as incarnations of the gods. Wander through a pet store of Egyptian animal gods. In the small room, by the big window, find Anubis, a

jackal in a toga. In the curved room, find the lioness, the fierce goddess Sekhmet. The clever baboon is the god of wisdom, Thoth. At the end of the curved hall on your right is Bes (the small white marble statue), the patron of pregnant women (and beer-bellied men).

• *Continue into the darkened wing and proceed to the third room (Room VIII), pausing at the glass case, which contains small, brown clay tablets.*

Sumerian Writing

Even before Egypt, civilizations flourished in the Middle East. The Sumerian culture in Mesopotamia (the ancestors of the ancient Babylonians and of today's Iraqis) invented writing in about

3000 BC. People wrote on clay tablets by pressing into the wet clay with a wedge-shaped (cuneiform) pen. The Sumerians also rolled cylindrical seals into soft clay to make an impression that authenticated documents and marked property.

• *Pass through the next room, and then turn left, to a balcony with a view of Rome through the window. You're in what was originally the Belvedere Palace—the pope's summer palace, on a hill, with a breeze and fine views.*

GREEK AND ROMAN SCULPTURE
(500 BC-AD 500)

This palace wouldn't be here, this sculpture wouldn't be here, and our lives would likely be quite different if it weren't for a few thousand Greeks in a small city about 450 years before Christ. Athens set the tone for the rest of the West. Democracy, theater, economics, literature, and art all flourished in Athens during a 50-year Golden Age. Greek culture was then appropriated by Rome, and revived again 1,500 years later, during the Renaissance. The Renaissance popes built and decorated these papal palaces, re-creating the glory of the classical world.

• *Enter the* **Octagonal Courtyard.** *In 1506, the Vatican Museums were born here as a place for popes to entertain VIPs and guests with their fine collection of art. The galleries opened to the public around 1800.*

Find the statue of Apollo Belvedere, *on your left as you enter.*

Apollo Belvedere

Apollo, the god of the sun and of music, is hunting. He's been running through the woods, and now he spots his prey. Keeping

his eye on the animal, he slows down and prepares to put a (missing) arrow into his (missing) bow. The optimistic Greeks conceived of their gods in human form...and buck naked.

This Apollo is a Roman copy (2nd century AD) of a Hellenistic original that followed the style of the great Greek sculptor Praxiteles. It fully captures the beauty of the human form. The anatomy is perfect, and his pose is natural. Instead of standing at attention, face-forward with his arms at his sides (Egyptian-style), Apollo is on the move, coming to rest with his weight on one leg.

The Greeks loved balance. A well-rounded man was both a thinker and an athlete, a poet and a warrior. In art, the *Apollo Belvedere* balances several opposites. He's moving, but not out of control. Apollo eyes his target, but hasn't attacked yet. He's realistic, but with idealized, godlike features. And the smoothness of his muscles is balanced by the rough folds of his cloak. The only sour note: his left hand, added in modern times. Could we try a size smaller?

During the Renaissance, when this Roman copy was discovered, it was considered the most perfect work of art in the world. The handsome face, eternal youth, and body that seems to float just above the pedestal made *Apollo Belvedere* seem superhuman, divine, and godlike, even for devout Christians. Remember this face when you see Jesus in Michelangelo's *Last Judgment* in the Sistine Chapel; clearly this Apollo inspired the artist.

• *In the neighboring niche to the right, a bearded old* **Roman river god** *lounges in the shade. This ancient statue also inspired Michelangelo. He used the river-god pose for the figure of Adam in the Sistine Chapel, reclining and reaching out to accept the spark of life from the finger of God.*

While there are a few fancy bathtubs in this courtyard, most of the carved boxes you see are sarcophagi—Roman coffins and relic holders, carved with the deceased's epitaph in picture form.

In the next niche is...

Laocoön

This man's agony captures the dramatic climax of the Trojan War. Laocoön (lay-AWK-oh-wahn), the high priest of Troy, had warned his fellow Trojans: "Beware of Greeks bearing gifts." The attacking Greeks had brought the Trojan Horse to the gates as a ploy to get inside the city walls, and Laocoön tried to warn his people not to bring it inside. But the gods wanted the Greeks to win, so they sent huge snakes to crush Laocoön and his two sons to death. We see them at the height of their terror, when they realize that, no matter how hard they struggle, they—and their entire race—are doomed. Laocoön's agonized face says it all: "Snakes...why'd it have to be snakes?"

The figures (carved from four blocks of marble pieced together seamlessly) are powerful, not light and graceful. The poses are as twisted as possible, accentuating every rippling muscle and bulging vein. Follow the line of motion from Laocoön's left foot, up his leg, through his body, and out his right arm (which some historians used to think extended straight out—until the elbow was dug up in the early 1900s). Goethe would stand here and blink his eyes rapidly, watching the statue flicker to life.

Laocoön was sculpted some four centuries after the Golden Age (5th-4th century BC), after the scales of "balance" had been tipped. Whereas *Apollo* is a balance between stillness and motion, this is textbook Hellenism...unbridled motion. *Apollo* is serene, graceful, and godlike, while *Laocoön* is powerful, emotional, and gritty.

Laocoön—the most famous Greek statue in ancient Rome and considered "superior to all other sculpture or painting"—was lost for more than a thousand years. Then, in 1506, it was unexpectedly unearthed in the ruins of Nero's Golden House near the Colosseum. The discovery caused a sensation. It was cleaned off and paraded through the streets in front of an awestruck populace (before landing here and becoming the first piece of this collection). No one had ever seen anything like its motion and emotion, having been raised on a white-bread diet of pretty-boy *Apollo*s. One of those who saw it was the young Michelangelo, and it was a revelation to him. Two years later, he started work on the Sistine Chapel, and the Renaissance was about to take another turn.

• *Leave the courtyard to the right of* Laocoön *and pause at the **Hall of Animals** (on the left), a Hellenistic zoo of beasts real and surreal. These animals are all ancient statues restored in the 18th century during the Enlightenment. (Can you find the camel?) Then continue to the limbless torso in the middle of the next large hall.*

Belvedere Torso

My experience with sculpting statues ends with snowmen. But standing face-to-face with this hunk of shaped rock makes you

appreciate the sheer physical labor involved in chipping a figure out of solid stone. It takes great strength but, at the same time, great delicacy.

This is all that remains of an ancient statue damaged by time. It shows a powerful man seated on an animal skin. Maybe it's Hercules with his lion skin, maybe a Cyclops—no one's quite sure. It's signed on the base by a sculptor named Apollonius, from the first century BC. Scholars think Apollonius may have copied an older statue, so it's clear that this subject was popular in the ancient world.

Michelangelo loved this old rock. He knew that he was the best sculptor of his day. The ancients were his only peers—and his rivals. He'd caress this statue lovingly and tell people, "I am the pupil of the Torso." To him, it contained all the beauty of classical sculpture. But it's not beautiful. Compared with the pure grace of the *Apollo*, it's downright ugly.

But Michelangelo, an ugly man himself, was looking for a new kind of beauty—not the beauty of idealized gods, but the innate beauty of every person, even so-called ugly ones. With its knotty lumps of muscle, the Torso has a brute power and a distinct personality despite—or because of—its rough edges. Michelangelo's Jesus in *The Last Judgment* mimics the Torso's slightly turned pose.

• *So, in the Sistine Chapel, Jesus has the body of the Torso and the face of Apollo, and Adam reclines like a river god. It's apparent that Michelangelo loved the ancients. Now, enter the next, domed room.*

Etruscan Wing Highlights

Just before the rise of Rome, the Etruscan people of central Italy (who inhabited the area between today's Rome and Florence) had their own Golden Age of peace and prosperity. Their mix of Greek-style art and Roman-style customs helped lay a foundation of civilization for the flourishing of Rome. I've noted some high-lights in the Etruscan Wing (800-300 BC); browse the remaining dozen rooms if you wish. When you've had your fill, backtrack to the long hall (the Gallery of the Candelabra) leading to the Sistine Chapel and Raphael Rooms.

Room I

The chariot is from 550 BC, when the crude Romans were ruled by their more civilized neighbors to the north—the Etruscans. (The wooden portions are a reconstruction.) Imagine the chariot racing around the dirt track of the Circus Maximus, through the marshy valley of the newly drained Forum, or up Capitoline Hill to the Temple of Jupiter—all originally built by Rome's Etruscan kings.

Room II

The golden breastplate (*Pectoral,* 650 BC), decorated with tiny winged figures and animals, shows off the sophistication of the Etruscans. Though unwarlike and politically decentralized, these people were able to "conquer" all of central Italy around 650 BC through trade, offering tempting metalwork goods like this.

The Etruscan vases done in the Greek style remind us of the other great pre-Roman power—the Greek colonists who settled in southern Italy (Magna Graecia). The Etruscans traded with the Greeks, adopting their fashions. Rome, cradled between the two, grew up learning from both cultures.

Round Room

This room, modeled on the Pantheon interior, gives some idea of Roman grandeur. Romans took Greek ideas and made them bigger, like the big bronze statue of Hercules with his club, found near the Theater of Pompey (by modern-day Campo de' Fiori). The mosaic floor you're standing on is 1,700 years old—it once decorated the bottom of a pool in an ancient Roman bath. Admire its fantas-

A Greek-style bowl (far corner of the room) depicting a man and woman in bed together would have scandalized early Roman farmers. He's peeing in a chamber pot, she's blowing a flute. Etruscan art often showed husbands and wives at ease together, giving them a reputation among the Romans as immoral, flute-playing degenerates.

Room III

This bronze warrior (late 5th century BC), whose helmet was sawed off by lightning, has a rare in-  scription that's readable (on armor below the navel). It probably refers to the statue's former owner: "Aha! Trutitis gave [this] as [a] gift." Archaeologists understand the Etruscans' Greek-style alphabet and some individual words, but they've yet to fully crack the code. As you look around at beautiful bronze pitchers, candlesticks, shields, and urns, ponder yet another of Etruria's unsolved mysteries—no one is sure where these sophisticated people came from.

Room IV

Most of our knowledge of the Etruscans is from sarcophagi and art in Etruscan tombs. Their funeral art is solemn, but hardly morbid—check out the sarcopha-guy with the bulging belly, enjoying a banquet for all eternity.

The Etruscans' origins are obscure, but their legacy is clear. In 509 BC, the Etruscan king's son raped a Roman noblewoman. The king was thrown out, the republic was declared, Etruscan cities were conquered by Rome's legions, and their culture was swallowed up in Roman expansion. By Julius Caesar's time, the few remaining ethnic Etruscans were reduced to serving their masters as flute players, goldsmiths, surgeons, and street-corner preachers, like the one that Caesar brushed aside when he called out, "Beware the Ides of March..."

tic beasts and battle scenes. The enormous Roman basin/hot tub/birdbath/vase decorated Nero's place. It was made of a single block of purple porphyry marble stone imported from Egypt. (It's so big that this 18th-century room was built around it.) Purple was a rare, royal, expensive, and prestigious color in pre-Crayola days. This particular variety, called "imperial porphyry," came from a single mountain in Egypt and was the stone of emperors...and then of popes. Now that source is quarried out, and the only "imperial porphyry" available to anyone has been recycled.

• *Enter the next room.*

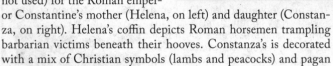

Sarcophagi

These two large porphyry marble coffins were made (though not used) for the Roman emperor Constantine's mother (Helena, on left) and daughter (Constanza, on right). Helena's coffin depicts Roman horsemen trampling barbarian victims beneath their hooves. Constanza's is decorated with a mix of Christian symbols (lambs and peacocks) and pagan

themes (Bacchuses harvesting grapes). Helena and Constanza were Christians—and therefore outlaws—until Constantine made Christianity legal in AD 313, and they became saints. Both sarcophagi were quarried and worked in Egypt. The technique for working this extremely hard stone (a special tempering of metal was required) was lost after this, and porphyry marble was not chiseled again until Renaissance times in Florence.

• *See how we've come full circle in this building—the Egyptian Rooms are ahead on your left. If you haven't seen Egypt yet, now's your chance. You probably can't enter the rooms from this exact spot, but if you go up the stairs, you'll find another set of stairs going down that will take you there.*

To continue our tour, from the precious purple porphyry, go upstairs. You'll find yourself at the head of a long hallway lined with statues. Prepare for the Long March to the Sistine Chapel.

Overachievers may first choose to pop into the Etruscan wing— labeled Museo Gregoriano Etrusco—*located a few steps up from the Long March level. (For a quick tour, see the sidebar.) Others have permission to save their aesthetic energy for the Sistine.*

THE LONG MARCH—SCULPTURE, TAPESTRIES, MAPS, AND VIEWS

This quarter-mile walk gives you a sense of the scale that Renaissance popes built on. Remember, this building was originally a series of papal palaces. The popes loved beautiful things—statues, urns, marble floors, friezes, stuccoed ceilings—and, as heirs of

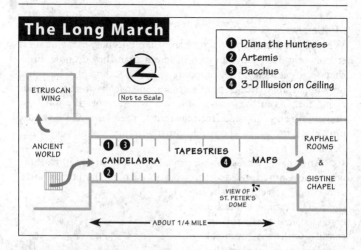

The Long March

1. Diana the Huntress
2. Artemis
3. Bacchus
4. 3-D Illusion on Ceiling

ETRUSCAN WING

ANCIENT WORLD

CANDELABRA

TAPESTRIES

MAPS

RAPHAEL ROOMS & SISTINE CHAPEL

VIEW OF ST. PETER'S DOME

Not to Scale

ABOUT 1/4 MILE

imperial Rome, they felt they deserved such luxury. The palaces and art represent both the peak and the decline of the Catholic Church in Europe. It was extravagant spending like this that inspired Martin Luther to rebel, starting the Protestant Reformation.

Gallery of the Candelabra (Galleria dei Candelabri): Classical Sculpture

About 30 yards along the long hall, stop at the statue of **Diana the Huntress** on the left. Here, the virgin goddess goes hunting. Roman hunters would pray and give offerings to statues like this to get divine help in their search for food.

Farmers might pray to another version of the same goddess, in her guise as **Artemis,** on the opposite wall. This billion-breasted beauty stood for fertility. "Boobs or bulls' balls?" Some historians say that bulls were sacrificed and castrated, with the testicles draped over the statues as symbols of fertility.

• *Shuffle along another 30 yards, remembering that, while the statues seem white and lifeless today, originally they were colorfully painted and had inlaid eyes. On the left is* **Bacchus,** *with a baby on his shoulders. Notice the fine floor— made of marble recycled from ancient baths.*

Fig Leaves

Why do the statues have fig leaves? Like Bacchus, many of these statues originally looked much different than they do now. First, they were painted, often in gaudy colors. Bacchus may have had brown hair, rosy cheeks, purple grapes, and a leopard-skin sidekick at his feet. Even the *Apollo Belvedere*, whose cool gray tones we now admire as "classic Greek austerity," may have had a paisley pink cloak for all we know. Also, many statues had glass eyes like Bacchus'.

And the fig leaves? Those came from the years 1550 to 1800, when the Church decided that certain parts of the human anatomy were obscene. (Why not the feet?) Perhaps Church leaders associated these full-frontal statues with the outbreak of Renaissance humanism that reduced their power in Europe. Whatever the cause, they reacted by covering classical crotches with plaster fig leaves, the same leaves Adam and Eve had used when the concept of "privates" was invented.

Note: The leaves could be removed at any time if the museum officials were so motivated. There are suggestion boxes around the museum. Whenever I see a fig leaf, I get the urge to pick-it. We could start an organ-ized campaign...

• *Cover your eyes in case they forgot a fig leaf or two, and continue to the...*

Tapestries

Along the left wall are tapestries designed by Raphael's workshop and made in Brussels (circa 1524). They show scenes from the life of Christ: Baby Jesus in the manger, being adored by shepherds, and so on. The tapestries were created by first painting the scene on paper—full size and full color. These "cartoons" were then sent to the famous weaving factories in Brussels, where they were cut up into manageable strips, and placed on the looms.

The Vatican tapestries are remarkable for their realism—almost like oil paintings. Notice the tiny details and subtle changes in color. In the weaving process, the vertical threads are a neutral color; the horizontal threads create the design. Imagine: The equivalent of each brushstroke had to be reproduced by thousands of short pieces of colored thread woven horizontally into exactly the right spot.

About two-thirds of the way down the hall, find the Resurrection tapestry (on the left), with Jesus striding out of the tomb. It's curiously interactive...as you walk, Jesus' eyes, feet, knee, and even the stone slab seem to follow you across the room. Next to it, *The Supper at Emmaus* (with Jesus sitting at a table) seems equally flexible.

Check out the beautiful sculpted reliefs on the ceiling. Admire the workmanship of this relief, then realize that it's not a relief at all—it's painted on a flat surface! Even the shadows are fake. Illusions like this were proof that painters had mastered the 3-D realism of ancient statues.

Map Gallery and View of Vatican City

This jaw-dropping gallery is the best place to appreciate the splendor of what this museum once was—the popes' palace. The crusted ceiling is pure papal splendor. The maps on the walls show the regions of Italy— "Sicilia," "Sardinia," and so on. Popes could take visitors on a tour of Italy, from the toe (entrance end) to the Alps (far end), with east Italy on the right wall, west on the left.

These maps functioned as the Vatican's official maps from 1582 (when they were painted) until the 19th century.

The colorful scenes on the ceiling complement the maps, portraying exciting moments in Church history in each of those regions. The ceiling is made of molded stucco (plaster) that's been painted. The decoration is based on ancient designs: lots of ornate garlands and intertwined vines, cupids, scallop shells, Roman vases, and winged nymphs. It's the so-called "grotesque" style, named for the excavated Roman grottoes they were discovered in.

Glance out the windows. This is your best look at the tiny country of Vatican City, officially established as an independent nation in 1929. It has its own radio station, as you see from the tower on the hill. What you see here is pretty much all there is—these gardens, the palaces you're in, and St. Peter's (for more on Vatican City, see the sidebar on page 236).

If you have the chance to lean out and look left, you'll see the dome of St. Peter's the way Michelangelo would have liked you to see it—without the bulky Baroque facade.

Near the end of the gallery (on the left) is the blue map of Liguria. On the far left side of the map, along the coast, find Levanto and Porto Venere. Between them lie the five little towns of the Cinque Terre, circa 1582. The map also depicts a chariot captained by Neptune himself as he takes Columbus (of Genoa) to the New World. A few steps farther along, the final maps feature all of Italy in the 16th century (left) and the Italian peninsula in ancient times (right). The one constant: The biggest city is Rome. Finally, before you exit the gallery, find the map of an Italian city situated on an island shaped like a fish—Venice.

• *Exit the map room. At this point, you may have to choose between two routes to the "Capella Sistina." One route makes a beeline to the Sistine. (Most tired and rushed cruise groups take this one.) But for our tour, turn left, toward the "Stanze di Raffaello"—the exquisite Raphael Rooms.*

Renaissance Wing

Papal Wallpaper

We've seen art from the ancient world; now we'll see its rebirth in the Renaissance. We're entering the living quarters of the great Renaissance popes—where they slept, worked, and worshipped. The rooms reflect the grandeur of their position. They hired the best artists—mostly from Florence—to paint the walls and ceilings, combining classical and Christian motifs.

Entering, you'll immediately see a huge 19th-century painting of the **liberation of Vienna.** It's 1683, and the Ottoman armies have surrounded Vienna—see their tents on the left. On the right, in the distance are the church spires of Christian Vienna. Just when the city is about to fall, it's saved—by King Jan Sobieski, who rides in at the center. He brings peace to the city, and a rainbow breaks through the clouds. The battle finally tipped the tide in favor of a Christian Europe. This is not by Raphael, but by Jan Matejko, a Polish painter who specialized in grand-scale historical epics like this one.

The second room commemorates the doctrine of the **Immaculate Conception,** establishing that Mary herself was born without sin. The elaborate bookcase in the center displays copies of the papal pronouncement that established the dogma. The room's frescoes show scenes of Mary, and the history of the idea through ancient and medieval times. The largest fresco depicts the moment when the doctrine became official, in 1854. Church leaders and secular VIPs gather below, while a heavenly host watches from above. In the center, the pope rises to proclaim the new doctrine. Notice how his inspiration comes straight from heaven: From the upper left corner of the painting, a thin ray of light beams directly down onto the pope.

• *Next, you'll pass along an outside walkway that overlooks a courtyard (the parking lot for some of the 4,000 people who commute to work here daily), finally ending up in the first of the Raphael Rooms, the Constantine Room (likely heavily scaffolded for a major restoration).*

RAPHAEL ROOMS
Constantine Room

These frescoes, painted between 1517 and 1524 (finished after Raphael's death by his assistants, notably Giulio Romano), celebrate the passing of the baton from one culture to the next. Remember, Rome was a pagan empire persecuting a new cult from the East—Christianity.

Then, on the night of October 27, AD 312 (left wall), as General Constantine (in gold, with crown) was preparing his troops for a coup d'état, he looked up and saw something strange. A cross appeared in the sky with the words, "You will conquer in this sign."

The next day (long wall), his troops raged victoriously into battle with the Christian cross atop their Roman eagle banners. There's Constantine in the center with a smile on his face, slashing through the enemy, while God's warrior angels ride shotgun overhead.

Constantine even stripped (right wall) and knelt before the pope to be baptized a Christian (some say). As emperor, he legalized Christianity and worked hand in hand with the pope, although the document in which he supposedly "gave" Rome to the pope (window wall) was later shown to be a forgery. When Rome fell, its glory lived on through the Dark Ages in the pomp, pageantry, and learning of the Catholic Church.

Look at the ceiling painting. A classical statue is knocked backward, crumbling before the overpowering force of the cross. Whoa! Christianity triumphs over pagan Rome. (This was painted, I believe, by Raphael's surrealist colleague, Salvadorus Dalio.)

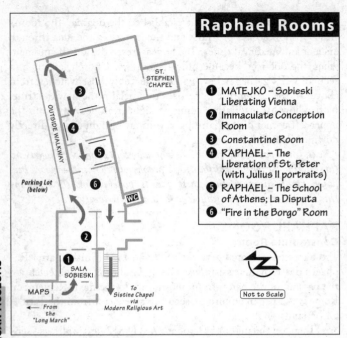

Raphael Rooms

1. MATEJKO – Sobieski Liberating Vienna
2. Immaculate Conception Room
3. Constantine Room
4. RAPHAEL – The Liberation of St. Peter (with Julius II portraits)
5. RAPHAEL – The School of Athens; La Disputa
6. "Fire in the Borgo" Room

ST. STEPHEN CHAPEL

OUTSIDE WALKWAY

Parking Lot (below)

WC

SALA SOBIESKI

MAPS

To Sistine Chapel via Modern Religious Art

← From the "Long March"

Not to Scale

VATICAN MUSEUMS

• *Continue on. In the next room you'll reach a room with frescoes arching over the windows (Room of Heliodorus, 1512–1514). Block the sunlight with your hand to see...*

The Liberation of St. Peter

Peter, Jesus' right-hand man, was thrown into prison in Jerusalem for his beliefs. In the middle of the night, an angel appeared and rescued him from the sleeping guards (Acts 12:5-12). The chains miraculously fell away (and were later brought to the St. Peter-in-Chains Church in Rome), and the angel led him to safety (right), while the guards took hell from their captain (left). This little "play" is neatly divided into three separate acts that make a balanced composition.

Raphael makes the miraculous event even more dramatic with the use of four kinds of light illuminating the dark cell—half-moonlight, the captain's torch, the radiant angel, and the natural light spilling through the museum's window. Raphael's mastery of realism, rich colors, and sense of drama made him understandably famous.

Raphael (1483-1520)

Raphael was only 25 when Pope Julius II invited him, in 1508, to paint the walls of his personal living quarters. Julius was so impressed by Raphael's talent that he had the work of earlier masters scraped off and gave Raphael free rein to paint what he wanted.

Raphael lived a charmed life. He was handsome and sophisticated, and soon became Julius' favorite. He painted masterpieces effortlessly. In a different decade, he might have been thrown out of the Church as a great sinner, but his love affairs and devil-may-care personality seemed to epitomize the optimistic pagan spirit of the Renaissance.

Raphael's paintings are bathed in an even light, with few shadows; his brushwork is smooth and blended, and colors are restrained. In group scenes, Raphael wants you to follow his subjects' gazes as they exchange glances or look off in different directions. This adds a sense of motion and psychological tension to otherwise well-balanced scenes.

Raphael's compositions always have a strong geometric template. Figures are arranged into a pyramid or a circle. Human bodies are composed of oval faces, cylindrical arms, and arched shoulders. Subconsciously, this creates the feeling that God's created world is geometrically perfect. But Raphael always lets a bit of messy reality spill over the lines so his scenes don't appear static. While always graceful, his works are never lightweight or frilly—they're strong, balanced, and harmonious in the best Renaissance tradition. When he died, at just 37 years old, the High Renaissance died with him.

Find portraits of Pope Julius II in several paintings in this room. Julius was the man who commissioned Raphael to paint these rooms, who browbeat Michelangelo into doing the Sistine ceiling, and who started construction of St. Peter's. You can make out gray-bearded Julius in the role of Peter in *The Liberation*, seated on the left in *The Expulsion of Heliodorus* (on the wall to the right), and as the kneeling pope in *The Mass of Bolsena* (opposite the *Liberation*).

• *Enter the next room (Room of the Segnatura, 1508–1511). Here in the pope's private study, Raphael painted...*

The School of Athens

In both style and subject matter, this fresco sums up the spirit of the Renaissance, which was not only the rebirth of classical art, but also of learning, discovery, and the optimistic spirit that man is a rational creature. Raphael pays respect to the great thinkers and scientists of ancient Greece, gathering them together at one time in a mythical school setting.

In the center are Plato and Aristotle, the two greatest Greeks. Plato points up, indicating his philosophy that mathematics and pure ideas are the source of truth, while Aristotle gestures down, showing preference for hands-on study of the material world. There's their master, Socrates (midway to the left, in green), ticking off arguments on his fingers. And in the foreground at right, bald Euclid bends over a slate to demonstrate a geometrical formula.

Raphael shows that Renaissance thinkers were as good as the ancients. There's Leonardo da Vinci, whom Raphael worshipped, in the role of Plato. Euclid is the architect Donato Bramante, who designed St. Peter's. Raphael himself (next to last on the far right, with the black beret) looks out at us. And the "school" building is actually an early version of St. Peter's Basilica (under construction at the time).

Raphael balances everything symmetrically—thinkers to the left, scientists to the right, with Plato and Aristotle dead center—showing the geometrical order found in the world. Look at the square floor tiles in the foreground. If you laid a ruler over them and extended the line upward, it would run right to the center of the picture. Similarly, the tops of the columns all point down to the middle. All the lines of sight draw our attention to Plato and Aristotle, and to the small arch over their heads—a halo over these two secular saints in the divine pursuit of knowledge.

While Raphael was painting this room, Michelangelo was at work down the hall in the Sistine Chapel. Raphael had just finished

The School of Athens when he got a look at Michelangelo's powerful figures and dramatic scenes. He was astonished. From this point on, Raphael began to beef up his delicate, graceful style to a more heroic level. He returned to *The School of Athens* and added one more figure to the scene—Michelangelo, the brooding, melancholy figure in front, leaning on a block of marble.

• *On the opposite wall is...*

La Disputa

As if to underline the new attitude that pre-Christian philosophy and Church thinking could coexist, Raphael painted *La Disputa* facing *The School of Athens*. Christ and the saints in heaven are overseeing a discussion of the Eucharist (the communion wafer)

by mortals below. The classical-looking character in blue and gold looks out as if to say, "The pagans had their *School of Athens,* but we Christians (pointing up) have the School of Heaven." These rooms were the papal library, so themes featuring learning, knowledge, and debate were appropriate.

In Catholic terms, the communion wafer miraculously becomes the body of Christ when it's consecrated by a priest, bringing a little bit of heaven into the material world. Raphael's painting also connects heaven and earth, with descending circles: Jesus in a halo floats above a circle surrounding the dove of the Holy Spirit, which radiates down toward the round communion wafer on the altar. Balance and symmetry reign, from the angel trios in the upper corners to the books littering the floor. Find Dante wearing his poet's laureate in the lower right. (Hint: He's the guy on your €2 coin, modeled after this detail of *La Disputa*.)

In these rooms, Raphael summed up the spirit of the Renaissance. He captures all that was good in the classical world and fuses it with Christian thought. The perfect symmetry echoes the geometrical order found in the world created by a perfect God. The paintings exude a spirit of learning, discovery, and the optimistic notion that man is a rational creature. In a way, this is the message of the entire Vatican Museums. By combining the classical and modern worlds, it's a celebration of both the divine and the divine creations of man.

• *Pass into the last Raphael Room (called the "Fire in the Borgo" Room, 1514-1517), done mostly by Raphael's students, who were influenced by the bulging muscles and bodybuilder poses of Michelangelo. Pause here—WCs are nearby.*

Next stop: the Sistine Chapel, just a 10-minute walk away. Exit the final Raphael Room through a passageway, bear right, and go down the stairs. At the foot of the stairs you'll find several quiet rooms with benches. Have a seat and read ahead before entering the hectic Sistine Chapel.

When you're ready to tackle the Sistine, stroll through the extensive (and impressive) **Modern Religious Art** *collection, following signs to the chapel. Near the end of the modern collection (starting with a large room of Matisse designs), you'll pass religious paintings by modern masters—Chagall, Dalí, Bacon, and others. (If you've downloaded my audio tour of the Sistine Chapel, plug into it now so you can just listen...and look.)*

The Sistine Chapel

The Sistine Chapel contains Michelangelo's ceiling and his huge Last Judgment. The Sistine is the personal chapel of the pope and the place where new popes are elected. (The small, old-fashioned stove that burns pope-vote ballots—which sends out puffs of tell-tale smoke—is near today's shortcut exit.)

When Pope Julius II asked Michelangelo to take on this important project, he said, "No, *grazie*." Michelangelo insisted he was a sculptor, not a painter. The Sistine ceiling was a vast undertaking, and he didn't want to do a half-vast job. But the pope pleaded, bribed, and threatened until Michelangelo finally consented, on the condition that he be able to do it all his own way.

Julius had asked for only 12 apostles along the sides of the ceiling, but Michelangelo had a grander vision—the entire history of the world until Jesus. He spent the next four years (1508-1512) craning his neck on scaffolding six stories up, covering the ceiling with frescoes of biblical scenes.

In sheer physical terms, it's an astonishing achievement: 5,900 square feet, with the vast majority done by his own hand. (Raphael only designed most of his rooms, letting assistants do the grunt work.)

First, he had to design and erect the scaffolding. Any materials had to be hauled up on pulleys. Then, a section of ceiling would be plastered. With fresco—painting on wet plaster—if you don't get it right the first time, you have to scrape the whole thing off and start over. And if you've ever struggled with a ceiling light fixture or worked under a car for even five minutes, you know how heavy

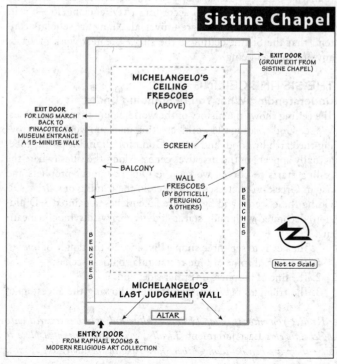

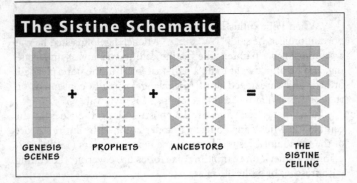

The Sistine Schematic

GENESIS SCENES   +   PROPHETS   +   ANCESTORS   =   THE SISTINE CEILING

your arms get. The physical effort, the paint dripping in his eyes, the creative drain, and the mental stress from a pushy pope combined to almost kill Michelangelo.

But when the ceiling was finished and revealed to the public, it simply blew 'em away. Like the *Laocoön* statue discovered six years earlier, it was unlike anything seen before. It both caps the Renaissance and turns it in a new direction. In perfect Renaissance spirit, it mixes Old Testament prophets with classical figures. But the style is more dramatic, shocking, and emotional than the balanced Renaissance works before it. This is a very personal work—the Gospel according to Michelangelo—but its themes and subject matter are universal. Many art scholars contend that the Sistine ceiling is the single greatest work of art by any one human being.

THE SISTINE CEILING
Understanding What You're Standing Under

The ceiling shows the history of the world before the birth of Jesus. We see God creating the world, creating man and woman, destroying the earth by flood, and so on. God himself, in his purple robe, actually appears in the first five scenes. Along the sides (where the ceiling starts to curve), we see the Old Testament prophets and pagan Greek prophetesses who foretold the coming of Christ. Dividing these scenes and figures are fake niches (a painted 3-D illusion) decorated with nude statue-like figures with symbolic meaning.

The key is to see three simple divisions in the tangle of bodies:
1. The central spine of nine rectangular biblical scenes;
2. The line of prophets on either side; and
3. The triangles between the prophets showing the ancestors of Christ.

• *Ready? You enter the chapel from the altar end, which is covered with Michelangelo's* Last Judgment. *Ideally, you'll find yourself a place to sit—there are benches along either side. Take in the scene. The room is big, and usually very crowded. Don't freak out. Get oriented by facing the altar with the big* Last Judgment *on the wall—more on that later. (If you're using this book's diagram of the ceiling on page 286, follow the "how to use this diagram" instructions carefully.) Now look up to the ceiling and find the central panel of...*

The Creation of Adam

God and man take center stage in this Renaissance version of creation. Adam, newly formed in the image of God, lounges

dreamily in perfect naked innocence. God, with his entourage, swoops in with a swirl of activity (which—with a little imagination—looks like a cross-section of a human brain...quite a strong humanist statement). Their reaching hands are the center of this work. Adam's is limp and passive; God's is strong and forceful, his finger twitching upward with energy. Here is the very moment of creation, as God passes the spark of life to man, the crowning work of his creation.

This is the spirit of the Renaissance. God is not a terrifying giant reaching down to puny and helpless man from way on high. Here they are on an equal plane, divided only by the diagonal bit of sky. God's billowing robe and the patch of green upon which Adam is lying balance each other. They are like two pieces of a jigsaw puzzle, or two long-separated continents, or like the yin and yang symbols finally coming together—uniting, complementing each other, creating wholeness. God and man work together in the divine process of creation.

• *This celebration of man permeates the ceiling. Notice the Adonises-come-to-life on the pedestals that divide the central panels.*

And then came woman.

The Garden of Eden

In one panel, we see two scenes from the Garden of Eden: *Temptation* and *Expulsion*. On

the left is the leafy garden of paradise where Adam and Eve lie around blissfully. But the devil comes along—a serpent with a woman's torso—and winds around the forbidden Tree of Knowledge. The temptation to gain new knowl-

VATICAN MUSEUMS

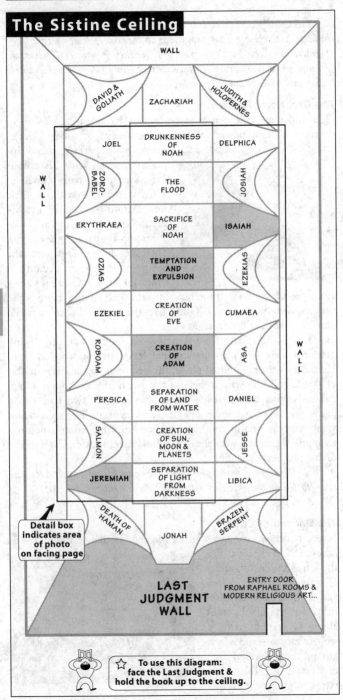

The Sistine Ceiling

WALL

VATICAN MUSEUMS

DAVID & GOLIATH

ZACHARIAH

JUDITH & HOLOFERNES

WALL

JOEL

DRUNKENNESS OF NOAH

DELPHICA

ZORO-BABEL

THE FLOOD

JOSIAH

ERYTHRAEA

SACRIFICE OF NOAH

ISAIAH

OZIAS

TEMPTATION AND EXPULSION

EZEKIAS

EZEKIEL

CREATION OF EVE

CUMAEA

ROBOAM

CREATION OF ADAM

ASA

WALL

PERSICA

SEPARATION OF LAND FROM WATER

DANIEL

SALMON

CREATION OF SUN, MOON & PLANETS

JESSE

JEREMIAH

SEPARATION OF LIGHT FROM DARKNESS

LIBICA

Detail box indicates area of photo on facing page

DEATH OF HAMAN

JONAH

BRAZEN SERPENT

LAST JUDGMENT WALL

ENTRY DOOR FROM RAPHAEL ROOMS & MODERN RELIGIOUS ART...

☆ To use this diagram: face the Last Judgment & hold the book up to the ceiling.

edge is too great for these Renaissance people. They eat the forbidden fruit.

At right, a sword-wielding angel drives them from Paradise into the barren plains. They're grieving, but they're far from helpless. Adam's body is thick and sturdy, and we know they'll survive in the cruel world. Adam firmly gestures to the angel, like he's saying, "All right, already! We're going!"

The Nine Scenes from Genesis
Take some time with these central scenes to understand the story that the ceiling tells. They run in sequence, starting at the front:

1. God, in purple, divides the light from darkness.
2. God creates the sun (burning orange) and the moon (pale white, to the right). Oops, I guess there's another moon.
3. God bursts toward us to separate the land and water.
4. God creates Adam.
5. God creates Eve, who dives into existence out of Adam's side.
6. Adam and Eve are tempted, then expelled, from the Garden of Eden.
7. Noah kills a ram and stokes the altar fires to make a sacrifice to God.
8. The great flood, sent by God, destroys the wicked, who desperately head for higher ground. In the distance, the ark carries Noah's family to safety. (The blank spot dates to 1793, when a nearby gunpowder depot exploded, shaking the building.)
9. Noah's sons see their drunken father. (Perhaps Michelangelo chose to end his work with this scene as a reminder that even the best of men are fallible.)

Prophets
Michelangelo depicted his favorite prophets as monumental, robed figures sitting on thrones. A typical one is Isaiah. He's near the lattice screen on the righthand side as you face the altar. He sits on a throne labeled Esaias. Compare him with others nearby: Each prophet has a completely different personality.

To the right of Isaiah (in the corner of the chapel) you'll find a female prophet, the so-called Delphic Sybil. She twists her body and looks out curiously, holding a scroll that prophesies the coming of Christ. The Delphic Sybil was not a Christian, but in Renaissance times, pagan priestesses and Old Testament prophets were all part of God's grand plan. Sprinkled among the prophets are the *ignudi*, or nudes, that lounge around the fake architecture.

You'll notice that all the figures at the far end of the chapel are a bit smaller than those over *The Last Judgment*. Michelangelo started at the far end, with the Noah scenes. By 1510, he'd finished the first half of the ceiling. When they took the scaffolding down

and could finally see what he'd been working on for two years, everyone was awestruck—except Michelangelo. As powerful as his figures are, from the floor they didn't look dramatic enough for Michelangelo. For the other half, he pulled out all the stops.

Compare the Noah scenes (far end), with their many small figures, to the huge images of God at the other end. Similarly, Isaiah (near the lattice screen, marked "Esaias") is stately and balanced, while Jeremiah ("Hieremias," in the corner by *The Last Judgment*) is a dark, brooding figure. This prophet who witnessed the destruction of Israel slumps his chin in his hand and ponders the fate of his people. Like the difference between the stately *Apollo Belvedere* and the excited *Laocoön*, Michelangelo added a new emotional dimension to Renaissance painting.

THE LAST JUDGMENT

In 1535, two decades after he had frescoed the ceiling, Michelangelo was asked to complete his Christian history of the world by painting the final event—the end of time. When he returned to the Sistine, the mood of Europe—and of Michelangelo—was completely different. The Protestant Reformation had forced the Catholic Church to clamp down on free thought, and religious wars raged. Rome had recently been pillaged by roving bands of mercenaries. The Renaissance spirit of optimism was fading. Michelangelo himself had begun to question the innate goodness of mankind.

It's Judgment Day, and Christ— the powerful figure in the center, raising his arm to spank the wicked—has come to find out who's naughty and who's nice. Beneath him, a band of angels blows its trumpets Dizzy Gillespie-style, giving a wake-up call to the sleeping dead. The dead at lower left leave their graves and prepare to be judged. The righteous, on Christ's right hand (the left side of the picture), are carried up to the glories of heaven. The wicked on the other side are hurled

down to hell, where demons wait to torture them. Charon, from the underworld of Greek mythology, waits below to ferry the souls of the damned to hell.

It's a grim picture. No one, but no one, is smiling. Even many of the righteous being resurrected (lower left) are either skeletons or cadavers with ghastly skin. The angels have to play tug-of-war with subterranean monsters to drag them from their graves.

Over in hell, the wicked are tortured by gleeful demons. One of the damned (to the right of the trumpeting angels) has an utterly lost expression, as if saying, "Why did I cheat on my wife?!" Two demons grab him around the ankles to pull him down to the bowels of hell, condemned to an eternity of constipation.

But it's the terrifying figure of Christ that dominates this scene. He raises his arm to smite the wicked, sending a ripple of fear through everyone. Even the saints around him—including Mary beneath his arm (whose interceding days are clearly over)—shrink back in terror from this uncharacteristic outburst from loving Jesus. His expression is completely closed, and he turns his head, refusing to even listen to the whining alibis of the damned. Look at Christ's

The Last Judgment

HEAVEN

THE **GOOD**

THE **BAD**

& THE **UGLY**

HELL

ENTRY DOOR TO SISTINE →

❶ Christ with Mary
❷ Trumpeting Angels
❸ Righteous Dead Ascending
❹ Damned Man

❺ Charon the Ferryman
❻ Demon/Critic Wrapped in Snake
❼ St. Bartholomew Holding Flayed Skin (Michelangelo's Face)

twisting upper body. If this muscular figure looks familiar to you, it's because you've seen it before—the *Belvedere Torso.*

When *The Last Judgment* was unveiled to the public in 1541, it caused a sensation. The pope is said to have dropped to his knees and cried, "Lord, charge me not with my sins when thou shalt come on the Day of Judgment."

And it changed the course of art. The complex composition, with more than 300 figures swirling around the figure of Christ, went far beyond traditional Renaissance balance. The twisted figures shown from every imaginable angle challenged other painters to try and top this master of 3-D illusion. And the sheer terror and drama of the scene was a striking contrast to the placid optimism of, say, Raphael's *School of Athens*. Michelangelo had Baroque-en all the rules of the Renaissance, signaling a new era of art.

With the Renaissance fading, the fleshy figures in *The Last Judgment* aroused murmurs of discontent from Church authorities. Michelangelo rebelled by painting his chief critic into the scene—in hell. He's the jackassed demon in the bottom-right corner, wrapped in a snake. Look at how Michelangelo covered his privates. Sweet revenge. (After Michelangelo's death, prudish Church authorities painted the wisps of clothing that we see today.)

Now move in close. Study the details of the lower part of the painting from right to left. Charon, with Dr. Spock ears and a Dalí moustache, paddles the damned in a boat full of human turbulence. Look more closely at the J-Day band. Are they reading music, or is it the Judgment Day tally? Before the piece was cleaned, these details were lost in murk.

The Last Judgment marks the end of Renaissance optimism epitomized in *The Creation of Adam*, with its innocence and exaltation of man. There, he was the wakening man-child of a fatherly God. Here, man cowers in fear and unworthiness before a terrifying, wrathful deity.

Michelangelo himself must have wondered how he would be judged—had he used his God-given talents wisely? Look at St. Bartholomew, the bald, bearded guy at Christ's left foot (our right). In the flayed skin he's holding is a barely recognizable face—the twisted self-portrait of a self-questioning Michelangelo.

• *To return to the museum's main entrance/exit, leave the Sistine through the side door next to the screen (on the left, with your back to the altar). You'll soon find yourself facing the* **Long March back to the museum's entrance** *(about 15 minutes away) and the Pinacoteca. Along this corridor (located one floor below the long corridor that you walked to get here), you'll see some of the wealth amassed by the popes, mostly gifts from royalty. Find your hometown on the 1529 map of the world: Look in the land labeled* "Terra Incognita." *The elaborately decorated library that branches off to the right contains rare manuscripts. The corridor eventually spills back outside. Follow signs to the Pinacoteca, where our tour picks up below.*

(Note: Another exit from the Sistine Chapel—at the rear, on the far right with your back to the altar—leads directly to St. Peter's Basilica, but this is reserved for official Vatican tour groups.)

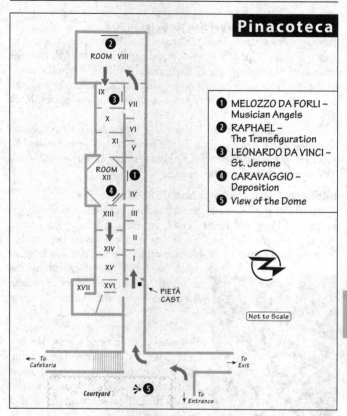

Pinacoteca

❶ MELOZZO DA FORLI – Musician Angels

❷ RAPHAEL – The Transfiguration

❸ LEONARDO DA VINCI – St. Jerome

❹ CARAVAGGIO – Deposition

❺ View of the Dome

Not to Scale

VATICAN MUSEUMS

Pinacoteca

Like Lou Gehrig batting behind Babe Ruth, the Pinacoteca (Painting Gallery) has to follow the mighty Sistine & Co. But after the Vatican's artistic feast, this little collection of paintings is a delicious 15-minute after-dinner mint.

See this gallery of paintings as you'd view the time-lapse blossoming of a flower, walking through the evolution of painting from medieval to Baroque. I've described just the most important stops.

• *Enter, passing a plaster cast of Michelangelo's* Pietà *(offering a handy close-up look), and stroll past a fine two-sided altarpiece by Giotto (in Room II) to Room IV.*

Melozzo da Forlì, *Musician Angels,* 1470s

Removed from the apse of a Roman church, this playful series of frescoes shows the delicate grace and nobility of Italy during the time known fondly as the Quattrocento (1400s). Notice the detail in the serene faces; the soothing primary colors; the bright and even light; and the classical purity given to these religious figures. Rock on.

• *Walk on to the end room (Room VIII), where precious Raphael-designed tapestries that once hung in the Sistine Chapel now surround the highlight of this collection. They've turned on the dark to let Raphael's* Transfiguration *shine. Take a seat.*

Raphael, *The Transfiguration,* 1516-1520

Christ floats above a stumpy mountaintop, visited in a vision by the prophets Moses and Elijah. Peter, James, and John, who wanted visual proof that Jesus was Lord, cower in awe under their savior, "transfigured before them, his face shining as the sun, his raiment white as light" (as described by the

evangelist Matthew—who can be seen taking notes in the painting's lower left).

Raphael composes the scene in three descending tiers: Christ, the holiest, is on top, then Peter-James-John, and finally, the nine remaining apostles surround a boy possessed by demons. They direct him and his mother to Jesus for healing.

Raphael died in 1520, leaving this final work to be finished by his pupils. The last thing Raphael painted was the beatific face of Jesus, perhaps the most beautiful Christ in existence. When Raphael was buried (in the Pantheon, at age 37), this work accompanied the funeral. The painting was displayed in St. Peter's Basilica until 1700, when it and other masterpieces were replaced by mosaic versions (so that the originals could be preserved away from the smoky church interior).

• *Heading back down the parallel corridor, stop in Room IX at the brown, unfinished work by Leonardo.*

Leonardo da Vinci, *St. Jerome,* c. 1482

Jerome squats in the rocky desert. He's spent too much time alone, fasting and meditating on his sins. His soulful face is echoed by his friend, the roaring lion.

This unfinished work gives us a glimpse behind the scenes at Leonardo's technique. Even in the brown undercoating, we see

the psychological power of Leonardo's genius. Jerome's emaciated body on the rocks expresses his intense penitence, while his pleading eyes hold a glimmer of hope for divine forgiveness. Leonardo wrote that a good painter must paint two things: "man and the movements of his spirit." (The patchwork effect is due to Jerome's head having been cut out and used as the seat of a stool in a shoemaker's shop.)

• *Roll on through the sappy sweetness of the Mannerist rooms into the gritty realism of Caravaggio (Room XII).*

Caravaggio, *Deposition,* c. 1600-1604

Christ is being buried. In the dark tomb, the faces of his followers emerge, lit by a harsh light. Christ's body has a deathlike color. We see Christ's dirty toes and Nicodemus' wrinkled, sunburned face.

Caravaggio was the first painter to intentionally shock his viewers. By exaggerating the contrast between light and dark, shining a brutal third-degree-interrogation light on his subjects,

and using everyday models in sacred scenes, he takes a huge leap away from the Raphael-pretty past and into the "expressive realism" of the modern world.

A tangle of grief looms in the darkness as Christ's heavy, dead body nearly pulls the whole group with him from the cross into the tomb. After this museum, I know how he feels.

• *As you emerge from the Pinacoteca, you're near the museum's entrance/ exit (to the left) and the cafeteria (left and downstairs). If interested in a bit more (stress-free) sightseeing, just beyond the cafeteria is a delightful public garden. Beyond that, steps lead into the **Carriage Pavilion** (Padiglione delle Carrozze), a peaceful exhibit showing off centuries of papal carriages, cars, and Popemobiles, including the one St. John Paul II was riding in when a would-be assassin shot him in 1981.*

Once you're ready to leave, enjoy one last view of the Vatican grounds and Michelangelo's magnificent dome. Then go in peace.

VATICAN MUSEUMS

BORGHESE
GALLERY TOUR

Galleria Borghese

More than just a great museum, the Borghese Gallery is a beautiful villa set in the greenery of surrounding gardens. You get to see art commissioned by the luxury-loving Borghese family displayed in the very rooms for which it was created. Frescoes, marble, stucco, and interior design enhance the masterpieces. This is a place where—regardless of whether you learn a darn thing—you can sit back and enjoy the sheer beauty of the palace and its art.

It's hard to believe that a family of cardinals and popes would display so many works with secular and sensual—even erotic—themes. But the Borgheses felt that all forms of human expression, including pagan myths and physical passion, glorified God.

Orientation

Cost: €15, covered by Roma Pass; advance reservation required (see below).

Hours: Tue-Sun 9:00-19:00, Thu until 21:00, closed Mon.

Information: Tel. 06-32810 (tickets and information), www.galleriaborghese.it.

Advance Reservations Required: Reservations are mandatory and simple to get. Every two hours, 360 people are allowed to enter the museum. Entry times are 9:00, 11:00, 13:00, 15:00, and 17:00 plus 19:00 on Thu. You'll get exactly two hours for your visit. The sooner you reserve, the better.

It's easiest to book online at www.tosc.it (€2/person booking fee; choose to pick up tickets at venue). You can also reserve with a real person over the telephone (€2/person booking fee, tel. 06-32810, press 2 for English, phones answered Mon-Fri 9:00-18:00, Sat 9:00-13:00, closed Sat in Aug and Sun year-round).

Arrive at the gallery 30 minutes before your appointed

time to pick up your ticket (remember to bring your reservation confirmation). After getting your ticket, check your bags (free and mandatory), then peruse the gift shop or relax in the café or courtyard before entering at the designated time. Don't cut it close—arriving late can mean forfeiting your reservation.

Free Entry: State museums in Italy, including the Borghese, are free to enter once or twice a month, usually on a Sunday. Check in advance and avoid going on a free day, which can attract huge crowds.

Getting There: The museum, at Piazzale del Museo Borghese 5, is set idyllically but inconveniently in the vast Villa Borghese Gardens (see page 77). To avoid missing your appointment,

allow yourself plenty of time to find the place. A taxi drops you 100 yards from the museum. Your destination is the Galleria Borghese, near Via Pinciana. Don't tell the cabbie "Villa Borghese," which is the park, not the museum.

To go by public transit, take bus #910 from Termini train station/Piazza della Repubblica to the Puccini stop, walk to the park, turn left, and use the first park entrance (but note that #910 runs back to Termini by a different, less convenient route). Bus #53 runs to the Via Pinciana stop from Largo Chigi (not far from Trevi Fountain) and the Barberini Metro station.

You can also go by foot (20 minutes) from the Barberini Metro stop: Walk 10 minutes up Via Veneto, enter the park, and turn right, following signs another 10 minutes to the Borghese Gallery. (The Spagna Metro stop is equally close, but involves a circuitous walk through underground passageways—a less-than-idyllic approach.)

Tours: Guided English tours are offered every day at 9:00 and 11:00 (€6.50; reserve online or by phone). Or consider the museum's excellent 1.5-hour audioguide (€5), which covers more than this chapter.

Length of This Tour: Two hours is all you get...and you'll want every minute. But if you have less time, focus on the ground-floor sculptures, especially Bernini.

Museum Strategy: Visits are strictly limited to two hours. Budget most of your time for the more interesting ground floor, but set aside 30 minutes for the paintings of the Pinacoteca upstairs (highlights are marked by the audioguide icons). Although my tour starts on the ground floor, you can avoid the crowds by seeing the Pinacoteca first. The fine bookshop is best visited outside your reservation window (it closes 30 minutes before the gallery).

Services: Baggage check is free, mandatory, and strictly enforced. Even small purses must be checked. The checkroom does not take coats. There's a WC in the staircase between the two floors.

Cuisine Art: A café/restaurant is on-site. A picnic-friendly park with benches is just in front of the museum (you can check your picnic with your bags and feast after your visit). The sandwich chain VyTA has a location at Casa del Cinema within the park, a pleasant 10-minute walk directly downhill from the museum, near the bike-rental stand.

Starring: Sculptures by Bernini and Canova; paintings by Caravaggio, Raphael, and Titian; and the elegant villa itself.

BACKGROUND

As you visit this palace-in-a-garden, consider its purpose. Cardinal Scipione Borghese (1576-1633) wanted to create a place just outside the city where he could showcase his fine art while wining and dining the VIPs of his age. He had the villa built, collected ancient works, and hired the best artists of his day. In pursuing the optimistic spirit of the Renaissance, they invented Baroque.

The cardinal was controversial because he was not religious. But as nepotism was routine in the 17th century, just being a nephew of the pope was justification enough to be made a cardinal. And the power of a cardinal could be parlayed into great wealth, still on incredible display here in the gallery.

The Tour Begins

• *Pick up your ticket. (Note that the entrance to the Borghese Gallery may be under renovation.) Begin the tour on the ground floor, in the main entry hall. If you want to start in the Pinacoteca, find the entrance at the far end of the basement and go directly upstairs to the second floor. (The first 100 people in line at the basement entrance are routed directly to the Pinacoteca.)*

GROUND FLOOR (SCULPTURE)
Main Entry Hall

The first room that guests saw upon entry was a "theater of the arts"—a multimedia and multi-era extravaganza of art treasures. Baroque frescoes on the ceiling, ancient statues along the walls,

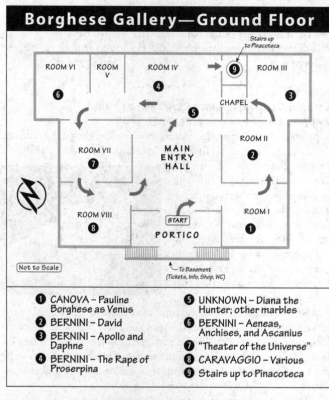

Borghese Gallery—Ground Floor

Stairs up
to Pinacoteca

ROOM VI | ROOM V | ROOM IV | ⑨ | ROOM III

6

4

CHAPEL

5

3

ROOM II

2

ROOM VII

MAIN ENTRY HALL

7

ROOM VIII

ROOM I

START

8

PORTICO

1

Not to Scale

↓ To Basement
(Tickets, Info, Shop, WC)

1 CANOVA – Pauline Borghese as Venus

2 BERNINI – David

3 BERNINI – Apollo and Daphne

4 BERNINI – The Rape of Proserpina

5 UNKNOWN – Diana the Hunter; other marbles

6 BERNINI – Aeneas, Anchises, and Ascanius

7 "Theater of the Universe"

8 CARAVAGGIO – Various

9 Stairs up to Pinacoteca

BORGHESE GALLERY

and Roman mosaics on the floor capture the essence of the collection—a gathering of beautiful objects from every age and culture inside a lavish 17th-century villa.

The cardinal was a man of power—gathering all this culture and showing it off added to his prestige. And with men of great culture like him, the glories of ancient Rome and Greece were being surpassed in their own time, and here that could be celebrated. So he made this palace not to live in but as a museum to flaunt his treasures.

Five fourth- and fifth-century mosaics from a private Roman villa adorn the floor with colorful, festive scenes of slaughter. Gladiators—as famous in their day as the sports heroes of our age—fight animals and each other with swords, whips, and tridents. The Greek letter Θ marks the dead. Notice some of the gladiators' pro-wrestler nicknames: "Cupid(-o)," "Serpent(-ius)," "Licentious(-us)." On the far left, a scene shows how "Alumnusvic" killed "Mazicinus" and left him lying upside down in a pool of blood.

High up on the wall is a thrilling first-century Greek sculpture of a horse falling. The Renaissance-era rider was added by Pietro Bernini, father of the famous Gian Lorenzo Bernini.

• *We'll tour this floor counterclockwise. From the entrance, turn right and head into...*

Room I
Antonio Canova, *Pauline Borghese as Venus (Paolina Borghese come Venere)*, 1808

Napoleon's sister went the full monty for the sculptor Canova, scandalizing Europe. ("How could you have done such a thing?!"

she was asked. She replied, "The room wasn't cold.") With the famous nose of her conqueror brother, she strikes the pose of Venus as conqueror of men's hearts. Her relaxed afterglow and slight smirk say she's already had her man. The light dent she puts in the mattress makes this goddess human.

Notice the contrasting textures that Canova (1757-1822) gets out of the pure white marble: the rumpled sheet versus her smooth skin, the satiny-smooth pillows and mattress versus the creases in them, her porcelain skin versus the waves of her hair. Canova polished and waxed the marble until it looked as soft and pliable as cloth.

The mythological pose, the Roman couch, the ancient hairdo, and the calm harmony make Pauline the epitome of the Neoclassical style.

Room II
Gian Lorenzo Bernini, *David*, 1624

Duck! David twists around to put a big rock in his sling. He purses his lips, knits his brow, and winds his body like a spring as his eyes lock onto the target: Goliath, who's somewhere behind us, putting us right in the line of fire.

The face of David is a self-portrait of the 25-year-old Bernini (1598-1680). Looking ready to take on the world, David is charged with the same fighting energy that fueled the missionaries and conquistadors of the Counter-Reformation.

Compared with Michelangelo's *David*, this is unvarnished realism—an unbalanced pose, bulging veins, determined face, and armpit hair. Michelangelo's *David* thinks, whereas Bernini's acts—biting his lips, eyes concentrating, and sling stretched. Bernini slays the pretty-boy *David*s of the Renaissance and prepares to invent Baroque.

Flanking David are two ancient sarcophagi carved with scenes from the *Labors of Hercules* (AD 160). The twisting bodybuilders' poses were the Hellenistic inspiration for Bernini's Baroque. The painting high on the wall between them, by a follower of Caravaggio, shows a triumphant David with the giant's head.

Room III
Bernini, *Apollo and Daphne (Apollo e Dafne)*, 1625

Apollo—made stupid by Cupid's arrow of love—chases after Daphne, who has been turned off by the "arrow of disgust." Just as

he's about to catch her, she calls to her father to save her. Magically, her fingers begin to sprout leaves, her toes become roots, her skin turns to bark, and she transforms into a tree. Frustrated Apollo is in for a rude surprise. (Notice the same scene, colorized, painted on the ceiling above.)

Stand behind the statue to experience it as Bernini originally intended. It's only when you circle around to the front that he reveals the story's surprise ending.

Walk slowly around the statue.

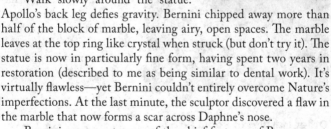

Apollo's back leg defies gravity. Bernini chipped away more than half of the block of marble, leaving airy, open spaces. The marble leaves at the top ring like crystal when struck (but don't try it). The statue is now in particularly fine form, having spent two years in restoration (described to me as being similar to dental work). It's virtually flawless—yet Bernini couldn't entirely overcome Nature's imperfections. At the last minute, the sculptor discovered a flaw in the marble that now forms a scar across Daphne's nose.

Bernini carves out some of the chief features of Baroque art. He makes a supernatural event seem realistic. He freezes the scene at its most dramatic, emotional moment. The figures move and twist in unusual poses. He turns the wind machine on, sending Apollo's cape billowing behind him. It's a sculpture group of two, forming a scene, rather than a stand-alone portrait. And the subject is classical. Even in strict Counter-Reformation times, there was always a place for groping, if the subject matter had a moral—this one taught you not to pursue fleeting earthly pleasures. And, besides, Bernini tends to show a lot of skin, but no genitals.

The cardinal's private **chapel** (between Rooms III and IV) is the only even vaguely religious room in the palace. It's relatively humble, a reminder that the cardinal probably didn't stop in here for much longer than tourists do today.

Room IV
Bernini, *The Rape of Proserpina* (*Il Ratto di Proserpina*), 1622

Pluto, King of the Underworld, strides into his realm and shows off his catch—the beautiful daughter of the earth goddess Ceres. His three-headed guard dog, Cerberus (who guards the gates of hell), barks triumphantly. Pluto is squat, thick, and uncouth, with knotted muscles and untrimmed beard. He's trying not to hurt Proserpina, but she pushes her divine molester away and twists to call out for help. Tears roll down her cheeks. She wishes she could turn into a tree.

Bernini, who carved this out of a single block of stone, was the master of marble. With this work, at the age of 24, he had discovered his Baroque niche. While Renaissance works were designed to be seen from the front, Baroque is theater-in-the-round—full of action, designed to be experienced from every angle as you walk around it. Look how Pluto's fingers dig into her frantic body as if it were real flesh. Bernini picked out this Carrara marble, knowing that its relative suppleness and ivory hue would lend itself to a fleshy statue.

Other Marbles in Room IV

The many ancient Roman statues and portrait busts of Roman emperors in this room were intended as a reminder that the pope was essentially a king, the successor to ancient Roman rulers of the past. (Until around 1800, popes held vast political—and even military—power.)

The statues in the niches are classical originals. *Diana the Hunter* is a rare Greek original, with every limb and finger intact, from the second century BC. The traditional *contrapposto* pose (weight on one leg) and idealized grace were an inspiration for

Gian Lorenzo Bernini
(1598-1680)

A Renaissance Man in Counter-Reformation times, Bernini al-

most personally invented the Baroque style, transforming the city of Rome. When visiting Rome, you *will* see Bernini's work.

Bernini was a child prodigy in his father's sculpting studio, growing up among Europe's rich and powerful. His flamboyant personality endeared him to his cultured employers—the popes in Rome, Louis XIV in France, and Charles I in England. He was extremely prolific, working fast and utilizing an army of assistants.

Despite the fleshiness and sensuality of his works, Bernini was a religious man, seeing his creativity as an extension of God's. In stark contrast to the Protestant world's sobriety, Bernini shamelessly embraced pagan myths and nude goddesses, declaring them all part of the "catholic"—that is, universal— church.

Bernini, a master of multimedia, was a...

- Sculptor (Borghese Gallery and *St. Teresa in Ecstasy*, pictured above and described on page 97)
- Architect (elements of St. Peter's—see "Bernini Blitz," page 253, and the Church of Sant'Andrea al Quirinale)
- Painter (Borghese Gallery)
- Interior decorator (the *baldacchino* canopy and other works in St. Peter's)
- Civic engineer (he laid out St. Peter's Square, and he designed and renovated Rome's fountains in Piazza Navona, Piazza Barberini, Piazza di Spagna, and more).

Even works done by other artists a century later (such as the Trevi Fountain) can be traced indirectly to Bernini, the man who invented Baroque, the "look" of Rome for the next two centuries.

Neoclassical artists such as Canova, who grew tired of Bernini's Baroque bombast.

Appreciate the beauty of the different types of marble in the room: Bernini's ivory Carrara, purple porphyry emperors and the granite-like columns supporting them, wood-grained pilasters on the walls, and the various colors on the floor—green, red, gray, lavender, and yellow, some grainy, some "marbled" like a steak. Some of the world's most beautiful and durable things have been made from the shells of sea creatures layered in sediment, fossilized into limestone, then baked and crystallized by the pressure of the earth—marble.

• *Before leaving this room, notice the staircase in the corner. You'll later return here to reach the Pinacoteca upstairs. But for now, continue through Room V and into...*

Room VI
Bernini, *Aeneas, Anchises, and Ascanius,* 1618-1619

Aeneas' home in Troy is in flames, and he escapes with the three most important things: his family (elderly father Anchises on his

shoulder, baby boy Ascanius at his leg), his household gods (the statues in Dad's hands), and the Eternal Flame (carried by his son). They are the refugees of antiquity: all in shock, lost in thought, facing an uncertain future. Aeneas isn't even looking where he's going; he just puts one foot in front of the other. Little do they know that eventually they'll wind up in Italy, where—according to legend—Aeneas will house the flame in the Temple of Vesta and found the city of Rome (and the Borghese dynasty). Study the statue from behind and think about the timeless and universal experience of caring for an aging loved one.

Bernini was just 20 when he started this, his first major work for Cardinal Borghese. Bernini was probably helped by his dad, who nurtured the child prodigy much like Leopold mentored Mozart, but without the rivalry. Bernini's portrayal of human flesh—from baby fat to middle-aged muscle to sagging decrepitude—is astonishing. Still, the flat-footed statue just stands there—it lacks the Baroque energy of his more mature work. More lively are the reliefs up at the ceiling, with their dancing, light-footed soldiers with do-si-do shields.

Room VII
The "Theater of the Universe"

The room's decor sums up the eclectic nature of the villa. You've got everything here—your Greek statues, your Roman mosaics, even your fake "Egyptian" sphinxes and hieroglyphs (perfectly symmetrical, in good Neoclassical style). Look out the window past the sculpted gardens at the mesh domes of the aviary, once filled with exotic birds. Cardinal Borghese's vision was to make a place where art, history, music, nature, and science from every place and time would come together in "a theater of the universe."

Room VIII
Caravaggio

This room holds the greatest collection of Caravaggio paintings anywhere. Michelangelo Merisi (1571-1610), nicknamed "Caravaggio" after his hometown (near Milan), brought Christian saints down to earth with gritty realism. Caravaggio's straightforwardness can be a refreshing change in a museum full of (sometimes overly) refined beauty.

Circling the room clockwise, trace the course of his brief, dramatic, and sometimes messy life. *Self-Portrait as Bacchus* shows twentysomething Caravaggio as he first arrived in Rome, a poor bohemian enjoying the wild life.

On the facing wall, *Boy with a Fruit Basket* dates from when he eked out a living painting minor figures in other artists' paintings. His specialty? Fruit. Ultrarealistic fruit.

In 1600, Caravaggio completed his first major commission (not on display in this gallery), a painting of St. Matthew for San Luigi dei Francesi, a church across town (see page 150). Overnight, Caravaggio was famous.

In the next 10 years, Caravaggio pioneered a new age in painting, much as Bernini soon would in sculpture. Caravaggio's unique style combined two striking elements: uncompromising realism and strong light-dark contrasts. His models were ordinary people—*St. John the Baptist* is a nude teenager with dirty feet, whose belly fat wrinkles up as he turns. His depiction of *St. Jerome* is balding and wrinkled. The *Madonna of Palafrenieri* (the largest painting in the room) was forbidden to hang in St. Peter's because the boy Jesus was buck naked, and because the Madonna's likeness was inspired by Rome's best-known prostitute. Caravaggio's figures emerge from a dark background, lit by a harsh, unflattering light, which highlights part of the figure, leaving the rest in deep shadows.

Now rich and famous, Caravaggio led a reckless, rock-star existence—trashing hotel rooms and picking fights. In 1606, he killed a man (the details are sketchy) and had to flee Rome to escape prosecution. In one of Caravaggio's last paintings, David sticks Goliath's severed head right in our face—and "Goliath" is the artist himself. From exile, Caravaggio appealed to Cardinal Borghese (one of his biggest fans) to get him a pardon. But while returning to Rome, Caravaggio died under mysterious circum-

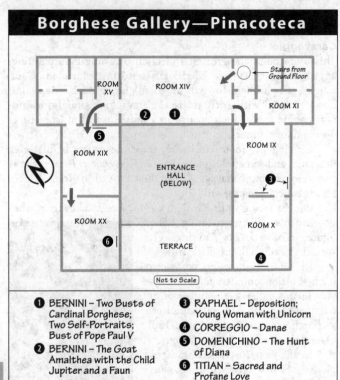

Borghese Gallery—Pinacoteca

Stairs from
Ground Floor

ROOM XV

ROOM XIV

ROOM XI

❷ ❶

❺

ROOM XIX

ENTRANCE
HALL
(BELOW)

ROOM IX

❸

ROOM XX

ROOM X

❻

TERRACE

❹

Not to Scale

❶ BERNINI – Two Busts of
Cardinal Borghese;
Two Self-Portraits;
Bust of Pope Paul V

❷ BERNINI – The Goat
Amalthea with the Child
Jupiter and a Faun

❸ RAPHAEL – Deposition;
Young Woman with Unicorn

❹ CORREGGIO – Danae

❺ DOMENICHINO – The Hunt
of Diana

❻ TITIAN – Sacred and
Profane Love

stances. Although he lived only to 38, in his short life he'd rocked
the world of art.

• *Caravaggio is the perfect transition between the elegant sculpture rooms
and the paintings upstairs, in the other half of the museum. To reach the
Pinacoteca, head through the main entry hall back to Room IV, find the
entry to the staircase in the far-right corner, and spiral up to the...*

PINACOTECA (PAINTING GALLERY)

You must visit the Pinacoteca within the two-hour window of
time printed on your Borghese Gallery ticket. Most visitors wait
until the last half-hour to see the Pinacoteca, so that's when it's
most crowded (and the ground floor is less crowded). If you see the
paintings first, remember to save most of your visit for the ground-
floor sculptures.

• *From the top of the stairs or elevator, step into the large Room XIV.
This fine room was once a loggia, with open spaces rather than windows.
Notice the ceiling and how painted statues literally raise the roof to let
in the sun. Along the long wall, you'll find the following statues and*

paintings by Bernini. First, look for the two identical white busts set on columns.

Room XIV
Bernini, Busts of Cardinal Borghese, 1632

Say *grazie* to the man who built this villa, assembled the collection, and hired Bernini to sculpt masterpieces. The cardinal is caught

turning as though to greet someone at a party. There's a twinkle in his eye, and he opens his mouth to make a witty comment. This man of the cloth was, in fact, a sophisticated hedonist.

Notice that there are two identical versions of this bust. The first one started cracking along the forehead (visible) just

as Bernini was finishing it. *No problema*—Bernini whipped out a replacement in just two weeks.

• *Between the busts, find these paintings...*

Bernini, Self-Portraits (*Autoritratto Giovanile* and *Autoritratto in età Matura*) 1623, 1630-1635

Bernini was a master of many media, including painting. The younger Bernini (age 25) looks out a bit hesitantly, as if he's still finding his way in high-class society. His jet-black eyes came from his southern Italian mother who, it's said, also gave him his passionate personality.

In his next self-portrait (roughly age 35), with a few masterpieces under his belt, Bernini shows himself with more confidence and facial hair—the dashing, vibrant man who would rebuild Rome in Baroque style, from St. Peter's Square to the fountains that dot the piazzas.

• *On the table below, find the smaller...*

Bust of Pope Paul V, 1618

The cardinal's uncle was a more sober man. As pope, Paul V ruled over the artistic era of Caravaggio and Bernini. He reopened an ancient aqueduct, helped steer St. Peter's toward completion, and personally met with Galileo to discuss the heliocentrism controversy.

He was also a patron of the arts with a good eye for talent, who hired Bernini's father. When Paul saw sketches made by little Gian Lorenzo, he announced, "This boy will be the Michelangelo of his age."

• *To the right of the Borghese busts, find a small statue of...*

The Goat Amalthea with the Child Jupiter and a Faun (La Capra Amaltea con Giove Bambino e un Faunetto), 1609/1615

Bernini was barely entering puberty when he made this. (That's about the age when I mastered how to make a Play-Doh snake.) But already its arrangement takes what would become one of Bernini's trademark forms: the sculptural ensemble. The two kids are milking a goat and drinking it. The kids lean one way, the goat the other, with the whole composition contained neatly in a circle of good fun.

• *Backtrack to the staircase/elevator and turn right to find...*

Room IX
Raphael (Raffaello Sanzio), *Deposition (Deposizione)*, 1507

Jesus is being taken from the cross. The men struggle heroically to support him while the women support Mary (in purple), who

has fainted. Mary Magdalene rushes up to take Christ's hand. The woman who commissioned the painting had recently lost her son. She wanted to show the death of a son and the grief of a mother. We see two different faces of grief—mother Mary faints at the horror, while Mary Magdalene still can't quite believe he's gone.

Enjoy the rich colors—solid reds, greens, blues, and yellows—that set off Christ's porcelain-skin body. Note Mary's face: She's fainted and is the same deathly gray as her dead son. Notice also the hand of Mary Magdalene holding Jesus' hand—the pink of the living on the gray of the dead. In true Renaissance style, Raphael (1483-1520) orders the scene with geometrical perfection. The curve of Jesus' body is echoed by the swirl of Mary Magdalene's hair, and then by the curve of Calvary Hill, where Christ met his fate.

• *Also in Room IX, to your left as you face the* Deposition, *is...*

Raphael, *Portrait of Young Woman with Unicorn (Ritratto di Giovane Donna con un Unicorno),* c. 1506

Raphael's genius as a portrait painter was his ability to simultaneously portray his subjects with masterful photorealism, yet also show them in their best light.

This is likely a wedding portrait. The blonde teenager poses, cradling her little dog (transformed later into a unicorn). Her body faces formally in one direction. Meanwhile, her eyes turn the other way, as if someone had just interrupted the sitting, capturing an unplanned moment. And the colors! Her rich red clothes, accented by the ruby pendant; her porcelain skin; and her delicate face, framed perfectly by the scene behind, with its pale blue atmosphere. It's little wonder that Raphael's sweet style dominated painting for a century, until the coming of Caravaggio.

• *Continue into...*

Room X
Correggio, *Danae,* c. 1531

Cupid strips Danae as she spreads her legs to receive a trickle of

gold from the smudgy cloud overhead—this was Zeus' idea of intercourse with a human. The sheets are rumpled, and Danae looks right where the action is with a smile on her face (most unladylike for the time).

• *Backtrack through the room with the two cardinal busts, continue through Room XV, then turn left in the small room to get to...*

Room XIX
Domenichino, *The Hunt of Diana (La Caccia di Diana),* 1616-1617

Half-naked Greek nymphs are frolicking under the watchful eye of the goddess of the hunt, Diana (with her crescent-moon diadem). Notice the archer's fine marksmanship with arrows in the post, the ribbon, and the bird. All eyes turn to see that one of the nymphs has successfully shot the bird. The playful scene is enlivened by the girl sprawled backward with abandon in the pond. She's made eye contact with an intruder—and it's you. No one should look at Diana and her nymphs, but we've been spotted.

(Psst—see the two Peeping Toms on the right?)
• *Continue into the next room.*

Room XX
Titian (Tiziano Vecellio), *Sacred and Profane Love* *(Amor Sacro e Amor Profano),* **c. 1515**
While you might guess that the naked woman on the right embod-

ies profane love, that's actually represented by the material girl on the left—with her box of treasures, fortified castle, and dark, claustrophobic landscape. Sacred love is represented by the naked woman who has nothing to hide and enjoys open spaces filled with light, life, a church in the distance, and even a couple of lovers in the field.

The clothed woman at left has recently married, and she cradles a vase filled with jewels representing the riches of earthly love. Her naked twin on the right holds the burning flame of eternal, heavenly love. Baby Cupid, between them, playfully stirs the waters.

Symbolically, the steeple on the right points up to the love of heaven, while on the left, soldiers prepare to "storm the castle" of the new bride. Miss Heavenly Love looks jealous.

This exquisite painting expresses the spirit of the Renaissance—that earth and heaven are two sides of the same coin. And here in the Borghese Gallery, that love of earthly beauty can be spiritually uplifting—as long as you feel it within two hours.

BORGHESE GALLERY

NATIONAL MUSEUM OF ROME

Museo Nazionale Romano •
Palazzo Massimo

Rome lasted a thousand years...and so do most Roman history courses. But if you want a breezy overview of this fascinating society, there's no better place than the National Museum of Rome, which displays the city's best collection of ancient Roman statuary.

Rome took Greek culture and wrote it in capital letters. Thanks to this lack of originality, ancient Greek statues were preserved for our enjoyment today. But the Romans also pioneered a totally new form of art—sculpting painfully realistic portraits of emperors and important citizens.

Think of this museum as a walk back in time. As you gaze at the same marble statues that the Romans swooned over, the history of ancient Rome comes alive—from Julius Caesar's murder to Caligula's incest to Vespasian's Colosseum to the coming of Christianity.

Orientation

Cost: €10, €12 combo-ticket valid for three days, includes entry into three lesser National Museum branches: the nearby Museum of the Bath (lackluster ancient inscriptions), Palazzo Altemps (so-so sculptures), and Crypta Balbi (medieval art). The price can vary depending on special exhibits.

Hours: Tue-Sun 9:00-19:45, closed Mon, last entry one hour before closing.

Information: Tel. 06-3996-7701, www.museonazionaleromano.beniculturali.it.

When to Go: The museum is seldom crowded outside of sporadic free days. Since it has a convenient and free bag check (even for backpacks and suitcases), consider a visit en route from the train station.

Getting There: The museum is at Largo di Villa Peretti 2, a few minutes' walk from either the Repubblica or Termini Metro stop. As you leave Termini, it's the sandstone-brick building a block up on your left. Enter at the far (west) end.

Tours: Audioguides cost €5 and last two hours, covering much more than this chapter.

Length of This Tour: Allow two hours. If you have less time, at least do the ground floor and the first floor as far as the discus thrower statue.

Starring: Roman emperor busts, the discus thrower, original Greek statues, and fine Roman copies.

OVERVIEW

The museum is rectangular, with rooms and hallways built around a central courtyard. The ground-floor sculptures follow Rome's history as the city changes from a republic to a dictatorial empire. The first-floor exhibits take Rome from its peak through its slow decline. The second floor houses rare frescoes and fine mosaics, and the basement presents coins and everyday objects. Take advantage of the thoughtfully written information panels throughout. As you tour this museum, note that in Italian, "room" is *sala* and "hall" is *galleria*.

The Tour Begins

GROUND FLOOR: FROM SENATORS TO CAESARS

• *Buy your ticket and pass through the turnstile, where you'll find...*

Minerva

It's big, it's gaudy, it's a weird goddess from a pagan cult. Welcome to the Roman world. It's also a good reminder that all the statues in this museum—now missing limbs, scarred by erosion, or weathered down to bare stone—were once whole, and colored or painted to look as lifelike as possible.

• *Continue straight ahead into the courtyard. The first corridor—called Gallery I—is lined with portrait busts.*

National Museum—Ground Floor

ROOM III

ROOM II

ROOM I

STAIRS ELEV.

BAGGAGE CHECK

WC

GALLERY I

TICKETS

ENTRY

GALLERY II

ROOM IV

ROOM V

Open-air Courtyard

STEPS

BOOK SHOP

GALLERY III

ROOM VI

ROOM VII

ROOM VIII

STAIRS UP TO FIRST FLOOR

WC

← To Termini Train Station

To Piazza Repubblica →

Not to Scale

1 Minerva
2 Portrait Heads
3 Julius Caesar (?)
4 Augustus as Pontifex Maximus

5 Livia
6 Caligula
7 Alexander the Great
8 Socrates

9 Dying Niobid
10 The Boxer at Rest & Hellenistic Prince

Gallery I
Portrait Heads from the Republic, 500-1 BC

Stare into the eyes of these stern, hardy, no-nonsense farmer-stock people who founded Rome. The wrinkles and crags of these original "ugly republicans" tell the story of Rome's roots as a small agricultural tribe, fighting for survival with neighboring bands.

These faces are brutally realistic, unlike more idealized Greek statues. Romans honored their ancestors and worthy citizens in the "family" *(gens)* of Rome. They wanted lifelike statues to remember them by, and to instruct the young with their air of moral rectitude.

In its first 500 years, Rome was a republic ruled by a Senate of wealthy landowners. But as Rome expanded throughout Italy, and the economy shifted from farming to booty, changes became necessary.

• *Enter Room I (Sala I). Along the left wall, find the portrait bust that may (or may not) be Julius Caesar.*

Room I
Julius Caesar? (labeled *Rilievo con ritratto di uomo anziano*)

Some scholars have identified this bust as representing Rome's most famous citizen. Others point out that it doesn't resemble any of the known images of him. Regardless of who's right, take this as a good moment to reflect on Caesar's life.

Julius Caesar (c. 100-44 BC)—with his prominent brow, high cheekbones, and male-pattern baldness with the forward comb-over—changed Rome forever.

When this charismatic general swept onto the scene, Rome was in chaos. Rich landowners were fighting middle-class plebs, who wanted their slice of the plunder. Slaves such as Spartacus were picking up hoes and hacking up masters. And renegade generals—the new providers of wealth and security in an economy of plunder—were becoming dictators. (Notice the **life-size statue** with a shaved-off head, of an unknown but obviously once-renowned general.)

Caesar was a people's favorite. He conquered Gaul (France), then sacked Egypt, then impregnated Cleopatra. He defeated rivals and made them his allies. He gave great speeches. Chicks dug him.

With the army at his back and the people in awe, he took the reins of government, instituted sweeping changes, made himself the center of power...and antagonized the Senate.

A band of republican assassins surrounded him in a Senate meeting. He called out for help as one by one they stepped up to take turns stabbing him. The senators sat and watched in silence. One of the killers was his adopted son, Brutus, and Caesar—astonished that even he joined in—died saying, *"Et tu, Brute?"*

• *At the end of Gallery I, turn left and enter the large glassed-in Room V, with a life-size statue of Augustus.*

Room V
Augustus as Pontifex Maximus
(Augusto Pontefice Massimo)

Julius Caesar died, but his family name, his politics, and his flamboyance lived on—his descendants would rule Rome for a century after his death, turning the surname "Caesar" into a title. Julius had adopted his grandnephew, Octavian, who united Rome's warring factions and took the name and title "Augustus," meaning "venerable" or "protected by the gods."

Here, Emperor Augustus has taken off his armor and laurel-leaf crown. He has pulled his toga over his head to assume his role as pontifex maximus—highest priest—of the city of Rome. He's retiring to a desk job after a lifetime of fighting to reunite Rome. He killed Brutus and eliminated his rivals, Mark Antony and Cleopatra. For the first time in almost a century of fighting, one general reigned supreme. Augustus became the first of the emperors who would rule Rome for the next 500 years.

In fact, Augustus was a down-to-earth man who lived simply, worked hard, read books, listened to underlings, and tried to restore traditional Roman values after the turbulence of Julius Caesar's time. He outwardly praised the Senate, while actually reducing it to a rubber-stamp body. Augustus' reign marked the start of 200 years of peace and prosperity, the Pax Romana.

See if the statue matches this description of Augustus by a contemporary, the historian Suetonius: "He was unusually handsome. His expression was calm and mild. He had clear, bright eyes, in which was a kind of divine power. His hair was slightly curly and somewhat golden." Any variations were made by sculptors who idealized his features to make him almost godlike.

Augustus proclaimed himself a god—not arrogantly or blasphemously, as Caligula later did, but as the honored "father" of the "family" of Rome. As the empire expanded, the vanquished had to worship statues like this one as a show of loyalty.

• *Here in Room V, in the hallway, and possibly in Room IV, look for busts of other members of his powerful family. To Julius Caesar's right are two busts of his wife, Livia.*

Rome's First Emperors (c. 50 BC-AD 68)

Livia

Augustus' wife, Livia, was a major power behind the throne. Her stern, thin-lipped gaze withered rivals at court. Her hairstyle—bunched up in a peak, braided down the center, and tied in back—

became the rage throughout the empire, as her face appeared everywhere, from statues to coins. Notice that by the next generation, a simpler bun was chic. And by the following generation, the trend was tight curls. Empresses dictated fashion the way emperors dictated policy.

Livia bore Augustus no sons. She lobbied hard for Tiberius, her own son by a first marriage, to succeed as emperor. Augustus didn't like him, but Livia was persuasive. He relented, ate some bad figs, and died—the gossip was that Livia poisoned him to seal the bargain. The pattern of succession was established—adopt a son from within the extended family—and Tiberius was proclaimed emperor. (We'll visit the fine frescoed walls of Livia's country villa upstairs on the top floor later.)

• *Now look in the hallway for a small glass case, with the small bust of...*

Caligula *(Caligola)*, ruled AD 37-41

This emperor had sex with his sisters, tortured his enemies, made off with friends' wives during dinner parties and then returned to rate their performance in bed, crucified Christians, took cuts in line at the Vatican Museums, and ordered men to kneel before him as a god. Caligula has become the archetype of a man with enough power to act out his basest fantasies.

Politically, he squandered Rome's money, then taxed and extorted from the citizens. Perhaps he was made mad by illness, perhaps he was the victim of vindictive historians, but still, no one mourned when assassins ambushed him and ran a sword through his privates. Rome was tiring of this family dynasty's dysfunction.

• *Turn left into Gallery III.*

Gallery III: Rome's Greek Mentors

Rome's legions easily conquered the less-organized but more-cultured Greek civilization that had dominated the Mediterranean for centuries. Romans adopted Greek gods, art styles, and fashions, and sophisticates sprinkled their conversation with Greek phrases.

• *Find the bronze head and marble head of Alexander the Great (outside Room VI).*

Alexander the Great *(Alessandro Magno)*

Alexander the Great (356-323 BC) single-handedly created a Greek-speaking empire by conquering, in just a few short years, lands from Greece to Egypt to Persia. Later, when the Romans conquered Greece (c. 200 BC), they inherited this preexisting collection of cultured Greek cities ringing the Mediterranean.

Alexander's handsome statues set the standard for those of later Roman emperors. His features were chiseled and youthful, and his statues adorned with pompous decorations, like a golden sunburst aura (fitted into the holes). The greatest man of his day, he ruled the known world by the age of 30.

Alexander's teacher was none other than the philosopher Aristotle. Aristotle's teacher was Plato, whose mentor was Socrates.

• *Gallery III is filled with the busts of Greeks whom Romans admired, including...*

Socrates *(Socrate)*

This nonconformist critic of complacent thinking is the father of philosophy. The Greeks were an intellectual, introspective, sensitive, and artistic people. The Romans were practical, no-nonsense soldiers, salesmen, and bureaucrats. Many a Greek slave was more cultured than his master, reduced to the role of warning his boss not to wear a plaid toga with a polka-dot robe.

• *Backtrack and enter Room VI.*

Room VI: Greek Beauty in Originals and Copies
Dying Niobid *(Niobide Morente)*, 440 BC

The Romans were astonished by the beauty of Greek statues. The smooth skin of this Niobid (the term for any child of the goddess

Niobe) contrasts with the rough folds of her clothing. She twists naturally around an axis running straight up and down. This woman looks like a classical goddess awakening from a beautiful dream, but...

Circle around back. The hole bored in her back, right in that itchy place you can't quite reach, once held a golden arrow. The woman has been shot by Artemis, goddess of hunting, because her mother dared to boast to the gods about her kids. The Niobid reaches back in vain, trying to remove the arrow before it drains her of life.

Romans ate this stuff up: the sensual beauty, the underplayed pathos, the very Greekness of it: They crated up centuries-old statues like this and brought them home to their gardens and palaces. Soon there weren't enough old statues to meet the demand. Crafty Greeks began cranking out knockoffs of Greek originals for mass consumption. Rooms VII and VIII contain both originals (like the Niobid) and copies—some of extremely high quality, others resembling cheesy fake *David*s in a garden store. Appreciate the beauty of the world's rare, surviving Greek originals.

Rome conquered Greece, but culturally the Greeks conquered the Romans.

• *Move next door to see...*

Room VII: Hellenistic and Classical Bronzes
The Boxer at Rest *(Pugilatore)*, first century BC

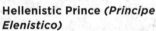

An exhausted boxer sits between rounds and gasps for air. Check out the brass knuckles-type Roman boxing gloves. Textbook Hellenistic, this pugilist is realistic and full of emotion. His face is scarred, his back muscles are knotted, and he's got cauliflower ears. He's losing.

Slumped over, he turns with a questioning look ("Why am I losing again?"), and eyes that once held glass now make him look empty indeed. "I coulda been a contender."

Hellenistic Prince *(Principe Elenistico)*

Back then, everyone wanted to be like Alexander the Great. This restored bronze statue—naked and leaning on a spear—shows a prince (probably Attalus II of Pergamon) in the style of a famous statue of his hero from the second century BC.

• *We've covered Rome's first 500 years. At the end of the hall are the stairs up to the first floor.*

NATIONAL MUSEUM

FIRST FLOOR: ROME'S PEAK AND SLOW FALL

As we saw, Augustus' family did not always rule wisely. Under Nero (ruled AD 54-68), the debauchery, violence, and paranoia typical of the Julio-Claudians festered to a head. When the city burned in the great fire of 64, the Romans suspected Nero of torching it himself to clear land for his enormous luxury palace.

Enough. Facing a death sentence, Nero committed suicide with the help of a servant. An outsider was brought in to rule—Vespasian, from the Flavian family.

National Museum—First Floor

1. Vespasian
2. Domitian
3. Domitia (?)
4. Nerva
5. Trajan
6. Hadrian
7. Aphrodite Crouching
8. Discus Thrower
9. Hermaphrodite Sleeping
10. Apollo
11. Nemi Ships
12. Septimius Severus
13. Caracalla
14. Sarcophagus with Processional Scene
15. Christ Teaching

• *At the top of the stairs, enter Room I (in front of you) and then move into the hallway on the left. To your left is a Flavian family reunion.*

Flavian Family
Vespasian *(Vespasianus)*, ruled AD 69-79

Balding and wrinkled, with a big head, a double chin, and a shy smile, Vespasian was a common man. The son of a tax collector, he rose through the military ranks with a reputation as a competent drudge. As emperor, he restored integrity, raised taxes, started the Colosseum, and suppressed the Jewish rebellion in Palestine.

Domitian *(Domitianus)*, ruled AD 81-96

Vespasian's son, Domitian, used his father's tax revenues to construct the massive Imperial Palace on Palatine Hill, home to emperors for the next three centuries. Shown with his lips curled in a sneer, he was a moralistic prude who executed several Vestal ex-Virgins, while in private he took one mistress after another. Until...

Domitia?

...his stern wife found out and hired a servant to stab him in the groin. Domitia's hairstyle is a far cry from the "Livia" cut, with a high crown of tight curls.

Nerva, ruled AD 96-98

Nerva realized that the Flavian dynasty was no better than its predecessors. Old and childless, he made a bold, farsighted move—he adopted a son from outside of Rome's corrupting influence.

• *Go back to Room I and head straight to Room II, where you'll find Trajan ("Traiano") on the left wall.*

Room II: A Cosmopolitan Culture
Trajan *(Traianus-Hercules)*, ruled AD 98-117

Born in Spain, this conquering hero pushed Rome's borders to their greatest extent, creating a truly worldwide empire. The spoils of three continents funneled into a city of a million-plus people. As in this statue, Trajan could dress up in a lion's skin, presenting himself as a "new Hercules," and no one found it funny. Romans, in the words of Livy the historian, felt a spirit of Manifest Destiny: "The gods desire that the City of Rome shall be the capital of all the countries of the world"—the Caput Mundi.

• *On the opposite wall (look for "Adriano") is...*

Hadrian *(Hadrianus)*, ruled AD 117-138

Hadrian was a fully cosmopolitan man. His trim beard—the first we've seen on an emperor—shows his taste for foreign things; he poses like the Greek philosopher he imagined himself to be.

Hadrian was a voracious tourist, personally visiting almost every corner of the vast empire, from Britain (where he built Hadrian's Wall) to Egypt (where he sailed the Nile), from Jerusalem (where he suppressed another Jewish revolt) to

Athens (where he soaked up classical culture). He scaled Sicily's Mount Etna just to see what made a volcano tick. Back home, he beautified Rome with the Pantheon and his villa at Tivoli, a microcosm of places he'd visited.

Hadrian is flanked here by the two loves of his life. His wife, **Sabina** (right), with modest hairstyle and scarf, kept the home fires burning for her traveling husband. Notice the traces of original paint in her veil and imagine the statues here all enlivened with color. Hadrian was 50 years old when he became captivated by a teenage boy named **Antinous** (left), with his curly hair and full, sensual lips. Together they traveled the Nile, where Antinous drowned. Hadrian wept. Statues of Antinous subsequently went up throughout the Empire, much to the embarrassment of the stoic Romans.

Hadrian spent his last years at his lavish villa outside Rome, surrounded by buildings and souvenirs that reminded him of his traveling days (see the Tivoli chapter).

• *Backtrack through Room I and into the gallery, then turn right, down the hall that leads into the large Room V.*

Rooms V and VI: Rome's Grandeur

Pause at Rome's peak to admire the things the Romans found beautiful. Imagine these statues as they originally stood—in the pleasure gardens of the Roman rich, surrounded by greenery with the splashing sound of fountains, all painted in bright, lifelike colors. Though executed by Romans, the themes are mostly Greek, with godlike humans and human-looking gods.

• *At the beginning of Room V is...*

Aphrodite Crouching *(Afrodite al Bagno Accovacciata)*

The goddess of beauty crouches while bathing, then turns to admire herself. This sets her whole body in motion— one thigh goes down, the other up; her head turns clockwise while her body goes in reverse—yet she's perfectly still. The crouch creates a series of symmetrical love handles, molded by the sculptor into the marble-like wax. Hadrian had good taste—he ordered a copy of this Greek classic for his bathroom.

• *At the far end of the room, look for the...*

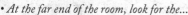

Discus Thrower (Discobolo)

An athlete winds up, about to unleash his pent-up energy and hurl the discus. The sculptor has frozen the moment for us so that we

can examine the inner workings of the wonder called Man. The perfect pecs and washboard abs make this human godlike. Geometrically, you could draw a perfect circle around him, with his hipbone at the center. He's natural yet ideal, twisting yet balanced, moving while at rest. For the Greeks, the universe was a rational place, and the human body was the perfect embodiment of the order found in nature.

This statue is the best-preserved Roman copy (not one member is missing—I checked) of the original Greek work by Myron (450 BC). (The subtle nubs on his head were aids for a measuring device used when making copies.) Statues of athletes like this commonly stood in the baths, where Romans cultivated healthy bodies, minds, and social skills, hoping to lead well-rounded lives. *The Discus Thrower,* with his geometrical perfection and godlike air, sums up all that is best in the classical world.

• *Continue into...*

Room VII

Hermaphrodite Sleeping (Ermafrodito Dormiente)

Imagine that after leaving the baths, a well-rounded Roman headed off to an orgy, where he saw a reclining nude like this. Titillated, he circled around for a closer look, and said, "Hey! *(Insert your own reaction here)*!"

From the back, this nude, lying on its stomach, possesses the perfect, lithe female form. But as you can see from the front, she/he is equipped with both breasts and a penis. It's the Greek/Roman god Hermaphroditus—the child of Hermes and Aphrodite, and protector of intersex people.

Apollo (Apollo del Tevere)

The god of light appears as a slender youth, not as some burly, powerful, autocratic deity. He stands *contrapposto*—originally he was leaning against the tree—in a relaxed and very human way. His curled hair is tied with a headband, strands tumbling down

his neck. His muscles and skin are smooth. (The rusty stains come from the centuries the statue spent submerged in the Tiber.) Apollo is in a reflective mood, and the serenity and intelligence in his face show off classical Greece as a nation of thinkers.

• *Take a detour into Room X (behind Apollo) for a special exhibit about the ancient...*

Nemi Ships

The emperor Caligula had at least two floating palaces—the larger one about 70 meters long, complete with marble temples and bronze fittings. The ships were intentionally sunk in AD 41 in Lake Nemi, to the south of Rome. A fascinating short video explains how archeologists long knew about the fabulous ships, but they were only excavated when the lake was drained in the 1920s. Appreciate the fine bronze fittings—like the exquisitely detailed wild animals holding rings for mooring—on display in this room.

• *Back in Room VII, exit at the far end, cut through Gallery II, and make your way to Room XIII, where you'll find the bust of Septimius Severus.*

Room XIII: Beginning of the End

Septimius Severus, ruled AD 193-211

Rome's sprawling empire was starting to unravel, and it took a disciplined emperor-warrior like this African to keep it together. Severus' victories on the frontier earned him a grand triumphal arch in the Forum, but here he seems to be rolling his eyes at the chaos growing around him.

• *Near Severus is his son...*

Caracalla, ruled AD 211-217

The stubbly beard, cruel frown, and glaring eyes tell us that Severus' son was bad news. He murdered his little brother to seize power, then proceeded to massacre thousands of loyal citizens on a whim. The army came to distrust rulers whose personal agenda got in their way, and Caracalla was stabbed in the back by a man whose brother had just been executed. Rome's long slide had begun.

• *Move next door into...*

Room XIV: The Fall

There are a lot of serious faces in this room. People who grew up in the lap of luxury and security were witnessing the unthinkable—the disintegration of a thousand years of tradition. Rome never recovered from the chaos of the third century. Disease, corruption, revolts from within, and "barbarians" pecking away at the borders were body blows that sapped Rome's strength.

Sarcophagus with Processional Scene
(Sarcofago con Corteo), AD 270

A parade of dignitaries, accompanying a new Roman leader, marches up Capitoline Hill. They huddle together, their backs to

the wall, looking around suspiciously for assassins. Their faces reflect the fear of the age.

By the third century, the Roman army could virtually handpick an emperor to be their front man. At one point, the office of emperor was literally auctioned to the highest bidder. In the space of 40 years, 15 different emperors were saluted, then murdered, at the whims of soldiers of fortune.

Rome would stagger on for another 200 years, but the glory of old Rome was gone. The city was becoming a den of thugs, thieves, prostitutes, barbarians...and Christians.

• Farther along, on the right-hand wall, find the small...

Christ Teaching (Cristo Docente), AD 350

Christ sits like a Roman senator—in a toga, holding a scroll, dispensing wisdom like the law of the land.

The statuette (beardless, as Jesus was portrayed in ancient times) dates from the time when formerly persecuted Christians could now "come out" and worship in public. Emperor Constantine (ruled AD 306-337) legalized Christianity, and within two generations it was Rome's official religion.

Whether Christianity invigorated or ruined Rome is debated, but the fall was inevitable. Rome's once-great legions backpedaled, until even the city itself was raped and plundered by foreigners (410). In 476, the last emperor sold his title for a comfy pension plan, "Rome" became just another dirty city with a big history, and the artistic masterpieces now in this museum were buried under rubble.

REST OF THE MUSEUM
• *A special treat awaits on the top floor.*

Second Floor
This floor contains frescoes and mosaics that once decorated the walls and floors of Roman villas of the aristocracy—the one percent of ancient Rome. They're remarkably realistic and unstuffy, featuring everyday people, animals, flowery patterns, and geometrical designs showing off the finest paintings from ancient Rome outside of Pompeii. The **Villa Farnesina frescoes**—in

black, red, yellow, and blue—are mostly architectural designs, with fake columns, friezes, and garlands.

The highlight of this collection is the frescoed underground dining room of the **Villa di Livia.** Imagine you've been invited to a dinner party with Livia, the wily wife of Augustus. Stepping down, out of the heat of the summer, you're suddenly immersed in a leafy green garden full of birds and fruit trees, symbolizing the gods. The only presence of man is the delicate wicker fence. It's an illusion of nature with birds chirping and flowers blooming. You can almost feel the breeze moving the branches.

Basement (Floor -2)
The **"Luxury in Rome"** rooms give a peek into the lives of Rome's well-to-do citizens, featuring fine jewelry and common everyday objects. The mummified body of an eight-year-old girl born in the second century AD, found in a stone sarcophagus near Rome in 1964, is a highlight; a doll buried with the girl is also on display.

Next, enter the extensive **coin collection.** Find your favorite emperor or empress on the coins: Julius Caesar (case 8, #41-44), Augustus (case 8, #65-69, and case 9, #1-38), Augustus' system of denars (case 10), Tiberius (case 10, #1-16), Caligula (case 10, #17-28), and Nero (case 11, #2-33). Evaluate Roman life by studying how Diocletian tweaked the gold standard (glass case 21). In AD 300, one denar bought one egg. The rest of the displays trace Italy's money from denars to euros. Exhibit 59 shows off the early history of a more recent monetary unit, the old Italian lira. And finally, case 62 brings us up to date with the Italian versions of Rome's latest coinage, the euro.

PILGRIM'S ROME TOUR

Pilgrimage Churches

Rome is the "capital" of the world's 1.2 billion Catholics. In Rome, you'll rub elbows with religious pilgrims from around the world—Nigerian nuns, Bulgarian theology novices, students from Notre Dame, extended Mexican families, and everyday Catholics returning to their religious roots.

The pilgrim industry helped shape Rome after the fall of the empire. Ancient Rome's population peaked at about 1.2 million. After Rome fell in AD 476, barbarians cut off the water supply by breaking the aqueducts, Romans fled the city, and the mouth of the Tiber River filled with silt and became a swamp.

During the Dark Ages, mosquitoes ruled over a pathetic village of 20,000...bad news for pilgrims, bad news for the papacy. Back then, the Catholic Church was the Christian Church. (Catholic means "universal," and being a Catholic was the only allowable way to be a Christian.) Centuries later, during the Renaissance, popes sought to project an image of prestige and authority. The Church revitalized the city, creating a place fit for pilgrimages. Owners of hotels and restaurants cheered.

In the late 1580s, Pope Sixtus V reconnected aqueducts and built long, straight boulevards connecting the great churches and pilgrimage sites. Obelisks were moved to serve as markers. As you explore the city, think like a pilgrim. Look down long roads and you'll see either a grand church or an obelisk (from which you'll see a grand church).

Pilgrims to Rome try to visit four great basilicas: St. Peter's Basilica, of course (covered in the 📖 St. Peter's Basilica Tour chapter in this book and on my 🎧 free audio tour), St. Paul's Outside the Walls (see page 114), Santa Maria Maggiore, and San Giovanni in Laterano. The last two are covered in this chapter, as well as two

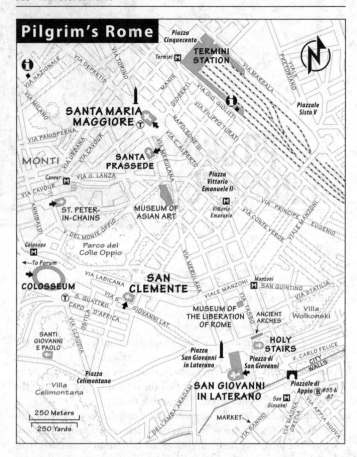

Pilgrim's Rome

other "honorable mentions": The Church of Santa Prassede and the
fascinating and central San Clemente.

Orientation

Planning Your Time: Depending on your time and interest, you
may want to hit every sight described in this chapter—or just
one or two of the churches. **Santa Maria Maggiore** (and nearby **Santa Prassede**) have mosaics dating back to the first days
of Christian Rome. **San Giovanni in Laterano** is grandiose
and historic, and its Holy Stairs are a one-of-a-kind experience. **San Clemente**'s church-beneath-church layout leads you
down—layer by mysterious layer—to a pagan Mithraic temple. To link this chapter's sights efficiently, check their opening hours (Santa Prassede and San Clemente close for several
hours at midday, as does the chapel at the Holy Stairs—the

Holy Stairs themselves do not) and decide whether to travel on foot, by taxi, or on public transit.

Getting to the Churches: Santa Maria Maggiore and San Giovanni in Laterano, this chapter's two biggies, are just a few minutes' walk from Metro stops on line A. Santa Maria Maggiore is on Piazza di Santa Maria Maggiore (Metro: Termini or Vittorio Emanuele), and San Giovanni in Laterano is on Piazza di San Giovanni in Laterano (Metro: San Giovanni).

Santa Maria Maggiore is a block from Santa Prassede; from there, it's about a 15-minute walk (or €6 taxi ride) to San Clemente, or a 20-minute walk to San Giovanni in Laterano. To avoid the walk from Santa Maria Maggiore to San Giovanni in Laterano, catch bus #16, #117, or #714 (along Via Merulana), or take a taxi.

San Clemente (Metro: Colosseo) is an easy 15-minute walk from San Giovanni in Laterano, or a quick hop on tram #3 or bus #87 or #117. (The useful #87 connects Largo Argentina, Piazza Venezia, the Colosseo Metro stop, San Clemente, and San Giovanni in Laterano.)

Church of Santa Maria Maggiore: Free, daily 7:00-18:45.

Church of Santa Prassede: Free (but bring €0.50 and €1 coins for lights), daily 7:00-12:00 & 15:00-18:30, no visits during Mass (Mon-Sat 7:30 and 18:00; Sun 8:00, 10:00, 11:30, and 18:00).

Church of San Clemente: Upper church—free, lower church—€10, both open Mon-Sat 9:00-12:30 & 15:00-18:00, Sun 12:15-18:00. Last entry to the lower church is at 17:30.

Church of San Giovanni in Laterano: Church—free, daily 7:00-18:30; cloister—€5, daily 9:00-18:00; church audioguide available (donation requested, or pay €10 for combo-ticket that includes audioguide and entry to cloister and Holy Stairs chapel, ID required as deposit; pick up at info desk near the main door, either inside or outside).

The **Holy Stairs** (Scala Santa), in a building across the street from the church, are free (Mon-Sat 6:30-19:00, Sun 7:00-19:00, Oct-March closes daily at 18:30). The chapel at the Holy Stairs costs €3.50 (Mon-Sat 9:30-12:40 & 15:00-17:10, closed Sun).

Dress Code: Modest dress is recommended (knees and shoulders covered).

The Tour Begins

Four churches are covered in this tour. You can visit all four or pick and choose the ones that interest you most. See "Getting to the Churches," earlier, for details on linking these sights.

CHURCH OF SANTA MARIA MAGGIORE

The basilica of Santa Maria celebrates Holy Mary, the mother of Jesus. One of Rome's oldest and best-preserved churches, it was built (AD 432) while Rome was falling around it. The city had been sacked by Visigoths (410), and the emperors were about to check out (476). Increasingly, popes stepped in to fill the vacuum of leadership. The fifth-century mosaics give the church the feel of the early Christian community. The general ambience of the church really takes you back to ancient times.

❶ Exterior

Start your visit by standing directly in front of the church next to the ornate column in the square. From here you can make out

the earlier medieval church and bell tower (the tower was built in the late 14th century and is the tallest in Rome). The 13th-century mosaics of the medieval church survive behind the newer Rococo facade, which welcomes you like open theater curtains. The wings to the left and right were added for Vatican offices.

Like Santa Maria Maggiore, most churches in Rome are much older than their facades. During the Baroque age, many were given facelifts.

Turn around and gape up. Mary's column originally stood in the Forum's Basilica of Constantine. This fifth-century church, built in her honor, proclaims she was indeed the Mother of God—a point disputed by hair-splitting theologians of the day.

When you step inside the church, you'll be entering Vatican property—the church, although on Italian territory, has similar status to an embassy. The "Maggiore" in the church's name indicates that it is one of the Catholic Church's four "major" basilicas (all of them in Rome; the others are St. Peter's, San Giovanni in Laterano, and St. Paul Outside the Walls).

❷ Nave

Despite the Renaissance ceiling and Baroque crusting, you still feel like you're walking into an early Christian church. You can feel the joy and lightness typical of early churches that were built before the heavier medieval styles took hold. The stately rows of columns, the simple basilica layout (nave flanked by side aisles), the cheery colors, the spacious nave—it's easy to imagine worshippers finding an oasis of peace here as the Roman Empire crashed around them. (The 15th-century coffered ceiling is gilded with gold—perhaps brought back from America.)

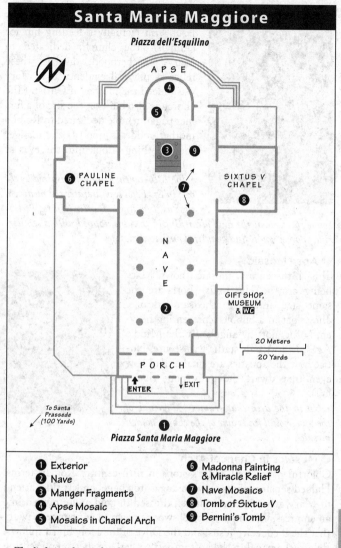

Santa Maria Maggiore

Piazza dell'Esquilino

APSE

④

⑤

③ ⑨

⑥ PAULINE
CHAPEL

⑦

SIXTUS V
CHAPEL

⑧

N
A
V
E

GIFT SHOP,
MUSEUM
& WC

②

20 Meters

20 Yards

PORCH

↑ ENTER   ↓ EXIT

To Santa
Prassede
(100 Yards)

①

Piazza Santa Maria Maggiore

① Exterior	⑥ Madonna Painting & Miracle Relief
② Nave	⑦ Nave Mosaics
③ Manger Fragments	⑧ Tomb of Sixtus V
④ Apse Mosaic	⑨ Bernini's Tomb
⑤ Mosaics in Chancel Arch	

• *The lighting boxes for three zones are in the back of the nave. If you put euro coins in each of the three slots, you give everyone two minutes of gorgeous art (and become the saint of light). In the center of the church is the main altar, under a purple and gold canopy. Underneath the altar, in a lighted niche, are...*

❸ Manger Fragments

A kneeling Pope Pius IX (who established the dogma of the Immaculate Conception in the 19th century) prays before a glass case with an urn that contains several pieces of wood, bound by

iron—these pieces are said to be from Jesus' crib (actually a feeding bin for animals). The church, dedicated to Mary's motherhood, displays these relics as physical evidence that Mary was indeed the mother of Christ. (The church is also built on the site of a former pagan temple dedicated to Rome's mother goddess, Juno.) Is the manger the real thing? Look into the eyes of pilgrims who visit.

• *The 18th-century canopy, inspired by the one in St. Peter's, obliterates the medieval apse as if to draw all attention to the Baroque spectacle at the high altar. But in the apse, topped with a semicircular dome, you'll find beautiful medieval mosaics.*

❹ Apse Mosaic

This 13th-century mosaic shows Mary being crowned by Jesus—both are the same size and share the same throne. They float in a bubble representing heaven, borne aloft by angels. By the Middle Ages, Mary's cult status was secure. Notice how the apostles are smaller and how even they dwarf the puny pope (lower left).

• *Up in the arch that frames the outside of the apse, you'll find some of the church's oldest mosaics.*

❺ Mosaics in Chancel Arch

Colorful panels tell Mary's story in fifth-century Roman terms. Haloed senator-saints in white togas (top panel on left side) attend to Mary, who sits on a throne, dressed in gold and crowned like an empress. The angel Gabriel swoops down to announce to Mary that she'll conceive Jesus, and the Dove of the Holy Spirit follows. Below (the panel in the bottom-left corner) are sheep representing the apostles, entering the city of Jerusalem ("HIERVSALEM").

• *In the separate chapel to your left, over the altar, you'll see a...*

❻ Madonna Painting and Miracle Relief

This chapel is a 17th-century Baroque addition to the church. Its altar, a geologist's delight, is adorned with jasper, agate, amethyst, lapis lazuli, and gold angels. Amid it all is a simple icon of the lady this church is dedicated to: Mary.

Above the painting is a bronze relief panel showing a pope,

with amazed bystanders, shoveling snow. One hot August night in the year 358, Mary appeared to Pope Liberius in a dream, saying: "Build me a church where the snow falls." The next morning, they discovered a small patch of snow here on Esquiline Hill—on August 5—and this church, dedicated to Santa Maria, was begun. The grandiose tombs of two grandiose popes fill the chapel's sides.

• *Back out in the nave, on the other side of the altar, take a look at the...*

❼ Nave Mosaics

The church contains some of the world's best-preserved mosaics from early Christian Rome. If the floodlights are on, those with good eyesight or binoculars will enjoy watching the story of Moses unfold in a series of surprisingly colorful and realistic scenes—more sophisticated than anything that would be seen for a thousand years.

The small, square mosaic panels are above all the columns, on the right side of the nave. Start at the altar and work back toward the entry.

1. This is a later painting—skip it.
2. Pharaoh's daughter (upper left) and her maids take baby Moses from the Nile.
3. Moses (lower half of panel) sees a burning bush that reconnects him with his Hebrew origins. (Now leap the arch to #4.)
4. A parade of Israelites (left side) flees Egypt through a path in the Red Sea, while Pharaoh's troops drown.
5. Moses leads them across the Sinai desert (upper half), and God provides for them with a flock of quail (lower half).
6. Moses (upper half) sticks his magic rod in a river to desalinate it.
7. The Israelites battle their enemies while Moses commands from a hillside.
8. Skip this one, too.
9. Moses (upper left) brings the Ten Commandments, then goes with Joshua (upper right) to lie down and die.
10. Joshua crosses the (rather puny) Jordan River...
11. ...and attacks Jericho...
12. ...and then the walls come a-tumblin' down.

• *Head back toward the altar to see whether the gate to the right transept is open. If so, enter the late-Renaissance chapel (late 1500s); otherwise, skip ahead to Bernini's Tomb. On the right wall of the chapel is a statue of a praying pope, atop the...*

❽ Tomb of Sixtus V

The Rome we see today is due largely to Pope Sixtus V (or was it Fiftus VI?). This energetic pope (1585-1590) leveled shoddy medieval Rome and erected grand churches connected by long, broad boulevards spiked with obelisks as focal points (such as the obelisk in Piazza dell'Esquilino behind Santa Maria Maggiore). Today the city of Rome has 13 Egyptian obelisks (and the ancient city had many more)—whereas all of Egypt has only five.

The centerpiece of this chapel (called the "Sistine Chapel," but it's not the more famous one) shows four angels carrying a gilded model of the new St. Peter's dome, which was designed by Michelangelo. Finishing this project was a major part of Pope Sixtus' legacy.

The white carved-marble relief panels decorating the pope's tomb celebrate more of his accomplishments in reviving Rome (like the obelisks he raised and the buildings he commissioned).

• *Back in the main nave, on the closest (right) side of the main altar, look down for an inscription on the first step between two white columns. This marks...*

❾ Bernini's Tomb

The plaque reads, *"Ioannes Laurentivs Bernini"*—Gian Lorenzo Bernini (1598-1680)—"who brought honor to art and the city, here humbly rests." Next to it is another plaque to the *"Familia Bernini."* It's certainly humble...a simple memorial for the man who grew up in this neighborhood, then went on to remake Rome in the ornate Baroque style. (For more on Bernini, see page 303.)

• *After looking around Santa Maria Maggiore, fans of mosaics, Byzantines, and the offbeat should consider a visit to the nearby Church of Santa Prassede, about 100 yards away.*

Exiting Santa Maria Maggiore, find the obelisk in the distance (which would have directed medieval pilgrims down Via Merulana to the next big stop on their trail: the Church of San Giovanni in Laterano). Head in that direction just a few steps and follow a lane to the right, leading to a low-key side door where you enter Santa Prassede.

CHURCH OF SANTA PRASSEDE

The mosaics at the Church of Santa Prassede, from AD 822, are the best Byzantine-style mosaics in Rome. The Byzantine Empire, with its capital in Constantinople (ancient Istanbul), was the eastern half of the Roman Empire. Unlike the western half, it didn't "fall," and its inhabitants remained Christian, Greek-speaking, and cultured for a thousand years while their distant cousins in Italy were fumbling for the light switch in the Dark Ages. Byzantine craftsmen preserved the techniques of ancient Roman mosaicists (who decorated floors and walls of villas and public buildings), then reinfused this learning into Rome during the city's darkest era. Take the time to let your eyes adjust, and appreciate the Byzantine glory glowing out of the dark church.

Bring €0.50 and €1 coins to buy floodlighting and enjoy the

full sparkle of the mosaics. Popping a coin into the box in the Chapel of St. Zeno (described later) saves you a trip to Ravenna, in northern Italy (famous for its Byzantine mosaics).

• *The best mosaics are in the apse (behind the main altar; note another Baroque-era, "look-at-me" canopy over the high altar, like at Santa Maria Maggiore) and in the small Chapel of St. Zeno along the right (north) side of the nave.*

Apse Mosaics

On a blue background is Christ, standing in a rainbow-colored river, flanked by saints. Christ has commanded Peter (to our

right of Christ, with white hair and beard) to spread the Good News to all the world. Beneath Christ, 12 symbolic sheep leave Jerusalem's city gates to preach to the world. Peter came here, to what was the world's biggest city, to preach love...and was met with a hostile environment. He turns his palm up in a plea for help. Persecuted Peter was taken in by a hospitable woman named Pudentia (next to him) and her sister, Praxedes (to the left of Christ, between two other saints), whose house was located on this spot. (The church is named for Praxedes.)

The saint on the far left (with the square halo, indicating he was alive at the time this was made) is Pope Paschal I, who built the church in the 800s in memory of these early sisters, hiring the best craftsmen in the known world to do the mosaics. Pope Paschal was also responsible for evacuating the bones of the early martyrs from the endangered catacombs outside the city walls and building several churches to contain them within the safety of downtown.

Chapel of St. Zeno

The ceiling is gold, representing the Byzantine heaven. An icon-like Christ emerges from the background, supported by winged angels in white, with lipstick and red cheeks. On the walls are saints walking among patches of flowers. In the altar niche, Mary and the child Jesus are flanked by the sisters Praxedes and Pudentia. On the side wall, the woman with the square blue halo is Theodora, the mom of the pope who built this. And in an-

other niche is a supposed relic of the pillar upon which Christ was whipped on his way to Golgotha.

The chapel, covered completely with mosaics, may be underwhelming to our modern eyes, but in the darkness of Rome's medieval era, it was known as the "Garden of Paradise."

CHURCH OF SAN GIOVANNI IN LATERANO

Imagine the jubilation when this church—the first Christian church in the city of Rome—was opened in about AD 318. Christians could finally "come out" and worship openly without fear of reprisal. (Still, most Romans were pagan, so this first great church was tucked away from the center of things, near the city wall.) After that glorious beginning, the church served as the center of Catholicism and the home of the popes until the Renaissance renovation of St. Peter's and the expansion of the Vatican. Until 1870, all popes were "crowned" here. Even today, it's the home church of the Bishop of Rome—the pope. Like Santa Maria Maggiore, it's Vatican property.

• *To reach the church from the San Giovanni Metro station, exit to the right onto Via Magna Grecia, then head toward the old city walls. Before you leave the square, look left to find the* **Via Sannio market**, *which sells clothing and some handicrafts every morning except Sunday. Then pass through the archways, hugging the left side of the street, to approach San Giovanni's white, statue-topped facade.*

❶ Exterior

The massive facade is 18th century, with Christ triumphant on the top. The blocky peach-colored building adjacent on the right is the

Lateran Palace, standing on the site of the old Papal Palace—residence of popes until about 1300. Across the street to your right are the pope's private chapel and the Holy Stairs (Scala Santa), popular with pilgrims (we'll see the stairs later). To the left is a well-preserved chunk of the ancient Roman wall. Pass the three-foot-high granite posts surrounding the church to leave Italy and enter the Vatican State—*carabinieri* must leave their guns at the door.

• *Step inside the portico and look left.*

❷ Statue of Constantine

It's October 28, AD 312, and Constantine—sword tucked under his arm and leaning confidently on a (missing) spear—has conquered Maxentius and liberated Rome. Constantine marched to

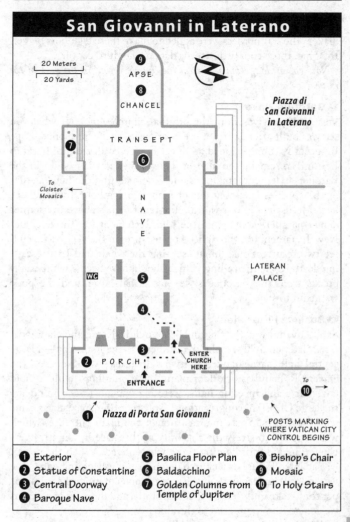

San Giovanni in Laterano

20 Meters
20 Yards

9 APSE

8 CHANCEL

7

To Cloister Mosaics ←

TRANSEPT

6

N A V E

WC

LATERAN PALACE

5

4

3 ENTER CHURCH HERE

2 PORCH

ENTRANCE

Piazza di San Giovanni in Laterano

To **10** →

1 *Piazza di Porta San Giovanni*

POSTS MARKING WHERE VATICAN CITY CONTROL BEGINS

1 Exterior
2 Statue of Constantine
3 Central Doorway
4 Baroque Nave
5 Basilica Floor Plan
6 Baldacchino
7 Golden Columns from Temple of Jupiter
8 Bishop's Chair
9 Mosaic
10 To Holy Stairs

this spot where his enemy's personal bodyguards lived, trashed their pagan idols, and dedicated the place to the god who gave him his victory—Christ. The holes in Constantine's head once held a golden, halo-like crown for the emperor who legalized Christianity. In the relief above the statue, you'll see a beheaded John the Baptist.

• *In the portico, take a look at the...*

3 Central Doorway

These tall green bronze doors, with their floral designs and acorn studs, are the original doors from ancient Rome's Senate House (Curia) in the Forum. The Church moved these here in the 1650s to remind people that, from now on, the Church was Europe's law-maker. The star borders were added to make these big doors bigger. Imagine, those cool little acorns date to the third century.

• *Now go inside the main part of the church. Stand in the back of the nave.*

❹ Baroque Nave

Very little survives from the original church—most of what you see was built after 1600. In preparation for the 1650 Jubilee, Pope Innocent X commissioned architect Francesco Borromini (rival to Bernini) to remake the interior. He redesigned the basilica in the Baroque style, reorganizing the nave and adding the huge statues of the apostles (stepping out of niches to symbolically bring ce-lestial Jerusalem to our world). The relief panels above the statues depict parallel events from the Old Testament (on the left) and New Testament (on the right). For instance, in the very back you'll see two resurrections: Jonah escaping the whale and Jesus escap-ing death. Only the ceiling (which should have been a white vault) breaks from the Baroque style—it's Renaissance, and the pope wanted it to stay.

❺ Basilica Floor Plan

San Giovanni was the first public church in Rome and the model for all later churches, including St. Peter's. The floor plan—a large central hall (nave) flanked by two side aisles—was based on the ancient Roman basilica floor plan. These buildings, built to hold law courts and meeting halls, were big enough to accommodate the large Christian congregations. Note that Roman basilicas came with two apses. You came in through the main entrance, which was designed to stress the authority of the place by slightly over-whelming and intimidating those who entered. When the design was adapted for use as a church, a grand and welcoming entry (the west portal) replaced one of the apses. Upon entering, the worship-per could take in the entire space instantly, and the rows of columns welcomed him to proceed to the altar.

• *The canopy over the altar is called the...*

❻ Baldacchino

In the upper cage are two silver statues of Sts. Peter (with keys) and Paul (sword), which contain pieces of their heads. The gossip buzz-ing among Rome's amateur archaeologists is that the Vatican tested DNA from Peter's head (located here) and from his body (located at St. Peter's)...and they didn't match.

• *Standing in the left transept are the...*

❼ Golden Columns from Temple of Jupiter

Tradition says that these gilded bronze columns once stood in pagan Rome's holiest spot—the Temple of Jupiter, which was dedicated to the king of all gods, on the summit of Capitoline Hill (c. 50 BC). Now they support a triangular pediment inhabited by a bearded, Jupiter-like God the Father.

• *In the apse, you'll find the...*

❽ Bishop's Chair

The chair (called a "cathedra") reminds visitors that this is the cathedral of Rome...and the pope himself is the bishop who sits here. Once elected, the new pope must actually sit in this chair to officially become the pope. The ceremonial sitting usually happens within one month of election—Pope Francis took his seat on April 7, 2013.

• *Under the semicircular dome of the apse, take a close look at the...*

❾ Mosaic

The original design dates from about 450 (although it was made in the 13th century and heavily restored in the 19th century).

You'll see a cross, animals, plants, and the River Jordan running along the base. Mosaic, of course, was an ancient Roman specialty adapted by medieval Christians. The head of Christ (above the cross) must have been a glorious sight to early worshippers. It was one of the first legal images of Christ ever seen in formerly pagan Rome.

• *Fans of cosmatesque marble-inlay floor (c. 1100-1300) may want to buy a ticket to visit the cloister (enter near left transept).*

The Holy Stairs are outside the church in a building across the street. To get there, exit the church, turn left, and cross the street to the nondescript building.

❿ Holy Stairs (Scala Santa)

In 326, Emperor Constantine's mother (St. Helena) brought home the 28 marble steps of Pontius Pilate's residence in Jerusalem. According to tradition, Jesus climbed these steps on the day he was sentenced to death. Each day, hundreds of faithful penitents climb these steps on their knees while reciting a litany of prayers.

Covered with walnut wood spotted with small glass-covered holes showing stains from Jesus' blood, the steps lead to the "Holy of Holies" (Sancta Sanctorum), the private chapel of the popes in the Middle Ages. With its world-class relics, this chapel was considered the holiest place on earth. The relics were moved to the Vatican in 1905.

You can climb the tourist staircases along the sides. At the top, you can look inside the "Holy of Holies" through the grated windows (you can see essentially the entire chapel through the grates, but if you'd like to go inside, you'll have to buy a ticket at the ticket desk downstairs, near the entrance).
You can also buy a souvenir at the gift shop (at the top floor, on the left). Or you're welcome to climb the stairs on your knees (pick up the €2 booklet at the gift shop that gives the proper prayer for each of the 28 steps). If you've done a lot of praying in your life, but never accompanied your prayers with a little pain—actually a lot of pain—give this a try.

Nearby: After exiting the steps, look right and notice the broken arch of the **Claudian Aqueduct** (1st century AD), which once carried water to the city from more than 40 miles away. The **Museum of the Liberation of Rome** isn't far behind it, just a few blocks down Via Tasso (see page 102). Then head toward the center of Piazza di San Giovanni in Laterano—straight ahead with your back to the Holy Stairs—for a look at the world's tallest obelisk, dating from the 15th century BC. (This is also the departure point for bus #16, which runs up Via Merulana to the Church of Santa Maria Maggiore.)

CHURCH OF SAN CLEMENTE

Here, like nowhere else, you'll enjoy the layers of Rome—a 12th-century basilica sits atop a fourth-century Christian basilica, which sits atop a second-century Mithraic temple and some even earlier Roman buildings.

Upper Church: 12th Century

The church (at today's ground level) is dedicated to the fourth pope, Clement, who shepherded the small Christian community when the religion was at best, tolerated, and at worst, a capital offense. Clement himself was martyred by drowning in about AD 100—tied to an anchor by angry Romans and tossed overboard. You'll see his symbol, the anchor, around the church. The painting on the ceiling shows Clement being carried aloft to heaven.

While today's main entry is on the side, the original entry was through the **courtyard** in back, a kind of defensive atrium common in medieval times. To reach the original entry, go in through today's main entrance, walk diagonally toward the right, and exit again into this courtyard. Turn around and face the original entry.

(This courtyard is inviting for a cool quiet break, as I imagine it was for a visiting medieval pilgrim.)

Back inside the church, step up to the carved marble **choir**—an enclosure in the middle of the church (Schola Cantorum) where the cantors sat. About 1,200 years ago, it stood in the old church beneath us, before that church was looted and destroyed by invading Normans.

In the apse (behind the altar), study the fine 12th-century mosaics. The delicate Crucifixion—with Christ sharing the cross with a dozen apostles as doves—is engulfed by a Tree of Life richly inhabited by deer, birds, and saints. The message is clear: All life springs from God in Christ. Above it all, a triumphant Christ, one hand on the Bible, blesses the congregation.

St. Catherine Chapel

The chapel in the back corner near the side (tourist) entrance—considered one of the first great Renaissance masterpieces—is ded-

icated to St. Catherine of Alexandria, a noblewoman martyred for her defense of persecuted Christians. The fresco on the left wall—which shows an early-Renaissance three-dimensional representation of space—is by the Florentine master Masolino (1428), perhaps aided by his young assistant, Masaccio. Studying the left wall, working from left to right, you can follow her story:

1. Catherine (lower-left panel), in black, confronts an assembly of the pagan Emperor Maxentius and his counselors. She bravely ticks off arguments on her fingers why Christianity should be legalized. Her powerful delivery silences the crowd.
2. Under the rotunda of a pagan temple (above, on the upper-left panel), Catherine, in blue, points up at a statue and tells a crowd of pagans, "Your gods are puny compared to mine."
3. Catherine, in blue (upper-right panel, left side), is thrown in prison, where she's visited by the emperor's wife (in green). Catherine converts her.
4. Emperor Maxentius, enraged, orders his own wife killed. The

executioner (upper panel, right side), standing next to the empress' decapitated corpse, impassively sheaths his sword.

5. In the best-known scene (the middle panel on the bottom), Maxentius, in black, looks down from a balcony and condemns Catherine (in black) to be torn apart between two large, spiked wheels turned by executioners. But suddenly, an angel swoops in with a sword to cut her loose.

6. Catherine is eventually martyred (lower-right panel). Now dressed in green, she kneels before the executioner, who raises his sword to finish the job.

7. Finally, on the top of holy Mount Sinai (same panel, upper-right corner), two angels bear Catherine's body to its final resting place.

Taking a few steps back, look up at the arch that frames the chapel, topped by the delightful Annunciation fresco (top of the arch) by Masolino. Also notice the big St. Christopher, patron saint of travelers (left pillar), with 500-year-old graffiti scratched in by pilgrims—now covered with glass.

Lower Church: Fourth Century

Buy a ticket in the bookshop, and descend 1,700 years to the time when Christians were razzed on their way to church by pagan neighbors. The first room you enter was the original atrium (entry hall)—the nave extends to the right. (Everything you'll visit from here on was buried until the 19th century.)

• *Most of the way down the atrium, look for the "reversible" stone set into a metal rack that you can rotate.*

Pagan Inscription

This two-sided recycled marble burial slab—one side (with leafy decorations) for a Christian, the other for a pagan—shows how the two Romes lived side by side in the fourth century.

• *Go through the nearby door into the nave, and walk to the far end. Five yards before the altar, on the left wall, look for the...*

Fresco of St. Clement and Sisinnius

Clement (center) holds a secret Mass for early Christians back when it was a capital crime. Theodora, a prominent Roman (in yellow, to the right), is one of the undercover faithful. Her pagan husband, Sisinnius, has come to retrieve and punish her when—*zap!*—he's struck blind and has to be led away (right side).

But Sisinnius is still unconvinced. When Clement cures his blindness, Sisinnius (very faded, lower panel, far right) orders two servants to drag Clement off to the authorities. But through a miraculous intervention, the servants mistake a column for Clement (see the shadowy black log) and drag that out of the house instead. The inscription (crossword-style on right, waist-high, very faded) is famous among Italians because it's one of the earliest examples of the transition from Latin to Italian. Sisinnius encourages his servants by yelling *"Fili dele pute, traite!"* ("You sons of bitches, pull!")

• *In the far-left corner of the lower church (in the room behind the fresco you just saw), near the staircase leading down, is the...*

Presumed Burial Place of St. Cyril

Cyril, who died in AD 869 (see the modern, icon-like mosaic of him), was an inveterate traveler who spread Christianity to the Slavic lands and Russia—today's Russian Orthodox faithful. Along the way, he introduced the Cyrillic alphabet still used by Russians and many other Slavs. Thanks to their tireless missionary work, Cyril and his brother Methodius are considered the most important figures in Slavic Christianity.

• *Now descend farther to the dark, dank Mithraic temple (Mithreum; through a door immediately to the right of the altar and down steps). Nowhere in Rome is there a better place to experience this weird cult.*

Temple of Mithras (Mithreum): Second Century

• *The barred room to the left is the...*

Worship Hall

Worshippers of Mithras—men only—reclined on the benches on either side of the room. At the far end is a small statue of the god

Mithras, in a billowing cape. In the center sits an altar carved with a relief showing Mithras fighting with a bull that contains all life. A scorpion, a dog, and a snake try to stop Mithras, but he wins, running his sword through the bull. The blood spills out, bringing life to the world.

Mithras' fans gathered here, in this tiny microcosm of the universe (the ceiling was decorated with stars), to celebrate the victory with a ritual meal. Every spring, Mithras brought new life again, and so they ritually kept track of the seasons—the four square shafts in the corners of the ceiling represent the seasons, the seven round ones were the great constellations. Initiates went through hazing rituals representing the darkness of this world, and then emerged into the light-filled world brought by Mithras.

Rome's official pagan religion had no real spiritual content and did not offer any concept of salvation. As the empire slowly crumbled, people turned more and more to Eastern religions (including Christianity), in search of answers and comfort. The cult of Mithras, stressing loyalty and based on the tenuousness of life, was popular among soldiers. Part of its uniqueness and popularity (in this very class-conscious society) was due to its belief that all were equal before God. It dates back to the time of Alexander the Great, who brought it from Persia. In 67 BC, sol-

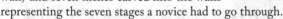

diers who had survived the bloody conquest of Asia Minor returned to Rome swearing by Mithras. When Christians gained power, they banished the worship of Mithras.

Facing the barred room are two rectangular Corinthian columns supporting three arches of the temple's entryway, decorated with a fine stucco coffered ceiling.

At the far end of the hallway, another barred door marks the equivalent of a Mithraic Sunday school room. Peek inside to see a faded fresco of bearded Mithras (right wall) and seven niches carved into the walls representing the seven stages a novice had to go through.

Head back the way you came. On your right, watch for a very narrow ancient alleyway separating Roman walls barely three feet across. If it's open, step in and imagine the first Western city to reach one million residents. Forget the two churches above you, and imagine standing on this exact spot and looking up at the sky 2,000 years ago. Now climb back through the centuries to today's street level.

TRASTEVERE WALK

From the Tiber to the Church of Santa Maria in Trastevere

Trastevere—the colorful neighborhood across the river from downtown—is *the* place to immerse yourself in the crustier side of Rome. This half-mile walk from the Tiber *(Tevere)* River to the Church of Santa Maria in Trastevere is designed to train your eye to see Rome more intimately.

Trastevere (trahs-TAY-veh-ray) literally means "across the *Tevere*"—the other side of the Tiber River—and it presents another side of Rome. Here you'll discover a secret, hidden city. Along with the usual churches, statues, and mosaics, there's the Rome of today—apartments with rooftop terraces, kids playing soccer in the piazza, and narrow lanes draped with drying underwear. It's a world of lovers kissing on Vespas, party-loving bankers, and feisty "Trasteverini"—old-timers who pride themselves on never setting foot on the opposite bank of the river.

Orientation

Length of This Walk: Allow 1.5 hours. To see Trastevere in less time, taxi directly to Santa Maria in Trastevere (the square where this walk ends). You'll still capture plenty of ambience.

When to Go: This walk can work well at any time of day, but starting around 10:00 allows you to see the Church of Santa Cecilia and the Villa Farnesina (except Sun). Mornings are cool and relatively quiet. Strolling through Trastevere at dusk is especially atmospheric. Consider combining this walk with a meal or as a prelude to my Heart of Rome Walk.

Getting There: This walk starts at the island in the Tiber River, just across from Rome's Jewish ghetto and within walking distance of the Capitoline Hill, Piazza Venezia, and Campo de' Fiori. From Piazza Venezia or Largo Argentina, tram #8 can speed your trip—get off at Piazza Belli. Except on Sunday, express bus #H runs to Trastevere from Termini train station and Piazza della Repubblica (on the northeast side of the square, near the entrance to the Baths of Diocletian)—get off at the Sonnino/S. Gallicano stop. From the Vatican, take bus #23 from Piazza Risorgimento or Leone IV to the Lungotevere Alberteschi stop. From the Colosseum area, take a bus to Piazza Venezia, then tram #8; or ride tram #3, which drops you about 15 minutes from the start of this walk (Min. P. Istruzione stop).

Church of Santa Cecilia: Church—free, daily 10:00-13:00 & 16:00-19:00; crypt—€2.50, same hours as church; choir loft with frescoes—€2.50, Mon-Sat 10:00-12:30, closed Sun; tel. 06-589-9289.

Church of Santa Maria in Trastevere: Free, daily 7:30-21:00 (except Aug 8:00-12:00 & 16:00-21:00).

Villa Farnesina: €10, Mon-Sat 9:00-14:00, closed Sun (except open 9:00-17:00 on second Sun of the month).

Tours: ∩ Download my free Trastevere Walk audio tour.

Eateries: Several recommended restaurants are on the map and described in the Eating in Rome chapter.

The Walk Begins

• *Start at Isola Tiberina—the "island in the Tiber River." We'll begin on the bridge called Ponte Cestio that leads from downtown Rome to the Trastevere neighborhood. (Note that the bridge is called Ponte Fabricio on the left bank of the river.) From atop Ponte Cestio, take in the island and the river.*

❶ Isola Tiberina and the Tiber River

Rome got its start 3,000 years ago along the Tiber River at this point. This was as far upstream as big boats could sail and the first

place the river could be crossed by bridge. As a center of river trade, Rome connected the interior of the Italian peninsula with the Mediterranean. The area below you would have been bustling in ancient times. Look down and imagine small ports, water mills, ramshackle boats, and platforms for fishing.

The **island** itself was once the site of a temple dedicated to Asclepius, the god of medicine. Ancient Romans who were ill spent the night here and left little statues of their healed body parts (feet,

TRASTEVERE

livers, hearts…) as thank-you notes. This tradition survives: Today, throughout Italy, Catholic altars are often encrusted with votive offerings, symbolizing gratitude for answered prayers. During plagues and epidemics, the sick were isolated on the island. These days, the island's largest building is the Fatebenefratelli, the public hospital favored by Roman women for childbirth. The island's reputation for medical care lives on.

The high point of the **bridge** (upon which you're probably leaning) is an ancient stone with a faded inscription dating from about AD 370, when this then-400-year-old bridge was rebuilt. The eroding plaque is stapled into the balustrade like a piece of recycled scrap. Run your fingers over the word "Caesar" (top line, just right of center).

This part of the Tiber River flooded frequently, which devalued the land on the north bank; in time it would become the site of the Jewish ghetto—started in the 16th century, but now long gone, though Rome's synagogue remains. (For a tour of this area, take my Jewish Ghetto Walk, available 📖 as a chapter in this book and 🎧 as a free audio tour.)

In the 1870s, the Romans removed the threat of flooding by practically walling off the Tiber, building the tall, anonymous embankments that continue to isolate the river from the city today.

• *Head south to leave the bridge. If open, the green riverside **Sora Mirella** kiosk on the right (run by Mirella's son, Stefano) is the most famous vendor of Rome's summer refresher called a* grattachecca *(pronounced grah-tah-kek-kah, €4), a concoction of shaved ice with fruit-flavored syrup and chopped fruit (similar to a granita). Cross the street and go down the 12 steps into the car-filled piazza.*

❷ Piazza in Piscinula

As you descend and enter the square, look directly ahead. Rising up among the buildings is a cute little church bell tower. Dating from 1069, this is the oldest working bell tower in the city. Study the brown building on the riverside and spot faint traces of Renaissance decoration. Today's earth-tone shades of the city echo this original Roman brown.

• *Facing the tower, turn right and exit the trapezoid-shaped square from the far corner, opposite where you entered, going uphill on Via dell'Arco de' Tolomei. At the top of the small slope, pause and look around.*

❸ Via dell'Arco de' Tolomei

Except for the parking garage, the buildings around you are mostly apartments. The ochre-and-yellow buildings, with green or brown shutters and draped with vines, are characteristic of Trastevere and many Roman neighborhoods. Find the olive trees in planters, and look up at the plant-covered rooftop terraces—the Roman equiva-

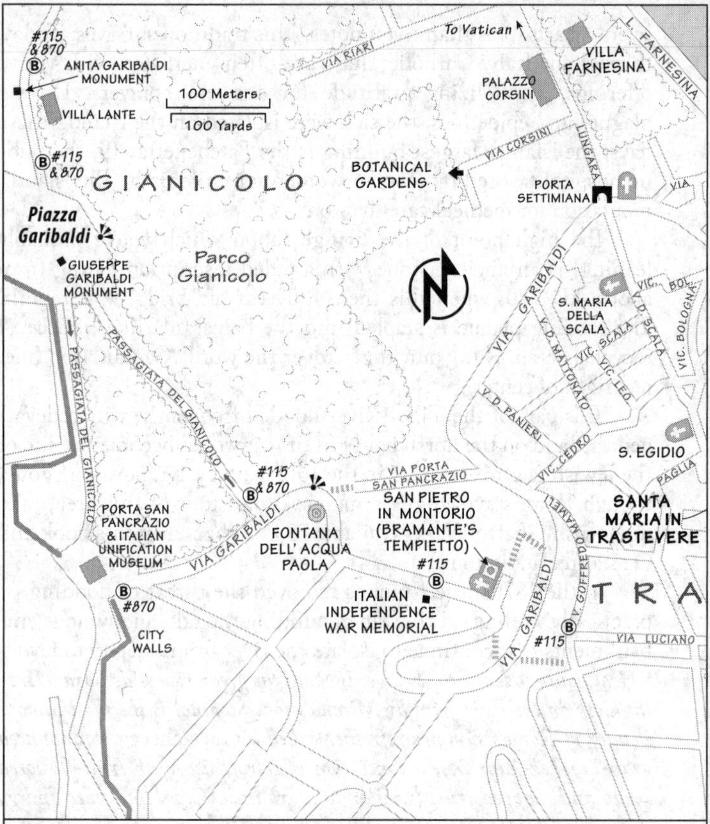

To Vatican
#115 & 870
ANITA GARIBALDI MONUMENT
VILLA LANTE
100 Meters
100 Yards
VIA RIARI
VILLA FARNESINA
L. FARNESINA
PALAZZO CORSINI
VIA CORSINI
LUNGARA
#115 & 870
GIANICOLO
BOTANICAL GARDENS
PORTA SETTIMIANA
VIA
Piazza Garibaldi
GIUSEPPE GARIBALDI MONUMENT
Parco Gianicolo
VIA GARIBALDI
S. MARIA DELLA SCALA
VIC. BOL.
V. D. SCALA
VIC. BOLOGNA
VIC. SCALA
V. D. MATTONATO
VIC. LEO
V. D. PANIERI
VIC. CEDRO
S. EGIDIO
PAGLIA
PASSAGIATA DEL GIANICOLO
#115 & 870
VIA PORTA SAN PANCRAZIO
SAN PIETRO IN MONTORIO (BRAMANTE'S TEMPIETTO)
SANTA MARIA IN TRASTEVERE
V. GOFFREDO MAMELI
PORTA SAN PANCRAZIO & ITALIAN UNIFICATION MUSEUM
VIA GARIBALDI
FONTANA DELL' ACQUA PAOLA
#115
ITALIAN INDEPENDENCE WAR MEMORIAL
TRA
#870
CITY WALLS
VIA GARIBALDI
#115
VIA LUCIANO

1. Isola Tiberina & Tiber River
2. Piazza in Piscinula
3. Via dell'Arco de' Tolomei
4. Via dei Salumi
5. Vicolo dell'Atleta
6. Church of Santa Cecilia
7. Walking Along Via dei Genovesi
8. Viale di Trastevere
9. Via della Lungaretta
10. Piazza di Santa Maria in Trastevere
11. Church of Santa Maria in Trastevere

lent of a leafy backyard. An *attico con terrazzo* (penthouse with a terrace) is every Roman's dream.

Glancing up, you'll notice an elegantly restored, freshly painted **tower** incorporated into the apartments. In medieval times, the city skyline had 300 of these towers (about 50 survive). Each noble family competed for the tallest one until, in about 1250, city authorities got fed up and had them all lopped off. Later (mainly Baroque) construction incorporated most of the remaining "stumps," and you can still see these remnants of medieval Rome all over the old center. Incorporating old structures into new ones was always considered more economical and practical than demolishing and starting again from scratch. In the Middle Ages, Rome had re-

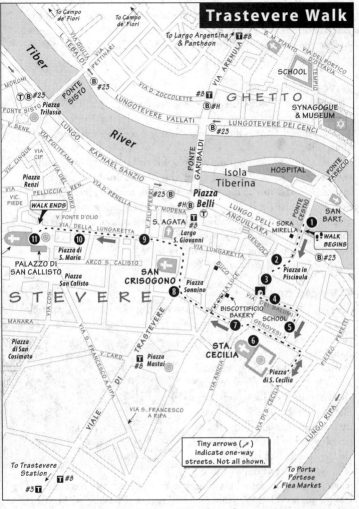

gressed to being a big village; any idea of town planning was lost until the Renaissance.

Now look down the lane ahead of you, where there's a low-arched passageway. Lots of aristocratic buildings were connected by these elevated passages. Imagine herds of sheep shuffling through here in medieval times

while smoke billowed from the windows and doors of homes that lacked chimneys.

• *Continue on, passing through the arched lane. Turn left immediately, and walk a few steps along...*

❹ Via dei Salumi

This is called "Cold Cuts Street." Here (as elsewhere in Mediterranean countries), many streets were named after the businesses that clustered there. The streets—rarely paved—were clogged by shop stalls.

The red-brown building on your right (pretty ugly unless you're a fascist) is a **school from the Mussolini era.** The fascist leader believed in the classical motto *mens sana in corpore sano* ("a healthy mind in a healthy body"), and loved being seen fencing, boxing, swimming, and riding. He endowed school buildings with lots of gyms. It's still a school, and you might hear the cheerful noise of kids pouring out the windows.

• *After passing the school, turn right again, heading up...*

❺ Vicolo dell'Atleta

This little "Alley of the Athlete" is too narrow for cars—only people and a few scooters. Notice how quiet this makes things. Check out the latest fashions in underwear hanging out to dry. Apartments in Rome tend to be quite small, and electricity is more expensive than in the US, so few have clothes dryers. The small apartments also explain why young people tend to hang around outside in streets like this.

Notice the variety of doorways in this unplanned community. Some structures have ancient fragments recycled ingloriously into medieval buildings. Halfway down the alley on the right (at #14) is a restaurant that, a thousand years ago, was a **synagogue.** Find the Hebrew faintly inscribed on the base of the columns of the exposed brick structure (on the upper floor). A large part of Rome's Jewish community, the most ancient outside Palestine, lived in Trastevere until the popes moved them into the ghetto on the other side of the river in the 1500s.

• *Continue, turning left on Via dei Genovesi, then go right on Via di S. Cecilia to reach Piazza di Santa Cecilia. Here you'll find the Church of Santa Cecilia by passing through the impressive, white, Neoclassical structure that encloses the convent courtyard. Enter the courtyard and take a moment to sit by the fountain.*

❻ Church of Santa Cecilia

The church stands on a spot where Christians have worshipped as far back as the second and third centuries. Trastevere had early

Christian churches like Santa Cecilia because foreigners tended to settle here, including early Christians from Greece and Judaea.

Notice the church's eclectic exterior. Its mismatched columns were recycled from pagan temples. The typical medieval bell tower sports an 18th-century facade.

The church was supposedly built atop what was St. Cecilia's home. Cecilia was a pagan Roman (third century) from a wealthy family, who converted to Christianity in a time when Christians were intensely persecuted. Cecilia revealed her faith to her pagan husband only on their wedding night and told him of her aspiration to remain chaste (uh-oh...). An angel appeared to reason with the frustrated groom. Once converted, he devoted himself to carrying out Christian burials in the catacombs, until he himself was killed. Cecilia was soon condemned as well. The Romans tried unsuccessfully for three days to suffocate her with steam in her bath to make it appear accidental. They finally lost patience and beheaded her.

Before her death, Cecilia had used her lavish house to host Mass, as churches were forbidden. She bequeathed the house to the neighborhood community, and it's been a place of worship since then. A church was built here soon after her death, although the structure we see today dates mostly from the early ninth century and was extensively restored in the 18th century.

Inside the Church: If the church is open, head inside and enjoy the cool elegance of the white-and-gold nave.

Cecilia is the patron saint of musicians and singers (notice the fine organ on the left). Legend says she sang at her own wedding. Ever since, the church named for her has been popular for weddings. Of Rome's 40 medieval churches, many have two-year waiting lists for weekend weddings. Most young Roman couples favor the more sober elegance of medieval churches over Baroque, which they dismiss as *troppo pesante*—"too heavy." (On the other hand, there's nothing understated about the typical Italian wedding gown.)

The white-marble **canopy** above the altar (dating from the 1200s) is by Arnolfo di Cambio. Its innovative fusion of Roman styles (realistic statues) and French Gothic architecture (pinnacles and rows of flamboyant "flames") shows that the artist knew his classics and had also been to Paris.

The **mosaic** in the apse dates from the ninth century. It shows Pope Paschal—the man who built the current church—on the left; he holds a little model of it in his hands. His square halo (the "halo of the living") signifies that he was alive when the mosaic was made.

The church's highlight is the evocative **statue of St. Cecilia** by Stefano Maderno (in the case below the altar). In the 1600s, Cecilia's long-buried remains were discovered. When her tomb was opened, Maderno himself was present. He claimed, along with other bystanders, to have seen her body perfectly preserved for an unforgettable instant before it turned to dust. He created this touching statue from his memory of that scene.

It shows Cecilia as she would have appeared just after her martyrdom. She lies with her face turned and hidden, the violence of her death suggested only by the gash in her neck. She died professing her faith. Notice the position of her fingers—showing three fingers on one hand (including the thumb, which Italians today also count with) and one on the other. Three in one—the oneness of the Trinity.

Maderno's statue—though made of hard stone—captures the limpness of Cecilia's lifeless body and the softness of her intricately folded robe and head scarf. It's typical of Counter-Reformation art—charged with great emotional impact to enhance faith.

More Church Sights: The **crypt** contains the so-so remains of a complex of ancient buildings (an *insula* or apartment house) that includes what is thought to have been Cecilia's house (a *domus*). The series of rooms is extensive but pretty bare. You'll see ancient fragments of sarcophagi with inscriptions and early Christian iconography (crosses, shepherds, anchors, doves). You'll walk over patches of original mosaic floors. One room was used for grain storage; you'll see holes in the floor where the grain was stored (entrance at the bookstore located to the left as you enter the church).

The **choir loft** *("Il Coro"),* where cloistered nuns would view the Mass while hidden behind a screen, contains a fragmentary but extraordinary Last Judgment fresco painted by Pietro Cavallini, a contemporary of Giotto (c. 1300). Scholars debate who influenced whom: Giotto or Cavallini. But there's no debate that the art here shows cutting-edge realism in the expressive faces of the apostles who sit believably in their chairs (accessed from outside the church through a doorway to the left of the facade; press the buzzer, and the sisters will let you in). If you're here at 18:00 on a Wednesday, you're welcome to read the Lectio Divina with the nuns.

• *Leaving the church, backtrack left, and take the first left onto Via dei Genovesi. From here we'll walk straight along this street several blocks to the busy boulevard of Viale di Trastevere.*

❼ Walking Along Via dei Genovesi

This is one of Trastevere's main streets, yet it's barely wide enough for a single car (as you'll notice whenever you have to step aside to let one pass). Buildings, people, and cars compete for the precious little available space. Strolling here, you'll understand why the Italian language has no word for "privacy" (they use our word and roll the *r*). Reading a letter on the Metro attracts a crowd. If someone has a fight (or a particularly good orgasm), the entire neighborhood knows. Young lovers with no place to go are adept at riding *motorini*...while parked.

As you walk, you'll pass the back side of the Mussolini-era school we saw earlier. Looking to the right, you'll see the low arch we walked under near Via dei Salumi.

After another 100 yards or so, detour right at Via della Luce. Walk a half-block to #21 (on the right) and pop into **Biscottificio Artigiano Innocenti,** a traditional cookie-and-pastry bakery that's been here since the 1940s. In the face of modern efficiency, humble Stefania Innocenti, who was "artisanal" long before it was cool, continues to bake the seasonal cookies that Italians love to eat.

• *Return to Via dei Genovesi, turn right, and continue straight ahead to where it meets a busy street.*

❽ Viale di Trastevere

The wide, modern boulevard called Viale di Trastevere bisects Trastevere, which was otherwise spared most of the demolishing and rebuilding suffered by other traditional neighborhoods when Rome became the capital of a united Italy in 1870.

Across the street, notice the four big, red columns on the facade of the venerable Basilica di San Crisogono (fifth century). Also notice the convenient #8 tram that passes along Viale di Trastevere. It can take you back to Largo Argentina or Piazza Venezia after our tour is over.

• *Cross to the other side of Viale di Trastevere and turn right, then left into the square called Largo San Giovanni de Matha. Pass by the textbook Baroque facade of the faded yellow church (Sant'Agata) and continue along...*

TRASTEVERE

❾ Via della Lungaretta

Here you'll notice a change in atmosphere—the quiet, mystical charm of the first part of your walk has given way to livelier, more colorful, more touristy (and higher-rent) surroundings.

A small crafts market is often open along here, and street-corner artists display their work. You'll pass lots and lots of restaurants and boutiques and swim amid a sea of strolling people—tourists and locals alike.
• *Walk several blocks until Via della Lungaretta opens up into the big square. Take a seat on the fountain steps.*

❿ Piazza di Santa Maria in Trastevere

You're in the heart of the neighborhood. Piazza di Santa Maria in Trastevere—in the shadow of the big brick bell tower of the Church of Santa Maria in Trastevere—is the district's most important meeting place. With its broad and inviting steps, the 17th-century fountain was actually designed to be the "sofa" of the neighborhood. During major soccer games, a large screen is set up here so that everybody can share in the tension and excitement. At other times, children gather here with a ball and improvise matches of their own (one reason for the window grates).
• *Dominating the square is the...*

⓫ Church of Santa Maria in Trastevere

One of Rome's oldest church sites, this building stands where early Christians worshipped illegally in a home until the year 313. It was made a basilica—probably the first church in Rome dedicated to the Virgin Mary—in the fourth century, when Christianity was legalized. The tower survives from the 12th century, when the entire church was rebuilt.

Step into the portico (the covered area just outside the door). It's decorated with ancient stone fragments, some from the earlier church. Filled with early Christian symbolism such as the dove and olive branch, many of these stones were lids to burial niches from catacombs. In one fragment (just left of the church door), notice how early Christians prayed with both hands raised, as evangelical Christians do today.

TRASTEVERE

Now go inside. Make a U-turn left (just around the column), and look up to find a gold-and-white **plaque** on the wall dedicated to "Fons Olei." This "fountain of oil" refers to a small petroleum deposit discovered here in 30 BC. The black liquid was almost magical in its ability to power lamps and was incorporated into the lore of this church.

Grab a pew. Most of what you see dates from around the 12th century, although the granite columns are from ancient Roman buildings. Later architects tried hard to match them, but notice how the capitals are mismatched (some have tiny pagan heads of Egyptian gods), and the shorter columns have taller bases. The ancient basilica floor plan (and ambience) survives. The intricate coffered ceiling has an image of Mary in the center that's painted on copper.

Approach the main altar (on the left side) for a closer look at the fine mosaics in the apse. Pop a coin in the box to light them.

The central scene is one of the few surviving examples of an early medieval mosaic (8th-10th century) in Rome. It's rich in symbolism. Christ and Mary sit side by side, enthroned in majesty. They wear rich gold robes, and Mary has a crown. Notice the stature Mary is given. Tour guides claim this is the first mosaic to show her at the throne with Jesus in heaven. He has his arm around his mother as if introducing her to us. Christ's almond eyes and the elaborate folds in the robes show the influence of Byzantine icons. Flanking Christ and Mary are early bishops of Rome, including the first one, St. Peter (in gray). Beneath them, the row of sheep is not just any flock—it represents Jesus in the middle (marked by a halo with a cross in it) and the 12 apostles. Sitting on the ground below all of these mosaics is the throne-like chair of the bishop, giving legitimacy to the Church leadership.

The mosaic panels below the sheep show scenes from the life of Mary. These more "modern" mosaics (from the late 1300s, also by Cavallini, who did the Last Judgment at Santa Cecilia) are impressively realistic and expressive, yet predate the Renaissance by a hundred years. The first panel (far left, facing out from the curved apse) shows Mary (in the lower corner of the scene) as a baby. A servant prepares to bathe her, but first she checks the temperature of the water with her hand, introducing an element of human tenderness almost unheard of in medieval art. The next panel shows the angel arriving to announce Jesus' coming to Mary (and Mary asking, "Who, me?!"). Next, Mary reclines, having just given birth

Soccer: The National Obsession

One of Rome's most local "sights" is a soccer match. Winston Churchill said that Italians lose wars as if they were soccer matches and soccer matches as if they were wars. Soccer (calcio) is the national obsession; Everyone, regardless of age or social class, is

an expert, quick with an opinion on a coach's lousy decision or a referee's unprofessional conduct. Fans love to insult officials: A favorite is *"arbitro cornuto!"*—the referee is a cuckold (i.e., his wife sleeps around).

Rome has a special passion for soccer. It has two teams, Roma (representing the city) and Lazio (the region), and the rivalry is fanatical. When Romans are introduced, they ask each other, *"Laziale o romanista?"* The answer can compromise a relationship. Both Roma (jersey: yellow and red; symbol: she-wolf) and Lazio (jersey: light blue and white; symbol: imperial eagle) claim to be truly Roman. Lazio is older (founded in 1900), but Roma has more supporters. Lazio is supposed to be more upper-class, Roma more popular, but the social division is blurred.

The most eagerly awaited sporting event of the year is the derby, when the two teams fight it out at the Olympic Stadium (Stadio Olimpico). All of Italy acknowledges that team spirit is most fervent in Rome. Fans prepare months in advance, and on

to Jesus in a stable, while shepherds arrive to admire him. Next comes the Three Kings, who kneel to adore the babe, followed by the presentation of the child Jesus in the temple. The final scene shows Mary's eternal sleep (not "death"). The gold mosaic backgrounds show buildings that, while not fully realistic, are a good step toward accurate 3-D representation.

The incredibly expensive 13th-century **floor** is a fine example of Cosmati mosaic work. The Cosmati family specialized in piecing together different colors of stone (in this case, made with marble scavenged from Roman ruins) to make intricate interlacing patterns of geometric shapes: circles, squares, triangles, and diamonds. The Cosmatis' work set the tone for the pavement in the rest of the church.

As you leave, spend a moment with **St. Anthony** (the statue in the back corner of the nave, opposite the "Fons Olei" plaque). He was a favorite of the poor and is inundated with prayer requests on scraps of paper. The Community of St. Egidio operates from this

TRASTEVERE

the day of the match they fill the entire stadium with team colors, flags, banners, and smoke candles.

Witty slogans on banners work like dialogues: A Roma banner proclaimed, "Roma: Only the sky is higher than you." The Lazio banner replied, "In fact, the sky is blue and white" (like its team colors). The exchange revealed that there had been a Lazio informer on the Roma side, which traumatized Roma fans for weeks. Tourists go to a match  more for the action in the stands than the action on the field—for some, it's the most Roman of all experiences.

Both teams call the Olympic Stadium home, so you can catch a game most weekends from September to May (Metro line A to Flaminio, then catch tram #2 to the end of the line, Piazza Mancini, and cross the bridge to the stadium). If you're coming from Termini train station, take bus #910; from the Vatican, take bus #32 from Piazza Risorgimento.

It's best to buy tickets in advance (which is often the only way to get them) through the teams' official websites, at www. sportsevents365.com, or via resale websites such as StubHub.

church. They feed the local poor and care for young drug addicts. Each Christmas they take out all the pews, move in tables and chairs, and put on a huge dinner for those in need.

• *From here, enjoy exploring Rome's most colorful district. Saunter around the streets to the left of the church as you leave. The farther you venture from the square, the less touristy and more rustic the neighborhood becomes. Wandering the back lanes and pondering the earthy enthusiasm people seem to have for life here, I can imagine that bygone day when proud Trastevere locals would brag that they never crossed the river.*

To get back to downtown Rome by public transportation, backtrack along Via della Lungaretta to Viale di Trastevere to catch tram #8. Or keep going straight down Via della Lungaretta to reach Ponte Cestio and Isola Tiberina, where our Trastevere walk began.

Extending the Walk

If you'd like to soak up expansive views of the city and interesting architecture, you can extend this walk from Piazza di Santa Maria up to the **Gianicolo Hill park** and viewpoint (see page 107).

Or, to cap off your Trastevere stroll with one more sight, visit **Villa Farnesina,** a Renaissance villa decorated by Raphael (see page 104 for a self-guided tour). To get there, face the Church of Santa Maria in Trastevere and leave the piazza by walking along the right side of the church, following Via della Paglia to Piazza di S. Egidio. Turn right and exit the piazza near the church—you'll be on Via della Scala. Follow through the Porta Settimiana, where the street changes names to Via della Lungara. On your right, you'll pass John Cabot University. Look for a white arch that reads Accademia dei Lincei (#230). The villa is through this gate.

Another way to extend this walk is to head to the river, cross the Ponte Sisto pedestrian bridge, and make your way to Campo de' Fiori, where my **Heart of Rome Walk** begins (see that chapter for details).

ANCIENT APPIAN WAY TOUR

Via Appia Antica

The wonder of its day, the Appian Way was the largest, widest, fastest road ever, called the "Queen of Roads." Begun in 312 BC and named after Appius Claudius Caecus (a Roman official), it connected Rome with Capua (near Naples), running in a straight line for much of the way and ignoring the natural contours of the land. Eventually, this most important of Roman roads stretched 430 miles to the port of Brindisi—the gateway to the East—where boats sailed for Greece and Egypt. Twenty-nine such roads fanned out from Rome. Just as Hitler built the autobahn system in anticipation of empire maintenance, the expansion-minded Roman government realized the military and political value of good roads.

The Hollywood image of the Appian Way as lined with the crucified bodies of Spartacus and his slave rebels is only partially accurate. While Spartacus was killed in battle, not crucified, historians do believe that after his defeat in 71 BC, 6,000 slaves were crucified on crosses spaced about 30 yards apart along the length of the Appian Way—a distance of more than 100 miles. As a warning to other slaves, their bodies were left to hang for several months. Imagine the eerie welcome this provided visitors arriving in Rome.

After the Christian faith permeated Rome, the Appian Way became a popular underground burial place for Christians. It later falsely entered Romantic lore as a place where Christians hid from persecution. Today the road and the landscape around it are preserved as a cultural park.

The Appian Way offers three attractions: the road itself, with its ruined monuments; the two major Christian catacombs; and a peaceful atmosphere (a respite from the city). Be aware that the road today is quite treacherous in spots—very narrow, with almost no shoulder, and busy with traffic. Following this tour's route helps you avoid the worst of the traffic, making it pleasant for strolling or biking.

Orientation

Length of This Tour: Budget five hours to get to and from the Appian Way, to walk or bike the stretch of sights, and to visit one of the catacombs.

When to Go: Visit in the morning or midafternoon (note that the Catacombs of San Callisto shut down from 12:00 to 14:00), but don't go too late; the last tours at both catacombs depart at 16:30 (and other sights close as early as 16:00). All the recommended sights are open on Tuesday, Thursday, Friday, and Saturday. On Monday several sights are closed, including the Tomb of Cecilia Matella and the Circus and Villa of Maxentius. On Wednesday, the Catacombs of San Callisto and the pedestrian path through the park are closed. On Sunday, the Catacombs of San Sebastiano are closed, but the Appian Way is closed to most car traffic, making it a great day for walking or biking (see "Bike Rental," later).

Getting There: You can reach the Appian Way by taxi or public transportation. This chapter's map shows bus stops, though locations can change. There are only a few places to buy bus tickets on the Appian Way (including the TI and the shop at the Catacombs of San Sebastiano)—have one in hand for your return trip.

A **taxi** will get you from Rome to the starting point of our tour, the Tomb of Cecilia Metella, for about €20. However, to return by taxi, you'll have to summon one (either over the phone or with the MyTaxi app); there are no taxi stands on the Appian Way.

To ride **public transit** to the Tomb of Cecilia Metella, take Metro line A to the Colli Albani stop, then take bus #660 (2/hour) 15 minutes to the last stop—Cecilia Metella/Via Appia Antica (at the intersection of Via Cecilia Metella and Via Appia Antica). Alternatively, it's a bumpy ride on bus #118 from downtown Rome to the Catacombs of San Sebastiano; from there, walk 500 yards (less than 10 minutes) south to the Tomb of Cecilia Metella. Ask at a TI for the latest information on where to catch the #118, as its route changes.

Returning to downtown Rome is easy by bus. Bus #118 is the quickest option from the end of our tour. It runs along the Appian Way at the road's north end; catch it at the Domine Quo Vadis Church. It stops at Circo Massimo Metro station, near the Forum and Palatine Hill, as well as other downtown locations. Bus #218 is another option. Hop on at

Sebastiano vs. Callisto

Which of the two catacombs is the best? They're actually quite similar. Both include a half-hour tour that takes you underground to see the niches where early Christians were buried (but no bones). Both have some faded frescoes and graffiti with Christian symbols. Both have small chapels and a few memorial statues. Most people pick one catacomb to visit, and either will fit the bill.

I lean slightly in favor of San Callisto, but only because of its historical importance, not because it's inherently more interesting. San Sebastiano tends to be less crowded, is historic in its own right (as the relics of Sts. Peter and Paul and St. Sebastian were kept here), and—most significantly—offers an experience with a bit more variety, since it also includes several remarkably well-preserved pagan Roman tombs and a Baroque church with a bust by Gian Lorenzo Bernini.

(Note that the **Catacombs of Priscilla**—more intimate and less crowded than these two more famous ones—can be found at the other end of town, northeast of the Villa Borghese Gardens; see page 90.)

Domine Quo Vadis Church or the west entrance of the Catacombs of San Callisto and ride to San Giovanni in Laterano, where you can pick up the Metro.

Tomb of Cecilia Metella: €5, includes entry to the Villa dei Quintili, valid for two consecutive days, free first Sun of month Oct-March and a few days in high season (check online); open Tue-Sun 9:00-19:00, closes earlier Oct-March, closed Mon year-round, last entry one hour before closing; tel. 06-3996-7700, www.coopculture.it.

Circus and Villa of Maxentius: Free but donations accepted, Tue-Sun 10:00-16:00, closed Mon, www.villadimassenzio.it.

Catacombs of San Sebastiano: €8, includes 35-minute tour, 2/hour; Mon-Sat 10:00-17:00, closed Sun and Dec; tel. 06-785-0350, www.catacombe.org.

Catacombs of San Callisto: €8, includes 30-minute tour, at least 2/hour; Thu-Tue 9:00-12:00 & 14:00-17:00, closed Wed and late Jan-late Feb; tel. 06-513-0151, www.catacombe.roma.it.

Domine Quo Vadis Church: Free, daily 8:00-19:00, until 20:00 in summer, tel. 06-512-0441.

Visitor Information: The **Via Appia Antica TI** near Domine Quo Vadis Church is a resource for the entire park, which stretches east and south of the visit outlined here (daily 9:30-18:00, rents bikes, sells good map, Via Appia Antica 58, tel. 06-513-5316, www.parcoappiaantica.it).

The archaeological site of **Capo di Bove** has a small info center that sits deep in a tranquil, inviting garden surrounding an ancient thermal complex (daily 9:00-18:30, until 17:00 in winter, good place for discreet picnic, clean WCs, Via Appia Antica 222, tel. 06-780-6686).

Bike Rental: Some may find the old paving stones too bumpy for biking. But if you'd like to try it, the best day for biking is Sunday, when the Appian Way is closed to traffic (though a few cars with special permission still sneak through). You can rent a bike from either end of my tour route. **Appia Antica Caffè** is near the tour's start, at the Tomb of Cecilia Metella (€4/1 hour, €7/2 hours, €10/3 hours, daily 9:00-sunset, closes earlier Mon, Via Appia Antica 175, on corner with Via Cecilia Metella, tel. 06-8987-9575, www.appiaanticacaffe.it). You can also rent a bike at the **Via Appia Antica TI,** near the church, and cycle to the beginning of the tour (€4/hour, €16/day, RS%—20 percent with "rickstevesrome" code at checkout; see "Visitor Information," earlier). I don't recommend biking all the way from downtown; it's a long ride with heavy traffic.

Services: Free WCs are at the San Sebastiano and San Callisto catacombs and at Capo di Bove, and WCs for paying customers are at the Tomb of Cecilia Metella and the Appia Antica Caffè. There are several fountains along the way for refilling water bottles.

Eating: Appia Antica Caffè (see "Bike Rental," above) makes big salads and abundant sandwiches and has a shaded, restful seating area in back; tucked even farther back in their garden is a fine little *gelateria* (closed off-season). If you've brought your own food, great picnic spots are just a half-mile farther south from here.

Several pricey restaurants are along the stretch between the Catacombs of San Sebastiano and the Tomb of Cecilia Metella. The Catacombs of San Sebastiano has a handy café, and you might find a sandwich-and-drinks cart by there, too.

Starring: An old road, crumbling tombs, and underground Christian cemeteries.

OVERVIEW

Our tour begins near the Tomb of Cecilia Metella, at the far (southern) end of the sightseeing highlights, and works northward for a mile-and-a-half to Domine Quo Vadis Church, toward the center of Rome. Sightseers share the road with speeding drivers talking on mobile phones (except on Sundays, when it's off limits to most cars). We'll avoid the worst stretch—between the Catacombs of San Sebastiano and Domine Quo Vadis Church—by taking a pedestrian path through a quiet park that parallels the busy road (except on Wednesdays, when the path is closed).

The Tour Begins

• *From the Tomb of Cecilia Metella, head south (away from downtown) 200 yards, where you walk (or rattle your bike) over a stretch of the...*

Original Paved Road

Huge basalt stones formed the sturdy base of a road 14 feet across. In its heyday, a central strip accommodated animal-powered vehicles, and elevated sidewalks served pedestrians. The first section (near Rome) was perfectly straight and lined with tombs and funerary monuments.

Return the way you came, and as you near the entrance to the Tomb of Cecilia Metella, look for the original **mile marker III**, one of more than 400 such stones that counted the distance from Rome to Brindisi. Rome's leaders knew that a fine network of roads was key to expanding and administering the republic—and later the empire. This road, from c. 312 BC, kicks off the expansion period.

• *On the right, you can't miss the...*

Tomb of Cecilia Metella
(Mausoleo di Cecilia Metella)

This massive cylindrical tomb, one of the best preserved of the many tombs of prominent Romans that line the road, was built in the time of Augustus (c. 30 BC) for the daughter-in-law of Crassus, Rome's richest man. Faced with white travertine and situated on the crest of a hill, the tomb was an imposing sight. This grand tomb in the suburbs rivaled Augustus' own round mausoleum in the city center.

Since no one was allowed to be buried inside the city walls, the Appian Way was a popular place to have a tomb where everyone could see and admire it. Later, Christians were buried here, although not in tombs (they preferred to be buried underground). Picture a funeral procession passing under the pines and cypresses, past a long line of pyramids, private mini temples, altars, and tombs.

In the 1300s, the area was turned into a fortified compound for an aristocratic family. The circular tomb was used as a tower (notice the crenellation on top) and a wall continued across the

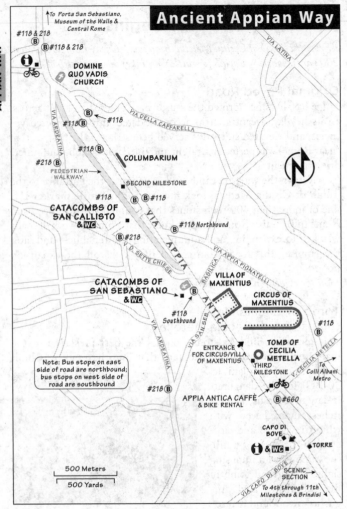

Ancient Appian Way

To Porta San Sebastiano,
Museum of the Walls &
Central Rome

VIA LATINA

B #118 & 218
B #118 & 218

DOMINE
QUO VADIS
CHURCH

VIA ARDEATINA

VIA DELLA CAFFARELLA

B #118
#118 B ← #118

#118 B

COLUMBARIUM

#218 B

PEDESTRIAN
WALKWAY

SECOND MILESTONE

#118
CATACOMBS OF
SAN CALLISTO
& WC

B #118

VIA APPIA

#118 Northbound
B

B #218

V. D. SETTE CHIESE

VIA APPIA PIGNATELLI

CATACOMBS OF
SAN SEBASTIANO
& WC

B

BASILICA

VILLA OF
MAXENTIUS

CIRCUS OF
MAXENTIUS

#118
Southbound

VIA APPIA ANTICA

#118
B

VIA ARDEATINA

VIA SAN SEB.

ENTRANCE
FOR CIRCUS/VILLA
OF MAXENTIUS

TOMB OF
CECILIA
METELLA

THIRD
MILESTONE

To
Colli Albani
Metro

V. CECILIA METELLA

#218 B

APPIA ANTICA CAFFÈ
& BIKE RENTAL

B #660

Note: Bus stops on east
side of road are northbound;
bus stops on west side of
road are southbound

CAPO DI
BOVE

& WC

TORRE

SCENIC
SECTION

500 Meters

500 Yards

VIA CAPO DI BOVE

To 4th through 11th
Milestones & Brindisi

N

street, enclosing the newly built church and other structures (since destroyed).

If you pay to go inside, you'll see the tomb's eerily hollow interior *(il sepolcro)*; a few statues of deceased Romans that once adorned tombs; and, in the cellar, a former paving-stone quarry with a preserved wagon-wheel groove.

• *About 200 yards farther along (north) from the tomb, on the right, are the ruins of the...*

Circus and Villa of Maxentius
(Circo e Villa di Massenzio)

This was the suburban home of the emperor who was eventually defeated by Constantine in AD 312. The main sight to see here

is a whole lot of nothing—that is, the expansive stretch of open space contained by this huge former chariot racetrack. You can walk between the entrance towers to the long central spine, and imagine chariots racing around it while 10,000 fans cheered.

Maxentius watched from the building rising up above the bleachers, where the chariots made their hairiest turn. At the far end of the 260-yard track is the triumphal arch under which the winner rode to receive his reward.

Also, just down the Appian Way from this circus is a square wall of ruins enclosing a modern building. Behind that modern building, you can glimpse the circular mausoleum of Maxentius' son, Romulus.

• *About 300 yards farther down the road (on the left) are the...*

▲▲Catacombs of San Sebastiano

This underground cemetery is named for the Christian soldier who was tied to a column and shot through with arrows because of his faith—a subject depicted by many artists throughout history. A guide takes you below ground to see burial niches, frescoes, and graffiti. It's said that the bodies of Peter and Paul were kept here for several decades in the third century. You'll also see the underground chapel (in its original location, but spiffed up in the 17th

century) where the relics of St. Sebastian were originally kept. But what distinguishes this from other catacombs experiences is the chance to also see some pagan Roman tombs, which provide an interesting contrast and a fascinating finale to the tour.

Besides the catacombs, the site also has a basilica (free) containing various relics. In the first chapel to the left are St. Sebastian's supposed remains, marked with a statue of an arrow-pierced corpse. On the opposite side of the nave, a chapel displays an arrow he was shot with, a section of the column he was tied to, and the (supposedly) original

Catacombs

The catacombs are burial places for (mostly) Christians who died in ancient Roman times. By law, no one was allowed to be buried within the walls of Rome. While pagan Romans were into cremation, Christians preferred to be buried (so that they could be resurrected when the time came). But land was expensive, and most Christians were poor. A few wealthy, landowning Christians allowed their properties to be used as burial places.

The 40 or so known catacombs are scattered outside the ancient walls of Rome. *Catacombe* means, literally, "near the quarry"—as some of these were dug into the exposed walls of existing quarries. From the first through the fifth centuries, Christians dug an estimated 375 miles of tomb-lined tunnels, with networks of galleries as many as five layers deep. The volcanic tuff that Rome sits atop—which is soft and easy to cut, but hardens when exposed to air—was perfect for the job. The Christians burrowed many layers deep for two reasons: to get more mileage out of the donated land, and to be near martyrs and saints already buried there. Bodies were wrapped in linen (like Christ's). Since they figured the Second Coming was imminent, there was no interest in embalming the body. They called this place a *dormitorio*—a "place to sleep" while awaiting the rapture. After each corpse was laid to rest, it was covered with a stone slab—though most of these are now long-gone, shattered by looters and vandals.

When Emperor Constantine legalized Christianity in AD 313, Christians had a new, interesting problem: There would be no more recently persecuted martyrs to bind them together and inspire them. Instead, the early martyrs and popes assumed more importance, and Christians began making pilgrimages to their burial places in the catacombs.

In the 800s, when barbarian invaders started ransacking the

footprints from the Domine Quo Vadis legend (explained later). Nearby stands a curly-haired bust of *The Savior (Il Salvatore)* by Bernini—his final creation, carved when he was in his eighties.

• *The stretch of the Appian Way beyond the Catacombs of San Sebastiano is the least interesting and most crowded (and dangerous). Avoid it by taking the pedestrian and bike path, which begins just past the Catacombs of San Sebastiano, at the intersection with Via delle Sette Chiese. To reach the path, go through the arch at #126. The quiet path parallels the Appian Way and takes you directly to the Catacombs of San Callisto. On Wednesdays, when the gate is closed, you'll have to stay straight on Via Appia Antica, being careful of traffic.*

▲▲Catacombs of San Callisto

Named for the first caretaker, St. Callixtus, this was the official cemetery for Rome's early Christians and the burial place of nine

tombs, Christians moved the relics of saints and martyrs to the safety of churches in the city center. For a thousand years, the catacombs were forgotten. In early modern times, they were excavated and became part of the Romantic Age's Grand Tour of Europe.

When abandoned plates and utensils from ritual meals were found, 18th- and 19th-century Romantics guessed that persecuted Christians hid out in these candlelit galleries. The popularity of this legend grew, even though it was untrue: By the second century, more than a million people lived in Rome, and the 10,000 early Christians didn't need to camp out in the catacombs. They hid in plain view, melting into obscurity within the city itself.

The underground tunnels, while empty of bones, are rich in early Christian symbolism, which functioned as a secret language. The dove represented the soul. You'll see it quenching its thirst (worshipping), with an olive branch (at rest), or happily perched (in paradise). Peacocks, known for their purportedly "incorruptible flesh," embodied immortality. The shepherd with a lamb on his shoulders was the "good shepherd," the first portrayal of Christ as a kindly leader of his flock. The fish was used because the first letters of these words—"Jesus Christ, Son of God, Savior"—spelled "fish" in Greek. The combination of an X and a P was actually a chi and a rho—the first two letters of CHRist's name in the Greek alphabet. And the anchor, a cross in disguise, symbolized how true believers felt anchored by their faith. Some fragments were stamped with the hallmark of the mason who created it. A second-century bishop had written on his tomb, "All who understand these things, pray for me." You'll see pictures of people praying with their hands raised—the custom at the time.

third-century popes, other bishops of Rome, and various martyrs. The most famous martyr was St. Cecilia, patron saint of music, a Roman noble who was killed for converting to Christianity. Her tomb is marked with a copy of a famous Maderno statue. For more on Cecilia and the statue, see page 352.)

Buy your ticket and wait for your language to be called. They move lots of people quickly. If one group seems ridiculously large (more than 50 people), wait for the next tour in English.

• *From the catacombs, continue along the pedestrian path another three-quarters of a mile, where you'll spill out at a busy three-way intersection. There you'll find the small...*

Domine Quo Vadis Church

The tiny ninth-century church (redone in the 17th) was built on the spot where Peter, while fleeing the city to escape Nero's persecution, saw a vision of Christ. Peter asked Jesus, "Lord, where are you going?" (*"Domine quo vadis?"* in Latin), to which Christ replied, "I am going to Rome to be crucified again." This miraculous sign gave Peter faith and courage and caused him to return to Rome. Inside the nave of the church, stumble over the stone marked with the supposed footprints of Jesus. You'll see a fresco of Peter on the left wall and one of Jesus on the right. A bust depicts Nobel Prize-winning Polish author Henryk Sienkiewicz, who wrote a historical novel that was the basis for the 1951 Hollywood movie *Quo Vadis*. The church is also called Santa Maria in Palmis.

• *The tour is over.* "Quo vadis, *pilgrim?*"

If you rented a bike at Appia Antica Caffè, near the beginning of the tour, pedal back to the starting point; from there you can return to Rome via bus #660 and the Metro.

Without a bike, catch a bus from the stop about 75 yards past Domine Quo Vadis Church (beyond the TI and across the street). Bus #118 makes several interesting stops on its way to the center (see "Sights on Bus #118 Route Back to Rome" at the end of this chapter); bus #218 goes to San Giovanni in Laterano, where you can change to the Metro.

For those with more energy, there's more to see, especially if you're renting a bike and want to get away from it all.

More of the Appian Way

Heading south away from downtown Rome and from the Tomb of Cecilia Metella, you'll find the best-preserved part of the Appian Way—quieter, less touristed, and lined with cypresses, pines, and crumbling tombs. It's all downhill after the first few hundred yards. On a bike, you'll travel over lots of rough paving stones (or dirt sidewalks) for about 30 minutes to reach a big pyramid-shaped ruin on its tiny base, and then five minutes more to the back side of Villa dei Quintili. Usually, you can't enter the villa from here, but you can admire the semicircular nymphaeum, or fake grotto. Enjoy a picnic, then turn around and pedal up that long hill to return your bike. Bus #118 also serves the Villa dei Quintili, stopping at the main entrance (far side) on the Via Appia Nuova.

Sights on Bus #118 Route Back to Rome

On the way back, about a half-mile from Domine Quo Vadis Church, the bus stops alongside Rome's ancient city wall at **Porta San Sebastiano**. Here, the **Museum of the Walls** (Museo delle Mura) offers an interesting look at Roman defenses and a chance to scramble along a stretch of the ramparts (free, Tue-Sun 9:00-14:00, closed Mon, Via di Porta San Sebastiano 18, bus stop: Porta San Sebastiano, www.museodellemuraroma.it). The Aurelian Wall (c. AD 270) was built in five years because of the threat of invasions. At 12 miles around, it was the biggest building project ever undertaken within the city of Rome.

A few minutes farther on, the bus stops near the **Baths of Caracalla** (described on page 120). Next, it makes a stop at the east end of the **Circus Maximus** (the Circo Massimo Metro stop is nearby). Assuming it is following its usual route, the bus continues on to Piazza Venezia before looping back to the Colosseum.

SLEEPING IN ROME

Choosing the right neighborhood in Rome is as important as choosing the right hotel. All of my recommended accommodations are in safe areas convenient to sightseeing. Most central hotels near **ancient Rome** are close to the Colosseum and Roman Forum. The most romantic ambience is in neighborhoods near the **Pantheon,** which encompass the Campo de' Fiori and the Jewish Ghetto. Hotels near **Vatican City** put St. Peter's and the Vatican Museums at your doorstep. The **Termini train station** neighborhood is handy for public transit and services, although not particularly charming. Finally, the bohemian **Trastevere neighborhood** is a good choice for living like a Roman when in Rome for a few days.

My recommendations include everything from €25 bunks to deluxe €350 doubles, although most of the hotels listed here cluster around €170. Cheaper doubles (around €100) are available, but I favor these pricier options because intense Rome is easier to enjoy with a welcoming oasis to call home. It's common for hotels in Rome to lower their prices 10-50 percent in the off-season, although prices at hostels and cheaper hotels won't fluctuate much. Room rates are lowest in sweltering August. Book any accommodations well in advance, especially if you'll be traveling during peak season (April-June and Sept-early Nov) or if your trip coincides with a major holiday or festival (see page 589).

I rank accommodations from **$** budget to **$$$$** splurge. To get the best deal, contact my family-run accommodations directly by phone or email. When you book direct, the owner avoids a roughly 20 percent commission and may be able to offer you a discount. For some travelers, short-term, Airbnb-type rentals can be a good alternative; search for places in my recommended hotel neighborhoods. For information and tips on rates and deals, making reservations, finding a short-term rental, and more, see the "Sleeping" section in the Practicalities chapter.

Sleeping at Convents: Rome has many convents that rent out rooms. At convents, the beds are twins and English is often in short supply, but the price is right. I've listed four nun-run places in this chapter: Casa Il Rosario (near Piazza Venezia), the expensive but divine Casa di Santa Brigida (near Campo de' Fiori), Casa per Ferie Santa Maria alle Fornaci (near the Vatican), and Suore di Santa Elisabetta (near Termini Station). For a longer list of convents, see the Church of St. Patrick's website (www.stpatricksamericanrome. org)—select "Resources" and then "Convent Accommodations."

NEAR ANCIENT ROME

This area is central, so you'll find these hotels are a short walk from the Colosseum and Roman Forum, as well as restaurants and shopping in the Monti district (see pages 391 and 430). All except Hotel Lancelot are within a 10-minute walk of the Cavour Metro stop.

$$$$ Hotel Lancelot is a comfortable refuge—a 60-room hotel with an elegant feel at a fair price. Located in a pleasant, low-key residential neighborhood a 10-minute stroll from the Colosseum, it's quiet and safe, with a shady courtyard, restaurant, bar, and tiny communal sixth-floor terrace. It's well-run by the Khan family, who serve a good €25 dinner—a tasty way to connect with your hotel neighbors and the friendly staff. No wonder it's popular with returning guests (family rooms, some view rooms, air-con, elevator, wheelchair-accessible, cheap parking, 10-minute walk behind Colosseum near San Clemente Church at Via Capo d'Africa 47, tel. 06-7045-0615, www.lancelothotel.com, info@lancelothotel.com). Faris and Lubna speak the Queen's English.

$$$$ Nerva Boutique Hotel is a snazzy slice of tranquility with 20 small, stylish, and often discounted rooms. It sits on a quiet, ideally located side street that faces the Roman Forum and backs onto the enjoyable Monti neighborhood (RS%—use code "RICKSTEVES," air-con, elevator, Via Tor de' Conti 3, tel. 06-678-1835, www.hotelnerva.com, info@hotelnerva.com, Antonio and Paolo).

$$$ Nicolas Inn Bed & Breakfast, a delightful little four-room place with thoughtful touches, is spacious and bright, and right on busy Via Cavour. Staying here can make you feel like you have caring friends in Rome (RS%, cash only, air-con, Via Cavour 295, mobile 328-555-3004, www.nicolasinn.it, info@nicolasinn.it).

Hotels & Restaurants near Ancient Rome

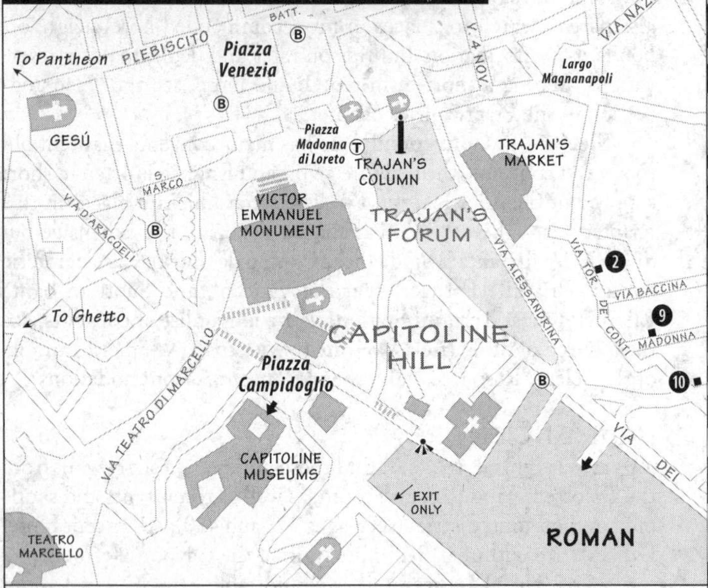
BATT.
VIA NAZIONALE
PLEBISCITO
To Pantheon
Piazza Venezia
V. 4 NOV.
Largo Magnanapoli
GESÚ
Piazza Madonna di Loreto
TRAJAN'S COLUMN
TRAJAN'S MARKET
S. MARCO
VIA D'ARACOELI
VICTOR EMMANUEL MONUMENT
TRAJAN'S FORUM
VIA ALESSANDRINA
VIA TOR DE CONTI
VIA BACCINA
MADONNA
To Ghetto
CAPITOLINE HILL
Piazza Campidoglio
VIA TEATRO DI MARCELLO
VIA DEI
CAPITOLINE MUSEUMS
EXIT ONLY
ROMAN
TEATRO MARCELLO

Accommodations

1. Hotel Lancelot
2. Nerva Boutique Hotel
3. Nicolas Inn B&B & Hotel Rosetta
4. Hotel Paba
5. Casa Il Rosario
6. Hotel Antica Locanda

Eateries

7. Barzilai Bistrot
8. Taverna Romana
9. Taverna dei Fori Imperiali
10. Alle Carrette Pizzeria
11. Trattoria da Valentino
12. Antico Forno ai Serpenti
13. Enoteca Cavour 313
14. Analemma & Pizzeria la Boccaccia
15. Fafiuché
16. Zia Rosetta
17. Fatamorgana Gelateria
18. Trattoria Luzzi
19. Rist. Pizzeria Naumachia
20. Li Rioni
21. Il Pentagrappolo
22. Hostaria da Nerone & Caffè dello Studente

$$$ Hotel Paba is homey, chocolate-box-tidy, and lovingly cared for by Alberta Castelli. It's just two blocks from the Forum. You'll take a vintage elevator to reach the seven rooms. Although some overlook busy Via Cavour, it's quiet enough (RS%, email reservations preferred, big beds, breakfast served in room, air-con, elevator, Via Cavour 266, second floor, tel. 06-4782-4497, www.hotelpaba.com, info@hotelpaba.com).

$$$ Casa Il Rosario is a peaceful, well-run Dominican convent renting 40 rooms with monastic simplicity to both pilgrims

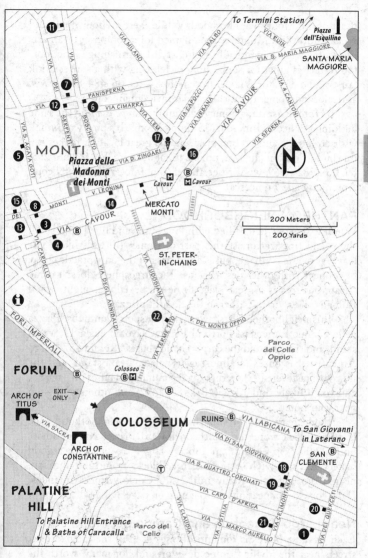

and tourists in a steep but pleasant corner of the Monti neighborhood. Doubles have two single beds that can be pushed together (RS%—use code "ricksteves," cheaper single rooms with shared bath, reserve several months in advance, some rooms with air-con and others with fans, elevator, small garden and rooftop terrace, midnight curfew, near bottom of Via Nazionale at Via Sant'Agata dei Goti 10, bus #40 or #170 from Termini, tel. 06-679-2346, www.casailrosarioroma.it, info@casailrosarioroma.it).

$$ Hotel Antica Locanda is a gem on a small street in the heart of the Monti neighborhood. While there are four floors and no elevator, the 15 rooms—each named for a composer or an artist—come with romantically rustic, stylish furnishings. The rooftop terrace is great for sunbathing or relaxing with a sunset drink (air-con, no elevator, Via del Boschetto 84, tel. 06-484-894, www. anticalocandaroma.it, anticalocandaroma@gmail.com).

$ Hotel Rosetta, a homey and family-run *pensione* in the same building as Nicolas Inn, rents 15 simple rooms. It's pretty minimal, with no lounge and no breakfast, but its great location makes it a fine budget option (air-con, up one flight of stairs, Via Cavour 295, tel. 06-4782-3069, www.rosettahotel.com, info@rosettahotel.com, Antonietta and Francesca).

PANTHEON NEIGHBORHOOD

Winding, narrow lanes filled with foot traffic and lined with small shops and tiny trattorias...this part of Rome still feels like a village. As in a real village, buses and taxis are the only practical way to connect with other destinations. The atmosphere doesn't come cheap, but this is a great place to be—especially at night, when Romans and tourists gather in the floodlit piazzas.

This neighborhood has two main transportation hubs: Piazza delle Cinque Lune (just north of Piazza Navona) has a TI, a taxi stand, and (just around the corner) handy buses #81 and #87. Largo Argentina has buses to almost everywhere, a taxi stand, and the tram to Trastevere (#8). Peruse my recommended buses on page 36, and you'll likely find a few (#81, #87, #492, and others) that stop near your hotel.

There are two **Co-op supermarkets** in the neighborhood. One is a half-block from the Pantheon toward Piazza Navona (daily until 22:00, Via Giustiniani 18b). A larger Co-op, with a good bakery and sandwich section, is three blocks from the Pantheon, near Largo Argentina (daily until 21:00, Corso Vittorio Emanuele II 42; for Co-op locations see the map on page 398).

Near Largo Argentina and Campo de' Fiori

Each of these places is romantically set deep in the tangled back streets near the idyllic Campo de' Fiori and, for many, worth the extra money. This area is connected to Termini Station by bus along Via Nazionale (#40 or #64). From the airport, consider taking the regional train to Trastevere Station and then the #8 tram to Largo Argentina.

$$$$ Relais Teatro Argentina, a six-room gem, is steeped in tasteful old-Rome elegance, but has all the modern comforts. It's cozy and quiet like a B&B and couldn't be more centrally located (air-con, 3 flights of stairs, breakfast in room or on balcony, Via

Hotels in the Pantheon Neighborhood

1. Relais Teatro Argentina
2. Arch Rome Suites
3. Casa di Santa Brigida
4. Hotel Smeraldo
5. Hotel Nazionale
6. Albergo Santa Chiara
7. Hotel Portoghesi
8. Hotel Due Torri

del Sudario 35, tel. 06-9893-1617, www.relaisteatroargentina.com, info@relaisteatroargentina.com, kind Paolo).

$$$ Arch Rome Suites, in a tranquil palace on the site of the former Baths of Agrippa, is just a few steps from the Pantheon and near the Jewish Ghetto. It rents 12 spacious, modern, and cozy rooms—some with balconies and views (family rooms, air-con, elevator, Via dell'Arco della Ciambella 19, tel. 06-4549-8947, www.archromesuites.it, info@archromesuites.com, friendly Marika and Omar).

$$$ Casa di Santa Brigida overlooks the elegant Piazza Farnese. With soft-spoken sisters gliding down polished hallways and pearly gates instead of doors, this lavish 20-room convent makes exhaust-stained Roman tourists feel like they've died and gone to heaven. You won't have a double bed or a TV in your room, but you can luxuriate in the inn's public spaces or on its lovely roof terrace (book well in advance, air-con, elevator, tasty €25 dinners—reserve ahead, roof garden, plush library, Via di Monserrato 54, tel. 06-6889-2596, www.brigidine.org, piazzafarnese@brigidine.org, many of the sisters are from India and speak English—pray you get to work with wonderful sister Gertrude).

$$$ Hotel Smeraldo, with 66 rooms, is clean and a reasonable deal in a good location. Sixteen of the rooms are in an annex across the street, but everyone has breakfast in the main building (air-con, elevator, roof terrace, midway between Campo de' Fiori and Largo Argentina at Via dei Chiavari 20, tel. 06-687-5929, www.smeraldoroma.com, info@smeraldoroma.com, Massimo and Walter).

Close to the Pantheon

These places are buried in the pedestrian-friendly heart of ancient Rome, each within about a five-minute walk of the Pantheon. They're an easy walk from many sights, but are a bit distant from the major public transportation arteries (though buses do run nearby). To get close, arrive and depart by taxi.

$$$$ Hotel Nazionale, a four-star landmark, is a 16th-century palace that shares a well-policed square with the Italian Parliament building. Its 100 rooms are accentuated by lush public spaces, fancy bars, a uniformed staff, and a marble-floored breakfast room. It's a big, stuffy hotel, but it's a worthy splurge if you want security, comfort, and the heart of Rome at your doorstep (RS%—use code "RICK," family rooms, air-con, elevator, Piazza Montecitorio 131, tel. 06-695-001, www.hotelnazionale.it, info@hotelnazionale.it).

$$$$ Albergo Santa Chiara, in the old center, is big, solid, and hotelesque. Flavia, Silvio, and their fine staff offer marbled elegance (but basic furniture) and all the hotel services. Its ample public lounges are dressy and professional, and its 96 rooms are quiet and spacious (RS%—use code "RICK," family rooms, air-con, elevator, behind the Pantheon at Via di Santa Chiara 21, tel. 06-687-2979, www.albergosantachiara.com, info@albergosantachiara.com).

$$$$ Hotel Portoghesi is a classic hotel with 27 colorful rooms in the medieval heart of Rome. It's peaceful, quiet, and comes with a delightful roof terrace—though you pay for the location (family rooms, breakfast on roof, air-con, elevator, Via dei Portoghesi 1, tel. 06-686-4231, www.hotelportoghesiroma.it, info@hotelportoghesiroma.it).

$$$ Hotel Due Torri, hiding out on a tiny quiet street, is beautifully located. It feels professional yet homey, with an accommodating staff, generous public spaces, and 26 rooms (the ones on upper floors are smaller but have views). While the location and lounge are great, the rooms are overpriced unless you score a discount (family rooms, air-con, elevator, a block off Via della Scrofa at Vicolo del Leonetto 23, tel. 06-6880-6956, www. hotelduetorriroma.com, info@hotelduetorriroma.com, Cinzia and her daughter Giorgia).

Near the Spanish Steps

$$$$ Hotel San Carlo is buried in the thick of Rome's bustling pedestrian-friendly "shopping triangle," close to the Spagna Metro stop. It has 47 rooms connected by a treehouse floor plan (RS%, air-con, elevator, Via delle Carrozze 92—see the "Dolce Vita Stroll" map on page 83, tel. 06-678-4548, www.hotelsancarloroma.com, info@hotelsancarloroma.com).

NEAR VATICAN CITY

Sleeping near the Vatican costs a little more, but some enjoy calling this relaxed, residential neighborhood home. The tree-lined streets are wider than in the historical center, so it feels less claustrophobic. Although it's handy to the Vatican, everything else is a long way away. Fortunately, it's well-served by public transit, especially the Metro (line A). Most of these listings are within a 10-minute walk of either the Cipro or Ottaviano Metro stops.

$$$$ Hotel Alimandi Vaticano, facing the Vatican Museums, is beautifully designed. Run by the Alimandi family (Nico and Germano), it features four stars, 24 spacious rooms, and all the modern comforts you can imagine (air-con, elevator, Viale Vaticano 99, tel. 06-3974-5562, www.alimandi.com, alimandivaticano@ alimandi.com).

$$$$ Hotel dei Consoli, family-run with 28 rooms, is a lesser value pleasantly located on a side street. Breakfast is served on its leafy rooftop terrace, with a view to St. Peter's—a nice way to start the day (RS%, air-con, elevator, Via Varrone 2D, tel. 06-6889-2972, www.hoteldeiconsoli.com, info@hoteldeiconsoli.com, friendly Laura and mom Amalia).

$$$$ Hearth Hotel, a block from the Vatican wall, has 22 small, modern, efficient, and characterless rooms (RS%—use code "rick steves," air-con, elevator, Via Santamaura 2, tel. 06-3903-8383, www.hearthhotel.com, info@hearthhotel.com).

$$$ Hotel Museum is located steps from the Vatican Museums and run by another branch of the entrepreneurial Alimandi family—Luca, Irene, and Barbara. It has 31 modest but comfortable rooms and large public spaces, including a piano lounge, pool table, and rooftop terrace where the grand buffet breakfast is

SLEEPING

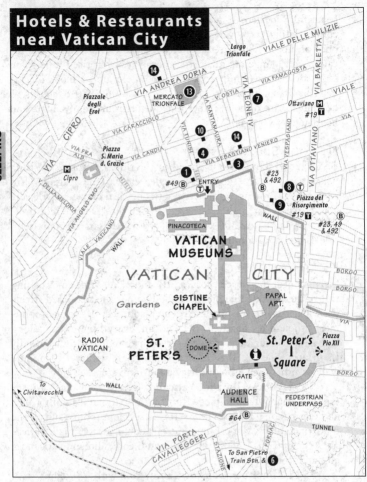

Hotels & Restaurants near Vatican City

served (family rooms, air-con, elevator, down the stairs directly in front of Vatican Museums, Via Tunisi 8, tel. 06-3972-3941, www. hotelmuseum.it, info@hotelmuseum.it).

$$ Casa Valdese is a well-managed, Protestant church-run hotel that's a good value and feels a bit institutional. Its 33 recently renovated—but basic—rooms come with the bonus of two breezy, communal roof terraces with incredible views (family rooms, air-con, elevator, Via Alessandro Farnese 18, Metro: Lepanto, tel. 06-321-5362, www.casavaldeseroma.it, reception@casavaldeseroma.it, Matteo).

$$ Casa per Ferie Santa Maria alle Fornaci is simple and efficient, housing pilgrims and secular tourists just a five-minute walk south of the Vatican in a dull, high-rise residential zone. Its 54 utilitarian rooms are mostly twin-bedded. Reserve at least three

SLEEPING

Accommodations
1. Hotel Alimandi Vaticano
2. Hotel dei Consoli
3. Hearth Hotel
4. Hotel Museum
5. Casa Valdese
6. To Casa per Ferie Rooms

Eateries & Other
7. Il Colibrì
8. L'Insalata Ricca & Duecento Gradi
9. Gelateria Old Bridge
10. Forno Feliziani
11. Tre Pupazzi
12. Vecchio Borgo
13. Mercato Trionfale
14. Supermarket (2)

months in advance (air-con, elevator; take bus #64 from Termini train station to San Pietro train station, then walk 100 yards north along Via della Stazione di San Pietro to Piazza Santa Maria alle Fornaci 27; or from the airport, take the train to Trastevere Station, then transfer to San Pietro Station; tel. 06-3936-7632, www. santamariafornaci.com, Carmine).

NEAR TERMINI STATION

While this neighborhood is not as atmospheric as other areas of Rome, the hotels near Termini train station are less expensive, and the Metro and buses link you easily to the rest of the city. My recommendations are within a 10-minute walk of the station (some are actually closer to the Repubblica Metro stop).

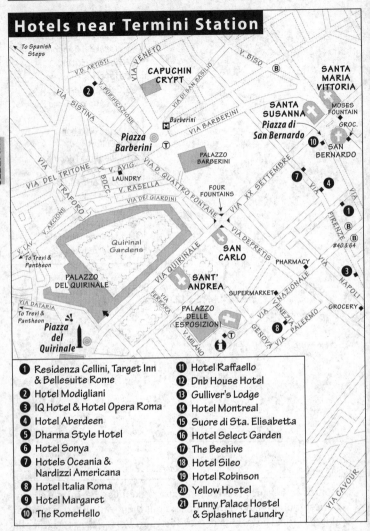

Hotels near Termini Station

To Spanish Steps

V.D. ARTISTI
VIA VENETO
V. BISO
V. SISTINA
V. PURIFICAZIONE
CAPUCHIN CRYPT
V. DI SAN BASILIO

SANTA MARIA VITTORIA

Barberini
VIA BARBERINI
Piazza Barberini
M Barberini
T
SANTA SUSANNA
Piazza di San Bernardo
MOSES FOUNTAIN
GROC.
SAN BERNARDO

VIA DEL TRITONE
V. AVIG.
V. BOCC.
VIA D. QUATTRO FONTANE
LAUNDRY
PALAZZO BARBERINI
FOUR FOUNTAINS
VIA XX SETTEMBRE
VIA TRAFORO
V. ARCIONE
V. RASELLA
VIA DEI GIARDINI
VIA DEPRETIS
VIA FIRENZE

V. LAV.
Quirinal Gardens
VIA QUIRINALE
SAN CARLO
PHARMACY
VIA NAZIONALE
VIA NAPOLI
GROCERY
B
#40 & 64
B

To Trevi & Pantheon
PALAZZO DEL QUIRINALE
SANT' ANDREA
SUPERMARKET
VIA DATARIA
VIA FERRATA
PALAZZO DELLE ESPOSIZIONI
VIA MILANO
V. VENEZIA
VIA GENOVA
VIA PALERMO
To Trevi & Pantheon
Piazza del Quirinale
T
i

① Residenza Cellini, Target Inn & Bellesuite Rome
② Hotel Modigliani
③ IQ Hotel & Hotel Opera Roma
④ Hotel Aberdeen
⑤ Dharma Style Hotel
⑥ Hotel Sonya
⑦ Hotels Oceania & Nardizzi Americana
⑧ Hotel Italia Roma
⑨ Hotel Margaret
⑩ The RomeHello

⑪ Hotel Raffaello
⑫ Dnb House Hotel
⑬ Gulliver's Lodge
⑭ Hotel Montreal
⑮ Suore di Sta. Elisabetta
⑯ Hotel Select Garden
⑰ The Beehive
⑱ Hotel Sileo
⑲ Hotel Robinson
⑳ Yellow Hostel
㉑ Funny Palace Hostel & Splashnet Laundry

West of the Station

Most of these hotels are on or near Via Firenze, a safe, handy, central, and relatively quiet street that's a 10-minute walk from Termini and the airport train, and two blocks beyond Piazza della Repubblica. The Defense Ministry is nearby, so you've got heavily armed guards watching over you all night.

The neighborhood is served by two Metro stops: Repubblica (line A), and Termini (intersection of lines A and B). Virtually all the city buses that rumble down Via Nazionale (#60, #64, #70, and the #40 express) take you to Piazza Venezia (near the Forum).

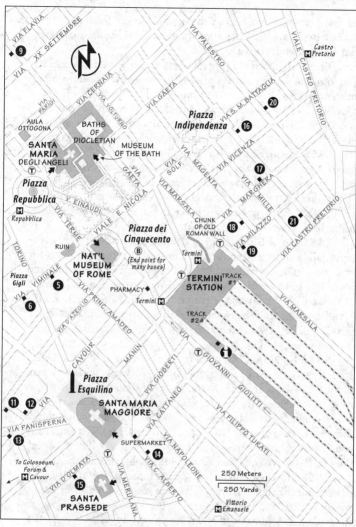

From Piazza Venezia, bus #64 (jammed with people and thieves) and the #40 express bus continue to Largo Argentina (for the Pantheon and Campo de' Fiori) and the Vatican area. Or, at Piazza Venezia, you can transfer to tram #8 to Trastevere (get off at first stop after crossing the river). Bus #H also runs directly to Trastevere, leaving from Piazza della Repubblica (on the northeast side of the square, near the entrance to Baths of Diocletian; none on Sun). If you're staying near the Santa Susanna and Santa Maria della Vittoria churches, buses from nearby Largo Santa Susanna (#62, #85, and #492) wind through the city center (leaving from the Bissolati stop; returning, the stop name is Largo S. Susanna). It's actually a pleasant downhill walk from these hotels to the Pantheon (about 25 minutes along Via Rasella and past the Trevi Fountain); save the bus for the uphill return journey.

These neighborhood supermarkets are all open daily until late (for locations see the map on page 410): **Co-op** (Via Nazionale 213, at the corner of Via Venezia), **Simply** (behind Santa Maria Maggiore Church at Piazza Santa Maria Maggiore 5B, in the basement), and **Sapori & Dintori** (downstairs from the inner atrium at Termini Station). There are many smaller grocery stores as well.

$$$$ Residenza Cellini feels like the guest wing of a gorgeous Neoclassical palace. It offers 13 rooms, "ortho/anti-allergy beds," four-star comforts and service, and a small, breezy terrace (RS%, breakfast extra, air-con, elevator, Via Modena 5, third floor, tel. 06-4782-5204, www.residenzacellini.it, info@residenzacellini. it; Barbara, Gaetano, and Donato).

$$$$ Hotel Modigliani, a delightful 23-room place, is energetically run in a clean, bright, minimalist yet in-love-with-life style that its artist namesake would appreciate. It has a vast and plush lounge, a garden, and a newsletter introducing you to each of the staff (RS%, air-con, elevator; from Tritone Fountain on Piazza Barberini, go 2 blocks up Via della Purificazione to #42; tel. 06-4281-5226, www.hotelmodigliani.com, info@hotelmodigliani. com, Giulia and Marco).

$$$$ IQ Hotel, in a modern blue building facing the Opera House, feels almost Scandinavian in its efficiency, without a hint of the Old World. It lacks charm, but more than compensates with modern amenities. Its 90 rooms are fresh and spacious, the roof garden comes with a play area and foosball, and vending machines dispense bottles of wine (RS%, family rooms, breakfast extra, air-con, elevator, cheap self-service laundry, gym, Via Firenze 8, tel. 06-488-0465, www.iqhotelroma.it, info@iqhotelroma.it, Diego).

$$$$ Hotel Aberdeen, which combines quality and friendliness, is warmly run by Annamaria, with support from sister Laura, cousin Cinzia, and staff member Costel. The 37 comfy rooms, on the ground floor and one floor up, are a fine value (RS%—use "Rick Steves reader reservations" link, family rooms, air-con, Via Firenze 48, tel. 06-482-3920, www.hotelaberdeen.it, info@hotelaberdeen. it).

$$$ Dharma Style Hotel spreads its 40 stylish rooms and suites across a few floors of a big palazzo, with elegant furnishings and room to breathe (RS%, family rooms, air-con, elevator, Via del Viminale 8, reception at #10, tel. 06-482-4460, www. dharmastylehotel.it, booking@dharmastylehotel.it).

$$$ Hotel Opera Roma, with contemporary furnishings and marble accents, boasts 15 spacious, modern, and thoughtfully appointed rooms. It's quiet and just a stone's throw from the Opera

House (air-con, elevator, Via Firenze 11, tel. 06-487-1787, www. hoteloperaroma.com, info@hoteloperaroma.com; Reza, Litu, and Federica).

$$$ Hotel Sonya offers 40 well-equipped rooms in varied sizes, a hearty breakfast, and decent prices (RS%—see the "Special Offers" page, family rooms, air-con, elevator, some rooms face the Opera House at Via Viminale 58, tel. 06-481-9911, www. hotelsonya.it, info@hotelsonya.it, Francesca and Simone).

$$$ Target Inn is a sleek, practical seven-room place next to Residenza Cellini (listed earlier). It's owned by the same people who run the recommended Target Restaurant nearby (air-con, elevator, Via Modena 5, third floor, tel. 06-474-5399, www.targetinn. com, info@targetinn.com).

$$$ Hotel Oceania is a peaceful slice of air-conditioned heaven. The 24 rooms are spacious, quiet, and tastefully decorated, and the elegant sitting room has a manor-house feel. Stefano runs a fine staff, serves wonderful coffee, provides lots of thoughtful extra touches, and works hard to maintain a caring family atmosphere (RS%—use code "RICKSTEVES," family rooms, elevator, TV lounge, Via Firenze 38, third floor, tel. 06-482-4696, www. hoteloceania.it, info@hoteloceania.it; Anna, Kira, and Roberto round out the staff).

$$ Bellesuite Rome offers seven small but nice rooms that are worth considering for the location—in the same fine building as Residenza Cellini and Target Inn (family rooms, air-con, elevator, Via Modena 5, third floor, tel. 06-9521-3049, www.bellesuiterome. com, mail@bellesuiterome.com, Martina).

$$ Hotel Nardizzi Americana, with a small rooftop terrace, 40 standard rooms, and a laid-back atmosphere, is another decent value (RS%—email reservation for discount, family rooms, aircon, elevator, Via Firenze 38, fourth floor, tel. 06-488-0035, www. hotelnardizzi.it, info@hotelnardizzi.it; friendly Stefano, Fabrizio, Mario, and Giancarlo).

$$ Hotel Italia Roma, in a busy and handy locale, is located safely on a quiet street next to the Ministry of the Interior. It has 35 modest but comfortable rooms plus four newer, more expensive "residenza" rooms on the third floor (RS%, family rooms, air-con, elevator, Via Venezia 18, just off Via Nazionale, tel. 06-482-8355, www.hotelitaliaroma.it, info@hotelitaliaroma.it; Andrea, Sabrina, Abdul, and Eleonora). They offer eight similar annex rooms across the street for the same price as the main hotel.

$$ Hotel Margaret offers few frills and 11 simple rooms at a fair price (family rooms, air-con, elevator, north of Piazza Repubblica at Via Antonio Salandra 6, fourth floor, tel. 06-482-4285, www.hotelmargaretrome.com, info@hotelmargaret.net).

¢ The RomeHello hostel is, as their slogan brags, "more than just a bed." Recently opened, it's a modern, quiet, and friendly hostel run with a mission to employ locals and provide a comfortable home for travelers, with about 200 beds in doubles, triples, and dorms. The public areas and guest kitchen feel like a computer-generated image of a hostel utopia (Via Torino 45, tel. 06-9686-0070, www.theromehello.com, ciao@theromehello.com).

Southwest of the Station

These good-value places cluster around the Basilica of Santa Maria Maggiore. Most are a five-minute walk from the Cavour Metro stop.

$$$ Hotel Raffaello, with its courteous and professional staff, offers 41 rooms in a grand 19th-century building on the edge of the Monti district. This formal hotel comes with generous public spaces and a breakfast room fit for aristocrats (family rooms, air-con, elevator, Via Urbana 3, tel. 06-488-4342, www.hotelraffaello.it, info@hotelraffaello.it).

$$ Dnb House Hotel, owned by the Oblate Sisters of Baby Jesus, is a spacious, pristine, and institutional-feeling hotel. The 38 high-ceilinged rooms are modest yet classy, and guests have access to a peaceful and leafy courtyard garden (RS%, air-con, elevator, expensive pay parking, Via Cavour 85A, tel. 06-4782-4414, www.dnbhotel.com, info@dnbhotel.com).

$$ Gulliver's Lodge has four colorful rooms on the ground floor of a large, secure building. Although it's on a busy street, the rooms are quiet. The public spaces are few, but in-room extras like Netflix make it a fine home base (RS%, price includes breakfast at nearby bar, cash only, air-con, Via Cavour 101, tel. 06-9727-3787, www.gulliverslodge.com, info@gulliverslodge.com, Stella and Gianluca).

$$ Hotel Montreal is a basic three-star place with 27 rooms on a big, noisy street a block southeast of Santa Maria Maggiore (RS%, family rooms, air-con, elevator, small garden terrace; Via Carlo Alberto 4, 1 block from Metro: Vittorio Emanuele, 3 blocks from Termini train station, tel. 06-445-7797, www.hotelmontrealroma.it, info@hotelmontrealroma.it, Fabrizio).

$ Suore di Santa Elisabetta is a heavenly Polish-run convent with a serene garden, roof terrace with grand views, and 37 rooms. All doubles have twin beds. Often booked long in advance, with such tranquility it's a super value (family rooms, cheaper rooms with shared bath, fans but no air-con, elevator for top floors, guest kitchen, Wi-Fi in lounge only, 23:00 curfew; a block southwest of Santa Maria Maggiore at Via dell'Olmata 9, Metro: Termini or Vittorio Emanuele; tel. 06-488-8271, www.csse-roma.com, select "Casa per ferie" for English, ist.it.s.elisabetta@libero.it).

SLEEPING

Sleeping Cheaply, Northeast of the Station

The cheapest beds in town are beyond Termini train station, to the northeast: Standing so that the tracks dead-end into your back, this neighborhood is to your right (Metro: Termini). The streets quiet down a block or so away from the station, and these hotels feel plenty safe. The **Splashnet** launderette is handy (offers full-service laundry, daily 8:30-23:00, just off Via Milazzo at Via Varese 33, tel. 06-4470-3523).

$$ Hotel Select Garden, a modern and comfortable 21-room hotel run by the cheery Picca family, boasts lively modern art adorning the walls and a beautiful lemon-tree garden. It's a safe, tranquil, and welcoming refuge just a couple of blocks from the train station (air-con, Via V. Bachelet 6, tel. 06-445-6383, www. hotelselectgarden.com, info@hotelselectgarden.com, Cristina and Maurizia).

$ The Beehive gives vagabonds—old and young—a cheap, clean, and comfy home in Rome. Thoughtfully and creatively run by friendly Americans Steve and Linda and their hardworking staff, the place offers a variety of great-value artsy-mod rooms. There's a mix of private rooms and less-expensive ones with shared baths, plus a dorm in the main building and more rooms in an annex a block away (air-con in some rooms, breakfast extra, private garden terrace, dinner several times weekly, cooking classes, 2 blocks from Termini train station at Via Marghera 8, tel. 06-4470-4553, www. the-beehive.com, info@the-beehive.com).

$ Hotel Sileo, with shiny chandeliers in dim rooms, is a homey little place renting 10 basic rooms. It's worn, but run with warmth by friendly Alessandro and Maria Savioli (who don't speak English) and their daughter Anna (who does); their other daughter, Stefania, painted the wall murals (RS%, air-con, elevator, Via Magenta 39, fourth floor, tel. 06-445-0246, www.hotelsileo.com, info@hotelsileo.com).

$ Hotel Robinson is just a few steps from the station, but tucked away from the commotion. Set on an interior courtyard, it has 20 small and simple rooms—handsomely decorated with dark-wood accents—that are a good value (RS%—includes breakfast and air-con when you pay in cash, apartment also available, Via Milazzo 3, tel. 06-491-423, www.hotelrobinsonrome.com, info@ hotelrobinsonrome.com).

¢ Yellow Hostel rents 220 beds to 18- through 45-year-olds only (I'd skip their 16 private rooms, which are basic and overpriced). Hip yet sane, it's well-run with fine facilities, including a café/late-night bar, and loads of activities (reserve online—no telephone reservations accepted, breakfast extra, elevator, no curfew, 6 blocks from station, just past Via Vicenza at Via Palestro 44,

#115 & 870
ANITA GARIBALDI MONUMENT
VILLA LANTE
To Vatican
VILLA FARNESINA
VIA RIARI
PALAZZO CORSINI
L. FARNESINA

100 Meters
100 Yards

#115 & 870
GIANICOLO
BOTANICAL GARDENS
VIA CORSINI
PORTA SETTIMIANA
LUNGARA
VIA

Piazza Garibaldi
GIUSEPPE GARIBALDI MONUMENT
Parco Gianicolo
N
VIA GARIBALDI
S. MARIA DELLA SCALA
VIC. BO.
10
8
VIC. BOLOGNA
VIC. SCALA
V. D. MATTONATO
V. D. PANIERI
VIC. LEO.
7
6
VIC. CEDRO
S. EGIDIO

PASSAGGIATA DEL GIANICOLO
PASSAGGIATA DEL GIANICOLO
#115 & 870
#115 & 870
VIA PORTA SAN PANCRAZIO
SAN PIETRO IN MONTORIO (BRAMANTE'S TEMPIETTO)
#115
FAGLIA
SANTA MARIA IN TRASTEVERE
PORTA SAN PANCRAZIO & ITALIAN UNIFICATION MUSEUM
VIA GARIBALDI
FONTANA DELL' ACQUA PAOLA
ITALIAN INDEPENDENCE WAR MEMORIAL
TRA
#870
CITY WALLS
VIA GARIBALDI
VIA GOFFREDO MAMEL
#115
VIA LUCIANO

Accommodations

1 Residenza Arco dei Tolomei & Arco del Lauro B&B
2 Hotel Santa Maria
3 Hotel San Francesco

Eateries & Other

4 Taverna Trilussa
5 Dar Sor Olimpio al Drago
6 Trattoria de Gli Amici

7 Trattoria da Lucia
8 La Prosciutteria Cantina dei Papi
9 Pizzeria "Ai Marmi"
10 Pizzeria Dar Poeta
11 Trapizzino Vineria di Roma
12 Grattachecca Stand
13 Almost Corner Bookshop
14 Open Door Bookshop

tel. 06-446-3554, www.yellowhostel.com, questions@the-yellow.com).

¢ **Funny Palace Hostel**—adjacent to Splashnet and run by the same entrepreneurial owner, Mabri—rents dorm beds in quiet four- and five-person rooms and more expensive but clean private rooms. It's far less convivial than Yellow Hostel, but good for introverts (cash only, includes breakfast in café, elevator, guest kitchen, reception at Splashnet launderette—described earlier, Via Varese 33, tel. 06-4470-3523, www.funnyhostel.com, funnypalace031@gmail.com).

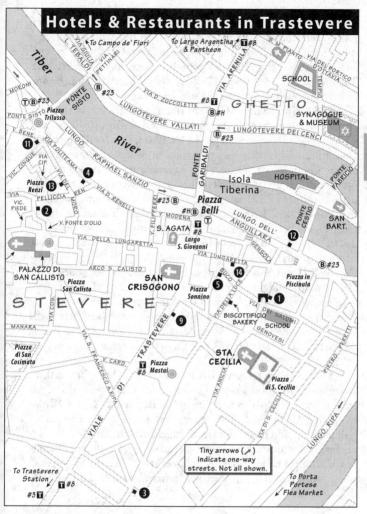

Hotels & Restaurants in Trastevere

To Campo de' Fiori

To Largo Argentina & Pantheon

Tiber

PONTE SISTO

Piazza Trilussa

PONTE SISTO

River

GHETTO

SCHOOL

SYNAGOGUE & MUSEUM

Isola Tiberina

HOSPITAL

PONTE FABRICIO

SAN BART.

Piazza Renzi

Piazza Belli

S. AGATA

Largo S. Giovanni

PALAZZO DI SAN CALLISTO

Piazza San Calisto

SAN CRISOGONO

STEVERE

Piazza Sonnino

Piazza in Piscinula

BISCOTTIFICIO BAKERY

SCHOOL

GENOVESI

Piazza di San Cosimato

Piazza Mastai

STA. CECILIA

Piazza di S. Cecilia

To Trastevere Station

To Porta Portese Flea Market

Tiny arrows (↗) indicate one-way streets. Not all shown.

TRASTEVERE

Colorful and genuine, with uneven cobbles and remnants of its tumbledown past, Trastevere is a treat for travelers looking for a more residential, bohemian atmosphere. The heart of Rome and its ancient ruins are just across the river, and tram #8 makes getting there and back a snap. Convenient bus #23 runs to the Vatican area, bus #H runs directly to Termini (none on Sun), and tram #3 goes to the Colosseum. From the airport, you can reach these listings by taking the regional train to Trastevere train station, and the #8 tram downhill from there.

$$$$ **Residenza Arco dei Tolomei** is your most poetic Traste-

vere experience imaginable, with six small, unique, antique-filled rooms, some boasting fragrant balconies. In this quiet and elegant setting, you can pretend you're visiting aristocratic relatives (reserve well in advance, from Piazza Piscinula a block up Via dell'Arco de' Tolomei at #27, tel. 06-5832-0819, www.bbarcodeitolomei.com, info@bbarcodeitolomei.com, Marco and Gianna Paola).

$$$$ **Hotel Santa Maria** sits like a lazy hacienda in the middle of Trastevere. Surrounded by a medieval skyline, you'll feel as if you're on some romantic stage set. Its 20 small but well-equipped, air-conditioned rooms—former cells in a cloister—are mostly on the ground floor, as are a few suites for up to six people. The rooms circle a gravelly courtyard of orange trees and stay-awhile patio furniture (RS%, family rooms, email reservations preferred, free loaner bikes, face church on Piazza Maria Trastevere and go right down Via della Fonte d'Olio 50 yards to Vicolo del Piede 2, tel. 06-589-4626, www.hotelsantamariatrastevere.it, info@hotelsantamaria.info).

$$$ **Hotel San Francesco,** big and blocky yet welcoming, stands practically and efficiently at the far end of all the Trastevere action. It rents 24 trim rooms and comes with an inviting roof terrace. It's fine, but a bit more distant than the others listed here (email reservations preferred, air-con, elevator, Via Jacopa de' Settesoli 7, tel. 06-5830-0051, www.hotelsanfrancesco.net, hotelsanfrancesco@gmail.com).

$$$ **Arco del Lauro B&B** rents six tight, whitewashed, straightforward rooms around a dim, quiet back courtyard. Consider it the less expensive version of the Residenza Arco dei Tolomei, which is upstairs. The lower prices make up for the lack of public spaces and mostly offsite management (one family room, includes small breakfast at nearby café, air-con, from Piazza Piscinula a block up Via dell'Arco de' Tolomei at #29, tel. 06-9784-0350, www.arcodellauro.it, info@arcodellauro.it, Lorenza and Daniela).

EATING IN ROME

Romans take great pleasure in dining well. Embrace this passion over a multicourse meal at an outdoor table, watching a parade of passersby while you sip wine with loved ones.

In ancient times, the dinner party was the center of Roman social life. It was a luxurious affair, set in the *triclinium* (formal dining room). Guest lists were small (3-9 people), and the select few reclined on couches during the exotic multicourse meal. Today the couches are gone, and the fare may not include jellyfish, boiled tree fungi, or flamingo, but the *cucina romana* influence remains. It's fair to say that while French cuisine makes an art of the preparation, Italian (and Roman) cuisine is simpler and all about the ingredients.

Roman meals are still lengthy social occasions. Simple, fresh, seasonal ingredients dominate the dishes. The *cucina* is robust, strongly flavored, and unpretentious—much like the people who've created it over the centuries. It is said that Roman cooking didn't come out of emperors' or popes' kitchens, but from the *cucina povera*—the home cooking of the common people. This may explain the Romans' fondness for meats known as the *quinto quarto* ("fifth quarter"), such as tripe, tail, brain, and pigs' feet, as well as their interest in natural preservatives like chili peppers and garlic.

Rome belongs to the warm, southern region of Lazio, which produces a rich variety of flavorful vegetables and fruit that are the envy of American supermarkets. Rome's proximity to the Mediterranean also allows for a great variety of seafood.

EATING TIPS

I rank eateries from $ budget to $$$$ splurge. For more advice on eating in Italy, including details on ordering, tipping, and Italian cuisine and beverages, see the "Eating" section of the Practicalities chapter.

Kitchens close at most restaurants between lunch and dinner; if it's a quality restaurant, it won't reopen before 19:00. If a smaller restaurant is booked up later in the evening (from 20:30 or so), they may accommodate walk-ins if you're willing to eat quickly.

Choosing Restaurants: I've listed restaurants that I enjoy. Many are in characteristic and touristy (and therefore pricey) areas such as Piazza Navona, Campo de' Fiori, and Trastevere. Others are tucked away from the tourist crush.

I'm impressed by how small the price difference can be between a mediocre Roman restaurant and a fine one. You can pay about 20 percent more for double the quality. If I had $100 for three meals in Rome, I'd spend $50 for one and $25 each for the other two, rather than $33 on all three. For splurge meals, I'd consider (in this order): Gabriello (near the Spanish Steps), Fortunato (near the Pantheon), and Taverna Trilussa (in Trastevere; all described later).

Rome's fabled squares—most notably Piazza Navona, near the Pantheon, and Campo de' Fiori—are lined with the outdoor tables of touristy restaurants with enticing menus and formal-vested waiters. The atmosphere is super romantic. I, too, like the idea of dining under floodlit monuments, amid a constantly flowing parade of people. But you'll likely be surrounded by tourists and hawkers, and awkward interactions can kill the ambience...leaving you with just a forgettable and overpriced meal. Restaurants in these areas are notorious for surprise charges, forgettable food, microwaved ravioli, and bad service.

I enjoy the view by savoring just a drink or dessert on a famous square, but I dine with locals on nearby low-rent streets, where the proprietor needs to serve a good-value meal and nurture a local following to stay in business.

If you're set on eating—or just drinking and snacking—on a

famous piazza, you don't need a guidebook listing to choose a spot; enjoy the ritual of slowly circling the square, observing both the food and the people eating it, and sit where the view and menu appeal to you. (Pizza is probably your best value and least risky bet.)

The *Aperitivo* **Tradition:** For a budget, light meal, consider partaking in an *aperitivo* buffet. Bars all over town serve up a buffet of small dishes, from about 18:00 to 21:00, and anyone buying a drink (generally €8-12) gets to eat "for free." While the food is generally forgettable, it's cheap and the atmosphere can be great. Some places limit you to one plate; others allow refills. Either way, if you want a quick, light dinner with a drink, it's a great deal.

Picnicking: Another cheap way to eat is to assemble a picnic and dine with Rome as your backdrop. Buy ingredients for your picnic at one of Rome's open-air produce markets (mornings only; see page 434), an *alimentari* (corner grocery store), a *rosticcerie* (cheap food to go), or a *supermercato*, such as Conad or Co-op. You'll find handy late-night supermarkets near the Panthe-

on (Via Giustiniani), Spanish Steps (Via Vittoria), Trevi Fountain (Via del Bufalo), and Campo de' Fiori (Via di Monte della Farina). Note that Rome discourages people from picnicking or drinking at historic monuments (such as at the Pantheon) in the old center. Violators can be fined. You'll be OK if you eat *with* a view rather than *in* the view and remain discreet.

ANCIENT ROME: NEAR THE COLOSSEUM AND FORUM

Within a block of the Colosseum and Forum, you'll find convenient eateries catering to weary sightseers, most offering neither memorable food nor good value. To get your money's worth, stick with one of my recommendations, even if it means a 10-minute walk from the ruins. For locations, see the map on page 372.

Monti

Behind the Imperial Forums, nestled in the tight and cobbled lanes between Via Nazionale and Via Cavour, is the characteristic (and recently trendy) Monti neighborhood. It's just a few steps farther from the ancient sites than the battery of forgettable touristy restaurants, but that extra effort opens up a world of characteristic dining experiences. From the Forum, head up Via Cavour and then

392 Rick Steves Rome

left on Via dei Serpenti; the action centers on Piazza della Madonna dei Monti and nearby lanes. For more on this area, see page 66.

$$ Barzilai Bistrot, a wine bar with a kitchen under stout timbers, feels like the neighborhood hangout. The bar is inviting if you just want a nice glass of wine with a plate of meat and cheese. It's family-run, with a fun menu ranging from pastas to burgers. Granny's meatloaf is a hit (daily, no reservations, Via Panisperna 44, tel. 06-487-4979).

$$ Taverna Romana is small, simple, and a bit chaotic—with an open kitchen and hams and garlic hanging from the ceiling. This family-run eatery's *cacio e pepe* (cheese-and-pepper pasta) is a favorite. Arrive early, as they take no reservations (daily 12:30-14:45 & 19:00-22:45, Via della Madonna dei Monti 79, tel. 06-474-5325).

$$ Taverna dei Fori Imperiali serves typical, slightly higher-priced Roman cuisine in a snug interior that bustles with energy (Wed-Mon 12:30-15:00 & 19:30-22:30, closed Tue, reserve for dinner, Via della Madonna dei Monti 9, tel. 06-679-8643, www.latavernadeiforiimperiali.com).

$$ Alle Carrette Pizzeria—simple, rustic, and family-friendly—serves great wood-fired pizza just 200 yards from the Forum. It's cheap and fast (daily 12:00-15:30 & 19:00-24:00, Vicolo delle Carrette 14, tel. 06-679-2770).

$ Trattoria da Valentino is a classic time warp hiding under its historic (and therefore protected) *Birra Peroni* sign. They specialize in *scamorza* (grilled cheese with various toppings; about €10), list the day's pastas on a chalkboard, and serve a variety of meat dishes (Mon-Sat 13:00-14:45 & 19:30-23:00, closed Sun, Via del Boschetto 37, tel. 06-488-0643).

$ Antico Forno ai Serpenti, a hip bakery with a few simple tables, puts out a small selection of *panini,* baked potatoes, and lasagna. They also bake good bread and pastries and do breakfasts (order at the counter, daily 8:00-23:00, closes at 22:00 on Sun, Via dei Serpenti 122, tel. 06-4542-7920).

$$ Enoteca Cavour 313 is a quality wine bar with a menu ranging from Lazio specialties and salads to high-quality *affettati* (cold cuts) and cheese. You'll be served with a mellow ambience under lofts of wine bottles, enjoying spacious-for-Rome seating (Mon-Sat 12:30-14:45 & 18:00-23:30, closed Sun, 100 yards off Via dei Fori Imperiali at Via Cavour 313, tel. 06-678-5496, Angelo).

Monti *Aperitivo:* Look for bars hosting the *aperitivo*—happy hours where, for the cost of a drink (€8-12), you get access to a buffet of simple dishes. It's a basic dinner (the Italian equivalent of macaroni and cheese, Spam, and Jello) in a fun scene with a drink. A good example, just a block off Monti's main square, is

Analemma, which has a casual, youthful scene and a nightly buffet with a drink for €10 (18:30-22:00, Via Leonina 77).

Monti Food Crawl

The streets of Monti are crowded with fun and creative places offering inexpensive quality snacks and light meals to eat on tiny informal tables or to take away. For a fun movable feast, drop in for a bite to whatever casual places you see that appeal. Here are some ideas:

Wine with *Aperitivo* (dinner only): **$$ Fafiuché** is an intimate yet vibrant family-run wine bar with a fun-loving vibe and no pretense. They serve a broad selection of wines and beers inside or at tables on the cobblestones outside. Andrea, Maria, and their son Gianmarco offer serious dishes from Apulia and Piedmont. And, if you're assembling a mobile dinner, they put out an inviting buffet for your choice of €3 tapas plates (Mon-Sat 18:30-21:00, closed Sun, Via della Madonna dei Monti 28).

Pizza by the Slice on the Square: The hole-in-the-wall **$ Pizzeria la Boccaccia** is good for a takeaway slice. Point at what you like and mime how big of a rectangle you want (pricing by the *etto*, or 100 grams, daily, Via Leonina 73). Take it a block away to the main square (Piazza della Madonna dei Monti), buy a beer at the convenience store (top of the square), and make the piazza scene.

Gourmet Sandwich and Veggie Juice: Gourmet *rosette*, sandwiches on rose-shaped buns, are the specialty at **$ Zia Rosetta**. At €3-4 for the tiny ones or €6-7 for the standard size, they're perfect for a light bite—either to take away or eat in. A fun, healthy, and creative menu includes salads and €4 *centrifughe*—fresh-squeezed, vitamin-bomb fruit and veggie juices (Mon-Thu 11:00-16:00, Fri-Sun until 22:00, Via Urbana 54).

Gelato: Hiding on the welcoming little square just above Zia Rosetta, **Fatamorgana** features the most creative gelato combinations I've seen in Italy, along with more conventional flavors. Portions are small but good quality—everything is organic and gluten-free (long hours daily, Piazza degli Zingari 5).

Behind the Colosseum

A pleasant little residential zone just up the street from the back of the Colosseum (the opposite direction from the Forum) features a real neighborhood feel and a variety of restaurants that capably serve tired and hungry sightseers.

$ Trattoria Luzzi is a well-worn, no-frills eatery serving simple food in a high-energy—sometimes chaotic—environment (as they've done since 1945). With good prices, big portions, and proximity to the Colosseum, it draws a crowd, so reserve ahead or

Roman Cuisine

Here are some of the specialties worth seeking out on the menu. For more on Italian food, including salumi, cheeses, pizza, and pasta, see the "Eating" section of the Practicalities chapter.

Antipasti (Appetizers)

Antipasto misto: Marinated or grilled vegetables (eggplant, artichokes, peppers, mushrooms), cured meats, cheeses, or seafood (anchovies, octopus).

Bruschetta: Toasted bread brushed with olive oil and garlic, topped with chopped tomatoes, mushrooms, or other tidbits.

Fritti: Battered or breaded fried snacks—often olives stuffed with meat, potato croquettes, or mozzarella balls. Other classics are *suppli* (rice balls with tomato sauce and mozzarella) and *fiori di zucca* (squash blossoms filled with mozzarella and anchovies).

Prosciutto e melone: Cantaloupe wrapped in thin-sliced ham.

Primo Piatto (First Course)

Bucatini all'amatriciana: Thin pasta tubes with a sauce of tomatoes, onion, pancetta, and pecorino cheese.

Gnocchi alla romana: Dumplings made from semolina (not potatoes) and baked with butter and cheese.

Penne all'arrabbiata: Spicy tomato sauce with chili peppers (peperoncini) and garlic over penne.

Rigatoni con la pajata: Pasta topped with a stew of calf intestines.

Spaghetti alla carbonara: Eggs, pancetta or *guanciale* (cured pork cheek), cheese (*pecorino romano* or *parmigiano reggiano*), and black pepper over pasta.

Spaghetti alle vongole veraci: Pasta served with small clams in the shell.

Stracciatella alla romana: Meat broth with whipped eggs, topped with parmesan.

Secondo Piatto (Second Course)

Abbacchio alla scottadito: Baby lamb chops grilled and eaten as finger food.

Anguillette in umido: Stewed baby eels from Lake Bracciano.

Coda alla vaccinara: Oxtail braised with garlic, wine, tomato, and celery.

Filetti di baccalà: Battered and fried salt cod (like fish-and-chips minus the chips).

Involtini di vitello al sugo: Veal cutlets rolled with prosciutto, celery, and cheese in a tomato sauce.

Saltimbocca alla romana: "Jump-in-the-mouth"—thinly sliced veal layered with prosciutto and sage, then lightly fried.

Trippa alla romana: Tripe braised with onions, carrots, and mint.

Contorni (Side Dishes)

You may want to order a side dish if your second course is not served with a vegetable. Note that if you order a salad, olive oil and wine vinegar are the only dressings.

Carciofi: Artichokes served either *alla romana* (simmered with garlic and mint) or *alla giudia* (flattened and fried).

Fave al guanciale: Fava beans simmered with cured pork cheek and onion.

Misticanza: Mixed green salad of arugula *(rucola)* and curly endive *(puntarelle)*.

Dolci (Desserts)

Dessert can be a seasonal fruit, such as *fragole* (strawberries) or *pesche* (peaches), or even cheese, such as *pecorino romano* (made from ewe's milk) or *caciotta romana* (combination of ewe's and cow's milk).

Bignè: Cream puff-like pastries filled with *zabaione* (egg yolks, sugar, and Marsala wine).

Crostata di ricotta: A cheesecake-like dessert with ricotta, sweet Marsala wine, cinnamon, and bits of chocolate.

Grattachecca: Sweetened shaved ice. Vendors at little booths scrape shavings off ice blocks, then flavor them with syrups, such as *limoncocco* (lemon and coconut with fresh chunks of coconut).

Tartufo: Rich dark-chocolate gelato ball with a cherry inside, sometimes served *con panna* (with whipped cream).

Roman Pizza

Roman-style pizza is made with a very thin and crispy dough called *scrocchiarella* (thinner and less chewy than Neapolitan-style pizza). In Rome, *pizza bianca* (white pizza) can mean a pizza made without tomato sauce, but can also simply mean a chunk of flat, crispy bread, or a sandwich made with that bread (similar to what's called a *panino* in other parts of Italy).

Local Wines

Rome is located in the region of Lazio, which produces several pleasant white wines and a few reds. Frascati, probably the best-known wine of the region, is an inexpensive dry white made from trebbiano (from the hills just south of Rome) and malvasia grapes. Castelli Romani, light and fairly dry, is made from trebbiano grapes and is similar to Marino, Colli Albani, and Velletri wines. Torre Ercolana is a dense, balanced, medium-bodied red made from the regional cesanese grape, as well as cabernet and merlot (known as Lazio's best-quality red, aged at least five years).

expect a short wait at lunch and after 19:30 (Thu-Tue 12:00-24:00, closed Wed, Via Celimontana 1, tel. 06-709-6332).

$$ Ristorante Pizzeria Naumachia is a good second bet if Trattoria Luzzi next door is jammed up. It's a bit more upscale and serves good-quality pizza and pastas at decent prices (Via Celimontana 7, tel. 06-700-2764).

$$ Li Rioni, a pizzeria, is open only for dinner, when its over-the-rooftops interior and terrace out front are jammed with Romans watching the busy chef plunge dough into its wood-fired oven, then pull out crispy-crust Roman-style pizzas (Wed-Mon 19:30-24:00, closed Tue, Via dei SS. Quattro 24, tel. 06-7045-0605).

$$ Il Pentagrappolo is an intimate *enoteca*, serving light meals (proudly, no pasta) to go with their selection of quality wines, many organic. Their €12 lunches include water, and on some nights there's live music (see "Jazz" in the Nightlife in Rome chapter). The location is convenient to the Forum and Colosseum (food served Mon-Fri 12:00-15:00, also Tue-Sun 18:00-24:00, best to reserve on weekends, three blocks east of the Colosseum at Via Celimontana 21, www.ilpentagrappolo.com, tel. 06-709-6301).

Between the Colosseum and St. Peter-in-Chains Church

You'll find these places across the street and up the hill from the Colosseum. They're more convenient than high cuisine, though they work fine in a pinch.

$$ Hostaria da Nerone is a traditional place serving hearty classics, including tasty homemade pasta dishes. Their *antipasti* plate—with a variety of veggies, fish, and meat—is a good value for a quick lunch. While the *antipasti* menu indicates specifics, you can have a plate of whatever's out—just direct the waiter to assemble the €10 *antipasti* plate of your lunchtime dreams (Mon-Sat 12:00-15:00 & 19:00-23:00, closed Sun, indoor/outdoor seating, Via delle Terme di Tito 96, tel. 06-481-7952).

$ Caffè dello Studente, a normal neighborhood bar popular with tourists and students attending the nearby Sapienza University, is run by Pina, her cheerful daughter Simona, and son-in-law Emiliano. I'd skip the microwaved pasta and stick to toasted sandwiches and salad. If it's not busy, show this book when you order at the bar and sit at a table without paying extra (daily 7:30-20:00, closed Sun Nov-March, Via delle Terme di Tito 95, mobile 320-854-0333).

JEWISH QUARTER

The former Jewish Ghetto sits between Capitoline Hill and Campo di' Fiori, just across the river from Trastevere. Eating here goes well with my self-guided tour of the neighborhood (see the Jewish Ghetto Walk chapter). The main drag, Via del Portico d'Ottavia, is lined with busy, traditional, touristic kosher restaurants with fine outdoor tables. It's tempting to grab a table (or picnic on a bench, or a slice of kosher pizza to go from Pizzeria Alice) here to watch the action. For eatery locations, see the map on page 225.

$$ Sora Margherita, hiding on a cluttered square, has been a rustic neighborhood favorite since 1927. Amid picturesque commotion, guests chow down on basic old-time Roman and Jewish dishes. Eat here for the experience rather than fine food. Reservations are strongly advised. While lunch (12:30-15:00) is open, for dinner there are two seatings: 20:00 and 21:30 (closed Sun for dinner, closed second half of Aug; just south of Via del Portico d'Ottavia at Piazza delle Cinque Scole 30—look for the red curtain; tel. 06-687-4216, www.soramargherita.com).

$$$ Beppe e i Suoi Formaggi is entirely dedicated to the fine wines, cold cuts, pastas—and above all the cheeses—of the Piedmont region of northern Italy. Its sleek, woody, and elegant wine-crate dining room is designed for foodies with money who are interested in the best of that region's organic cuisine (€28 cheese plate for two, €20 daily specials, wine by the glass, Mon-Sat 12:00-22:30, closed Sun, Santa Maria del Pianto 11, tel. 06-6819-2210, www.beppeeisuoiformaggi.it).

$ Fast Lunch Options Near the Main Intersection: Via del Portico d'Ottavia hits Via Reginella at the Ghetto's main intersection, with three good options. **Pollaria** is delightfully situated with outdoor tables overlooking the action (salads, sandwiches, and vegan fare; lunch and dinner). **Ristorante Sheva** has a good *aperitivo* deal—munchies free with a drink—nightly at 18:00, and of course there's the **Ghetto bakery.** Just beyond that, on Via di Santa Maria del Pianto, is a line of fast, casual eateries including a kosher burger joint **(Fonzie)** and a "fast kosher kebab" shop **(Yesh).**

PANTHEON NEIGHBORHOOD

I've listed the restaurants in this central area based on which landmark they're closest to: Campo de' Fiori, Piazza Navona, the Trevi Fountain, or the Pantheon itself.

On and near Campo de' Fiori

By day, Campo de' Fiori hosts a colorful fruit-and-veggies market (with an increasing number of tourist knickknacks; Mon-Sat until around 13:30, closed Sun). Combined with a sandwich and a sweet from **Forno Campo de' Fiori,** the bakery in the west corner of the square (behind the fountain), you can assemble a nice picnic.

In the evening, Campo de' Fiori offers a characteristic setting—although it can be overrun by tourists out drinking. The

EATING

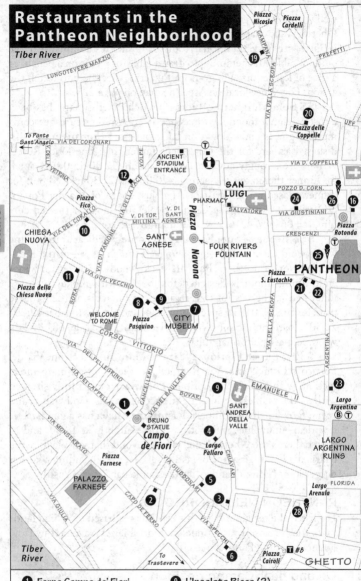

Restaurants in the Pantheon Neighborhood

1. Forno Campo de' Fiori
2. Enoteca L'Angolo Divino
3. Antico Forno Roscioli
4. Trattoria der Pallaro
5. Filetti di Baccalà
6. Open Baladin Pub
7. Vivi Bistrot
8. Cul de Sac
9. L'Insalata Ricca (2)
10. Rist. Pizzeria "da Francesco"
11. Pizzeria da Baffetto
12. Chiostro del Bramante
13. To Hostaria Romana
14. Origano
15. L'Antica Birreria Peroni
16. Ristorante da Fortunato & Wine Bar

EATING

17 Enoteca Corsi, Pane Pane Vino ar Vino & L'Antico Caffee della Pigna

18 Trattoria dal Cavalier Gino

19 Ristorante la Campana

20 Osteria delle Coppelle & Osteria da Mario

21 Ginger

22 Miscellanea

23 Frullati Pascucci

24 Supermarket (2)

25 Crèmeria Monteforte

26 San Crispino Gelateria

27 Giolitti Gelateria

28 Gelateria Artigianale Corona

square is lined with popular and interesting bars, pizzerias, and small restaurants—all great for people-watching over a glass of wine. Later at night, any charm is smothered by a younger clubbing crowd, but romance lives on the nearby quieter streets.

$$ Enoteca L'Angolo Divino is an inviting little wine bar run by Massimo Crippa, a sommelier who beautifully describes a fine array of wines along with the best accompanying meats, cheeses, and pastas. With tiny tables, a tiny menu, great wines by the glass, intriguing walls of wine bottles, smart advice, more locals than tourists, and a smooth jazz vibe, this place can leave you with a life-long memory (daily 17:00-24:00, also Tue-Sat 11:00-14:00, a block off Campo de' Fiori at Via dei Balestrari 12, tel. 06-686-4413).

$ Antico Forno Roscioli is an attractive upscale bakery with a few stools, selling a tempting array of breads, pizzas, and pastries (Mon-Sat 7:00-20:00, Sun 8:00-19:00, Via dei Chiavari 34).

$$ Trattoria der Pallaro, an eccentric and well-worn eatery that has no menu, has a slogan: "Here, you'll eat what we want to feed you." Paola Fazi—with a towel wrapped around her head turban-style—and her gang dish up a five-course meal of homey Roman food. You have three menu choices: €25 for the works; €20 for appetizers, *secondi*, and dessert; or €16 for appetizers and pasta. Any option is filling and includes wine. The service can be odd and the food is, let's say...rustic, but the experience is fun (daily 12:00-16:00 & 19:00-24:00, reserve if dining after 20:00, cash only, indoor/outdoor seating on quiet square, a block south of Corso Vittorio Emanuele, down Largo del Chiavari to Largo del Pallaro 15, tel. 06-6880-1488).

$ Filetti di Baccalà is a cheap and basic Roman classic, where nostalgic regulars cram in at wooden tables and savor €6 fried cod finger-food fillets and raw, slightly bitter *puntarelle* greens (slathered with anchovy sauce, available in spring and winter). Study what others are eating, and order from your grease-stained server by pointing at what you want. Sit in the fluorescently lit interior or try to grab a seat out on the little square, a quiet haven a block east of Campo de' Fiori (Mon-Sat 17:00-23:00, closed Sun, Largo dei Librari 88, tel. 06-686-4018). If you're not into greasy spoons, avoid this place.

$$ Open Baladin is a busy, modern, and spacious brewpub featuring a few dozen Italian craft beers on tap and a menu of burgers, salads, and freshly cooked potato chips. As burger bars are trendy in Italy, prices are somewhat high. It's a nice break if you're parched and ready for pub grub (daily 12:00-24:00, Via degli Specchi 5, tel. 06-683-8989).

Near Piazza Navona

Piazza Navona and the streets just to the west are jammed with an amazing array of restaurants. The places lining the piazza itself are traditional and touristy. Instead, survey the scene on the two streets heading west from the square. Here are my favorites in that zone:

$$ Vivi Bistrot is in the Museum of Rome building at the south end of Piazza Navona, with two window tables overlooking the square. This cheery and modern little restaurant serves salads, pastas, and burger plates with a focus on organic ingredients (Tue-Sun 10:00-24:00, closed Mon, Piazza Navona 2, tel. 06-683-3779).

$$ Cul de Sac, a long and skinny trattoria lined with wine bottles, is packed with an enthusiastic crowd enjoying a wide-ranging menu, from pasta to homemade pâté. They have fun sampler plates of *salumi* and cheese, good wines by the glass, and fine outdoor seating. It's jammed with regulars, and they don't take reservations—come early to avoid a wait (daily 12:00-24:00, a block off Piazza Navona on Piazza Pasquino 73, tel. 06-6880-1094).

$$ L'Insalata Ricca, a popular local chain, specializes in filling salads and also serves pasta and €12 meal deals. A small branch is at Piazza Pasquino 72 (tel. 06-6830-7881), and a more spacious and enjoyable location is a couple of blocks toward Largo Argentina, just across busy Corso Vittorio Emanuele (Largo dei Chiavari 85, tel. 06-6880-3656). Both are open daily 12:00-24:00.

$$$ Ristorante Pizzeria "da Francesco," bustling and authentic, has a 50-year-old tradition, a hardworking young waitstaff, great indoor seating, and a few tables stretching along the quiet street. Their blackboard explains the daily specials (daily 12:00-15:30 & 19:00-24:00, Piazza del Fico 29, tel. 06-686-4009, www.dafrancesco.it). While a bit overpriced, it's very popular. Reservations are required for evening seatings at 19:00, 20:30, or 22:00.

$ Pizzeria da Baffetto is famous among visiting Italians and therefore generally comes with a ridiculous line. The pizzas are great, the service is surly, and the tables are tightly arranged amid the mishmash of sketches littering the walls. The pizza-assembly kitchen keeps things energetic, and the pizza oven keeps the main room warm. Streetside tables are less congested and sweaty, but also less memorable (daily 12:00-15:30 & 18:30-late, cash only, order "M" or "D"—medium or large, Via del Governo Vecchio 114, tel. 06-686-1617).

$$ Chiostro del Bramante ("Bramante's Cloister") is a museum café serving light lunches in a unique setting—overlooking the tranquil open-air *chiostro*. Gaze out as the Renaissance master Bramante brings symmetry to your meal. With not a hint of tourism, it's a refined and elegant place, and fine for a predinner drink too. Enter just to the left of the church entrance and tell the ticket-window staff that you're just going to the café (daily 10:00-20:00, meals served 12:00-15:00, Arco della Pace 5, tel. 06-6880-9035).

Near the Trevi Fountain

The streets surrounding the Trevi Fountain are littered with mediocre restaurants catering exclusively to tourists. Skip them and walk a few blocks away to one of these. Also consider nearby **Hostaria Romana,** behind the fountain near the Palazzo del Quirinale (walk along Via Rasella to reach the restaurant; see the listing on page 409).

$$$ Origano is a bustling, modern bistro (and café) located three blocks away from the Trevi Fountain. It serves well-priced traditional Roman specialties and wood-fired pizza in an often chaotic setting (daily 12:00-24:00, Via di Sant'Andrea delle Fratte 25/26, tel. 06-699-20907, Germana).

$$ L'Antica Birreria Peroni is Rome's answer to a German beer hall. Serving hearty mugs of the local Peroni beer and lots of just plain fun beer-hall food and Italian classics, the place is a hit with Romans for a cheap night out (Mon-Sat 12:00-24:00, closed Sun, midway between Trevi Fountain and Capitoline Hill, a block off Via del Corso at Via di San Marcello 19, tel. 06-679-5310).

Close to the Pantheon

Eating on the square facing the Pantheon is a temptation, and I'd consider it for breakfast or just to relax and enjoy the Roman scene over a drink. But if you walk a block or two away, you'll get less view and better value. Here are some suggestions:

$$$$ Ristorante da Fortunato is an Italian classic, with white-coated, black-tie career waiters politely serving good meat and fish to politicians, foreign dignitaries, and well-heeled tourists. Peruse the photos of their famous visitors—everyone from Prince Charles to Bill Clinton are pictured with the late Signore Fortunato, who started this restaurant in 1975 and was a master of simple edible elegance. (His son Jason now runs the show.) The outdoor seating is fine for people-watching, but the elegance is inside (figure €50/person, daily 12:30-16:00 & 18:30-23:30, in front of Pantheon at Via del Pantheon 55, tel. 06-679-2788, www. ristorantefortunato.it). The **Fortunato Wine Bar** is a classy place for a glass of fine wine with a plate of properly paired cold meats and cheeses. For a fun wine option, you can run up a tab from the bar's tasting machine while dining next door.

$$ Enoteca Corsi, a wine shop that grew into a thriving restaurant, is a charming local scene with the family table in back, where the kids do their homework. The Paiella family serves straightforward, traditional cuisine to an appreciative crowd of office workers. The board lists daily specials (gnocchi on Thursday, fish on Friday, and so on). Friendly Manuela and her staff offer fine wine at a third of the price you'd pay in normal restaurants—buy from their shop and pay a corking fee. Show this book for a free glass of homemade

Resources for Foodies

For those looking to take their Roman culinary endeavors seriously, there's no shortage of in-depth advice. Books and blogs on Roman cuisine abound, and several local companies run food- and wine-themed tours. (While Testaccio lends itself to a food walk, I find Trastevere is too crowded and touristy.) Here is a sampling:

KatieParla.com: Food author Katie Parla's website has all the latest on the Roman food scene. She also offers private tours and top-notch tastings and has an easy-to-use app, Katie Parla's Rome (works without internet connection).

Eat Italy: Food writer Elizabeth Minchilli's excellent app lists a wide range of good eateries and food-oriented shops. It covers many cities—including Rome (and works without internet connection). Her website also features recipes and private food tours (www.elizabethminchilliinrome.com).

Eating Italy Food Tours: This tour company leads fun and insightful walks almost daily through Rome's colorful Testaccio neighborhood, interspersing history, tradition, and local food culture while giving you a glimpse into daily life in less-seen parts of the city. Each group of about a dozen people makes about 10 tasty stops (€79-99, RS%—10 percent discount with promo code "ricksteves," 3-4 hours, several morning and evening departures Mon-Sat, www.eatingitalyfoodtours.com). They also offer cooking classes.

Vino Roma: This small wine "school" is run by several sommeliers who offer evening tasting classes (€50/person) designed to help you understand and enjoy Italian wine. They also lead several neighborhood walks (www.vinoroma.com).

Local Aromas: Giuliana and her daughters Benedetta and Valeria offer excellent food and market tours (€55/person), wine and craft beer tours (€65), and cooking classes (€86) from a view penthouse two blocks from the Vatican Museums (www.localaromas.com).

Buon appetito, e salute!

EATING

limoncello for dessert (Mon-Sat 12:00-15:30, Wed-Fri also 19:00-22:30, closed Sun, a block toward the Pantheon from the Gesù Church at Via del Gesù 87, tel. 06-679-0821).

$$ Next to Enoteca Corsi are two other good lunch-only options popular with local office workers: **Pane Pane Vino ar Vino** is a creative little sandwich bar with a delightful menu (Via del Gesù 84) and **L'Antico Caffee della Pigna** is a timeless old café serving pastas, salads, and sandwiches (Piazza della Pigna 57).

$$ Trattoria dal Cavalier Gino, tucked away on a tiny street behind the Parliament, has been a favorite since 1963. Photos on the wall recall the days when it was the haunt of big-time politicians. English-speaking siblings Carla and Fabrizio serve up traditional Roman favorites. They offer four seatings a day: 13:00, 14:30, 20:00, and 22:00. Reserve ahead, even for lunch, as you'll be packed in with savvy locals (Mon-Sat, closed Sun, behind Piazza del Parlamento and just off Via di Campo Marzio at Vicolo Rosini 4, tel. 06-687-3434).

$$$ Ristorante la Campana is a classic—an authentic slice of old Rome appreciated by well-dressed locals. Claiming a history dating to 1518, this place feels unchanged over the years. It serves typical Roman dishes and daily specials, plus it has a self-service *antipasti* buffet, which makes a nice €12 lunch (Tue-Sun 12:30-15:00 & 19:30-23:00, closed Mon, inside seating only, just off Via della Scrofa and Piazza Nicosia at Vicolo della Campana 18, tel. 06-687-5273, www.ristorantelacampana.com).

$$ Osteria delle Coppelle, a slapdash, trendy place, serves traditional dishes to a local crowd and a fun selection of €3 *cicchetti* (small plates) that lets you enjoy a variety of Roman dishes as tapas. It has a rustic interior and jumbled exterior seating, with a much classier dining section in the back (daily 12:30-15:30 & 19:00-late, Piazza delle Coppelle 54, tel. 06-4550-2826). They run a fun "speakeasy" bar which opens nightly at 22:00—but don't tell anyone. On the same charming square, the more old-school **Osteria da Mario,** with classic tables inside or out, is also worth considering.

$$ Ginger is a crisp, modern restaurant one block from the Pantheon, with a spacious and bright interior and seating on a delightful square. The menu selection—pastas, *panini*, salads, and smoothies—is healthy, organic, and a bit pricey (daily 8:00-23:00, Piazza di S. Eustachio 54, tel. 06-6830-8559). A second location is four blocks in front of the Spanish Steps (see listing later, under "North Rome").

$$ Miscellanea is run by much-loved Miki, who's on a mission to keep foreign students well-fed. He offers €4 sandwiches, pizza-like bruschetta, and a long list of hearty salads, along with pasta and other staples—it's a good value for a cheap and filling dinner in a convenient location. Miki (and his son Romeo) often tosses in a fun little extra (like their "sexy wine") if you have this book on the table (daily 9:00-24:00, just behind the Pantheon at Via della Palombella 37, tel. 06-6813-5318).

Picnicking Close to the Pantheon

It's fun to picnic with a view of the Pantheon. (Remember to be discreet.) Here are some options:

$ Frullati Pascucci, a hole-in-the-wall convenient for take-away, has been making refreshing €4-5 fruit *frullati* and frappés (like smoothies and shakes), plus fruit salads, for more than 80 years. Add a €4 sandwich to make a healthy light meal (Mon-Sat 6:00-23:00, closed Sun, north of Largo Argentina at Via di Torre Argentina 20, tel. 06-686-4816).

For picnic goodies, try the **Co-op** supermarket. There's one a half block from the Pantheon (daily 8:30-22:00, Via Giustiniani 18b) and another one three blocks away (daily until 21:00, Corso Vittorio Emanuele II 42).

Gelato Close to the Pantheon

Several fine *gelaterie* are within three or four blocks of the Pantheon.

Crèmeria Monteforte is known for its traditional gelato and super-creamy sorbets *(cremolati)*. The fruit flavors are especially refreshing—think gourmet slushies (closed Mon, faces the west side of the Pantheon at Via della Rotonda 22).

San Crispino serves small portions of tasty gourmet gelato. Because of their commitment to natural ingredients, the colors are muted; ice cream purists know that bright colors are artificial and used to attract children (a block in front of the Pantheon at Piazza della Maddalena 3).

Giolitti is Rome's most famous and venerable ice-cream establishment (although few would say it has the best gelato). Takeaway prices are reasonable, and it has elegant Old World seating (just off Piazza Colonna and Piazza Montecitorio at Via Uffici del Vicario 40).

Gelateria Artigianale Corona feels like a time warp and is nothing fancy, but it's got some of the finest homemade gelato in town, with an array of creative flavors (just south of Largo Argentina at Largo Arenula 27).

NEAR VATICAN CITY

As in the Colosseum area, some eateries near the Vatican prey on exhausted tourists. Avoid the restaurant pushers handing out fliers: They're usually hawking places with bad food and expensive menu tricks. Instead, tide yourself over with a slice of pizza or at any of these eateries (see map on page 378), and save your euros for a better meal elsewhere.

Handy Lunch Places near Piazza Risorgimento

These listings are a stone's throw from the Vatican wall. They're mostly fast and cheap, with a good *gelateria* nearby.

$$ Il Colibrì, run by the Ricci brothers, has noisy streetside seating and a quiet interior (daily 10:30-15:30 & 17:00-24:00, at corner of Via Leone IV and Via Famagosta 69, tel. 06-3751-4767).

$ L'Insalata Ricca is another branch of the popular chain that serves hearty salads and pastas (daily 12:00-23:30, across from the Vatican walls at Piazza Risorgimento 5, tel. 06-3973-0387).

$ Duecento Gradi is a good bet for fresh and creative sandwiches—though at €5-8 they're expensive by Roman standards. Munch your lunch sitting down (€1 extra) or take it away (daily 11:00-24:00, Piazza Risorgimento 3, tel. 06-3975-4239).

Gelateria Old Bridge scoops up hearty portions of fresh gelato for tourists and nuns alike—join the line (just off Piazza Risorgimento across from the Vatican walls at Viale dei Bastioni di Michelangelo 3).

Other Options in the Vatican Area

Most of these listings are near the Vatican Museums and Cipro Metro stop. The Borgo Pio eateries are near St. Peter's Basilica.

Viale Giulio Cesare and **Via Candia:** These streets are lined with cheap *pizza rustica* shops and self-serve places. **$ Forno Feliziani** (closed Sun, Via Candia 61) is a fancy version with nicely presented pizza by the slice and simple cafeteria-style dishes that you can eat in or take out.

Covered Market: Turn your nose loose in the wonderful **Mercato Trionfale,** one of the city's best market halls. It's more of a sight than a place to eat. Almost completely untouristy (with lots of vendors, but no real prepared-food stands aside from a bakery and a sandwich counter), it's located just three blocks north of the Vatican Museums (Mon-Sat roughly 7:00-14:00, Tue and Fri some stalls stay open until 19:00, closed Sun, corner of Via Tunisi and Via Andrea Doria). If the market is closed, try one of these grocery stores (both open daily until 20:30): **Co-op,** with a big bakery section and tables where you can eat pizza by the slice (to the northwest at Via Andrea Doria 46), or the smaller **Carrefour Express** (closer to the Vatican at Via Sebastiano Veniero 16).

Eating Close to St. Peter's: The pedestrian-only Borgo Pio—a block from Piazza San Pietro—has restaurants worth a look, such as the traditional **$$ Tre Pupazzi** (Mon-Sat 12:00-15:00 & 19:00-23:00, closed Sun, at corner of Via Tre Pupazzi and Borgo Pio, tel. 06-6880-3220). At **$ Vecchio Borgo,** across the street, you can get pasta, pizza by weight, and veggies to go or to eat at simple tables (daily 9:30-22:30, Borgo Pio 27a).

NORTH ROME: NEAR THE SPANISH STEPS AND ARA PACIS

To locate these restaurants, see the map on page 83.

$$$$ Ristorante il Gabriello is inviting and small—modern under medieval arches—and provides a peaceful and local-feeling respite from all the top-end fashion shops in the area. Claudio serves with charisma, while his brother Gabriello cooks creative Roman cuisine using fresh, organic products from his wife's farm. Italians normally just trust their waiter and say, "Bring it on." Tourists are understandably more cautious, but you can be trusting here. Invest €55—not including wine—in "Claudio's Extravaganza," created especially for my readers (not on the menu). Specify whether you'd prefer fish, meat, or both. (Be warned: Romans think raw shellfish is the ultimate in fine dining. If you don't, make that clear.) While you're likely to dine surrounded by my readers here (especially if eating before 21:00), the atmosphere is fun and convivial (dinner only, Mon-Sat 19:00-23:00, closed Sun, reservations smart, air-con, dress respectfully—no shorts, 3 blocks from Spanish Steps at Via Vittoria 51, tel. 06-6994-0810, www.ilgabriello.com).

$$ Ginger, four blocks in front of the Spanish Steps, is modern and bright, with an emphasis on sustainable and healthy ingredients (daily 8:00-23:00, Via Borgognona 43, tel. 06-9603-6390). A sister location near the Pantheon is described earlier.

$$$ Caffè Vitti, delightfully set on a fine traffic-free square, has been serving its neighborhood for over a century. The food won't win any awards—and you pay for the location—but it offers a delightful chance to enjoy a meal (good salads, pizza) or a cocktail on a quiet and characteristic square. Sit outside and people-watch amidst a professional Roman crowd. The cocktails come with a little tray of munchies (daily 6:30-24:00, Piazza San Lorenzo in Lucina 33, tel. 06-687-6304).

Via della Croce Stand-Up Food Crawl

Two blocks north of the Spanish Steps, touristy Via della Croce is a fun street to graze for a light meal or snack. As you peruse this street from Via del Corso, you'll pass these enticing stops for a bite:

Grano Frutta e Farina (#49) sells hard-to-resist pizza by the weight. Consider a tasting plate with a tiny bit of each pizza.

Focacci Deli (#43) makes sandwiches on request. Choose from their long, enticing counter of meats and cheeses.

Antica Enoteca (#76) is an inviting bar for a glass of wine in wonderful surroundings.

Salsamenteria F.lli Fabbi (#28) is a classic *alimentari* (corner grocery/deli). They'll make a sandwich to your specs and price it by weight.

Venchi (#25) can make your gelato and chocolate dreams come true.

Pompi (#82), the self-proclaimed "kingdom of tiramisù," features several flavors (classic, strawberry, pistachio, chocolate-banana, and more) in €4 portions.

Pastificio (#8), with a history going back to World War I, serves up two fresh €4 pasta dishes each day; a glass of water or wine is included when you eat at the stools along the wall.

EATING

NEAR TERMINI STATION

With a constant swarm of hungry, well-worn travelers, Rome's train station and the streets on either side of it are a nightmare of mostly low-end eateries. A few places stand out as options to consider:

At the Station

From near track 15, ride the escalator up to a food court called **$ Terrazza Termini.** It's bright, spacious, and safe-feeling, with several decent mall-type eateries, free Wi-Fi and charging stations, and plenty of places to sit. You'll notice competing *aperitivo* deals (17:00-20:00, €7 for a drink and access to buffet, **Eccellenze della Costiera** is best). There are also large self-service **cafeterias** on the ground floor.

The upscale **Mercato Centrale** (about 200 yards up track 24 facing Via Giovanni Giolitti) is a thriving and slick food market hall with a great vibe and plenty of **$$** foodie options (daily 8:00-24:00).

Around Recommended Via Firenze Area Hotels

$$$ Target Restaurant seems to be the favorite recommendation of every hotel receptionist on Via Firenze. It has a sleek and dressy ambience, capable service, and food that's reliably good, but pricey (free *aperitivo* with this book, daily 12:00-15:30 & 19:00-24:00, closed Sun at lunch, reserve to specify seating outside or inside—avoid getting seated in basement, Via Torino 33, tel. 06-474-0066, www.targetrestaurant.it).

$$ Café Pasticceria Dagnino, a time-warp from the 1960s set in a tired old arcade, has a big selection at its *tavola calda* counter. It's known for its fine pastry section and Sicilian treats from *arancini* to cannoli. A hit with local office workers, it's fast, reasonably priced, and reliable, with good seating inside, upstairs, and outside in the mall. Their €12 "Granpiatto Dagnino" lunch special is a big mixed plate of your choice from the *tavola calda* with water and coffee (daily 7:00-23:00, Galleria Esedra, enter at Via Torino 95, tel. 06-481-8660).

$ Caffè Torino Tavola Calda is another workers' favorite for a quick, cheap lunch. They have good, fresh, hot dishes ready to go for a fine price. Head back past the bar to peruse their enticing display, point at what you want, then grab a seat and the young waitstaff will serve you (Mon-Fri 6:00-18:00, closed Sat-Sun, Via Torino 40, tel. 06-487-0000).

$ Il Forno degli Amici, handy if your hotel is on Via Firenze, is a little dive selling salads by the weight, pizza by the slice, sandwiches, and bakery items (Mon-Sat until 21:00, closed Sun, Via Firenze 51).

Around Via Flavia

For a serious meal near the station, it's worth walking 10 minutes to the quiet and residential-feeling Via Flavia, where you'll find almost no tourism and a cluster of fine dining options. As these places are each distinct and within 100 yards of each other (and there are several other fine options not listed here), I'd show up, survey the scene, and eat at the spot that makes your stomach leap.

$$$ Ristorante la Pentolaccia, upscale and romantic, is a dressy but still tourist-friendly place with tight seating and traditional Roman cooking—consider their daily specials. This is a local hangout, and reservations are smart (daily 12:00-15:00 & 18:00-23:00, a block off Via XX Settembre at Via Flavia 38, tel. 06-483-477, www.lapentolaccia-restaurant.it, Vincenzo gives a warm welcome). To start things off with a free bruschetta, leave this book on the table.

$$$ La Bottega Ristorante, in the Punturi family since 1919, is a bright, contemporary, and easygoing place serving Roman and Mediterranean cuisine, and good wine by the glass (nightly from 17:00, Via Flavia 46, tel. 06-487-0391). They run the adjacent pizzeria.

$ Pietro Punturi Tavola Calda is a *rosticceria* cooking up super casual dishes sold by the weight and eaten on plastic at its fast-food-type seating (Mon-Sat 8:30-20:30, closed Sun, Via Flavia 46).

$$ Pizzeria Annicinquanta, big and modern, is a neighborhood fixture, serving Neapolitan-style pizzas in a calm ambience with outdoor seating (daily 12:00-15:30 & 19:30-24:00, Via Flavia 3, tel. 06-4201-0460).

$$$ I Colori del Vino Enoteca is a classy wine bar that feels like a laboratory of wine appreciation. It has woody walls of bottles, vinyl records playing, a creative menu of *affettati* (cold cuts) and cheeses with different regional themes, and a great list of fine wines by the glass. Helpful, English-speaking Marco carries on a long family tradition of celebrating the fundamentals of good nutrition: fine wine, cheese, meat, and bread (Mon-Sat 12:00-15:00 & 18:00-23:00, closed Sun, Via Aureliana 15 at corner of Via Flavia, tel. 06-474-1745). This is a great stop after dinner for a dessert wine (which comes with a plate of cookies).

Between Piazza Barberini and Trevi Fountain

$$$ Hostaria Romana, near the Quirinale, is a busy bistro with a hustling and fun-loving gang of waiters and makes a good choice on your way to or from Trevi Fountain. The upstairs is a tight, tidy, glassed-in terrace, while the cellar has noisy walls graffitied by happy eaters. As its menu specializes in traditional Roman dishes, it's a good place to try *saltimbocca alla romana* or *bucatini*

EATING

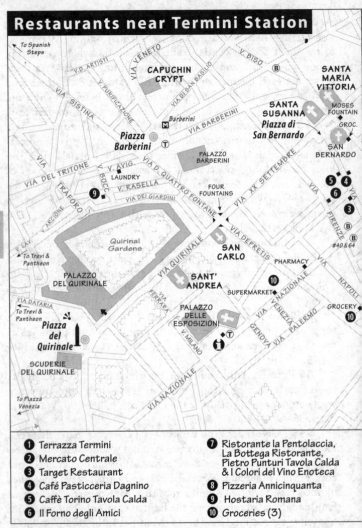

Restaurants near Termini Station

1 Terrazza Termini

2 Mercato Centrale

3 Target Restaurant

4 Café Pasticceria Dagnino

5 Caffè Torino Tavola Calda

6 Il Forno degli Amici

7 Ristorante la Pentolaccia,
La Bottega Ristorante,
Pietro Punturi Tavola Calda
& I Colori del Vino Enoteca

8 Pizzeria Annicinquanta

9 Hostaria Romana

10 Groceries (3)

all'amatriciana. Their €12 antipasti della casa plate, with a variety of vegetables and cheeses, makes a hearty start to your meal (Mon-Sat 12:30-15:00 & 19:15-23:00, closed Sun and Aug, reservations smart, midway between Piazza Barberini and Trevi Fountain at Via del Boccaccio 1, tel. 06-474-5284, www.hostariaromana.it).

TRASTEVERE

Restaurants line the streets of colorful Trastevere. It's a favorite dining neighborhood for both Romans and tourists—more rustic than the downtown zone, but just a short walk across the river. While it's become extremely touristy, if you venture away from the

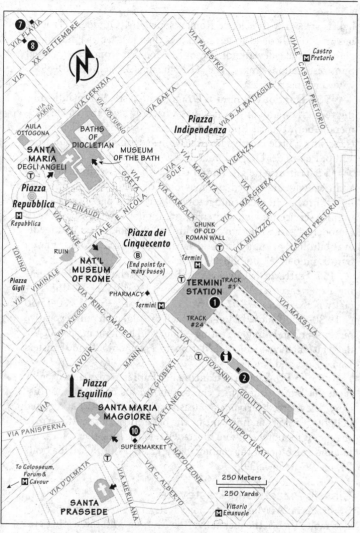

central square (Piazza di Santa Maria in Trastevere) into the back streets you'll find places that serve with sincerity and charm. For locations, see the map on page 387.

$$$$ Taverna Trilussa is your best bet for dining well in Trastevere. Brothers Massimo and Maurizio offer quality without pretense. With a proud 100-year-old tradition, this place has the right mix of style and informality. The service is fun-loving (they're happy to let you split plates into smaller portions to enjoy a family-style meal), yet professional. The menu celebrates local classics and seasonal specials—as well as their award-winning *pasta amatriciana*—and comes with a big wine selection. The spacious dining hall is strewn with eclectic Roman souvenirs. Outdoors, Trilussa has an actual hedged-in terrace rather than just tables jumbled together on the sidewalk (dinner only, Mon-Sat from 19:30, closed Sun, reservations smart, Via del Politeama 23, tel. 06-581-8918, www.tavernatrilussa.it).

$$$ Dar Sor Olimpio al Drago, with a small, romantic dining room (no outdoor seating), has a friendly staff and an enticing menu—both typical Roman and modern Italian. The chef enjoys exercising a little creative license (Mon-Sat from 18:00, Sun from 12:00, Piazza del Drago 2, mobile 339-885-7574).

$$ Trattoria de Gli Amici employs people with mental disabilities (who are helped and mentored by volunteers) to offer delightful meals in a charming atmosphere. Be a part of that community service mission and enjoy traditional Roman cuisine with a modern twist while surrounded by contemporary art in a medieval building or on a romantic square (daily 12:00-23:00, Piazza Sant'Egidio 6, tel. 06-580-6033).

$$ Trattoria da Lucia is your basic old-school Trastevere dining experience, family-run since before World War II. The specialty is *spaghetti alla Gricia,* with pancetta (Tue-Sun 12:30-15:30 & 19:30-23:00, closed Mon and much of Aug, cash only, evocative outdoor or comfy indoor seating—but avoid back room, just off Via del Mattonato at Vicolo del Mattonato 2, tel. 06-580-3601; sisters Livia, Zoe, and Elisa).

$$ La Prosciutteria Cantina dei Papi is a cozy and friendly place celebrating the wine, cheese, and meats of Lazio and Tuscany. They serve hearty *taglieri* (easily splittable boards) of regional delights (€5-15) and fine wine by the big or little bottle. If you're in the mood for porchetta and mortadella, look no further. Nothing's hot and you order at the counter (daily 12:00-24:00, Via della Scala 71, tel. 06-6456-2839).

Classic Pizzerias in Trastevere

$$ Pizzeria "Ai Marmi" is a noisy festival of pizza. Tight marble-slab tables (hence the nickname "the Morgue") fill the seating area in front of the oven and pizza-assembly line. It's a classic Roman scene whether you enjoy the chaos inside, sit at a sidewalk table, or take the famously good, thin, and crispy €8-9 pizza home. They also serve fried cod, rice balls with mozzarella *(supplì)*, and bean dishes. Expect brusque service and a long line between 20:00 and 22:00 (Thu-Tue 18:30 until very late, closed Wed, cash only, tram #8 from Piazza Venezia to first stop over bridge, just beyond Piazza Sonnino at Viale di Trastevere 53, tel. 06-580-0919).

$$ Pizzeria Dar Poeta, tucked in a back alley and a hit with local students, cranks out €9 wood-fired pizzas and calzones. These pizzas are easily splittable and, if you're extra hungry, pay an extra euro for *pizza alta* (thicker crust). Choose between their sloppy, cramped interior or the lively tables outside on the cobblestones (daily 12:00-24:00, call to reserve, arrive before 19:00 or expect a wait, 50 yards directly in front of Santa Maria della Scala Church at Vicolo del Bologna 45, tel. 06-588-0516).

$ Trapizzino Vineria di Roma is a modern cousin to these classic pizzerias. It's a bar with just two items on the menu: a variety of €4 *trapizzini* (pizza-like wraps with delicious freshly toasted crusts) and €2 *supplì* (the Roman answer to *arancini*—Sicily's fried rice balls). They serve a good variety of Lazio wine and play classic American pop music (daily 10:00 until late, Piazza Trilussa 46, tel. 06-581-7312). It's a fast and cheap option if you're in the mood for something like pizza—but a bit different. Another location is in the Testaccio area (described below).

TESTACCIO

To eat far from the crowds in a typical Roman neighborhood, take the Metro (to Piramide), tram (#3), or bus (#83 from Piazza Venezia) to Testaccio. Once a working-class slaughterhouse district, Testaccio has gentrified, but still isn't too touristy. Its bustling market hall has been renovated, and Testaccio has become a favorite spot for local chefs and international foodies. Combine a meal here with a stroll through the neighborhood. To learn even more about the neighborhood, consider the Eating Italy Food Tour (described in the "Resources for Foodies" sidebar, earlier in this chapter). Note that the flagship location of the Eataly food hall chain is in this neighborhood.

Testaccio Market

This is a fun place for foodies (Mon-Sat until 14:00, closed Sun). Buy a drink or light meal, grab a spot under the open skylight where you'll find inviting tables open to all, and be part of the scene. **Caffè in Piazzetta** is a cheery, authentic old bar facing the food court seating in the center of the market.

On the side of the market closest to Via Beniamino Franklin, search out a few favorites for a light lunch: At **Mordi & Vai** (#15), Sergio makes tasty €3-4 sandwiches; locals love the *trippa* (tripe), but I prefer the *panino con allesso* (boiled beef with the bread dipped in broth) and *picchiapò* (stewed beef in a mildly spicy tomato sauce). Survey his dozen or so sandwich fillings and choose. As this is a popular place, you'll need to take a number. They have simple seating across the lane.

Nearby (around #45) are several other tempting stalls: Along with places dishing up pizza by the slice, there's **Zoé,** serving up a little bit of California with fruit, smoothies, and salads made to order. And several bakery stalls will satisfy your sweet tooth with creative pastries.

Near Testaccio Market

For locations of the following restaurants, see the map on page 110.

$$ Agustarello has been serving Roman cuisine since 1957, but their restaurant feels up-to-date and without pretense—the emphasis is on the food. As this family-run place is quite small and very lively, reservations are smart (Mon-Sat 12:30-15:00 & 19:30-24:00, closed Sun, Via Giovanni Branca 98, tel. 06-574-6585).

$ Trapizzino, next door (at #88), serves tasty little pizza wraps for a quick light bite (daily 12:00-late, tel. 06-4341-9624). Another location of this upscale street food chain is in Trastevere (and described earlier).

$$ Flavio al Velavevodetto, partially set inside Monte Testaccio (windows reveal the ancient stacked pottery shards), is a good place to try nose-to-tail classics like *coda alla vaccinara* (oxtail) as well as less adventurous options (daily 12:30-15:00 & 19:45-23:00, reservations smart for dinner, Via di Monte Testaccio 97, tel. 06-574-4194, www.ristorantevelavevodetto.it).

$$ Pizzeria Remo—the humble pizza joint with the huge mob of locals out front late into the evening—is a favorite for Roman-style (thin, crispy-crust) pizza and deep-fried appetizers. It's inexpensive, busy, and crowded. If people are jamming the entrance, muscle your way inside and put your name on the list; there's ample seating, and table turnover is brisk (Mon-Sat 19:00-24:00, closed Sun, Piazza Santa Maria Liberatrice 44, tel. 06-574-6270).

$$$ Volpetti Taverna is a crisp and modern restaurant featuring reinvented classic dishes with seasonal ingredients and a serious wine list. Popular with local office workers for a quick lunch, it turns pricey for dinner (Tue-Sun 11:00-23:00, closed Mon, Via V. Volta 8, tel. 06-574-4306, Matteo).

$ Volpetti Salumeria is a venerable deli—a cheese-and-meat sensory extravaganza—and sells pizza, calzones, and bakery items to go (closed Sun, Via Marmorata 47, tel. 06-574-2352).

$$ Perilli is the neighborhood's classic, old-school eating house—rollicking with tight tables of local families since 1911 (indoor seating only, Thu-Tue 12:30-15:00 & 19:30-23:15, closed Wed, Via Marmorata 39, tel. 06-575-5100).

$$ L'Oasi della Birra ("Beer Oasis") is well known among Roman beer lovers, as it stocks more than 500 Italian and international brews. The main floor is a bottle shop and classy grocery, while the nondescript cellar and the terrace out front serve as a popular bar for locals to hang out and dine on pub grub. This is not a place for a fine meal or special ambience, but rather, to enjoy a beer and the lively local scene. During happy hour (17:30-20:30) just €10 buys you a beer and access to their light dinner spread (open daily 8:00-13:30 & 16:00-24:00, Piazza Testaccio 38, tel. 06-574-6122).

ROME WITH CHILDREN

Sorry, but Rome is not a great place for little kids. Parks are rare. Kid-friendly parks are rarer. Most museums are low-tech and lack hands-on fun.

But there is some good news. Rome's many squares are traffic-free, with plenty of space to run and pigeons to feed while Mom and Dad enjoy coffee at an outdoor table.

Italians love strolling the streets in the evening, and your kids and teens will, too. It can be worth adjusting your sightseeing schedule to allow a siesta in the hot mid-afternoon so your kids have energy to stay up later than they normally do. For a suggested strolling route, see page 82.

Italians are openly fond of kids, so you'll probably get lots of friendly attention. Rome's huge ancient sites (I'm thinking the Colosseum and Pantheon) instill awe in travelers of any age—especially if they can conceive of just how old these structures are. And you won't get many complaints about the cuisine: pizza and gelato. *Buona fortuna!*

Trip Tips

PLAN AHEAD
Involve your kids in trip planning. Have them read about the places that you may include in your itinerary (even the hotels you're considering), and let them help with your decisions.

Where to Stay
- Minimize hotel changes by planning three-day stays or consider renting an apartment through an Airbnb-type service (for more info on short-term rentals, see page 553).

- Aim for hotels with restaurants, so older kids can go back to the room while you finish a pleasant dinner.
- Rome's hotels often give price breaks for kids. Most have some sort of crib you can use.
- Your kids will thank you for avoiding the few remaining hotels without air-conditioning.

What to Bring

- Bring your own drawing supplies and English-language picture books, as these supplies are pricey in Italy.
- For a touch of home at the hotel, bring some favorite movies.

EATING

Rome offers plenty of food options for children.

What to Eat (and Drink)

- Kid-friendly foods found everywhere include fresh bread *(pane)* and pasta (plain is *"pasta bianca"* and pasta with butter is *"pasta al burro"*; grated cheese will be served on the side). Pizza is another popular favorite—kids like *margherita* (tomato, basil, and cheese) and the slightly spicy Italian version of pepperoni *(diavola, salsiccia piccante, or salame piccante).*
- Popular drinks are *granitas* (slushies), *frullati* (smoothies), frappés (shakes), *aranciata* (orange soda), *limonata* (lemonade), *spremuta d'arancia* (fresh-squeezed orange juice), and *cioccolata calda* (hot chocolate).
- The official drinking age in Italy is 18. Teens are sometimes offered wine or beer in restaurants, especially when accompanied by a parent. It's best to decide on a family policy beforehand.

When and Where to Eat

- For a refreshing respite from the midday heat, take a gelato break or go to a casual, air-conditioned place for lunch.
- Eat dinner "early" (at about 19:00) to dodge the romantic crowd. Restaurants are less kid-friendly after 21:00.
- Skip the famous places. Look instead for self-service cafeterias, bars (children are welcome), or fast-food restaurants where kids can move around without bothering others.
- Eating *al fresco* is fun; try places on squares where kids can

run free while you dine, but avoid historical monuments in the city center. Picnic lunches and dinners work well—stop by the market and bakery at Campo de' Fiori, get your fixings at the *alimentari* and *frullati* shop near the Pantheon, or try the sandwich shops on Via della Croce. *Pizza rustica* shops sell cheap takeout pizza, and of course gelato provides some of the best high-calorie memories in town. See the Eating in Rome chapter for these and other ideas.

SIGHTSEEING

The key to a successful Roman family vacation is to slow down and incorporate your child's interests into each day's plans.

Planning Your Time

- Let your kids make some decisions, such as choosing lunch spots or deciding which stores or museums to visit. Deputize your child to lead you on my self-guided walks and museum tours.
- Don't overdo it. Tackle only one or two key sights a day (Vatican Museums, or Colosseum and Forum). Force your kids to endure an hour to see a sight, then relent if they've had enough.
- Get kids engaged in age-appropriate museum fun. Younger kids might enjoy a scavenger hunt approach: Buy postcards of sights in the museum gift shop (or give them this book with its photos) and let them find the art. Museum audioguides are great for older children.
- Balance your museum-going with fun and energetic activities, like climbing up St. Peter's Dome or Castel Sant'Angelo, biking the Borghese Gardens, or running around Piazza Navona.

Successful Sightseeing

- Ask at Rome's TIs about kid-friendly activities. TIs sometimes have a helpful "kid's pack."
- Italy's national museums generally offer free admission to children under 18—always ask before buying tickets for your kids.
- Follow this book's crowd-beating tips. Kids don't want to stand in a long line for a museum (which they might not even want to see). If you get a Roma Pass, be aware that kids get to skip the line with parents who have the pass.
- Public WCs are hard to find: Try museums, bars, gelato shops, and fast-food restaurants.

Making or Finding Quality Souvenirs

- Buy your child a trip journal, and encourage him or her to write down observations, thoughts, and favorite sights and

Books and Films for Kids

Get your kids into the spirit of the Eternal City with these books and movies.

City Trails—Rome (Lonely Planet Kids, 2016). Follow Marco and Amelia as they find odd and wonderful secrets that give quirky insights into the sights and history of Rome.

Classic Myths to Read Aloud: The Great Stories of Greek and Roman Mythology (William F. Russell, 1988). This thoughtful introduction to the tales of the ancient past is sure to captivate children five and up.

Julius Caesar (1953). Portraying the dramatic story of Julius Caesar's assassination and its aftermath, this classic film brings history to life.

Kids' Travel Guide—Rome (Flying Kids, 2019). In this activity travel guide, kids can explore Rome with a mix of interactive quizzes, tips, and coloring pages alongside their personal tour guide, Leonardo.

The Last Legion (2007). In this adventure film, brave 12-year-old Romulus Augustus takes bold action to save the Roman Empire from rebels in AD 470.

The Lizzie McGuire Movie (2003). A middle-school class trip to Rome is an adventure filled with comedy, drama, and romance.

Mission Rome: A Scavenger Hunt Adventure (Catherine Aragon, 2014). Young travelers will have hands-on fun discovering the city in this spy-themed scavenger hunt.

The Pink Panther 2 (2009). Bumbling Inspector Jacques Clouseau heads to Rome with detectives from around the globe in a case of stolen world treasures.

Rome: Panorama Pops (Kristyna Litten, 2013). This accordion-style pop-up book takes you through sites like St. Peter's Basilica and Villa Borghese.

The Thieves of Ostia (Caroline Lawrence, 2001). In ancient Rome, a young ship captain's daughter joins three friends to solve a mystery. This is the first book in Lawrence's *The Roman Mysteries* series.

This is Rome (Miroslav Sasek, 1960). History comes alive in this charming picture book of Rome through the ages. The 2007 edition includes a section about the modern-day city.

CHILDREN

memories. This journal could end up being your child's favorite souvenir.

- For a group project, keep a family journal. Pack a small diary and a glue stick. While relaxing over a gelato, take turns writing or drawing about the day's events and include mementos such as ticket stubs from museums and postcards.

- Teens might love shopping (or even window-shopping). See the Shopping in Rome chapter for fun areas.

MONEY AND SAFETY

Before your trip gets underway, talk to your kids about safety and money.

- If you allow kids to explore a museum or neighborhood on their own, be sure to establish a clear meeting time and place.
- Give your child a money belt and an expanded allowance; you are on vacation, after all. Let your children budget their funds by comparing and contrasting the dollar and euro.
- It's good to have a "what if" procedure in place in case something goes wrong. Give your kids your hotel's business card, your phone number (if you brought a mobile phone), and emergency taxi fare. Let them know to ask to use the phone at a hotel if they are lost.

STAYING CONNECTED AND TRANSPORTATION

- If your kids have mobile phones, show them how to make calls in Italy. If traveling with older kids, you can help them keep in touch with friends at home with cheap texting plans and by email.
- Hotel guest computers and Wi-Fi hotspots are a godsend. Readily available Wi-Fi (at hotels, some cafés, and all Starbucks and McDonald's) makes bringing a mobile device worthwhile.
- Most parents find it worth the peace of mind to buy a supplemental messaging plan for the whole family: Adults can stay connected to teenagers while allowing them maximum independence (see page 572).
- Children under age 10 travel free on Rome's public transit system when accompanied by an adult.
- If you're taking the train to another city, check for family discounts; see page 581.

Sights and Activities

ANCIENT SITES, CHURCHES, AND MUSEUMS

While some ancient sites, such as the **Colosseum,** are naturally captivating for kids, others, like the Roman Forum, may be a snooze. To keep them engaged, consider picking up a copy of *Rome: Past and Present,* a book with plastic overlays showing how the ruins used to look. It's available online and at stalls near the entrance of ancient sites (prices are soft, so negotiate).

Catacombs of Priscilla

These spooky tunnels just outside the walls of the ancient city are goblin pleasers. Kids will get a thrill out of descending into this underground tomb and seeing some of the 40,000 burial niches carved for Christians from the second to the fifth century. Visits are by 30-minute guided English-language tours. See listing on page 90.

Capuchin Crypt

The most macabre place in Rome is decorated with bones; it's fascinating for children and adults alike (may be too creepy for younger kids). In the basement below the Church of Santa Maria della Immacolata Concezione, bones of about 4,000 friars who died in the 1700s decorate a series of six crypts. Your introduction to the place is the Crypt of the Three Skeletons, where the ceiling is decorated with a scythe-wielding skeleton, a bony chandelier, and floral motifs made of ribs and vertebrae. Other chambers are named for the type of bones that line them: Crypt of the Tibia and Fibia, Crypt of the Hips, and Crypt of the Skulls are a few that'll keep you awake at night. For more information, see page 80.

St. Peter's Basilica Dome

In Vatican City, the climb to the top of St. Peter's is great for its dizzy railing view into the church from halfway up the dome—plus the hike will tire out young adventurers. ☐ See the St. Peter's Basilica Tour chapter for detailed information.

Vatican Museums

These extensive museums feature mummies, sarcophagi, ancient statues and armor, old maps, and the bedrooms of Renaissance popes. There's an audioguide designed for families. ☐ See the Vatican Museums Tour chapter for detailed information.

Castel Sant'Angelo

This emperor's tomb-turned-castle has one of the best views of Rome from the rooftop—including striking vistas of the Vatican. The weapon displays will appeal to young knights. See listing on page 74.

Church of Sant'Ignazio

This church's riot of Baroque illusions will intrigue kids. The colorful ceiling fresco fools the eye into thinking you're looking up at a dome—including false two-dimensional columns that look like extensions of the real columns below. Kids might also get a kick out of seeing the headquarters of the Carabinieri police force, across the street. Sant'Ignazio is included in the ☐ Pantheon Tour chapter; see page 158.

CHILDREN

Pyramid of Gaius Cestius

Your children can get a whiff of Egypt by visiting Rome's funky little pyramid. Also check out the cat hospital in the adjacent park and climb on the chunk of old Roman wall across the street (Via Raffaele Persichetti, Metro: Piramide). See page 110.

Bocca della Verità

At the legendary "Mouth of Truth" at the Church of Santa Maria in Cosmedin, kids can test their truthfulness—and bravery—by sticking their hands in the mouth of the stone face in the church's porch wall. Liars will have their hands gobbled up. Expect hordes of tourists and long waits. See page 47.

Montemartini Museum

Its location in an old power plant may be even more interesting to young visitors than the ancient statuary featured in this unusual museum. Kids can inspect the defunct centrifuges, boilers, and steam turbines that mingle with the statues of muses and satyrs. An added plus: no crowds. For details, see page 114.

Explora

This children's museum is a hands-on wonderland for kids 12 and under. The interactive exhibits will have your little ones doing the shopping, pulling toy carrots in the garden, puttering in the kitchen, creating cartoons, and experimenting with weights and measures, among many other fun activities. Descriptions are in Italian (with some English), but kids probably won't care.

Cost and Hours: €5 for kids 1-3, €8.50 for kids 3-99, parent must accompany child; visit limited to two hours with entry Tue-Sun at 10:00, 12:00, 15:00, and 17:00, closed Mon; confirm times in advance, reservations required on weekends, helpful English-speaking staff; 10-minute walk north of Piazza del Popolo at Via Flaminia 82, Metro: Flaminio, tel. 06-361-3776, www.mdbr.it.

OUTDOOR FUN

Rome feels safe at night, and you can easily take your kids on the **walks** suggested in this book, such as my "Dolce Vita Stroll" on page 82. On my Heart of Rome Walk, children like slurping up chocolate gelato at the Tre Scalini *gelateria* on Piazza Navona and tossing coins in the Trevi Fountain. Consider letting your child act as tour guide for an hour by leading one of the walks.

CHILDREN

These other outdoor activities will also amuse your young and active travel companions.

Villa Borghese Gardens

These sprawling gardens are Rome's version of Central Park. This may be your best bet in Rome to get your kid pedaling in a leafy, bike-friendly area. (For an overview of the park, see the map on page 77.) The best kids' zones are near Porta Pinciana, where you'll find rental bikes, pony rides, and other amusements. Summer weekends at the gardens, sure to be a hit with kids, include classic Roman puppet shows at Teatro dei Burattini. Rome's **zoo,** Bioparco, in the northern section of the park, houses about 900 animals including the endangered black lemur, pygmy hippopotamus, and Gila monster.

Cost and Hours: Gardens—free to enter; Bioparco—free for kids "under 1 meter tall," €13 for kids over 1 meter and under age 10, €16 for adults; daily 9:30-18:00, Nov-March until 17:00, last entry one hour before closing; café and picnic areas; Piazzale del Giardino Zoologico 1—take bus #910 from Termini to Pinciana stop, or tram #19 from Metro: Ottaviano to Bioparco stop; tel. 06-360-8211, www.bioparco.it.

Beaches

Beyond the ruins of Ostia Antica, the sandy beaches of modern Ostia are easily accessible via a combination Metro and suburban train ride. As elsewhere in Italy, most of the shoreline is occupied by private "clubs" *(stabilimenti balneare)* that charge a fee to use their facilities. Clubs lay out rows of beach chairs and umbrellas, and most have cafés, WCs, changing rooms, lockers, and lifeguards on duty. Some even have full-service restaurants and swimming pools. Bring a towel and picnic, and expect to be surrounded by a thoroughly local scene. Expect to pay around €5 for beach-club entry in peak season (free and uncrowded off-season), and about €10 for each chair and umbrella (swimming pools usually cost extra, beach clubs open roughly May-Sept).

Any club will work. **Belsito** (on Facebook as "Stabilimento Belsito") and its neighbor to the north, **Il Capanno** (www.ilcapanno.net) are nice and unpretentious choices. They are a 15-minute walk south from the public pier (or 5-minute walk from the Stella Polare train station described on the next page—head straight for the water and turn right).

Next to Il Capanno, there's a small, free **public beach** that's usually packed, especially on weekends. Other public beaches are few and far between. Public beaches are free year-round.

Getting There: The journey is covered by a normal Metro ticket (passes valid) and takes about an hour from central Rome. Take Metro line B to the Piramide stop, which is linked to the

Roma Porta San Paolo train station. Follow signs to *Lido:* Go up the escalator, turn left, and go down the steps to reach the Roma-Lido train line. From here, it's easy—all trains depart in the direction of Lido, leaving every 15 minutes. Look for the information board that reads something like, *"Treno in partenza, 13.25, bin 3,"* which means that there's a train departing at 13:25, track 3. Hop on and ride for about 45 minutes (no need to validate your Metro ticket again).

You can get off at either of two stations a half-mile apart: Lido Centro or Stella Polare. Stella Polare is a five-minute walk from the beach clubs mentioned earlier. The Lido Centro station is near downtown Ostia; it's about a 15-minute walk through town (past stores selling food and beach gear), to the public pier (Pontile di Ostia) and surrounding clubs. The way is not well marked; don't hesitate to ask for directions.

Hydromania Water Park

Just outside Rome, cool off at this big water park with looping slides, several swimming pools, terraces of chaise lounges with umbrellas, and a snack bar. A great change of pace from museums and churches, this alternative is perfect for a hot Italian summer day.

Cost and Hours: €24, cheaper for kids 12 and under and anyone arriving after 14:00; open in summer Mon-Fri 9:30-18:30, Sat-Sun until 19:00, closed early Sept-May; Vicolo del Casale Lumbroso 200, exit 33 off ring freeway west of the city, tel. 06-6618-3183, www.hydromania.it.

SHOPPING IN ROME

Rome is a wonderful city to shop in. Even if you're not aiming to buy anything, exploring popular shopping areas provides a break from stressful, clogged tourist sights and an excuse to lose yourself on a charming street. Sometimes window-shopping, rather than museum-going, is the best way to connect with the contemporary life of a city. And that's certainly true in Rome.

Traditionally, shops are open from roughly 9:00 to 13:00 and from 15:30 or 16:00 to 19:00 or 19:30. They're often closed on Sundays, summer Saturday afternoons, and winter Monday mornings. But in the city center, you'll find that many are now staying open through lunch (generally 10:00-19:00). Shop early if you intend to hit Rome's produce or flea markets (described at the end of this chapter)—with the exception of the weekend Mercato Monti market, they typically close by 13:30.

For information on VAT refunds and customs regulations, see page 542.

Shopping Neighborhoods

I've described four of Rome's most engaging and easy-to-reach shopping zones: the heart of Rome near Piazza Navona and Campo de' Fiori; the Jewish Ghetto; the Monti district, convenient to the ancient sites; and Rome's most famous (and, arguably, least characteristic) shopping zone, the "shopping triangle" along Via del Corso and near the Spanish Steps. Turnover is rampant, so some places I mention may have changed hands by the time you visit. Explore and make discoveries of your own.

The following shopping areas are also worth a look: **Via Nazionale** has a range of reasonably priced shops, especially for clothes and shoes. The back lanes of **Trastevere** have a similar feel to Monti, with offbeat boutiques. **Via Cola di Rienzo,** near the Vatican, is good for midrange clothes.

HEART OF ROME

Although right in the tourist-clogged center, the streets near Piazza Navona and Campo de' Fiori are surprisingly less crowded—and the shops less tacky—than along the main thoroughfares connecting Rome's top squares. Heavy on antiques and home furnishings, this area may be better for window shopping than buying, but you can find souvenirs here as well. Everything mentioned here is within about a 15-minute walk of each other.

Near Piazza Navona

The main shopping street here—and one of the most charming streets in all of Rome, with cobblestones, leafy planters, and little to no traffic—is the straight-shot **Via dei Coronari,** between Piazza Navona and the bend in the river. To find it, pop out the north end of Piazza Navona and turn left. This is the place to browse antiques and daydream about furnishing a Roman apartment. Stampe Antiche "Trincia" Restauro (#15) is a fascinating shop that specializes in painstaking restoration of works of art, with antique prints that will fit in your suitcase. This street also boasts several fine clothing and shoe stores, such as Superga (#18), the classic Italian athletic shoe brand (which also makes designer heels). Made (#25) is a "creative bakery" with bagel sandwiches and delicate cupcakes.

After Piazzetta di San Simeone, there are fewer antiques and more clothes—stylish yet accessible. Tucked in the little square on the left, Spazio IF (#44a) features eye-catching Sicilian style—mostly women's fashion, including handbags and scarves. Dimorae Design (#57) sells trendy Italian home furnishings. At Pastori Antichi (#110), an army of military miniatures from around the world stands watch. Lisa Corti Home Textile Emporium (#197, part of a small Italian chain) fills its showroom with colorful fabrics, while Le Tele di Carlotta (#228) charms with hand-embroidered towels and handkerchiefs.

At the end of Via dei Coronari, you could angle right one block to Castel Sant'Angelo. Or, to make your walk a loop, hook left at the big square and Alimentari Coronari (gourmet sandwiches) onto **Via di Panico.** You'll pass a few more shops along here—including Kromatika Lab (#14), with striking design.

From here, turn right on Via degli Orsini; one block later, turn left onto **Via del Governo Vecchio.** Passing the Penny Lane shop (#4, with youthful vintage wear), you'll be greeted by a street with fashion, home decor, textiles, and plenty of cute boutiques (casual wear and accessories—mostly women's, but some men's as well). The closer you get to Piazza Navona, the more crowded the street becomes, with souvenir stands and tourist-trap restaurants mixed in with boutiques. When the street opens up into a square, bear left up narrow Via di Pasquino to reach Piazza Navona.

Near Campo de' Fiori

Two worthwhile parallel shopping streets run northwest (toward the river) from Piazza Farnese, just a block south of Campo de' Fiori: Via Monserrato/Via dei Banchi Vecchi and Via Giulia. (Streets in the opposite direction—to the southeast—are sleepier, with fewer shops.)

Heading away from Piazza Farnese on low-key **Via Monserrato,** you'll see several antique, furniture, and home-decorating shops. Hollywood (#107) is a treat for cinephiles, with movie posters and rare DVDs; their sister store, at #110, sells movie-themed embroidered T-shirts. Between these two, at #108, is a fascinating old-time cobbler, with a crowded workbench crammed into a tiny shop. Estremi (#101) has inspiring retro furniture, while Antichi Kimono (#43b) features Asian-themed dresses and fabrics.

Farther along, Via Monserrato becomes **Via dei Banchi Vecchi,** with antiques of varying aesthetics—from mothballed grannies to hipster vintage. Banchievecchi Pellami (#40) is an old-school leather shop, with belts and wallets. And Restore (#51) is packed with housewares, home furnishings, and kitchen gadgets.

When Via dei Banchi Vecchi dead-ends at the big cross street, loop left around the block to stroll more atmospheric **Via Giulia**— narrower, cobbled, and mostly traffic-free. Here you'll find fewer shops and more offices. House Kitchen & Design, near the start of the street at #101, is a cramped hole-in-the-wall with cooking gadgets; farther down, Magie di Casa (#140c) has a nice selection of linens, from tea towels to aprons.

One more street near Campo de' Fiori may be worth exploring: **Via Giubbonari,** which stretches southeast from the square. More heavily trafficked (and more touristy), it has dozens of stores selling affordable apparel aimed mainly at a younger crowd.

JEWISH GHETTO

In addition to its gorgeous synagogue, evocative history, and bustling restaurants, Rome's Jewish ghetto is also a great place to browse. My 📖 Jewish Ghetto Walk provides a natural spine for shopping explorations.

Near the start of that walk, just around the corner from the synagogue, the Leone Limentani housewares and dishware shop feels like a well-stocked mini warehouse—this is where Roman couples register for wedding gifts (walk away from the river, and turn left at the ruins onto Via del Portico d'Ottavia; it's at the corner on the left at #47).

Shopping in Rome

Shopping Areas
1. Via dei Coronari
2. Via del Governo Vecchio
3. Via Monserrato
4. Via dei Banchi Vecchi
5. Via Giulia
6. Via Giubbonari
7. Via della Reginella
8. Via del Boschetto & Via dei Serpenti
9. Via Leonina, Via Urbana & Mercato Monti
10. Shopping Triangle: Via del Corso to Via del Babuino
11. Piazza Borghese
12. Via Margutta
13. Piazza Pio XII

Shops
14. La Rinascente (2)
15. Galleria Alberto Sordi
16. UPIM (3)
17. Oviesse/OVS (2)

Markets
18. Porta Portese Flea Market
19. Via Sannio Flea Market
20. Mercato Trionfale
21. Mercato Esquilino
22. Mercato di Testaccio
23. Piazza delle Coppelle
24. Via Balbo
25. Via della Pace

SHOPPING

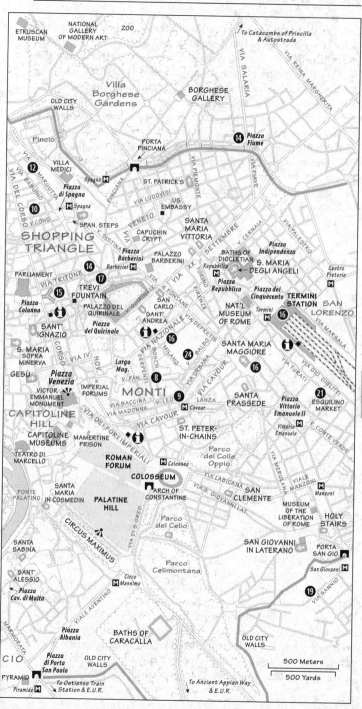

Farther along Via del Portico d'Ottavia, Mondo di Laura (#6) sells artisan cookies. Just beyond, turn right up **Via della Reginella,** lined with cute boutiques: Giuseppe Casetti's funky shop (#8a), with vintage photos, stacks of yellowing books, and other artsy objects; L'Officinaturale (at #3), a natural-products shop with oils, soaps, perfumes, and health foods; takeawaygallery, which is a mod art boutique (#11); and, at the end of the street (#30), Peperita, run by sisters who combine their passions for olive oil and all manner of hot peppers. Their products—powders, pastes, and infused oils—are ranked on a spiciness scale of 1 to 17; generous samples let you test your limits.

Back on the main drag is a long row of food stands, kosher butchers, and a few Judaica shops. Less than a 10-minute walk straight ahead is the Campo de' Fiori shopping zone described earlier.

MONTI, NEAR THE ROMAN FORUM

Located between Via Cavour and Via Nazionale, behind the Imperial Forums, the Monti neighborhood is a delight for exploring, dining, and shopping (and described in more detail on page 66). Monti has Rome's closest thing to a hipster aesthetic: gourmet foodie shops and funky boutiques alongside very traditional neighborhood stores. Get oriented from the main square, Piazza della Madonna dei Monti. Then explore four nearby streets—Via del Boschetto, Via dei Serpenti, Via Leonina, and Via Urbana—always returning to this charming center of the Monti neighborhood.

Via del Boschetto and Via dei Serpenti: This little loop takes you up and down the parallel main drags of Monti. From the top of Piazza della Madonna dei Monti, head left down Via del Boschetto. You'll pass several little boutiques and jewelry shops. Along the way, watch for: a tea house, a vinyl records shop, a kids' clothing store, Gallina Smilza (colorful plastic dishes and housewares), and Pulp (women's casual fashion).

After two blocks, circle left on Via Panisperna. Walk downhill on Panisperna, noticing—on the corner—Macelleria Stecchiotti, a classic Roman butcher (where, reportedly, VIPs from the president to the pope get their meat), the neighborhood's favorite hangout bar (Ai Tre Scalini), and (at the corner) a popular bakery.

Turn left on Via dei Serpenti, which leads back to the piazza where you started. Along the way, browse past a funky collection of shops, including: Podere Vecciano (at #33)—"a farm in the city" selling enticing Tuscan (not Roman) goods, including wines, olive oils, gifty edibles, and wood-carved items; a characteristic jewelry store; a tempting *alimentari* (grocery); and a neighborhood fixture dating from the days when vintage wasn't yet vintage. The aptly named Di Tutto di Più ("Everything and More," at #4) is a general store stuffed to the gills with everything you could possibly need.

Via Leonina and Via Urbana: For more of the same, browse from Piazza della Madonna dei Monti up Via Leonina, which leads to Via Urbana. Heading up Via Leonina, you'll pass some fun little galleries, a chocolatier (La Bottega del Cioccolato), and lots of creative hole-in-the-wall eateries. The big garage on the right opens its doors on weekends to host the lively Mercato Monti (see "Flea Markets," below).

After passing the entrance to Cavour Metro station, the street swings left and becomes Via Urbana. At the gap with the parking lot, look high on the left to spot the recommended Fatamorgana *gelateria* (see map on page 372). Farther along, you'll pass the Studio Cassio mosaics workshop (#98), a fascinating *orologiaio* (clock shop, #103a), more boutiques, and Aromaticus (at #134), which sells nothing but fresh herbs.

THE SHOPPING TRIANGLE, NEAR VIA DEL CORSO AND THE SPANISH STEPS

Via del Corso runs south, from Piazza del Popolo to the heart of Rome, and the little streets that poke east off the main drag—toward the Spanish Steps—form an area nicknamed the "shopping triangle." This zone has big international chains to suit every budget—from Dolce & Gabbana to the Gap—along with some very famous designers...all of which makes it less funky and colorful than the neighborhoods described previously. Nevertheless, a few quirky shops hide out here as well.

Streets Between Via del Corso and Via del Babuino

The following streets branch off of Via del Corso. Starting at Piazza del Popolo, these are listed from north to south and are to the left as you walk (the streets to the right have fewer shops). Via del Babuino, which angles off parallel to Via del Corso, has mostly pricey international chains (Tiffany, Chanel, Dolce & Gabbana, and so on). See the "Dolce Vita Stroll" map on page 83 for specific locations of these streets.

Via Laurina, two blocks from Piazza del Popolo, has some funkier shops, including several with youth fashions; halfway down at #10 is the recommended Fatamorgana *gelateria*, and classier galleries and antiques sit at the far end.

Via di Gesù e Maria, running along its namesake church, has fewer stores. Discount dell'Alta Moda (at #16a, literally "Discount on High Fashion," where last year's designer duds are marked down by half) is a hit with bargain shoppers, while sports fans peruse the store with merchandise promoting the local Lazio soccer team. **Via di San Giacomo,** on the other side of the church, is also fairly sleepy—though it's fun to peek in the windows of the art school to see the artisans and craftspeople of the 21st century hard at work.

Via del Greci has a sheet music store, antiques, fashion boutiques, and a fragrant flower stall.

Via Vittoria and **Via della Croce** are major thoroughfares for reaching the Spanish Steps, with fewer interesting shops and more touristy crowds (although the historic stationery shop Vertecchi, at #70, is a favorite); however, Via della Croce *is* a great place to browse for a meal (see suggestions on page 407). The recommended Pastificio (near the end of the street, at #8) is, true to its name, a pasta factory, where you can buy dry pasta as an edible souvenir.

Some of the streets that run parallel to Via del Corso along here are also fun to wander. **Via Mario de' Fiori** is crammed with upscale boutiques but tucked amidst the glitz is the appealing c.u.c.i.n.a. shop (at #65), where you can stock up on Italian-style kitchen gadgets and crockery.

Via delle Carrozze is fun to browse, with shops carrying specialties from other parts of Italy (handy if Rome is your only destination): The Santa Maria Novella perfume shop (#87) stocks scents from that famous church-run perfume works in Florence; Il Cerichio dei Goloso (#19) serves delicate pastries—and sells colorful plates—from Sicily; and La Peonia (#85) specializes in products from Sardinia. Also along this stretch, look in the window of the old-time tailor, Attilio Roncaccia (#12).

From **Via dei Condotti,** you can see the Spanish Steps hovering in the distance. This busy, glamorous strip has the same type of high-roller international shops found on Via del Babuino.

For the simpler side of this area, find your way a few blocks west (on Via dei Condotti *away* from the Spanish Steps—toward the river, just south of Ara Pacis) to **Piazza Borghese.** This sleepy little square is filled with green kiosks selling prints, antique books, and curios.

Via Margutta

Hiding parallel to Via del Corso and Via del Babuino is one of the most chic addresses in town, **Via Margutta.** (To find it, go down Via della Fontanella, near the top of Via del Corso; or head up from the Spanish Steps.) Here you'll find exclusive-feeling designer boutiques, big-ticket antiques, home-decorating galleries, day spas, fashion eyewear, jewelers, wedding planners, and other places where you must ring the bell to be let inside. Tucked along here is one holdover from simpler times: La Bottega del Marmoraro (#53), where Sandro busily carves marble in a cramped hole-in-the-wall.

Department Stores, Souvenirs, and Markets

If all you need are souvenirs, a surgical strike at any gift shop will do. Otherwise, stop at a department store, scout near the Vatican or in the Jewish Ghetto for religious items, hit the flea market and produce markets, or—if you're in a pinch—pick up some mementos at the airport on your way out of town.

Department Stores

The shopping complex under Termini train station is a convenient place to peruse clothes, bags, shoes, and perfume at several major Italian chain stores (most open daily 8:00-22:00).

A good upscale department store is **La Rinascente** (Via del Tritone 61). Besides deluxe brands, it has a fine design section with great and often affordable ideas for gifts, a magnificent rooftop terrace for a romantic *aperitivo,* good restaurants, free bathrooms, and a section of an ancient aqueduct in the basement (worth a quick visit). You'll find another branch on Piazza Fiume (east of the Borghese Gallery).

The **Galleria Alberto Sordi** is an elegant 19th-century "mall" (across from Piazza Colonna). **UPIM** is a popular midrange department store (many branches, including inside Termini train station, Via Nazionale 111, and Piazza Santa Maria Maggiore). **Oviesse/OVS,** a cheap clothing outlet, is near the Vatican Museums (on the corner of Via Candia and Via Mocenigo, Metro: Cipro) and also near Piazza Barberini (Via del Tritone 172, Metro: Barberini).

Religious Souvenirs

Rome is a magnet for pilgrims, who find no shortage of shops near the Vatican—in the area directly in front of St. Peter's Square (on and around **Piazza Pio XII**), or along nearby Via Borgo Pio. Several shops in the Jewish Ghetto sell Judaica, Jewish-themed art, and other souvenirs.

Flea Markets

For antiques and fleas, the granddaddy of markets is the **Porta Portese** *mercato delle pulci* (flea market). This Sunday-morning market is long and spindly, running between the actual Porta Portese (a gate in the old town wall) and the Trastevere train station. Starting at Porta Portese, walk through the long, tacky parade of stalls selling cheap bras and shoes. Along the way, check out the con artists with the shell games. Each has shills in the crowd "winning big money" to get suckers involved. Hang on to your wallet—literally, in your front pocket, or better yet, use a money belt and make sure it's safely tucked under your clothes. This is a den of thieves. The heart of the market for real flea-market junk (hiding a few little antique treasures) is the square in the center near Via Cesare Pas-

carella. I find that a slow stroll through the entire market and back to the Porta Portese takes about an hour and a half. While the shopping gets old (and the vendor food shouldn't be consumed), the people-watching is endlessly entertaining (6:30-13:00 Sun only, on Via Portu-ense and Via Ippolito Nievo; to get to the market, catch bus #75 from Termini train station or tram #8 from Piazza Venezia, get off on Viale di Trastevere, and walk toward the river—and the noise).

At the **Via Sannio** market, you'll find new and used clothing and leather goods, some handicrafts, and random items that were probably stolen. You won't find antiques (Mon-Sat 9:00-13:30, closed Sun, behind Coin department store, just outside the walls of San Giovanni in Laterano, Metro: San Giovanni).

For something a bit hipper, visit the weekend **Mercato Monti** in the Monti district. This flea market has an emphasis on vintage clothes and housewares and up-and-coming designers (Sat-Sun 10:00-20:00, closed July-Aug, Hotel Palatino, Via Leonina 46, Metro: Cavour, www.mercatomonti.com).

Open-Air Produce Markets

For a fun and colorfully authentic experience, wander through the easygoing neighborhood produce markets that clog certain streets and squares every morning (7:00-13:30) except Sunday. Consider the huge **Mercato Trionfale** (three blocks north of Vatican Museums at Via Andrea Doria). Another great food market is the **Mercato Esquilino** (near Termini Station at Via Filippo Turati, Metro: Vittorio Emanuele). The covered **Mercato di Testaccio** sells produce and housewares and is a hit with photographers and people-watchers (Metro: Piramide; for more on the market, see page 113). Smaller but equally charming slices of everyday Roman life are at markets on these streets and squares: **Piazza delle Coppelle** (near the Pantheon), **Via Balbo** (near Termini train station and recommended hotels off Via Nazionale), and **Via della Pace** (near Piazza Navona). And **Campo de' Fiori,** despite having become quite touristy, is still a fun scene.

Shopping at Fiumicino Airport

Rome's main airport (a.k.a. Leonardo da Vinci Airport) sells Italian specialty foods vacuum-packed to clear US customs. Most shops are near the departure gates (after you check your bags and pass through security). Try *parmigiano reggiano* cheese, dried porcini mushrooms or peppers, and better olive oil than you can buy at home. Don't bother buying any salami or prosciutto unless it's canned; you're not allowed to bring fresh meat into the US (and even canned beef products are prohibited). Remember, if you're flying to the US and transferring before your final destination, you'll likely be required to pack purchased liquids in your checked luggage after clearing customs (a potential recipe for disaster). You'll have better odds of carrying it onto a connecting flight if the vendor seals it in a "STEB"—a secure, tamper-evident bag.

NIGHTLIFE IN ROME

Romans get dressed up and eat out in casual surroundings for their evening entertainment. For most visitors, the best after-dark activity is simply to grab a gelato and join in the *passeggiata*, the evening stroll through the medieval lanes that connect Rome's romantic, floodlit squares and fountains. Head for Piazza Navona, the Pantheon, Campo de' Fiori, Trevi Fountain, the Spanish Steps, Via del Corso, Trastevere (around the Santa Maria in Trastevere Church), or Monte Testaccio.

For a great evening stroll, 📖 see my Heart of Rome Walk chapter or my "Dolce Vita Stroll" (on page 82).

PERFORMANCES AND FILM

Check out the current listings of concerts, operas, dance, and films. Posters around town also advertise upcoming events. For the most up-to-date events calendar, check these English-language websites: www.inromenow.com, www.wantedinrome.com, and www.angloinfo.com.

Contemporary Music Scene

Music lovers will seek out the mega-music complex of the Rome **Auditorium** (Auditorium Parco della Musica), designed by contemporary architect Renzo Piano and hosting concerts by both Italian and international artists (€20-60 tickets, check availability in advance—concerts often sell out, Viale Pietro de Coubertin 30, take Metro to Flaminio and then catch tram #2 to Apollodoro, from there it's a 5-minute walk east, just beyond the elevated road, tram/metro runs until 23:30, box office tel. 02-6006-0900, www.auditorium.com). Also called the "Park of Music," it's a place where many Romans go just for the scene—music store, restaurants, cafés, and fresh modern architecture with three state-of-the-art auditoriums (known as "the beetles" for their appearance). If you want to see today's Romans enjoying the modern culture of their city, an evening here is the best you'll do.

Classical Music and Opera

The **Teatro dell'Opera** has an active schedule of opera and classical concerts. In the summer, the productions move to the Baths of Caracalla, where ancient ruins make an evocative backdrop. You'll brush shoulders with locals in all their finery, so pull your fanciest outfit from your backpack (tickets from €25, online reservations encouraged, box office takes phone reservations beginning 5 days prior at tel. 06-4816-0255; Via Firenze 72, a block off Via Nazionale, Metro: Repubblica; www.operaroma.it).

Opera da Camera di Roma is a cute, tourist-oriented, greatest-hits-of-opera performance in the Palazzo Albertoni Spinola. While their advertising may make the show seem grander than it is, it's still a charming hour-plus of music—and it comes with a glass of wine. In a pretty little hall, with a string trio, piano, and two singers (soprano and tenor), you'll enjoy a touristy revue of the most popular Italian arias and Neapolitan songs in a casual and fun-loving atmosphere. It's your chance to hear some of the most beloved works of Verdi, Rossini, Puccini, Bellini, and Vivaldi in a very intimate space—much as the Italian nobility would have heard them in private concerts. The organizers are very proud of the acoustics of the little hall, and there is no reason to pay for more than the cheapest seats. Book direct: Buy the cheapest tickets and request the Rick Steves upgrade (RS%, performances Tue-Sun at 19:30, none on Mon, near the Jewish quarter at Piazza Capizucchi 6; call for ticket info, mobile 320-530-7112).

Tourist-oriented musical events take place at the Episcopal **Church of St. Paul's Within the Walls.** The music ranges from orchestral concerts (usually Tue and Fri at 20:30) to full operatic performances (usually Sat at 20:30). Some Sunday evenings at 18:30, the church hosts hour-long candlelit "Luminaria" concerts. Check the church website (under "Music") to see what's on (€10-30, same-day tickets usually available, arrive 30-45 minutes early for best seat, Via Napoli 58 at corner of Via Nazionale, Metro: Repubblica, tel. 06-482-6296, www.stpaulsrome.it).

Jazz

Rome has a small but vibrant jazz scene. **Alexanderplatz** is the venerable club in town, with performances most evenings (Sun-Thu concerts at 21:45, Fri-Sat at 22:30, closed in summer, Via Ostia 9, Metro: Ottaviano, tel. 06-3972-1867, alexanderplatzjazzclub.com).

Il Pentagrappolo is a recommended *enoteca* (see listing on page 396) that hosts live music (usually jazz) many Friday and Saturday evenings starting at 22:00 from September to June—check

NIGHTLIFE

under "Eventi musicali" on their website to confirm (best to reserve on weekends, three blocks east of the Colosseum at Via Celimontana 21, www.ilpentagrappolo.com, tel. 06-709-6301).

TramJazz, a creative venture by the public transit company, combines dinner, music, and a journey through the city in a vintage cable car for a mostly local crowd (€65, daily at 21:00, 3 hours, leaves from Piazza di Porta Maggiore—reached by tram #5 or #14 from Termini Station, book at least a week in advance, www. tramjazz.com).

Movies
Movies in their original language are scarce in Rome, but not impossible to come by (look for v.o.—*versione originale*). For a list of what's showing in English, check www.inromenow.com and www. romereview.com. The most reliable theater for English-language films is the **Nuovo Olimpia** (3 blocks north of Piazza Colonna, just off Via del Corso at Via in Lucina 16, tel. 06-686-1068). **Multisala Barberini** occasionally has v.o. screenings as well (Piazza Barberini, barberini.18tickets.it).

EVENING SIGHTSEEING
Sound-and-Light Shows
The Imperial Forums area hosts two atmospheric and inspirational sound-and-light shows that give you a chance to fantasize about the world of the Caesars. Consider one or both of the similar and adjacent evening experiences. During each of these "nighttime journeys through ancient Rome" you spend about an hour with a headphone dialed to English, listening to an artfully crafted narration synced with projections on ancient walls, columns, and porticos. Each show is distinct, working in its own way to bring the rubble to life and take you back 2,000 years. The final effect is worth the price tag (€15, both for €25, nightly mid-April-mid-Nov—bring your warmest coat, tickets sold online and at the gate, shows can sell out on busy weekends, tel. 06-0608, www.viaggioneifori.it). If you plan to see both, do Caesar first and allow 80 minutes between starting times.

Caesar's Forum Stroll: Starting at Trajan's Column, this tour leads you to eight stops along a wooden sidewalk of a few hundred yards, while an hour's narration tells the dramatic story of Julius Caesar. You'll be on the ground level of an archaeological site that is otherwise closed to the public, giving you views you'd never see otherwise. The tour departs every 20 minutes from dark until nearly midnight.

Forum of Augustus Show: From your perch on wooden bleachers overlooking the remains of a vast forum, you'll learn the story of Augustus through images projected on an ancient firewall that survives to provide a fine screen for modern-day spectacles. Showings are on the hour from dark until 22:00 or 23:00. Enter on Via dei Fori Imperiali just before Via Cavour (you'll see the bleachers along the boulevard).

Museums and Art Exhibitions

Some **museums** have later opening hours (especially on Sat in summer), offering a good chance to see art in a cooler, less-crowded environment. See the "Rome at a Glance" sidebar on page 56 for suggestions.

Both the **Scuderie del Quirinale** and the nearby **Palazzo delle Esposizioni** stay open late when they're hosting major art exhibitions (typically €10-12 each; both open Sun-Thu 10:00-20:00 except the Palazzo is closed Mon, Fri-Sat until 22:30; may open—and stay open—much later in summer; last entry one hour before closing; tel. for both 06-3996-7500; Scuderie—Via XXIV Maggio 16, www.scuderiequirinale.it; Palazzo—Via Nazionale 194, www.palazzoesposizioni.it).

BARS AND NIGHTSPOTS

I've listed some fun neighborhoods worth exploring after dark, along with a few bars and *enoteche* (wine bars) in each. All of these places are recommended in the Eating in Rome chapter, where you'll find more details on each.

Heart of Rome, near the Pantheon

The scene here is touristy but delightful. The monuments—especially the Pantheon and Trevi Fountain—are magically floodlit at night. Not far from the Trevi Fountain, **L'Antica Birreria Peroni** is a big, boisterous beer hall. Farther south, Campo de' Fiori and the surrounding streets become one big, rude street party around 22:00. One good place to sample the youthful energy, as well as some craft beers, is the rollicking **Open Baladin** pub. (For more on these places, see their listings under "Pantheon Neighborhood" on page 397.)

North Rome, near the Spanish Steps and Via del Corso

A babel of international tourists, this glitzy zone is bustling after dark. For many, just hanging out around the Spanish Steps is enough to fill an evening. For nearby dining options, see page 406.

Near the Colosseum and Forum, in Monti

The best plan in this lively village-Rome zone is to pop the top off a brew and hang out at the fountain on Piazza della Madonna dei Monti. To join the after-dark scene, buy a drink at the shop on the uphill side of the square (cheap bottles of wine with plastic glasses,

NIGHTLIFE

beer, fruit, and munchies) and be part of what becomes the hottest bar in the area. There are plenty of makeshift benches around the fountain (this scene is described on page 66).

For more details, see the "Monti" section of the Eating in Rome chapter.

Trastevere

After hours in this youthful district, students and younger tourists drink beer, eat late-night pizza-by-the-slice, and lick cones of gelato as they prowl the cobbles.

Near Termini Station

This is a pretty sleepy area at night, though there's often some activity around Piazza della Repubblica. To sip wine in a sophisticated setting, stroll over to **I Colori del Vino Enoteca** on Via Flavia (see page 409).

Testaccio

Some find this district a bit seedy after dark, but young Romans don't seem to mind. Beer pilgrims flock to **L'Oasi della Birra,** with hundreds of microbrews (see listing on page 414). **Monte Testaccio,** once an ancient trash heap, is now a small hill whose cool caves house funky restaurants and trendy clubs. And the area around Monte Testaccio is a hotspot for club-hopping—after 21:00, just follow the noise.

Pub Crawls

Offered year-round by several companies, these attract a boisterous crowd. I tried one and had never seen 50 young, drunk people having so much fun (or seen so many locals roll their eyes). Look for fliers locally. Late on Friday and Saturday evenings, entire quarters of old Rome seem to be overtaken by young beer-drinking revelers.

NIGHTLIFE

ROME CONNECTIONS

Rome is well connected with the rest of the planet: by train, plane, bus, car, and cruise ship. This chapter explains the various options for your arrival and departure from the city.

By Train

Rome's primary train station, centrally located **Termini,** has high-speed connections to other Italian cities and fast trains to the airport. Rome's other major station is called **Tiburtina.** Most trains you'll encounter depart from Termini. But it's always smart to confirm whether your train departs from Termini or Tiburtina (or one of Rome's even smaller stations).

Buying Tickets: Italy has two train companies: Trenitalia, with most connections (tel. 06-6847-5475, www.trenitalia.it), and Italo, with high-speed routes between larger cities (no rail passes accepted, tel. 06-8937-1892, www.italotreno.it).

For travel within Italy, there's no reason to stand in line at a ticket window. It's quick and easy to buy tickets online; with a smartphone, you can even purchase them minutes before the train departs. If you buy tickets at the station, take advantage of the ticket *(biglietti)* machines that display schedules, issue tickets, and even make reservations for rail-pass holders (found under the "Global Pass" ticket type). Some take only credit cards; others take cards and cash. Using them is easy—just select "English." Both Trenitalia and Italo have bright-red machines, so be sure you use the right one, and be aware that ticket machines only sell tickets for Italian destinations. Note that an open ticket (generally for a *regionale* train) bought from a ticket desk or machine must be validated before you board (stamp it in the machine near the track). Be aware that people offering help are likely pickpockets: Watch your belongings.

For some international destinations, you'll need to either go to a ticket window or visit a travel agency in Rome (also helpful if you need assistance buying tickets). For general information on train travel in Italy—including ticket-buying options—see page 577.

TERMINI TRAIN STATION

Termini, Rome's main train station (www.romatermini.com), is indeed a bustling terminus but gets its name from the nearby Baths *(terme)* of Diocletian. Like much of modern Rome, the station sits atop ancient Roman ruins. The biggest surviving chunk of the impressive 2,300-year-old Servian Wall is just outside (look right as you exit). There are even wall remnants in the McDonald's on the basement level.

The station is a buffet of tourist services. At the head of the tracks are two atriums. The inner atrium, open at both ends, houses shops and eateries. The outer atrium, with glass walls, houses ticket windows and ticket machines plus a good-sized bookstore. (Note that ticket windows can be jammed with travelers—find the small red kiosk, take a number, and wait.) Outside the station is a large square where city buses depart. A basement shopping area extends beneath both atriums. Various services (outlined below) are located in halls along the sides of the tracks.

For security, entry to the train platforms themselves is restricted to ticket holders. Entrances are from the inner atrium and from the halls to the sides of the tracks. You may need to show your ticket, but there are no metal detectors and lines are generally short.

Eating: In general, the best places in the station to sit are in its eateries (open long hours daily). A snack bar and a good self-service cafeteria (Ciao) are perched one floor above the ticket windows in the outer atrium, accessible from the side closest to track 24. For good-quality sandwiches to go, try VyTA in the inner atrium across from track 1. The large Sapori & Dintori supermarket is on the basement shopping level, below the inner atrium (go down the escalators on the Via Marsala side).

For something more substantial, try the Terrazza Termini food court near track 15 (good, clean WCs), or the Mercato Centrale food counters near track 24 (see listings on page 408).

Services: In the hall along Via Giovanni Giolitti, on the southwest side of the station (near track 24), you'll find the TI (daily 8:00-18:45), a travel agency, a car-rental desk, a medical center, and baggage storage (*deposito bagagli;* paying €12 daily rate

CONNECTIONS

rather than hourly allows you to skip the line; daily 6:00-23:00). The Leonardo Express train to Fiumicino Airport runs from track 23 or 24 on this side of the station (see "By Plane," later).

In the hall along Via Marsala, on the northeast side of the station (near track 1), you'll find a pharmacy. Pay WCs are down the escalators from the inner atrium and inside the Mercato Centrale (near track 24).

The station has some sleazy sharks with official-looking business cards; avoid anybody selling anything unless they're in a legitimate shop at the station. Other shady characters linger around the ticket machines—offers to help usually come with the expectation of a "tip." There are no official porters; if someone wants to carry your bags or help you find your platform, they are simply angling for some cash.

Getting Between Termini and Rome Hotels

From Termini, many of my recommended hotels are easily accessible by foot or by Metro (for those in the Colosseum and Vatican neighborhoods). The Termini Metro station, where Metro lines A and B intersect, is beneath the station. City buses leave from the square directly in front of the outer atrium. Buses to the airport leave from the streets on both sides of the station. Taxis queue in front and outside exits on both the north and south sides; if there's a long taxi line in front, try a side exit instead. Avoid con men hawking "express taxi" services in unmarked cars (only use official white taxis with the maroon *Roma Capitale* logo).

Train Connections

Unless otherwise specified, the following connections are for Trenitalia.

From Termini by Train to: Fiumicino Airport (Leonardo Express; 2/hour, 32 minutes—see details under "By Plane," later), **Venice** (Trenitalia: hourly, 4 hours, 1 direct night train, 7 hours; Italo: 4/day, 3.5 hours), **Florence** (Trenitalia: 2-3/hour, 1.5 hours; Italo: 2/hour, 1.5 hours), **Siena** (1-2/hour, 1 change, 3-4 hours), **Orvieto** (every 1-2 hours, 1.5 hours; regional trains are half the price and only slightly slower than Intercity trains), **Assisi** (4/day direct, 2 hours; more with change in Foligno), **Pisa** (1-2/hour, 3 hours, some change in Florence), **La Spezia** (7/day direct, 3-4 hours), **Milan** (Trenitalia: 1-3/hour, 3.5 hours; Italo: 11/day nonstop, 3 hours, more with stops), **Naples** (Trenitalia: 1-4/hour, 1 hour on Frecciarossa, 2 hours on Intercity, 2.5 hours and much cheaper on regional trains; Italo: hourly, 70 minutes), **Sorrento** (Italo train/bus combination, 2/day, 3.5 hours), **Civitavecchia** cruise-ship port (regional trains roughly hourly, 80 minutes; faster but pricier trains every 2 hours, 40-50 minutes), **Brindisi** (3/day, 5 hours), **Bern** (3/day, 6.5 hours, change in Milan), **Munich** (4/

day, 10 hours, change in Verona or Padua; 1 direct night train, 11.5 hours), **Nice** (2/day, 9 hours, change in Milan), **Paris** (2/day, 11.5 hours, change in Turin; 1 night train, 13.5 hours, change in Milan), **Vienna** (3/day, 12 hours, 1-2 changes; 1 direct night train, 14 hours).

TIBURTINA TRAIN STATION

Tiburtina, Rome's second-largest train station (www. stazioneromatiburtina.it), sits next to the Tiburtina Metro station in the city's northeast corner, and across the road from Rome's bus station. It's a pass-through station: Fast trains along the Milan-Naples line stop here and continue on quickly. A few of these fast trains now stop only at Tiburtina, but most stop at both Tiburtina and Termini. Use the station that's most convenient for you.

Getting Between Tiburtina and Downtown Rome: Tiburtina is on Metro line B, four stops from Termini. Note that when going to Tiburtina, Metro line B splits—you want a train signed *Rebibbia*, not *Jonio*. Bus #492 runs conveniently between Tiburtina, several city-center stops (including Piazza Barberini, Piazza Venezia, and Piazza Navona), and the Vatican neighborhood (as you emerge from the train station's front door, the city bus stop is just to the left).

SMALLER STATIONS

Rome has about a dozen small train stations that are usually only useful if you're staying nearby. These stations are served mostly by slow regional trains (for example, from coastal destinations such as Civitavecchia, where cruise ships dock), and slow trains from the airport. The ones you're most likely to use are **San Pietro** (south of Vatican City; bus #64 connects it to Piazza Venezia and Termini; if you're staying near the Vatican and taking a regional train, get off here); **Trastevere** (a few minutes' ride on tram #8 from Trastevere and Piazza Venezia); and **Ostiense** (5 minutes from the Piramide Metro stop via an underground walkway). **Porta San Paolo Station,** directly at the Piramide Metro stop, is part of the Metro rather than the national rail system; suburban trains (Metro tickets valid) to Ostia Antica and Rome's Lido (beach) leave from here.

By Bus

ROME'S BUS STATION: AUTOSTAZIONE TIBURTINA

Long-distance buses use Autostazione Tiburtina, 200 yards from the Tiburtina train and Metro station. Buses are slower than trains, but fares are cheap (as little as €5 to Naples or Florence). Buses are also handy for destinations poorly served by rail. To reach the bus station from either Tiburtina station, don't follow the *Bus* signs, which lead to the city bus stop. Instead, exit the station, cross the street under the elevated freeway, and look for the fenced-in area with bus platforms. The station is chaotic and crowded, with nowhere to sit. Ticket-window lines can be slow, so buy your ticket online in advance if possible. If your bus departure platform isn't listed on the digital board, ask one of the drivers for help.

From Rome by Bus to: Siena (9/day, 3 hours, https://global.flixbus.com), **Sorrento** (1-2/day, 4 hours; this is a cheap and easy way to go straight to Sorrento, buy tickets at www.marozzivt.it—in Italian only, at the Tiburtina ticket office, travel agencies, or on board for a €3.50 surcharge; tel. 080-579-0111), **Naples** (every 1-2 hours, 3 hours, https://global.flixbus.com), **Florence** (every 1-2 hours, 4 hours, https://global.flixbus.com), **Assisi** (2/day, 3 hours, www.sulga.it—the train makes much more sense).

By Plane

Rome's two airports—**Fiumicino** (a.k.a. Leonardo da Vinci, code: FCO) and the small **Ciampino** (code: CIA)—share the same website (www.adr.it).

FIUMICINO AIRPORT

Rome's major airport is manageable. Terminals T1, T2, and T3 are all under one roof—walkable end to end in 20 minutes. T5 is a separate building requiring a short shuttle trip. (T4 is still being built.) The T1-2-3 complex has ground transport, a TI (in T3, daily 9:00-17:30, longer in summer), ATMs, banks, luggage storage, shops, and bars. For airport information, call 06-65951.

Getting Between Fiumicino Airport and Downtown Rome

In either direction, give yourself lots of time to allow for traffic delays, travel between your hotel and the train/bus station, finding your train or bus, and walking to the terminal.

By Train: Trenitalia's slick, direct, first-class-only Leonardo Express train connects the airport train station (called Fiumicino Aeroporto) and Rome's central Termini Station in 32 minutes for €14. At either station, buy your ticket from a Trenitalia machine, a ticket office *(biglietteria)*, or a newsstand near the platform. Machines sell open tickets that can be used on any train. (You know you're in Italy when the machine makes you choose a departure time—even though you're allowed to take any train.) You must validate your ticket before boarding by stamping it in a green-and-gray machine near the track. Trains run at least twice hourly in both directions from roughly 6:00 to 23:00 (up to 4/hour in busy times).

From the airport's arrival gate, follow signs to the train icon or *Stazione/Railway Station*. Make sure the train you board is going to the central "Roma Termini" station, as trains from the airport serve other destinations too.

Returning from Termini train station *to* the airport, trains usually depart from track 23 or 24. Check the departure boards for "Fiumicino Aeroporto" and confirm with an official or a local on the platform that the train is indeed going to the airport.

You can access most of the airport's terminals from the airport train station. If your flight leaves from terminal T5 (where most American air carriers flying direct to the US depart), catch the T5 shuttle bus *(navetta)* on the sidewalk in front of T3—it's too far to walk with luggage.

Cheaper (€8) local trains also run between the airport and some of Rome's smaller train stations (including Trastevere, Ostiense, and Tiburtina). If you're staying in Trastevere or the Pantheon area, it can be simpler and cheaper to take the local train to Trastevere station, then walk out to the street and take the #8 tram downhill to your hotel. The train to Tiburtina is useful if you have a long-distance bus to catch.

Only a couple of long-distance trains per day serve the airport. To connect to other Italian cities, you'll usually have to change at Termini or Tiburtina.

By Bus: Four bus companies—Terravision (www.terravision. eu), SIT (www.sitbusshuttle.com), T.A.M. (www.tambus.it), and Schiaffini (www.romeairportbus.com)—connect Fiumicino and Termini train station. The SIT bus also stops near the Vatican. I'd just hop on whichever one is departing first (every 10-15 minutes at peak times). While cheaper than the train (about €7 one-way), buses take twice as long (about an hour, depending on traffic) and can fill up (allow plenty of extra time). At the airport, the bus station is at the far end of terminal T3. At Termini, T.A.M. and Schiaffini depart from the south side of the station; Terravision and SIT from the north side.

By Airport Shuttle: Shared shuttle van services can be economical for one or two people. Consider Rome Airport Shuttle (€25 for one person, extra people—€6 each, by reservation only, tel. 06-4201-4507 or 06-4201-3469, www.airportshuttle.it).

By Taxi: A taxi between Fiumicino and downtown Rome takes 45 minutes in normal traffic (for taxi tips, see page 36) and costs exactly €48. (Add a €2-5 tip for good service.) From the airport, be sure to catch an official taxi at the taxi stand. Avoid unmarked, unmetered taxis; these guys will try to tempt you away from the taxi-stand lineup by offering an immediate (rip-off) ride. Rome's official taxis are white, with a "taxi" sign on the roof and a ma-roon *Roma Capitale* logo on the door. By law, taxi drivers can only charge €48 for the ride to anywhere in the historic center (within the old city walls, where my recommended hotels are located). The fare covers up to four people with normal-size bags (to save money, try teaming up with any tourist also just arriving—most are head-ing for hotels near yours). An official taxi will have the fare amount clearly posted on its door.

Cabs based in Fiumicino (the town near the airport) are al-lowed to charge €60 for the ride to downtown Rome. Signs stat-ing the Rome and Fiumicino price caps are posted next to the taxi stand. It's best to use the Rome city cabs and establish the price before you get in. If your driver tries to point to the price for Fi-umicino-based cabs or otherwise charge you more than the official rate, say, *"Quarant'otto euro—è la legge"* (kwah-RAHNTOH-toe AY-oo-roh—ay lah LEJ-jay; which means, "Forty-eight euros—it's the law"), and they should back off.

When departing Rome, your hotel can arrange a taxi to the airport at any hour. Alternatively, they sometimes work with com-parably priced private car services, which are usually just fine (if not nicer than a regular cab).

CIAMPINO AIRPORT

Rome's smaller airport (tel. 06-6595-9515) handles charter flights and some budget airlines (including most Ryanair flights).

Getting Between Ciampino Airport and Downtown Rome: Bus companies Terravision, Schiaffini, and SIT will take you to Rome's Termini train station (about €5, 2/hour, 45 minutes). Atral runs a quicker route (25 minutes, www.atral-lazio.com) to the Anagnina Metro stop, where you can connect to the stop nearest your hotel (departs every 40 minutes). City bus #520 runs from Ciampino to the Subaugusta Metro stop for a single transit ticket.

The fixed price for any official **taxi** (with the maroon *Roma Capitale* logo on the door) is €30 to downtown (within the old city walls, including most of my recommended hotels).

Rome Airport Shuttle also offers shared van rides to and from Ciampino (€25 for one person, listed earlier).

By Car

DRIVING AND PARKING IN ROME

A car is a worthless headache in Rome. If you're visiting Rome as part of a longer trip, avoid a pile of stress and save money by parking at the huge, easy, free, and relatively safe lot behind the train station in the hill town of Orvieto (follow *P* signs from the autostrada) and catching a cheap *regionale* train to Rome (every 1-2 hours, 1.5 hours).

Alternatively, use one of the more than two dozen park-and-ride lots at Rome's outlying Metro stations (€5/24 hours). These vary in size and convenience; one of the largest is at the Anagnina Metro station, just inside Rome's ring expressway along the Via Tuscolana (southeast of downtown). For details, search for "park and ride" *(parcheggi di scambio)* at www.atac.roma.it.

If you must park closer in, there's a large underground garage at the Villa Borghese Gardens near the Spagna Metro station, just outside the restricted downtown zone (€18/day, Viale del Galoppatoio 33, www.sabait.it). The recommended Hotel Lancelot, though not cheap, is a rare hotel with private parking (see the Sleeping in Rome chapter).

During most of the week, you need a special permit to drive in the old center of Rome. The restricted zone is roughly bounded by Piazza del Popolo, Termini Station, the Colosseum, and the river, plus Trastevere, and on Friday and Saturday nights. Testaccio is off-limits too (for details, go to www.romamobilita.it and search for "LTZ" in English or "ZTL" in Italian). Without a permit, you'll be photographed and fined. Your hotel can help you get one if you absolutely must drive or park downtown.

If you do need to drive into Rome, it helps to time your journey for Friday evening or the weekend. It's a good idea to check online for events that might limit access to certain areas of the city (www.060608.it). A ring-shaped expressway (the Grande Raccordo Anulare) circles greater Rome. This ring road has spokes that lead you into the center. Take the Settebagni exit, then follow the ancient Via Salaria, then *Centro* signs to enter the city from the north. Avoid rush hour and drive defensively: Roman cars stay in their lanes like rocks in an avalanche.

By Cruise Ship

CONNECTIONS

ROME'S CRUISE PORT: CIVITAVECCHIA

Hundreds of cruise ships dock each year at the small, manageable port city of Civitavecchia (chee-vee-tah-VEH-kyah), about 45 miles northwest of Rome.

Civitavecchia is historic: With foundations dating back to Etruscan times, this "Ancient Town" (as its name means) was built up by Emperor Trajan, then favored by the popes with "free port" status. By the 20th century, it had become Rome's main port before being leveled by Allied bombs in World War II, and later rebuilt. Today, this town of 50,000 has little for visitors to see. Virtually every cruise passenger disembarking at Civitavecchia is headed for Rome.

Civitavecchia's large port area stretches west from its main crossroads, a square called Largo Plebiscito. It's a huge commercial port, and ferries to Sardinia, Sicily, and Tunisia also dock here. Cruise ships dock in the middle of the hubbub, and passengers are not allowed to walk out of the secured port area. Nearby is the stout 16th-century Michelangelo Fortress (Forte Michelangelo,

partially designed by the master), which stands where the port area meets the town.

Tourist Information: A **TI** desk is at the Largo della Pace transit center, where the cruise shuttle-bus stops, with free maps and good advice (daily 6:00-19:00 during cruise season).

Sights in Civitavecchia: Civitavecchia's humble three-floor **National Archaeological Museum,** at Largo Plebiscito in the city center, focuses on its ancient past, with a small exhibit described in English (free, Tue-Sun until 19:30, closed Mon). For some **beach** time, handy little Pirgo Beach is directly in front of the train station.

For more details, see my *Rick Steves Mediterranean Cruise Ports* guidebook.

Getting to Rome: As road traffic between Civitavecchia and Rome is terrible, generally the fastest (and most economical) way to day-trip into Rome is to take the **train.** Trains connect Civitavecchia with several stations in Rome, including Ostiense (two Metro stops from the Colosseum), San Pietro (a short walk from Vatican City), or Termini (the main transit hub, but farther from key sights). Trains depart frequently for Rome and take 40-80 minutes. You can buy train tickets at Civitavecchia's station, or the "Tourist Information" travel agency at the station, which also sells other transportation tickets. To reach Civitavecchia's train station, take a free shuttle bus from your ship to the Largo della Pace transit hub. City bus service from the hub to the train station is fast and reliable (€2, 6/hour, 10 minutes, buy tickets from kiosk before boarding). Or you can walk (about 25 minutes) or take a taxi to the station (€15-20, triple the fair metered rate).

Regional Trains: These trains (marked *REG*) stop at San Pietro (45-60 minutes), Ostiense (55-70 minutes), and Termini stations (65-80 minutes). If you're taking a regional train round-trip, save money and time by getting the good-value €12 **BIRG ticket** (five-zone version). This day pass covers second-class round-trip train travel between Civitavecchia and Rome as well as unlimited travel on Rome's buses, Metro (subway), and trams. You can buy the BIRG ticket at the train station (newsstand, Food Village café, "Tourist Information" travel agency, and the ticket counter but not at machines).

Intercity trains: These trains (marked *IC*) stop at Ostiense (40-50 minutes) and Termini (50-60 minutes), but are not covered by the BIRG pass. Expect to pay about €11 on the Intercity. You can avoid the long ticket-window lines by using the station's easy self-service machines.

Seasonal Express Train for Cruisers: When there are enough ships in port to justify it, there's also a special **"Vatican Express" to San Pietro Station,** offering one daily round-trip designed for cruise travelers (generally departs Civitavecchia 9:30, arrives San Pietro 10:15; return trip: departs San Pietro 15:50, arrives Civitavecchia 16:30). While much more expensive (€25 round-trip), the ride is comfortable, air-conditioned, and limited to cruise passengers only (so it's not as crowded as regular trains often are), and it can save you up to 20 minutes each way. The train is operated by a private company without a website, but you can check its status with the TI at Largo della Pace or at the train station. Buy tickets at the station's ticket window (not available at self-service machines), at the station's "Tourist Information" travel agency, or on the train.

Le Frecce: This fast train runs from Civitavecchia to Roma Termini in less than an hour. But it runs less frequently than other trains, and reservations are mandatory.

More Options: Other options for getting into Rome include a cruise-ship excursion package, a taxi, organized tours run by private tour companies, or a private bus. A **taxi** into Rome takes about 1.5 hours and costs around €150-200 one-way, though many cabbies inflate their prices (avoid unlicensed taxis offering a huge price break; you can be fined for taking one). **Organized tours** into Rome are offered by Can't Be Missed Tours (RS%, mobile 329-129-8182, www.cantbemissedtours.com) and Miles & Miles Private Tours (see page 40). Several private companies offer cheap **bus transfers** from the transit hub to Rome or Rome's airports (try Civita Tours, mobile 346-217-7803, www.civitatours.com).

DAY TRIPS

Ostia Antica • Tivoli •
Naples & Pompeii

There's so much to see and do in Rome that you could easily fill a vacation without ever leaving the city limits. But here are several nearby sights that might match your particular interests.

Ostia Antica is similar to Pompeii, but without the crowds. This excavated ancient Roman city is located an easy 30 minutes by suburban train from Rome's Piramide Metro station. Or stay on the train another 15 minutes and enjoy Ostia's beaches.

Tivoli is doable but cumbersome by public transportation;

Day Trips from Rome

consider seeing it via private tour, or hire your own driver for the day. The trip rewards you with the evocative ruins of Hadrian's Villa and with the lush gardens and restored fountains of a Renaissance mansion, the Villa d'Este.

Thanks to Italy's excellent train system, it's 70 minutes to **Naples** on a direct high-speed train that lands you right in the middle of town (or 2.5 hours on cheaper trains). In Naples, see ancient statues and mosaics at the wonderful Archaeological Museum, stroll colorful Spaccanapoli street, and have lunch in the city where pizza was born, sampling the exotic chaos of southern Italy.

History hounds can venture another 35 minutes south of Naples by train to see the ultimate in ruined Roman cities—**Pompeii**—frozen in time by the eruption of Mt. Vesuvius.

Arrive back in Rome for a late dinner at a sidewalk café to recount your busy day over a glass of wine.

Italy's fast trains put other cities within day-trip range, including **Orvieto** (1-1.5 hours by inexpensive regional train), **Assisi** (4/ day direct, 2 hours; more with a change in Foligno), and **Florence** (1.5 hours on fast but expensive trains). For in-depth information on Orvieto and Assisi, see *Rick Steves Italy*, and for Florence, see *Rick Steves Florence & Tuscany*.

OSTIA ANTICA

For an exciting day trip, pop down to the Roman port of Ostia, which is similar to Pompeii but a lot closer and, in some ways, more interesting. Because Ostia was a working port town, it offers a more complete and gritty look at Roman life than wealthier Pompeii. Wandering around today, you'll see warehouses, apartment flats, mansions, shopping arcades, and baths that served a once-thriving port of 60,000 people. With more than 70 peaceful parklike acres to explore and relatively few crowds, it's a welcome break from the bustle of Rome.

GETTING THERE

Getting to Ostia Antica from downtown Rome is a snap—it's a 45-minute combination Metro/train ride. (Since the train is part of the Metro system, it only costs one Metro ticket each way.)

In Rome, take Metro line B to the Piramide stop, which is attached to the Roma Porta San Paolo train station. The train tracks are just a few steps from the Metro tracks: Follow signs to *Lido* (beach)—go up the escalator, turn left, and go down the steps to reach the Roma-Lido train line. All trains depart in the direction of Lido, leave every 15 minutes, and stop at Ostia Antica along the way. The lighted schedule will read something like *"Treno in partenza, 13.25, bin 3,"* meaning that a train is departing at 13:25 from track 3. Look for the next train, hop on, ride for about 30 minutes (no need to stamp your Metro ticket again, but keep it handy in case they decide to check), and get off at the Ostia Antica stop.

Leaving the train station in Ostia Antica, cross the road via the blue skybridge and walk straight down Via della Stazione di Ostia Antica, continuing straight (through a small parking lot) until you reach the larger parking lot for the site. The entrance is to your left.

Orientation

Cost: €10 for the site and museum, €12 during special exhibits; free to enter (and crowded) once or twice a month, usually on a Sun. Check in advance and avoid going on a free day.

Hours: April-Aug Tue-Sun 8:30-19:15, Sept until 19:00, most of Oct until 18:30, late Oct-mid-Feb until 16:30, mid-Feb-March until 17:00, closed Mon year-round, last entry one hour before closing. The small museum closes one hour before the site does.

Information: Tel. 06-5635-0215. The official website is www.ostiaantica.beniculturali.it; a helpful website run by friends of the ruins is www.ostia-antica.org.

Visitor Information: A map of the site with suggested itineraries is available for €2 from the ticket office.

Tours: €5 **audioguide;** choose between a short version (lasts 3 hours) or a longer one (7 hours). ID required.

⌒ Download my free Ostia Antica **audio tour.**

Length of This Tour: Allow two to three hours inside the site. Add in the round-trip train ride, and it's at least a four-hour excursion from Rome.

Services: There are WCs at the entrance, near the cafeteria, and (often the cleanest of all) in the modern building behind the marble chunks, east of the cafeteria.

Eating: You'll pass a few cafés and restaurants as you walk to the site. The only option inside is a small **$$** cafeteria with sandwiches and hot dishes next to Ostia's museum. Ostia is a great place for a discreet picnic among the ruins.

Sightseeing Tip: Maximize sightseeing efficiency by visiting south Rome sights on your return. The Piramide Metro stop—where you'll catch the suburban train—really *is* next to a pyramid, and also near the colorful Testaccio neighborhood. Farther south are St. Paul's Outside the Walls, E.U.R., and the Montemartini Museum.

Beach Time: The train line that leads to Ostia also connects Romans to their beaches. To combine some beach time with your sightseeing, see page 423.

BACKGROUND

Located at (and named for) the mouth *(ostium)* of the Tiber, Ostia was founded in the fourth century BC. Gobbled up early by Rome, it's often called Rome's first colony. Originally its main industry was salt gleaned from nearby salt flats (salt was a precious preserver

Ostia Antica

400 Meters
400 Yards

TOUR BEGINS

Former Course of Tiber River

Tiber River

MODERN OFFICES

SQUARE OF THE GUILDS

ASPHALT ROAD

MAP

ENTRANCE

V. DEGLI SCAVI
V. STAZIONE
V. DELLA

To Ostia Station

CAFETERIA & SHOP

MUSEUM

DECUMANUS MAXIMUS

PORTA ROMANA

To Rome

CAPITOL-IUM

FORUM

CURIA

BASILICA

LATRINE

TEMPLE OF ROMA

FORUM BATHS

COURSE OF ANCIENT CITY WALLS

VIA CALZA (SR-296)

VIA DEL MARE (S-8)

TRAIN LINE

To Ostia Stn. & Rome's Porta San Paolo Station

VIA TOR BOCCIANA

To Lido d'Ostia (Beach)

THEATER

1 Necropolis
2 Porta Romana
3 Republican Warehouses
4 Baths of Neptune
5 Theater
6 Square of the Guilds
7 Mill
8 Via Casa di Diana
9 Forum
10 Forum Baths
11 Ostia Museum

of meat in ancient times). Ostia next served as a naval base, protecting Rome from any invasion by river. By 150 BC, when Rome had secured control of the Mediterranean, Ostia's importance became commercial rather than military. At its peak, Ostia was vital to the Roman Empire. Most of what the city of Rome consumed—and that was a lot by historical standards—came in through this port.

Rome eventually outgrew Ostia, and a vast new port was dug a little farther north (where Rome's airport now stands). But Ostia remained a key administrative and warehousing center, busy with the big business of keeping more than a million Romans fed and in sandals.

Eventually things really soured for Ostia. Rome fell. The river changed course. The port was abandoned, silted up, became a malaria-infested swamp, and was eventually forgotten. The mud that buried Ostia actually protected it from the ravages of time—it lay safely buried until it was excavated and opened to the public.

The Tour Begins

Consider your visit a three-part affair:

1. Follow this tour (with this chapter or my 🎧 free audio tour). You'll go straight down Decumanus Maximus (the town's main drag), with a couple of slight detours, finishing at the forum (the main square).

2. Pop into the museum, and consider getting a bite to eat at the cafeteria.

3. Explore the back lanes—going on a visual scavenger hunt—as you wander your way back to the entry point.

• *Find the* **map** *(30 yards inside the gate, on the right) for an orientation: We're entering at the far right (near Porta Romana and the necropolis) and then heading down the main street, labeled* Decumano Massimo, *to the center of town—the forum, labeled* Foro. *The blue Tiber River borders the top. It once spilled into the sea at the far left. The pale green to the right of the Tiber shows the former flow of the river, which left the city's businesses high and dry when it changed*

course. Notice how the core of Ostia is basically a rectangle, dating from its origins as a Roman military camp, with two major roads crossing at the forum. One of the four city gates lies ahead. But first, immediately on your left is the...

❶ Necropolis

As you pass by row after row of brick foundations, you might think that these ruins are former homes in a great city. Oh, this *was* a city—but a city of the dead. These are not homes, but tombs.

Ancient Romans buried their dead outside the city walls. Ostia was a famously pagan town, slow to become Christian. To a pagan, the closest thing to an afterlife was to be remembered. If their families could afford it, they'd place the tomb

on the roadside with a thumbnail bio carved into the stone that all could read as they came and went (for example, "My name was Caius. I was a baker."). This area was called a necropolis (city of the dead); Christians preferred the term cemetery (from the Greek for resting place).

Also lining the road, you'll see a few sarcophagi (small stone "coffins" where remains were placed) and statues, which honored the dead.

Burial practices changed over the years. In BC times, the remains were placed in these room-like tombs. After the first century AD, cremation became popular, so this necropolis also has some family sepulchers (marked by arches) lined with niches for ash-filled urns. In the second and third centuries AD, the Romans here buried their dead in marble and terra-cotta sarcophagi, placed in the tombs.

• *Ahead (where the road narrows), look for a section of a low brick wall with a few marble fragments tacked on. This is where you enter the ancient city of Ostia, through the scant remains of the gate called...*

❷ Porta Romana

This gate was part of a wall that surrounded the city on three sides. The fourth "wall" of defense was the river. The gate, locked at night, was one of Ostia's grandest entrances, receiving travelers from Rome. (Just as Rome's Porta San Paolo faced Ostia, Ostia's Porta Romana faced Rome.)

Pass through the gate and imagine entering the city. You'd immediately enter a grand square called **Piazzale della Vittoria.** You could water your animals at the huge water basin on the left—the low, rectangular brickwork structure. Nearby, a statue of Victory *(Vittoria)* greeted visitors (this one's a copy of the original). You could store your goods in the warehouse on the right (the maze of brick foundations below street level). Immediately to the left (under an umbrella pine), find a low wall with marble panels. The Latin inscription proclaimed to all who entered: "The Senate ("...[SE]NATUS...") and the people of the colony of Ostia constructed the walls." The "colony" reference is a reminder that Ostia was the first acquisition of the Roman Empire.

From here, Decumanus Maximus leads straight to the forum, where this walk ends. Note that this road was elevated above some buildings' foundations. Over the centuries, Ostia's ground level rose. You can actually identify buildings from the republic (centuries before Christ) and the empire (centuries after Christ) by their level. Anything you walk down into is from the earlier period.

• *Continue up Decumanus Maximus, passing (on the right) still more of the brick ruins of the...*

❸ Republican Warehouses (Magazzini Repubblicani)

In the first century BC, this city bustled in its role as a river port. Walking along the main street, you pass its vast warehouses. The

goods of the port, such as grain from Sicily, Egypt, and all of North Africa, were processed and stored in warehouses here (which had elevated floors to keep things dry) before being consumed by Rome.

About 100 yards ahead, immediately past a lone gray column, pause at the stubby brick

columns on the right. These are the remains of a roofed portico that once provided a shaded walkway into town. It stood two stories tall, was lined with shops, and had a popular tavern in back. Notice the bricks—generally, rough bricks are original, while smooth bricks are part of the reconstruction. Ostia has been picked clean since ancient times. The port's treasures ended up gracing buildings as far away as Constantinople.

• *Continue straight another 100 yards to the **little well** in the road. This well is not ancient, but a remnant from medieval squatters who found shelter in these ruins. In ancient times, Ostia had a far more sophisticated water system, with aqueducts providing plenty of fresh drinking water and water for the baths. Speaking of which...from here, you'll see a viewpoint (with railings), above on the right. Climb up for a view of the...*

❹ Baths of Neptune (Terme di Nettuno)

The complex of ruins stretching below was a bathhouse. Examine the fine mosaics. The largest one depicts Neptune riding four

horses through the sea. He's surrounded by a menagerie of sea creatures: fish, crustaceans, and serpents with the heads of horses, goats, and rams. At the top, Triton blows his long horn. The mosaic is dominated by serpent-like creatures with other animals' heads. Apart from the cupid riding the dolphin, the sea looks frightening—which it was.

Romans came to these baths on a daily basis—to clean, swim, exercise, and socialize. They'd work up a sweat in the steam room, move to the next room (with another mosaic) to take a cold plunge, then cool down in a medium-temperature room. The large open-air square to the left of the mosaic would have been busy with people wrestling, stretching, doing jumping jacks, and getting rubdowns. The niches that ring the square housed small businesses.

• *Climb back down to the main drag, and continue to the right until you reach the theater on your right. Ideally, enter the theater through its main central gate. If that's blocked by scaffolding, find a staircase up into the theater seats, with a view of the stage.*

❺ Theater (Teatro)

As men entered the theater, they would bid farewell to their women (before the women went to sit in the higher seats—typical of the gender division in public Rome).

Take a seat. Before you is the stage. Up to 4,000 residents could gather here. The musicians (and some actors) performed on the semicircular floor, called the orchestra. Romans also used a wooden stage—the five-foot-tall brick wall you can see once formed its lip. A wall rose behind the stage (there's a fragment on the right), where scenery could be hung. Some plays featured actors in masks—notice the carved stone masks on display to the left of the stage. Each face shows a particular emotion, and the mouths are oversized so actors could speak clearly through them.

Plays were rowdy daytime events—like going to a day game at the ballpark—with lots of audience participation. And heaven help a bad actor. The three rows of marble steps near the orchestra were reserved for the chairs of big shots. Even today, this place—one of the oldest brick theaters anywhere—is used for concerts.

Looking beyond the stage, notice that the theater is just one part of this typically Roman complex, mixing religion, business, and entertainment: a grand theater facing a temple surrounded by a commercial square.

• *Let's explore that square. From the theater, continue (farther away from the main street) behind the stage. Head to the right and walk counterclockwise around the square. We'll end back at the theater.*

❻ Square of the Guilds (Piazzale delle Corporazioni)

This grand square evolved from a simple place where businessmen would stroll and powwow together to a monumental square lined with more than 60 offices of ship owners and traders. This was the bustling center of Rome's import-export industry.

As you walk along the sidewalk on the right side (circling the square counterclockwise), admire the second-century AD **mosaics.** These advertised the services offered by the businesses inside. Some are in Latin, but most use pictures for illiterate sailors or non-Latin-reading foreigners—for instance, *naviculari* means shipping company.

A few steps farther, you'll see the most common motif—ships. Next comes a barrel. Businesses here included grain importers, tanners, and fish wholesalers. Dolphin mosaics indicate a business associated with the sea. The elephant marks the office of Libyan traders who dealt in ivory or perhaps in exotic animals (great for parties, private spectacles, and Colosseum events). Check out the many mosaics of Roman ships, with their elaborate sails and rudders. Roman ingenuity enabled boats to tack and sail against the wind. Commerce moved more readily, making the Mediterranean a thriving Roman free-trade zone.

Reaching the end of the right side, continue working counterclockwise to find the chess-board-like mosaic. In the lower right, this mosaic has one of the most common symbols of all: the lighthouse. (It's the squat tower with flames coming out the top. Fueled by an oven below, it directed ships into Ostia's port.) The lighthouse became the sign of the port of Ostia.

Continuing on, notice the many statues of notable local guild members and business leaders that decorated the courtyard. The temple in the center was likely related to Ceres, the goddess of harvest and abundance (prosperity from good business).

Turning the corner again (back toward the theater), find another lighthouse mosaic. Next comes an amphora (pointed jug) between palm trees—likely marking an importer of palm oil.

As you arrive back at the theater, look immediately to the right. The small white **altar** *(Sacello dell' Ara di Romolo e Remo)* was dedicated to Rome's legendary founders—find Romulus and Remus suckling the she-wolf on the bottom of the relief. This altar would have been used to sacrifice animals—such as the rams carved into the corners—to ask for favor from the gods. The entrails would be read to divine the future and to determine whether the gods were for or against a particular business venture. This altar is a copy; the original is in Rome. (Consider the burden on Italy of protecting and preserving what is actually the cultural heritage of all of Europe against illegal digging, exportation, vandalism, weather, and pollution. There's a special branch of the Carabinieri dedicated to art theft.)

• *Continue down the main street. About two blocks down, you reach the intersection with Via dei Molini. Turn right and walk about a block and a half down Via dei Molini, keeping a sharp eye out for our next sight (look for the* Molino del Silvano *sign on the left among the ruins). Step inside.*

❼ Mill (Molino)

This mill and bakery building *(panificio)* dates from AD 120. The lava millstones in front of you were used to grind grain. Study the workings: The grain was ground between two stones. At bottom is a bowl-like stone. On top of that rests a cylindrical upper section with holes in it. Wood poles were inserted into these holes to turn the mill. Grain would be sprinkled in from a sack

hanging from the ceiling. Then, mules or workers would power the grinding by walking in circles, pushing on the wood poles to turn the cylindrical crushing stone. Eventually, powdery flour (with not much grit) would tumble out the bottom. They'd walk it next door to make bread.

• *If you need a break before we continue, notice that we're not far from the museum, cafeteria, and WC. Now, backtrack half a block down Via dei Molini in the direction of the main street. Take the first right onto Via Casa di Diana. The street is unmarked, but it's distinctive—lined with taller-than-usual buildings.*

❽ Via Casa di Diana

About 75 yards down the street (on the left), step into the **Insula of the Thermopolium** *(Termopolio)*—an ancient tavern. Go past the grooved threshold— which once held a slid- ing wooden door—and make yourself at home. You'll see a couple of dis- play shelves where they stacked food and drinks for sale, and a small sink. A cute fresco on the wall advertised the tavern's of-

ferings: food (the dish), drink (the cup), and music (the castanets). Too smoky and noisy? Step out back and enjoy the quiet courtyard with the fountain.

Next, cross the street to the **Insula of the Paintings.** Find the staircase (a few steps down the road) and climb all the way to the open rooftop for a good view.

Imagine life as an apartment dweller in ancient Rome. An *insula* was a multistoried apartment complex where the lower-middle class lived. These held miserable, cramped units crammed into buildings up to 10 floors high (the average was 5 floors). To reach their rooms on the higher floors, people climbed treehouse-type stairs. Plumbing didn't exist. It was stinky. "Windows" covered with shutters or cloth curtains dipped in grease did little to cut the street din.

Buildings were made cheaply of wood, with weak foundations, so many burned or collapsed. The apartments had no heat and no kitchen, so residents cooked or purchased food elsewhere. They tossed garbage out the windows. Because chariot and cart traffic was allowed only after dark, there was lots of night noise.

The wealthier classes, on the other hand, lived in sprawling and luxurious homes. These were generally built on one floor, with a series of rooms facing a central open courtyard. Decorative pools collected rainwater. Statues, mosaics, and frescoes were everywhere. Rome's wealthy were as comfortable as the poor were wretched.

From this **rooftop perch,** you have a great view over the entire site. Find the museum—the pink-and-white building. Behind the museum, see modern pleasure boats parked alongside where today's Tiber leaves Ostia. Now find the row of umbrella pines stretching to the right of the museum. This marks the original channel of the river, before it changed course, abandoning the town and leaving the harbor to silt up. Ostia declined and was slowly buried, leaving this field of rubble you see today.

• *Before leaving, face the museum and turn 90 degrees left to see the enormous brick ruin—as tall as you are. This is the Capitolium temple, where we're headed next. Descend to street level, and continue to the end of the street, toward the brick wall of the Capitolium, and then left into Ostia's forum. For the best view, head for the center of the forum, where there's a round (well-like) brick monument dedicated to the emperor's guardian angels. From here, take in the sights.*

❾ Forum

You're standing at the center of ancient Ostia. As in Italian cities today, Ostia's main gathering place was a central piazza. This forum had a large rectangular open space surrounded by columns supporting arcades and buildings.

At one end of the square is the grandest structure—the temple called the **Capitolium** (from AD 120), with its grand staircase. The mar-

ble veneer was scavenged in the Middle Ages, leaving only the core brickwork. Note the reinforcement arches in the brick. The Capitolium (named after the original atop Capitoline Hill in Rome) was dedicated to the pagan trinity of Jupiter, Juno, and Minerva. A forum dominated by a Capitolium temple was a standard feature of colonies throughout the empire. The purpose: to transport the Roman cult of Jupiter, Juno, and Minerva to the newly conquered population.

On the opposite side of the square, distinguished by its lone sawed-off column, is the **Temple of Roma and Augustus.** Its position is powerfully symbolic. The power of the emperor stands equal, facing the power of the Capitolium Triad.

The town's **basilica** was also on the forum square. As you face the Capitolium, it's to your left and consists of little more than the footprint of the building. Dating from about AD 100, this was where legal activities and commercial business took place. Its central nave and two side aisles lead to the "high altar," where the judge sat.

Under your feet runs Decumanus Maximus, one of the town's two main streets that intersect at the forum. Whenever possible, Rome imposed a grid road plan on its conquered cities. From its beginnings, this spot was the original center of Roman Ostia. After Rome conquered Ostia in about 400 BC, it built a military camp, or *castrum*—a rectangular fort with east, west, north, and south gates and two main roads converging on the forum. Throughout the empire, Romans found comfort in this familiar city plan. While people found it no fun to be conquered, the empire brought order and stability to their lives through laws and the creation of grid-planned cities and grand squares such as this one.

Standing at the center of the forum, plan your next move after our tour ends. You could visit the **museum**—it's the pink-and-white building behind the Capitolium. For more sightseeing, the Decumanus Maximus continues west into a vast urban expanse, great for simply wandering (see "Archaeological Scavenger Hunt" at the end of this chapter). Or the Decumanus can take you east directly back to the entrance/exit—a 15-minute walk away.

• *But first, make one more stop. Walk to the Temple of Roma and Augustus. As you're facing it, look left and find a brick arch over a street. Pass through that arch, and after a dozen steps, stop. You're standing between the forum baths (right) and latrine (left).*

⓾ Forum Baths (Terme del Foro) and Latrine (Forica)

Start with the **baths**—they're sometimes open to walk through, or you may have to view them from the street. Try to imagine this huge complex peopled, steaming, and busy. Government-subsidized baths were a popular social and business meeting place in any Roman city. Roman engineers were experts at radiant heat. A huge furnace heated both the water and air that flowed through pipes under the floors and in the walls (you might see the hollow bricks in the walls). There were fine marble steps—great for lounging—that led into the pools. Bathers used olive oil rather than soap to wash, so the water needed to be periodically skimmed by servants. Like at a high-end spa, there was a *laconicum* (sweating room), two *tepidariae* (where Romans were rubbed down by masseuses), and the once-steamy *caldarium* with three pools.

Now turn your attention to the **latrine.** The 20 holes with seats make it obvious that this was once a public toilet. In the door-

way, find the pivot hole in the floor that supported its revolving entrance door. The cutout below each seat was to accommodate the washable sponge on a stick, which was used rather than toilet paper. Rushing water below each seat (brought in by aqueduct) did the flushing. So much for privacy—even today, there's no word in Italian for it.

⓫ Ostia Museum

This small museum offers a delightful look at some of Ostia's finest statuary. Without worrying too much about exactly what's what, just wander and imagine these fine figures—tangled wrestlers, kissing cupids, playful gods—adorning the courtyards of wealthy Ostian families. Most of the statues are second- and third-century AD Roman pieces inspired by rare and famous Greek originals. The portrait busts are of real people—the kind you'd sit next to in the baths (or on the toilets).

Roman sculptors excelled at realistic busts. Roman religion revered the man of the house (and his father and grandfather). Statues of daddy and grandpa were common in the corner of any proper house. And with the emperor considered a god, you'd find his bust in classrooms, at the post office, and so on. The sarcophagi (marble coffins) generally show mythological scenes.

The grandest statue is the one that greets you as you go in—the Minerva as Victory that once stood by the Porta Romana, where we entered Ostia. Perhaps the most interesting room (to the left as you enter, just before the steps) features statuary from religions of foreign lands. Being a port town, Ostia accommodated people (and their worship needs) from all over the known world. The large statue of a man sacrificing a bull is a Mithraic altarpiece (see page 343).

The **cafeteria, WC,** and **shop** are in a modern building just behind the museum.

Archaeological Scavenger Hunt

As you return to the entry gate, get off the main drag and explore Ostia's back streets. Wandering beyond the forum and then taking the back lanes as you return to the entry, see if you can find:

- Tarp- and sand-protected mosaic flooring.
- White cornerstones put into buildings to fend off wild carts and reflect corners in the dark.
- Fast-food fish joint (on Decumanus Maximus, just beyond the forum).
- Hidden bits of fresco (clue: under hot tin roofs).
- Republican buildings and buildings dating from the empire.
- Stucco roughed up for fresco work (before applying the wet plaster of a fresco, the surface needs to be systematically gouged so the plaster can grip the wall).
- Millstones for grinding grain (Ostia's big industry).
- Floor patterns made colorful with inlaid marble.
- A *domus*—a single-family dwelling facing a fancy, central, open-air courtyard.

TIVOLI

Villa d'Este • Hadrian's Villa

At the edge of the Sabine Hills, 18 miles east of Rome, sits the medieval hill town of Tivoli, a popular retreat since ancient times. Today, it's famous for two very different villas: Hadrian's Villa, the ruins of a Versailles-like seat of government—outside but still near the capital—from which the emperor ruled, and the restored Villa d'Este, the lush and watery 16th-century residence of a cardinal in exile. These two sights complement each other well: While Hadrian's Villa ("Villa Adriana" in Italian) is about evocative ruins that ache with an untold history, Villa d'Este is simply beautiful, carefree, and relaxing—a pure confection.

Getting to Tivoli, you'll likely travel along the Via Tiburtina. The road was initially built by the ancient Romans; today it takes you through sections of uninteresting concrete sprawl. Famous for its thermal baths (smell the sulfur?), the area also contains the travertine quarries that supplied Rome with material for many of its buildings, including the Colosseum. While you're in the countryside, keep an eye out for the many olive groves (this area bottles up the prized Sabina olive oil), as well as flocks of sheep that produce the local *pecorino romano* cheese.

PLANNING YOUR TIME

Villa d'Este is in the center of the town of Tivoli, while Hadrian's Villa is about 2.5 miles outside of town. Because public transportation connections are a bit complicated and time-consuming, consider a tour or driver and give yourself the better part of a day for the trip to Tivoli, especially if you plan to see both villas. Note that Hadrian's Villa is open daily, Villa d'Este is closed on Monday, and buses are limited on Sunday.

If visiting both villas, see Villa d'Este first, then Hadrian's Villa. Those with limited time should focus on Hadrian's Villa.

GETTING TO TIVOLI
With a Tour or Driver

Several Rome tour companies—including Context Rome and Through Eternity—offer private tours of the villas (see websites for specifics; tour companies listed on page 39). You can also hire a driver for the day to make the trip there and back faster and easier (drivers are recommended on page 41).

On Your Own

Reaching the town of Tivoli and Villa d'Este is easy. Getting to Hadrian's Villa is more of a challenge and requires patience. The directions given here rely on local buses (Tivoli's train station isn't convenient to either sight).

From Rome, take a Metro/bus combination. Ride Metro line B to Ponte Mammolo (20 minutes from Termini Station; make sure to take a train going to Rebibbia, not Jonio). At Ponte Mammolo, catch the local blue Cotral bus to Tivoli (€2.20, 2/hour; check monitor for departure schedule, then buy bus tickets at the bar or newsstand downstairs—they're €7 if you buy them on the bus, easiest to buy return ticket at the same time; buses leave upstairs and can be crowded, be prepared to stand, validate ticket on board, direction: Tivoli, www.cotralspa.it).

To go straight to **Hadrian's Villa,** ride the Cotral bus roughly 45 minutes to the stop for Villa Adriana (ask the driver or fellow passengers which stop you need for the *"scavi"*—excavations). You'll hop off shortly after passing the quarries and walk approximately 20 minutes through a residential area. The route is not well-signed, so don't be shy about asking locals for directions.

For **Villa d'Este,** stay on the bus another 10 minutes to reach downtown Tivoli. Get off near the central square and the big park with the playground (start paying attention as the bus winds up the hill—your stop is shortly after it levels out; ask the driver, "Villa d'Este?"). The round TI kiosk is just uphill to the right. The entrance to the villa is across the square, past the modern-art arch—follow the signs (for about a block downhill).

From Tivoli, to backtrack to **Hadrian's Villa,** catch the gray "CAT" city bus #4 or #4X at the bus stop near the playground. Buy your ticket at a tobacco shop—there's one right where you got off the Cotral bus—or newsstand (€1.30, about 2/hour Mon-Sat, hourly Sun morning, no buses Sun after 12:45, 10-minute ride, drops you near the villa entrance—tell driver "Villa Adriana," schedules at TI or www.catbustivoli.com). A taxi is €15 (look for one near the arch in the main square under the pine trees; confirm price before getting in).

From Hadrian's Villa, to return to **Rome,** either walk 20 minutes back to the main road (Via Tiburtina) or catch bus #4 or #4X (direction: Tivoli) and get off at the main road (buy tickets in advance; schedules and tickets may be available at the entrance to the ruins). At the main road, change to a Cotral bus to Rome (confirm destination with bus driver—ask *"per Roma?"*).

Orientation to Tivoli

TIVOLI

The town of Tivoli, with Villa d'Este in its center, is about 2.5 miles from Hadrian's Villa. Modern Tivoli was heavily reconstructed after being bombed during World War II, when it was a Nazi stronghold. While most of Tivoli blankets the hilltop in less-than-charming concrete, a more rustic and picturesque quarter clings to the cliffs above a gorge on the back side of town. This area, anchored by the sleepy Piazza Rivarola, has a few evocative ancient ruins of its own and the steep Villa Gregoriana park. Strolling the main pedestrian drag gives you a glimpse of a small, unembellished Italian town.

Tourist Information: The TI is on Piazza Garibaldi, near the bus stop, and has bus schedules (daily 9:30-17:30, tel. 0774-313-536).

Sights in Tivoli

▲Villa d'Este

Clinging to a steep hillside just below Tivoli's main square, this Renaissance-era palace has a dull interior but a spectacularly entertaining garden, divinely land-scaped and punctuated by pools, streams, waterfalls, and thundering fountains that harness the natural hydro power of the Aniene River. If you can handle the many stairs (it's more vertical than horizontal), exploring these gardens is a peaceful and picturesque experience.

Cost and Hours: €12, more with special exhibits; Tue-Sun 8:30-19:45, Mon from 14:00, closes as early as 17:00 off-season, last villa entry one hour before closing, last garden entry two hours before sunset; audioguide—€4, tel. 0774-335-850 or 0774-332-920, www.villadestetivoli.info.

Background: Ippolito d'Este's grandfather was Pope Alexander VI, and from birth Ippolito was fast-tracked for church service. He became a cardinal, but his claim to fame was his pleasure palace at Tivoli. In the 1550s, he destroyed a Benedictine monastery to

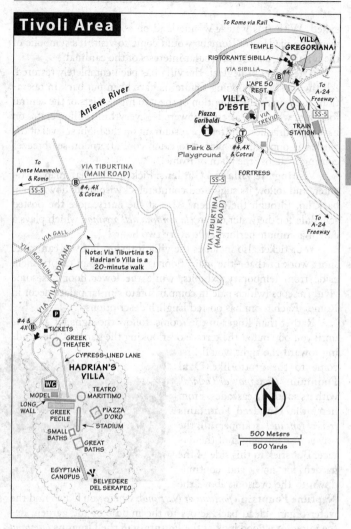

Tivoli Area

To Rome via Rail →

Aniene River

To Ponte Mammolo & Rome

VILLA GREGORIANA

TEMPLE

RISTORANTE SIBILLA

VIA SIBILLA

L'APE 50 REST.

VILLA D'ESTE

TIVOLI

Piazza Garibaldi

Park & Playground

VIA TIBURTINA (MAIN ROAD)

#4, 4X & Cotral

SS-5

#4, 4X & Cotral

VIA TREVIO

TRAIN STATION

FORTRESS

To A-24 Freeway

SS-5

VIA TIBURTINA (MAIN ROAD)

To A-24 Freeway

VIA GALL

VIA ROSALINA

VIA VILLA ADRIANA

Note: Via Tiburtina to Hadrian's Villa is a 20-minute walk

#4 & 4X

P

TICKETS

GREEK THEATER

CYPRESS-LINED LANE

HADRIAN'S VILLA

WC

MODEL

LONG WALL

GREEK PECILE

TEATRO MARITTIMO

PIAZZA D'ORO

STADIUM

SMALL BATHS

GREAT BATHS

EGYPTIAN CANOPUS

BELVEDERE DEL SERAPEO

N

500 Meters

500 Yards

build this fanciful late-Renaissance residential estate. Its gardens feature hundreds of Baroque fountains, all gravity-powered. The Aniene River, frazzled into countless threads, weaves its way entertainingly through the property. At the bottom of the garden, the exhausted little streams once again team up to make a sizable river. Pirro Ligorio, Tivoli's architect, was also the archaeologist in charge of excavating Hadrian's Villa, and that site provided much in inspiration—and raw material—for the fancy fountains of Villa d'Este. Ligorio basically used Hadrian's Villa as a quarry to provide statuary and decorative stonework for his vision here.

The cardinal had a political falling-out with Rome, and he was exiled. With this watery wonderland on a cool hillside with fine views, he made sure Romans would come to visit. It's symbolic of the luxurious tastes and secular interests of the cardinal.

After years of neglect, the villa has been completely restored. All the most eye-popping fountains have been put back in operation, and—with the exception of the two highest jets of the central fountain, which are electric-powered—everything still operates on natural hydraulics. The terrace restaurant on the highest level of the garden is opportunely placed to catch cool afternoon sea breezes coming in across the plain of Rome.

Visiting the Villa and Gardens: Pick up the small map as you enter, and follow its suggested counterclockwise route down, then back up, through the garden. Also at the entry, note the posted schedule for the water organ *(la fontana dell'organo)*, which plays a cute five-minute performance every two hours.

Your ticket also includes the villa **interior,** but you can make short work of that—the main floor is essentially an empty shell, aside from temporary exhibits, while the lower floor has some vivid frescoes (which pale in comparison to similar palace decor in Rome). Each room has posted English descriptions.

Rather than linger in the rooms, follow the signs for *giardino* until you pop out at the terrace overlooking the gardens. Descend-

ing toward the right, you'll first come to the grotto-like **Oval Fountain** *(fontana dell'ovato)*, with its soothing cascades. From here, the **Hundred Fountains** *(cento fontane)* scamper all the way across the length of the terrace. But stick to this side of the garden for now, and continue down to the overlook above the **Neptune Fountain** *(fontana di Nettuno)*, where you'll also find the water organ. Head back across to the middle of the garden, descending for a good look at the **Fountain of the Dragons** *(fontana dei draghi)*. Then descend to the row of fishponds that stretches scenically in one direction to the bottom of the Neptune Fountain, and in the other to a viewpoint overlooking the countryside. The lowest level of the park has a few smaller fountains (including the many-breasted Artemis, along the bottom wall). When you're ready, huff your way back up to the top...and the exit.

▲Hadrian's Villa (Villa Adriana)

Built at the peak of Rome's power by Emperor Hadrian (ruled AD 117-138), this was a retreat from the political complexity of court life. The Spanish-born Hadrian—an architect, lover of Greek culture (nicknamed "The Little Greek"), and great traveler—envisioned the site as a microcosm of the lands he ruled, which at that point stretched from Britannia (England) to the Euphrates River and encompassed countless diverse cultures. In the spirit of Legoland, Epcot, and Las Vegas, he re-created famous structures from around the world, producing a kind of diorama of his empire

in the form of the largest and richest Roman villa anywhere. Just as Louis XIV governed France from Versailles rather than Paris, Hadrian ruled Rome from this villa of more than 300 evocative acres. He basically spent his last decade here. Regrettably, this "Versailles of Ancient Rome" was plundered by barbarians and Renaissance big shots who all wanted something classical in their courtyards. They even burned the marble to make lime for cement. The scavenged art wound up in the Vatican Museums, the Louvre, and other museums throughout Europe. Today, Hadrian's Villa is a harmonious blend of nature and ruins—ideal for wandering while pondering the legacy of a great civilization.

Cost and Hours: €10, more with special exhibits; daily 8:30-19:30 in summer, April and Sept until 19:00, closes as early as 17:00 off-season, last entry 1.5 hours before closing; audioguide-€5, tel. 0774-382-733, www.coopculture.it.

Visiting the Ruins: Information at the site is sparse, but occasional posted maps and English descriptions do help keep you on track. The area can be difficult to make sense of, so watching a reconstruction beforehand can be really useful—there are several good ones on YouTube. From the ticket booth, hike about 10 minutes up the main path through olive groves. You'll reach a field with a WC (hidden underground). In the nearby beige building is a **model** of the reconstructed site that's helpful for getting oriented.

Just beyond that, go through the high brick wall to enter the Athenian-style **Greek Pecile,** a long, enclosed courtyard with a tranquil, fish-stocked pond. This wall—and the pond—are all that remain of the original structure.

Beyond the left end of the pond is a cluster of other ruins, including the long stadium and the **Teatro Marittimo** (a circular palace built on a little island, Hadrian's favorite retreat, where he did his serious thinking). Continuing up through the ruins and to the left, you'll reach what's left of the palace itself; at the far corner is the vast **Piazza d'Oro,** which was once filled with fountains and flowing water.

Looping back around, you'll come to a dramatic overview of

the gigantic (and aptly named) **Great Baths** complex. Descending to explore this area, continue to the left to find the villa's highlight, the **Egyptian Canopus** (sanctuary of the god Serapis), a canal lined with statues.

At the far end of the canal, climb a few stairs up to the Belvedere del Serapeo **viewpoint.** To return to the entrance, head back along the path above (and parallel) to the pool, eventually passing the **Small Baths** on your way to the Pecile. When you reach the long wall, exit the same way you entered, and continue down the main path toward the parking lot to reach the **Greek Theater.**

TIVOLI

Villa Gregoriana Park

This steep park incorporates a landscape enjoyed from antiquity to the Romantic Age and today. Over a 1.5-mile network of trails, you'll descend into the Aniene River valley, passing views of waterfalls, trees, and raw wilderness. For those with more interest in nature than antiquity—although bits of the ancient villa remain—it offers a convenient alternative to Hadrian's Villa.

Cost and Hours: €8, daily 10:00-18:30, off-season until 16:00 and closed Mon, last entry one hour before closing, closed Jan-Feb, several hundred feet of elevation change over uneven steps—good shoes and knees helpful, tel. 0774-332-650, www.parcovillagregoriana.it.

Getting There: It's handy to access the park through its back entrance, adjacent to the recommended Ristorante Sibilla. From the exit/main entrance (on the other side of the ravine from where you entered), it's a 15-minute walk back to the center of town. Alternatively, bus #4 leaves sporadically from the piazza out front (Largo Sant'Angelo) and goes through the center of town on its way to Hadrian's Villa and beyond (best to have purchased tickets in advance; otherwise try the green newspaper kiosk or Flo's Bar).

Eating in Tivoli

Eateries catering to tourists cluster around the main square, Largo Garibaldi—but for more choices and a better look at this tidy, no-frills town, head up Via del Trevio (which eventually curves and becomes Via Palatina then Via Ponte Gregoriano). This also takes you to the more scenic, older part of Tivoli—well worth exploring.

About a 10-minute walk from Largo Garibaldi, you'll arrive at **$$ l'Ape 50** (on the left), a classy but unpretentious place serving big gourmet sandwiches at a reasonable price (Tue-Sun 12:30-15:00 & 18:30-24:00, closed Mon, seating inside or out, Via di Ponte Gregoriano 5, tel. 0774-556-471).

Farther on, angling left at Piazza Rivarola, you'll find the **$$$ Ristorante Sibilla.** It's been open since 1720 but boasts a trendy, modern ambience. The restaurant neighbors two ancient temples, provides a glimpse of the waterfalls from its spectacularly set terrace, and offers pricey but tasty traditional cuisine (Tue-Sun 12:30-15:00 & 19:30-22:30, closed Mon, reserve for outdoor seating, Via della Sibilla 50, tel. 0774-335-281, www.ristorantesibilla. com). The restaurant is adjacent to the back entrance to Villa Gregoriana Park.

NAPLES & POMPEII

Napoli • Pompeii

While the Eternal City can keep you busy for ages, here are two excuses to leave Rome for a day. The trip south to Naples and Pompeii is demanding (4-5 hours of train and bus travel round-trip). But you'll be rewarded with a chance to wander ancient Rome's most evocative ruins and go on an urban safari in what is perhaps Europe's most intense city.

If you have a week in Rome and are interested in maximum travel thrills, take a day trip to Naples and Pompeii. Note that Naples' Archaeological Museum is closed on Tuesday. Pompeii is open daily.

Naples

If you like Italy as far south as Rome, go farther south—it gets better. If Italy is getting on your nerves, stop at Rome. Italy intensifies as you plunge deeper. Naples is Italy in the extreme—its best (birthplace of pizza) and its worst (home of the Camorra, Naples' "family" of organized crime).

Before Italy unified in the late 1800s, Naples was the country's richest city. But Naples' fortunes nosedived when the capital of modern Italy was established in Rome. Things got so bad that many of its residents emigrated. The Italy America knows—pizza, spaghetti, and "O Sole Mio"/"Santa Lucia"—came from 19th-century Naples, as brought to the US by all those immigrants.

Today, Naples impresses visitors with one of Europe's top archaeological museums (showcasing the artistic treasures of Pompeii), fascinating churches, an underground warren of Greek and Roman ruins, fine works of art (including pieces by Caravaggio, who lived here for a time), and evocative Nativity scenes (called *presepi*). Of course, Neapolitans make great pizza and tasty pastries (try the crispy, ricotta-stuffed *sfogliatella*). But more than anything, Naples has a brash and vibrant street life—"Italy in your face" in ways both good and bad. Walking through its colorful old town is one of my favorite experiences anywhere in Europe.

Naples is southern Italy's leading city, the third-largest city in Italy, and Europe's most densely populated city, with more than one million people and few open spaces or parks. While in many ways it feels like an urban jungle, Naples surprises the observant traveler with its impressive knack for living, eating, and raising children with good humor and decency.

Naples doesn't get nearly as many tourists as it deserves. While the city has its problems, it has improved a lot in recent years. And even though it remains a bit edgy, I feel comfortable here. Naples richly rewards those who venture in.

PLANNING YOUR TIME

A blitz visit to Naples and Pompeii looks something like this:

7:35	Have breakfast on the early express train from Rome to Naples Centrale train station. Link to Pompeii by shuttle bus or commuter train.
10:00	Tour Pompeii, grab a quick lunch (it's best to bring a picnic), then catch the shuttle or commuter train back to Naples.
14:30	Visit Naples' Archaeological Museum during the heat of the day (closed Tue).
16:30	Take my self-guided "Naples Walk."
18:30	Finish with a pizza dinner as the city comes to life in the early evening.
20:30	Hop on the train back to Rome.
22:30	Arrive in Rome.

Orientation to Naples

Naples is set deep inside the large, curving Bay of Naples, with Mount Vesuvius looming just five miles away. Although Naples is a sprawling city, its fairly compact core contains the most interesting sights. The tourist's Naples is a triangle, with its points at the Centrale train station in the east, the Archaeological Museum to the west, and Piazza del Plebiscito (with the Royal Palace) and the port to the south. Steep hills rise above this historic core, including San Martino, capped with a mighty fortress.

TOURIST INFORMATION

Central Naples has multiple small TIs, none of them particularly helpful—just grab a map and browse the brochures. The handiest one is in **Centrale train station** (daily 8:30-19:30, in the main lobby, tel. 081-268-779). Two others are by the entrance to the **Galleria Umberto I** shopping mall, across from Teatro di San Carlo (Mon-Sat 9:00-17:00, Sun until 13:00, tel. 081-402-394), and on Spaccanapoli, across from the **Church of Gesù Nuovo** (same hours as Galleria Umberto I TI, tel. 081-551-2701). For information online, the best overall website is www.inaples.it.

ARRIVAL IN NAPLES

Express trains from Rome arrive at the slick, modern main station, **Napoli Centrale.** It has a small TI (next to the Trenitalia ticket office), a travel agency (on the left of the main lobby), a bookstore (La Feltrinelli, near track 24—beyond the pharmacy), and baggage check (*deposito bagagli*, run by Kipoint, near track 2). Pay WCs are down the stairs across from track 13. Shops and eateries are concentrated in the underground level. A good supermarket (Sapori & Dintorni) is out the front door and to the left. Immediately downstairs is the **Garibaldi** commuter rail station, which you'll use if you take a train to Pompeii. If you're taking the CitySightseeing shuttle bus to Pompeii, the bus stop is across the street from the main entrance.

Getting Downtown from the Station: Metro lines 1 and 2 are signposted throughout Centrale and Garibaldi. Line 1 is handy for city-center stops, including the cruise port (Municipio), the main shopping drag (Toledo and Dante), and the Archaeological Museum (Museo). Line 2 is slightly quicker for reaching the Archaeological Museum (ride it to the Cavour stop and walk 5 minutes). For tips on navigating the Metro, see "Getting Around Naples," later.

Long rows of white **taxis** line up out front. Ask the driver to charge you the fixed rate *(tariffa predeterminata)*, which should be around €9 for the old center. The TI in the station can tell you the going rate.

CONTINUING TO POMPEII

On a day trip, see Pompeii first, spending the afternoon and early evening in Naples. The two can be connected by a private shuttle bus or commuter train.

CitySightseeing Italy offers a convenient, clean, and stress-free shuttle bus from Naples to Pompeii. From Centrale Station, the bus stop is located across the street and to the left, next to the Hotel D'Anna. Tickets can be purchased online, but be aware that each bus has a specific return time about four hours after arrival at Pompeii; no return-trip changes are allowed. Departures from Centrale Station in summer are at 9:30, 10:15, and 11:15, with corresponding return trips leaving Pompeii at 13:20, 14:40, and 16:00; fewer departures off-season; 30-minute ride if traffic is light (€8 one-way, €15 round-trip, air-con, tel. 081-551-7279, www.citysightseeing.it).

For more flexibility, consider the **Circumvesuviana,** a rundown, crowded commuter train that's handy for tourists, commuters...and pickpockets. Note: When coming from Rome, don't be tempted to take a Trenitalia connection all the way to the stop called "Pompei," which leaves you at a station in Pompeii's ugly, modern city center—a long walk to the actual site. It's better to get off at Naples' Centrale Station and transfer to the Circumvesuviana.

There are two trains per hour to Pompeii—just take any train marked for Sorrento, and get off at the stop called Pompei Scavi-Villa dei Misteri; it's the stop after Villa Regina (about 35 minutes, €2.90 one-way, not covered by rail passes, no air-con, Italian-only website at www.eavsrl.it).

At Naples' Centrale Station, follow Circumvesuviana signs downstairs and down the corridor to the Circumvesuviana ticket windows and turnstiles (no self-service ticket machines or online sales—line up or buy at a newsstand). Buy your ticket, confirm time and track (usually departs from platform 3), insert your ticket at the turnstiles, and head down another level to the platforms. On the platform, double-check with a local that the train goes to Pompeii, as the Circumvesuviana has several lines that branch out to other destinations.

When returning to Naples on the Circumvesuviana, get off at the next-to-the-last station, Garibaldi (Centrale Station is just up the escalator). For more tips about riding the Circumvesuviana, see "Helpful Hints," next.

Pricier **Campania Express** trains, operated by the Circumvesuviana, use the same tracks and stations, but staff check tickets as you enter, so trains are much less crowded—and they have air-conditioning. But they run only four times a day from mid-March to October. On a day trip from Rome, it's possible to take the morning Campania Express to Pompeii, but if you want any quality time in Naples, you'll have to take a standard train back (€6 one-way, leaves at 9:09 but schedule can change, see http://ots.eavsrl.it).

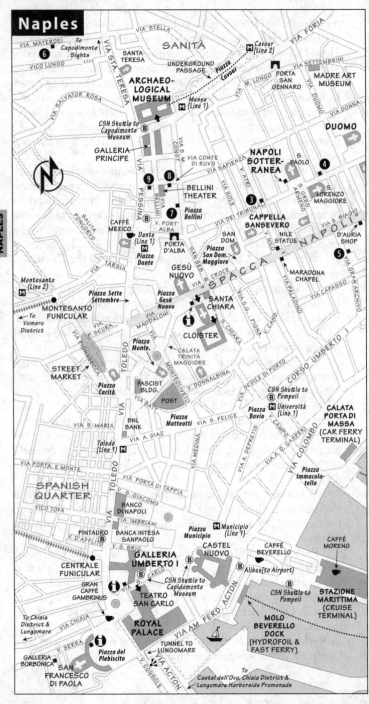

Naples

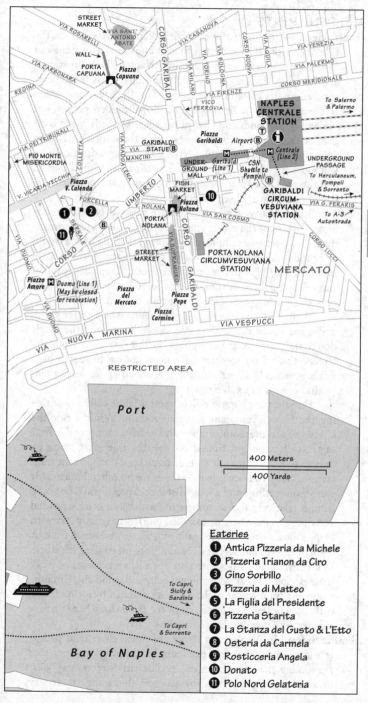

STREET MARKET

VIA ROSARELLI

VIA SANT' ANTONIO ABATE

WALL

PORTA CAPUANA

Piazza Capuana

VIA CARBONARA

REGINA

CORSO GARIBALDI

VIA CASANOVA

VIA CASANOVA

VIA BOLOGNA

VIA NUOVA

VIA AQUILA

VIA VENEZIA

VIA TORINO

VIA MILANO

VIA FIRENZE

VIA PALERMO

CORSO MERIDIONALE

VICO FERROVIA

NAPLES CENTRALE STATION

To Salerno & Palermo

VIA DEI TRIBUNALI

PIO MONTE MISERICORDIA

COLLETTA

VIA MADDALENA

UMBERTO I

VIA MANCINI

GARIBALDI STATUE

Piazza Garibaldi

Airport

Centrale (Line 2)

UNDERGROUND PASSAGE

V. VICARIA VECCHIA

Piazza V. Calenda

FORCELLA

UNDER GROUND MALL

Garibaldi (Line 1)

V. PICA

CSN Shuttle to Pompeii

GARIBALDI CIRCUM-VESUVIANA STATION

To Herculaneum, Pompeii & Sorrento

FISH MARKET

VIA NOLANA

Piazza Nolana

❿

VIA SAN COSMO

VIA G. FERARIS

To A-3 Autostrada

SENSALE

ⓐ

PORTA NOLANA

CORSO GARIBALDI

VIA SOPRAMURO

PORTA NOLANA CIRCUMVESUVIANA STATION

MERCATO

CORSO LUCCI

VIA DUOMO

CORSO

STREET MARKET

Piazza Amore

Duomo (Line 1) (May be closed for renovation)

Piazza del Mercato

Piazza Carmine

Piazza Pepe

VIA DUOMO

VIA NUOVA MARINA

VIA VESPUCCI

RESTRICTED AREA

Port

400 Meters

400 Yards

To Capri, Sicily & Sardinia

To Capri & Sorrento

Bay of Naples

NAPLES

Eateries
❶ Antica Pizzeria da Michele
❷ Pizzeria Trianon da Ciro
❸ Gino Sorbillo
❹ Pizzeria di Matteo
❺ La Figlia del Presidente
❻ Pizzeria Starita
❼ La Stanza del Gusto & L'Etto
❽ Osteria da Carmela
❾ Rosticceria Angela
❿ Donato
⓫ Polo Nord Gelateria

HELPFUL HINTS

Theft Alert: While most travelers visit Naples safely, err on the side of caution. Be aware that thieves and con-artists hang out close to where travelers tumble into Naples: the train station and the port. Although the train station itself has been nicely spruced up, its glow doesn't extend far. The areas nearby are frequented by some of Italy's most downtrodden people, but remember that poor and chaotic do not necessarily mean dangerous. Don't let your first impression of the station area get in your way of enjoying Naples—the city changes drastically as you move further away. Touristy Spaccanapoli, Capodimonte, and the posh Via Toledo shopping boulevard are more upscale, though you may still see panhandlers.

Stick to busy streets and beware the odd gang of hoodlums. A third of the city is unemployed, and past local governments have set an example of corruption that the Mafia would be proud of. As in most big cities, consider any jostle or commotion a possible thief-team smokescreen. Keep a low profile, carry only the bare minimum, and leave heavy bags in Rome or at the left-luggage office in Centrale Station.

Walk with confidence, as if you know where you're going and what you're doing. Use the sidewalk (even if the locals don't) and carry your belongings on the side away from the street—thieves on scooters have been known to snatch bags as they swoop by. Keep valuables buttoned up (or leave them behind at your hotel in Rome).

Perhaps your biggest risk of theft is while catching or riding the Circumvesuviana commuter train. While I ride the Circumvesuviana comfortably and safely, each year I hear of travelers who get ripped off on this ride. You won't be mugged—but you may be conned or pickpocketed. At the train station, carry your own bags—there are no official porters. If you're connecting from a long-distance express, you'll be going from a relatively secure compartment into an often-crowded and dingy train, where disoriented tourists delicately mix with Naples' down-and-out. Be ready for this very common trick: A team of thieves blocks the door at a stop, pretending it's stuck. While everyone rushes to try to open it, an accomplice picks their pockets. Wear your money belt, and avoid the Circumvesuviana train late at night when it's plagued by intimidating ruffians. For peace of mind, sit in the front car, where there is a driver who may be able to monitor activity.

Traffic Safety: In Naples, red lights are timed short, and pedestrians need to be wary, particularly of motor scooters that zip among the cars. Even on "pedestrian" streets, stay alert to avoid being sideswiped by scooters that nudge their way through the crowds. Smart tourists jaywalk in the shadow of bold locals, who generally ignore crosswalks. Wait for a break in traffic, cross with confidence, and make eye contact with approaching drivers and motor scooters. The traffic will slow to let you pass.

GETTING AROUND NAPLES

Sightsee Naples with help from its subway (Metro), funiculars, and taxis. (There are also public buses but these generally aren't useful for travelers.) For general transit information, maps, and fares in English, visit www.unicocampania.it. The TI hands out a good free map showing Metro, funicular, and bus routes. For schedules, your only option is the Italian-only site www.anm.it. For journey planning, use maps.google.com.

Tickets and Passes: Most of Naples' public transportation system—Metro, funiculars, and buses—use the same ticket, which must be stamped as you enter (in yellow or blue machines). Tickets are sold at tobacco stores, some newsstands, clunky machines at Metro stations (coins and small bills only), and occasionally at station windows. Basically, anywhere you see a queue near the station, people are buying tickets.

A €1.10 single ticket *(corsa singola)* covers any ride on bus, funicular, or Metro line 1, with no transfers; for Metro line 2 you need the €1.30 version. (This ticket is a long, printed receipt with a QR code that needs to be punched at the machine—fold your ticket in half and insert.)

By Metro *(Metropolitana):* Naples' subway has three main lines *(linea).* Station entrances and signs to the Metro are marked by a red square with a white *M.*

Line 1 is handy for tourists. Starting from the train station (stop name: Garibaldi), it heads to Università (the university), Municipio (at Piazza Municipio, just above the harbor and cruise terminal), Toledo (south end of Via Toledo, near Piazza del Plebiscito), Dante (Piazza Dante), and Museo (Archaeological Museum).

Line 2 (part of the Italian national rail system) is most useful for getting quickly from the train station to Piazza Cavour (a 5-minute walk from the Archaeological Museum) or Montesanto (the top of the Spanish Quarter and Spaccanapoli street, and base of one funicular up to San Martino).

The under-construction **line 6** is unlikely to be of much use to tourists.

By Funicular: Central Naples' three funiculars *(funicolare)* carry commuters and sightseers into the hilly San Martino neighborhood just west of downtown. All three converge near Piazza Fuga, a short walk from the hilltop fortress and monastery/museum. The Centrale line runs from the Spanish Quarter, just near Pi-

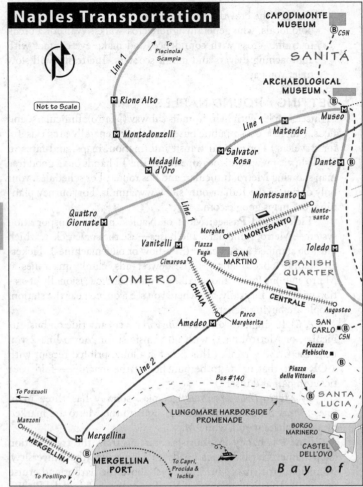

Naples Transportation

CAPODIMONTE
MUSEUM 🅱 CSN

SANITÁ

Ⓜ Rione Alto

Line 1

To
Piscinola/
Scampia

(Not to Scale)

ARCHAEOLOGICAL
MUSEUM 🅱

Museo Ⓜ

Ⓜ Montedonzelli

Line 1   Materdei Ⓜ

Ⓜ Salvator
Rosa

Medaglie
Ⓜ d'Oro

Dante Ⓜ 🅱

Montesanto Ⓜ

Quattro
Giornate Ⓜ

Morghen ○——○ Monte-
santo

MONTESANTO

Vanitelli Ⓜ

Piazza
Fuga   SAN
Cimarosa   MARTINO

Toledo Ⓜ

SPANISH
QUARTER

VOMERO

CHIAIA

CENTRALE

Augusteo ○

Amedeo Ⓜ   Parco
Margherita

SAN
CARLO 🅱
■ CSN

Piazza
Plebiscito ■

Line 2

Bus #140

Piazza
della Vittoria

Piazza
Plebiscito 🅱

🅱 SANTA
LUCIA

To Pozzuoli

Manzoni
○

MERGELLINA

LUNGOMARE HARBORSIDE
PROMENADE

🅱

Ⓜ Mergellina

🅱

BORGO
MARINERO

To Posillipo

🅱 MERGELLINA
PORT

To Capri,
Procida &
Ischia

CASTEL
DELL'OVO

Bay of

azza del Plebiscito and the Toledo Metro stop; the Montesanto line from the Montesanto Metro stop and Via Pignasecca market zone; and the Chiaia line from near the Piazza Amadeo Metro stop.

By Taxi: A short ride in town should cost €10-15. Always ask for the *tariffa predeterminata* (a fixed rate). For metered rides there are some legitimate extra charges (baggage fees, €2.50 supplement after 22:00 or all day Sun and holidays) but the destinations I recommend are covered by the *tariffa predeterminata*. Radio Taxi 8888 is one reputable company (tel. 081-8888).

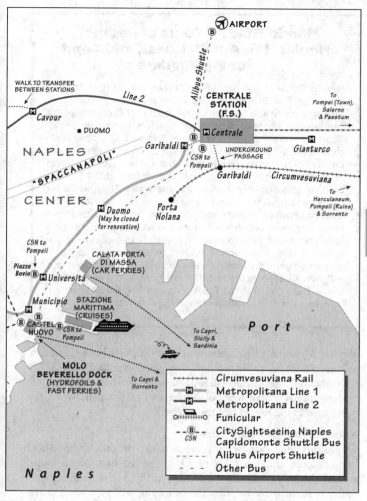

WALK TO TRANSFER
BETWEEN STATIONS

Line 2

Cavour

■ DUOMO

NAPLES

"SPACCANAPOLI"

CENTER

Garibaldi

Alibus Shuttle

✈ AIRPORT

CENTRALE
STATION
(F.S.)

Centrale

To
Pompei (Town),
Salerno
& Paestum

Gianturco

CSN to
Pompeii

UNDERGROUND
PASSAGE

Garibaldi

Circumvesuviana

To
Herculaneum,
Pompeii (Ruins)
& Sorrento

Duomo
(May be closed
for renovation)

Porta
Nolana

CSN to
Pompeii

Piazza
Bovio

Università

CALATA PORTA
DI MASSA
(CAR FERRIES)

Municipio

STAZIONE
MARITTIMA
(CRUISES)

CASTEL
NUOVO

CSN to
Pompeii

To Capri,
Sicily &
Sardinia

Port

MOLO
BEVERELLO DOCK
(HYDROFOILS &
FAST FERRIES)

To Capri &
Sorrento

NAPLES

Naples

Cirumvesuviana Rail
Metropolitana Line 1
Metropolitana Line 2
Funicular
CitySightseeing Naples
Capidomonte Shuttle Bus
Alibus Airport Shuttle
Other Bus

Tours in Naples

🎧 To sightsee on your own, download my free Rick Steves audio tours of the Naples Archaeological Museum and my Naples Walk.

Local Guides

Pina Esposito has a Ph.D. in ancient archaeology and art and does fine private walking and driving tours of Naples and the region (Pompeii, Capri, the Amalfi Coast, etc.), including Naples' Archaeological Museum (€60/hour, 2-hour minimum, 10 percent off with this book, additional discounts for full-day tours, mobile 338-763-4224, annamariaesposito1@virgilio.it).

The team at **Mondo Guide** offers private tours of the Archae-

Mondo Guide's Tours of Pompeii, Naples, the Amalfi Coast, and Capri for My Readers

Mondo Guide, a big Naples-based company, offers "shared tours" for Rick Steves readers. These include a private, professional guide at a fraction of the usual cost (because you're sharing the expense with other travelers using this book). Tours run April-October and include **Pompeii** (€15, doesn't include €15 Pompeii entry, daily at 11:00, 2 hours, meet in Pompeii at Hotel/Ristorante Suisse) and a walking tour of **Naples** (€25, daily at 15:00, 3 hours, meet at the steps of the Archaeological Museum—not included in the walk). They also offer shore excursions from Naples and Salerno, and full-day Amalfi Coast minibus tours and Capri boat trips (both departing from Sorrento). Reservations are required at www.sharedtours.com (use your credit card to reserve a spot, then pay cash to the guide). Tours depart only if at least six people sign up. You'll be sent an email confirmation as soon as they're sure your tour will run. Confirmed departures are continually updated on the website (tel. 081-751-3290, mobile 340-460-5254, www.mondoguide.it, sharedtours@mondoguide.com).

ological Museum (€120/2 hours) and city (€240/4 hours), and can provide guides or drivers throughout the region (tel. 081-751-3290, www.mondoguide.it, info@mondoguide.com). They also offer my readers special shared tours of Naples and of Pompeii, as well as other trips in the region (see the sidebar).

Hop-On, Hop-Off Bus Tours
CitySightseeing Napoli tour buses make two different hop-on, hop-off loops through the city. Only the red line, which loops around the historical center and stops at the Archaeological Museum, is particularly helpful. The bus route will give you a sense of greater Naples (€23, ticket valid 24 hours, 2/hour, buy from driver or from kiosk at Piazza Municipio in front of Castel Nuovo near the port, scant recorded narration, tel. 081-551-7279, www.napoli.city-sightseeing.it). The same company offers a shorter, more frequent route around the old center in an open-top minibus and shuttles to Pompeii (described earlier).

Cruise-Ship Excursions
Convenient for cruise-ship passengers, the **Can't Be Missed** tour company takes you from the port of Naples on an all-day, big-bus trip along the Amalfi Coast that includes a stop in Sorrento and a guided tour of Pompeii (€69, meet at 8:00 in front of port, bus leaves at 8:30, returns at 17:15, Pompeii ticket extra, mobile 329-

129-8182, www.cantbemissedtours.com, RS%—10 percent off when you use promo code "RICKSTEVES" on their website).

Capri Sightseeing offers shuttle service from the Naples cruise port to Pompeii, Herculaneum, and/or Vesuvius (www.caprisightseeing.com, info@caprisightseeing.com).

Archaeological Museum Tour

Naples' Archaeological Museum (Museo Archeologico), worth ▲▲▲, is one of the world's great museums of ancient art. It boasts

supersized statues as well as art and decorations from Pompeii and Herculaneum, the two ancient burgs that were buried in ash by the eruption of Mount Vesuvius in AD 79. For lovers of antiquity, this museum alone makes Naples a worthwhile stop. When Pompeii was excavated in the late 1700s, Naples' Bourbon

king bellowed, "Bring me the best of what you find!" The finest art and artifacts ended up here, leaving the ancient sites themselves barren (though still impressive). It's here at the Archaeological Museum that you can get up close and personal with the ancient world. This self-guided tour covers the highlights.

ORIENTATION

Cost and Hours: €18, sometimes more for temporary exhibits; Wed-Mon 9:00-19:30, closed Tue. Avoid lines by purchasing your ticket online. Early and temporary closures are noted on a board near the ticket office: Expect some rooms to be closed in July and August.

Free Entry: State museums in Italy are free to enter once or twice a month, usually on a Sunday. Check in advance and avoid going on a free day, which can attract huge crowds.

Getting There: From Centrale Station, you can reach the museum by Metro or taxi. **Metro** line 2 is quickest: At the station, buy a single €1.30 transit ticket at a newsstand or tobacco shop—specify you want line 2 since the price and ticket are different from line 1. Follow the signs for *Metro Linea 2,* then fold and punch your ticket in the small blue boxes near the escalator going down to the tracks. You're looking for trains heading in the direction of Pozzuoli (ticket attendants will ask and confirm which direction you're going). Ride one stop to Piazza Cavour. Follow *Museo* signs through the underground passage or exit and walk five minutes uphill through the park. Look for a grand old red building located up a flight of stairs at the top of the block.

You can also take the Metro's cheaper line 1 five stops from Centrale Station to Museo—it's only a little slower. Figure on around €13 for a **taxi** from the train station to the museum.

Information: The shop sells a worthwhile *National Archaeological Museum of Naples* guidebook for €12. Tel. 081-442-2149, www.museoarcheologiconapoli.it.

Tours: The self-guided tour in this chapter covers all the basics. For more detail, the decent audioguide (€5, leave ID at ticket desk) focuses largely on the provenance of the artifacts and how they ended up here. For a guided tour, book Pina Esposito (see "Tours in Naples," earlier).

∩ Download my free Archaeological Museum **audio tour.**

Baggage Check: Bag check is obligatory and free.

Eating: The museum has no café, but vending machines sell drinks and snacks. There are several good places to grab a meal within a few blocks; see page 509.

➲ SELF-GUIDED TOUR

Entering the museum, cross the atrium, and stand at the base of the grand staircase. To your right, on the ground floor, are the larger-than-life statues of the Farnese Collection, starring the *Toro Farnese* and the *Farnese Hercules*. Up the stairs on the mezzanine level are mosaics and frescoes from Pompeii, including the Secret Room of erotic art. On the top floor are more artifacts from Pompeii, a scale model of the doomed city, and bronze statues from Herculaneum. WCs are behind the staircase.

• *From the base of the* ❶ *grand staircase, turn right through the door marked* Collezione Farnese *and head for the far end, walking through a rich collection of ancient portrait* ❷ *busts.*

Pause at the busts of **Caracalla** *(a third of the way down, on the left), and marvel at how he evolved from idealistic youth to cruel tyrant (and nemesis of Russell Crowe in the movie* Gladiator*). Admire the* **Seated Agrippina** *(two-thirds of the way down) with her typical hairstyle, realistic face, and pensive look. Nearby, look in* **Vespasian**'s *right ear and see how the huge head was hollowed out in medieval times. Now, continue to the end, jog right, then left, entering Room 13.*

Ground Floor: The Farnese Collection

The Farnese Collection statues are not from Pompeii, but from Rome. Today they're displayed in this grand hall of huge, bright, and wonderfully restored statues excavated from Rome's Baths of Caracalla. Peruse the larger-than-life statues filling the hall. They

Naples Archaeological Museum

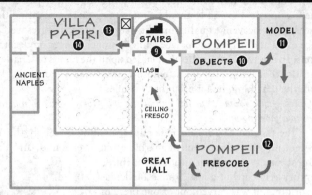

Second Floor (2)

Mezzanine (1)

⌧ Elevator

Not to Scale

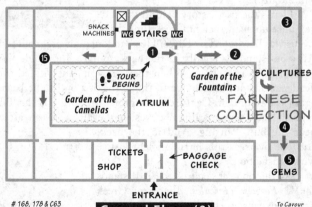

Ground Floor (0)

NAPLES

❶ Grand Staircase	❼ Dancing Faun & Battle of Alexander	⓫ Model of Pompeii
❷ Hall of the Busts	❽ Secret Room	⓬ Frescoes
❸ Toro Farnese	❾ Great Hall	⓭ Papyrus Scrolls
❹ Farnese Hercules	❿ Metal, Ivory & Glass Objects	⓮ Bronze Statues
❺ Farnese Cup		⓯ Doriforo
❻ Various Mosaics		

were dug up in the 1540s at the behest of Alessandro Farnese (by then Pope Paul III) while he was building the family palace on the Campo de' Fiori in Rome. His main purpose in excavating the baths was to scavenge quality building stone. The sculptures were a nice extra and helped the palace come in under budget on decorations. In the 1700s, the collection ended up in the hands of Charles, the Bourbon king of Naples (whose mother was a Farnese). His son, the next king, had it brought to Naples.

• *Quick—look down to the left end of the hall. There's a woman being tied to a snorting bull.*

The tangled ❸ *Toro Farnese* tells a thrilling Greek myth. At 13 feet, it's the tallest ancient marble group ever found, and the largest intact statue from antiquity. A third-century AD copy of a lost bronze Hellenistic original, it was carved out of one piece of marble. Michelangelo and others "restored" it at the pope's request—meaning that they integrated surviving bits into a new work. Some pieces were actually carved by Michelangelo: the head of the woman in back, the torso of the aunt under the bull, and the dog. (Imagine how the statue would stand out if it were thoughtfully lit and not surrounded by white walls.)

Here's the tragic story behind the statue: Once upon an ancient Greek time, King Lycus was bewitched by Dirce. He abandoned his pregnant wife, Antiope (standing regally in the background). The single mom gave birth to twin boys. When they grew up, they killed their deadbeat dad and tied Dirce to the horns of a bull to be bashed against a mountain. Captured in marble, the action is thrilling: cape flailing, dog snarling, hooves in the air. You can almost hear the bull snorting. And in the back, Antiope oversees this harsh ancient justice with satisfaction.

At the opposite end of the hall stands the ❹ *Farnese Hercules*. The great Greek hero is exhausted. He leans wearily on his club (draped with his lion skin) and bows his head. He's just finished the daunting Eleventh Labor, having traveled the world, fought men and gods, freed Prometheus from his rock, and carried Atlas' weight of the world on his shoulders. Now he's returned with the prize: the golden apples of the gods, which he cups behind his back. But, after all that, he's just been told he has to return the apples and do one final labor: descend into hell itself. Oh, man.

The 10-foot colossus is a third-century AD Roman marble copy (signed by "Glykon") of a fourth-century BC Greek bronze original (probably by Lysippos). The statue was enormously famous in its day. Dozens of copies—some marble, some bronze—have been found in Roman villas and baths. This version was unearthed in Rome's Baths of Caracalla in 1546, along with the *Toro Farnese*.

The *Farnese Hercules* was equally famous from the 16th to 18th century. Tourists flocked to Rome to admire it, art students studied it from afar in prints, Louis XIV made a copy for Versailles, and petty nobles everywhere put small-scale knock-offs in their gardens. This curly-haired version of Hercules became the modern world's image of the Greek hero.

• *Behind Hercules is a doorway into the impressive Farnese gem collection (Rooms 9 and 10). You'll see cameos and the ancient cereal-bowl-shaped* ❺ **Farnese Cup,** *which features a portrait thought to be of Cleopatra. When you're ready to move on, backtrack to the main entry hall with its grand staircase—perhaps stopping briefly to admire the magnificent sarcophagi in adjacent rooms, then head up to the mezzanine level (turn left at the lion and go under the* Mosaici *sign), and enter Room 57.*

Mezzanine: Pompeiian Mosaics and the Secret Room

These ❻ **mosaics**—mostly of animals, battle scenes, and geometric designs—were excavated from the walls and floors of Pompeii's ritzy villas. The *Chained Dog*

once graced a home's entryway. The colorful mosaic columns (to your right in adjoining Room 58) shaded a courtyard, part of an ensemble of wall mosaics and bubbling fountains. In Room 59, admire the realism of the tambourine-playing musicians, the drinking doves, and the skull—a reminder of impending death.

Continue a few steps into Room 60, with objects taken from one of Pompeii's greatest villas, the House of the Faun. The 20-inch-high statue was the house's delightful centerpiece, the ❼ *Dancing Faun.* This rare surviving Greek bronze statue (from the fourth century BC) is surrounded by some of the best mosaics of that age. (Find the little cat, who's caught a bird.)

A museum highlight, just beyond the statue, is the grand *Battle of Alexander,* a second-century BC copy of the now-lost original Greek fresco, done a century earlier. It decorated a floor in the

House of the Faun and was found intact. (The damage you see occurred as this treasure was moved from Pompeii to the king's collection here.) Alexander (left side of the scene, with curly hair and sideburns) is about to defeat the Persians under Darius (central figure, in chariot with turban and beard). This pivotal victory allowed Alexander to quickly over-run much of Asia (331 BC). Alexander is the only one without a helmet...a confident master of the battlefield while everyone else is fighting for their lives, eyes bulging with fear. Notice how the horses, already in re-treat, add to the scene's propaganda value.

Notice also the shading and perspective, which Renaissance artists would later work so hard to accomplish. (A modern reproduction of the mosaic is now back in Pompeii, at the House of the Faun.)

Farther on, the ❽ **Secret Room** (Gabinetto Segreto, Room 65) contains a sizable assortment of erotic frescoes, well-hung pottery, and perky statues that once decorated bedrooms, meeting rooms, brothels, and even shops at Pompeii and Herculaneum. These bawdy statues and frescoes—many of them once displayed in Pompeii's grandest houses—were entertainment for guests. (By the time they made it to this museum, in 1819, the frescoes could be viewed only with permission from the king—see the letters in the glass case just outside the door.) The Roman nobles commissioned the wildest scenes imaginable. Think of them as ancient dirty jokes.

At the entrance, you're enthusiastically greeted by big stone penises that once projected over Pompeii's doorways. A massive phallus was not necessarily a sexual symbol, but a magical amulet used against the "evil eye." It symbolized fertility, happiness, good luck, riches, straight A's, and general wellbeing.

Circulating counterclockwise through this section, look for the following: the fresco—high up—of a faun playfully pulling the sheet off a beautiful woman (#12), only to be surprised by both male and female plumbing (perhaps the original *"Mamma mia!"*). A few steps farther, see horny pygmies from Africa in action (#27). There's a toga with an embarrassing bulge (#34). A particularly high-quality statue depicts a goat and a satyr engaging in a sex act (#36). And, watching over it all with remarkable aplomb, is Venus, the patron goddess of Pompeii (#39).

The back room is furnished and decorated the way an ancient brothel might have been. The 10 frescoes on the wall functioned as both a menu of services offered and as a kind of *Kama Sutra* of sex positions. The glass cases contain more phallic art, including dangling mobiles used as party favors at rowdy banquets.

• *So, now that your travel buddy is finally showing a little interest in art…finish up your visit by climbing the stairs to the top floor.*

At the top of the stairs, pause and get oriented to our final sights. Directly ahead is a doorway (marked Salone Meridiana) that leads into a big, empty hall. To the left of this grand hall is a series of rooms with more artifacts from Pompeii. To the right are rooms of statues from Herculaneum. Keep this general layout in mind, because occasionally doorways and routes are altered, and you may have to improvise a bit to find your way.

Top Floor: Frescoes, Statues, Artifacts, and a Model of Pompeii

First, step into the Salone Meridiana. This was the ❾ **great hall** of the university (17th and 18th centuries) until the building became the royal museum, in 1777. Walk to the center. The sundial (from 1791) still works. Look up to the far-right corner of the hall and find the tiny pinhole. At noon (13:00 in summer), a ray of sun enters the hall and strikes the sundial, showing the time of the year… if you know your zodiac.

Now enter the series of rooms to the left of the grand hall, with ❿ **Metal, Ivory, and Glass Objects** found in Pompeii. You enter through a doorway marked *Vetri e Avori*, which leads into Room 89. Browse your way to the far end, with the stunning *Blue Vase* (Room 85), decorated with cameo Bacchuses harvesting grapes. Turn left, then right, to find the huge, room-filling ⓫ **model of Pompeii,** a 1:100 scale model of the ruins (Room 96). Face the model from the side labeled *plastico di Pompeii*. This is how tourists enter today, up the street, and spilling into the large rectangular forum with the Temple of Jupiter at one end. Farther up in the model are the city's two amphitheater-shaped theaters. This was all that had been excavated when the model was made in 1879. Another model (displayed on the wall) shows the site in 2004, after more excavations, when they'd dug up as far as the huge oval-shaped arena. Video screens capture images from the 1879 model and reconstruct buildings in 3D as they would have appeared before the eruption.

Continue on (through Rooms 83-80) and enter Room 75 (marked *affreschi*) to see the museum's impressive collection of (nonerotic) ⓬ **frescoes** taken from the walls of Pompeii villas. Pompeiians loved to decorate their homes with scenes from mythology (Hercules' labors, Venus and Mars in love), landscapes, everyday market scenes, and faux architecture. To the left (in Room 78), find the famous dual portrait of baker Terentius Neo and his wife—possibly two of the 2,000 victims when Vesuvius erupted.

• *Browse through more frescoes and objects from Pompeii in this labyrinth of rooms until, eventually, you end up back near the great hall.*

From here (facing the hall entrance), turn right and find the entrance to the wing labeled La Villa dei Papiri.

These artifacts came from the Herculaneum holiday home of Julius Caesar's father-in-law. In Room 114, find the glass cases holding two blackened examples of the 2,000  **⓭ papyrus scrolls** that gave the villa its name. The half-burned scrolls were unrolled and (with luck) read after excavation in the 1750s. Apparently Caesar's father-in-law was an educated man who appreciated everything from Greek philosophy to Latin history.

Continuing into Room 116, enjoy some of the villa's **⓮ bronze statues.** Look into the lifelike blue eyes of the intense *Corridore* (runners), bent on doing their best. The *Five Dancers,* with their inlaid-ivory eyes and graceful poses, decorated a portico. The next room (117) has more fine works: *Resting Hermes* (with his tired little heel wings) is taking a break. Nearby, the *Drunken Faun* (singing and snapping his fingers to the beat, a wineskin at his side) is clearly living for today. This statue epitomizes the *carpe diem* lifestyle of the Epicurean philosophy followed by Caesar's father-in-law and so many other Romans living in Herculaneum and Pompeii on that fateful morning of August 24, AD 79, when Vesuvius changed everything.

• *Ka-pow. The artistic explosion you've just experienced in this mighty museum is now over. To exit, return to the ground floor. To reach the exit, circle around the museum courtyard to the gift shop. But for extra credit, stop at one more sight on your way out.*

Doriforo

As you circle the courtyard toward the exit, find **⓯ Doriforo.** (If he's been moved, ask a guard, *"Dov'è il Doriforo?"*) This seven-foot-tall "spear-carrier" (the literal translation of *doriforo*) just stands there, as if holding a spear. What's the big deal about this statue, which looks like so many others? It's a marble replica made by the Romans of one of the most-copied statues of antiquity, a fifth-century BC bronze Greek original by Polyclitus. This copy once stood in a Pompeii gym, where it inspired ancient athletes by showing the ideal proportions of Greek beauty. So full of motion, and so realistic in

its *contrapposto* pose (weight on one foot), the *Doriforo* would later inspire Donatello and Michelangelo, helping to trigger the Renaissance. And so the glories of ancient Pompeii, once buried and forgotten, live on today.

Naples Walk

Naples, a living medieval city, is its own best sight. Couples artfully make love on Vespas surrounded by more smiles per cobblestone than anywhere else in Italy. Sure, Naples has its important sights. But to capture its essence, take this walk through the core of the city.

A SLICE OF NEAPOLITAN LIFE

This self-guided walk, worth ▲▲▲, takes you from the Archaeological Museum through the heart of town and back to Centrale Station. Allow at least two hours for the full two-part walk, plus time for pizza and sightseeing stops. If your time is short, you can end the walk at Piazza Carità and take the Metro back to the station.

🎧 You can also download my free Naples City Walk audio tour.

Part 1: Archaeological Museum to Piazza Carità

Start at the Archaeological Museum, at the top of Piazza Cavour (Metro: Cavour or Museo; for directions on getting here, see page 485). From here, we'll ramble down a fine boulevard before cutting into the medieval heart of the city.

❶ **Archaeological Museum:** The palatial building, built in the mid-1700s, captures the glory of Naples at its peak, and is a great introduction to the Naples we'll see. Back then, the city was rich from sea trade and home to eru-

dite nobles from abroad. They built a magnificent capital of buildings like this one. On this walk we'll see that grand city they built...and its remnants following centuries of decline.

• *From the door of the Archaeological Museum, cross the street, veer right, and enter the arched doorway of the beige-colored Galleria Principe di Napoli mall. (If the entrance is blocked, simply loop around the block to another entrance or pick up our walk behind the Galleria.)*

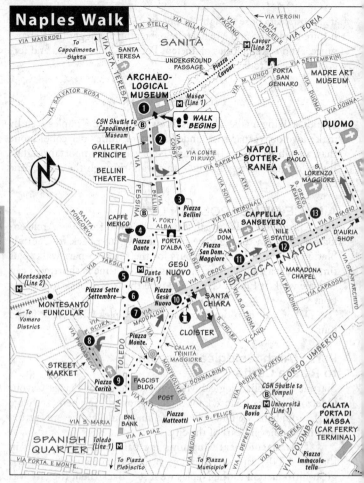

Naples Walk

❷ Galleria Principe di Napoli: There's no better example of Naples' grandeur—and decline—than this elegant 19th-century shopping mall. You'll enjoy a soaring skylight, carved woodwork, ironwork lanterns, playful cupids, an elegant atmosphere...and empty shops. Built with great expectations, the galleria was named for the first male child of the royal Savoy family, the Prince of Naples. Malls like these were popular in Paris and London. In the US, we call this decorative style Art Nouveau; in Italy it's "Liberty Style," named for a British department store that was in vogue at a time when Naples was nicknamed the "Paris of the South." Despite its grandeur, the mall never took off. Ambitious renovations in recent years have failed to attract much business, leaving the

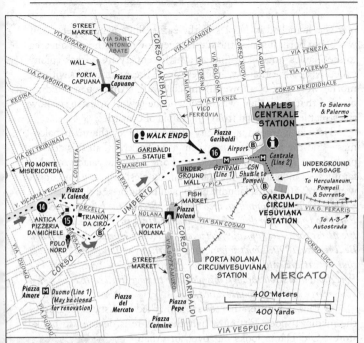

Part 1

❶ Archaeological Museum
❷ Galleria Principe di Napoli
❸ Piazza Bellini
❹ Piazza Dante
❺ Via Toledo
❻ Piazza Sette Settembre
❼ Spaccanapoli
❽ Via Pignasecca
❾ Piazza Carità

Part 2

❿ Piazza Gesù Nuovo
⓫ Piazza San Domenico Maggiore
⓬ Statue of the Nile
⓭ Via San Gregorio Armeno
⓮ Via Vicaria Vecchia
⓯ Eateries
⓰ Piazza Garibaldi

mall in a state of disrepair. Falling debris occasionally closes the entire structure.

• *Leaving the gallery through the opposite end, walk one block downhill on a pedestrian street. You'll pass alongside the palatial golden facade of the Academy of Fine Arts, fronted by tropical plants and (usually) busy with students at its outdoor cafés. At Via Conte di Ruvo, turn left, passing the fine* **Bellini Theater** *(also in Liberty Style). All along our walk, be sure to enjoy the architecture of the late 19th century, when Naples was the last stop on Romantic Age travelers' Grand Tour of Europe. After one block, turn right on Via Santa Maria di Costantinopoli. Walking between two grand churches, continue directly downhill to a small park with a statue in the center called...*

❸ **Piazza Bellini:** Suddenly you're in neighborhood Napoli. The statue honors the opera composer Vincenzo Bellini, whose career was launched in Naples in the early 1800s, when opera itself was being born. Just past the statue, peer down into the sunken area to see Naples' ancient origins as a fifth-century BC Greek colony called Neapolis—literally, "the new city." These tuff blocks without mortar were part of a tower in the city wall. (And you're standing on land that, back then, was outside of the town.) You can see how the street level has risen from the rubble of centuries.

Now look around at the city of today. Survey the many balconies—and the people who use them as a "backyard" in this densely packed city. The apartment blocks were originally the palaces of noble families, as indicated by the stately family crests above grand doorways. For 2,500 years, laundry has blown in the breeze right here.

· *Walk 30 yards downhill on the right side. Stop at the horseshoe-shaped* ***Port'Alba gate.*** *Spin slowly 360 degrees and take in the scene. The proud tile across the street (upstairs, between the two balconies) shows Piazza Bellini circa 1890. Don't ignore the graffiti; try to figure out the issues that artists are calling attention to. Pass through the gate, down Via Port'Alba, and stroll through this pleasant passage lined with book stalls. You emerge into a big square called...*

❹ **Piazza Dante:** This square is marked by a statue of Dante, the medieval poet. Fittingly, half the square is devoted to bookstores. Old Dante looks out over an urban area that was once grand, then chaotic, and is now slowly becoming grand again.

Along one side is a grandiose, orange-and-gray **pseudo-facade** of columns and statues designed by Luigi Vanvitelli, an architect who made his mark on the city in the late 1700s. Vanvitelli remade an existing Jesuit monastery into this new school, representing the power of the Bourbon monarchy when Naples was at its peak. Originally, a statue of the king stood in the square. But in 1799, the Bourbon monarchy was toppled when Napoleon invaded. The king's statue was removed and replaced with the generic figure of Dante. And note the name that was later added to the big facade—Victor Emmanuel. These suggest the next phase of Naples' history—its decline—which we'll see in just a bit.

The Neapolitan people are survivors. A long history of corrupt and greedy colonial overlords (German, Norman, French, Austrian, Spanish, Napoleon, etc.) has taught Neapolitans to deal creatively with authority. Many credit this aspect of Naples' past for the strength of organized crime here.

· *Before moving on, note the red "M" that Dante seems to be gesturing to. This marks the* ***Dante Metro station,*** *the best of Napoli's art-splashed*

NAPLES

Metro stations. (To take a look, go down three flights of escalators and then back up; you'll need a ticket, unless you can sweet-talk a guard.) Then, exit Piazza Dante at the far end, walking downhill on...

❺ Via Toledo: The long, straight street heading downhill from Piazza Dante is Naples' principal shopping drag. It originated as a military road built by the Spanish viceroys (hence the name) who made Naples great in the 16th century. Back then, Via Toledo skirted the old town wall to connect the Spanish military headquarters (now the museum where you started this walk) with the Royal Palace (down by the bay). As you stroll, peek into the many lovely atriums, which provide a break from the big street.

After a couple hundred yards, you'll reach the triangular **❻ Piazza Sette Settembre.** This public space recalls the event that precipitated Naples' swift decline. On September 7, 1860, from the white marble balcony of the Neoclassical building overlooking the square, the famous revolutionary Giuseppe Garibaldi celebrated his conquest of Naples. He declared Italy united and Victor Emmanuel II its first king. And a decade later, that declaration became reality when Rome also fell to unification forces. It was the start of a glorious new era for Italy, Rome, and the Italian people. But not for Naples.

Naples' treasury was confiscated to subsidize the industrial expansion of the north, and its bureaucrats were transferred to the new capital in Rome. Within a few decades, Naples went from being a thriving cultural and political capital to a provincial town, with its economy in shambles and its dialect considered backward.
• Continue straight on Via Toledo. A block past Piazza Sette Settembre, you'll come to Via Maddaloni, which marks the start of the long, straight, narrow street nicknamed...

❼ Spaccanapoli: Via Maddaloni is the modern name for the beginning of this thin street that, since ancient times, has

bisected the city. The name Spaccanapoli translates as "split Naples." Look left down the street (toward the train station), and right (toward San Martino hill), and you get a sense of how Spaccanapoli divides this urban jungle of buildings.
• At the Spaccanapoli intersection, go right (toward the church facade on the hill), heading up Via Pasquale Scura. After about 100 yards, you hit a busy intersection. Stop. You're on one of Naples' most colorful open-air market streets...

❽ Via Pignasecca: Take in the colorful scene at the intersection. Then, turn left down Via Pignasecca and stroll this colorful market strip. You'll pass fish stalls, tripe vendors, butchers, produce stands, cheap clothes stores, street-food vendors, and much more. There's more activity during the morning, but afternoon offers better light for photography.

This is a taste of Naples' famous **Spanish Quarter** (its center is farther down Via Toledo but this area provides a good sampling).

The Spanish Quarter is a classic world of *basso* (low) living. The streets—which were laid out in the 16th century for the Spanish military barracks outside the city walls—are unbelievably narrow (and cool in summer), and the buildings rise five stories high. In such tight quarters, life—flirting, fighting, playing, and loving—happens in the road. This is *the* cliché of life in Naples, as shown in so many movies. The Spanish Quarter is Naples at its most characteristic. The shopkeepers are friendly, and the mopeds are bold (watch out). Concerned locals will tug on their lower eyelids, warning you to be wary. Hungry? Pop into a grocery shop and ask the clerk to make you his best prosciutto-and-mozzarella sandwich (it should cost you about €4).

• *Turn left and follow Via Pignasecca as it leads back to Via Toledo at the square called...*

❾ Piazza Carità: This square, built for an official visit by Hitler to Mussolini in 1938, is full of stern, straight, obedient lines. The big building belonged to an insurance company. (For the best example of fascist architecture in town, take a slight detour from here: With your back to Via Toledo, leave Piazza Carità downhill on the right-hand corner and walk a block to the Poste e Telegrafi building. There you'll see several government buildings with stirring reliefs singing the praises of lobotomized workers and a totalitarian society.)

In Naples—long a poor and rough city—rather than being heroic, people learn from the cradle the art of survival. The modern memorial statue in the center of this square celebrates Salvo d'Acquisto, a rare hometown hero. In 1943, he was executed after falsely confessing to sabotage...saving 22 fellow Italian soldiers from a Nazi revenge massacre.

• *We're at the midpoint of this walk. Need a WC? Pop into the Burger King. Running out of time and energy? If you end the walk here, you'll find many cafés and wine bars nearby, and it's a short stroll down Via Toledo to the Toledo Metro station.*

To continue, from Piazza Carità veer northwest (past more fascist-style architecture) on Via Morgantini through Piazza Monteoliveto. Cross the busy street, then angle up Calata Trinità Maggiore to the fancy column in the piazza at the top of the hill.

Part 2: Piazza Gesù Nuovo to Centrale Station

• *You're back on the straight-as-a-Greek-arrow Spaccanapoli, former-ly the main thoroughfare of the Greek city of Neapolis. (Spaccanapoli changes names several times: Via Maddaloni, Via B. Croce, Via S. Bi-agio dei Librai, and Via Vicaria Vecchia.) Linger for a moment on...*

❿ Piazza Gesù Nuovo: This square is marked by a towering 18th-century Baroque monument to the Counter-Reformation.

Although the Jesuit order was powerful in Naples because of its Spanish heritage, locals never attacked Protestants here with the full fury of the Spanish In-quisition.

If you'd like, you can visit two bulky old churches, start-ing with the dark, fortress-like, 17th-century **Church of Gesù Nuovo,** followed by the simpler **Church of Santa Chiara** (in the courtyard across the street; both described under "Sights in Na-ples"). There's also a **TI** on this square.

• *Continue along the main drag for another 200 yards. Since this is a university district, you may see students and bookstores. As this neigh-borhood is also famously superstitious, look for incense-burning women with carts full of good-luck charms for sale.*

Passing Palazzo Venezia—the embassy of Venice to Naples when both were independent powers—you'll emerge into the next square...

⓫ Piazza San Domenico Maggiore: This square is marked by another ornate 17th-century monument built to thank God for ending the plague. From this square, you can detour left along the right side of the castle-like church, then follow yellow signs, tak-ing the first right and walking one short block to the remarkable Baroque **Cappella Sansevero** (described later, under "Sights in Naples").

• *After touring the chapel, return to Via B. Croce (a.k.a. Spaccanapoli), turn left, and continue your cultural scavenger hunt. At the intersection of Via Nilo, find the...*

⓬ Statue of the Nile (on the left): A reminder of the multi-ethnic makeup of Greek Neapolis, this statue is in what was the

Egyptian quarter. Locals like to call this statue *The Body of Naples*, with the overflowing cornucopia symbolizing the abundance of their fine city. (I once asked a Neapolitan man to describe the local women, who are famous for their beauty, in one word. He replied, simply, "Abundant.") This intersection is considered the center of old Naples.

• *Directly opposite the statue, inside of Bar Nilo, is the...*

"Chapel of Maradona": The small "chapel" on the right wall is dedicated to Diego Maradona, a soccer star who played for Na-

ples in the 1980s. Locals consider soccer almost a religion, and this guy was practically a deity. You can even see a "hair of Diego" and a teardrop from the city when he went to another team for more money. Unfortunately, his reputation has since been sullied by problems he's had with organized crime, drugs, and police. Perhaps inspired by Maradona's example, the coffee bar has posted a quadrilingual sign (though, strangely, not in English) threatening that those who take a picture without buying a cup of coffee may find their camera damaged...*Capisce?*

• *Continue on another 100 yards. You may pass gold and silver shops. Some say stolen jewelry ends up here, is melted down immediately, and gets resold in some other form as soon as it cools. Look for* compro oro *("I buy gold") signs—a sign of Naples' continuing tough economic times after the 2008 economic crisis. Continue to a tiny square at the intersection with Via San Gregorio Armeno.*

❸ **Via San Gregorio Armeno:** Stroll up this tiny lane toward the fanciful tower that arches over the street. The street is lined

with stalls selling lots of souvenir kitsch, as well as some of Naples' most distinctive local crafts. Among the many figurines on sale, find items relating to *presepi* (Nativity scenes). Just as many Americans keep an eye out year-round for Christmas-tree ornaments, Italians regularly add pieces to the family *prese-pe*, the centerpiece of their holiday decorations. You'll see elaborate manger scenes made of bark and moss, with niches to hold Baby Jesus or mother Mary. You'll also see lots of jokey figurines caricaturing local politicians, soccer stars, and other celebrities. (Some of the highest-quality *presepi* pieces are sold at the D'Auria shop, a little farther down Spaccanapoli, on the right at #87.

Another popular Naples souvenir sold here—and all over—is the *corno,* a skinny, twisted, red horn that resembles a chili pepper. The *corno* comes with a double symbolism for fertility: It's a horn of plenty, and it's also a phallic symbol turned upside-down. Neapolitans explain that fertility isn't sexual; it provides the greatest gift a person can give—life—and it ensures that one's soul will live on through the next generation.

• *Continue down Spaccanapoli another 100 yards until you hit busy Via Duomo. Consider detouring five minutes north (left) up Via Duomo to visit Naples'* **Duomo**; *just around the corner from that is the* **Pio Monte della Misericordia Church***, with a fine Caravaggio painting (both described later, under "Sights in Naples"). But for now, continue straight, crossing Via Duomo. Here, Spaccanapoli is named...*

❹ **Via Vicaria Vecchia:** Here along Via Vicaria Vecchia, the main "sight" is the vibrant street life. It's grittier, less touristy, but just as atmospheric as what we've been seeing. The street and side-street scenes intensify. The area is said to be a center of the Camorra (the Naples-based version of the Sicilian Mafia), but as a tourist, you won't notice. Paint a picture with these thoughts: Naples has the most intact street plan of any surviving ancient Greek or Roman city. Imagine this city during those times (and retain these images as you visit Pompeii), with streetside shop fronts that close up after dark, and private homes on upper floors. What you see today is just one more page in a 2,000-year-old story of a city: all kinds of meetings, beatings, and cheatings; kisses, near misses, and little-boy pisses.

You name it, it occurs right on the streets today, as it has since ancient times. People ooze from crusty corners. Black-and-white death announcements add to the clutter on the walls. Widows sell cigarettes from buckets. For a peek behind the scenes in the shade of wet laundry, venture down a few side streets. Buy two carrots as a gift for the woman on the fifth floor, if she'll lower her bucket to pick them up. The neighborhood action seems best at about 18:00.

At the tiny fenced-in triangle of greenery, hang out for a few minutes to just observe the crazy motorbike action and teen scene.
• *From here, veer right onto Via Forcella. You emerge into Piazza Vincenzo Calenda. Hungry? Turn right here, on Via Pietro Colletta, and close out the walk with three typical Neapolitan...*

❺ **Eateries:** Step into the North Pole at **Polo Nord Gelateria** (at #41). The oldest *gelateria* in Naples has had four generations of family working here since 1931. Before you order, sample a few flavors, including their *bacio*, or "kiss," flavor (named after the national chocolate-and-praline candy)—all are made fresh daily.

Two of Napoli's most competitive **pizzerias** are nearby. **Trianon da Ciro** (across the street from Polo Nord) has been serving them up hot and fast for almost a century. A half-block farther, on the right, is the place where some say pizza was born—at **Antica Pizzeria da Michele**. (For more on both, see "Eating in Naples," later.)

• *Our walk is over. It's easy to return to Centrale Station. Continue straight ahead, downhill, until you hit the grand boulevard, Corso Umberto I. Turn left here, and it's a straight 15-minute walk to Centrale Station. (Or cross the street and hop on a bus; they all go to the station.) You'll pass a gauntlet of purse/CD/sunglasses salesmen and shady characters hawking stolen mobile phones. You'll soon reach the vast* ⓰ *Piazza Garibaldi, with a modern canopy in the middle. On the far side is the station. You made it.*

Sights in Naples

Naples' best sights are the Archaeological Museum and my self-guided Naples Walk, both covered earlier. For extra credit, consider these sights.

CHURCHES ON OR NEAR SPACCANAPOLI
▲Church of Gesù Nuovo

This church's unique pyramid-grill facade survives from a fortified 15th-century noble palace. Step inside for a brilliant Neapolitan Baroque interior. The second chapel on the right features a much-adored **statue of St. Giuseppe Moscati** (1880-1927), a Christian doctor famous for helping the poor. In 1987, Moscati became the first modern doctor to be canonized. Sit and watch a steady stream of Neapolitans taking turns to kiss

and touch the altar, then hold the good doctor's highly polished hand.

Continue on to the third chapel (past his vertical tombstone) and enter the **Sale Moscati**. Look high on the walls of this long room to see hundreds of ex-votos—tiny red-and-silver plaques of thanksgiving for prayers answered with the help of St. Moscati (each has a symbol of the ailment cured). Naples' practice of using ex-votos, while incorporated into its Catholic rituals, goes back to its pagan Greek roots. Rooms from Moscati's nearby apartment are on display, and a glass case shows possessions and photos of the great doctor. As you leave the Sale Moscati, notice the big bomb casing that hangs high in the left corner. It fell through the church's dome in 1943, but caused almost no damage...yet another miracle.

Cost and Hours: Free, daily 6:45-13:00 & 16:00-19:30, Piazza del Gesù Nuovo, www.gesunuovo.it.

Church of Santa Chiara

Dating from the 14th century, this church is from a period of French royal rule under the Angevin dynasty. Consider the stark contrast between this church (Gothic) and the Gesù Nuovo (Baroque), across the street. Inside, look for the faded Trinity on the back wall (on the right as you face the door, under the stone canopy), which shows a dove representing the Holy Spirit between the heads of God the Father and Christ (c. 1414). This is an example of the fine frescoes that once covered the walls. Most were stuccoed over during Baroque times or destroyed in 1943 by Allied bombs. Continuing down the main aisle, you'll step over a huge inlaid-marble Angevin coat of arms on the floor. The altar is adorned with four finely carved Gothic tombs of Angevin kings. A chapel stacked with Bourbon royalty is just to the right.

Cost and Hours: Free, daily 7:30-13:00 & 16:30-20:00, Piazza del Gesù Nuovo, www.monasterodisantachiara.it. Its tranquil cloistered courtyard, around back, is not worth its €6 entry fee.

▲▲Cappella Sansevero

This small chapel is a Baroque explosion mourning the body of Christ, who lies on a soft pillow under an incredibly realistic veil.

It's also the personal chapel of Raimondo de Sangro, an eccentric Freemason, containing his tomb and the tombs of his family. Like other 18th-century Enlightenment figures, Raimondo was a wealthy man of letters, scientist and inventor, and patron of the arts—and he was also a grand master of the Freemasons of the Kingdom of Naples. His chapel—filled with Masonic symbolism—is a complex ensemble, with statues representing virtues such as self-control, religious zeal, and the Masonic philosophy of freedom through enlightenment. Though it's a pricey private enterprise, the chapel is worth a visit.

Cost and Hours: €7, buy tickets at office at the corner—or skip the long ticket-buying line by reserving ahead online (€2 fee); open Wed-Mon 9:30-18:30, closed Tue; Via de Sanctis 19, tel. 081-551-8470, www.museosansevero.it. The least crowded time to visit is after 16:00—the later the better. Pick up the free floor plan, which identifies each of the statues lining the nave.

▲Duomo

Naples' historic cathedral, built by imported French Anjou kings in the 14th century, boasts a breathtaking Neo-Gothic facade. Step into the vast interior to see the mix of styles along the side chapels— from pointy Gothic arches to rounded Renaissance ones to gilded Baroque decor. Explore the two largest side-chapels (flanking the nave, about halfway to the transept). Each is practically a church in its own right. On the right is the **Chapel of San Gennaro**—dedicated to the beloved patron saint of Naples—decorated with sil-

ver busts of centuries of bishops, and six paintings done on bronze (skip the €3 chapel audioguide). On the left, the **Chapel of Santa Restituta** stands on the site of the original, early-Christian church that predated the cathedral. The stairs beneath the altar take you to a **crypt** with the relics of St. Gennaro and a statue of the bishop who rescued the relics from a rival town and returned them to Naples.

Cost and Hours: Free, Mon-Sat 8:30-13:30 & 14:30-20:00, Sun 8:30-13:30 & 16:30-19:30, Via Duomo.

Pio Monte della Misericordia

This small church (near the Duomo, and run by a charitable foundation) displays one of the best works by Caravaggio, *The Seven Works of Mercy,* which hangs over the main altar in a darkened gray chapel. The painting is well lit, allowing Caravaggio's characteristically dark canvas to really pop. In one crowded canvas, the great early-Baroque artist illustrates seven virtues: burying the dead (the man carrying a corpse by the ankles); visiting the imprisoned and feeding the hungry (Pero breastfeeding her starving father—a scene from a famous Roman story); sheltering the homeless (a pilgrim on the Camino de Santiago, with his floppy hat, negotiates with an innkeeper); caring for the sick and clothing the naked (St. Martin offers part of his cloak to the injured man in the foreground); and giving drink to the thirsty (Samson chugs from a jawbone in the background)—all of them set in a dark Neapolitan alley and watched over by Mary, Jesus, and a pair of angels.

Cost and Hours: €7 (ticket booth across the street), includes audioguide, Thu-Tue 9:00-14:30, closed Wed, Via dei Tribunali 253, tel. 081-446-944, www.piomontedellamisericordia.it.

NEAR THE PORT
This cluster of important sights can be found between the big ceremonial square, Piazza del Plebiscito, and the cruise ship terminal. I've linked them with walking directions.

▲Piazza del Plebiscito
This square celebrates the 1861 vote (*plebiscito*, plebiscite) in which Naples chose to join Italy. Dominating the top of the square is the

Church of San Francesco di Paola, with its Pantheon-inspired dome and broad, arcing colonnades. If it's open, step inside to ogle the vast interior—a Neoclassical re-creation of one of ancient Rome's finest buildings.
• *Opposite is the...*

Royal Palace (Palazzo Reale)
Having housed Spanish, French, and even Italian royalty, this building displays statues of all those who stayed here. From the square in front of the palace, look for eight kings in the niches, each

from a different dynasty (left to right): Norman, German, French, Spanish, Spanish, Spanish, French (Napoleon's brother-in-law), and, finally, Italian— Victor Emmanuel II, King of Savoy. The statues were done at the request of V. E. II's son, so his dad is the most dashing of the group. As far as palaces go, the interior is relatively unimpressive.

Cost and Hours: €6, skip the painfully dry €3 audioguide (each room has excellent panel descriptions in English; Thu-Tue 9:00-20:00, closed Wed, last entry one hour before closing; tel. 848-082-408, www.coopculture.it).
• *Continue 50 yards past the Royal Palace (toward the trees) to enjoy a...*

Fine Harbor View

While boats busily serve Capri and Sorrento, Mount Vesuvius smolders ominously in the distance. Look back to see the vast "Bourbon red" palace—its color inspired by Pompeii. The hilltop above Piazza del Plebiscito is San Martino, with its Carthusian monastery-turned-museum and Castle of St. Elmo (the Centrale funicular to the top is just across the square and up Via Toledo). The promenade you're on continues to Naples' romantic harborfront—the fishermen's quarter (Borgo Marinaro)—a fortified island connected to the mainland by a stout causeway, with its fanciful, ancient Castel dell'Ovo (Egg Castle) and trendy harborside restaurants.

• *Head back through the piazza and pop into...*

Gran Caffè Gambrinus

This coffeehouse, facing the piazza, takes you back to the elegance of 1860. It's a classic place to sample a crispy *sfogliatella* pastry, or perhaps the mushroom-shaped, rum-soaked bread-like cakes called *babà*, which come in a huge variety. Stand at the bar *(banco)*, pay double to sit *(tavola)*, or just wander around as you imagine the café buzzing with the ritzy intellectuals, journalists, and artsy bohemian types who munched on *babà* here during Naples' 19th-century heyday (daily 7:00-24:00, Piazza del Plebiscito 1, tel. 081-417-582).

• *A block away, tucked behind the palace, you can peek inside the Neo-classical...*

Teatro di San Carlo

Built in 1737, 41 years before Milan's La Scala, this is Europe's oldest opera house and Italy's second-most-respected (after La Scala). The original theater burned down in 1816, and was rebuilt within the year. Guided 35-minute visits in English basically just show you the fine auditorium with its 184 boxes—each with a big mirror to reflect the candlelight (€6; tours Mon-Sat at 10:30, 11:30, 12:30, 14:30, 15:30, and 16:30; Sun at 10:30, 11:30, and 12:30; tel. 081-797-2331, www.teatrosancarlo.it).

• *Beyond Teatro di San Carlo and the Royal Palace is the huge, harborfront...*

Castel Nuovo

This imposing castle now houses government bureaucrats and the **Civic Museum.** It feels like a mostly empty shell, with a couple of dusty halls of Neapolitan art, but the views over the bay from the upper terraces are impressive (€6, Mon-Sat 8:30-19:00, closed Sun, last entry one hour before closing, tel. 081-795-7722, www.comune.napoli.it).

• *Head back to Teatro di San Carlo, cross the street, and go through the tall yellow arch into...*

▲Galleria Umberto I

This Victorian iron-and-glass shopping mall opened in 1890 to reinvigorate the district after a devastating cholera epidemic occurred here. Gawk up, then walk left to bring you back out on Via Toledo.

• Just up the street and behind Piazza del Plebiscito is an interesting subterranean experience.

▲Galleria Borbonica

Beneath Naples' Royal Palace was a vast underground network of caves, aqueducts, and cisterns that originated as a quarry in the 15th century. In the mid-1800s, when popular revolutions were threatening royalty across Europe, the understandably nervous king of Naples, Ferdinand II, had this underground world expanded to create an escape tunnel from the palace to his military barracks nearby. In World War II, it was used as an air-raid shelter; after the war, the police used it to store impounded cars and motorcycles. Today, enthusiastic guides take the curious on a fascinating 70-minute, 500-yard-long guided walk through this many-layered world littered with disintegrating 60-year-old vehicles upon which Naples sits.

Cost and Hours: €10 English-language tours leave Fri-Sun at 10:00, 12:00, 15:00, and 17:00; tel. 081-764-5808, www.galleriaborbonica.com. The most convenient entry is just behind Piazza del Plebiscito—up Via Gennaro Serra and down Vico del Grottone to #4 (to avoid that entrance's 90 steep steps, enter at Via Morelli 61).

Porta Nolana Open-Air Fish Market

Naples' fish market squirts and stinks as it has for centuries under the darkened Porta Nolana (gate in the city wall), four long blocks down from Centrale Station. Of the town's many boisterous outdoor markets, this will net you the most photos and memories. From Piazza Nolana, wander under the medieval gate and take your first left down Via Sopramuro, enjoying this wild and entirely edible cultural scavenger hunt (Tue-Sun 8:00-14:00, closed Mon). Stalls display the best catch of the day as water jets caress mounds of mussels and clams.

Eating in Naples

FANTASTIC, FAMOUS PIZZA

Naples is the birthplace of pizza. Its pizzerias bake just the right combination of fresh dough (soft and chewy, as opposed to Roman-style, which is thin and crispy), mozzarella, and tomatoes in traditional wood-burning ovens. You can head for the famous, venerable places, but these can have long lines stretching out the door, and half-hour waits for a table. An average one-person pie (usually the only size available) costs €6-9; most places

offer both takeout and eat-in, and pizza is often the only thing on the menu.

Near the Station

These two pizzerias—the most famous—are both a few long blocks from the train station, and near the end of my self-guided Naples Walk.

$ Antica Pizzeria da Michele is for pizza purists. Filled with locals (and tourists), it serves just two varieties: *margherita* (tomato sauce and mozzarella) and *marinara* (tomato sauce, oregano, and garlic, no cheese). Come early to sit and watch the pizza artists in action. A pizza with beer costs around €8. If there's a mob, head inside to get a number. If it's just too crowded to wait, the less-exceptional Pizzeria Trianon (described next) often has room (Mon-Sat 10:30-24:00, closed Sun; look for the vertical red *Antica Pizzeria* sign at the intersection of Via Pietro Colletta and Via Cesare Sersale at #1; tel. 081-553-9204).

$ Pizzeria Trianon da Ciro, across the street and left a few doors, has been da Michele's archrival since 1923. It offers more choices, higher prices, air-conditioning, and a cozier atmosphere. For less chaos, head upstairs. While waiting for your meal, you can survey the transformation of a humble wad of dough into a smoldering, bubbly feast in their entryway pizza kitchen (daily 11:00-15:30 & 19:00-23:00, Via Pietro Colletta 42, tel. 081-553-9426).

On and near Via dei Tribunali

This street, which runs a couple of blocks north of Spaccanapoli, is legendary for its pizzerias and fun eateries. It's packed with hungry strollers and long lines marking the most popular places.

$ Gino Sorbillo is a local favorite and is on all the "best pizza in Naples" lists...as you'll learn the hard way if you show up at peak mealtimes, when huge mobs crowd outside the front door waiting for a table (Mon-Sat 12:00-15:30 & 19:00-24:00, closed Sun, Via dei Tribunali 32, tel. 081-446-643). Relatives run similarly named places on the same street at #35 (a good option for its specialty: fried pizza) and #37.

$ Pizzeria di Matteo is popular for its fried takeout treats. People waiting out front line up at the little window to snack on deep-fried goodies—*arancini* (with rice, gooey cheese, peas, and sausage), *melanzane* (eggplant), *frittatine* (balls of mac and cheese plus sausage), and *crocché* (croquettes)—for €1 apiece or less (sometimes closed Sun, Via dei Tribunali 94, tel. 081-455-262).

$ La Figlia del Presidente sits a block and a half south of the two legendary joints listed above and is quickly establishing its own loyal clientele. Push your way through the locals gathered around the door to get a number, then patiently wait for a slice of heaven. With abundant and innovative toppings, this small pizzeria updates the Neapolitan classics (Tue-Sat 12:00-15:30 & 19:00-23:30, Mon 12:00-15:30, closed Sun, Via Grande Archivio 24, tel. 081-286-738).

Near the Archaeological Museum

If you've had enough of crowds at the museum, head a few blocks north for world-class pizza without the throngs of people.

$ Pizzeria Starita has been in business for over 100 years, first as a cantina (featured in a Sophia Loren flick) then offering pizza since the 1950s. The fourth generation currently runs this bustling, friendly eatery just off the normal tourist circuit (Tue-Sun 12:00-15:30 & 19:00 until late, closed Mon, no reservations—just show up and add your name to the wait list, from the museum walk 10 minutes up Via Santa Teresa degli Scalzi to the intersection with Via Materdei—the pizzeria is a few steps down on the left at #27, Metro: Museo, tel. 081-557-3682).

RESTAURANTS
Near the Archaeological Museum

$$ La Stanza del Gusto, two blocks downhill from the museum, tackles food creatively and injects crusty Naples with a little modern color and irreverence. The ground floor is casual, trendy, and playful, while the upstairs is more refined yet still polka-dotted. A few tables are on the sidewalk (weekday lunch specials, daily 12:00-23:30 except Sun until 17:30, Via Santa Maria di Constantinopoli 100, tel. 081-401-578).

$$ Osteria da Carmela serves up traditional Neapolitan classics only mama could make—like *ragù, polpetti,* and tasty fried fish—with a dash of Old World charm. Affordable house wine and fine cheeses complete the meal. Tables are limited, so reservations are smart (Mon-Sat 12:00-15:00 & 19:00-24:00, closed Sun, Via Conte di Ruvo 11, tel. 081-549-9738, www.osteriadacarmela.it).

$ L'Etto is fast, fun, and cheap, with tasty dishes constantly coming out of the kitchen to fill an inviting buffet line. Choose from 20 vegetable, meat, and fish options (perfect for vegetarians or vegans). It's self-serve—weigh and pay €2.50 per 100 grams (100 grams is an *etto,* hence the name). Bread and water are free at the table (daily 12:30-15:30 & 19:30-22:30, longer hours on weekends, facing Piazza Bellini at Via S. Maria di Costantinopoli 102, tel. 081-1932-0967).

$ Rosticceria Angela is a *tavola calda* with hot ready-to-eat dishes and a coffee bar, run by a team of older gentlemen. Pricing is honest and there's simple, peaceful, air-conditioned indoor seating. Next door is **Gastronomia,** a tiny meat, cheese, and bread shop with all you need for a cheap meal to go (*rosticceria* open Mon-Sat 7:30-21:00, closed Sun, 3 blocks below museum at Via Conte di Ruvo 21, between Via Pessina and Via Bellini, tel. 081-033-2928).

Near the Station

$$ Da Donato, an excellent, traditional, family-run trattoria on a glum street near the station, serves delicious food in an unpretentious atmosphere. The best approach is for two people to share the astonishing *antipasti* sampler—*degustazione "fantasia" della Casa Terra e Mare*—for €25. You'll get more than a dozen small portions, each more delicious than the last. A version without seafood is €15 (Tue-Sun 12:30-14:30 & 19:30-22:00, closed Mon, two blocks from Piazza Garibaldi—turn down Via Silvio Spaventa to #39, tel. 081-287-828).

Pompeii

Stopped in its tracks by the eruption of Mount Vesuvius in AD 79, Pompeii offers the best look anywhere at what life in Rome must have been like around 2,000 years ago.

A once-thriving commercial port of 20,000, Pompeii (worth ▲▲▲) grew from Greek and Etruscan roots to become an important Roman city. Then, on August 24, AD 79, everything changed. Vesuvius erupted and began to bury the city under 30 feet of hot volcanic ash. For the archaeologists who excavated it centuries later, this was a shake-

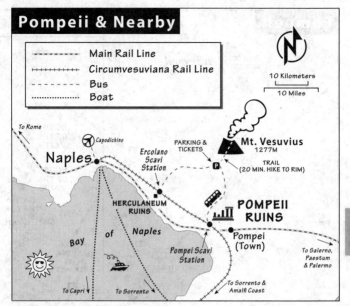

and-bake windfall, teaching them volumes about daily Roman life. Pompeii was accidentally rediscovered in 1599; excavations began in 1748.

GETTING THERE

By Train or Train-and-Bus Combo from Rome: It's possible to day-trip to Pompeii from Rome, if you start early and plan on a long day. You'll take an express train to Naples and transfer to a private shuttle bus or a commuter train at Naples' Centrale Station. For tips, see the "Planning Your Time" and "Continuing to Pompeii" sections at the beginning of this chapter. From the Pompei Scavi train station, it's just a two-minute walk to the Porta Marina entrance: Leaving the station, turn right and walk down the road about a block to the entrance (on your left).

Pompei vs. Pompei Scavi: Make sure you're taking the Circumvesuviana commuter train or Campania Express to Pompei Scavi (*scavi* means "excavations"), the station right next to the ancient site. Pompei is the name of a separate train station on the main national rail line that's a long, dull walk from the ruins. It serves the ugly modern city of Pompei (always with one "i").

When coming from Rome, it's better to transfer to the Circumvesuviana or the Campania Express at Naples' Centrale Station than to take the national rail straight to the Pompei city station and walk from there.

By Car: Parking is available at Camping Zeus, next to the

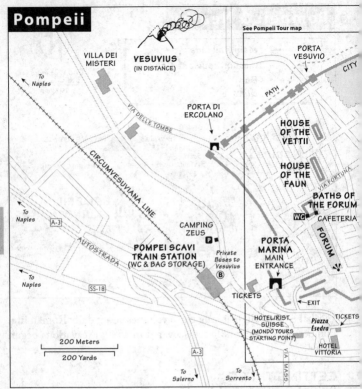

Pompei Scavi train station (€2.50/hour, €10/12 hours); several other campgrounds/parking lots are nearby.

ORIENTATION

Cost: €16, includes special exhibits.

Hours: Mon-Fri 9:00-19:30, Sat-Sun 8:30-19:30, Nov-March daily until 17:00, last entry 1.5 hours before closing.

Free Entry: Some state museums in Italy, including Pompeii, are free to enter once or twice a month, usually on a Sunday. Check in advance and avoid these free days—they're packed.

Information: Tel. 081-857-5347, general info at www.pompeiisites.org, tickets at www.ticketone.it.

Crowd-Beating Tips: To skip ahead of everyone, purchase your ticket online at www.ticketone.it (€2 surcharge). If you're buying onsite and there's a very long ticket line at the Porta Marina entrance, continue walking three minutes to the ticket booth near Hotel Vittoria (rarely a line). Buy your ticket, return to Porta Marina, and walk right in.

Closures: Some buildings and streets are bound to be closed for restoration when you visit. Make a point to use your map and

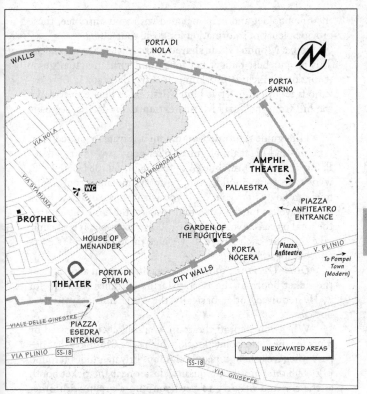

numbers to find your way. Street names and building numbers
are very clearly marked throughout the site.

Visitor Information: Admission includes a wonderful English
guide-booklet and map (be sure to get and use this). Ask for it
when you buy your ticket, or check at the info window to the
left of the WCs—the maps aren't available within the walls
of Pompeii. The bookshop sells a couple of books with plastic
overlays that allow you to re-create Pompeii from the ruins
(€16; if you buy from a street vendor, pay no more than that).
Another good book is the €6 *Pompeii (Brief) Guide,* with excellent photos and additional walking routes.

Ignore the "info point" kiosk at the train station, which is
a private agency selling tours.

Tours: Here are several ways to enjoy an organized and educational
visit to Pompeii.

Simply follow the **self-guided** tour in this chapter (or,
better, enjoy the audio version with my free ∩ Rick Steves
Audio Europe app). Both cover the basics and provide a good
framework for exploring the site on your own. Combined with

the fine booklet and map included with your entry fee, these provide plenty of information for do-it-yourselfers.

Join a **Mondo Guide shared tour** for Rick Steves readers. This is your best budget bet for a tour with an actual guide (€15, doesn't include €15 Pompeii entry, daily at 11:00, reservations required; meet at Hotel/Ristorante Suisse, just down the hill from the Porta Marina entrance; for details, see page 484).

Hire guide **Antonio Somma** for a private or shared tour. Antonio and his team of guides offer good two-hour tours of Pompeii for €120 (mobile 393-406-3824, tel. 081-850-1992, www.tourspompeiiguide.com, info@pompeitour.com). The tour can be just for you, or, if you wish, they can try to book other travelers for the same tour to share the cost. Either way, the total price is no more than €120. For example, if six people take the tour, each pays €20. (A nice tip for the guide's extra effort is appreciated.)

Other Options: Audioguides available from a kiosk near the ticket booth at the Porta Marina entrance (€8, €13 for 2, ID required) offer basically the same info as your free booklet.

When you step off the train, you'll likely be accosted by touts for the "info point" kiosk, which sells €15 tours that depart whenever enough people sign up. Private guides (around €120/2 hours) of varying quality cluster near the ticket booth at the site and may try to herd you into a group with other travelers, which is fine if it makes the price more reasonable. It's unethical for a guide to double charge by combining two groups into one tour. Instead, tourists should enjoy the savings and tip higher.

Rated Risqué: Parents, note that the ancient brothel and its sexually explicit frescoes are included on tours; let your guide know if you'd rather skip that stop.

Length of This Tour: Allow two hours, or three if you visit the theater and amphitheater. With less time, focus on the Forum, Baths of the Forum, House of the Vettii, House of the Faun, and brothel.

Baggage Check: Use the free baggage check near the turnstiles at the site entrance (just yards from the station). The train station also offers pay luggage storage (downstairs, by the WC).

Services: There's a pay WC at the train station. The Pompeii site has three WCs—one near the entrance, one in the cafeteria, and another near the end of this tour, uphill from the theaters.

Eating: These **$** eateries offer reasonably priced meals (though your cheapest bet may be to bring your own food for a discreet picnic). The **Ciao cafeteria,** within the site, serves good sandwiches, pizza, and pasta. You're welcome to picnic here if you buy a drink. **Bar Sgambati,** the café/restaurant at the train station, has air-conditioning, Wi-Fi, sandwiches to go, and pastas and pizzas. **Marius Juice Shop** (run by local guide Antonio Somma's family) sells sandwiches to go, and is located between Bar Sgambati and the Porta Marina entrance. A second cluster of eateries around the ticket booth near Hotel Vittoria dishes out handy slices of pizza, salads, and pasta.

Starring: Roofless (collapsed) but otherwise intact Roman buildings, plaster casts of hapless victims, some erotic frescoes, and the dawning realization that these ancient people were not that different from us.

BACKGROUND

Pompeii, founded in 600 BC, eventually became a booming Roman trading city. Not rich, not poor, it was middle class—a perfect example of typical Roman life. Most streets would have been lined with stalls and jammed with customers from sunup to sundown. Chariots vied with shoppers for street space. Two thousand years

ago, Rome controlled the entire Mediterranean—making it a kind of free-trade zone—and Pompeii was a central and bustling port.

There were no posh neighborhoods in Pompeii. Rich and poor mixed it up as elegant houses existed side by side with simple homes. While nearby

Herculaneum would have been a classier place to live (traffic-free streets, fancier houses, far better drainage), Pompeii was the place for action and shopping. It served an estimated 20,000 residents with more than 40 bakeries, 130 bars, restaurants, and hotels, and 30 brothels. With most of its buildings covered by brilliant white ground-marble stucco, Pompeii in AD 79 was an impressive town.

As you tour Pompeii, remember that its best art is safeguarded in the Archaeological Museum in Naples (described earlier in this chapter). Visiting the museum before or after going to Pompeii will help put this fascinating sight into context.

POMPEII

❷ SELF-GUIDED TOUR

• *Just past the ticket-taker, start your approach up to the...*

❶ Porta Marina

The city of Pompeii was born on the hill ahead of you. This was the original town gate. Before Vesuvius blew and filled in the harbor, the sea came nearly to here. Notice the two openings in the gate (ahead, up the ramp). Both were left open by day to admit major traffic. At night, the larger one was closed for better security.

• *Pass through the Porta Marina and continue up to the top of the street, pausing at the three large stepping-stones in the middle.*

❷ Pompeii's Streets

Every day, Pompeiians flooded the streets with gushing water to clean them. These stepping-stones let pedestrians cross without getting their sandals wet. Chariots traveling in either direction could straddle the stones (all had standard-size axles). A single stepping-stone in a road means it was a one-way street, a pair indicates an ordinary two-way, and three (like this) signifies a major thoroughfare. The basalt stones are the original Roman

pavement. The sidewalks (elevated to hide the plumbing—you'll see ancient plumbing revealed throughout the site) were paved with bits of broken pots (an ancient form of recycling) and studded with reflective bits of white marble. These "cats' eyes" helped people get around after dark, either by moonlight or with the help of lamps.

• *Continue straight ahead, don your mental toga, and enter the city as the Romans once did. The road opens up into the spacious main square: the Forum. Stand at the right end of this rectangular space and look toward Mount Vesuvius.*

❸ The Forum (Foro)

Pompeii's commercial, religious, and political center stands at the intersection of the city's two main streets. While it's the most ruined part of Pompeii, it's grand nonetheless. Picture the piazza surrounded by two-story buildings on all sides. The pedestals that

Pompeii Tour

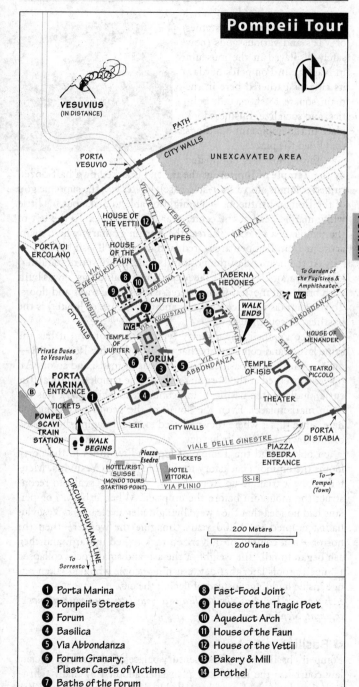

VESUVIUS (IN DISTANCE)

PATH

CITY WALLS

UNEXCAVATED AREA

PORTA VESUVIO

VIC. VETTII

VIA VESUVIO

VIA NOLA

HOUSE OF THE VETTII ⑫

PIPES

PORTA DI ERCOLANO

HOUSE OF THE FAUN ⑪

VIA MERCURIO

⑧

VIA FORTUNA

To Garden of the Fugitives & Amphitheater

⑨ ⑩

TABERNA HEDONES

WC

CAFETERIA

⑬

VIA CONSOLARE

VIA AUGUSTAL

⑦

⑭

WALK ENDS

CITY WALLS

WC

VIA ABBONDANZA

HOUSE OF MENANDER

TEMPLE OF JUPITER

⑥

FORUM

VIA TEATRI

VIA STABIANA

Private Buses to Vesuvius

②

③

⑤

VIA ABBONDANZA

TEMPLE OF ISIS

TEATRO PICCOLO

B

PORTA MARINA ENTRANCE

①

④

THEATER

PORTA DI STABIA

TICKETS

EXIT

CITY WALLS

POMPEII SCAVI TRAIN STATION

👣 **WALK BEGINS**

VIALE DELLE GINESTRE

PIAZZA ESEDRA ENTRANCE

Piazza Esedra

TICKETS

To→ Pompei (Town)

CIRCUMVESUVIANA LINE

HOTEL/RIST. SUISSE (MONDO TOURS STARTING POINT)

HOTEL VITTORIA

SS-18

VIA PLINIO

To Sorrento ↓

200 Meters

200 Yards

POMPEII

① Porta Marina
② Pompeii's Streets
③ Forum
④ Basilica
⑤ Via Abbondanza
⑥ Forum Granary; Plaster Casts of Victims
⑦ Baths of the Forum

⑧ Fast-Food Joint
⑨ House of the Tragic Poet
⑩ Aqueduct Arch
⑪ House of the Faun
⑫ House of the Vettii
⑬ Bakery & Mill
⑭ Brothel

line the square once held statues of VIPs and various gods (now safely displayed in the museum in Naples). In Pompeii's heyday, its citizens gathered here in the main square to shop, talk politics, and socialize. Business took place in the important buildings that lined the piazza.

The Forum was dominated by the **Temple of Jupiter,** at the far end (marked by a half-dozen ruined columns atop a stair-step base). Jupiter was the supreme god of the Roman pantheon—you might be able to make out his little white marble head at the center-rear of the temple. To the left of the temple is a fenced-off area, the **Forum granary,** where many artifacts from Pompeii are stored (and which we'll visit later).

At the near end of the Forum (behind where you're standing) is the **curia,** or City Hall. Like many Roman buildings, it was built with brick and mortar, then covered with marble walls and floors. To your left (as you face Vesuvius and the Temple of Jupiter) is the **basilica,** or courthouse.

Since Pompeii was a pretty typical Roman town, it has the same layout and components that you'll find in any Roman city—main square, curia, basilica, temples, axis of roads, and so on. All power converged at the Forum: religious (the temple), political (the curia), judicial (the basilica), and commercial (this piazza was the main marketplace). Even the power of the people was expressed here, since this is where they gathered to vote. Imagine the hubbub of this town square in its heyday.

Look beyond the Temple of Jupiter. Five miles to the north looms the ominous backstory to this site: **Mount Vesuvius.** Mentally draw a triangle up from the two remaining peaks to reconstruct the mountain before the eruption. When it blew, Pompeiians had no idea that they were living under a volcano, as Vesuvius hadn't erupted for 1,200 years. Imagine the wonder—then the horror—as a column of pulverized rock roared upward, and then ash began to fall. The weight of the ash and small rocks collapsed Pompeii's roofs later that day, crushing people who had taken refuge inside buildings instead of fleeing the city.

• *As you face Vesuvius, the basilica is to your left, lined with stumps of columns. Step inside.*

❹ Basilica

Pompeii's basilica was a first-century palace of justice. This ancient law court has the same floor plan later adopted by many Christian churches (which are also called basilicas). The big central hall (or nave) is flanked by rows of columns marking off narrower side aisles. Along the side walls are traces of the original stucco imitating marble.

The columns—now stumps all about the same height—were not ruined by the volcano. Rather, they were left unfinished when

Vesuvius blew. Pompeii had been devastated by an earthquake in AD 62, and was just in the process of rebuilding the basilica when Vesuvius erupted, 17 years later. The half-built columns show off the technology of the day. Uniform bricks were stacked around a cylindrical core. Once finished, they would have been coated with marble dust stucco to simulate marble columns—an economical construction method found throughout Pompeii (and the Roman Empire).

Besides the earthquake and the eruption, Pompeii's buildings have suffered other ravages over the years, including Spanish plunderers (c. 1800), 19th-century souvenir hunters, WWII bombs, creeping and destructive vegetation, another earthquake in 1980, and modern neglect. The fact that the entire city was covered by the eruption of AD 79 actually helped preserve it, saving it from the sixth-century barbarians who plundered many other towns into oblivion.

• *Exit the basilica and cross the short side of the square to where the city's main street hits the Forum. Stop at the three white stones that stick up from the cobbles.*

❺ Via Abbondanza

Glance down Via Abbondanza, Pompeii's main street. Lined with shops, bars, and restaurants, it was a lively, pedestrian-only zone.

The three "beaver-teeth" stones are traffic barriers that kept chariots out. On the corner at the start of the street (just to the left), take a close look at the dark travertine column standing next to the white one. Notice that the marble drums of the white column are not chiseled entirely round—another construction project left unfinished when Vesuvius erupted.

• *Our tour will eventually end a few blocks down Via Abbondanza after making a big loop. But now, head toward Vesuvius, cutting across the Forum. To the left of the Temple of Jupiter is the...*

❻ Forum Granary

A substantial stretch of the west side of the Forum was the granary and ancient produce market. Today, it houses thousands of artifacts excavated from Pompeii. You'll see lots of crockery, pots, pans, jugs, and containers used for transporting oil and wine. You'll also see casts of a couple of victims (and a dog) of the eruption. These casts show Pompeiians, eerily captured in their last moments, hands covering their mouths as they gasped

for air. They were quickly suffocated by a superheated avalanche of gas and ash, and their bodies were encased in volcanic debris. While excavating, modern archaeologists detected hollow spaces underfoot, created when the victims' bodies decomposed. By gently filling the holes with plaster, the archaeologists created molds of the Pompeiians who were caught in the disaster.

A few steps to the left of the granary is a tiny alcove that contained the Mensa Ponderaria, a counter where standard units (such as today's liter or gallon) were used to measure the quantities of liquid and solid food that were sold. And just to the right of the granary is the remains of a public toilet. You can imagine the many seats, lack of privacy, and constantly flushing stream running through the room.

• *Exit the Forum by crossing it again in front of the Temple of Jupiter and turning left. Go under the arch. In the road are more "beaver-teeth" traffic blocks. On the pillar to the right, look for the pedestrian-only road sign (two guys carrying an amphora, or ancient jug; it's above the REG VII INS IV sign). The modern cafeteria (on the left) is the only eatery inside the archaeological site. Twenty yards past the cafeteria, on the left-hand side at #24, is the entrance to the...*

❼ Baths of the Forum (Terme del Foro)

Pompeii had six public baths, each with a men's and a women's section. You're in the men's zone. The leafy courtyard at the entrance was the gymnasium. After working out, clients could relax with a hot bath *(caldarium)*, warm bath *(tepidarium)*, or cold plunge *(frigidarium)*.

The first big, plain room you enter served as the **dressing room.** Holes on the walls were for pegs to hang clothing. High up, the window (with a faded Neptune underneath) was originally

The Eruption of Vesuvius

At about 1:00 in the afternoon on August 24, AD 79, Mount Vesuvius erupted, sending a mushroom cloud of ash, dust, and rocks 12 miles into the air. It spewed for 18 hours straight, as winds blew the cloud southward. The white-gray ash settled like a heavy snow on Pompeii, its weight eventually collapsing roofs and floors, but leaving the walls intact. And though most of Pompeii's 20,000 residents fled that day, about 2,000 stayed behind. Then, at around 7:30 the next morning, a pyroclastic flow headed south and struck Pompeii, dealing a fatal blow to those who'd remained.

covered with a less-translucent Roman glass. Walk over the nonslip mosaics into the next room.

The *tepidarium* is ringed by mini statues or *telamones* (male caryatids, figures used as supporting pillars), which divided the lockers. Clients would undress and warm up here, perhaps relaxing on one of the bronze cow-footed benches near the bronze heater while waiting for a massage. Look at the ceiling—half crushed by the eruption and half intact, with its fine blue-and-white stucco work.

Next, admire the engineering in the steam-bath room, or **caldarium**. The double floor was heated from below—so it was nice

for bare feet (look into the grate across from where you entered to see the brick support towers). The double walls with brown terra-cotta tiles held the heat. Romans soaked in the big tub, which was filled with hot water. Opposite the big tub is a fountain, which spouted water onto the hot floor, creating steam. The lettering on the fountain reminded those enjoying the room which two politicians paid for it...and how much it cost them. (On the far right, the Roman numerals indicate they paid 5,250 *sestertii*). To keep condensation from dripping annoyingly from the ceiling, fluting (ribbing) was added to carry water down the walls.

• *Today's visitors exit the baths through the original entry (at the far end of the dressing room). Hungry? Immediately across the street is an ancient...*

❽ Fast-Food Joint

After a bath, it was only natural to want a little snack. So, just across the street is a fast-food joint, marked by a series of rectangular marble counters. Most ancient Romans didn't cook for themselves in their tiny apartments, so to-go places like this were commonplace. The holes in the counters held the pots for food. Each container was like a thermos, with a wooden lid to keep the soup hot, the wine cool, and so on. You could dine in the back or get your food to go. Notice the groove in the front doorstep and the holes out on the curb. The holes likely accommodated cords for stretching awnings over the sidewalk to shield the clientele from the hot sun, while the grooves were for the shop's folding accordion doors. Look at the wheel grooves in the pavement, worn

down through centuries of use. Nearby are more stepping-stones for pedestrians to cross the flooded streets.

• *Just a few steps uphill from the fast-food joint, at #5 (with a locked gate), is the...*

❾ House of the Tragic Poet (Casa del Poeta Tragico)

This house is typical Roman style. The entry is flanked by two family-owned shops (each with a track for a collapsing accordion door). The home is like a train running straight away from the street: atrium (with skylight and pool to catch the rain), den (where deals were made by the shopkeeper), and garden (with rooms facing it and a shrine to remember both the gods and family ancestors). In the entryway is the famous "Beware of Dog" *(Cave Canem)* mosaic.

When it's open, today's visitors enter the home by the back door (circle around to the left). On your way there, look for the modern exposed pipe on the left side of the lane; this is the same as ones used in the ancient plumbing system, hidden beneath the raised sidewalk. The richly frescoed dining room is off the garden. Diners lounged on their couches (the Roman custom) and enjoyed frescoes with fake "windows," giving the illusion of a bigger and airier room. Next to the dining room is a humble BBQ-style kitchen with a little closet for the toilet (the kitchen and bathroom shared the same plumbing).

• *Return to the fast-food place and continue about 10 yards downhill to the big intersection. From the center of the intersection, look left to see a giant arch, framing a nice view of Mount Vesuvius.*

❿ Aqueduct Arch—Running Water

Water was critical for this city of 20,000 people, and this arch was part of Pompeii's water-delivery system. A 100-mile-long aqueduct

carried fresh water down from the hillsides to a big reservoir perched at the highest point of the city wall. Since overall water pressure was disappointing, Pompeiians built arches like the brick one you see here (originally covered in marble) with hidden water tanks at the top. Located just below the altitude of the main tank, these smaller tanks were filled by gravity and provided each neighborhood with reliable pressure. Look closely at the arch and you'll see 2,000-year-old pipes (made of lead imported all the way from Cornwall in Britannia) embedded deep in the brick.

If there was a water shortage, democratic priorities prevailed: First the baths were cut off, then the private homes. The last to go were the public fountains, where all citizens could get drinking and cooking water.

• *If you're thirsty, fill your water bottle from the modern fountain. Then continue straight downhill one block (50 yards) to #2 on the left.*

⓫ House of the Faun (Casa del Fauno)

Stand across the street and marvel at the grand entry with *"HAVE"* (hail to you) as a welcome mat. Go in. Notice the two shrines above

the entryway—one dedicated to the gods, the other to this wealthy family's ancestors. (Contemporary Neapolitans still carry on this practice; you'll notice little shrines embedded in walls all over Naples.)

You are standing in Pompeii's largest home, where you're greeted by the delightful small bronze statue of the *Dancing Faun*, famed for its realistic movement and fine proportion. (The original, described on page 489, is in Naples' Archaeological Museum.) With 40 rooms and 27,000 square feet, the House of the Faun covers an entire city block. The next floor mosaic, with an intricate diamond-like design, decorates the homeowner's office. Note the pieces of multicolored stone that remain embedded in the floor, and think of how vibrant and luxurious this house would have seemed before the eruption. Beyond that, at the far end of the first garden, is the famous floor mosaic of the *Battle of Alexander*. (The original is also at the museum in Naples.) In 333 BC, Alexander the Great beat Darius and the Persians. Romans had great respect for Alexander, the first great emperor before Rome's. While most of Pompeii's nouveau riche had notoriously bad taste and stuffed their palaces with over-the-top, mismatched decor, this guy had class. Both the faun (an ancient copy of a famous Greek statue) and the Alexander mosaic show an appreciation for history.

The house's back courtyard is lined with pillars rebuilt after the AD 62 earthquake. Take a close look at the brick, mortar, and fake-marble stucco veneer.

• *Leave the House of the Faun through its back door in the far-right corner, past a tiny guard's station. (If closed, exit out the front and walk around to the back.) Turn right and walk about a block until you see metal cages over the sidewalk protecting exposed stretches of ancient lead water pipes. Continue east and take your first left, walking about 20 yards to the entrance (on your left) to the...*

⑫ House of the Vettii

This is Pompeii's best-preserved home, retaining many of its mosaics and frescoes. The House of the Vettii was the bachelor pad of two wealthy merchant brothers. In the entryway, it's hard to miss the huge erection. This was not pornography. This was a symbol of success: The penis and sack of money balance each other on the goldsmith scale above a fine bowl of fruit. Translation? Only with a balance of fertility and money can you enjoy true abundance.

Step into the atrium with its replica wooden ceiling open to the sky and a lead pipe to collect water for the house cistern. The pool was flanked by two large moneyboxes (one survives, the footprint of the other shows how it was secured to the ground). The brothers wanted all who entered to know how successful they were. A variety of rooms give an intimate peek at elegant Pompeiian life. The dark room to the right of the entrance (as you face out) is filled with exquisite frescoes. Notice more white "cat's eye" stones embedded in the floor. Imagine these glinting like little eyes as the brothers and their friends wandered around by oil lamp late at night, with their sacks of gold, bowls of fruit, and enormous...egos.

• *Our next stop, the Bakery, is located about 150 yards south (downhill) from here. To get there, return to the street in front of the House of the Vettii. Walk downhill along Vicolo dei Vetti. Go one block, to where you dead-end at a T-intersection with Via della Fortuna. Go a few steps left and then right at the first corner. Continue down this gently curving road to #22.*

⑬ Bakery and Mill

The stubby stone towers are flour grinders. Grain was poured into the top and donkeys or slaves, treading in a circle, pushed wooden bars that turned the stones that ground the grain. The powdered grain dropped out the bottom as flour—flavored with tiny bits of rock. Nearby, the thing that looks like a modern-day pizza oven was...a brick oven. Each neighborhood had a bakery just like this.

• *Continue down the curvy road to the next intersection. As you walk consider the destructive power of all the plants and vines that you see around. Also, notice the chariot grooves worn into the pavement. When the curvy road reaches the intersection with Via degli Augustali, turn left. Ahead, in 50 yards, at #44, is the Taberna Hedones, an ancient tavern with an original floor mosaic still intact. A few steps past that, turn right and walk downhill to #18—one of many Pompeii brothels.*

⓮ Brothel (Lupanare)

You'll find the biggest crowds in Pompeii at a place that was likely also quite popular 2,000 years ago—the brothel. Prostitutes were nicknamed *lupe* (she-wolves), alluding to the call they made when attracting business. The brothel was a simple place, with beds and pillows made of stone and then covered with mattresses. The ancient graffiti includes tallies and exotic names of the women, indicating the prostitutes came from all corners of the Mediterranean (it also served as feedback from satisfied customers). The faded frescoes above the cells may have been a kind of menu for services offered. Note the idealized women (white, which was considered beautiful; one wears an early bra) and the rougher men (dark, considered horny). The bed legs came with little disk-like barriers to keep critters from crawling up, the tiny rooms had curtains for doors, and the prostitutes provided sheepskin condoms.

• *Leaving the brothel, go right, then take the first left, and continue going downhill two blocks to return to Via Abbondanza. This walk is over. The Forum—and exit—are to the right. If you exit now, you'll be routed through the exhibition rooms—where you'll find a scale model of the city, an interesting video, and some artifacts—and the gift shop.*

   But before you leave, consider these extra stops—all worth the time and energy (if you have any left). To locate them, refer to your map.

MORE POMPEII STOPS
Temple of Isis

This temple served Pompeii's Egyptian community. The little white stucco shrine with the modern plastic roof housed holy water from the Nile. Isis, from Egyptian myth, was one of many foreign gods adopted by the eclectic Romans. Pompeii must have had a synagogue, too, but it has yet to be excavated.

Theater

Originally a Greek theater (Greeks built theirs with the help of a hillside), this was the birthplace of the Greek port here in 470 BC. During Roman times, the theater sat 5,000 people in three sets of seats: the five marble terraces up close (filled with romantic wooden seats for two), the main section, and the cheap nosebleed section (surviving only on the high end, near the trees).

House of Menander (Casa di Menandro)

Once owned by a wealthy Pompeiian, this house takes its current name from a fresco of the Greek playwright Menander on one of the walls. Admire the grand atrium (with frescoes depicting scenes from Homer's *Iliad* and *Odyssey,* and an altar to the family gods), the wall frescoes, and the mosaics. The cloister-like back courtyard leads to a room with skeletons (not plaster casts) of eruption victims from this house. Farther back, a passage leads to the servants' quarters.

Viewpoint

You're at ground level—post eruption. To the right (inland), the farmland shows how locals lived on top of the ruins for centuries without knowing what was underneath. To the left, you can see the entire ancient city of Pompeii spread out in front of you and appreciate the magnitude of the excavations.

Garden of the Fugitives

Archaeologists identified this house as belonging to a middle-class merchant family. Plaster casts of this fleeing ("fugitive") family are placed exactly as the bodies were found after the eruption: lined up in single file as they attempted to escape several cubic feet of already fallen ash. Their exit was stopped by a sudden wave of hot gas and volcanic material, likely traveling over 100 miles per hour.

Amphitheater

Climb to the upper level. With Vesuvius looming in the background, mentally replace the tourists below with gladiators and wild animals locked in com-  bat. Facing the other way, look for the bell tower that tops the roofline of the modern city of Pompei, where locals go about their daily lives in the shadow of the volcano, just as their ancestors did 2,000 years ago.

• *If it's too crowded to bear hiking back along uneven lanes to the entrance, you can slip out the site's "back door," which is next to the amphitheater. Exiting, turn right and follow the site's wall all the way back to the entrance.*

ROMAN HISTORY

Three Millennia in Nine Pages

HISTORY IN A HURRY
Ancient Rome lasted a thousand years (500 BC–AD 500), half as an expanding republic, half as a dominating empire. When Rome fell to invaders, all of Europe suffered a thousand years of poverty and ignorance (AD 500-1500), although Rome's influence could still be felt through the Catholic Church. Popes rebuilt Rome for pilgrims—in Renaissance, then Baroque and Neoclassical styles (1500-1800). As capital of a newly united Italy, Rome followed fascist Mussolini into World War II (and lost), but rebounded in Italy's postwar economic boom.

Want more?

LEGENDARY BIRTH (1200-500 BC)
Aeneas flees burning Troy (1200 BC), wanders like Odysseus, and finally finds a home along the Tiber. His descendants, Romulus and Remus—orphaned at birth, suckled by a she-wolf, and raised

by shepherds—grow up to steal wives and build a wall, thus founding Rome (753 BC).

Closer to fact, the local, Latin-speaking agrarian tribes were dominated by more sophisticated neighbors to the north (Etruscans) and south (Greek colonists). But their convenient location on the Tiber was perfect for a rise to power.

Sights
- Romulus' "huts" and wall (Palatine Hill)
- She-Wolf statue (Capitoline Museums)
- Frescoes of Aeneas and Romulus (National Museum of Rome)
- Bernini's Aeneas statue (Borghese Gallery)
- Etruscan wing (Vatican Museums)
- Etruscan Museum (in Villa Borghese Gardens)
- Etruscan legacy (the original Circus Maximus, the drained Forum)

THE REPUBLIC
(509-27 BC)

The city expands throughout the Italian peninsula (500-300 BC), then defeats Hannibal's North African Carthaginians (the Punic Wars, 264-146 BC) and Greece (168 BC). Rome is master of the Mediterranean, and booty and captured slaves pour in. Romans bicker among themselves over their slice of the pie, pitting the wealthy landowners (the ruling Senate) against the working class (plebs) and the rebellious slaves (Spartacus' revolt, 73 BC). In the chaos, charismatic generals like Julius Caesar, who can provide wealth and security, become dictators. Change is necessary...and coming.

Sights
- Forum's Curia, Temple of Saturn, Temple of Castor and Pollux, Rostrum, Basilica Aemilia, Temple of Julius Caesar, and Basilica Julia (all rebuilt later)
- Appian Way built, lined with tombs
- Aqueducts, which carry water to a growing city

- Portrait busts of citizens (National Museum of Rome)
- The republic's "S.P.Q.R." monogram and motto, seen today on statues, buildings, and even manhole covers: *Senatus Populusque Romanus,* or the "Senate and People of Rome." (Some northern Italians, who feel the South is dragging them down,

Rome Almanac

Population: Approximately 2.8 million people

Currency: Euro (€)

Nickname: The Eternal City

City Layout: Rome, the capital of Italy, is divided into 22 *rioni* (districts). Of the famous seven hills of Rome, you're most likely to see Palatine Hill (birthplace of the legendary founders of the city, Romulus and Remus), Capitoline Hill (topped by museums and a Michelangelo-designed square), and the Quirinale, one of the highest of the hills and the site of many of my recommended hotels.

Best Strolls: Two major thoroughfares are open to pedestrians and closed to traffic: the northern part of Via del Corso (best for strolling Mon-Sat around 17:00-19:00, earlier afternoon on Sun) and the southern part of Via dei Fori Imperiali (open to buses/taxis Mon-Sat, closed to all vehicles Sun). My two favorite walks in Rome take me through Trastevere, and through the heart of the city at night.

Tourist Tracks: The Colosseum attracts about six million visitors every year. About €3,000 is collected from the Trevi Fountain daily.

Culture Count: The vast majority of Romans are native-born Italians; only about 13 percent of the city's residents are immigrants, mostly from Romania, Bangladesh, the Philippines, and China. Rome's population is largely Roman Catholic.

Average Roman: The average Roman is 44 years old, has 1.4 children, and will live until the age of 82.

translate S.P.Q.R. as *Sono Porci Questi Romani*—"These Romans Are Pigs.")

THE EMPIRE: THE "ROMAN PEACE," OR PAX ROMANA (AD 1-200)

After Julius Caesar is killed by disgruntled republicans, his adopted son Augustus takes undisputed control, ends the civil wars, declares himself emperor, and adopts a family member to succeed him, setting the pattern of rule for the next 500 years.

Rome rules an empire of 54 million people, stretching from England to Africa, from Spain to Turkey. The city, with more than a million inhabitants, is decorated with Greek-style statues and monumental, marble-faced buildings...it is the marvel of the known world. The empire prospers on a (false) economy of booty, slaves, and trade, surviving the often turbulent and naughty behavior of emperors such as Caligula and Nero. You can see Roman history in the faces of the emperors by reading the 📖 National Museum of Rome Tour chapter.

Sights

- Colosseum
- Forum
- Palatine Hill palaces
- Ara Pacis ("Altar of Peace")
- Augustus' house (House of Livia and Augustus) on Palatine Hill
- Pantheon
- Trajan's Column and Forum
- Greek and Greek-style statues and emperors' busts (National Museum of Rome, Vatican Museums, Capitoline Museums)
- Piazza Navona (former stadium)
- Hadrian's Villa (Tivoli) and tomb (now Castel Sant'Angelo)

ROME FALLS
(200-476)

Corruption, disease, and the constant pressure of barbarians pecking away at the borders slowly drain the unwieldy empire. Despite Diocletian's division of the empire and Constantine's legalization of Christianity (313), the city is sacked (410), and the last emperor checks out (476). Rome falls like a huge col-  umn, kicking up dust that will plunge Europe into a thousand years of darkness.

Sights

- Arch of Constantine
- The Forum's Basilica of Constantine
- Baths of Diocletian
- Old Roman Wall (gates at Via Veneto or Piramide)

MEDIEVAL ROME
(500-1500)

The once-great city of a million people dwindles to a rough village of 20,000, with a corrupt pope, forgotten ruins, and malaria-carrying mosquitoes. Cows graze in the ruined Forum, and wolves prowl the Vatican at night. During the 1300s, even the popes leave Rome to live in France. What little glory Rome retains is in the pomp, knowledge, and wealth of the Catholic Church.

Sights
- The damage done to ancient Roman monuments, caused by disuse, barbarian looting, and pillaging for precut stones
- Early Christian churches built before Rome fell (Santa Maria Maggiore, San Giovanni in Laterano, and San Clemente)
- Churches of Santa Maria sopra Minerva and Santa Maria in Trastevere
- Castel Sant'Angelo

RENAISSANCE AND BAROQUE ROME (1500-1800)

As Europe's economy recovers, energetic popes rebuild Rome to attract pilgrims. The best artists decorate palaces and churches, carve statues, and build fountains. The city is not a great political force, but as the center of Catholicism during the

struggle against Protestants (c. 1520-1648), it is an influential religious and cultural capital.

Renaissance Sights
- Michelangelo: Sistine Chapel (Vatican Museums), dome of St. Peter's, *Pietà* (St. Peter's), *Moses* (St. Peter-in-Chains Church), Christ statue (Santa Maria sopra Minerva), Piazza del Campidoglio (Capitoline Hill Square), Santa Maria degli Angeli church (in former Baths of Diocletian)

- Raphael's *School of Athens* and *Transfiguration* (Vatican Museums)
- Paintings by Raphael, Titian, and others (Borghese Gallery)

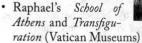

HISTORY

Church Architecture

History comes to life when you visit a centuries-old church. Even if you wouldn't know your apse from a hole in the ground, learning a few simple terms will enrich your experience. Note that not every church has every feature, and that a "cathedral" isn't a type of church architecture, but rather a designation for a church that's a governing center for a local bishop.

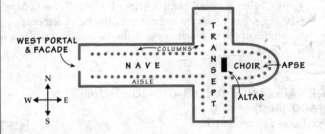

Aisles: The long, generally low-ceilinged arcades that flank the nave.

Altar: The raised area with a ceremonial table (often adorned with candles or a crucifix), where the priest prepares and serves the bread and wine for Communion.

Apse: The space beyond the altar, generally bordered with small chapels.

Barrel Vault: A continuous round-arched ceiling that resembles an extended upside-down U.

Choir: A cozy area, often screened off, located within the church nave and near the high altar, where services are sung in a more intimate setting.

Cloister: A square-shaped series of hallways surrounding an open-air courtyard, traditionally where monks and nuns got fresh air.

Facade: The outer wall of the church's main (west) entrance, viewable from outside and generally highly decorated.

Groin Vault: An arched ceiling formed where two equal barrel vaults meet at right angles. Less common usage: term for a medieval jock strap.

Narthex: The area (portico or foyer) between the main entry and the nave.

Nave: The long, central section of the church (running west to east, from the entrance to the altar) where the congregation stood through the service.

Transept: The north-south part of the church, which crosses (perpendicularly) the east-west nave. In a traditional Latin cross-shaped floor plan, the transept forms the "arms" of the cross.

West Portal: The main entry to the church (on the west end, opposite the main altar).

Baroque Sights

- St. Peter's Square and interior (largely by Bernini)
- Bernini statues (at Borghese Gallery; also *St. Teresa in Ecstasy* at Santa Maria della Vittoria church) and fountains (Piazza Navona, Piazza Barberini)
- Ancient obelisks erected in squares (Piazza del Popolo, Piazza Navona)
- Trevi Fountain and Spanish Steps
- Gesù and Sant'Ignazio churches
- Caravaggio's *Calling of St. Matthew* (San Luigi dei Francesi Church) and other paintings (Borghese Gallery and Vatican Museums)
- Baroque paintings (Borghese Gallery)
- Borromini's facade of Sant'Agnese Church (Piazza Navona)

MODERN ROME (1800-PRESENT)

Rome becomes the capital of a newly reunited Italy (1871) under King Victor Emmanuel II, is modernized by fascist Mussolini, and survives the destruction of World War II to become a republic. Italy's postwar "economic miracle" makes Rome a world-class city of cinema, banking, and tourism.

Sights

- Victor Emmanuel Monument, which honors the first king of a united Italy
- Mussolini: the balcony he spoke from (at Palazzo Venezia, on Piazza Venezia), his planned city (E.U.R.), grand boulevards (Via dei Fori Imperiali, Via della Conciliazione), his home (Villa Torlonia), and Olympic Stadium
- Cinecittà film studios and Via Veneto nightlife, which have faint echoes of Fellini's *La Dolce Vita*
- Subway system, broad boulevards, smog

ROME TODAY

After surviving the government-a-year turbulence and Mafia-tainted corruption of the postwar years, Rome started stabilizing. And the 21st century has seen a flurry of activity. Signature sights such as the Colosseum, Trevi Fountain, and Mausoleum of Augustus got million-euro upgrades. Bold new architecture was added:

Rome in World War II

By 1943, as bombs began falling just outside the walls of Rome, it was clear to all that Italy's alliance with Nazi Germany was a huge mistake, leading the country to ruin. The fascist Grand Council dismissed Mussolini, and the king ordered his arrest. The ex-dictator fled north, and fascism collapsed without violence. Rome was declared an "open city" (meaning a city with no military bases). Italy surrendered to the Allies. The king fled to Allied-occupied southern Italy, abandoning Rome to Nazi forces, which occupied it for nine terrible months. The Roman people and the Vatican joined forces to save some citizens from the Nazis.

The Gestapo demanded 50 kilos of gold from the Roman Jews, who, with great difficulty and help from non-Jews, succeeded in providing it. Regardless, more than 2,000 Jews were deported to concentration camps. After Italian partisans planted a bomb near the Trevi Fountain, killing 32 Germans, more than 300 people randomly chosen from Rome's prison were executed in retaliation. This tragic event—called the Fosse Ardeatine massacre, for the caves near the Appian Way where it took place—remains an important milestone in the Italian consciousness. As the Allies marched closer, they bombed Rome and its surroundings, but avoided striking the center.

Thankfully, Hitler granted the occupying Nazi troops permission to leave the city, which he declared a "place of culture" that should not be "the scene of combat operations." Pope Pius XII agreed, declaring, "Whoever raises a hand against Rome will be guilty of matricide to the whole civilized world and in the eternal judgment of God." Finally, the Germans marched out, the Americans marched in (through the gate of San Giovanni) on June 4, 1944, and the exhausted city welcomed them with joy and relief.

the Auditorium Parco della Musica (by Renzo Piano, 2002), the Ara Pacis museum (by Richard Meier, 2006), and MAXXI, a state-of-the-architecture museum of modern art (by Zaha Hadid, 2010). The long-awaited Metro line C started running, though it still hasn't reached the city center, and Rome's Tiburtina Station was renovated for high-speed rail.

But Italy's slow recovery from the Great Recession of the late 2000s lingers. Unemployment among Italy's youth is very high; many stay with their parents even into their 30s. They spend a lot of time being trendy and hanging out—you'll see them in Rome's piazzas, where the hot *vroom-vroom* motor scooter is their symbol; haircuts and fashion are follow-the-leader.

In 2016 Romans elected an anti-establishment candidate—Virginia Raggi—as their new mayor to shake things up. Rome's first female leader, Raggi immediately canceled a bid for the 2024 Summer Olympics, stating that Rome couldn't afford it. Popular at first, over time this political newbie has been blamed for everything from spotty garbage collection to potholes to broken-down buses. Some news reports said she even wanted to divert all the coins collected at Trevi Fountain from helping the poor to prop up the city government—a claim she denied. (It's a lot of coins—about €1.5 million annually.) With low approval ratings and a rising right-wing challenge, it's not clear how much longer Raggi can hang on.

The Vatican is buzzing, too. In 2013, Pope Benedict XVI shockingly took an early retirement and handed the keys to the kingdom over to a free-wheeling successor, the first Jesuit pope, Francis I. In his first years as pope, Francis won the hearts of Catholics and non-Catholics alike for his message of love, mercy, and compassion. But fallout from Catholic sex-abuse scandals has diminished his reputation recently.

Today's Rome is ready for pilgrims, travelers, and you to come and make more history.

For more on Roman history, consider *Europe 101: History and Art for the Traveler*, written by Rick Steves and Gene Openshaw (available at www.ricksteves.com).

HISTORY

PRACTICALITIES

This chapter covers the practical skills of European travel: how to get tourist information, pay for things, sightsee efficiently, find good-value accommodations, eat affordably but well, use technology wisely, and get between destinations smoothly. For more information on these topics, see www.ricksteves.com/travel-tips.

Tourist Information

Before your trip, scan the website of the Italian national tourist office (www.italia.it) for a wealth of travel information. If you have a specific question, try contacting one of their US offices (New York: Tel. 212/245-5618, newyork@enit.it; Chicago: Tel. 312/644-9335, chicago@enit.it; Los Angeles: Tel. 310/820-1898, losangeles@enit.it).

In **Rome,** you'll find about a dozen small tourist information kiosks and offices (abbreviated **TI** in this book) scattered through town. They have maps and sell sightseeing passes but are usually not worth a special trip. It's more helpful to visit their good website (www.060608.it) or utilize their call center (tel. 06-0608, answered daily 9:00-19:00, press 2 for English), which can answer many practical questions. For more details on Rome's TIs, see page 25.

Travel Tips

Travel Advisories: For updated health and safety conditions, including any restrictions for your destination, consult the US State Department's international travel website (travel.state.gov).

Emergency and Medical Help: For any emergency service—ambulance, police, or fire—call **112** from a mobile phone or landline. Operators, who generally speak English, will deal with your request or route you to the right emergency service. If you get sick, do as the locals do and go to a pharmacist for advice. Or ask at your hotel for help—they'll know the nearest medical and emergency services.

ETIAS Registration: The European Union may soon require US and Canadian citizens to register online with the European Travel Information and Authorization System (ETIAS) before entering Italy and other Schengen Zone countries (quick and easy process). For the latest, check www.etiasvisa.com.

Theft or Loss: To replace a passport, you'll need to go in person to an embassy. If your credit and debit cards disappear, cancel and replace them (see "Damage Control for Lost Cards" on page 541). File a police report, either on the spot or within a day or two; you'll need it to submit an insurance claim for lost or stolen rail passes or electronics, and it can help with replacing your passport or credit and debit cards. For more information, see www.ricksteves.com/help.

US Embassy: Tel. 06-46741, passport and nonemergency consular services by appointment only, walk-in emergency services Mon-Fri 8:30-12:00 (Via Vittorio Veneto 121), https://it.usembassy.gov.

Canadian Embassy: Tel. 06-854-441 (Via Zara 30), www.italy.gc.ca. After-hours emergency tel. in Ottawa 613-996-8885.

Time Zones: Italy, like most of continental Europe, is generally six/nine hours ahead of the East/West Coasts of the US. The exceptions are the beginning and end of Daylight Saving Time: Europe "springs forward" the last Sunday in March (two weeks after most of North America), and "falls back" the last Sunday in October (one week before North America). For a handy time converter, use the world clock app on your phone or download one (see www.timeanddate.com).

Business Hours: Traditionally, Italy used the siesta plan, with people generally working from about 9:00 to 13:00 and from 15:30 or 16:00 to 19:00 or 19:30, Monday through Saturday. Siesta hours are no longer required by law, so many shops stay open through lunch or later into the evening, especially larger stores in tourist areas. In Rome, stores are usually closed on Sundays, summer Saturday afternoons, and winter Monday mornings. Banking hours are generally Monday through Friday 8:30 to 13:30 and 15:30 to 16:30, but can vary wildly.

Watt's Up? Europe's electrical system is 220 volts, instead of North America's 110 volts. Most electronics (laptops, smartphones, cameras) and new hair dryers convert automatically, so you won't need a converter, but you will need an adapter plug with two round prongs, sold inexpensively at travel stores in the US. Sockets in Italy and Switzerland only accept plugs with slimmer prongs: Don't buy an adapter with the thicker ("Schuko" style) prongs—it won't work. Avoid bringing older appliances that don't automatically convert voltage; instead, buy a cheap replacement in Europe.

Discounts: Discounts for sights are generally not listed in this book. However, youths under 18 and students and teachers with proper identification cards (obtain from www.isic.org) can get discounts at many sights—always ask. Italy's national museums generally offer free admission to children under 18, but some discounts are available only for citizens of the European Union (EU).

Online Translation Tips: Google's Chrome browser instantly translates websites; Translate.google.com is also handy. The Google Translate app converts spoken or typed English into most European languages (and vice versa) and can also translate text it "reads" with your smartphone's camera.

Money

Here's my basic strategy for using money in Europe:

- Upon arrival, head for a cash machine (ATM) at the airport and withdraw some local currency, using a debit card with low international transaction fees.
- In general, pay for bigger expenses with a credit card and use cash for smaller purchases and tips. Use a debit card only for cash withdrawals.
- Keep your cards and cash safe in a money belt.

PLASTIC VERSUS CASH

Although credit cards are widely accepted in Europe, cash is sometimes the only way to pay for cheap food, bus fare, taxis, tips, and local guides. Some businesses (especially smaller ones, such as B&Bs and mom-and-pop cafés and shops) may charge you extra for using a credit card—or might not accept credit cards at all. Having cash on hand helps you out of a jam if your card randomly doesn't work.

I use my credit card to book and pay for hotel reservations, to buy advance tickets for events or sights, and to cover most other

---

Exchange Rate

1 euro (€) = about $1.20

To convert prices in euros to dollars, add about 20 percent: €20 = about $24, €50 = about $60. (Check www.oanda.com for the latest exchange rates.) Just like the dollar, one euro is broken down into 100 cents. Coins range from €0.01 to €2, and bills from €5 to €200 (bills over €50 are rarely used).

---

expenses. It can also be smart to use plastic near the end of your trip, to avoid another visit to the ATM.

WHAT TO BRING

I pack the following and keep it all safe in my money belt.

Debit Card: Use this at ATMs to withdraw local cash.

Credit Card: Handy for bigger transactions (at hotels, shops, restaurants, travel agencies, car-rental agencies, and so on), payment machines, and online purchases.

Backup Card: Some travelers carry a third card (debit or credit; ideally from a different bank), in case one gets lost, demagnetized, eaten by a temperamental machine, or simply doesn't work.

A Stash of Cash: I carry $100-200 as a cash backup, which comes in handy in an emergency (such as when the banks go on strike or if your ATM card gets eaten by the machine).

What NOT to Bring: Resist the urge to buy euros before your trip or you'll pay the price in bad stateside exchange rates. Wait until you arrive to withdraw money. I've yet to see a European airport that didn't have plenty of ATMs.

BEFORE YOU GO

Use this pre-trip checklist.

Know your cards. Debit cards from any major US bank will work in any standard European bank's ATM (ideally, use a debit card with a Visa or MasterCard logo). As for credit cards, Visa and MasterCard are universal, American Express is less common, and Discover is unknown in Europe.

Know your PIN. Make sure you know the numeric, four-digit PIN for all of your cards, both debit and credit. Request it if you don't have one, as it may be required for some purchases in Europe (see "Using Credit Cards," later), and allow time to receive the information by mail.

Report your travel dates. Let your bank know that you'll be using your debit and credit cards in Europe, and when and where you're headed.

Adjust your ATM withdrawal limit. Find out how much you

can take out daily and ask for a higher daily withdrawal limit if you want to get more cash at once. Note that European ATMs will withdraw funds only from checking accounts; you're unlikely to have access to your savings account.

Ask about fees. For any purchase or withdrawal made with a card, you may be charged a currency conversion fee (1-3 percent) and/or a Visa or MasterCard international transaction fee (less than 1 percent). If you're getting a bad deal, consider getting a new debit or credit card. Reputable no-fee cards include those from Capital One, as well as Charles Schwab debit cards. Most credit unions and some airline loyalty cards have low or no international transaction fees.

IN EUROPE
Using Cash Machines
European cash machines have English-language instructions and work just like they do at home—except they spit out local currency instead of dollars, calculated at the day's standard bank-to-bank rate.

In most places, ATMs are easy to locate—in Italy ask for a *bancomat*. When possible, withdraw cash from a bank-run ATM located just outside that bank. Ideally use the machine during the bank's opening hours so you can go inside for help if your card is munched.

If your debit card doesn't work, try a lower amount—your request may have exceeded your withdrawal limit or the ATM's limit. If you still have a problem, try a different ATM or come back later—your bank's network may be temporarily down.

Avoid "independent" ATMs, such as Travelex, Euronet, Moneybox, Your Cash, Cardpoint, and Cashzone. These have high fees, can be less secure than a bank ATM, and may try to trick users with "dynamic currency conversion" (see later).

Exchanging Cash
Avoid exchanging money in Europe; it's a big rip-off. In a pinch, you can always find exchange desks at major train stations or airports—convenient but with crummy rates. Anything over 5 percent for a transaction is piracy. Banks generally do not exchange money unless you have an account with them.

Using Credit Cards
Despite some differences between European and US cards, there's little to worry about: US credit cards generally work fine in Europe. I've been inconvenienced a few times by self-service payment machines that wouldn't accept my card, but it's never caused me serious trouble (I carry cash just in case).

European cards use chip-and-PIN technology; most chip cards issued in the US instead have a signature option. Some European card readers will accept your card as-is while others may generate a receipt for you to sign or prompt you to enter your PIN (so it's important to know the code for each of your cards). If a cashier is present, you should have no problems.

At self-service payment machines (transit-ticket kiosks, parking, etc.), results are mixed, as US cards may not work in some unattended transactions. If your card won't work, look for a cashier who can process your card manually—or pay in cash.

Drivers Beware: Be aware of potential problems using a US credit card to fill up at an unattended gas station, enter a parking garage, or exit a toll road. Always carry cash as a backup and be prepared to move on to the next gas station if necessary. When approaching a toll plaza, use the "cash" lane.

Dynamic Currency Conversion

If merchants offer to convert your purchase price into dollars (called dynamic currency conversion, or DCC), refuse this "service." You'll pay extra for the expensive convenience of seeing your charge in dollars. If an ATM offers to "lock in" or "guarantee" your conversion rate, choose "proceed without conversion." Other prompts might state, "You can be charged in dollars: Press YES for dollars, NO for euros." Always choose the local currency.

Security Tips

Pickpockets target tourists. Keep your cash, credit cards, and passport secure in your money belt, and carry only a day's spending money in your front pocket or wallet.

Before inserting your card into an ATM, inspect the front. If anything looks crooked, loose, or damaged, it could be a sign of a card-skimming device. When entering your PIN, carefully block other people's view of the keypad.

Don't use a debit card for purchases. Because a debit card pulls funds directly from your bank account, potential charges incurred by a thief will stay on your account while the fraudulent use is investigated by your bank.

To access your accounts online while traveling, be sure to use a secure connection (see the "Tips on Internet Security" sidebar, later).

Damage Control for Lost Cards

If you lose your credit or debit card, report the loss immediately to the respective global customer-assistance centers. With a mobile phone, call these 24-hour US numbers: Visa (tel. +1 303/967-1096), MasterCard (tel. +1 636/722-7111), and American Express (tel. +1

336/393-1111). From a landline, you can call these US numbers collect by going through a local operator. European toll-free numbers can be found at the websites for Visa and MasterCard.

You'll need to provide the primary cardholder's identification-verification details (such as birth date, mother's maiden name, or Social Security number). You can generally receive a temporary card within two or three business days in Europe (see www.ricksteves.com/help for more).

If you report your loss within two days, you typically won't be responsible for unauthorized transactions on your account, although many banks charge a liability fee.

TIPPING

Tipping in Italy isn't as automatic and generous as it is in the US. For special service, tips are appreciated, but not expected. As in the US, the proper amount depends on your resources, tipping philosophy, and the circumstances, but some general guidelines apply.

Restaurants: In Italy, a service charge *(servizio)* is usually built into your check (look at the bill carefully). If it is included, there's no need to leave an extra tip. If it's not included, it's common to leave about €1 per person (a bit more at finer restaurants) or to round up the bill. For more details on restaurant tipping, see page 558.

Taxis: For a typical ride, round up your fare a bit (for instance, if the fare is €4.50, pay €5). If the cabbie hauls your bags and zips you to the airport to help you catch your flight, you might want to toss in a little more. But if you feel like you're being driven in circles or otherwise ripped off, skip the tip.

Services: In general, if someone in the tourism or service industry does a super job for you, a small tip of a euro or two is appropriate...but not required. If you're not sure whether (or how much) to tip, ask a local for advice.

GETTING A VAT REFUND

Wrapped into the purchase price of your Italian souvenirs is a Value-Added Tax (VAT) of about 22 percent. You're entitled to get most of that tax back if you purchase more than €155 (about $185) worth of goods at a store that participates in the VAT-refund scheme. Typically, you must ring up the minimum at a single retailer—you can't add up your purchases from various shops to reach the required amount. (If the store ships the goods to your US home, VAT is not assessed on your purchase.)

Getting your refund is straightforward...and worthwhile if you spend a significant amount on souvenirs.

Get the paperwork. Have the merchant completely fill out the necessary refund document. You'll have to present your passport.

Get the paperwork done before you leave the store to ensure you'll have everything you need (including your original sales receipt).

Get your stamp at the border or airport. Process your VAT document at your last stop in the European Union (such as at the airport) with the customs agent who deals with VAT refunds. Arrive an additional hour before you need to check in to allow time to find the customs office—and wait. Some customs desks are positioned before airport security; confirm the location before going through security.

It's best to keep your purchases in your carry-on. If your item isn't allowed as carry-on (such as a knife), pack it in your checked bag and alert the check-in agent. You'll be sent (with your tagged bag) to a customs desk outside security; someone will examine your bag, stamp your paperwork, and put your bag on the belt. You're not supposed to use your purchased goods before you leave. If you show up at customs wearing your new Italian leather shoes, officials might look the other way—or deny you a refund.

Collect your refund. You can claim your VAT refund from refund companies, such as Global Blue or Planet, with offices at major airports, ports, or border crossings (either before or after security, probably strategically located near a duty-free shop). These services (which extract a 4 percent fee) can refund your money in cash immediately or credit your card. Otherwise, mail the stamped refund documents to the address given by the shop where you made your purchase.

CUSTOMS FOR AMERICAN SHOPPERS

You can take home $800 worth of items per person duty-free, once every 31 days. Many processed and packaged foods are allowed, including vacuum-packed cheeses, dried herbs, jams, baked goods, candy, chocolate, oil, vinegar, mustard, and honey. Fresh fruits and vegetables and most meats are not allowed, with exceptions for some canned items. As for alcohol, you can bring in one liter duty-free (it can be packed securely in your checked luggage, along with any other liquid-containing items).

To bring alcohol (or liquid-packed foods) in your carry-on bag on your flight home, buy it at a duty-free shop at the airport. You'll increase your odds of getting it onto a connecting flight if it's packaged in a "STEB"—a secure, tamper-evident bag. But stay away from liquids in opaque, ceramic, or metallic containers, which usually cannot be successfully screened (STEB or no STEB).

For details on allowable goods, customs rules, and duty rates, visit help.cbp.gov.

Sightseeing

Sightseeing can be hard work. Use these tips to make your visits to Rome's finest sights meaningful, fun, efficient, and painless.

MAPS AND NAVIGATION TOOLS

A good map is essential for efficient navigation while sightseeing. The maps in this book are concise and simple, designed to help you locate recommended destinations, sights, and local TIs, where you can pick up more in-depth maps.

You can also use a mapping app on your mobile device. Be aware that pulling up maps or looking up turn-by-turn walking directions on the fly usually requires a data connection: To use this feature, it's smart to get an international data plan. With Google Maps or City Maps 2Go, it's possible to download a map while online, then go offline and navigate without incurring data-roaming charges, though you can't search for an address or get real-time walking directions. A handful of other apps—including Apple Maps and Navmii—also allow you to use maps offline.

PLAN AHEAD

Set up an itinerary that allows you to fit in all your must-see sights. For a one-stop look at opening hours, see "Rome at a Glance" (page 56; also see the "Daily Reminder" on page 28). Most sights keep stable hours, but you can easily confirm the latest by checking with the TI or visiting museum websites. Or call sights in the morning and ask: "Are you open today?" (*"Aperto oggi?"*; ah-PER-toh OH-jee) and "What time do you close?" (*"A che ora chiude?"*; ah kay OH-rah kee-OO-day).

Don't put off visiting a must-see sight—you never know when a place will close unexpectedly for a holiday, strike, or restoration. Many museums are closed or have reduced hours at least a few days a year, especially on holidays such as Christmas, New Year's *(Capodanno)*, Italian Liberation Day (April 25), and Labor Day (May 1). A list of holidays is in the appendix; check for possible closures during your trip. In summer, some sights may stay open late. In the off-season, hours may be shorter.

Going at the right time helps avoid crowds. This book offers tips on the best times to see specific sights. Try visiting popular sights very early or very late. Evening visits (when possible) are usually peaceful, with fewer crowds. Late morning is usually the worst time to visit a popular sight.

If you plan to hire a local guide, reserve ahead by email. Popular guides can get booked up.

Study up. To get the most out of the self-guided tours and sight descriptions in this book, read them before you visit.

RESERVATIONS, ADVANCE TICKETS, AND PASSES

Given how precious your vacation time is, I recommend getting reservations for any must-see sight that offers them. For Rome, if you want to see the Colosseum or Borghese Gallery, you must make reservations in advance (see pages 162 and 296). It's also smart to reserve for the Roman Forum and the Vatican Museums (see page 259) as well.

To deal with lines, many popular sights sell advance tickets that guarantee admission at a certain time of day (for example, Rome's Vatican Museums), or that allow you to skip entry lines. Either way, it's worth giving up some spontaneity to book in advance. While hundreds of tourists sweat in long ticket-buying lines, those who've booked ahead are assured of getting in. In some cases, getting a ticket in advance simply means buying your ticket earlier on the same day. But for other sights, you may need to book weeks or even months in advance. As soon as you're ready to commit to a certain date, book it. To avoid surprises, make sure you are using an official site.

The advance-purchase price is often less expensive than what you would pay on-site (my listings include the online price, if available). And many museums offer convenient mobile ticketing. Simply buy your ticket online and send it to your phone, eliminating the need for a paper ticket.

Booking a guided tour can help you avoid lines at many popular sights. So can knowing what days to avoid. Italian state museums are free to enter (and often very crowded) one or two days a month, usually on a Sunday. Check museum websites for specifics and avoid free entry days when possible.

AT SIGHTS

Here's what you can typically expect:

Entering: You may not be allowed to enter if you arrive too close to closing time. And guards start ushering people out well before the actual closing time, so don't save the best for last.

Many sights have a security check. Allow extra time for these lines. Some sights require you to check day packs and coats. (If you'd rather not check your day pack, try carrying it tucked under your arm like a purse as you enter.) Pocketknives may not be allowed.

Photography: If the museum's photo policy isn't clearly posted, ask a guard. Generally, taking photos without a flash or tripod is allowed. Some sights ban selfie sticks; others ban photos altogether.

Audioguides and Apps: Many sights rent audioguides with excellent recorded descriptions in English. If you bring your own ear buds, you can often enjoy better sound. If you don't mind being tethered to your travel partner, you'll save money by bringing a Y-

PRACTICALITIES

jack and sharing one audioguide. Museums and sights often offer free apps that you can download to your mobile device (check their websites). And, I've produced free, downloadable audio tours for my Heart of Rome, Trastevere, Jewish Ghetto, and Naples neighborhood walks, and my tours of the Pantheon, St. Peter's Basilica, Roman Forum, Colosseum, Sistine Chapel, Vatican Museums, Ostia Antica, Naples Archaeological Museum, and Pompeii; look for the 🎧 in this book. For more on my audio tours, see page 21.

Temporary Exhibits: Museums may show special exhibits in addition to their permanent collection. Some exhibits are included in the entry price, while others come at an extra cost (which you may have to pay even if you don't want to see the exhibit).

Expect Changes: Artwork can be on tour, on loan, out sick, or shifted at the whim of the curator. Pick up a floor plan as you enter, and ask the museum staff if you can't find a particular item. Say the title or artist's name, or point to the photograph in this book and ask, *"Dov'è?"* (doh-VEH, meaning "Where is?").

Dates for Artwork: It helps to know the terms. Art historians and Italians refer to centuries by dropping a thousand years. The Trecento (300s), Quattrocento (400s), and Cinquecento (500s) were the 1300s, 1400s, and 1500s. The Novecento (900s) means modern art (the 1900s). In Italian museums, art is dated with *sec* for *secolo* (century, often indicated with Roman numerals), AC (*avanti Cristo*, or BC), and DC (*dopo Cristo*, or AD). OK?

Services: Important sights usually have a reasonably priced on-site café or cafeteria (handy places to rejuvenate during a long visit). The WCs at sights are free and generally clean.

Before Leaving: At the gift shop, scan the postcard rack or thumb through a guidebook to be sure that you haven't overlooked something that you'd like to see. Every sight or museum offers more than what is covered in this book. Use the information I provide as an introduction—not the final word.

FIND RELIGION

Churches offer some amazing art (usually free), a cool respite from heat, and a welcome seat.

A modest dress code—no bare shoulders or above-the-knee shorts or skirts for anyone, even kids—is strictly enforced at St. Peter's Basilica and the Sistine Chapel. To-the-knee shorts and skirts are usually permissible around the rest of Vatican City, in the Vatican Museums, and at Rome's major churches, such as St. Peter-in-Chains and St. Paul's Outside the Walls. The definition of what constitutes "modest" dress is at the discretion of church guards.

If you're most comfortable in shorts, carry a pair of lightweight pants or a skirt to pull on before entering places with stricter regulations. And anyone in a sleeveless shirt should carry a cover-up.

If you're caught by surprise, you can sometimes improvise, using maps to cover your shoulders and a jacket for your knees. A few major churches let you borrow or buy disposable ponchos to cover up in a pinch. (I wear a super-lightweight pair of long pants rather than shorts for my hot and muggy Italian sightseeing.) If your heart's set on seeing a certain church, err on the side of caution and dress appropriately. Note that major churches have security checks.

Some churches have coin-operated audioboxes that describe the art and history; just set the dial on English, put in your coins, and listen. Coin boxes near a piece of art illuminate the art. I pop in a coin whenever I can, to improve my experience (and photos), as a small contribution to that church, and as a courtesy to other visitors enjoying this great art. Whenever possible, let there be light.

Sleeping

Extensive and opinionated listings of good-value rooms are a major feature of this book's Sleeping sections. Rather than list accommodations scattered throughout a town, I choose hotels in my favorite neighborhoods that are convenient to your sightseeing.

My recommendations run the gamut, from dorm beds to fancy rooms with all of the comforts. I like places that are clean, central, relatively quiet at night, reasonably priced, friendly, small enough to have a hands-on owner or manager, and run with a respect for Italian traditions. I'm more impressed by a handy location and a fun-loving philosophy than flat-screen TVs and a fancy gym. Most of my recommendations fall short of perfection. But if I can find a place with most of these features, it's a keeper.

Book your accommodations as soon as your itinerary is set, especially if you want to stay at one of my top listings or if you'll be traveling during busy times. See the appendix for a list of major holidays and festivals in Italy.

RATES AND DEALS
I've categorized my recommended accommodations based on price, indicated with a dollar-sign rating (see sidebar). The price ranges suggest an estimated cost for a one-night stay in high season in a standard double room with a private toilet and shower, including breakfast, and assume you're booking directly with the hotel (not through a booking site, which extracts a commission). Room prices can fluctuate significantly with demand and amenities (size, views, room class, and so on), but relative price categories remain constant. Rome charges a hotel tax of €3-7 per person, per night, which must be paid in cash and is typically not included in the prices in this book. The only exemptions are for hostelers and children under age 10.

Sleep Code

Hotels are classified based on the average price of a standard double room with breakfast in high season.

$$$$	**Splurge:** Most rooms over €170
$$$	**Pricier:** €130-170
$$	**Moderate:** €90-130
$	**Budget:** €50-90
¢	**Backpacker:** Under €50
RS%	**Rick Steves discount**

Unless otherwise noted, credit cards are accepted, hotel staff speak basic English, and free Wi-Fi is available. Comparison-shop by checking prices at several hotels (on each hotel's own website, on a booking site, or by email). For the best deal, *book directly with the hotel*. Ask for a discount if paying in cash; if the listing includes **RS%**, request a Rick Steves discount.

Room rates are especially volatile at hotels that use "dynamic pricing" to set rates. Prices can skyrocket during festivals and conventions, while business hotels can have deep discounts on weekends when demand plummets. Of the many hotels I recommend, it's difficult to say which will be the best value on a given day—until you do your homework.

Booking Direct: Once your dates are set, compare prices at several hotels. You can do this by checking Hotels.com, Booking.com, and hotel websites. Then book directly with the hotel itself. Contact small family-run hotels directly by phone or email. When you go direct, the owner avoids the commission paid to booking sites, thereby leaving enough wiggle room to offer you a discount, a nicer room, or a free breakfast (if it's not already included). If you prefer to book online or are considering a hotel chain, it's to your advantage to use the hotel's website.

Booking directly also increases the chances that the hotelier will be able to accommodate any special needs or requests (such as shifting your reservation). Going through a middleman makes it more difficult for the hotel to adjust your booking.

Getting a Discount: Some hotels extend a discount to those who pay cash or stay longer than three nights. And some accommodations offer a special discount for Rick Steves readers, indicated in this guidebook by the abbreviation **"RS%."** Discounts vary: Ask for details when you reserve. Generally, to qualify for this discount, you must book direct (not through a booking site), mention this book when you reserve, show this book upon arrival, and sometimes pay cash or stay a certain number of nights. In some cases, you may need to enter a discount code (which I've provided in the listing) in the booking form on the hotel's website. Rick

Steves discounts apply to readers with either print or digital books. Understandably, discounts do not apply to promotional rates.

TYPES OF ACCOMMODATIONS
Hotels

In Rome, you can snare a spartan, clean, and comfortable double with breakfast and a private bath for about €100. You get near-elegance in peak season for €170. Rome's hoteliers are eager to fill their rooms in the off-season. Consider prices negotiable.

Some hotels can add an extra bed (for a small charge) to turn a double into a triple; some offer larger rooms for four or more people (I call these "family rooms" in the listings). If there's space for an extra cot, they'll cram it in for you. In general, a triple room is cheaper than the cost of a double and a single. Three or four people can economize by requesting one big room.

Arrival and Check-In: Hotels and B&Bs are sometimes located on the higher floors of a multipurpose building with a secured door. In that case, look for your hotel's name on the buttons by the main entrance. When you ring the bell, you'll be buzzed in.

Hotel elevators are common, though some older buildings still lack them. You may have to climb a flight of stairs to reach the elevator (if so, you can ask the front desk for help carrying your bags up). Elevators are typically very small—pack light, or you may need to send your bags up without you.

The EU requires that hotels collect your name, nationality, and ID number. When you check in, the receptionist will normally ask for your passport and may keep it for anywhere from a couple of minutes to a couple of hours. If you're not comfortable leaving your passport at the desk for a long time, ask when you can pick it up. Or, if you packed a color copy of your passport, you can generally leave that rather than the original.

If you're arriving in the morning, your room probably won't be ready. Check your bag safely at the hotel and dive right into sightseeing.

In Your Room: Traffic in Rome roars. Thanks to double-paned windows and air-conditioning, night noise is not the problem it once was. Even so, light sleepers who ask for a *tranquillo* room will likely get a room in the back...and sleep better. Once you actually see your room, consider the potential problem of night noise. Don't hesitate to ask for a quieter room.

Most hotel rooms have a TV, telephone, and free Wi-Fi (although in old buildings with thick walls, the Wi-Fi signal might be available only in the lobby). Simpler places rarely have a room phone. Pricier hotels usually come with a small fridge stocked with beverages, called a *frigo bar* (FREE-goh bar; pay for what you use).

More pillows and blankets are usually in the closet or avail-

Using Online Services to Your Advantage

From booking services to user reviews, online businesses play a greater role in travelers' planning than ever before. Take advantage of their pluses—and be wise to their downsides.

Booking Sites

Booking websites such as Booking.com and Hotels.com offer one-stop shopping for hotels. While convenient for travelers, they present a real problem for independent, family-run hotels. Without a presence on these sites, small hotels become almost invisible. But to be listed, a hotel must pay a sizeable commission... and promise that its own website won't undercut the price on the booking-service site.

Here's the work-around: Use the big sites to research what's out there, then book directly with the hotel by email or phone, in which case hotel owners are free to give you whatever price they like. Ask for a room without the commission mark-up (or ask for a free breakfast if not included, or a free upgrade). If you do book online, be sure to use the hotel's website. The price will likely be the same as via a booking site, but your money goes to the hotel, not agency commissions.

As a savvy consumer, remember: When you book with an online booking service, you're adding a middleman who takes roughly 20 percent. To support small, family-run hotels whose world is more difficult than ever, book direct.

Short-Term Rental Sites

Rental juggernaut Airbnb (along with other short-term rental sites) allows travelers to rent rooms and apartments directly from locals, often providing more value than a cookie-cutter hotel. Airbnb fans appreciate feeling part of a real neighborhood and getting into a daily routine as "temporary Europeans." Depending on the host, Airbnb can provide an opportunity to get to know a local person, while keeping the money spent on your accommo-

able on request. Towels and linens aren't always replaced every day. Some hotels use lightweight "waffle," or very thin, tablecloth-type towels; these take less water and electricity to launder and are preferred by many Italians.

Nearly all places offer private bathrooms, which have a tub or shower, a toilet, and a bidet (which Italians use for quick sponge baths). The cord over the tub or shower is not a clothesline. You pull it when you've fallen and can't get up.

Double beds are called *matrimoniale,* even though hotels aren't interested in your marital status. Twins are *due letti singoli.* Convents offer cheap accommodation but have more *letti singoli* than *matrimoniali.*

Breakfast and Meals: Italian hotels typically include break-

dations in the community.

Critics view Airbnb as a threat to "traditional Europe," saying it creates unfair, unqualified competition for established guest-house owners. In some places, the lucrative Airbnb market has forced traditional guesthouses out of business and is driving property values out of range for locals. Some cities have cracked down, requiring owners to occupy rental properties part of the year (and staging disruptive "inspections" that inconvenience guests).

As a lover of Europe, I share the worry of those who see residents nudged aside by tourists. But as an advocate for travelers, I appreciate the value and cultural intimacy Airbnb provides.

User Reviews

User-generated review sites and apps such as Yelp and TripAdvisor can give you a consensus of opinions about everything from hotels and restaurants to sights and nightlife. If you scan reviews of a restaurant or hotel and see several complaints about noise or a rotten location, you've gained insight that can help in your decision-making.

But as a guidebook writer, my sense is that there is a big difference between the uncurated information on a review site and the vetted listings in a guidebook. A user-generated review is based on the limited experience of one person, who stayed at just one hotel in a given city and ate at a few restaurants there. A guidebook is the work of a trained researcher who forms a well-developed basis for comparison by visiting many restaurants and hotels year after year.

Both types of information have their place, and in many ways, they're complementary. If something is well reviewed in a guidebook and it also gets good online reviews, it's likely a winner.

fast in their room prices. If breakfast is optional, you may want to skip it. While convenient, it's usually pricey for what you get: a simple continental buffet with (at its most generous) bread, croissants, ham, cheese, yogurt, and unlimited *caffè latte*. A picnic in your room followed by a coffee at the corner café can be lots cheaper.

Checking Out: While it's customary to pay for your room upon departure, it can be a good idea to settle your bill the day before, when you're not in a hurry and while the manager's in.

Hotelier Help: Hoteliers can be a good source of advice. Most know their city well, and can assist you with everything from public transit and airport connections to finding a good restaurant, the nearest launderette, or a late-night pharmacy.

Hotel Hassles: Even at the best places, mechanical break-

Making Hotel Reservations

Reserve your rooms as soon as you've pinned down your travel dates. For busy national holidays, it's wise to reserve far in advance (see the appendix).

Requesting a Reservation: For family-run hotels, it's generally best to book your room directly via email or phone. For business-class and chain hotels, or if you'd rather book online, reserve directly through the hotel's official website (not a booking website). Almost all of my recommended hotels take reservations in English.

Here's what the hotelier wants to know:
- Type(s) of rooms you want and size of your party
- Number of nights you'll stay
- Your arrival and departure dates, written European-style as day/month/year (for example, 18/06/21 or 18 June 2021);
- Special requests (en suite bathroom, cheapest room, twin beds vs. double bed, quiet room)
- Applicable discounts (such as a Rick Steves reader discount, cash discount, or promotional rate)

Confirming a Reservation: Most places will request a credit-card number to hold your room. If you're using an online reservation form, make sure it's secure by looking for the *https* or a lock icon at the top of your browser. If the hotel's website doesn't have a secure form where you can enter the number directly, it's best to share that confidential info via a phone call.

Canceling a Reservation: If you must cancel, it's courteous—and smart—to do so with as much notice as possible, especially for

downs occur: Sinks leak, hot water turns cold, toilets may gurgle or smell, the Wi-Fi goes out, or the air-conditioning dies when you need it most. Report your concerns clearly and calmly at the front desk.

To guard against theft in your room, keep valuables out of sight. Some rooms come with a safe, and other hotels have safes at the front desk. I've never bothered using one and, in a lifetime of travel, I've never had anything stolen out of my room.

For more complicated problems, don't expect instant results. Above all, keep a positive attitude. Remember, you're on vacation. If your hotel is a disappointment, spend more time out enjoying the place you came to see.

Bed-and-Breakfasts

B&Bs can offer good-value accommodations in excellent locations. Usually converted family homes or apartments, they can range from humble rooms with communal kitchens to high-end boutique accommodations with extra amenities. Boutique B&Bs can be an

From:	rick@ricksteves.com
Sent:	Today
To:	info@hotelcentral.com
Subject:	Reservation request for 19-22 July

Dear Hotel Central,

I would like to stay at your hotel. Please let me know if you have a room available and the price for:

- 2 people
- Double bed and en suite bathroom in a quiet room
- Arriving 19 July, departing 22 July (3 nights)

Thank you!
Rick Steves

smaller family-run places. Cancellation policies can be strict; read the fine print before you book. Many discount deals require pre-payment, with no cancellation refunds.

Reconfirming a Reservation: Always call or email to reconfirm your room reservation a few days in advance. For B&Bs or very small hotels, I call again on my day of arrival to tell my host what time to expect me (especially important if arriving late—after 17:00).

Phoning: For tips on calling hotels overseas, see page 574.

especially good option, as they are typically less expensive than a big hotel, but often newer and nicer, with more personal service. Because the B&B scene is constantly changing, it's smart to supplement this book's recommendations with your own research.

Be aware that B&Bs can suffer from absentee management. The proprietors often live off-site (or even in another town) and may be around only when they are expecting guests. Clearly communicate your arrival time, and after checking in, be sure you have your host's telephone number in case you need to reach them.

Short-Term Rentals

A short-term rental—whether an apartment, house, or room in a local's home—is an increasingly popular alternative, especially if you plan to settle in one location for several nights. For stays longer than a few days, you can usually find a rental that's comparable to—and even cheaper than—a hotel room with similar amenities. Plus, you'll get a behind-the-scenes peek into how locals live.

Many places require a minimum stay and have strict cancel-

Keep Cool

If you're visiting Italy in the summer, you'll want an air-conditioned room. Most hotel air-conditioners come with a control stick that generally has similar symbols and features: fan icon (click to toggle through wind power, from light to gale); temperature control (20 degrees Celsius is comfortable; louver icon (choose steady airflow or waves); snowflake and sunshine icons (cold air or heat); and clock ("O" setting: run X hours before turning off; "I" setting: wait X hours to start). When you leave your room for the day, turning off the air-conditioning is good form.

lation policies. And you're generally on your own: There's no hotel reception desk, breakfast, or daily cleaning service.

Finding Accommodations: Websites such as Airbnb, FlipKey, Booking.com, and the HomeAway family of sites (HomeAway, VRBO, and VacationRentals) let you browse a wide range of properties. Alternatively, rental agencies such as InterhomeUSA.com or RentaVilla.com, which list more carefully selected accommodations that might cost more, can provide more personalized service. Or try Cross-Pollinate, a booking service for private rooms and apartments in the old centers of Rome, Florence, and Venice; rates start at €30 per person (www.cross-pollinate. com). You can also browse through www.wantedinrome.com or other websites serving expats living in Rome.

Before you commit, be clear on the location. I like to virtually "explore" the neighborhood using the Street View feature on Google Maps. Also consider the proximity to public transportation, and how well connected the property is with the rest of the city. Ask about amenities (elevator, air-conditioning, laundry, Wi-Fi, parking, etc.). Reviews from previous guests can help identify trouble spots.

Think about the kind of experience you want: Just a key and an affordable bed...or a chance to get to know a local? There are typically two kinds of hosts: those who want minimal interaction with their guests, and hosts who are friendly and may want to interact with you. Read the promotional text and online reviews to help shape your decision.

Confirming and Paying: Many places require you to pay the entire balance before your trip. It's easiest and safest to pay through the site where you found the listing. Be wary of owners who want to take your transaction offline; this gives you no recourse if things go awry. Never agree to wire money (a key indicator of a fraudulent transaction).

Apartments: If you're staying in one place for four or more nights, it's worth considering an apartment (shorter stays aren't worth the hassle of arranging key pickup, buying groceries, etc.). Apartment rentals can be especially cost-effective for groups and families. European apartments, like hotel rooms, tend to be small by US standards. But they often come with laundry machines and small, equipped kitchens *(cucinetta)*, making it easier and cheaper to dine in.

Rooms in Private Homes: Renting a room in someone's home is a good option for those traveling alone, as you're more likely to find true single rooms—with just one single bed, and a price to match. Beds range from air-mattress-in-living-room basic to plush-B&B-suite posh. Some places allow you to book for a single night. While you can't expect your host to also be your tour guide—or even to provide you with much info—some may be interested in getting to know the travelers who come through their home.

Other Options: Swapping homes with a local works for people with an appealing place to offer (don't assume where you live is not interesting to Europeans). Good places to start are HomeExchange.com and LoveHomeSwap.com. To sleep for free, Couchsurfing.com is a vagabond's alternative to Airbnb. It lists millions of outgoing members, who host fellow "surfers" in their homes.

Hostels

A hostel provides cheap beds in dorms where you sleep alongside strangers for about €25-30 per night. Travelers of any age are welcome if they don't mind dorm-style accommodations and meeting other travelers. Most hostels offer kitchen facilities, guest computers, Wi-Fi, and a self-service laundry. Hostels almost always provide bedding, but the towel's up to you (though you can usually rent one for a small fee). Family and private rooms are often available.

Independent hostels tend to be easygoing, colorful, and informal (no membership required; www.hostelworld.com). You may pay slightly less by booking directly with the hostel. **Official hostels** are part of Hostelling International (HI) and share a booking site (www.hihostels.com). HI hostels typically require that you be a member or else pay a bit more per night.

If going the hostel route, consider the ones I list in the Sleeping in Rome chapter (within a 10-minute walk of Termini train station).

Convents

Nun-run places are common in Rome, offering cheap twin beds, little English, and an interesting experience. See the Sleeping in Rome chapter for listings.

Eating

The Italians are masters of the art of fine living. That means eating long and well. Lengthy, multicourse meals and endless hours sitting in outdoor cafés are the norm. Americans eat on their way to an evening event and complain if the check is slow in coming. For Italians, the meal is an end in itself, and only rude waiters rush you.

A highlight of your Italian adventure will be this country's cafés, cuisine, and wines. Trust me: This is sightseeing for your palate. Even if you liked dorm food and are sleeping in cheap hotels, your taste buds will relish an occasional first-class splurge. You can eat well without going broke. But be careful: You're just as likely to blow a small fortune on a disappointing meal as you are to dine wonderfully for €25. Rely on my recommendations in the Eating in Rome chapter.

In general, Italians eat meals a bit later than we do. Eating like a Roman means stopping at the neighborhood bar each morning for a light breakfast (coffee—usually cappuccino or espresso—and a pastry, often standing up at a café). Lunch (between 13:00 and 15:00) was traditionally the largest meal of the day, eaten at home, but work habits have changed this, and the family often doesn't come together until dinner. Instead, for lunch Italians grab a quick meal in a *tavola calda* bar (cafeteria) or buy a *panino* or *tramezzino* (sandwich). They eat a late dinner around 20:00-21:30, or maybe earlier in winter. To bridge the gap, people drop into a bar in the late afternoon for a *spuntino* (snack) and aperitif.

RESTAURANT PRICING

I've categorized my recommended eateries based on the average price of a typical main course, indicated with a dollar-sign rating (see sidebar). Obviously, expensive specialties, fine wine, appetizers, and dessert can significantly increase your final bill.

The categories also indicate the personality of a place: **Budget** eateries include street food, takeaway, order-at-the-counter shops, basic cafeterias, and bakeries selling sandwiches. **Moderate** eateries are nice (but not fancy) sit-down restaurants, ideal for a straightforward, fill-the-tank meal. Most of my listings fall in this category—great for a good taste of local cuisine at a reasonable price.

Pricier eateries are a notch up, with more attention paid to the setting, presentation, and (often inventive) cuisine. **Splurge** eateries are dress-up-for-a-special-occasion swanky—typically with an elegant setting, polished service, pricey and intricate cuisine, and an expansive (and expensive) wine list.

Restaurant Code

Eateries in this book are categorized according to the average cost of a typical main course. Drinks, desserts, and splurge items can raise the price considerably.

$$$$ **Splurge:** Most main courses over €20
$$$ **Pricier:** €15-20
$$ **Moderate:** €10-15
$ **Budget:** Under €10

Pizza by the slice and other takeaway food is **$**; a basic trattoria or sit-down pizzeria is **$$**; a casual but more upscale restaurant is **$$$**; and a swanky splurge is **$$$$**.

BREAKFAST

Italian breakfasts, like Italian bath towels, can be small: The basic, traditional version is coffee and a roll with butter and marmalade. Many places have yogurt and juice (the delicious red orange juice—*spremuta d'arancia rossa*—is made from Sicilian blood oranges), and possibly also cereal, cold cuts and sliced cheese, and eggs (typically hard-boiled; scrambled or fried eggs are less common). Small budget hotels may leave a basic breakfast in your room (stale croissant, roll, jam, yogurt, coffee).

If you want to skip your hotel breakfast, consider browsing for a morning picnic at a local open-air market. Or do as the Italians do: Stop into a bar or café to drink a cappuccino and munch a *cornetto* (croissant) while standing at the bar. While the *cornetto* is the most common pastry, you'll find a range of *pasticcini* (pastries, sometimes called *dolci*—sweets). Look for *otto* (an 8-shaped pastry, often filled with custard, jam, or chocolate), *sfoglia* (filo-dough crust that's fruit-filled, like a turnover), or *ciambella* (doughnut filled with custard or chocolate)—or ask about local specialties.

ITALIAN RESTAURANTS

While *ristorante* is self-explanatory, you'll also see other types of Italian eateries. A trattoria and an osteria (which can be more casual) are both generally family-owned places serving home-cooked meals, often at moderate prices. A *locanda* is an inn, a *cantina* is a wine cellar, and a *birreria* is a brewpub. *Pizzerie, ros-*

PRACTICALITIES

ticcerie (delis), *tavola calda* ("hot table") bars, *enoteche* (wine bars), and other alternatives are explained later.

I look for restaurants that are convenient to hotels and sight-seeing. When restaurant-hunting, choose a spot filled with locals, not the place with the big neon signs boasting, "We speak English and accept credit cards." Restaurants parked on famous squares generally serve bad food at high prices to tourists. Venturing even a block or two off the main drag leads to higher-quality food for less than half the price of the tourist-oriented places. Locals eat better at lower-rent locales. Family-run places operate without hired help and can offer cheaper meals.

Most restaurant kitchens close between their lunch and dinner service. Good restaurants don't reopen for dinner before 19:00. If you arrive at opening time, most restaurants will be empty and available—the main push of customers arrives later. Small restaurants with a full slate of reservations for 20:30 or 21:00 often will accommodate walk-in diners willing to eat a quick, early meal, but you aren't expected to linger.

When you want the bill, mime-scribble on your raised palm or request it: *"Il conto, per favore."* You may have to ask more than once. If you're in a hurry, request the check when you receive the last item you order.

Cover and Tipping

Avoid surprises when eating out by familiarizing yourself with two common Italian restaurant charges: *coperto* and *servizio.* You won't encounter them in all restaurants, but both charges, if assessed, by law must be listed on the menu.

The *coperto* (cover), sometimes called *pane e coperto* (bread and cover), is a minor fee (€1.50-3/person) covering the cost of the typical basket of bread, oil, salt, cutlery, and linens found on your table. It's not negotiable, even if you don't eat the bread. And it's not a tip (it goes to the owner)—think of it as entitling you to use the table for as long as you like.

The *servizio* (a 10- to 15-percent service charge) is similar to the mandatory gratuity that American restaurants often add for groups of six or more. You can consider it a "tourist tax," as you're most likely to encounter it in locations with lots of tourists. Because the service charge is sometimes built into your bill, look carefully at your check to see if you've already paid a tip—don't leave any tip beyond this.

If there is no *servizio* on the bill, a common **tip** at a simple restaurant or pizzeria is €1 per person at the table (or simply round up the bill). At a finer restaurant, leave a few euros per person. Don't leave the tip on the table; hand it directly to the server to make sure he or she receives it. Be prepared to tip with cash/coins, as credit/debit card receipts won't have a tip line as in the US.

Italian Menu Courses

A full Italian meal consists of multiple courses (all described below). For most travelers, it's simply too much food—and the euros can add up in a hurry. To avoid overeating (and to stretch your budget), share dishes. A good rule of thumb is for each person to order any two courses. For example, a couple can order and share one antipasto, one *primo*, one *secondo*, and one dessert; or two *antipasti* and two *primi;* or whatever combination appeals.

Small groups can mix *antipasti* and *primi* family-style (skipping *secondi*). If you do this right, you can eat well in better places for less than the cost of a tourist *menù* in a cheap place.

Some touristy restaurants serve a *piatto unico*, with smaller portions of each course on one dish (for instance, a meat, starch, and vegetable).

Antipasto: An appetizer such as bruschetta, grilled veggies, deep-fried tasties, thin-sliced meat (prosciutto or carpaccio), or a plate of olives, cold cuts, and cheeses. To get a sampler plate of cold cuts and cheeses in a restaurant, ask for *affettato misto* (mixed cold cuts), antipasto *misto* (cold cuts, cheeses, and marinated vegetables), or *tagliere* (a sampler "board"). This could make a light meal in itself.

Primo piatto: A "first dish" generally consisting of pasta but also rice or soup. If you think of pasta when you think of Italian food, you can dine well here without ever going beyond the *primo*.

Secondo piatto: A "second dish," equivalent to our main course, of meat or fish/seafood. Italians freely admit the *secondo* is the least interesting part of their cuisine.

Contorno: A vegetable side dish may come with the *secondo* but more often must be ordered separately. Typical *contorni* are *insalata mista*, spinach, roasted potatoes, or grilled veggies. This can be an interesting, if overlooked, part of the menu. Vegetarians can skip the *secondo* and order several *contorni* to make a meal.

Dolce: No meal is complete without a sweet. On most menus you'll find typical Italian desserts such as tiramisu and *panna cotta* as well as local favorites.

Ordering Tips

Seafood and steak may be sold by weight and priced by the *etto* (100 grams, 3.5 ounces) or the *kilo* (1,000 grams, 2.2 pounds). The abbreviation *s.q. (secondo quantità)* indicates an item is priced by weight (often used at antipasto buffets). Unless the menu indicates a fillet *(filetto)*, fish is usually served whole with the head and tail. However, you can always ask your server to select a small fish and fillet it for you. Sometimes, especially for steak, restaurants require a minimum order of four or five *etti* (which diners can share). Make sure you're clear on the price before ordering.

Some special dishes come in larger quantities meant to be shared by two people. The shorthand way of showing this on a menu is "X2" (for two), but the price listed could indicate the cost per person.

In a traditional restaurant, if you order a pasta dish and a side salad—but no main course—the server will bring the salad after the pasta (Italians prefer it this way, believing that it enhances digestion). If you want the salad with your pasta, specify *insieme* (een-see-EH-meh; together).

Because pasta and bread are both starches, Italians consider them redundant. If you order only a pasta dish, bread may not come with it; you can request it, but you may be charged extra. On the other hand, if you order a vegetable antipasto or a meat *secondo*, bread is often provided to balance the ingredients.

At places with counter service—such as at a bar or a freeway rest-stop diner—you'll order and pay at the *cassa* (cashier). Take your receipt to the counter to claim your food.

Fixed-Price Meals and Ordering à la Carte

You can save by getting a fixed-priced meal, which is frequently exempt from cover and service charges. Avoid the cheapest ones (often called a *menù turistico*). Look instead for a genuine *menù del giorno* (menu of the day), which offers diners a choice of appetizer, main course, and dessert. It's worth paying a little more for an inventive fixed-price meal that shows off the chef's creativity.

While fixed-price meals can be easy and convenient, galloping gourmets prefer to order à la carte with the help of a menu translator. When going to an especially good restaurant with an approachable staff, I like to find out what they're eager to serve. Sometimes I'll simply say, *"Mi faccia felice"* ("Make me happy") and set a price limit.

BUDGET EATING

Italy offers many budget options for hungry travelers.

Self-service cafeterias offer the basics without add-on charges. Travelers on a hard-core budget equip their room with a pantry stocked at the market (fruits and veggies are remarkably cheap), or pick up a sandwich or *döner kebab*, then dine in at picnic prices. Bars and cafés are also good places to grab a meal on the go.

Pizzerias

Pizza is cheap and readily available. Stop by a pizza shop for stand-up or takeout (many pizza places sell whole pies meant for one person; *pizza al taglio* means "by the slice"). Supermarkets usually have a pizza counter too.

Some shops feature *pizza rustica*—thick pizza baked in a large rectangular pan and sold by weight. If you simply ask for a piece, you may wind up

with a gigantic slab and be charged top euro. Instead, clearly indicate how much you want: 100 grams, or *un etto,* is a hot and cheap snack; 200 grams, or *due etti,* makes a light meal. Or show the size with your hands—*tanto così* (TAHN-toh koh-ZEE; this much). They'll often helpfully cut it up into smaller pieces. If you want your pizza warm, say *"si"* when they ask if you want it heated up (*riscaldare;* ree-skahl-DAH-ray). For a rundown of common types of pizza, see that section, later.

Bars/Cafés

Italian "bars" are not taverns, but inexpensive cafés. These neighborhood hangouts serve coffee, mini pizzas *(pizzette),* sandwiches, and drinks from the cooler. This budget choice is the Italian equivalent of English pub grub.

Many bars are small—if you can't find a table, you'll need to stand or find a ledge to sit on outside. Most charge extra for table service. All bars have a WC *(toilette, bagno)* in the back, and customers—and the discreet public—can use it.

Food: For quick meals, bars usually have trays of cheap, premade sandwiches (*panini,* on a baguette; *piadine,* on flatbread; or *tramezzini,* on crustless white bread)—some are delightful grilled. (Others have too much mayo.) In bigger cities, they'll have a variety of salads ready to serve up from under the glass counter. To save time for sightseeing and room for dinner, stop by a bar for a light lunch, such as a ham-and-cheese sandwich (called *toast*); have it grilled twice if you want it really hot.

Prices and Paying: You'll notice a two- or three-tiered pricing system. Drinking a cup of coffee while standing at the bar is cheaper than drinking it at an indoor table (you'll pay still more at an outdoor table). Many places have a *lista dei prezzi* (price list) with two columns—*al bar* and *al tavolo* (table)—posted somewhere by the bar or cash register. If you're on a budget, don't sit down without first checking out the financial consequences. Ask, "Same price if I sit or stand?" by saying, *"Costa uguale al tavolo o al banco?"* (KOH-stah oo-GWAH-lay ahl TAH-voh-loh oh ahl BAHN-koh). Throughout Italy, you can get cheap coffee at the bar of any establishment, no matter how fancy, and pay the same low, government-regulated price (generally a euro or less if you stand).

If the bar isn't busy, you can probably just order and pay when you leave. Otherwise: 1) Decide what you want; 2) find out the price by checking the price list on the wall, the prices posted near the food, or by asking the barista; 3) pay the cashier; and 4) give the receipt to the barista (whose clean fingers handle no dirty euros) and tell him or her what you want.

International Cuisine

A good bet for a cheap, hot meal is a *döner kebab* (Middle Eastern-style rotisserie meat wrapped in pita bread). Look for little hole-in-the-wall kebab shops (especially around Termini Station and Santa Maria Maggiore), where you can get a hearty takeaway dinner—either as a sandwich or a wrap—for about €3. Asian restaurants, although not as common as in northern Europe, can also be a good value.

Tavola Calda Bars and *Rosticcerie*

For a fast and cheap lunch, find an Italian variation on the corner deli: a *rosticceria* (specializing in roasted meats and accompanying *antipasti*) or a *tavola calda* bar (a "hot table" point-and-shoot cafeteria with a buffet spread of meat and vegetables). For a healthy light meal, ask for a mixed plate of vegetables with a hunk of mozzarella (*piatto misto di verdure con mozzarella;* pee-AH-toh MEE-stoh dee vehr-DOO-ray). Don't be limited by what's displayed. If you'd like a salad with a slice of cantaloupe and a hunk of cheese, they'll whip that up for you in a snap. Belly up to the bar; with a pointing finger, you can assemble a fine meal. If something's a mystery, ask for *un assaggio* (oon ah-SAH-joh) to get a little taste. To have your choices warmed up, ask for them to be heated (*riscaldare;* ree-skahl-DAH-ray).

Wine Bars

Wine bars *(enoteche)* are a popular, fast, and inexpensive option for lunch. Surrounded by the office crowd, you can get a salad, a plate of meats (cold cuts) and cheeses, and a glass of good wine (see blackboards for the day's selection and price per glass). A good *enoteca* aims to impress visitors with its wine, and will generally feature excellent-quality ingredients for the simple dishes it offers with the wine (though the prices add up—be careful with your ordering to keep this a budget choice). The area around the Pantheon and Piazza del Parlamento (popular with politicians and bureaucrats) has plenty of *enoteche* handy for a sightseeing lunch break or evening destination. For more on Italian cocktails and wines, see page 570.

Aperitivo Buffets

The Italian term *aperitivo* means a pre-dinner drink, but it's also used to describe their version of what we might call happy hour: a light buffet that many bars serve to customers during the pre-dinner hours (typically around 18:00 or 19:00 until 21:00). The drink itself may not be cheap (typically around €8-12), but bars lay out an enticing array of meats, cheeses, grilled vegetables, and other *antipasti*-type dishes, and you're welcome to nibble to your heart's content while you nurse your drink. While it's intended as an appetizer course before heading out for a full dinner, light eaters could discreetly turn this into a small meal. Bars advertising *"apericena"* (*cena* means dinner) tend to have buffets hearty enough to pass as dinner. Drop by a few bars around this time to scope out their buffets before choosing.

Markets, Groceries, and Delis: Assembling a Picnic

Picnicking saves lots of euros and is a great way to sample regional specialties. A picnic can even be an adventure in high cuisine. Be daring. Try the fresh ricotta, *presto* pesto, shriveled olives, and any regional specialties the locals are excited about.

Markets: For the most colorful experience, gather your ingredients in the morning at a produce market. Towns big and small have markets selling everything imaginable for a fantastic picnic, including cheese, meat, bread, sweets, and prepared foods. You'll often find street-food stalls tucked into the marketplace as well (note that many stalls close in the early afternoon).

Groceries and Delis: Another budget option is to visit a supermarket (look for the Conad, Carrefour, and Co-op chains), *alimentari* (neighborhood grocery), or *salumeria* (delicatessen) to pick up cold cuts, cheeses, and other picnic supplies. Some grocery stores, *salumerie,* and any *paninoteca* or *focacceria* (sandwich shop) can make a sandwich to order. Just point to what you want, and they'll stuff it into a *panino*. Almost every grocery store has a deli case with prepared items like stuffed peppers, lasagna, olives, or chicken, all usually sold by weight; if you want it reheated, remember the word *riscaldare* (ree-skahl-DAH-ray). And *rosticcerie* sell cheap food to go—you'll find options such as lasagna, rotisserie chicken, and sides including roasted potatoes and spinach. For more on *salumi* and cheeses, see those sections, later.

Ordering: A typical picnic might be fresh rolls, *un etto* (quarter-pound) of cheese, and *un etto* of meat (sometimes ordered by the slice—*fetta*—or piece—*pezzo*).

For two people, I might also get *un etto* of prosciutto and *due pezzi* of bread. Add two tomatoes, three carrots, two apples, yogurt, and a liter box of juice. Total cost: about €10.

If ordering *antipasti* (such as grilled or marinated veggies) at a deli counter, you can ask for *una porzione* in a takeaway container *(contenitore)*. Use gestures to show exactly how much you want. To set a price limit on what you order, say *"Da __ euro, per favore."* The word *basta* (BAH-stah; enough) works as a question or as a statement.

Shopkeepers are happy to sell small quantities of produce, but it's customary to let the merchant choose for you. Say *"per oggi"* (pehr OH-jee; for today) and he or she will grab you something ready to eat. To avoid being overcharged, know the cost per kilo, study the weighing procedure, and do the arithmetic. Remember that a kilo is 2.2 pounds.

ITALIAN CUISINE STAPLES

Much of your Italian eating experience will likely involve the big five: pizza, pasta, *salumi*, cheese, and gelato. For a look at cuisine you'll likely find in Rome, see the sidebar on page 394. For more food help, try a menu translator, such as the *Rick Steves Italian Phrase Book & Dictionary*, which has a menu decoder and plenty of useful phrases for navigating the culinary scene.

Pizza

Here are some of the pizzas you might see at restaurants or at a pizzeria. Note that if you ask for pepperoni on your pizza, you'll get *peperoni* (green or red peppers, not sausage); request *diavola*, *salsiccia piccante*, or *salame piccante* instead (the closest thing in Italy to American pepperoni).

Bianca: White pizza with no tomatoes

Capricciosa: Prosciutto, mushrooms, olives, and artichokes—literally the chef's "caprice"

Funghi: Mushrooms

Margherita: Tomato sauce, mozzarella, and basil—the red, white, and green of the Italian flag

Marinara: Tomato sauce, oregano, garlic, no cheese

Eating with the Seasons

Italian cooks love to serve fresh produce and seafood at its tastiest. Each region in Italy has its seasonal specialties, which you'll see displayed in open-air markets. To get a plate of the freshest veggies at a fine restaurant, request *"Un piatto di verdure della stagione, per favore."* ("A plate of seasonal vegetables, please."). Italians take fresh, seasonal ingredients so seriously that a restaurant cooking with frozen ingredients *(congelato)* must note it on the menu. Here are a few examples of what's fresh when:

April-May: Romanesco (similar to cauliflower), fava beans, green beans, artichokes

April-May and Sept-Oct: Black truffles

April-June: Asparagus, zucchini flowers, zucchini

May-June: Mussels, cantaloupe, loquats, strawberries

May-Aug: Eggplant, clams

July-Sept: Figs

Oct-Nov: Mushrooms, white truffles, persimmons, chestnuts

Nov-Feb: Cardoon (wild artichoke), *puntarelle* (chicory shoots)

Napoletana: Mozzarella, anchovies, and tomato sauce
Ortolana or *vegetariana:* "Greengrocer-style," with vegetables
Quattro formaggi: Four different cheeses
Quattro stagioni: Different toppings on each of the four quarters

Pasta

While we think of pasta as a main dish, in Italy it's considered a *primo piatto*—first course. There are more than 600 varieties of Italian pasta, and each is specifically used to highlight a certain sauce, meat, or regional ingredient. Most pastas in Italy are made fresh.

Italian pasta falls into two broad categories: *pasta lunga* (long pasta) and *pasta corta* (short pasta).

Pasta lunga can be round, such as *capellini* (thin "little hairs"), *vermicelli* ("little worms"), and *bucatini* (long and hollow), or it can be flat, such as *linguine* (narrow "little tongues"), *fettuccine* (wider "small ribbons"), *tagliatelle* (even wider), and *pappardelle* (very wide, best with meat sauces).

The most common *pasta corta* are tubes, such as *penne, rigatoni, ziti, manicotti,* and *cannelloni;* they come either *lisce* (smooth) or *rigate* (grooved—better to catch and cling to sauce). Many short pastas are named for their shapes, such as *conchiglie* (shells), *farfalle* (butterflies), or *cavatappi* (corkscrews).

Here's a list of common pasta toppings and sauces. On a menu, these terms are usually preceded by *alla* (in the style of) or *in* (in):

Aglio e olio: Garlic and olive oil

Alfredo: Butter, cream, and parmesan

Amatriciana: Pork cheek, *pecorino romano* cheese, and tomato

Arrabbiata: "Angry," spicy tomato sauce with chili peppers

Bolognese: Meat and tomato sauce

Boscaiola: Mushrooms and sausage

Burro e salvia: Butter and sage

Cacio e pepe: *Pecorino romano* cheese and ground pepper.

Carbonara: Bacon, egg, cheese, and pepper

Carrettiera: Spicy and garlicky, with olive oil and little tomatoes

Diavola: "Devil-style," spicy hot

Frutti di mare: Seafood

Genovese: Basil ground with *parmigiano* cheese, garlic, pine nuts, and olive oil; a.k.a. pesto

Gricia: Cured pork cheek and *pecorino romano* cheese

Marinara: Usually tomato, often with garlic and onions, but can also be a seafood sauce ("sailor's style")

Norma: Tomato, eggplant, and ricotta cheese

Pajata: Calf intestines (also called *pagliata*)

Pescatora: Seafood ("fisherman style")

Pomodoro: Tomato only

Puttanesca: "Harlot-style" tomato sauce with anchovies, olives, and capers.

Ragù: Meaty tomato sauce

Scoglio: Mussels, clams, and tomatoes

Sorrentina: "Sorrento-style," with tomatoes, basil, and mozzarella (usually over gnocchi)

Sugo di lepre: Rich sauce made of wild hare

Tartufi: Truffles (also called *tartufate*)

Umbria: Sauce of anchovies, garlic, tomatoes, and truffles

Vongole: Clams and spices

Salumi

Salumi (cured meats), also called *affettati* (sliced meats), are an Italian staple. While most American cold cuts are cooked, in Italy they're far more commonly cured by air-drying, salting, and smoking. (Don't worry; these so-called "raw" meats are safe to eat, and you can really taste the difference.)

The two most familiar types of *salumi* are *salame* and *pro-*

sciutto. Salame is an air-dried, sometimes-spicy sausage that comes in many varieties. When Italians say *"prosciutto,"* they usually mean *prosciutto crudo*—the raw ham that air-cures on the hock and is then thinly sliced. Produced mainly in the north of Italy, *prosciutto* can be either *dolce* (sweet) or *salato* (salty). Purists say the best is *prosciutto di Parma*.

Other *salumi* may be less familiar:

Bresaola: Air-cured beef

Capocollo: Peppery pork shoulder (also called *coppa*)

Culatello: High quality, slow-cured prosciutto

Finocchiona: *Salame* with fennel seeds

Lonzino: Cured pork loin

Mortadella: A finely ground pork loaf, similar to our bologna

Pancetta: Salt-cured, peppery pork-belly meat, similar to bacon

Guanciale: Tender pork cheek

Salame di Sant'Olcese: What we'd call "Genoa salami"

Salame piccante: Spicy hot, similar to pepperoni

Speck: Smoked pork shoulder

If you've got a weak stomach, avoid *testa in cassetta* (head-cheese—organs in aspic) and *lampredotto* (cow stomach).

Cheese

When it comes to cheese *(formaggio),* you're probably already familiar with most of these Italian favorites:

Asiago: Hard cow cheese that comes either *mezzano* (young, firm, and creamy) or *stravecchio* (aged, pungent, and granular)

Burrata: A creamy mozzarella

Fontina: Semihard, nutty, Gruyère-style mountain cheese

Gorgonzola: Pungent, blue-veined cheese, either *dolce* (creamy) or *stagionato* (aged and hard)

Mascarpone: Sweet, buttery, spreadable dessert cheese

Mozzarella di bufala: Made from the milk of water buffaloes

Parmigiano-reggiano: Hard, crumbly, sharp, aged cow cheese with more nuanced flavor than American parmesan; *grana padano* is a less expensive variation

Pecorino: Either *fresco* (fresh, soft, and mild) or *stagionato* (aged and sharp, sometimes called *pecorino romano*)

Provolone: Rich, firm, aged cow cheese

Ricotta: Soft, airy cheese made by "recooking" leftover whey

Scamorza: Similar to mozzarella, but often smoked

Gelato

American ice cream and Italian gelato are similar but decidedly not the same. Gelato is denser and creamier (even though it has less butterfat than ice cream), and connoisseurs swear it's more flavorful.

A key to gelato appreciation is sampling liberally and choosing flavors that go well together. At a *gelateria*, ask, as Italians do, for a taste: *"Un assaggio, per favore?"* (oon ah-SAH-joh pehr fah-VOH-ray). You can also ask what flavors go well together: *"Quali gusti stanno bene insieme?"* (KWAH-lee GOO-stee STAH-noh BEH-nay een-see-EH-may).

Most *gelaterie* clearly display prices and sizes. But in the textbook *gelateria* scam, the tourist orders two or three flavors—and the clerk selects a fancy, expensive chocolate-coated waffle cone, piles it high with huge scoops, and cheerfully charges the tourist €10. To avoid rip-offs, point to the price or say what you want—for instance, a €3 cup: *"Una coppetta da tre euro"* (OO-nah koh-PEH-tah dah tray eh-OO-roh).

The best *gelaterie* display signs reading *artigianale, nostra produzione,* or *produzione propria,* indicating that the gelato is made on the premises. Seasonal flavors are also a good sign, as are mellow hues (avoid colors that don't appear in nature). Gelato stored in covered metal tins (rather than white plastic) is more likely to be homemade. Gourmet gelato shops are popping up all over Italy, selling exotic flavors. Unless it's a gelato emergency, avoid the chain called Grom—it's the Starbucks of gelato in Italy.

Gelato variations or alternatives include *sorbetto* (sorbet—made with fruit, but no milk or eggs); *granita* or *grattachecca* (a cup of slushy ice with flavored syrup); and *cremolata* (a gelato-*granita* float).

Classic gelato flavors include:

After Eight: Chocolate and mint
Bacio: Chocolate hazelnut, named for Italy's popular "kiss" candies
Cassata: With dried fruits
Cioccolato: Chocolate
Crema: Vanilla
Croccantino: "Crunchy," with toasted peanut bits
Fior di latte: Sweet milk
Fragola: Strawberry
Macedonia: Mixed fruits
Malaga: Similar to rum raisin
Riso: With actual bits of rice mixed in
Stracciatella: Vanilla with chocolate shreds
Tartufo: Super chocolate
Zabaione: Named for the egg yolk-and-Marsala wine dessert
Zuppa inglese: Sponge cake, custard, chocolate, and cream

BEVERAGES

Italian bars serve great drinks—hot, cold, sweet, caffeinated, or alcoholic.

Water, Juice, and Cold Drinks

Italians are notorious water snobs. At restaurants, your server just can't understand why you wouldn't want good water to go with your good food. It's customary and never expensive to order a *litro* or *mezzo litro* (half-liter) of bottled water. *Acqua leggermente effervescente* (lightly carbonated water) is a mealtime favorite. Or simply ask for *con gas* if you want fizzy water and *senza gas* if you prefer still water. You can ask for *acqua del rubinetto* (tap water) in restaurants, but your server may give you a funny look. Chilled bottled water—still *(naturale)* or carbonated *(frizzante)*—is sold cheap in stores. Half-liter bottles of mineral water are available everywhere for about €1. (I refill my water bottle with tap water.)

Juice is *succo*, and *spremuta* means freshly squeezed. Order *una spremuta* (don't confuse it with *spumante*, sparkling wine)—it's usually orange juice *(arancia)*, and from February through April it's almost always made from Sicilian blood oranges *(arance rosse)*.

In grocery stores, you can get a liter of O.J. for the price of a Coke or coffee. Look for *100% succo* or *senza zucchero* (without sugar) on the label—or be surprised by something diluted and sugary sweet. Hang on to your water bottles. Buy juice in cheap liter boxes, then drink some and store the extra in your water bottle.

Tè freddo (iced tea) is usually from a can—sweetened and flavored with lemon or peach. Lemonade is *limonata*.

Coffee and Other Hot Drinks

The espresso-based style of coffee so popular in the US was born in Italy. If you ask for *"un caffè,"* you'll get a shot of espresso in a little cup—the closest thing to American-style drip coffee is a *caffè americano*. Most Italian coffee drinks begin with espresso, to which they add varying amounts of hot water and/or steamed or foamed milk. Milky drinks, like cappuccino or *caffè latte*, are served to locals before noon and to tourists any time of day (to an Italian, cappuccino is a morning drink; they believe having milk after a big meal or anything with tomato sauce impairs digestion). If they add any milk after lunch, it's just a splash, in a *caffè macchiato*. Italians like their coffee only warm—to get it very hot, request *"Molto caldo, per favore"* (MOHL-toh KAHL-doh pehr fah-VOH-ray). Any coffee drink is available decaffeinated—ask for it *decaffeinato* (deh-kah-feh-NAH-toh).

If you want a hot drink other than coffee, *cioccolato* is hot chocolate, and *tè* is hot tea.

Cappuccino: Espresso with foamed milk on top (*cappuccino freddo* is iced cappuccino)

Caffè latte: Espresso mixed with hot milk, no foam, in a tall glass (ordering just a "latte" gets you only milk)

Caffè macchiato: Espresso "marked" with a splash of milk, in a small cup

Latte macchiato: Layers of hot milk and foam, "marked" by an espresso shot, in a tall glass. Note that if you order simply a "*macchiato,*" you'll probably get a *caffè macchiato.*

Caffè corto/lungo: Concentrated espresso diluted with a tiny bit of hot water, in a small cup

Caffè americano: Espresso diluted with even more hot water, in a larger cup

Caffè corretto: Espresso "corrected" with a shot of liqueur (normally *grappa, amaro,* or *sambuca*)

Marocchino: "Moroccan" coffee with espresso, foamed milk, and cocoa powder; the similar *mocaccino* has chocolate instead of cocoa

Caffè freddo: Sweet and iced espresso

Caffè hag: Instant decaf

Alcoholic Beverages

Beer: While Italy is traditionally considered wine country, in recent years there's been a huge and passionate growth in the production of craft beer *(birra artigianale).* Even in small towns, you'll see microbreweries slinging their own brews. You'll also find local brews (Peroni and Moretti), as well as imports such as Heineken. Italians drink mainly lager beers. Beer on tap is *alla spina.* Get it *piccola* (33 cl, 11 oz), *media* (50 cl, about a pint), or *grande* (a liter). A *lattina* (lah-TEE-nah) is a can and a *bottiglia* (boh-TEEL-yah) is a bottle.

Cocktails and Spirits: Italians appreciate both *aperitivi* (palate-stimulating cocktails) and *digestivi* (after-dinner drinks designed to aid digestion). Popular *aperitivo* options include Campari (dark-colored bitters with herbs and orange peel), Americano (vermouth with bitters, brandy, and lemon peel), Cynar (bitters flavored with artichoke), and Punt e Mes (sweet red vermouth and red wine). Widely used vermouth brands include Cinzano and Martini.

Digestivo choices are usually either strong herbal bitters or something sweet. Many restaurants have their own secret recipe for a bittersweet herbal brew called *amaro;* popular commercial brands are Fernet Branca and Montenegro. If your tastes run sweeter, try any of these flavored liqueurs: *amaretto* (almond), Frangelico (hazelnut), *limoncello* (lemon), *nocino* (walnut), *sambuca* (anise), or a sweet Marsala wine. *Grappa* is a brandy distilled from grape skins and stems; *stravecchio* is an aged, mellower variation.

Wine: The ancient Greeks who colonized Italy more than 2,000 years ago called it Oenotria—land of the grape. Centuries later, Galileo wrote, "Wine is light held together by water." Wine *(vino)* is certainly a part of the Italian culinary trinity—grape, olive, and wheat.

Ordering Wine

To order a glass of red or white wine, say, *"Un bicchiere di vino rosso/bianco."* House wine comes in a carafe; choose from a quarter-liter pitcher (8.5 oz, *un quarto*), half-liter pitcher (17 oz, *un mezzo*), or one-liter pitcher (34 oz, *un litro*). When ordering, have some fun, gesture like a local, and you'll have no problems speaking the language of the *enoteca*. *Salute!*

English	Italian
wine	*vino* (VEE-noh)
house wine	*vino della casa* (VEE-noh DEH-lah KAH-zah)
glass	*bicchiere/calice* (bee-kee-EH-ray/KAH-lee-chay)
bottle	*bottiglia* (boh-TEEL-yah)
carafe	*caraffa* (kah-RAH-fah)
red	*rosso* (ROH-soh)
white	*bianco* (bee-AHN-koh)
rosé	*rosato* (roh-ZAH-toh)
sparkling	*spumante/frizzante* (spoo-MAHN-tay/freed-ZAHN-tay)
dry	*secco* (SEH-koh)
fruity	*fruttato* (froo-TAH-toh)
full-bodied	*corposo/pieno* (kor-POH-zoh/pee-EH-noh)
sweet	*dolce* (DOHL-chay)

(I'd add gelato.) Ideal conditions for grapes (warm climate, well-draining soil, and an abundance of hillsides) make the Italian peninsula a paradise for grape growers, winemakers, and wine drinkers.

Even if you're clueless about wine, the information on an Italian wine label can help you choose something decent. Terms you

may see on the bottle include *classico* (from a defined, select area), *annata* (year of harvest), *vendemmia* (harvest), and *imbottigliato dal produttore all'origine* (bottled by producers).

In general, Italy designates its wines by one of four official categories:

Vino da Tavola (VDT) is table wine, the lowest grade, made from grapes grown anywhere in Italy. It's often inexpensive, but Italy's wines are so good that, for many people, a basic *vino da tavola* is just fine with a meal. Many restaurants, even modest ones, take pride in their house wine *(vino della casa)*, bottling their own or working with wineries.

Hurdling the Language Barrier

Many Italians—especially those in the tourist trade and in big cities—speak English. Still, you'll get better treatment if you learn and use Italian pleasantries. In smaller, nontouristy towns, Italian is the norm. Italians have an endearing habit of talking to you even if they know you don't speak their language—and yet, thanks to gestures and thoughtfully simplified words, it somehow works. Don't stop them to tell them you don't understand every word—just go along for the ride. For a list of survival phrases, see the appendix.

Note that Italian is pronounced much like English, with a few exceptions, such as: c followed by e or i is pronounced ch (to ask, *"Per centro?"* "To the center?" you say, pehr CHEHN-troh). In Italian, ch followed by e or i is pronounced like the hard c in Chianti (*chiesa*—church—is pronounced kee-AY-zah). Adding a vowel to the English word often gets you close to the Italian one. Give it your best shot. Italians appreciate your efforts.

For more tips on hurdling the language barrier, consider the *Rick Steves Italian Phrase Book* (available at www. ricksteves.com).

Denominazione di Origine Controllata (DOC) meets national standards for high-quality wine. Made from grapes grown in a defined area, it's usually quite affordable and can be surprisingly good. Hundreds of wines have earned the DOC designation.

Denominazione di Origine Controllata e Guarantita (DOCG), the highest grade, meets national standards for the highest-quality wine (made with grapes from a defined area whose quality is "guaranteed"). These wines can be identified by the pink or green label on the neck...and the scary price tag on the shelf. They're generally a good bet if you want a quality wine, but you don't know anything else about the winemaker. (*Riserva* indicates a DOC or DOCG wine that's been aged for even longer than required.)

Indicazione Geografica Tipica (IGT) is a broad group of wines that don't meet the standard for DOC or DOCG status, but have been designated as "typical" of a particular region.

Staying Connected

One of the most common questions I hear from travelers is, "How can I stay connected in Europe?" The short answer is: more easily and cheaply than you might think.

The simplest solution is to bring your own device—mobile phone, tablet, or laptop—and use it just as you would at home (following the money-saving tips below, such as getting an international plan or connecting to free Wi-Fi whenever possible). Another option is to buy a European SIM card for your US mobile phone. Or you can use European landlines and computers to connect. Each of these options is described next, and more details are at www.ricksteves.com/phoning. For a very practical one-hour talk covering tech issues for travelers, see www.ricksteves.com/mobile-travel-skills.

USING A MOBILE PHONE IN EUROPE
Here are some budget tips and options.

Sign up for an international plan. To stay connected at a lower cost, sign up for an international service plan through your carrier. Most providers offer a simple bundle that includes calling, messaging, and data. Your normal plan may already include international coverage (T-Mobile's does).

Before your trip, call your provider or check online to confirm that your phone will work in Europe, and research your provider's international rates. Activate the plan a day or two before you leave, then remember to cancel it when your trip's over.

Use free Wi-Fi whenever possible. Unless you have an un-limited-data plan, you're best off saving most of your online tasks for Wi-Fi. You can access the internet, send texts, and even make voice calls over Wi-Fi.

Most accommodations in Europe offer free Wi-Fi, but some—especially expensive hotels—charge a fee. Many cafés (including Starbucks and McDonald's) have free hotspots for customers; look for signs offering it and ask for the Wi-Fi password when you buy something. You'll also often find Wi-Fi at TIs, city squares, major museums, public-transit hubs, airports, and aboard trains and buses. In Rome, you can browse free for an hour a day on any tram (and at tram stops) with an "ATAC Wi-Fi" logo.

Minimize the use of your cellular network. The best way to make sure you're not accidentally burning through data is to put your device in "airplane" mode (which also disables phone calls and texts), turn your Wi-Fi back on, and connect to networks as needed. When you need to get online but can't find Wi-Fi, simply turn on your cellular network (or turn off airplane mode) just long enough for the task at hand.

Even with an international data plan, wait until you're on Wi-Fi to Skype, download apps, stream videos, or do other mega-byte-greedy tasks. Using a navigation app such as Google Maps over a cellular network can take lots of data, so do this sparingly or offline.

Limit automatic updates. By default, your device constantly checks for a data connection and updates apps. It's smart to disable these features so your apps will only update when you're on Wi-Fi.

How to Dial

International Calls

Whether phoning from a US landline or mobile phone, or from a number in another European country, here's how to make an international call. I've used one of my recommended Florence hotels as an example (tel. 055-213-154).

Initial Zero: Drop the initial zero from international phone numbers—except when calling Italy.

Mobile Tip: If using a mobile phone, the "+" sign can replace the international access code (for a "+" sign, press and hold "0").

US/Canada to Europe

Dial 011 (US/Canada international access code), country code (39 for Italy), and phone number.

▶ To call the Florence hotel from home, dial 011-39-055-213-154.

Country to Country Within Europe

Dial 00 (Europe international access code), country code, and phone number.

▶ To call the Florence hotel from Germany, dial 00-39-055-213-154.

Europe to the US/Canada

Dial 00, country code (1 for US/Canada), and phone number.

▶ To call from Europe to my office in Edmonds, Washington, dial 00-1-425-771-8303.

Domestic Calls

To call within Italy (from one Italian landline or mobile phone to another), simply dial the phone number, including the initial 0 if there is one.

▶ To call the Florence hotel from Rome, dial 055-213-154.

Also change your device's email settings from "auto-retrieve" to "manual" (or from "push" to "fetch").

Use Wi-Fi calling and messaging apps. Skype, WhatsApp, FaceTime, and Google Hangouts are great for making free or low-cost calls or sending texts over Wi-Fi worldwide. Just log on to a Wi-Fi network, then connect with any of your friends or family members who use the same service. If you buy credit in advance, with some of these services you can call or text anywhere for just pennies.

Some apps, such as Apple's iMessage, will use the cellular network for texts if Wi-Fi isn't available: To avoid this possibility, turn off the "Send as SMS" feature.

Buy a European SIM Card. If you anticipate making a lot of local calls or need a local phone number, or if your provider's

More Dialing Tips

Toll and Toll-Free Numbers: It's generally not possible to dial Italian toll or toll-free numbers from a US mobile or land-line (although you can sometimes get through using Skype). Look for a direct-dial number instead.

More Phoning Help: See www.howtocallabroad.com.

European Country Codes		Ireland & N. Ireland	353/44
Austria	43	Italy	39
Belgium	32	Latvia	371
Bosnia-Herzegovina	387	Montenegro	382
Croatia	385	Morocco	212
Czech Republic	420	Netherlands	31
Denmark	45	Norway	47
Estonia	372	Poland	48
Finland	358	Portugal	351
France	33	Russia	7
Germany	49	Slovakia	421
Gibraltar	350	Slovenia	386
Great Britain	44	Spain	34
Greece	30	Sweden	46
Hungary	36	Switzerland	41
Iceland	354	Turkey	90

PRACTICALITIES

international data rates are expensive, consider buying a SIM card in Europe to replace the one in your (unlocked) US phone or tablet.

In Italy, buy SIM cards at mobile-phone shops. You'll be required to register the SIM card with your passport as an antiterrorism measure (which may mean you can't use the phone for the first hour or two).

There are no roaming charges when using a European SIM card in other EU countries, though to be sure you get this "roam-like-at-home" pricing, ask if this feature is included when you buy your SIM card.

Tips on Internet Security

Make sure that your device is running the latest versions of its operating system, security software, and apps. Next, ensure that your device and key programs (like email) are password-protected. On the road, use only secure, password-protected Wi-Fi hotspots. Ask the hotel or café staff for the specific name of their Wi-Fi network, and make sure you log on to that exact one.

If you must access your financial info online, use a banking app rather than accessing your account via a browser. A cellular connection is more secure than Wi-Fi. Avoid logging onto personal finance sites on a public computer.

Never share your credit-card number (or any other sensitive information) online unless you know that the site is secure. A secure site displays a little padlock icon, and the URL begins with *https* (instead of the usual *http*).

WITHOUT A MOBILE PHONE

It's less convenient but possible to travel in Europe without a mobile device. You can make calls from your hotel and check email or get online using public computers.

Most **hotels** charge a fee for placing calls—ask for rates before you dial. You can use a prepaid international phone card (*carta telefonica prepagata internazionale*—usually available at newsstands, tobacco shops, and train stations) to call out from your hotel. Dial the toll-free access number, enter the card's PIN code, then dial the number.

You'll only see **public pay phones** in a few post offices and train stations. Most don't take coins but instead require insertable phone cards, which you can buy at a newsstand, convenience store, or post office. Except for emergencies, they're not worth the hassle.

Some hotels have **public computers** in their lobbies for guests to use; otherwise you may find them at public libraries (ask your hotelier or the TI for the nearest location). On a European keyboard, use the "Alt Gr" key to the right of the space bar to insert the extra symbol that appears on some keys. If you can't locate a special character (such as @), simply copy and paste it from a web page.

MAIL

You can mail one package per day to yourself worth up to $200 duty-free from Europe to the US (mark it "personal purchases"). If you're sending a gift to someone, mark it "unsolicited gift." For details, visit www.cbp.gov, select "Travel," and search for "Know Before You Visit." The Italian postal service works fine, but for quick transatlantic delivery (in either direction), consider services such as DHL (www.dhl.com).

Transportation

If your trip will cover more of Italy than just Rome, you may need to take a long-distance train or bus, rent a car, or fly. Buses are an alternative to trains (and may be your only option for reaching some small Italian towns), but they are generally slower and less efficient. Renting a car is great for touring the small hill towns of Umbria and Tuscany north of Rome. I give some specifics on trains, buses, and flights here. For more detailed information on transportation throughout Europe, including trains, flying, buses, renting a car, and driving, see www.ricksteves.com/transportation.

TRAINS

To travel by train affordably within Italy, you can simply buy tickets as you go. For travelers ready to lock in dates and times weeks or months in advance, buying nonrefundable tickets online can cut costs in half. Note that the Italy rail pass is generally not a good value, but if your travel extends beyond Italy, there are multicountry rail passes that might be worth checking into. For advice on figuring out the smartest train-ticket or rail-pass options for your trip, visit the Trains & Rail Passes section of my website at www.ricksteves.com/rail.

Types of Trains

Most trains in Italy are operated by the state-run **Trenitalia** company (www.trenitalia.com, a.k.a. Ferrovie dello Stato Italiane, abbreviated FS). Ticket prices depend on the speed of the train, so it helps to know the different types of trains: pokey Regionale (R or REG); medium-speed Regionale Veloce (RV); fast InterCity (IC) and EuroCity (EC); and super-fast Frecce trains. All Frecce trains, many EuroCity and InterCity trains, and most international trains require reservations.

Regional trains offer only open seating (no assigned seats); all other classes of service come with an assigned seat. If you're traveling with a rail pass, you'll need to reserve a seat for any service but regional trains (see "Rail Passes," later).

The private train company **Italo** (www.italotreno.it) runs fast trains on major routes in Italy. Italo is focused on two corridors:

Italy's Public Transportation

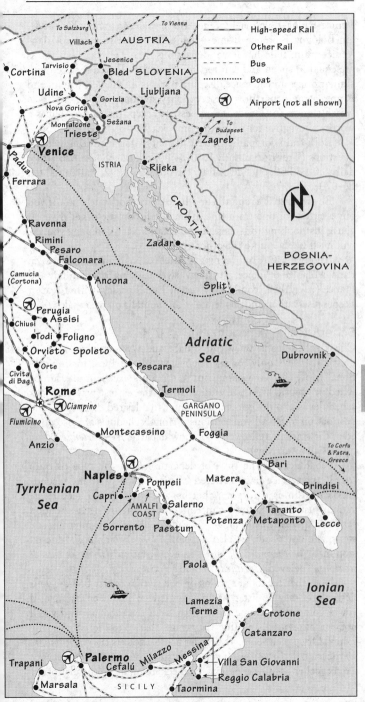

Venice-Padua-Bologna-Florence-Rome-Salerno and Turin-Milan-Bologna-Florence-Rome-Naples. They also run a useful Milan-Venice train. Italo has fewer departures than Trenitalia but trains are equal in speed and comfort to Trenitalia's Frecce service, with similar prices and advance discount options. In Naples, Milan, and Rome, some departures use secondary stations—pay attention to which station you need. Italo does not accept rail passes, but is a worthy alternative for point-to-point tickets.

Both train companies have call centers for answering general questions (**Trenitalia:** daily 7:00-24:00, tel. 06-6847-5475; **Italo:** daily 6:00-23:00, outside of Italy tel. 06-8937-1892, Italian toll tel. 06-0708).

Be aware that Trenitalia and Italo don't cooperate at all. If you buy a ticket for one train line, it's not valid on the other. Even if you're just looking for schedule information, the company you ask will most likely ignore the other's options.

Another private train company, **Thello,** runs night trains between Paris, Milan, and Venice, plus a few daytime trains between Italy and France (www.thello.com). They accept Eurail passes (with a seat or sleeper reservation) and cooperate with Trenitalia on ticket sales.

Schedules

Check schedules at www.trenitalia.it and www.italotreno.it (domestic journeys only) or use their smartphone apps; for international trips, use www.bahn.com (Germany's excellent all-Europe schedule website). At the train station, the easiest way to check schedules is at a ticket machine. Enter the desired date, time, and destination to see all your options. Printed schedules are also posted at the station (yellow posters show departures—*partenze;* white posters show arrivals).

Schedules list the time of departure *(ora)*, the type of train *(treni)*, and service classes offered *(classi servizi)*—first- and second-class cars, dining car, *cuccetta* berths, and whether you need reservations (usually denoted by an R in a box). The train's destination *(principali fermate destinazioni)* is shown, along with intermediate stops, and notes such as "also stops in..." *(ferma anche a...),* "doesn't stop in..." *(non ferma a...),* "stops in every station" *(ferma in tutte le stazioni),* "delayed..." *(ritardo...),* and so on.

Note that for today's trains on the station reader boards, your destination may be listed as an intermediate stop. For example, if you're going from Rome to Orvieto, scan the schedule and you'll notice that regional and InterCity trains that go to Florence usually stop in Orvieto en route. The reader board also lists the track *(binario)* the train departs from. If you're not sure, confirm the *binario* with a ticket seller or railway official, or check monitors on the platform.

Point-to-Point Tickets

Train tickets are a good value in Italy. Typical fares are shown on the map on page 583, though ticket prices can vary for the same journey, mainly depending on the time of day, the speed of the train, and advance discounts.

Classes of Service: Frecce and Italo trains each offer several classes of service (e.g., Standard, Premium, Business, Executive) where all seats are reserved. Other trains offer standard first- and second-class seating (with first class costing up to 50 percent more than second). Buying up gives you a little more elbow room, a snack, or perhaps a better chance at seating a group together, if you're buying on short notice.

Advance Discounts: Ticket price levels are Base (full fare, easily changeable or partly refundable before scheduled departure), Economy (one schedule change allowed before departure, for a fee), and Super Economy or Low Cost (sells out quickly, no refunds or exchanges). For example, traveling Standard class from Rome to Florence on the fastest train costs €50 for a Base fare, €39 for an Economy fare, or €28 at the Super Economy rate. Discounted fares typically sell out several weeks before departure. Fares labeled *servizi abbonati* are available only for locals with monthly passes—not tourists. Regional trains don't offer advance discounts or seat assignments, so there's little need to buy those tickets in advance.

Speed vs. Savings: For point-to-point tickets, you'll pay more the faster you go. Spending a modest amount of extra time in transit can save money. On longer, mainline routes, fast trains save more time and provide most of the service. For example, a one-way ticket between Rome and Civitavecchia costs €16 on a Frecce train (45 minutes each way), but €5 on a regional train (80 minutes each way). Super-fast Rome-Venice trains run hourly, cost €92 in second class, and make the trip in less than 4 hours, while infrequent InterCity trains (only 1-2/day) cost €56 and take 6 hours.

Age-Based Discounts: Discounts for kids don't usually beat the Super Economy rate described above. If the cheapest tickets are no longer available, look for deals like "Bimbi Gratis" and "Offerta Famiglia." Other discounts for youths and seniors require purchase of a separate card (€40 Carta Verde for ages 12-26, €30 Carta Argento for ages 60 and over), but the ticket discount is so minor (10-15 percent respectively for domestic travel), it's not worth it for most.

Buying Point-to-Point Tickets

You can buy tickets online, with a smartphone app, at train station ticket windows, from ticket machines, or at travel agencies. For long-haul runs or travel on a busy weekend or holiday, it can be cheaper to buy tickets in advance. But because most Italian trains run frequently and there's no deadline to buy tickets, for the most part I prefer to keep my travel plans flexible by purchasing tickets as I go. (You can buy tickets for several trips when you are ready to commit.)

It's easy to buy tickets **online** at Trenitalia.com or ItaloTreno.it. On either website, choose English and be sure to read the pricing info, as many of the cheaper tickets are not refundable or changeable. You can keep the ticket on your mobile device (either as a PDF or in a "ticketless" format with a booking code), or you can print it out.

Or download the Trenitalia or Italo app to your **smartphone**—both have English versions. If using the Trenitalia app to buy tickets, do so as a guest (a log-in isn't necessary—or possible—if you don't live in Italy).

If you instead go to the train station to buy tickets, you can avoid ticket-office lines by using the ticket machines in station halls. You'll be able to easily purchase tickets for travel within Italy, make seat reservations, and even book a *cuccetta* (koo-CHEH-tah; overnight berth). If you do use the ticket windows (e.g., to buy international tickets), be sure you're in the correct line. Key terms: *biglietti* (general tickets), *prenotazioni* (reservations), *nazionali* (domestic), and *internazionali*.

Trenitalia's **ticket machines** are user-friendly and found in all but the tiniest stations in Italy. You can pay with cash (change given when indicated) or by debit or credit card (even for small amounts, but you may need to enter your PIN). Select English, then your destination. If you don't immediately see the city you're traveling to, keep keying in the spelling until it's listed. You can choose from first- and second-class seats, request tickets for more than one traveler, and pick seats, when applicable. Don't select a discount rate without being sure that you meet the criteria (for example, Americans are not eligible for certain EU or resident discounts).

To buy tickets at the station for **Italo** trains, look for a dedicated service counter (in most major stations) or a red ticket machine labeled *Italo*.

Some **international tickets** can't be bought online or from machines; for these tickets and anything else that requires a real person, you must go to a ticket window at the station. A good alternative, though, is to drop by a local travel agency. Agencies sell domestic and international tickets and make reservations. They charge a small fee, but the language barrier (and the lines) can be smaller than at the station's ticket windows.

Rail Passes

The single-country Eurail Italy Pass may save you money if you take several long train rides or prefer first-class travel, but for most people it's not a good value. Most train travelers in Italy take relatively short rides on the Milan-Venice-Florence-Rome circuit. For these

Rail Pass or Point-to-Point Tickets?

Will you be better off buying a rail pass or point-to-point tickets? It pays to know your options and choose what's best for your itinerary.

Rail Passes

A Eurail Italy Pass lets you travel by train in Italy for three to eight days (consecutively or not) within a one-month period. Italy is also covered (along with most of Europe) by the classic Eurail Global Pass.

Discounted rates are offered for seniors (age 60 and up) and youths (ages 12-27). Up to two kids (ages 4-11) can travel free with each adult-rate pass (but not with senior rates). All rail passes offer a choice of first or second class for all ages.

Rail passes are best purchased outside Europe (through travel agents or Rick Steves' Europe). For more on rail passes, including current prices, visit RickSteves.com/rail.

Point-to-Point Tickets

Italian train tickets are relatively cheap, and most include seat reservations, making them the best deal for most travelers. Use this map to add up approximate pay-as-you-go fares for your itinerary, and compare that to the price of a rail pass plus reservations. Keep in mind that significant discounts on point-to-point tickets may be available with advance purchase.

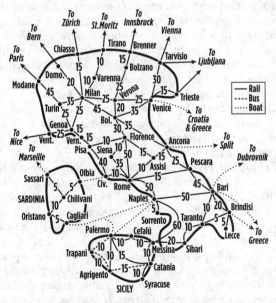

Map shows approximate costs, in US dollars, for one-way, second-class tickets on faster trains.

trips, it can be cheaper to buy point-to-point tickets. Remember that rail passes are valid on Trenitalia trains but not on Italo trains.

Furthermore, a rail pass doesn't offer much hop-on convenience in Italy, since even with a rail pass, seat reservations are required for InterCity, EuroCity, and Frecce trains (€5-10 each; make seat reservations at station ticket machines or windows). Most regional trains (such as Florence-Pisa-Cinque Terre service) don't require (or offer) reservations. Reservations for berths on overnight trains cost extra and aren't covered by rail passes.

If you're also traveling by train in other countries, consider a Eurail Global Pass. Although it covers most of Europe, prices can work for trips as short as three travel days or as long as three months. For more info, see the sidebar.

Train Tips

Validating Tickets: If your ticket includes a seat reservation on a specific train *(biglietto con prenotazione)*, you're all set and can just get on board. The same is true for any ticket bought online or with the Trenitalia or Italo smartphone apps (whether open or reserved seating); these tickets are considered already validated.

An open ticket (generally for a *regionale* train) bought from a ticket desk or machine must be validated (date-stamped) before you board (the ticket may say *da convalidare* or *convalida*). To validate it, before getting on the train, stamp your ticket in the machine near the platform (usually marked *convalida biglietti* or *vidimazione*). Once you validate a ticket, you must complete your trip within the timeframe stamped on the ticket (usually about four hours). If you forget to validate your ticket, go right away to the train conductor—before they come to you—or you'll pay a fine.

Getting a Seat: If you're taking an unreserved *regionale* train that originates at your departure point (e.g., you're catching the Rome-Assisi train in Rome), arriving at least 15 minutes before the departure time will help you snare a seat.

Baggage Storage: Many Italian stations have *deposito bagagli* where you can safely leave your bag for a standardized but steep price (€6/5 hours, €12/12 hours, €17/24 hours, payable when you pick up the bag, double-check closing hours; they may ask to photocopy your passport). Due to security concerns, no Italian stations have lockers.

Theft Concerns: In big cities, exercise caution and prudence at train stations to avoid thieves and con artists. Homeless and marginalized people lurk around the station trying to skim tips (or worse) from unsuspecting tourists. If someone helps you to find your train or carry your bags, be aware that they are not an official porter; they are simply hoping for some cash. And if someone other than a uniformed railway employee tries to help you use the ticket machines, politely refuse.

Italian trains are famous for their thieves. Never leave a bag unattended. Police do ride the trains, cutting down on theft. Still, for an overnight trip, I'd feel safe only in a *cuccetta* (a bunk in a special sleeping car with an attendant who keeps track of who comes and goes while you sleep—approximately €40 or more).

Strikes: Strikes, which are common, generally last a day (often a Friday). Train employees will simply explain, *"Sciopero"* (SHOH-peh-roh, strike). But in actuality, a minimum amount of "essential" main-line service is maintained (by law) during strikes. When a strike is pending, travel agencies, savvy hoteliers, and remaining station personnel can check to see when the strike will go into effect and which trains will continue to run. Revised schedules may be posted online and in Italian at stations. See www.trenitalia.com, choose English, then "Information and Contacts," and then "In Case of Strike."

If your train is cancelled, your reserved-seat ticket will likely be accepted on any similar train running that day (either earlier or later than the original departure time) but you won't have a seat assignment. Tickets for cancelled trains should also be exchangeable without penalty ahead of the original departure time, or can be refunded (have an agent mark it "unused," and check refund deadlines). A rail pass works on any train still operating, but partially used rail passes can't be refunded—so make full use of any pass you have to continue your trip.

BUSES

You can usually get anywhere you want in Italy by bus, as long as you're not in a hurry and plan ahead using bus schedules (pick up at local TIs or bus stations). For reaching small towns, buses are sometimes the only option if you don't have a car.

Long-distance buses are catching on in Italy as an alternative to the train. They are usually cheaper, modern, and often (unlike trains) have free Wi-Fi. They're especially useful on routes poorly served by train. Some of the operators you'll see are Flixbus (https://global.flixbus.com) and Marozzi (www.marozzivt.it). In general, orange buses are local city buses, and blue buses are for long distances.

Larger towns have a (usually chaotic) long-distance bus station *(stazione degli autobus)*, with ticket windows and several stalls (usually labeled *corsia, stallo,* or *binario*)—but to save time, buy your ticket at a travel agent or online, and print it out. Smaller towns—where buses are more useful—often have a central bus stop *(fermata)*, likely along the main road or on the main square, and maybe several more scattered around town. In small towns, buy bus tickets at newsstands or tobacco shops (with the big *T* signs). When buying your ticket, confirm the departure point *("Dov'è la fermata?")*.

Before boarding, confirm the destination with the driver. You are expected to stow big backpacks underneath the bus (open the luggage compartment yourself if it's closed). Upon arrival, double-check that the posted schedule lists your next destination and departure time.

Traveling by bus on Sundays and holidays can be problematic; even from large cities, schedules are sparse, departing buses are jam-packed, and ticket offices are often closed. Plan ahead and buy your ticket in advance. Most travel agencies book bus (and train) tickets for a small fee.

TAXIS AND RIDE-BOOKING SERVICES

Most Italian taxis are reliable and cheap. In many cities, two people can travel short distances by cab for little more than the cost of bus or subway tickets. If you like ride-booking services such as Uber, their apps usually work in Europe just like they do in the US: Request a car on your mobile phone (connected to Wi-Fi or data), and the fare is automatically charged to your credit card. In Italy, however, Uber faces legal challenges, and may not be consistently available. In Rome, the MyTaxi app is a local alternative that connects you with regular city taxis. After you enter your credit-card number, the app charges you regular taxi fares and lets you add a tip. For more about taxis in Italy, see page 36.

FLIGHTS

To compare flight costs and times, begin with an online travel search engine: Kayak is the top site for flights to and within Europe, easy-to-use Google Flights has price alerts, and Skyscanner includes many inexpensive flights within Europe. To avoid unpleasant surprises, before you book be sure to read the small print about refunds, changes, and the costs for "extras" such as reserving a seat, checking a bag, or printing a boarding pass.

Flights to Europe: Start looking for international flights about four to six months before your trip, especially for peak-season travel. Depending on your itinerary, it can be efficient and no more expensive to fly into one city and out of another. If your flight requires a connection in Europe, see my hints on navigating Europe's top hub airports at www.ricksteves.com/hub-airports.

Flights Within Europe: Flying between European cities is surprisingly affordable. Before buying a long-distance train or bus ticket, check the cost of a flight on one of Europe's airlines, whether a major carrier or a no-frills outfit like Easyjet or Ryanair. Be aware that flying with a discount airline can have drawbacks, such

PRACTICALITIES

as minimal customer service and time-consuming treks to secondary airports.

Flying to the US and Canada: Because security is extra tight for flights to the US, be sure to give yourself plenty of time at the airport. Charge your electronic devices before you board in case security checks require you to turn them on (see www.tsa.gov for the latest rules).

Resources from Rick Steves

Begin Your Trip at RickSteves.com

My mobile-friendly **website** is *the* place to explore Europe in preparation for your trip. You'll find thousands of fun articles, videos, and radio interviews; a wealth of money-saving tips for planning your dream trip; travel news dispatches; a video library of my travel talks; my travel blog; my latest guidebook updates (www.ricksteves.com/update); and my free Rick Steves Audio Europe app. You can also follow me on Facebook, Instagram, and Twitter.

Our **Travel Forum** is a well-groomed collection of message boards where our travel-savvy community answers questions and shares their personal travel experiences—and our well-traveled staff chimes in when they can be helpful (www.ricksteves.com/forums).

Our **online Travel Store** offers bags and accessories that I've designed to help you travel smarter and lighter. These include my popular carry-on bags (which I live out of four months a year), money belts, totes, toiletries kits, adapters, guidebooks, and planning maps (www.ricksteves.com/shop).

Our website can also help you find the perfect **rail pass** for your itinerary and your budget, with easy, one-stop shopping for rail passes, seat reservations, and point-to-point tickets (www.ricksteves.com/travel-tips/transportation/trains).

Rick Steves' Tours, Guidebooks, TV Shows, and More

Small Group Tours: Want to travel with greater efficiency and less stress? We offer more than 40 itineraries reaching the best destinations in this book...and beyond. Each year about 30,000 travelers join us on about 1,000 Rick Steves bus tours. You'll enjoy great guides and a fun bunch of travel partners (with small groups of 24 to 28 travelers). You'll find European adventures to fit every vacation

length. For all the details, and to get our tour catalog, visit www.ricksteves.com/tours or call us at 425/608-4217.

Books: *Rick Steves Rome* is just one of many books in my series on European travel, which includes country and city guidebooks, Snapshots (excerpted chapters from bigger guides), Pocket Guides (full-color little books on big cities), "Best Of" guidebooks (condensed, full-color country guides), and my budget-travel skills handbook, *Rick Steves Europe Through the Back Door*. A complete list of my titles—including phrase books; cruising guides; travelogues on European art, history, and culture; and more—appears near the end of this book.

TV Shows and Travel Talks: My public television series, *Rick Steves' Europe,* covers Europe from top to bottom with over 100 half-hour episodes—and we're working on new shows every year (watch full episodes at my website for free). My free online video library, Rick Steves Classroom Europe, offers a searchable database of short video clips on European history, culture, and geography (classroom.ricksteves.com). And to raise your travel I.Q., check out the video versions of our popular classes (covering most European countries as well as travel skills, packing smart, cruising, tech for travelers, European art, and travel as a political act—www.ricksteves.com/travel-talks).

Audio Tours on My Free App: I've produced dozens of free, self-guided audio tours of the top sights in Europe. For those tours and other audio content, get my free **Rick Steves Audio Europe app,** an extensive online library organized by destination. For more on my app, see page 21.

Radio: My weekly public radio show, *Travel with Rick Steves,* features interviews with travel experts from around the world. It airs on 400 public radio stations across the US. An archive of programs is available at RickSteves.com/radio.

Podcasts: You can enjoy my travel content via several free podcasts. The podcast version of my radio show brings you a weekly, hour-long travel conversation. My other podcasts include a weekly selection of video clips from my public television show, my audio tours of Europe's top sights, and live recordings of my travel classes (RickSteves.com/watch-read-listen/audio/podcasts).

APPENDIX

Holidays and Festivals

In Italy, where every town has a festival honoring its patron saint, holidays seem to strike without warning. In Rome, the Vatican Museums close for a multitude of Catholic holidays; check the schedule at www.museivaticani.va.

This list includes selected festivals in Rome, plus national holidays observed throughout Italy. Many sights and banks close on national holidays—keep this in mind when planning your itinerary. Before planning a trip around a festival, verify the dates with the festival website, TI sites for Italy and Rome (www.italia.it and www.turismoroma.it), or my "Upcoming Holidays and Festivals in Italy" web page (www.ricksteves.com/europe/italy/festivals).

In Rome, hotels get booked up on Easter weekend, Liberation Day, Labor Day, Ascension Day, Sts. Peter and Paul feast day, All Saints' Day, and on Fridays and Saturdays year-round. Some hotels require you to book the full three-day weekend around a holiday.

Jan 1	New Year's Day
Jan 6	Epiphany
Early April	Rome Marathon (www.maratonadiroma.it)

April	Easter weekend (Good Friday-Easter Monday: April 2-5, 2021)
April 21	City Birthday
April 25	Italian Liberation Day
May 1	Labor Day
June 2	Anniversary of the Republic
June	Feast Day of Corpus Christi (June 3, 2021)
June 24	St. John the Baptist Day
June 29	Sts. Peter and Paul Day
Mid-July	Trastevere's Noantri Festival
Aug 10	St. Lawrence's Day
Aug 15	Feast of the Assumption (Ferragosto)
Sept 19	St. Januarius Day, Naples
Nov 1	All Saints' Day
Dec 8	Feast of the Immaculate Conception
Dec 25	Christmas
Dec 26	St. Stephen's Day

Books and Films

To learn more about Italy past and present, and specifically Rome, check out a few of these books and films. For kids' recommendations, see page 419.

Nonfiction

Absolute Monarchs (John Julius Norwich, 2011). This warts-and-all illustrated guide to the most significant popes in history is a readable best seller.

Ancient Rome: The Rise and Fall of an Empire (Simon Baker, 2007). Baker chronicles the rise and demise of the great Roman Empire and its powerful leaders.

City: A Story of Roman Planning and Construction (David Macaulay, 1974). Macaulay's illustrated book about the Eternal City will please both kids and adults.

A Day in the Life of Ancient Rome (Alberto Angela, 2007). Travel back to the world of gladiators and grand banquets in this 24-hour journey through the ancient city.

Italian Journey (Johann Wolfgang von Goethe, 1786). In this 18th-century collection of writings, Goethe describes his travels to Rome, Sicily, and Naples.

A Literary Companion to Rome (John Varriano, 1992). Roman sites associated with Ibsen, Dickens, Woolf, Wilde, and other great writers are explained in 10 self-guided walking tours.

Michelangelo and the Pope's Ceiling (Ross King, 2003). The story behind the Sistine Chapel includes Michelangelo's technical difficulties, personality conflicts, and money troubles.

The Pope's Elephant (Silvio A. Bedini, 1997). Pope Leo X's favorite pet was an albino elephant named Hanno, and his story is also an account of the end of Rome's Golden Age.

Rome and a Villa (Eleanor Clark, 1952). This masterful collection of vignettes by the wife of Robert Penn Warren touches such diverse topics as Rome's Protestant Cemetery and Hadrian's Villa.

Saints & Sinners (Eamon Duffy, 1997). Everything you always wanted to know about the popes, but were afraid to ask.

SPQR: A History of Ancient Rome (Mary Beard, 2015). This is a fresh take on the history of Rome by the prominent classics scholar who also wrote and narrated the popular BBC series *Meet the Romans*.

The Seasons of Rome (Paul Hofmann, 1997). A former *New York Times* bureau chief reveals the eccentricities of Rome often overlooked by tourists.

The Secrets of Rome: Love and Death in the Eternal City (Corrado Augias, 2005). Augias takes readers back through 27 centuries of Roman history, secrets, and conspiracies.

The Smiles of Rome: A Literary Companion for Readers and Travelers (Susan Cahill, 2005). This collection of essays, stories, and poems about Rome by everyone from Ovid to Federico Fellini includes a guide to visiting these most-loved places.

When in Rome (Robert Hutchinson, 1998). A lapsed (sometimes irreverent) Catholic discovers the roots of Christianity in Vatican City.

Fiction

The Agony and the Ecstasy (Irving Stone, 1958). Stone fictionalizes Michelangelo's struggle to paint the Sistine Chapel (also a 1965 movie starring Charlton Heston).

Angels & Demons (Dan Brown, 2000). The *Da Vinci Code* author's page-turner about a secret society and a time bomb in the Vatican (also a 2009 movie starring Tom Hanks).

Clash of Civilizations Over an Elevator in Piazza Vittorio (Amara Lakhous, 2006). The multicultural community of a Roman apartment building confronts the death of one of its members.

The Decameron (Giovanni Boccaccio, 1348). Boccaccio's collection of 100 hilarious, often bawdy tales is a masterpiece of Italian literature and inspired Chaucer, Keats, and Shakespeare.

The First Man in Rome (Colleen McCullough, 1990). The author of

APPENDIX

The Thorn Birds describes the early days of the Roman Republic, in the first of a best-selling series of historical fiction.

I, Claudius (Robert Graves, 1934). This brilliant history of ancient Rome is told by Claudius, the family's laughingstock who becomes emperor himself. The sequel is *Claudius the God* (1935).

Lucrezia Borgia (Maria Bellonci, 1939). In this historically based tale of court intrigue, a daughter of Pope Alexander VI navigates passions, plots, and controversy in Renaissance Rome.

My Brilliant Friend (Elena Ferrante, 2012). The first of four titles in the Neapolitan Novels series traces two girls' coming of age in mid-20th-century Naples.

Pompeii (Robert Harris, 2003). The engineer responsible for Pompeii's aqueducts has a bad feeling about Mount Vesuvius in this historical novel.

The Roman Spring of Ms. Stone (Tennessee Williams, 1950). A wealthy American widow and former stage actress haunts the Eternal City in the years after World War II, seeking purpose amid its grandeur.

A Soldier of the Great War (Mark Helprin, 1991). A young Roman lawyer falls in love with an art student, but World War I rips them apart.

That Awful Mess on the Via Merulana (Carlo Emilio Gadda, 1957). This detective story about a murder and a burglary in an apartment building in central Rome shines a harsh light on fascist Italy.

The Woman of Rome (Alberto Moravia, 1949). This classic tale of obsession and betrayal set against the backdrop of Mussolini's fascist regime follows a young model who attracts destructive passions.

Film and TV

Ben-Hur (1959). At the height of the Roman Empire, a Jewish prince is enslaved by a friend, and later seeks revenge in a stunning chariot race (the film won a record 11 Oscars).

Bicycle Thieves (1948). A poor man looks for his stolen bicycle in busy Rome in this inspirational classic of Italian Neorealism.

Caterina in the Big City (2003). A teenager whose family moves to Rome from a small town is the focus of this bitter comedy about the crisis of contemporary Italian society.

La Dolce Vita (1961). Director Federico Fellini tells a series of stories that capture the hedonistic days of early 1960s Rome.

Gladiator (2000). An enslaved Roman general (Russell Crowe) fights his way back to freedom in Ridley Scott's Oscar winner.

The Great Beauty (2013). This thoughtful movie, named best foreign film at the 2014 Academy Awards, showcases Rome in all of its decadence and splendor.

Massacre in Rome (1973). Richard Burton and Marcello Mastroianni star in this historical drama, which recounts one of the bloodiest events during the Nazi occupation of Rome.

Mid-August Lunch (2008). A broke Roman bachelor gets more than he bargained for when he agrees to take care of an elderly lady during a summer holiday to pay off a debt.

Quo Vadis (1951). A Roman general falls in love with a Christian hostage in this epic that includes the burning of Rome, the crucifixion of St. Peter, and the madness of Nero.

Rome, Open City (1945). Roberto Rossellini's war drama is set in the Eternal City during the WWII Nazi occupation.

Roman Holiday (1953). Audrey Hepburn plays a princess who escapes her royal minders, falls for an American newspaperman (Gregory Peck), and discovers Rome on the back of his scooter.

Spartacus (1960). In this epic directed by Stanley Kubrick, a gladiator (Kirk Douglas) leads a slave revolt in the last days of the Roman Republic.

A Special Day (1977). On the day of Hitler's visit to Rome, the wife (Sophia Loren) of a militant fascist has a fateful meeting with a persecuted journalist (Marcello Mastroianni).

Conversions and Climate

Numbers and Stumblers

- Europeans write a few of their numbers differently than we do. 1 = 1, 4 = 4, 7 = 7.
- In Europe, dates appear as day/month/year, so Christmas 2021 is 25/12/21.
- Commas are decimal points and decimals are commas. A dollar and a half is $1,50, one thousand is 1.000, and there are 5.280 feet in a mile.
- When counting with fingers, start with your thumb. If you hold up your first finger to request one item, you'll probably get two.
- What Americans call the second floor of a building is the first floor in Europe.
- On escalators and moving sidewalks, Europeans keep the left "lane" open for passing. Keep to the right.

Metric Conversions

A **kilogram** equals 1,000 grams (about 2.2 pounds). One hundred **grams** (a common unit at markets) is about a quarter-pound. One **liter** is about a quart, or almost four to a gallon.

A **kilometer** is six-tenths of a mile. To convert kilometers to miles, cut the kilometers in half and add back 10 percent of the original (120 km: 60 + 12 = 72 miles). One **meter** is 39 inches—just over a yard.

1 foot = 0.3 meter	1 square yard = 0.8 square meter
1 yard = 0.9 meter	1 square mile = 2.6 square kilometers
1 mile = 1.6 kilometers	1 ounce = 28 grams
1 centimeter = 0.4 inch	1 quart = 0.95 liter
1 meter = 39.4 inches	1 kilogram = 2.2 pounds
1 kilometer = 0.62 mile	32°F = 0°C

Roman Numerals

In the US, you'll see Roman numerals—which originated in ancient Rome—used for copyright dates, clocks, and the Super Bowl. In Italy, you're likely to observe these numbers chiseled on statues and buildings. If you want to do some numeric detective work, here's how: In Roman numerals, as in ours, the highest numbers (thousands, hundreds) come first, followed by smaller numbers. Many numbers are made by combining numerals into sets: V = 5, so VIII = 8 (5 plus 3). Roman numerals follow a subtraction principle for multiples of fours (4, 40, 400, etc.) and nines (9, 90, 900, etc.). The number four, for example, is written as IV (1 subtracted from 5), rather than IIII. The number nine is IX (1 subtracted from 10).

Big numbers such as dates can look daunting at first. The easiest way to handle them is to read the numbers in discrete chunks. For example, Michelangelo was born in MCDLXXV. Break it down: M (1,000) + CD (100 subtracted from 500, or 400) + LXX (50 + 10 + 10, or 70) + V (5) = 1475. It was a very good year.

M = 1000	XL = 40
CM = 900	X = 10
D = 500	IX = 9
CD = 400	V = 5
C = 100	IV = 4
XC = 90	I = duh
L = 50	

Clothing Sizes

When shopping for clothing, use these US-to-European comparisons as general guidelines (but note that no conversion is perfect).

Women: For pants and dresses, add 36 in Italy (US 10 = Italian 46). For blouses and sweaters, add 8 for most of Europe (US 32 = European 40). For shoes, add 30-31 (US 7 = European 37/38).

Men: For shirts, multiply by 2 and add about 8 (US 15 = European 38). For jackets and suits, add 10. For shoes, add 32-34.

Children: Clothing is sized by height—in centimeters (2.5 cm = 1 inch), so a US size 8 roughly equates to 132-140. For shoes up to size 13, add 16-18, and for sizes 1 and up, add 30-32.

Rome's Climate

First line—average daily high; second line—average daily low; third line—average days without rain. For more detailed weather statistics for Rome (as well as the rest of the world), check www.wunderground.com.

J	F	M	A	M	J	J	A	S	O	N	D
55°	57°	63°	68°	75°	84°	90°	86°	81°	73°	64°	59°
37°	37°	43°	46°	55°	63°	66°	64°	61°	54°	46°	39°
24	22	24	21	24	26	28	31	24	23	22	22

Fahrenheit and Celsius Conversion

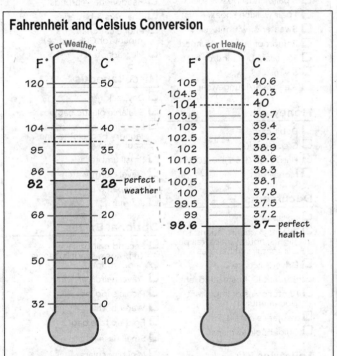

Europe takes its temperature using the Celsius scale, while we opt for Fahrenheit. For a rough conversion from Celsius to Fahrenheit, double the number and add 30. For weather, remember that 28°C is 82°F—perfect. For health, 37°C is just right. At a launderette, 30°C is cold, 40°C is warm (usually the default setting), 60°C is hot, and 95°C is boiling. Your air-conditioner should be set at about 20°C.

Packing Checklist

Whether you're traveling for five days or five weeks, you won't need more than this. Pack light to enjoy the sweet freedom of true mobility.

Clothing

- ☐ 5 shirts: long- & short-sleeve
- ☐ 2 pairs pants (or skirts/capris)
- ☐ 1 pair shorts
- ☐ 5 pairs underwear & socks
- ☐ 1 pair walking shoes
- ☐ Sweater or warm layer
- ☐ Rainproof jacket with hood
- ☐ Tie, scarf, belt, and/or hat
- ☐ Swimsuit
- ☐ Sleepwear/loungewear

Money

- ☐ Debit card(s)
- ☐ Credit card(s)
- ☐ Hard cash (US $100-200)
- ☐ Money belt

Documents

- ☐ Passport
- ☐ Tickets & confirmations: flights, hotels, trains, rail pass, car rental, sight entries
- ☐ Driver's license
- ☐ Student ID, hostel card, etc.
- ☐ Photocopies of important documents
- ☐ Insurance details
- ☐ Guidebooks & maps

Toiletries Kit

- ☐ Basics: soap, shampoo, toothbrush, toothpaste, floss, deodorant, sunscreen, brush/comb, etc.
- ☐ Medicines & vitamins
- ☐ First-aid kit
- ☐ Glasses/contacts/sunglasses
- ☐ Sewing kit
- ☐ Packet of tissues (for WC)
- ☐ Earplugs

Electronics

- ☐ Mobile phone
- ☐ Camera & related gear
- ☐ Tablet/ebook reader/laptop
- ☐ Headphones/earbuds
- ☐ Chargers & batteries
- ☐ Phone car charger & mount (or GPS device)
- ☐ Plug adapters

Miscellaneous

- ☐ Daypack
- ☐ Sealable plastic baggies
- ☐ Laundry supplies: soap, laundry bag, clothesline, spot remover
- ☐ Small umbrella
- ☐ Travel alarm/watch
- ☐ Notepad & pen
- ☐ Journal

Optional Extras

- ☐ Second pair of shoes (flip-flops, sandals, tennis shoes, boots)
- ☐ Travel hairdryer
- ☐ Picnic supplies
- ☐ Water bottle
- ☐ Fold-up tote bag
- ☐ Small flashlight
- ☐ Mini binoculars
- ☐ Small towel or washcloth
- ☐ Inflatable pillow/neck rest
- ☐ Tiny lock
- ☐ Address list (to mail postcards)
- ☐ Extra passport photos

Italian Survival Phrases

English	Italian	Pronunciation
Good day.	Buongiorno.	bwohn-**jor**-noh
Do you speak English?	Parla inglese?	**par**-lah een-**gleh**-zay
Yes. / No.	Sì. / No.	see / noh
I (don't) understand.	(Non) capisco.	(nohn) kah-**pees**-koh
Please.	Per favore.	pehr fah-**voh**-ray
Thank you.	Grazie.	**graht**-see-ay
You're welcome.	Prego.	**preh**-go
I'm sorry.	Mi dispiace.	mee dee-spee-**ah**-chay
Excuse me.	Mi scusi.	mee **skoo**-zee
(No) problem.	(Non) c'è problema.	(nohn) cheh proh-**bleh**-mah
Good.	Va bene.	vah **beh**-nay
Goodbye.	Arrivederci.	ah-ree-veh-**dehr**-chee
one / two	uno / due	**oo**-noh / **doo**-ay
three / four	tre / quattro	tray / **kwah**-troh
five / six	cinque / sei	**cheeng**-kway / **seh**-ee
seven / eight	sette / otto	**seh**-tay / **oh**-toh
nine / ten	nove / dieci	**noh**-vay / dee-**ay**-chee
How much is it?	Quanto costa?	**kwahn**-toh **koh**-stah
Write it?	Me lo scrive?	may loh **skree**-vay
Is it free?	È gratis?	eh **grah**-tees
Is it included?	È incluso?	eh een-**kloo**-zoh
Where can I buy / find...?	Dove posso comprare / trovare...?	**doh**-vay **poh**-soh kohm-**prah**-ray / troh-**vah**-ray
I'd like / We'd like...	Vorrei / Vorremmo...	voh-**reh**-ee / voh-**reh**-moh
...a room.	...una camera.	**oo**-nah **kah**-meh-rah
...a ticket to ____.	...un biglietto per ____.	oon beel-**yeh**-toh pehr ____
Is it possible?	È possibile?	eh poh-**see**-bee-lay
Where is...?	Dov'è...?	doh-**veh**
...the train station	...la stazione	lah staht-see-**oh**-nay
...the bus station	...la stazione degli autobus	lah staht-see-**oh**-nay **dehl**-yee **ow**-toh-boos
...tourist information	...informazioni per turisti	een-for-maht-see-**oh**-nee pehr too-**ree**-stee
...the toilet	...la toilette	lah twah-**leh**-tay
men	uomini / signori	**woh**-mee-nee / seen-**yoh**-ree
women	donne / signore	**doh**-nay / seen-**yoh**-ray
left / right	sinistra / destra	see-**nee**-strah / **deh**-strah
straight	sempre dritto	**sehm**-pray **dree**-toh
What time does this open / close?	A che ora apre / chiude?	ah kay **oh**-rah **ah**-pray / kee-**oo**-day
At what time?	A che ora?	ah kay **oh**-rah
Just a moment.	Un momento.	oon moh-**mehn**-toh
now / soon / later	adesso / presto / tardi	ah-**deh**-soh / **preh**-stoh / **tar**-dee
today / tomorrow	oggi / domani	**oh**-jee / doh-**mah**-nee

In an Italian Restaurant

English	Italian	Pronunciation
I'd like...	Vorrei...	voh-**reh**-ee
We'd like...	Vorremmo...	vor-**reh**-moh
...to reserve...	...prenotare...	preh-noh-**tah**-ray
...a table for one / two.	...un tavolo per uno / due.	oon **tah**-voh-loh pehr **oo**-noh / **doo**-ay
Is this seat free?	È libero questo posto?	eh **lee**-beh-roh **kweh**-stoh **poh**-stoh
The menu (in English), please.	Il menù (in inglese), per favore.	eel meh-**noo** (een een-**gleh**-zay) pehr fah-**voh**-ray
service (not) included	servizio (non) incluso	sehr-**veet**-see-oh (nohn) een-**kloo**-zoh
cover charge	pane e coperto	**pah**-nay ay koh-**pehr**-toh
to go	da portar via	dah **por**-tar **vee**-ah
with / without	con / senza	kohn / **sehnt**-sah
and / or	e / o	ay / oh
menu (of the day)	menù (del giorno)	meh-**noo** (dehl **jor**-noh)
specialty of the house	specialità della casa	speh-chah-lee-**tah deh**-lah **kah**-zah
first course (pasta, soup)	primo piatto	**pree**-moh pee-**ah**-toh
main course (meat, fish)	secondo piatto	seh-**kohn**-doh pee-**ah**-toh
side dishes	contorni	kohn-**tor**-nee
bread	pane	**pah**-nay
cheese	formaggio	for-**mah**-joh
sandwich	panino	pah-**nee**-noh
soup	zuppa	**tsoo**-pah
salad	insalata	een-sah-**lah**-tah
meat	carne	**kar**-nay
chicken	pollo	**poh**-loh
fish	pesce	**peh**-shay
seafood	frutti di mare	**froo**-tee dee **mah**-ray
fruit / vegetables	frutta / legumi	**froo**-tah / lay-**goo**-mee
dessert	dolce	**dohl**-chay
tap water	acqua del rubinetto	**ah**-kwah dehl roo-bee-**neh**-toh
mineral water	acqua minerale	**ah**-kwah mee-neh-**rah**-lay
milk	latte	**lah**-tay
(orange) juice	succo (d'arancia)	**soo**-koh (dah-**rahn**-chah)
coffee / tea	caffè / tè	kah-**feh** / teh
wine	vino	**vee**-noh
red / white	rosso / bianco	**roh**-soh / bee-**ahn**-koh
glass / bottle	bicchiere / bottiglia	bee-kee-**ehr**-ay / boh-**teel**-yah
beer	birra	**bee**-rah
Cheers!	Cin cin!	cheen cheen
More. / Another.	Di più. / Un altro.	dee pew / oon **ahl**-troh
The same.	Lo stesso.	loh **steh**-soh
The bill, please.	Il conto, per favore.	eel **kohn**-toh pehr fah-**voh**-ray
Do you accept credit cards?	Accettate carte di credito?	ah-cheh-**tah**-tay **kar**-tay dee **kreh**-dee-toh
tip	mancia	**mahn**-chah
Delicious!	Delizioso!	day-leet-see-**oh**-zoh

For more user-friendly Italian phrases, check out *Rick Steves Italian Phrase Book & Dictionary* or *Rick Steves French, Italian, & German Phrase Book*.

INDEX

INDEX

MAP INDEX

Our website enhances this book and turns

Explore Europe

At ricksteves.com you can browse through thousands of articles, videos, photos and radio interviews, plus find a wealth of money-saving travel tips for planning your dream trip. And with our mobile-friendly website, you can easily access all this great travel information anywhere you go.

TV Shows

Preview the places you'll visit by watching entire half-hour episodes of Rick Steves' Europe (choose from all 100 shows) on-demand, for free.

your travel dreams into affordable reality

Radio Interviews

Enjoy ready access to Rick's vast library of radio interviews covering travel tips and cultural insights that relate specifically to your Europe travel plans.

Travel Forums

Learn, ask, share! Our online community of savvy travelers is a great resource for first-time travelers to Europe, as well as seasoned pros.

Travel News

Subscribe to our free Travel News e-newsletter, and get monthly updates from Rick on what's happening in Europe.

Classroom Europe

Check out our free resource for educators with 300+ short video clips from the Rick Steves' Europe TV show.

Rick's Free Travel App

Get your FREE **Rick Steves Audio Europe**™ app to enjoy...

- Dozens of self-guided tours of Europe's top museums, sights and historic walks
- Hundreds of tracks filled with cultural insights and sightseeing tips from Rick's radio interviews
- All organized into handy geographic playlists
- For Apple and Android

With Rick whispering in your ear, Europe gets even better.

Find out more at ricksteves.com

Gear up for your next adventure at ricksteves.com

Light Luggage

Pack light and right with Rick Steves' affordable, custom-designed rolling carry-on bags, backpacks, day packs and shoulder bags.

Accessories

From packing cubes to moneybelts and beyond, Rick has personally selected the travel goodies that will help your trip go smoother.

Shop at ricksteves.com

Save time and energy

This guidebook is your independent-travel toolkit. But for all it delivers, it's still up to you to devote the time and energy it takes to manage the preparation and logistics that are essential for a happy trip. If that's a hassle, there's a solution.

Rick Steves Tours

A Rick Steves tour takes you to Europe's most interesting places with great

with minimum stress

guides and small groups of 28 or less. We follow Rick's favorite itineraries, ride in comfy buses, stay in family-run hotels, and bring you intimately close to the Europe you've traveled so far to see. Most importantly, we take away the logistical headaches so you can focus on the fun.

Join the fun

This year we'll take 33,000 free-spirited travelers— nearly half of them repeat customers—along with us on 50 different itineraries, from Athens to Istanbul. Is a Rick Steves tour the right fit for your travel dreams?

Find out at ricksteves.com, where you can also request Rick's latest tour catalog. Europe is best experienced with happy travel partners. We hope you can join us.

See our itineraries at **ricksteves.com**

BEST OF GUIDES

Full-color guides in an easy-to-scan format. Focused on top sights and experiences in the most popular European destinations

Best of England
Best of Europe
Best of France
Best of Germany
Best of Ireland
Best of Italy
Best of Scotland
Best of Spain

COMPREHENSIVE GUIDES

City, country, and regional guides printed on Bible-thin paper. Packed with detailed coverage for a multi-week trip exploring iconic sights and venturing off the beaten path

Amsterdam & the Netherlands
Barcelona
Belgium: Bruges, Brussels, Antwerp & Ghent
Berlin
Budapest
Croatia & Slovenia
Eastern Europe
England
Florence & Tuscany
France
Germany
Great Britain
Greece: Athens & the Peloponnese
Iceland
Ireland
Istanbul
Italy
London
Paris
Portugal
Prague & the Czech Republic
Provence & the French Riviera
Rome
Scandinavia
Scotland
Sicily
Spain
Switzerland
Venice
Vienna, Salzburg & Tirol

THE BEST OF ROME

...me, Italy's capital, is studded with ...man remnants and floodlit-fountain ...ares. From the Vatican to the Colos-...m, with crazy traffic in between, Rome ...onderful, huge, and exhausting. The ...rds, the heat, and the weighty history

of the Eternal City where Caesars walked can make tourists wilt. Recharge by taking siestas, gelato breaks, and after-dark walks, strolling from one atmospheric square to another in the refreshing evening air.

...red **Pantheon**—which ...gest dome until the ...rly 2,000 years old ...day over 1,500).

...of Athens in the **Vat**-...dies the humanistic ...nce.

...gladiators fought ...another, entertaining

Rick Steves books are available from your favorite bookseller. Many guides are available as ebooks.

POCKET GUIDES

Compact color guides for shorter trips

Amsterdam
Athens
Barcelona
Florence
Italy's Cinque Terre
London
Munich & Salzburg

Paris
Prague
Rome
Venice
Vienna

SNAPSHOT GUIDES

Focused single-destination coverage

Basque Country: Spain & France
Copenhagen & the Best of Denmark
Dublin
Dubrovnik
Edinburgh
Hill Towns of Central Italy
Krakow, Warsaw & Gdansk
Lisbon
Loire Valley
Madrid & Toledo
Milan & the Italian Lakes District
Naples & the Amalfi Coast
Nice & the French Riviera
Normandy
Northern Ireland
Norway
Reykjavík
Rothenburg & the Rhine
Scottish Highlands
Sevilla, Granada & Southern Spain
St. Petersburg, Helsinki & Tallinn
Stockholm

CRUISE PORTS GUIDES

Reference for cruise ports of call

Mediterranean Cruise Ports
Scandinavian & Northern European
 Cruise Ports

Complete your library with...

TRAVEL SKILLS & CULTURE

Study up on travel skills and gain insight on history and culture

Europe 101
Europe Through the Back Door
Europe's Top 100 Masterpieces
European Christmas
European Easter
European Festivals
For the Love of Europe
Travel as a Political Act

PHRASE BOOKS & DICTIONARIES

French
French, Italian & German
German
Italian
Portuguese
Spanish

PLANNING MAPS

Britain, Ireland & London
Europe
France & Paris
Germany, Austria & Switzerland
Iceland
Ireland
Italy
Spain & Portugal

Credits

RESEARCHERS
To help update this book, Rick and Gene relied on...

Virginia Agostinelli

Virginia was born and raised in Abruzzo, in central Italy. After graduation she moved to Seattle, where she taught Italian studies at the University of Washington while finishing her doctorate. Besides travel and teaching, Virginia has a passion for Italian cinema and detective fiction. When not leading a Rick Steves' Europe tour, she spends her time in the Pacific Northwest swimming, reading, and sipping a cappuccino at the nearest coffeehouse.

Robert Wright

Raised in Memphis, Robert funded his first dream trip to Europe in 1998 by selling his entire *Star Wars* collection—proof that where there's a will, there's a way. He fell in love with Italy, Spain, and Portugal and constantly returned, all while living for 14 years in Argentina. Robert recently married a *sevillano* and moved to Spain. He continues to enjoy Iberian architecture and loves uncovering forgotten connections between Spain and Portugal's intertwined history.

Acknowledgments
Thanks to our friends in Rome, Francesca Caruso and Ilaria Ceccarelli, for their invaluable help in updating this edition.

Photo Credits
Front Cover: Roman Forum © Alessandro Saffo / Sime / eStock Photo

Back Cover (left to right): © F11photo, © Dsanchezpaniagua, © Griffisgigi. Dreamstime.com

Title Page: Colosseum © Dominic Arizona Bonuccelli

Alamy: 90 The Picture Art Collection, 105 (bottom) Heritage Image Partnership Ltd, 107 Adam Eastland, 287 Bailey-Cooper Photography, 309 (bottom) Archivart, 310 (bottom) Artepics, 503 National Geographic Image Collection, 534 World History Archive

Dreamstime: 6 (top right) Robynmac, 16 (bottom) Dzianis Rabtsevich, 289 (top right) Andrei Stancu

Public Domain via Wikimedia Commons: 11 (bottom)

Additional Photography: Dominic Arizona Bonuccelli, Ben Cameron, Orin Dubrow, Trish Feaster, Cameron Hewitt, David C. Hoerlein, Heather Lawless, Gene Openshaw, Rhonda Pelikan, Rick Steves, Molly Verlin, Ian Watson. Photos are used by permission and are the property of the original copyright owners.

Avalon Travel
Hachette Book Group
1700 Fourth Street
Berkeley, CA 94710

Printed in Canada by Friesens
22nd Edition. First printing January 2021

ISBN 978-1-64171-295-8

For the latest on Rick's talks, guidebooks, tours, public television series, and public radio show, contact Rick Steves' Europe, Inc., 130 Fourth Avenue North, Edmonds, WA 98020, 425/771-8303, www.ricksteves.com, rick@ricksteves.com.

Rick Steves' Europe

Managing Editor: Jennifer Madison Davis
Assistant Managing Editor: Cathy Lu
Special Publications Manager: Risa Laib
Editors: Glenn Eriksen, Suzanne Kotz, Rosie Leutzinger, Teresa Nemeth, Jessica Shaw, Carrie Shepherd, Meg Sneeringer
Editorial & Production Assistant: Megan Simms
Editorial Intern: Maxwell Eberle
Researchers: Virginia Agostinelli, Robert Wright
Graphic Content Director: Sandra Hundacker
Maps & Graphics: David C. Hoerlein, Lauren Mills, Mary Rostad
Digital Asset Coordinator: Orin Dubrow

Avalon Travel

Senior Editor and Series Manager: Madhu Prasher
Associate Managing Editors: Jamie Andrade, Sierra Machado
Copy Editor: Maggie Ryan
Proofreaders: Kelly Lydick, Rachael Sablik
Indexer: Stephen Callahan
Production & Typesetting: Lisi Baldwin, Jane Musser, Ravina Schneider
Cover Design: Kimberly Glyder Design
Maps & Graphics: Lohnes and Wright, Kat Bennett, Mike Morgenfeld

COLOR MAPS

*Rome • West Rome • East Rome • South Rome
• Rome Public Transportation*

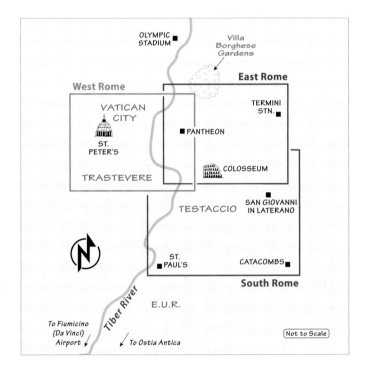

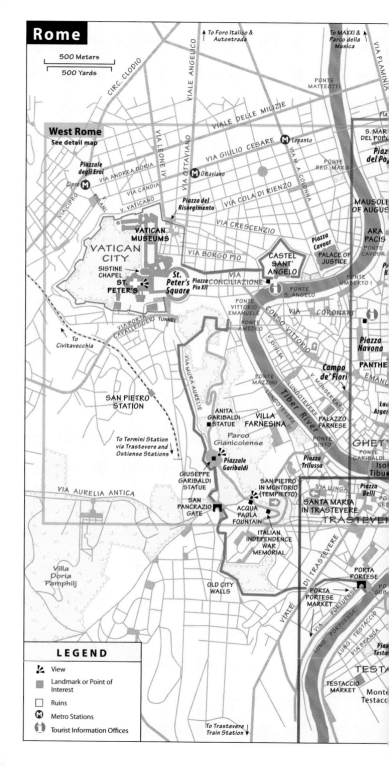

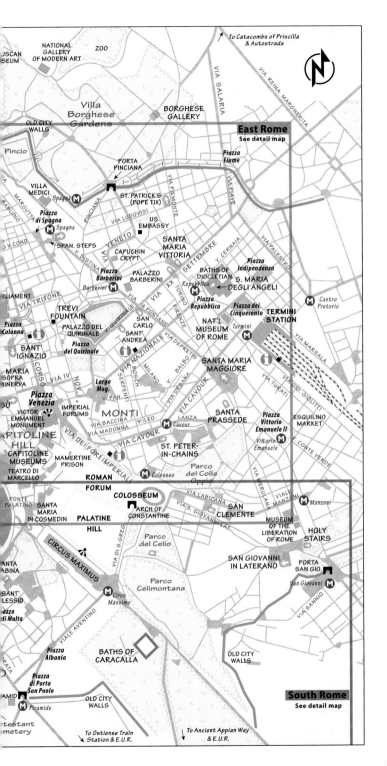

West Rome

Piazzale degli Eroi

MERCATO TRIONFALE **3**

VIA ANDREA DORIA

VIA TOLEMAIDE

VIA F. CARACCIOLO

VIA CANDIA

VIALE GIULIO CESARE

Ⓜ Ottaviano

VIA PISANI

VIA FAMAGOSTA

VIA LEONE IV

VIA

VIA OTTAVIANO

DEGLI

SCIPIONI

GERMANICO

V LUIGI RIZZO

VENTICINQUE CIPRO

V. SEBASTIANO ZIANI

V. RIALTO

VIA GIORGIO SCALIA

VIA DELLA MELORIA

V. R. FIORE

VIA F. SIVORI

VIA PISANI

VIA MOCENIGO

V. SEB. VENIERO

VIALE VATICANO

VASPASIANO

VIA DEI CATONE

VIA DEGRA

Cipro Ⓜ

Piazza S.Maria d. Grazie

VIA ANGELO EMO

Ⓑ Ⓣ **10**

VIA VATICANO

Piazza Risorgimento Ⓣ

Ⓑ

VATICAN MUSEUMS

PINACOTECA

VATICANO

V.S. PO

BORGO ANGELI

ITALIAN POST

V. D. PORTA ANGELICA

V. D. MASCHERINO

BOR

BOR

Vatican Gardens

VATICAN CITY

V. D. BELVEDERE

4

V. DEI CORRI

SISTINE CHAPEL

7

St. Peter's Square

9

Piazza Pio XII

8

ST. PETER'S BASILICA

ⓘ

→ To Via Aurelia & Ring Freeway

VIALE

VATICAN WALL

VATICANO

VIA NICOLÒ V

AUDIENCE HALL

PEDESTRIAN UNDERPASS

Ⓑ

VIA AURELIA

V. PORTA CAVALLEGGERI

GAL. PRINCIPE AMEDO SAVOIA AOSTA

V. PAOLO III

VIA VILLA ALBERICI

ALESSANDRO III

(TUNNEL)

URBANO VIII

To Civitavecchia

Piazza Gregorio VII

ANCIENT CITY WALLS

VIA D.S.M. MEDIATRICE

V.D.Y.C. AGLIARDI

VIA D. STAZIONE

A. DE GASPERI

VIA DELLE FORNACI

Ⓝ

VIA DEL COTTOLENGO

V.D. GELSOMINO

VII

CLIVO DI MONTE DEL GALLO

GREGORIO

DI MONTE DEL GALLO

CROCIFISSO NICOLO III

VIA PAOLO II

To Via Aurelia & Ring Freeway

VIA

VIC DEL GELSOMINO

V.S. SILVERO

MONTE

DEL

DELLA CAVA

V.D. LAGO TERRIONE

SAN PIETRO STATION

VIA DELLE FORNACI

VIALE DELLE MURA AURELIE

G. ROSSO

ANITA GARIBALDI MONUMENT

VIL

LA

VIA NUOVA DELLE FORNACI

Piazz Garib

GIUSEPPE GARIBALDI MONUMENT

lorem ipsum

To Termini

m ipsum

SIGHTS

1. Castel Sant'Angelo
2. Gianicolo Hill Viewpoint
3. Mercato Trionfale
4. Papal Apartments
5. Ponte Sant'Angelo
6. Santa Maria in Trastevere Church
7. Sistine Chapel
8. St. Peter's Basilica
9. St. Peter's Square & Obelisk
10. Vatican Museums (Entrance/Main Exit)
11. Villa Farnesina

LEGEND

- Pedestrian-Friendly Area
- Popular Shopping Area
- ‖‖‖ Stairway
- ▪ Landmark or Point of Interest (sight number marks entrance)
- ▭ Ruins
- ⫩⫩ Obelisks, Columns
- Ⓜ Ⓣ Metro Stations, Taxi Stands,
- Ⓑ Ⓣ Bus Hubs, Tram Stops
- ⓘ Tourist Information Offices

| 300 meters |
| 300 yards |

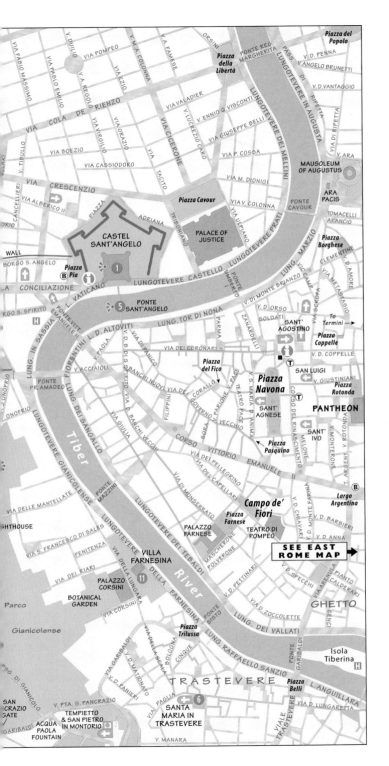

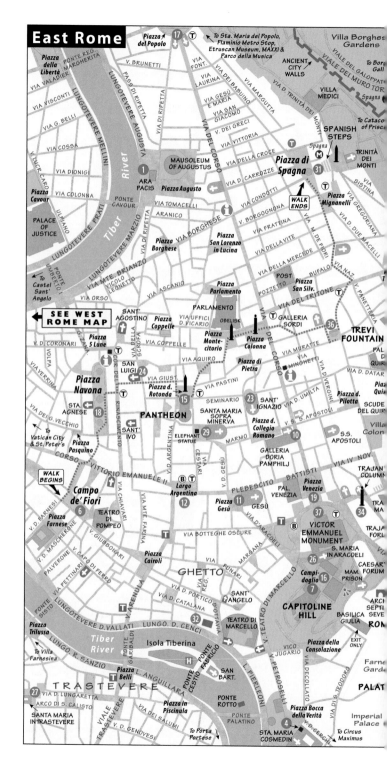

East Rome

Villa Borghese Gardens

Piazza del Popolo

To Sta. Maria del Popolo, Flaminio Metro Stop, Etruscan Museum, MAXXI & Parco della Musica

ANCIENT CITY WALLS

VILLA MEDICI

VIALE DEL GALOPPAT
VIALE DEI MURO TOR

To Borg
Gall

Spagna

Piazza della Libertà

PONTE REG. MARGHERITA

V. VALADIER

LUNGOTEVERE MELLINI

PASS DI RIPETTA

V. BRUNETTI

VIA FONT.

VIA LAURINA

VIA DEI BABUINO

VIA GESÙ E MARIA

VIA SAN GIACOMO

VIA DEI GRECI

VIA MARGUTTA

VIA D. TRINITÀ DEI MONT

SPANISH STEPS

To Cataco of Prisc

VIA VISCONTI

VIA G. BELLI

VIA COSSA

V. LUCR. CARO

VIA DIONIGI

VIA COLONNA

Piazza Cavour

PONTE CAVOUR

Tiber River

PONTE CAVOUR

LUNGOTEVERE MARZIO

MAUSOLEUM OF AUGUSTUS

ARA PACIS

Piazza Augusto

Piazza Augusto

VIA DELLA CROCE

VIA D. CARROZZE

VIA CONDOTTI

Spagna

TRINITÀ DEI MONTI

VIA SISTINA

Piazza di Spagna

Piazza Mignanelli

VIA GREGORIANA

VIA D. DUE MACELLI

PALACE OF JUSTICE

LUNGOTEVERE PRATI

PONTE UMBERTO I

To Castel Sant'Angelo

VIA TOMACELLI

ARANICO

VIA DI RIPETTA

VIA MTE. BRIANZO

VICOLO LEONETTO

VIA BORGHESE

Piazza Borghese

V. BORGOGNONA

VIA FRATTINA

VIA M. DE' FIORI

WALK ENDS

VIA DELLAVITE

VIA DELLA MERCEDE

Piazza San Lorenzo in Lucina

VICOLO ORSO

VIA ORSO

VIA ASCANIO

Piazza Parlamento

POST

PIAZZETTA

Piazza San Silv.

BUFALO

VIA NAZ.

V. PANETTERIA

SEE WEST ROME MAP

SANT' AGOSTINO

Piazza 5 Lune

V. D. CORONARI

V. D. SCROFA

VIA DELLA SCROFA

Piazza Coppelle

VIA COPPELLE

PARLAMENTO

VIA UFFICI D. VICARIO

VIA AQUIRO

OBELISK

Piazza Montecitorio

Piazza Colonna

GALLERIA SORDI

VIA DEL CORSO

VIA DEL TRITONE

TREVI FOUNTAIN

PAL D QUIR

VOLFA

VIA VERRINA

V. DEI CORONARI

Piazza Navona

STA. AGNESE

V. DI G. VECCHIO

To Vatican City & St. Peter's

CORSO

Piazza Pasquino

SANT' LUIGI

VIA GIUST.

Piazza d. Rotonda

PANTHEON

SANT' IVO

VIA PASTINI

SEMINARIO

SANTA MARIA SOPRA MINERVA

ELEPHANT STATUE

SANT' IGNAZIO

Piazza d. Collegio Romano

GALLERIA DORIA PAMPHILJ

Piazza d. Pietra

V. S. S. APOSTOLI

Piazza d. Pilotta

SCUDE DEL QUIR

S.S. APOSTOLI

Villa Colon

VIA MURATTE

VIA D. VERGIN

Piaz Quir

VIA D. DATAR

VIA IV NOV

TRAJAN COLUMN

WALK BEGINS

Campo de' Fiori

VITTORIO EMANUELE II

Piazza Farnese

VIA CHIAVARI

TEATRO DI POMPEO

Largo Argentina

V. D. GESÙ

PLEBESCITO

PAL. VENEZIA

GESÙ

Piazza Venezia

VICTOR EMMANUEL MONUMENT

TRA MA

TRAJAN FORL

V. MTE. FARINA

V. D. FARNESI

V. DI MASCHERONE

PALVERONE

V. CAPO DI FERRO

V. PETTINARI

Piazza Gesù

Piazza Cairoli

VIA BOTTEGHE OSCURE

VIA D'ARACOELI

VIA FUNARI

Piazza Cairoli

GHETTO

VIA MARGANA

S. MARIA IN ARACOELI

CAESAR' MAM. FORUM PRISON

Campidaglio

CAPITOLINE HILL

ARC SEPTI SEVE ROM

PONTE SISTO

LUNGOTEVERE D. VALLATI

V. ARENULA

SANT' ANGELO

VIA D. PORTICO D'OTTAVIA

VIA D. CATALANA

TEATRO DI MARCELLO

V. TEATRO DI MARCELLO

Piazza della Consolazione

EXIT ONLY

BASILICA GIULIA

Farne Gard

PALAT

Piazza Trilussa

LUNGO. D. CENCI

Isola Tiberina

PONTE FABRICIO

VICO JUGARIO

VIA DECOLLATO

Tiber River

LUNGO. R. SANZIO

To Villa Farnesina

Piazza L. Anguillara

PONTE GARIBALDI

SAN BART.

PONTE CESTIO

PONTE PALATINO

PALATINO

L. PIERLEONI

VIA DI S. TEODORO

Imperial Palace

TRASTEVERE

VIA D. LUNGARETTA

ARCO DI S. CALISTO

SANTA MARIA IN TRASTEVERE

VIALE TRASTEVERE

V. DEI GENOVESI

V. DEI SALUMI

Piazza in Piscinula

PONTE ROTTO

To Porta Portese

STA. MARIA COSMEDIN

Piazza Bocca della Verità

V. D' CERCHI

To Circus Maximus

SIGHTS

- Ara Pacis
- Arch of Constantine
- Baths of Diocletian
- Bocca della Verità
- To Borghese Gallery
- Campo de' Fiori
- Capitoline Museums
- Capuchin Crypt
- Colosseum
- Galleria Doria Pamphilj

11 Gesù Church
12 Largo Argentina
13 Nat'l Museum of Rome
14 Palatine Hill
15 Pantheon
16 Piazza del Campidoglio
17 Piazza del Popolo
18 Piazza Navona
19 Piazza Venezia
20 Roman Forum

21 St. Peter-in-Chains Church
22 San Clemente Church
23 Sant'Ignazio Church
24 San Luigi dei Francesi Church
25 S. Maria della Vittoria Church
26 S. Maria in Aracoeli Church
27 S. Maria in Trastevere Church
28 S.Maria Maggiore Church
29 S. Maria sopra Minerva Church
30 Santa Susanna Church

31 Spanish Steps
32 Synagogue & Jewish Museum
33 Termini Train Station
34 Trajan's Column
35 Trajan's Market & Museum of the Imperial Forums
36 Trevi Fountain
37 Victor Emmanuel Monument

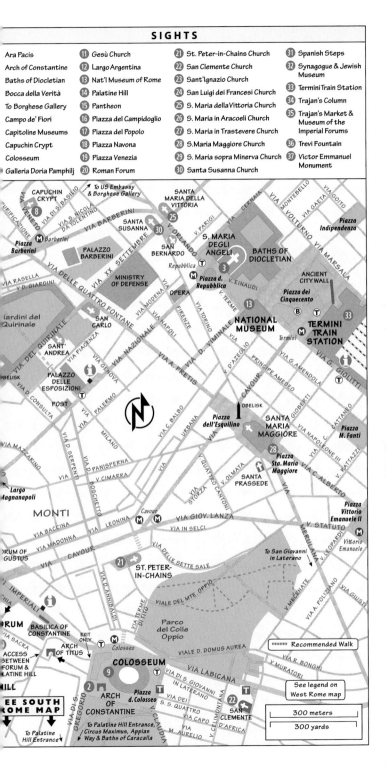

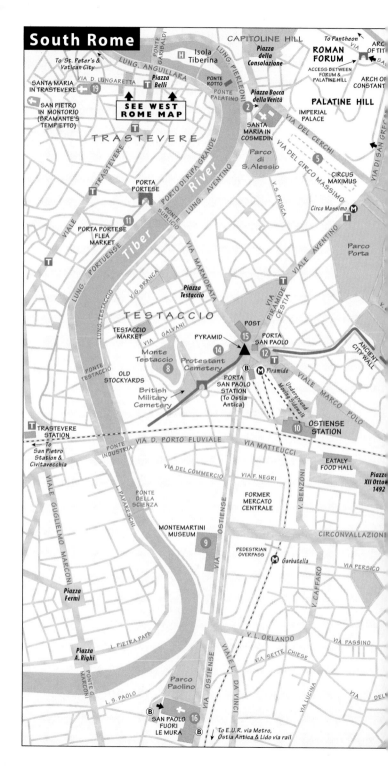

South Rome

To Pantheon

CAPITOLINE HILL

ARC OF TIT

ROMAN FORUM

ACCESS BETWEEN FORUM & PALATINE HILL

ARCH OF CONSTANT

Isola Tiberina

Piazza della Consolazione

LUNG. ANGUILLARA

PONTE GARIBALDI

To St. Peter's & Vatican City

SANTA MARIA IN TRASTEVERE **19**

VIA D. LUNGARETTA

Piazza Belli

SEE WEST ROME MAP

PONTE ROTTO
PONTE PALATINO

Piazza Bocca della Verità **2**

SANTA MARIA IN COSMEDIN

PALATINE HILL

IMPERIAL PALACE

VIA DEL CERCHIO

SAN PIETRO IN MONTORIO (BRAMANTE'S TEMPIETTO)

TRASTEVERE

Parco di S.Alessio

VIA DEL CIRCO MASSIMO **5**

CIRCUS MAXIMUS

VIA DI SAN GRE

PORTA PORTESE

PORTO DI RIPA GRANDE

LUNG. AVENTINO

V.S PRISCA

Circo Massimo **M**

Parco Porta

PORTA PORTESE FLEA MARKET **11**

PONTE SUBLICIO

Tiber River

VIA MARMORATA

Viale AVENTINO

LUNG. PORTUENSE

LUNG. TESTACCIO

V.G. BRANCA

Piazza Testaccio

TESTACCIO

POST

PYRAMID **14**

15 PORTA SAN PAOLO

VIA PIRAMIDE CESTIA

TESTACCIO MARKET

VIA GALVANI

Monte Testaccio **8**

Protestant Cemetery

PORTA SAN PAOLO **12**

Piramide **M**

ANCIENT CITY WALL

PONTE TESTACCIO

OLD STOCKYARDS

British Military Cemetery

PORTA SAN PAOLO STATION (To Ostia Antica)

VIALE MARCO POLO

Underground Moving Sidewalk

OSTIENSE STATION **10**

TRASTEVERE STATION

To San Pietro Station & Civitavecchia

VIA D. PORTO FLUVIALE

VIA MATTEUCCI

PONTE INDUSTRIA

VIA DEL COMMERCIO

VIA F. NEGRI

V. BENZONI

EATALY FOOD HALL

Piazz XII Otto 1492

VIALE GUGLIELMO MARCONI

PONTE DELLA SCIENZA

L. PAPARESCHI

FORMER MERCATO CENTRALE

CIRCONVALLAZIONI

MONTEMARTINI MUSEUM **9**

VIA OSTIENSE

PEDESTRIAN OVERPASS

Garbatella **M**

V. CAFFARO

VIA PERSICO

Piazza Fermi

VIA L. ORLANDO

VIA PASSINO

Piazza A. Righi

L. PIETRA PAPA

VIA SETTE CHIESE

VIA LUCINA

PONTE G. MARCONI

VIALE L. DA VINCI

VIA DEL

Parco Paolino

SAN PAOLO FUORI LE MURA **16**

VIA OSTIENSE

To E.U.R. via Metro, Ostia Antica & Lido via rail

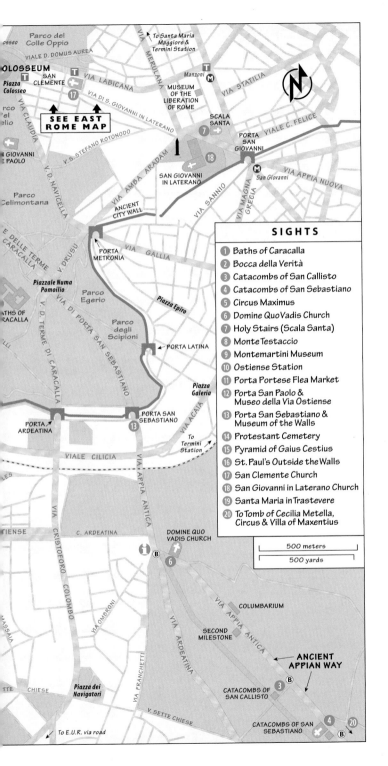

Parco del
Colle Oppio
VIALE D. DOMUS AUREA
Parco del 0550
VIA MERULANA
To Santa Maria
Maggiore &
Termini Station

COLOSSEUM
Piazza
Colosseo
SAN
CLEMENTE
VIA LABICANA
Manzoni
M
VIA STATILIA

arco
el
elio
VIA CLAUDIA
17
VIA DI S. GIOVANNI IN LATERANO
MUSEUM
OF THE
LIBERATION
OF ROME

SEE EAST ROME MAP

V. S. STEFANO ROTONODO
SCALA
SANTA
7
VIALE C. FELICE

I GIOVANNI
E PAOLO
V. D. NAVICELLA
18
PORTA
SAN GIOVANNI
M
San Giovanni
VIA APPIA NUOVA

Parco
Celimontana
SAN GIOVANNI
IN LATERANO
VIA SANNIO
VIA MAGNA GRECIA

ANCIENT
CITY WALL

E DELLE TERME
CARACALLA
VIA AMBA ARADAM
PORTA
METRONIA
VIA GALLIA
V. DRUSU

Piazzale Numa
Pomoilio
Parco
Egerio
Piazza Epiro

SIGHTS

1 Baths of Caracalla
2 Bocca della Verità
3 Catacombs of San Callisto
4 Catacombs of San Sebastiano
5 Circus Maximus
6 Domine Quo Vadis Church
7 Holy Stairs (Scala Santa)
8 Monte Testaccio
9 Montemartini Museum
10 Ostiense Station
11 Porta Portese Flea Market
12 Porta San Paolo &
   Museo della Via Ostiense
13 Porta San Sebastiano &
   Museum of the Walls
14 Protestant Cemetery
15 Pyramid of Gaius Cestius
16 St. Paul's Outside the Walls
17 San Clemente Church
18 San Giovanni in Laterano Church
19 Santa Maria in Trastevere
20 To Tomb of Cecilia Metella,
   Circus & Villa of Maxentius

ATHS OF
RACALLA
V. D. TERME DI CARACALLA
VIA DI PORTA SAN SEBASTIANO
Parco
degli
Scipioni
PORTA LATINA
Piazza
Galeria

PORTA
ARDEATINA
PORTA SAN
SEBASTIANO
13
VIA ACAIA
To
Termini
Station

VIALE CILICIA

VIA APPIA ANTICA

500 meters
500 yards

TIENSE
VIA CRISTOFORO COLOMBO
C. ARDEATINA
DOMINE QUO
VADIS CHURCH
i
B
6

MASSA
VIA OMBRONI
Piazza dei
Navigatori
VIA ARDEATINA
COLUMBARIUM
SECOND
MILESTONE
VIA APPIA ANTICA

To E.U.R. via road
V. SETTE CHIESE
VIA FRANCHETTI
**ANCIENT
APPIAN WAY**

TTE
CHIESE
CATACOMBS OF
SAN CALLISTO
3
B

CATACOMBS OF SAN
SEBASTIANO
4
20
B

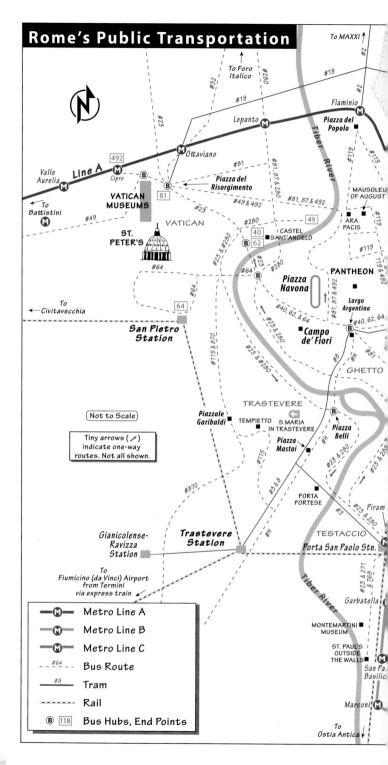

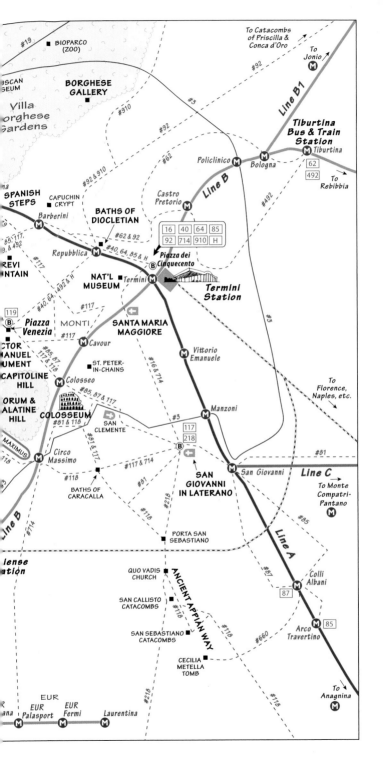

Keep on Travelin'

Your trip
doesn't need
to end.

Follow Rick on
social media!

Your trip doesn't need to end.

Follow Rick on social media!